AF545023

Melle Smets & Joost van Onna

turtle 1 building a car in Africa

L: Smets and van Onna visit the Ford plant at Highland Park, Detroit, 2011.
R: Model T Chassis Inspection, Ford plant, Highland Park, Detroit, 1914.

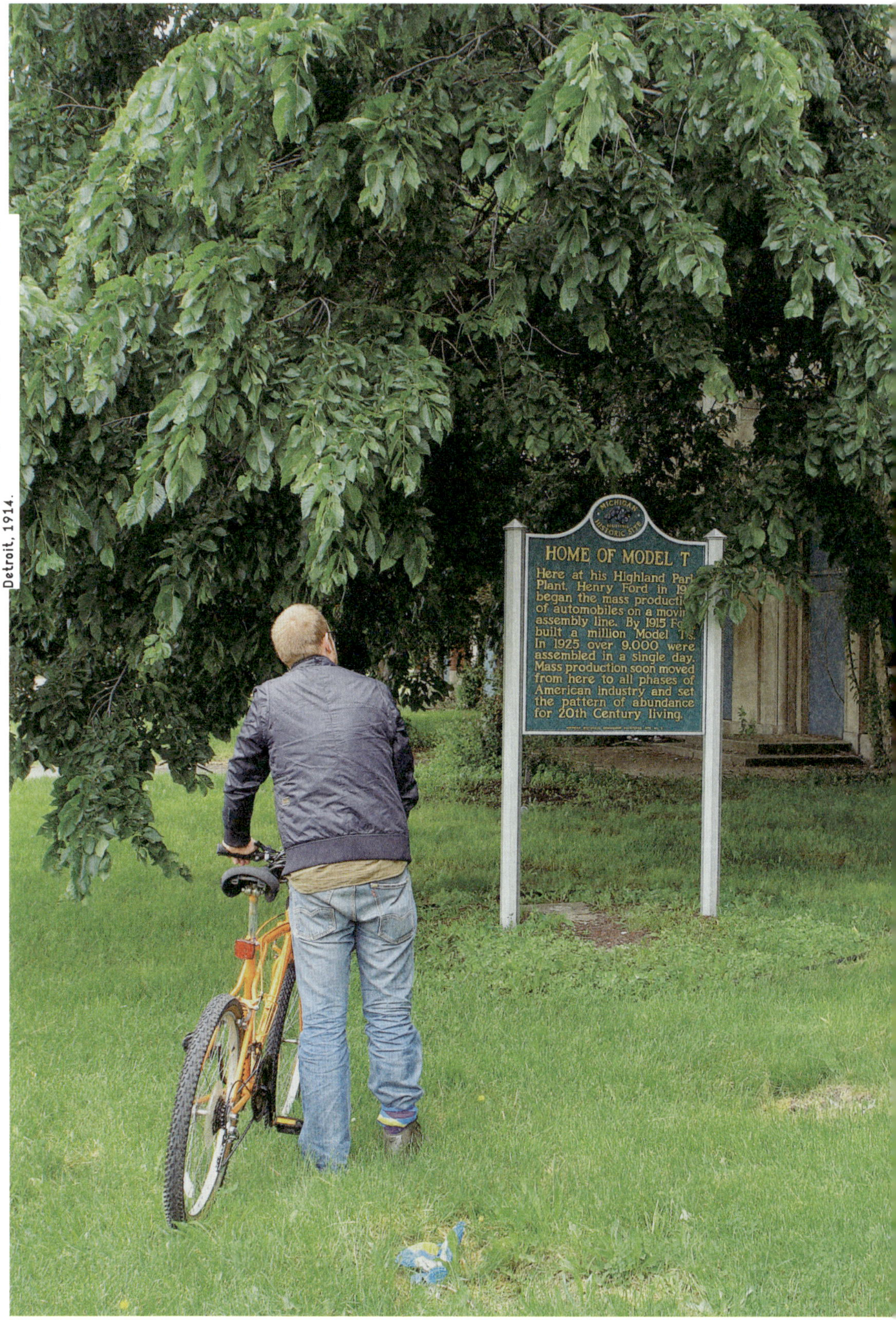

fordism

t1 | 5

L: Excerpt from the American magazine *Modern Mechanix*, September 1956.
R: Advertisement for the Fiat 500, ca 1960.

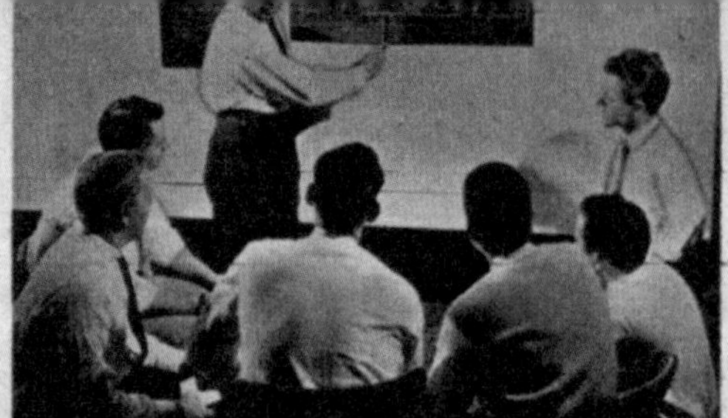

First step in the building of Club de Mer was to decide what type of car was wanted.

How to Dream Up a Car

The creation of Pontiac's Club de Mer dream car took years of work.

PONTIAC'S Club de Mer is the stuff that dreams are made of—dreams that result from years of painstaking planning and hard work by stylists and engineers at GM's lush new Technical Center. A dream car begins when vice-president in charge of styling, Harley Earl, and other top executives decide what type of car is to be created. In

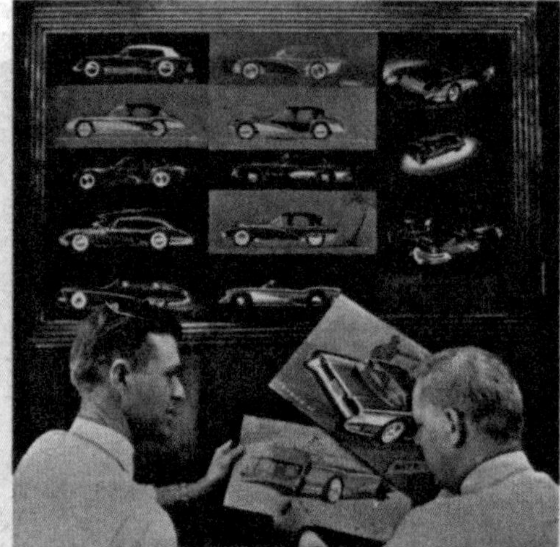

Thousands of sketches are made. Basic design will incorporate features from them.

Club de Mer has a Cerulean blue body of brushed aluminum.

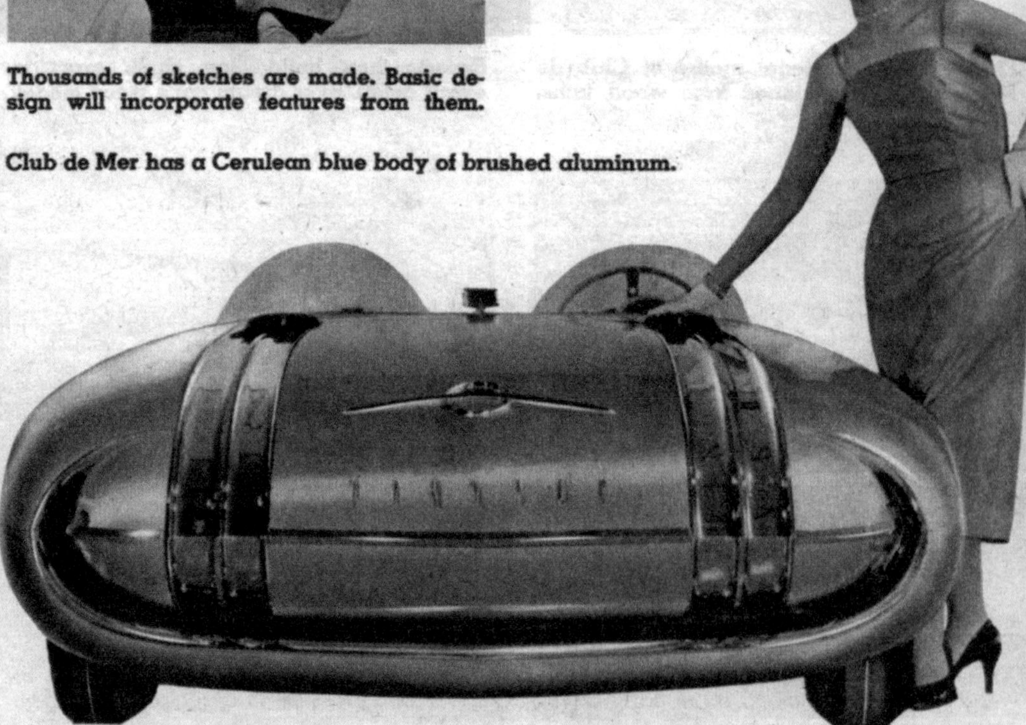

99

L: Detail from advertisement for the BMW X6, 2015.
R: Detail from advertisement for the Land Rover Defender, 2012.

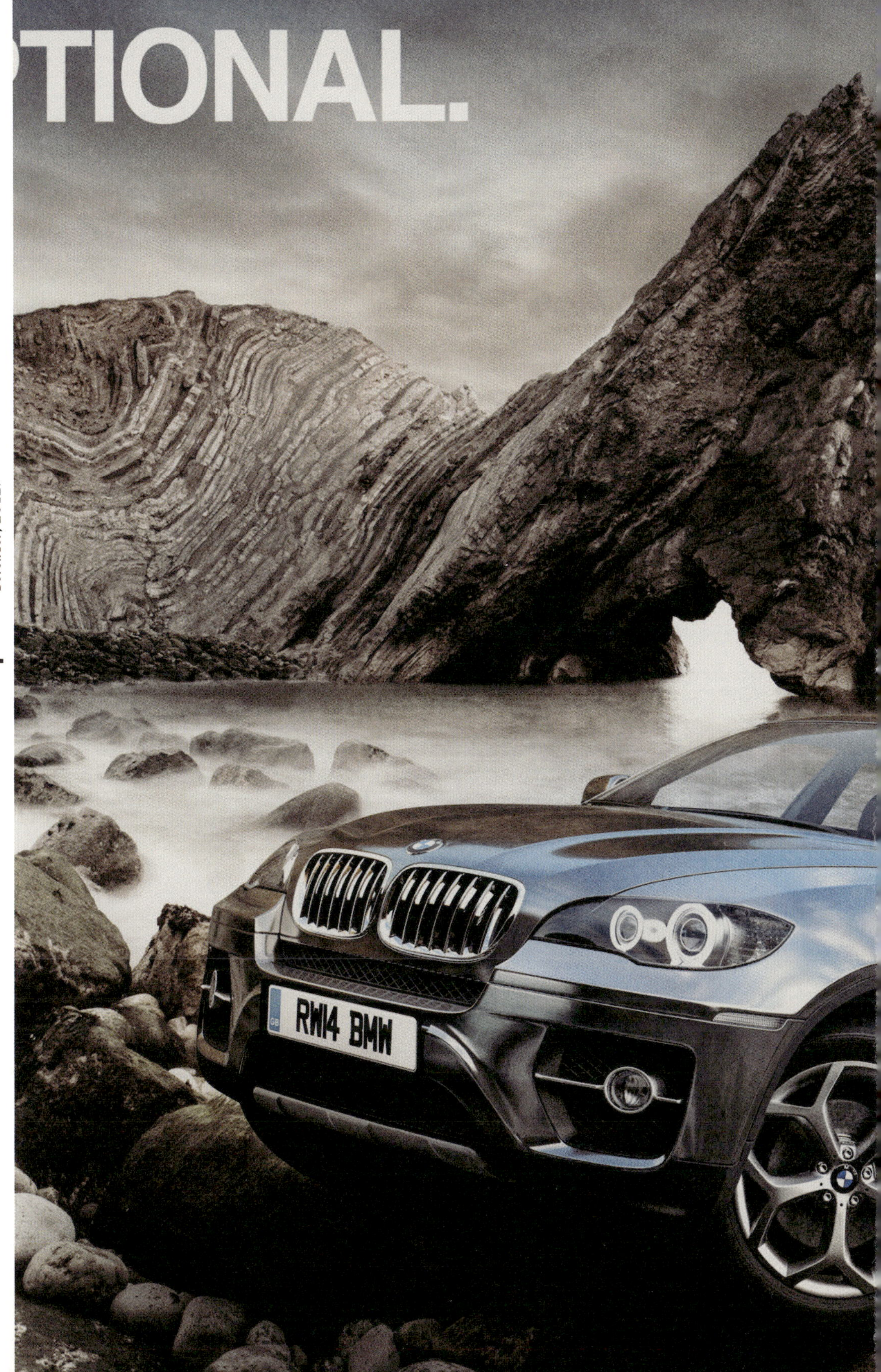

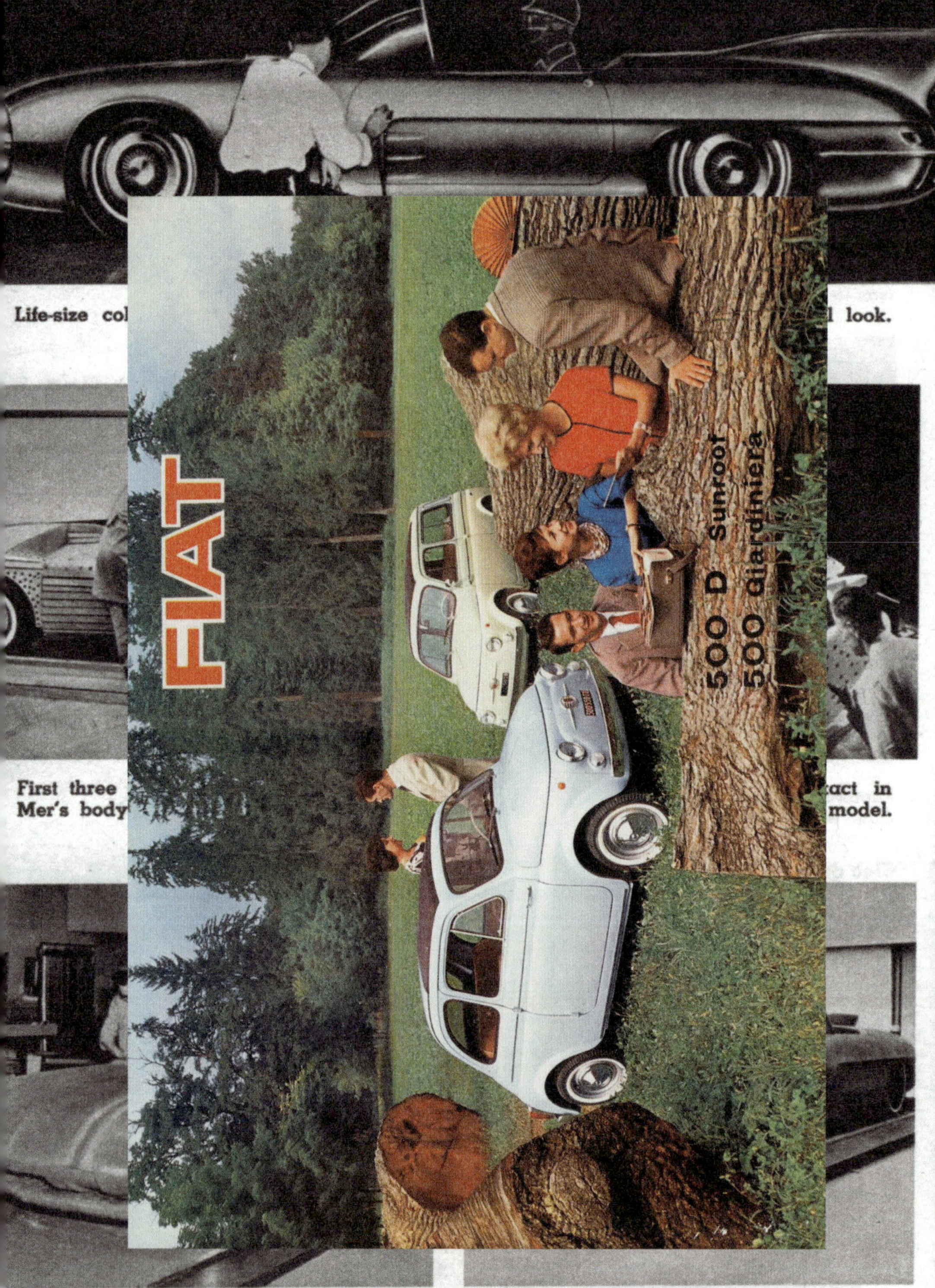

Life-size col… l look.

First three … act in
Mer's body … model.

After hours of tedious detail work the "clay buck" takes on lines of car's body.

Finished clay model will be duplicated in metal or Fiberglas through plaster molds.

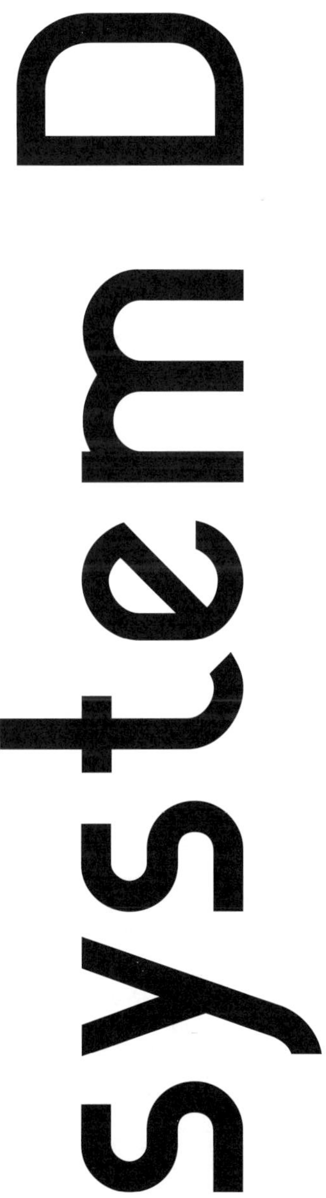

In an informal economy, economic activities take place out of sight and beyond the reach of governments. The more governments are able to maintain rules, the more difficult it is to develop informal activities. Across the world there are great differences in the size and visibility of informal economic activities. In the West, they are often small and concealed, but in large parts of the world they are omnipresent. Hundreds of millions of people find work in these wondrous spaces. Here civilians and entrepreneurs have to find solutions to the same problems that civilians and entrepreneurs face in formal systems, but without government support, oversight or control: how to organise workers, gain knowledge, create a market, build up a clientele, buy products, attract investments and resolve conflicts. The informal economy is also known as Système D, where D stands for the French words débrouille or débrouillard, which implies resourcefulness and ingenuity.[3]

Informal economies are usually characterised by small companies that use labour-intensive and low-tech processes. Entry requirements (in terms of capital and education) are low and training usually takes place outside the formal setting. Often such systems have a small-scale set-up, but they can also develop into complex, refined and efficient systems of self-organisation. The public transport system in the Peruvian capital Lima is a good example of a vibrant and complex informal system: until recently, an estimated 80,000 buses made 8.5 million trips per day, with hardly any government interference. Then there is Mumbai's famous Dabbawala lunch delivery system, as part of which 5,000 deliverymen deliver around 200,000 meals a day. The system has a tiny margin of error that is thought to be just one in six million. The term "informal economy" was coined in 1973 by the British anthropologist Keith Hart in a scientific article in which he described how the Frafras, a population group in northern Ghana, try to find work outside the formal framework in the capital Accra.[4] Today, 40 years on, the world may have changed, but the Frafras still live and work in this way. Many of them live in Suame Magazine, where they have become scrapyard bosses.

3 Neuwirth, R. 2012. Stealth of Nations: *The Global Rise of the Informal Economy.* New York: Random House.
4 Hart, K. 1973. *Informal Income Opportunities and Urban Employment in Ghana,* Journal of Modern African Studies, 11: 61-89.

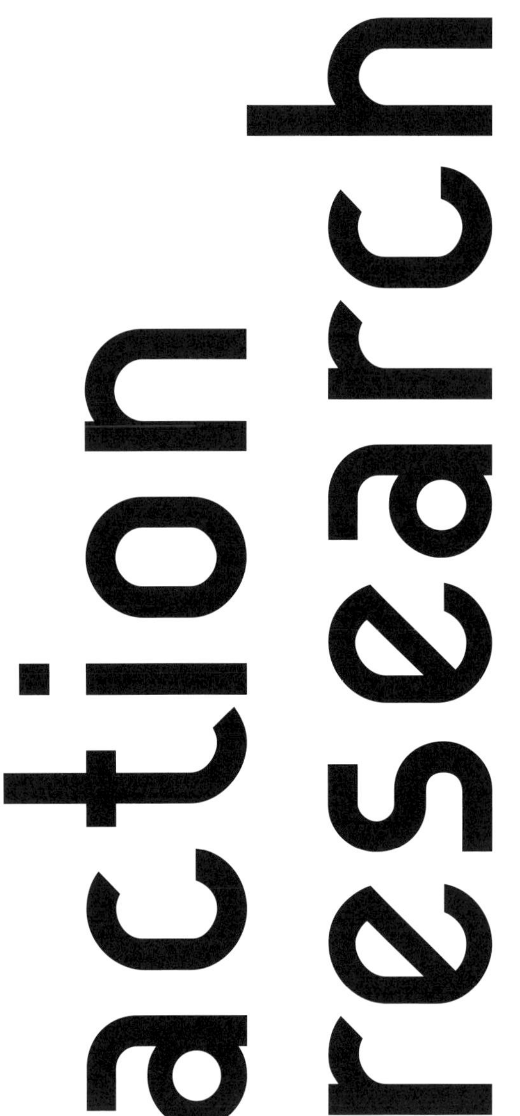

There is a long tradition of action research, in which research is conducted during the course of an action that effects change. Our sources of inspiration included the classic study on unemployment in the Austrian town of Marienthal. Researchers lived and worked there for months as collectors and distributors of second-hand clothing in order to better understand the effects of the closure of a local factory on the population.**5** We also drew on the study by De Soto et al. They mapped the world of informal entrepreneurs in Peru, Egypt and the Philippines and worked with them to establish legal companies in order to demonstrate how difficult it is to follow all the steps and meet the many hundreds of administrative requirements. Through "learning by doing", these researchers tangibly mapped the resilience of an environment.**6** Action research has a special place in the palette of research types. Important characteristics include the researchers' special personal involvement, their active participation and the close cooperation with the local population, on terms that are as equal as possible. In addition, the experimental set-up and active influencing distinguish this method from other forms of qualitative data collection where researchers try to limit their influence on their research environment as much as possible and are usually passive observers.**7**

We did not want to carry out our research from a purely scientific or artistic point of view. We wanted to approach and document the binding link – the experiment and the research – through different disciplines, from various angles and using a range of artistic and scientific documentation methods in the hope that they would complement and strengthen each other.**8**

5 Jahoda, M., P.F. Lazarsfeld, & H. Ziesel. 1971. *Marienthal. The Sociography of an Unemployed Community.* London: Transaction Publishers.
6 De Soto, H. 1989. *The Other Path: The Invisible Revolution in the Third World.* New York: HarperCollins. De Soto, H. 2000. *The Mystery of Capital: Why Capitalism Triumphs in the West and Fails Everywhere Else.* New York: Basic Books.
7 Onna, van J.H.R. 2013. *Sharing ideas en putting pressure. Criminologische inzichten uit actie-onderzoek naar informeel ondernemerschap in de grootste autowijk ter wereld* ('Sharing Ideas and Putting Pressure. Criminological Insights from Action-research in Informal Entrepreneurship in the Largest Car-related Industrial Cluster in the World'). Cahiers Politiestudies, 29: 147-170.
8 We were inspired by Liebenberg, L. 1990. *The Art of Tracking. The Origin of Science.* Claremont: David Philip Publishers.

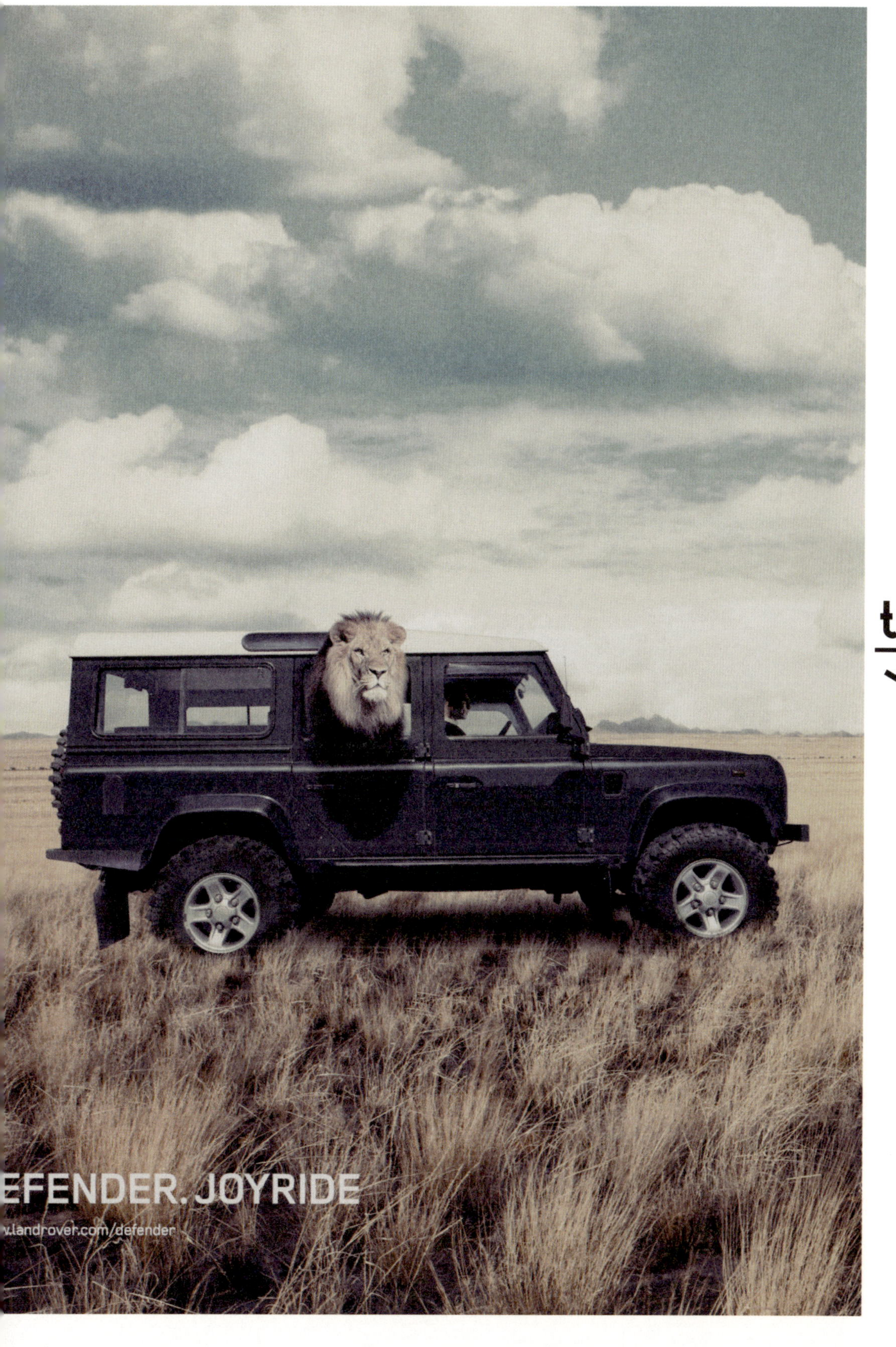
EFENDER. JOYRIDE
v.landrover.com/defender

10

Robotic arms weld the frame of a Chevrolet Corsa Classic sedan on an assembly line at the General Motors manufacturing plant in Sao Jose dos Campos, Brazil, 2010.

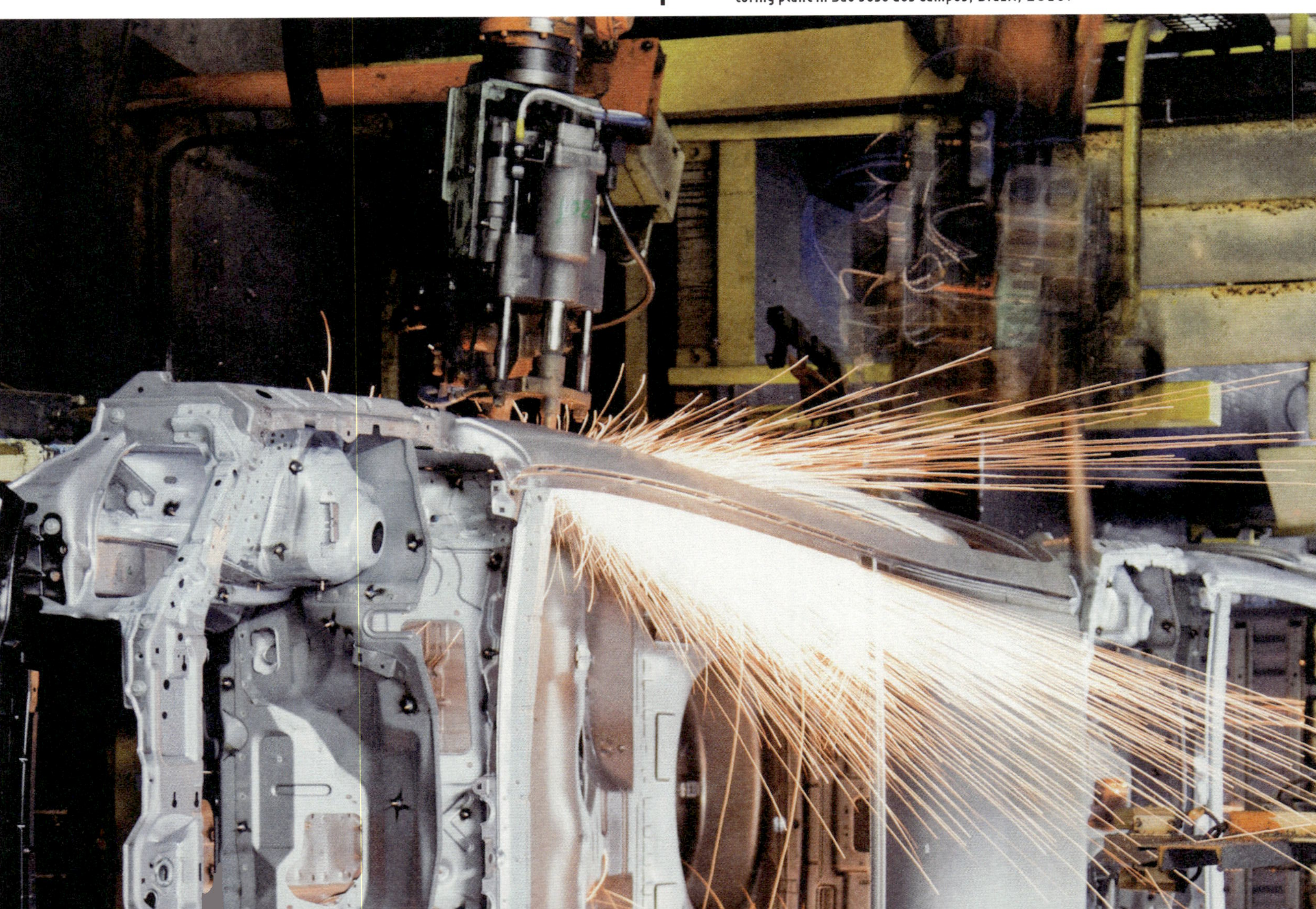

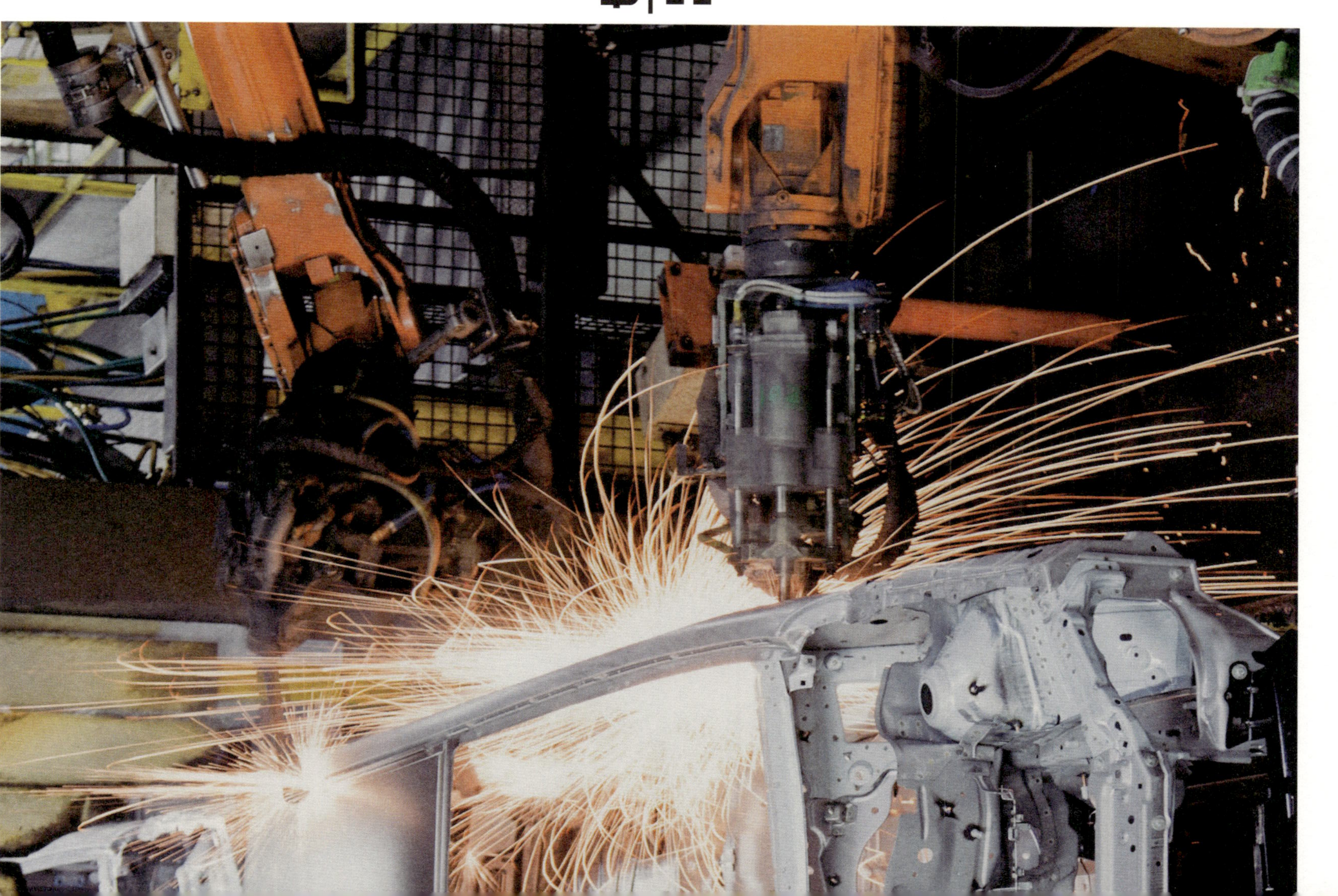

The deserted Packard Automotive factory, Detroit, 2011.

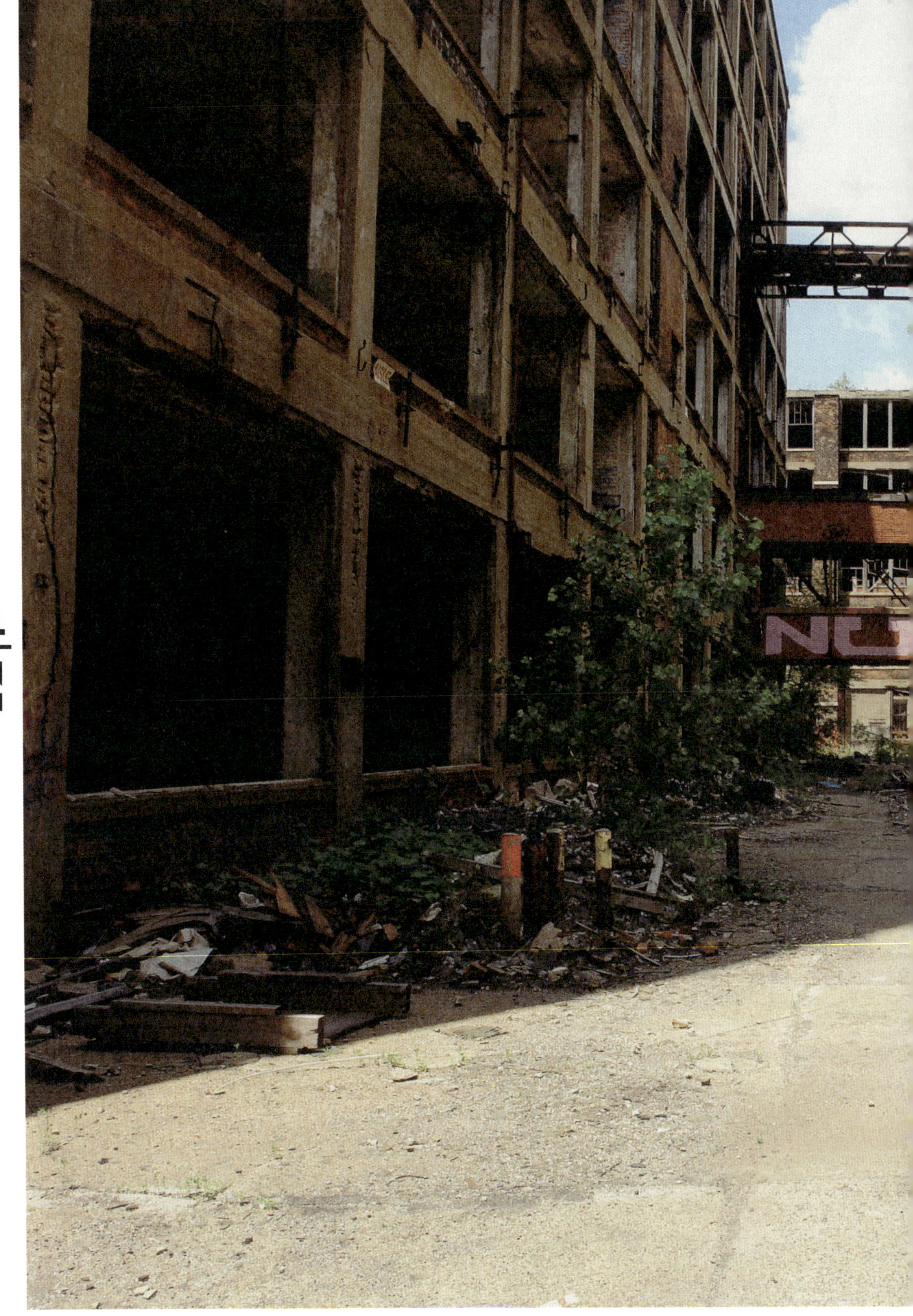

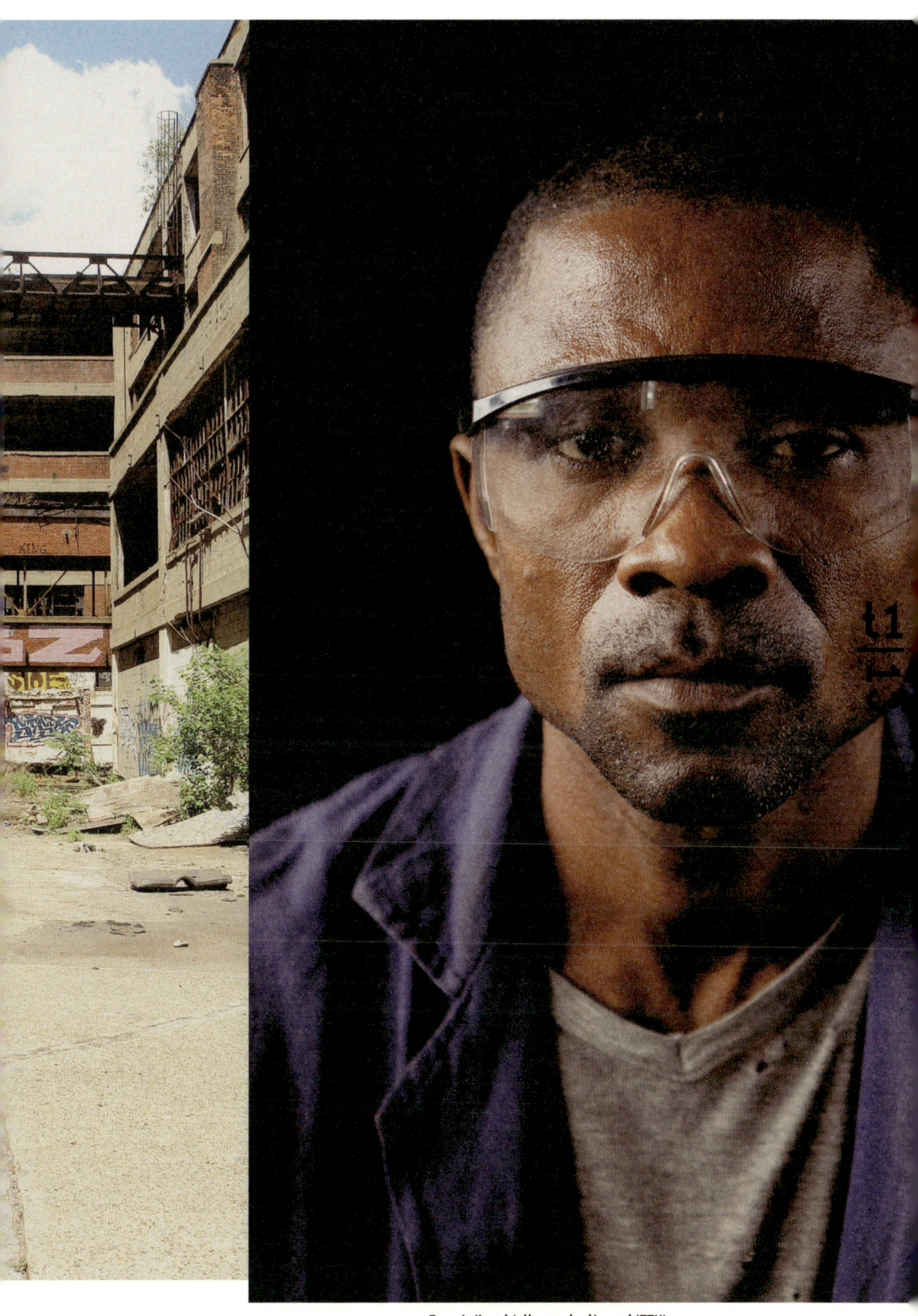

Francis Kuyol (all-round artisan at ITTU)

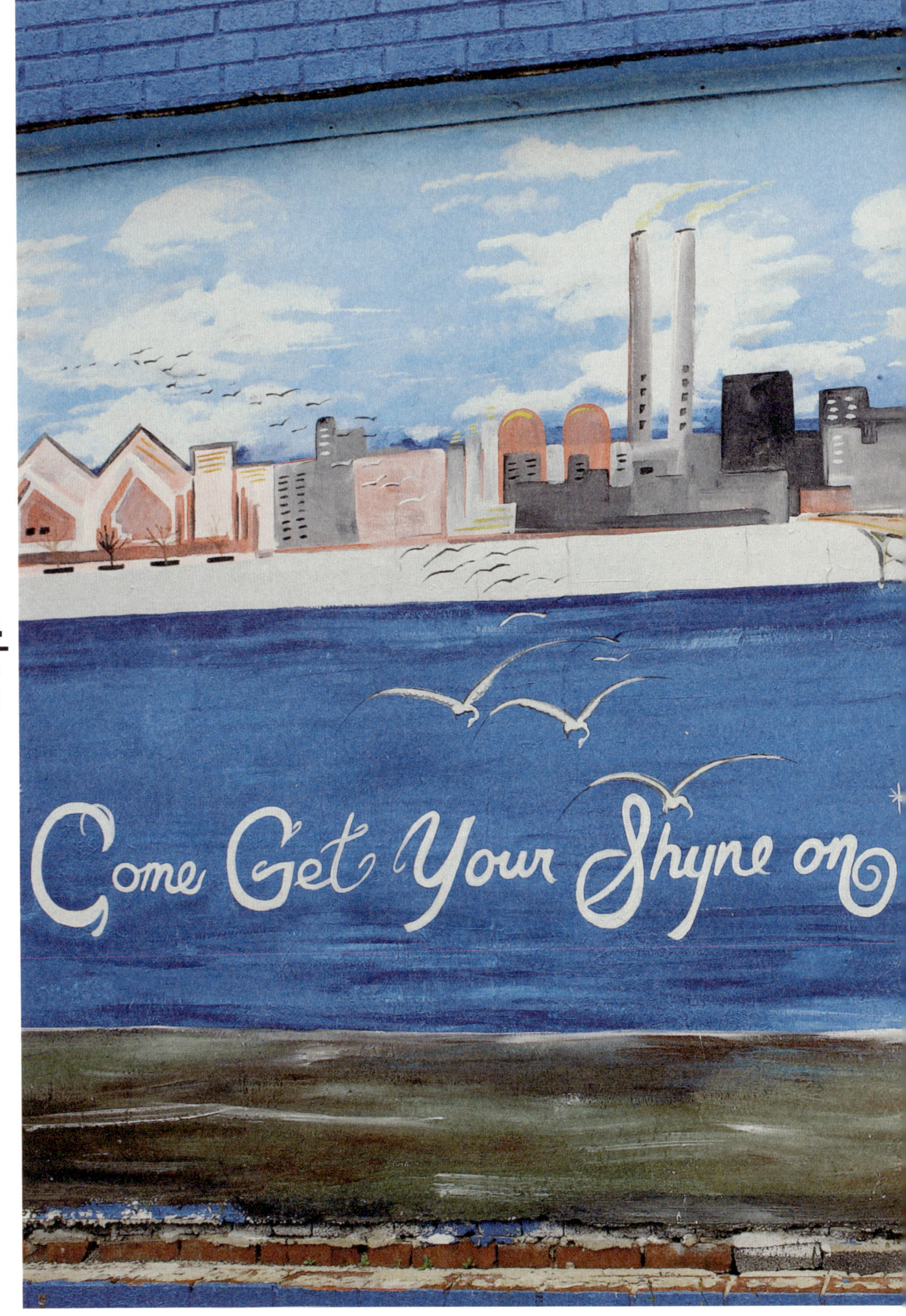

Billboard for a car wash, Detroit, 2011.

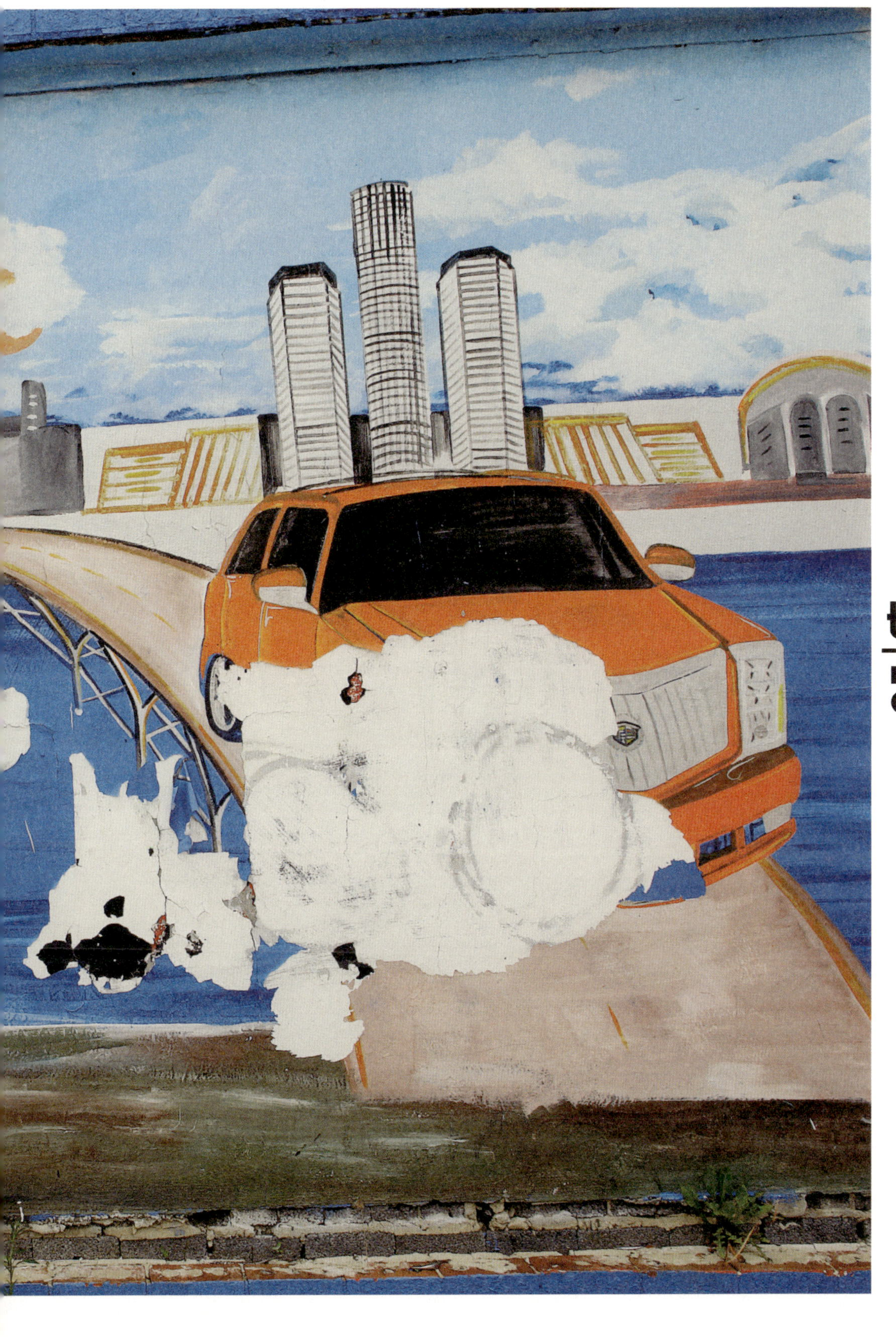

Modern cars run on chips and computers. It makes it very difficult to recycle the parts of discarded cars in Africa. If the electronics break down, the car becomes e-waste.

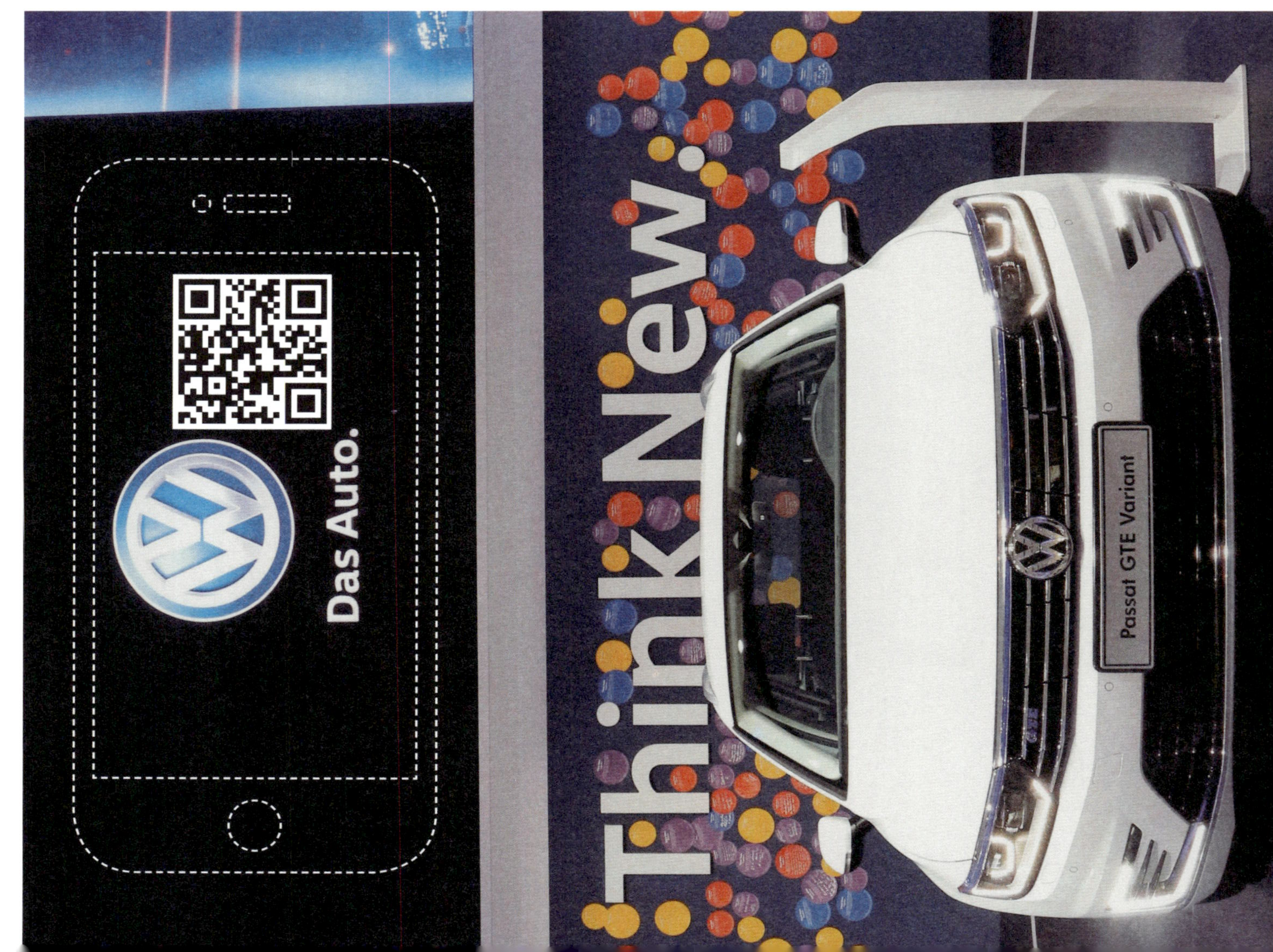

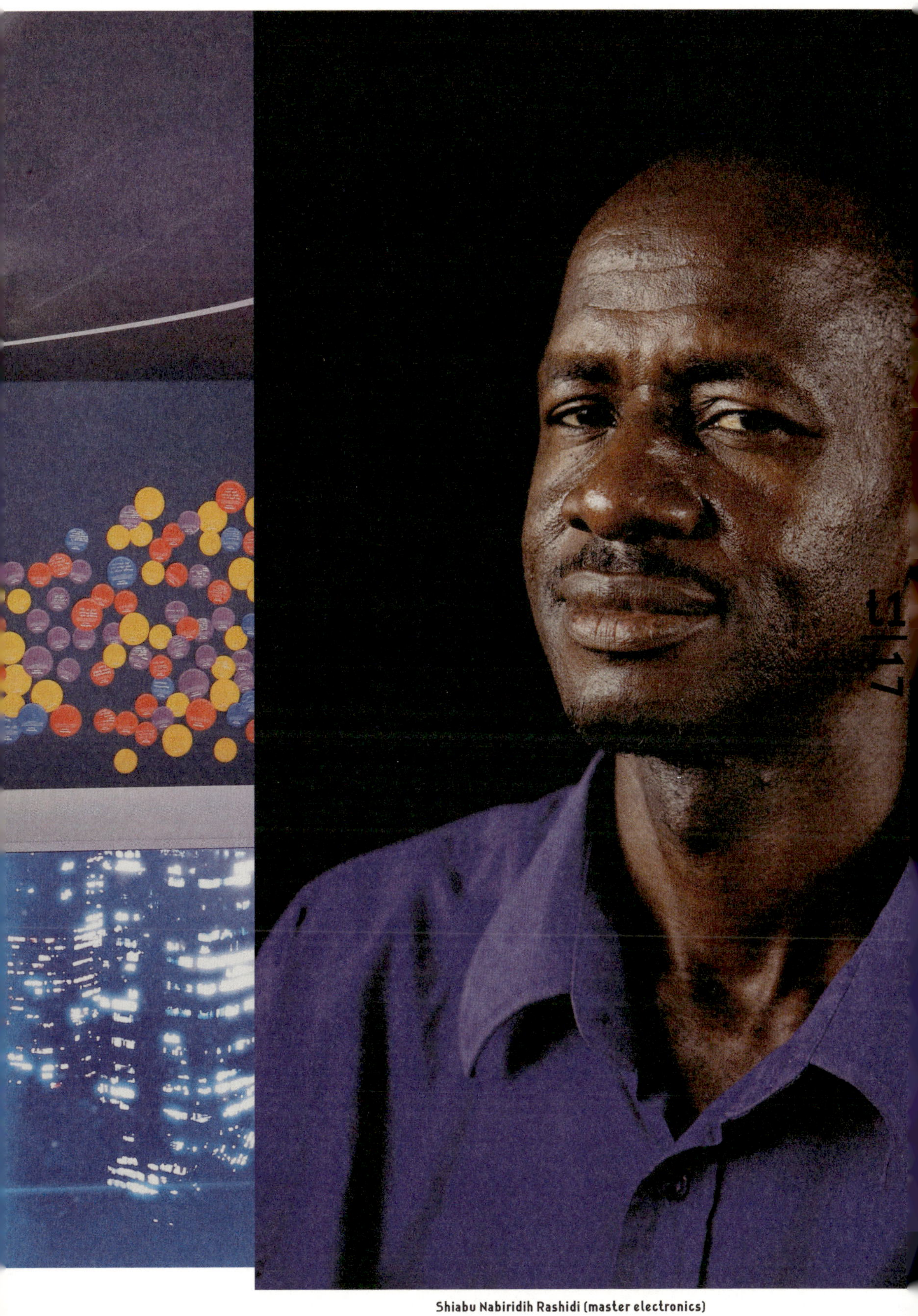

Shiabu Nabiridih Rashidi (master electronics)

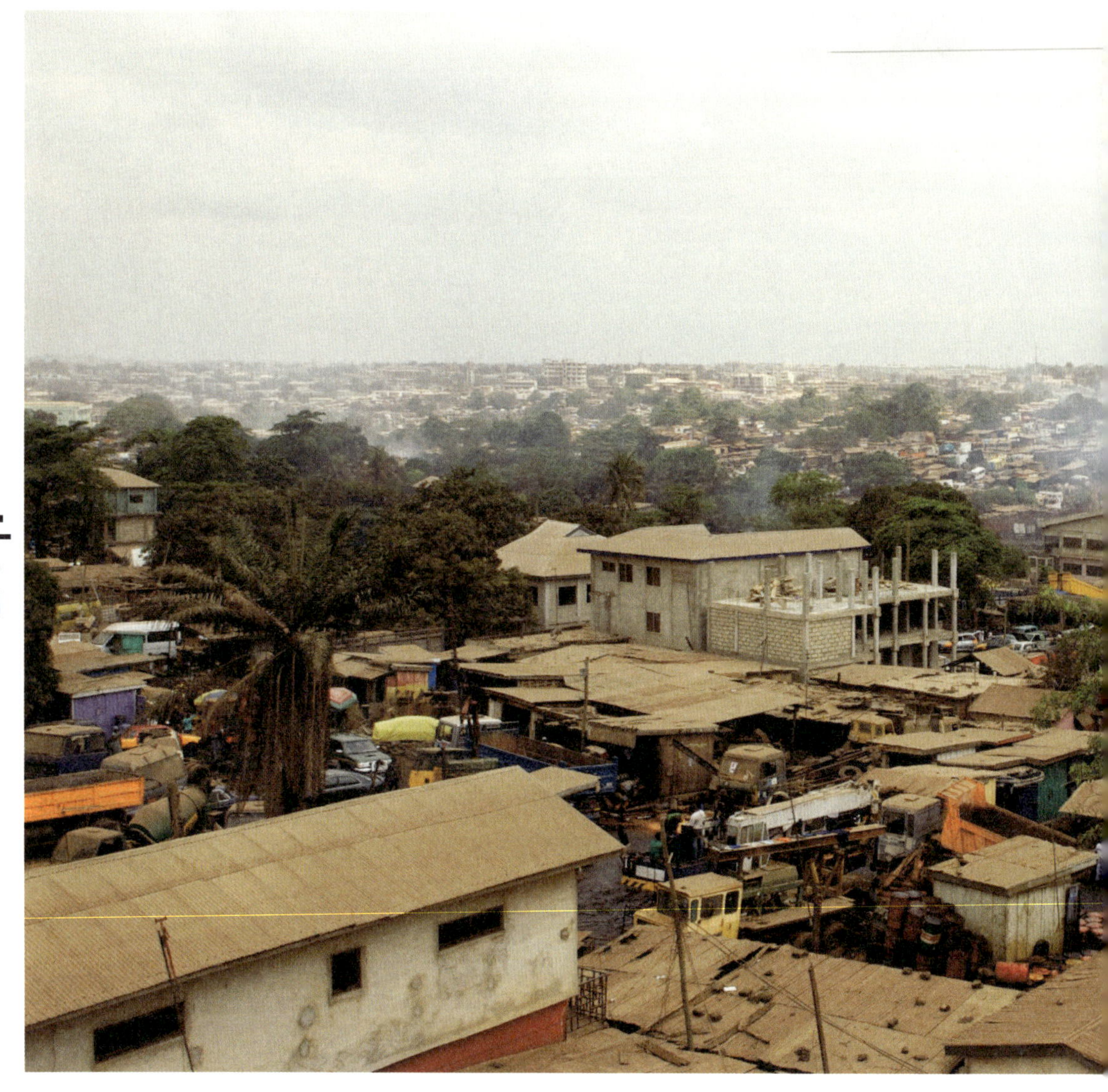

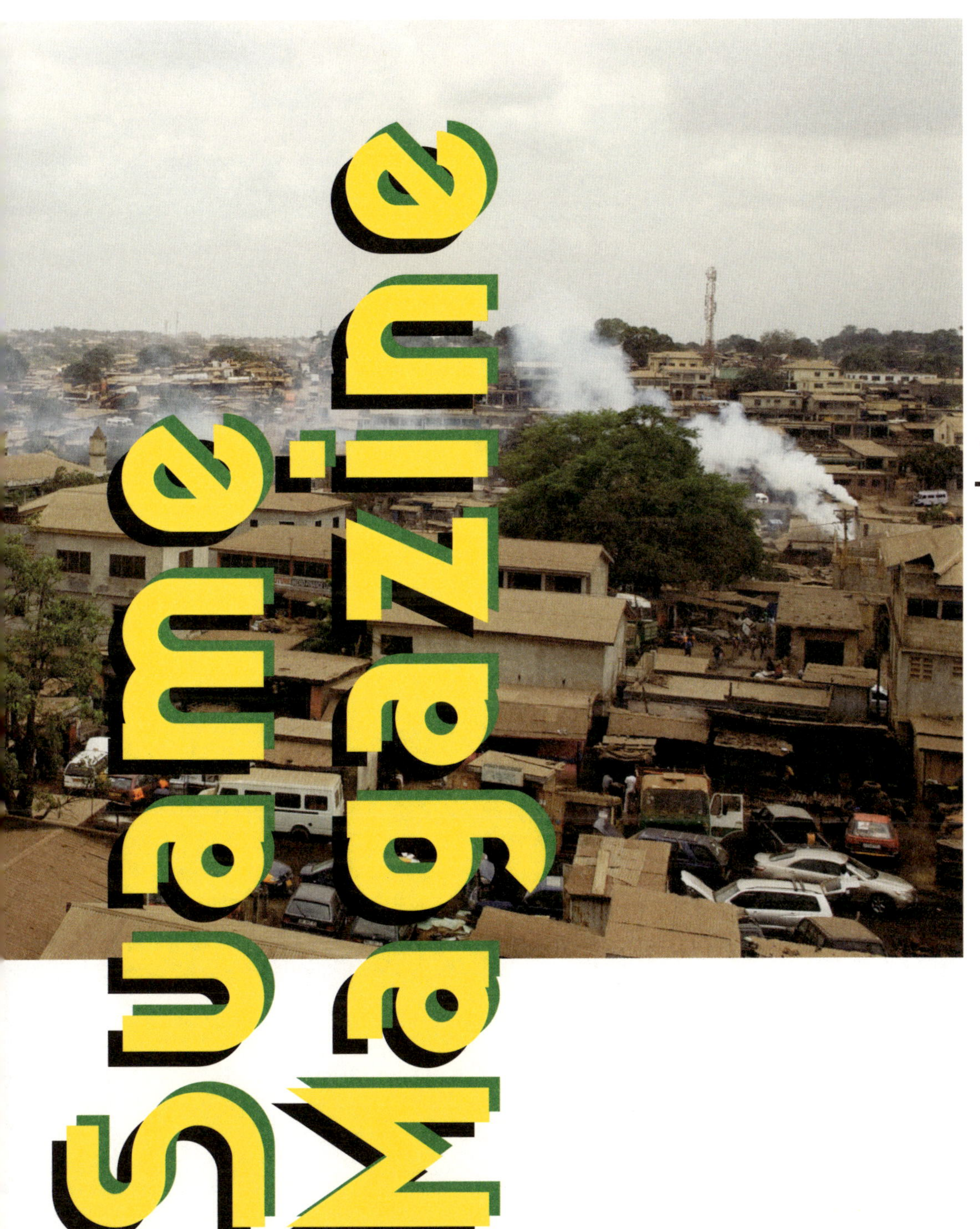

t1|19

GH // AM-12 // 02.2013

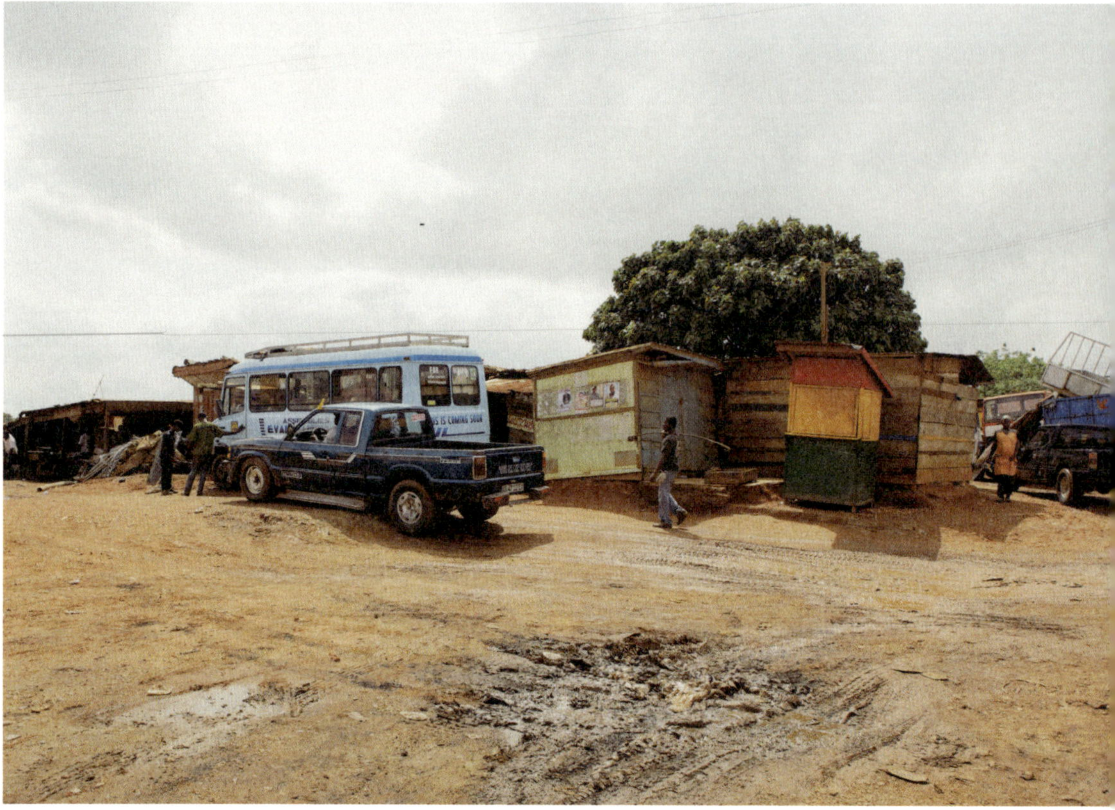

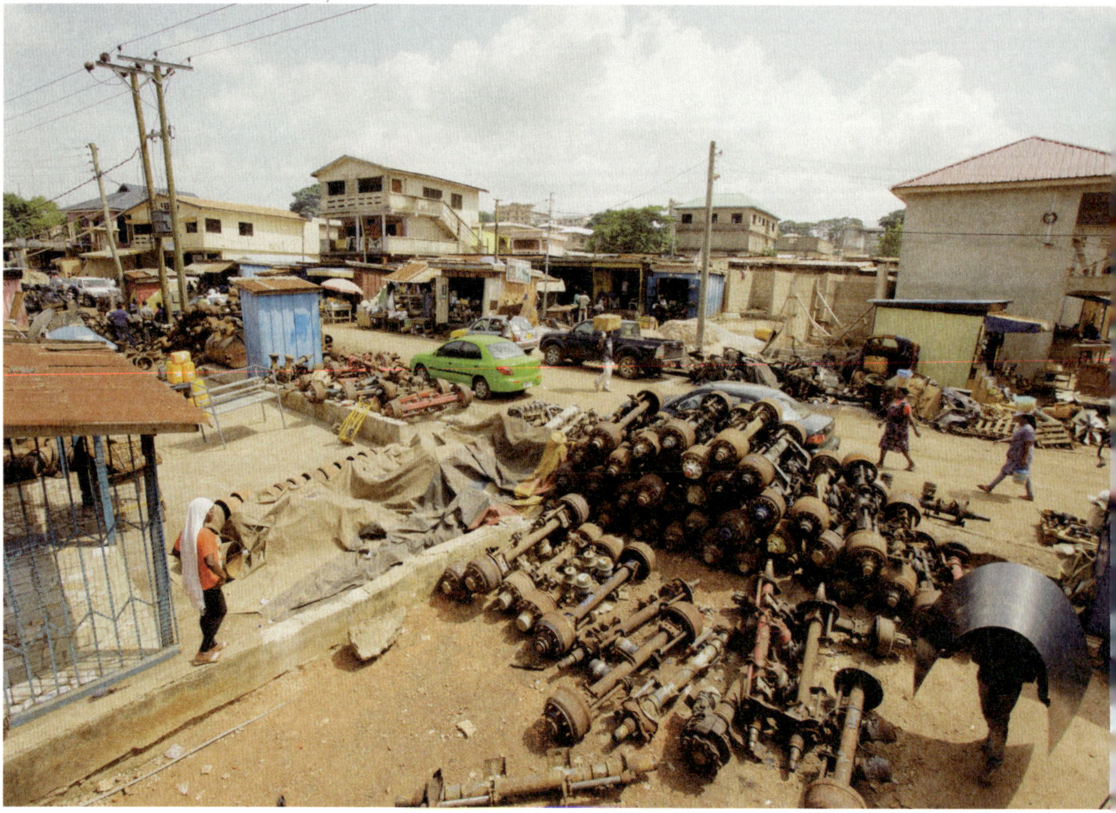

GH // NS // 04.2013
GH // AM-11 // 05.2015

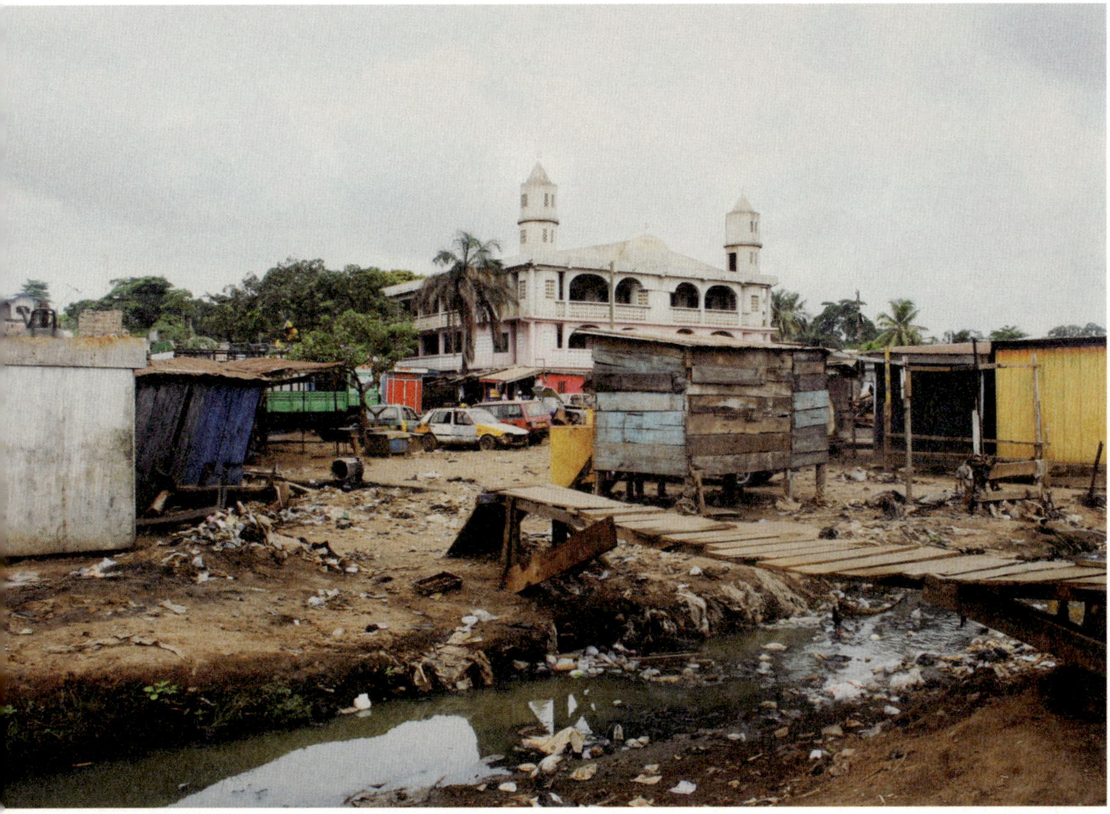

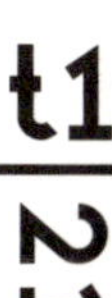

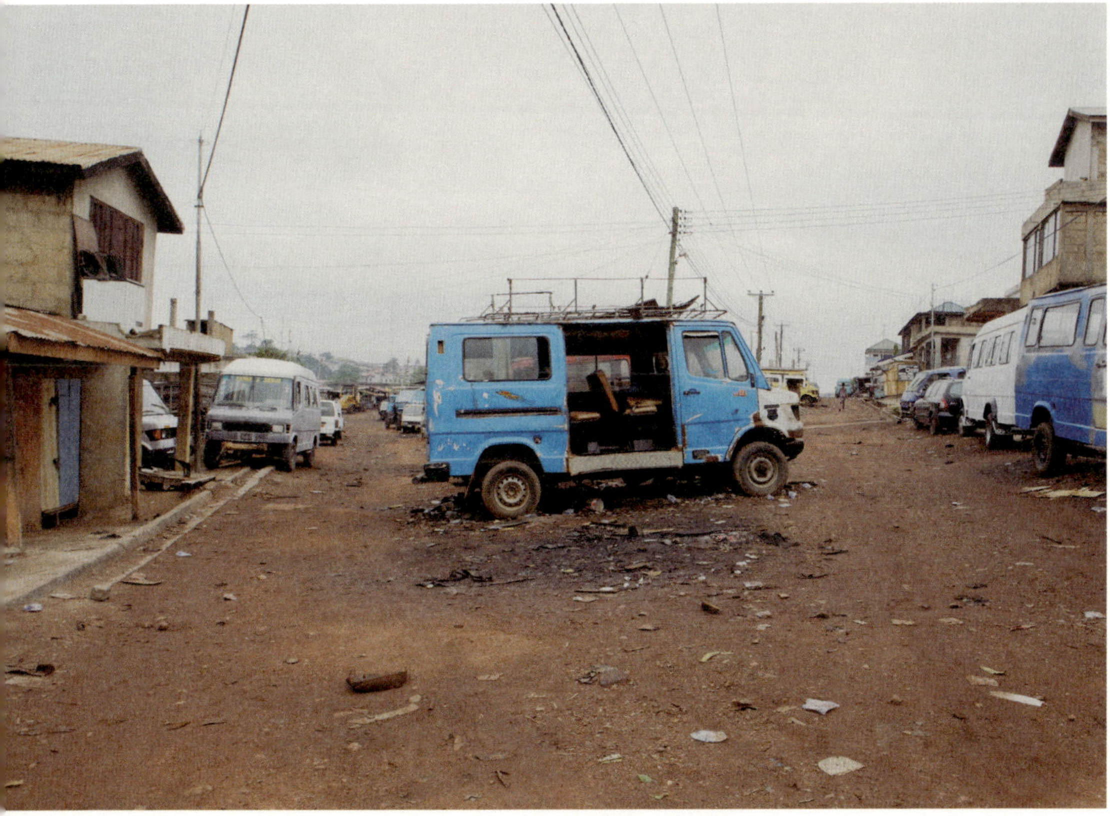

GH // AP-11 // 04.2012
GH // NS // 03.2013

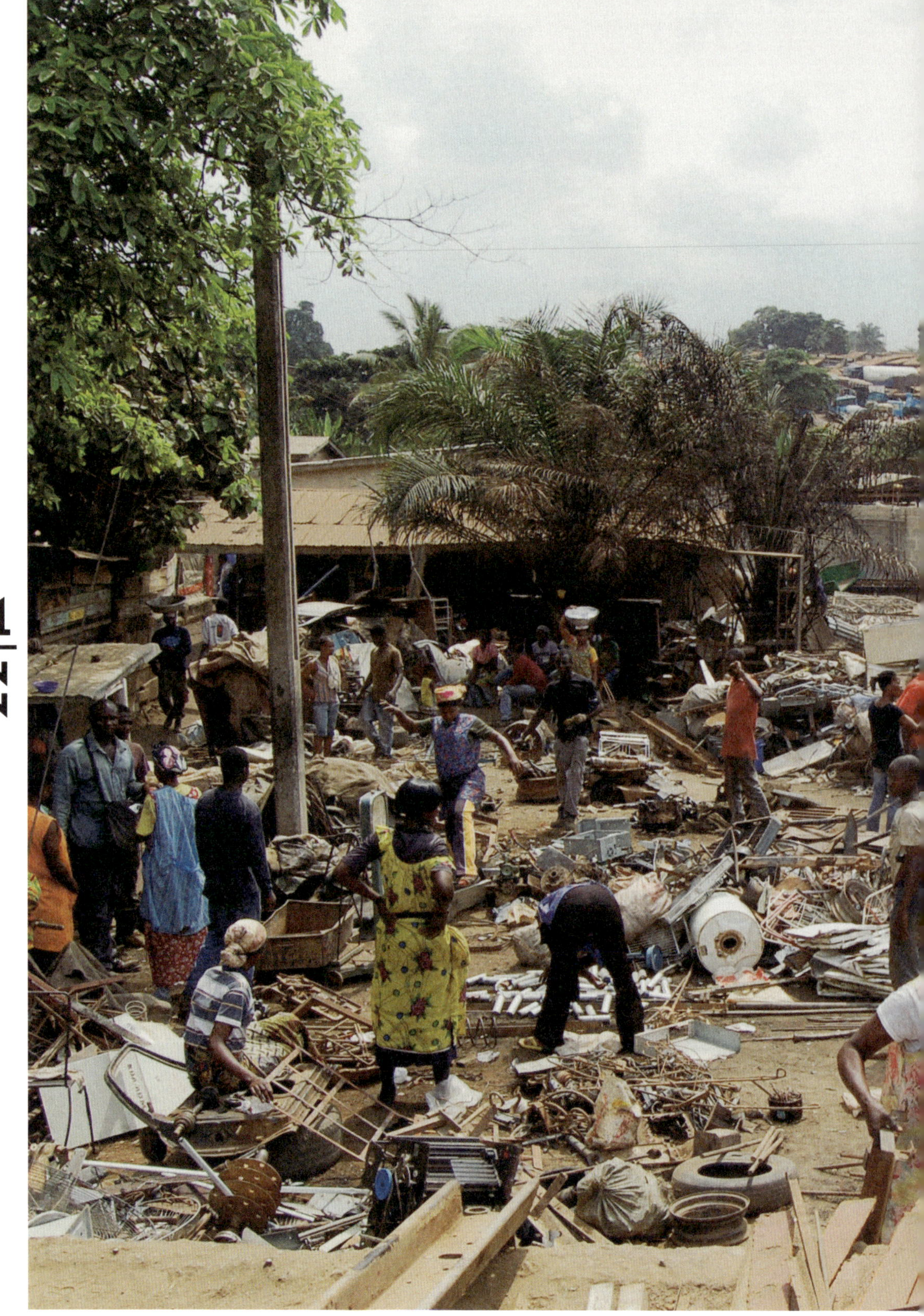

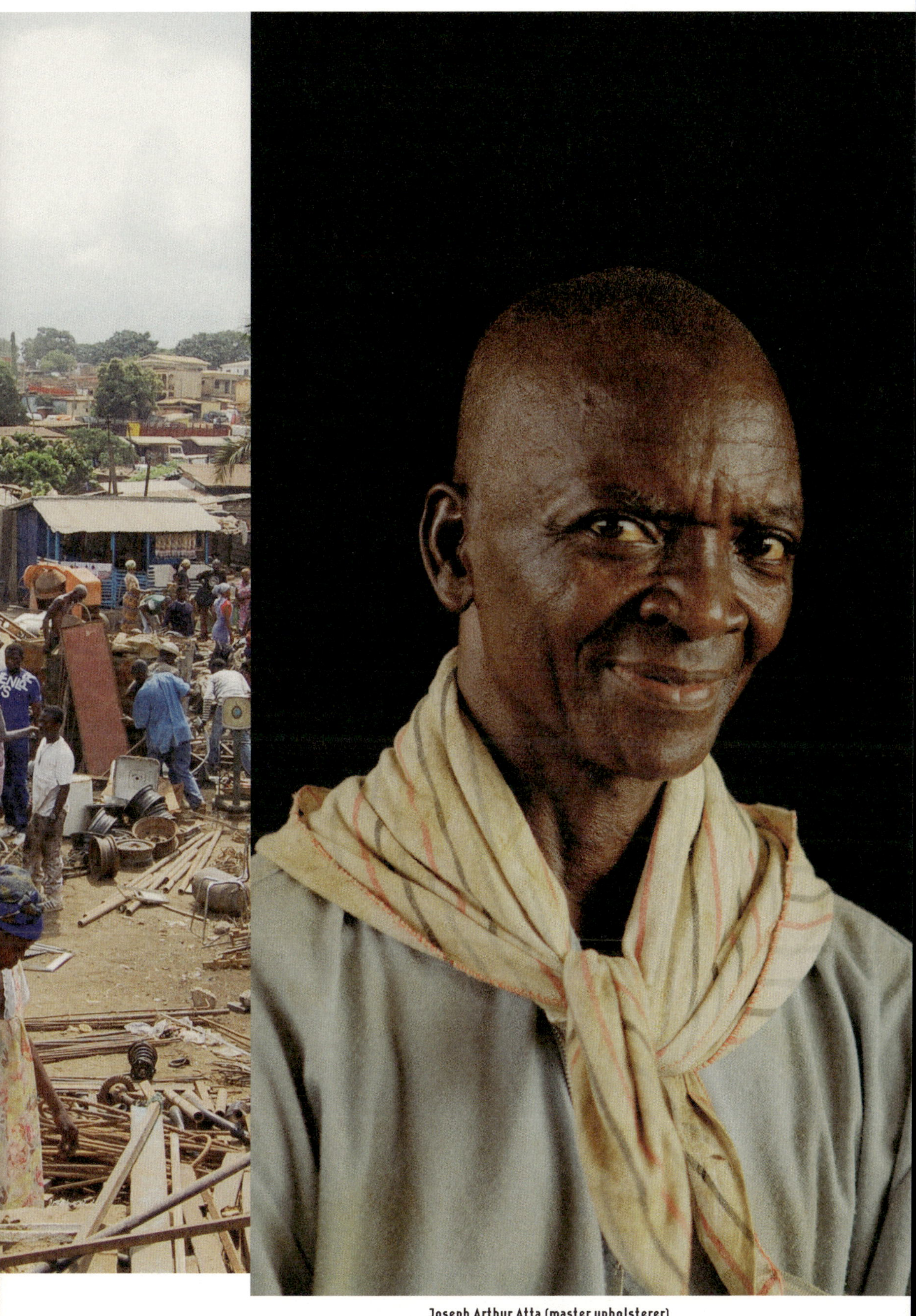

Joseph Arthur Atta (master upholsterer)

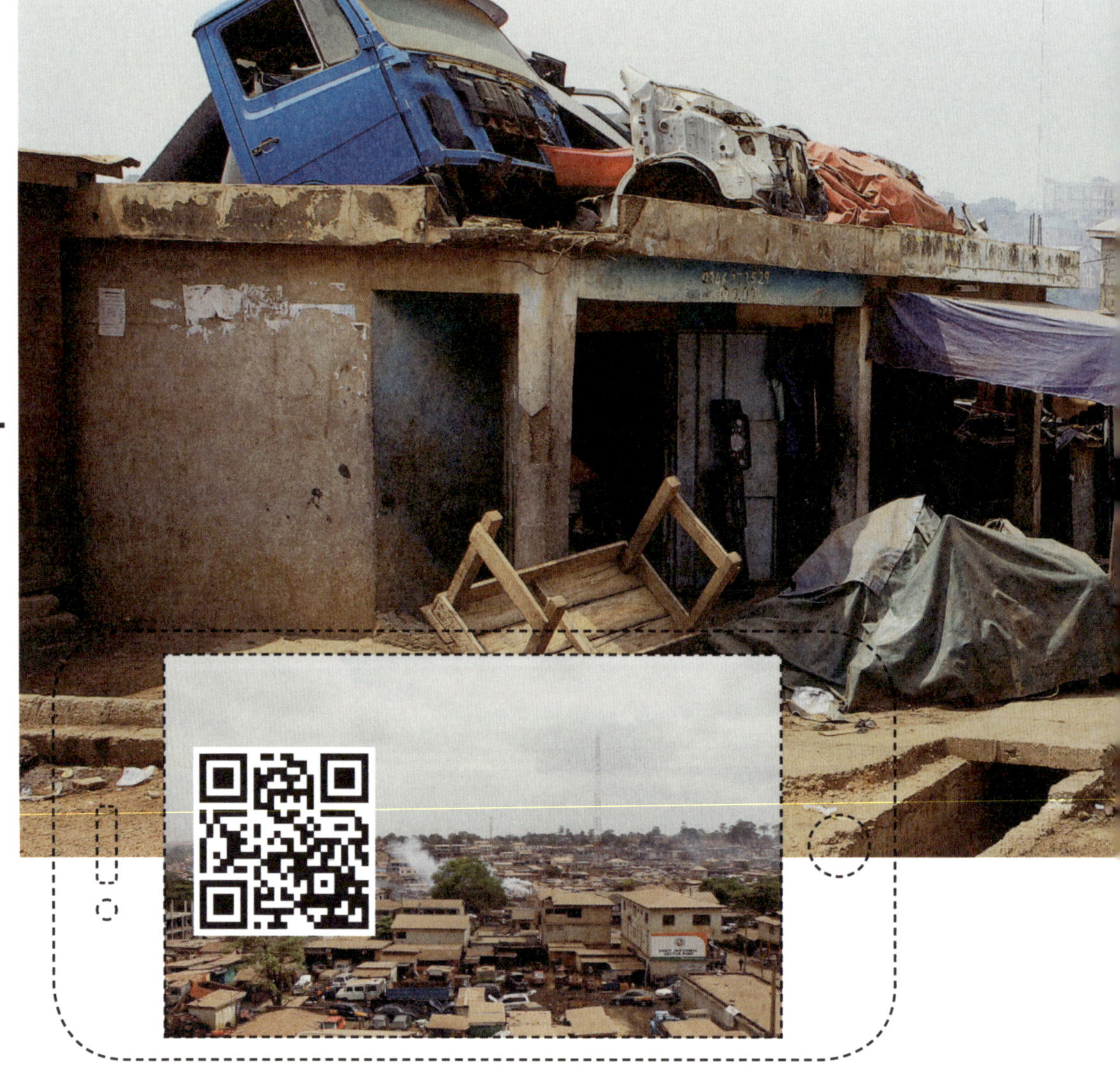

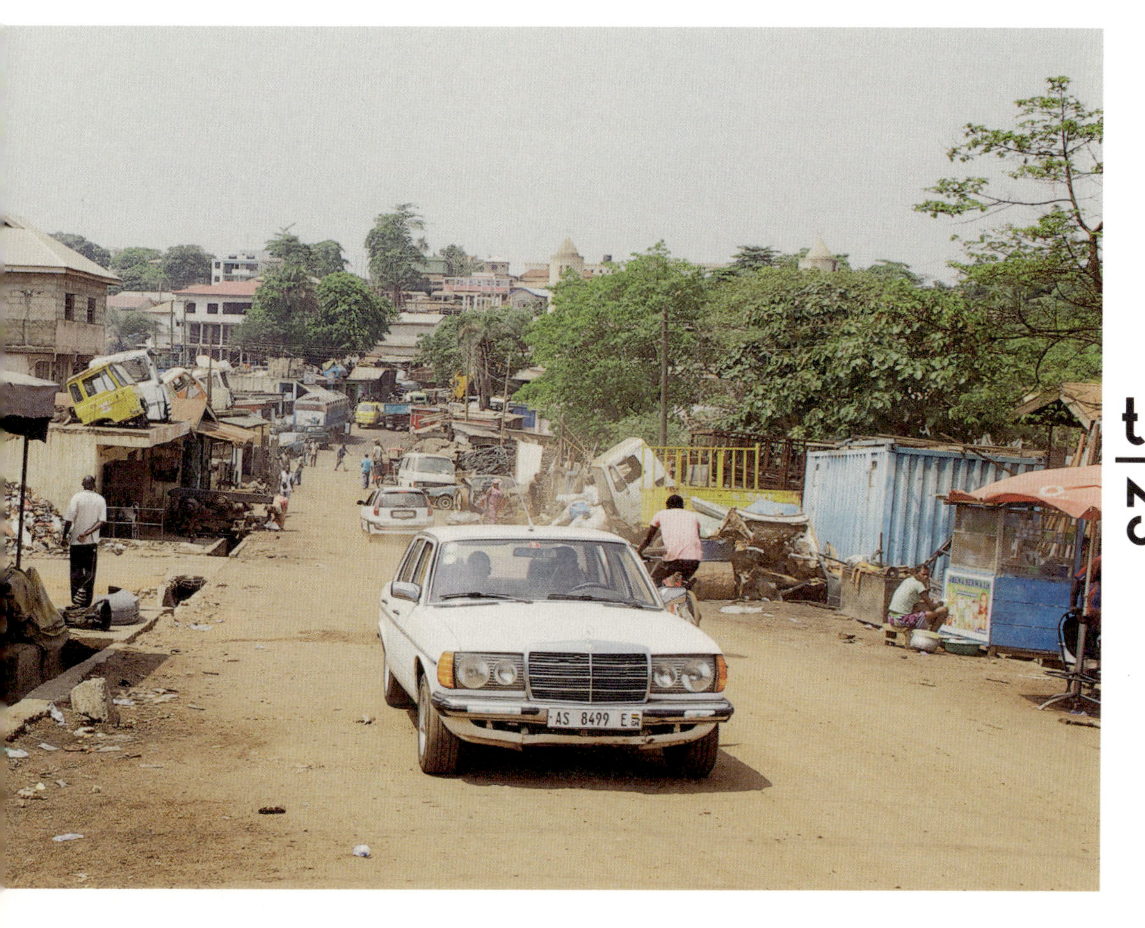
AS 8499 E

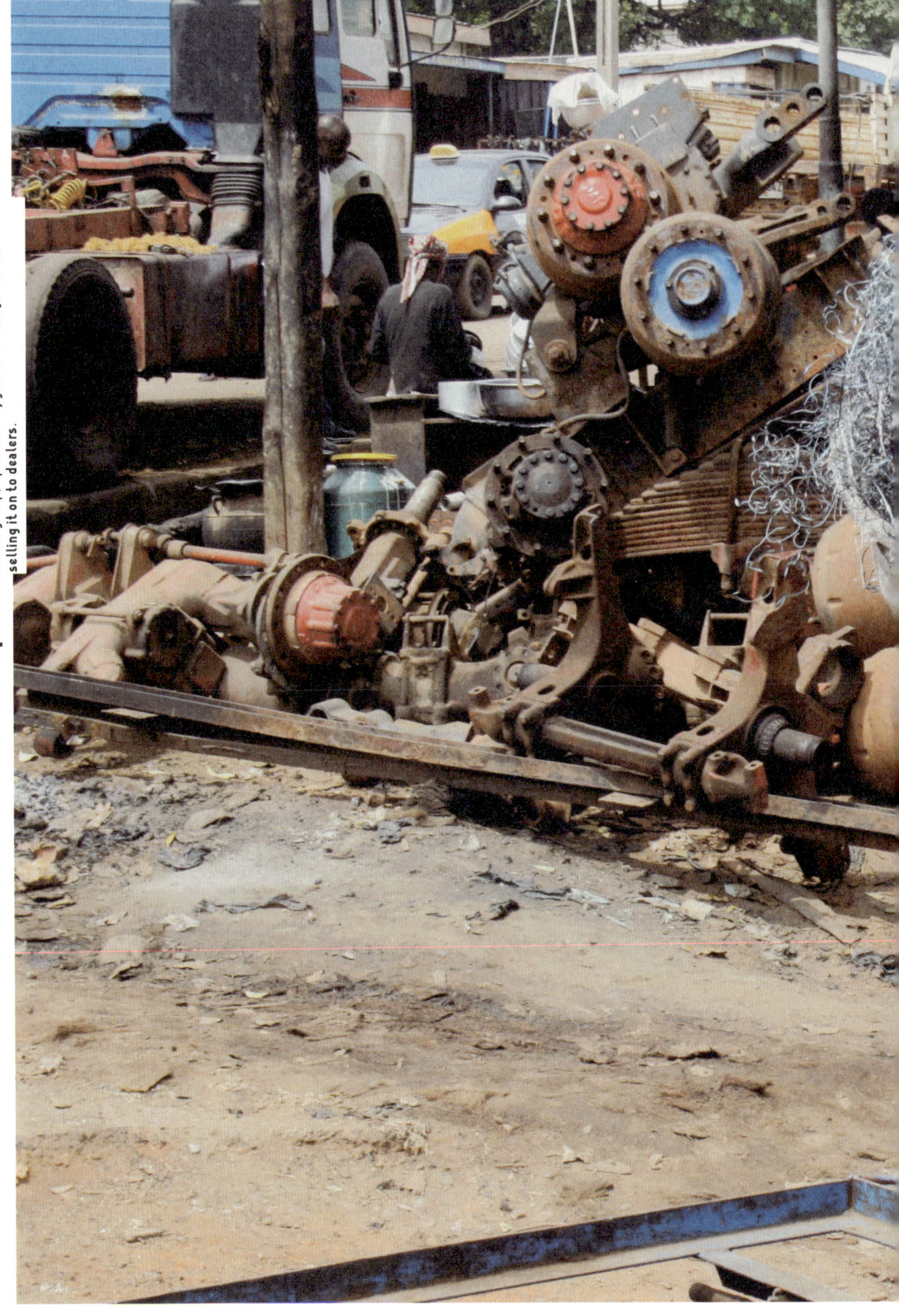

As iron is expensive in Suame Magazine, not a single sliver is wasted. Scrappers, who form a separate professional group, spend all day just collecting iron and selling it on to dealers.

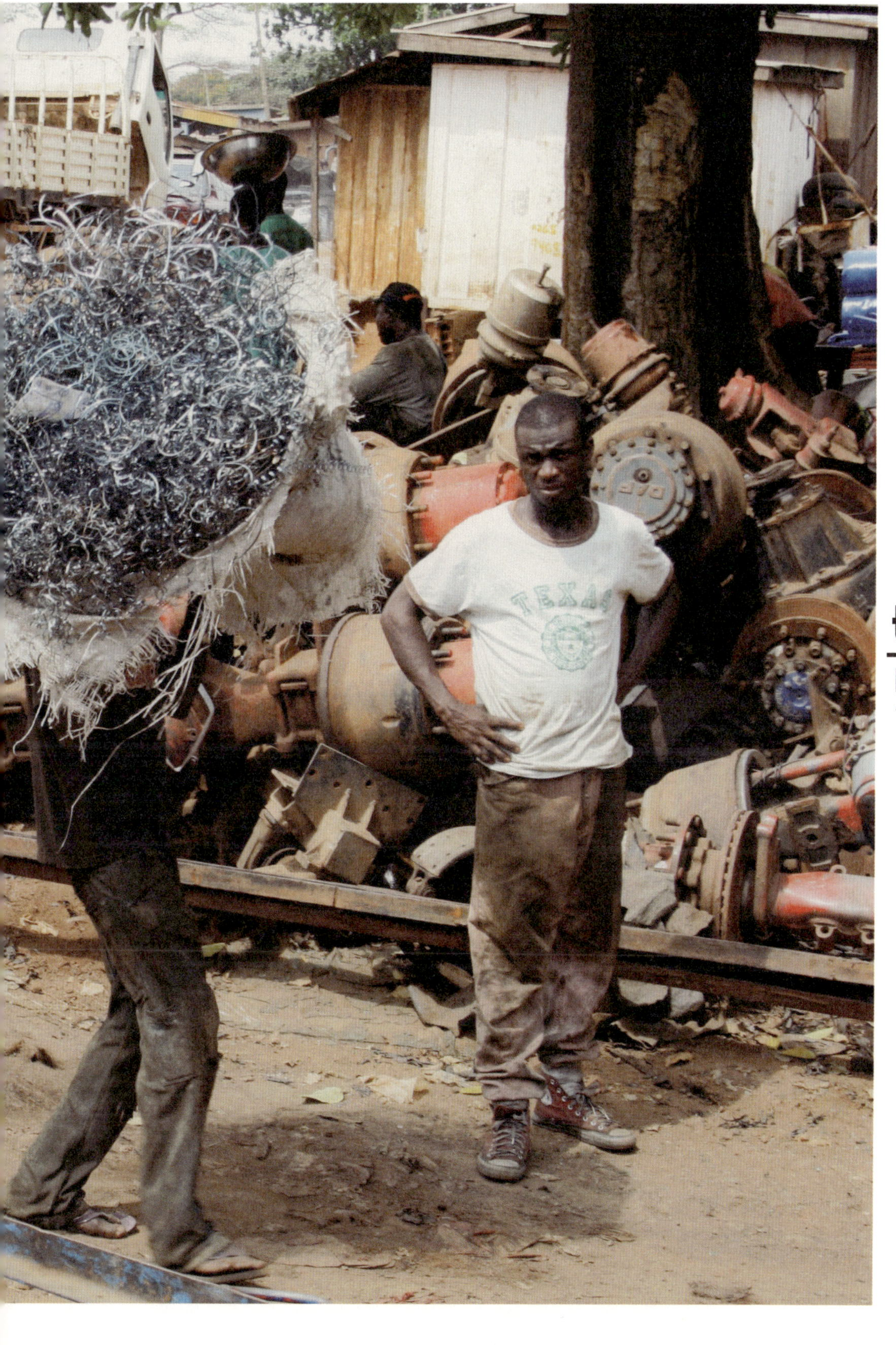
TEXAS

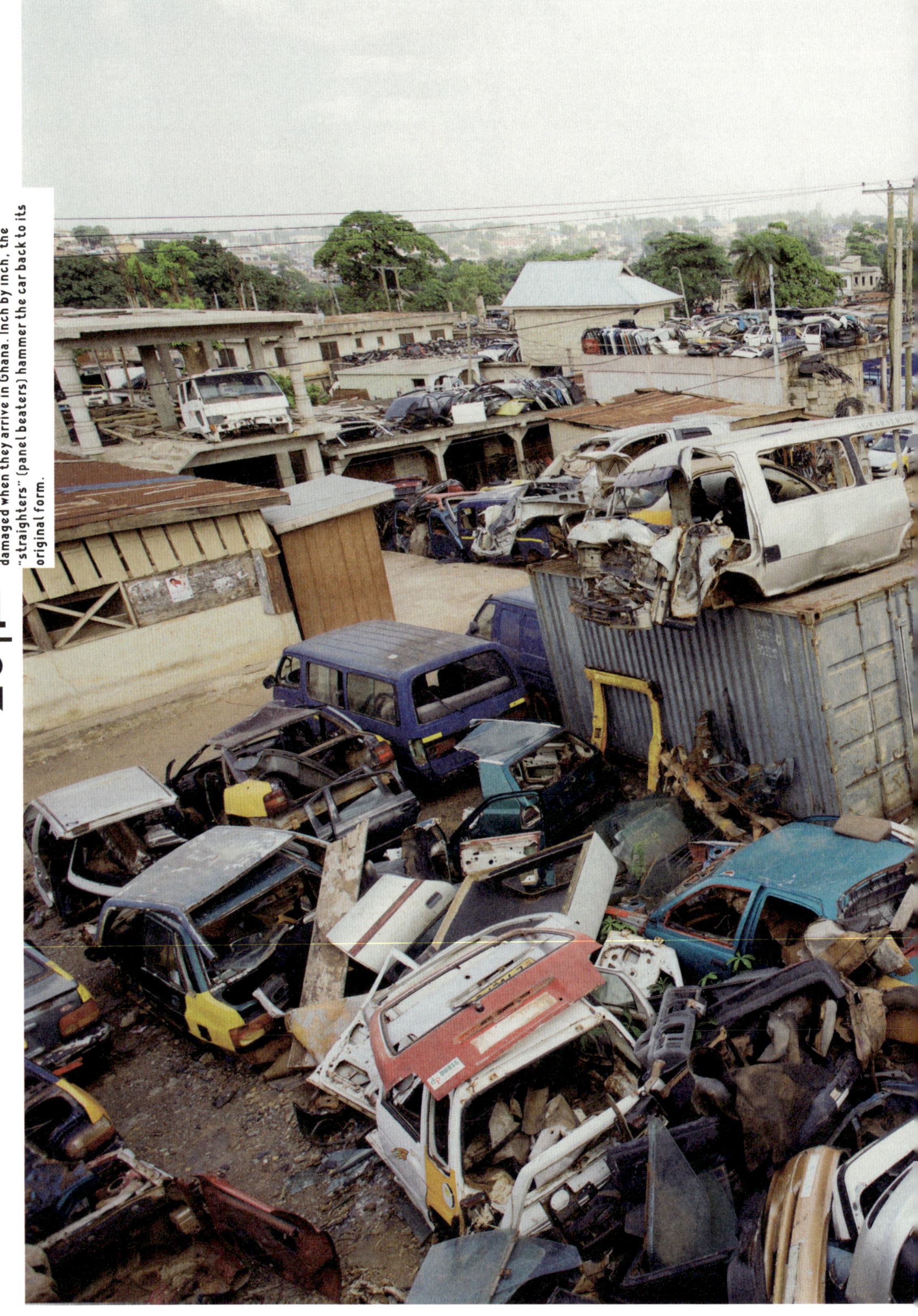

Straighter (dent removal) workshops are the most common workshops in Suame Magazine. Cars are often heavily damaged when they arrive in Ghana. Inch by inch, the "straighters" (panel beaters) hammer the car back to its original form.

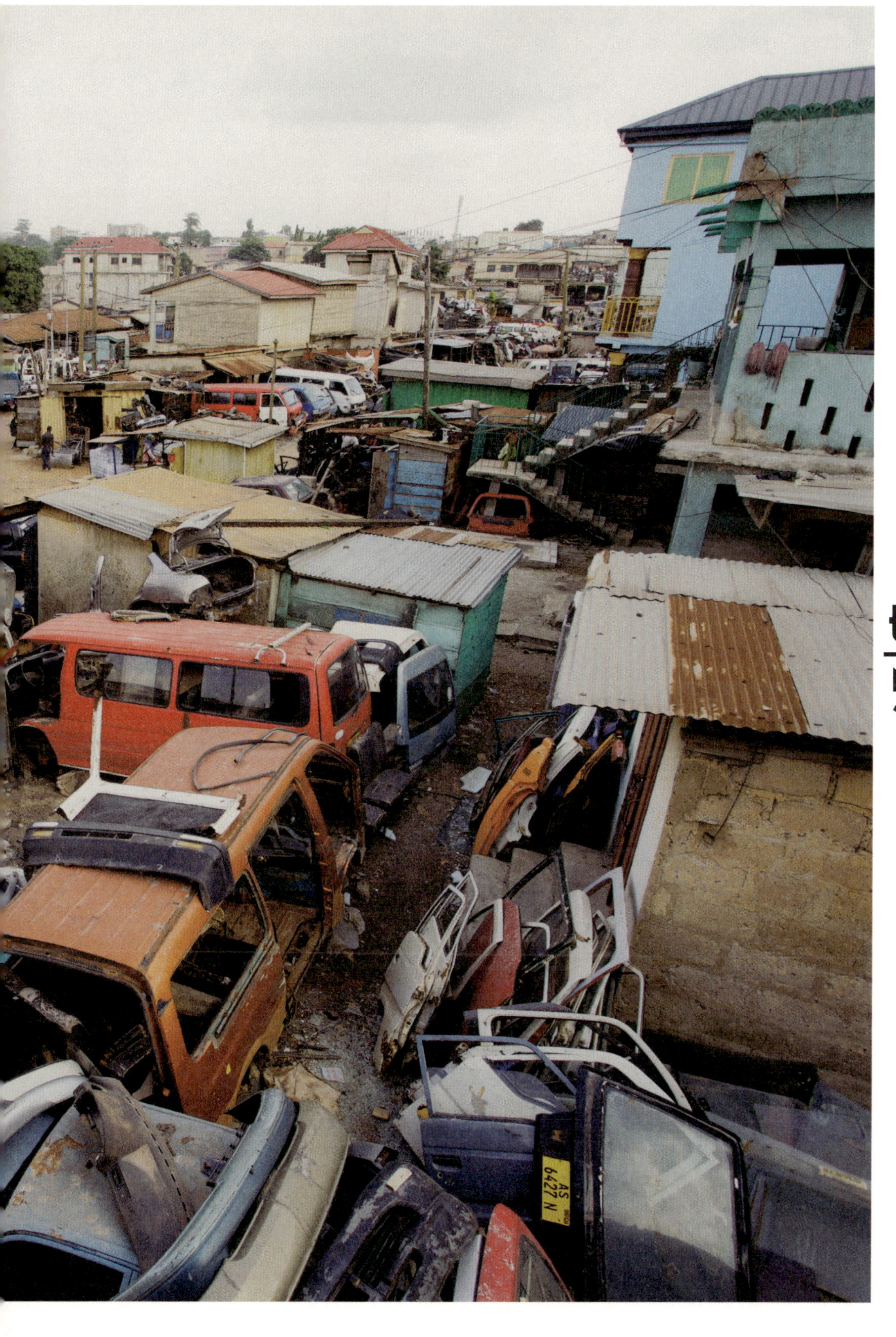
AS
6427 N

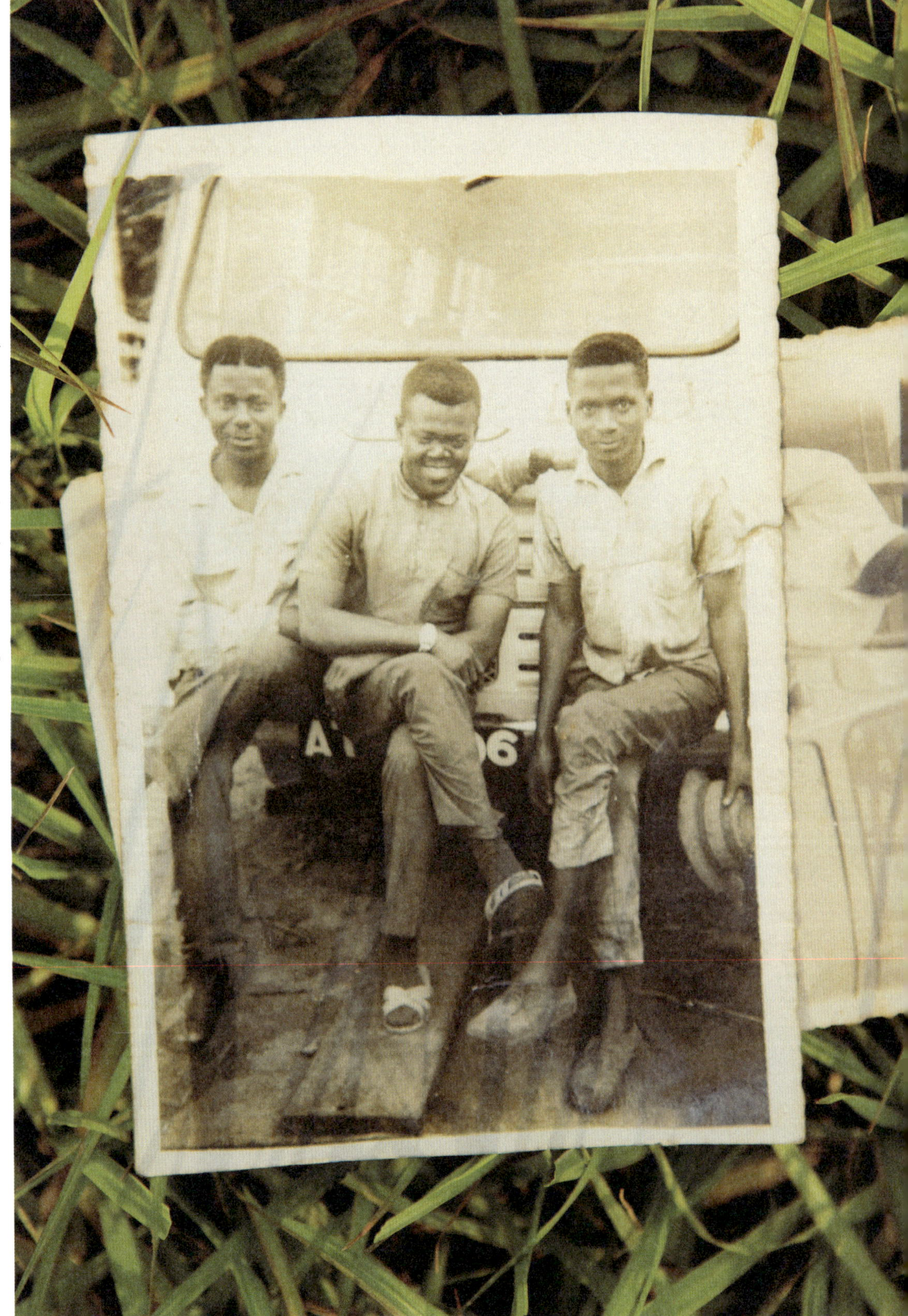

Suame Magazine has a long history: discarded cars have found their way here since the birth of the auto industry at the beginning the of the 20th century.

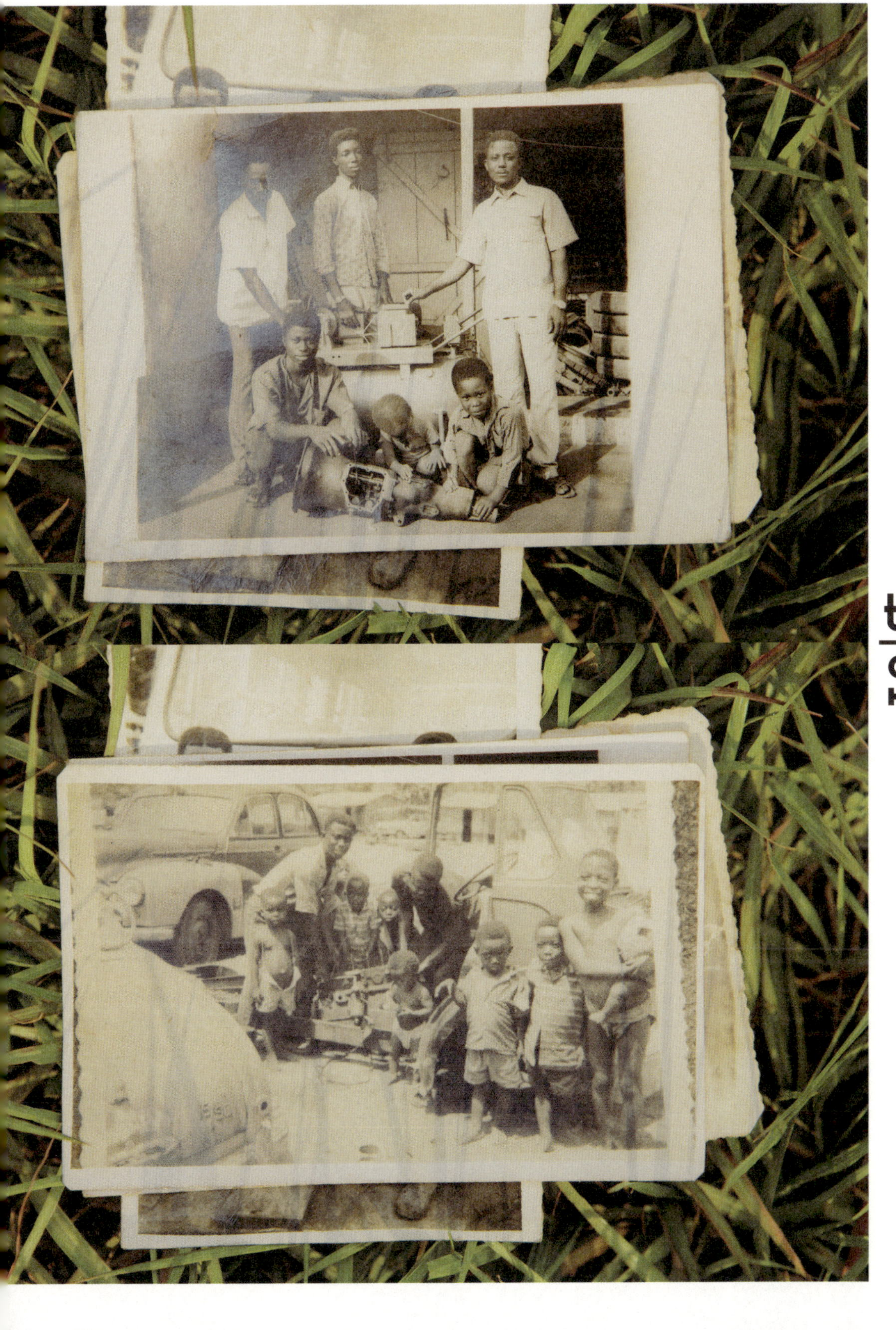

Suame Magazine is more than an industrial cluster. It is a neighbourhood where people work and live. Funerals are important social gatherings in Ghana. Every guild has its own funerary rituals. The tow-truckers' guild carries the coffin of the deceased driver to the grave with his own tow truck. The gas cutters' guild shoot carbide cannons for an entire week after a colleague is buried.

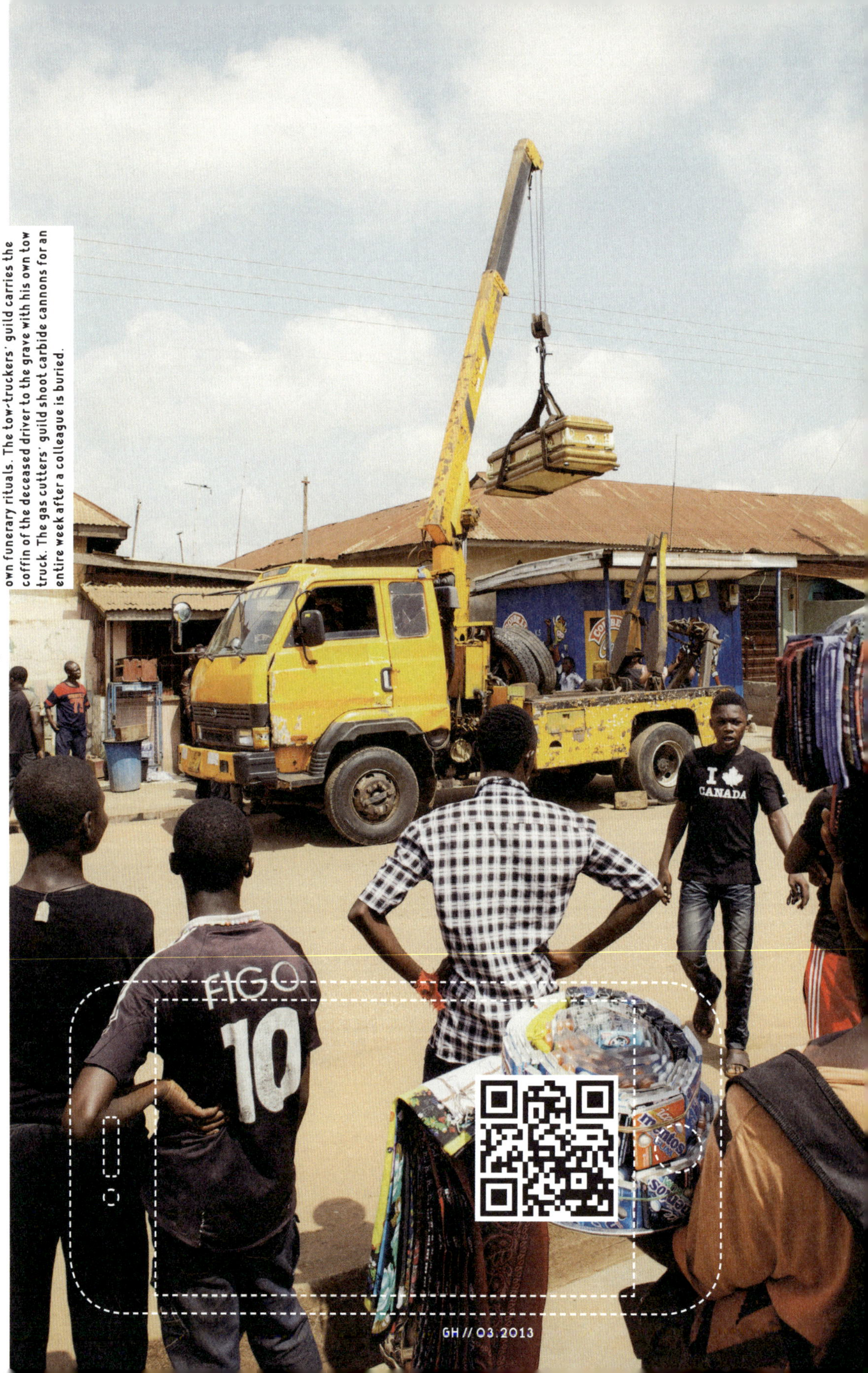

FIGO
10
I CANADA
GH // 03.2013

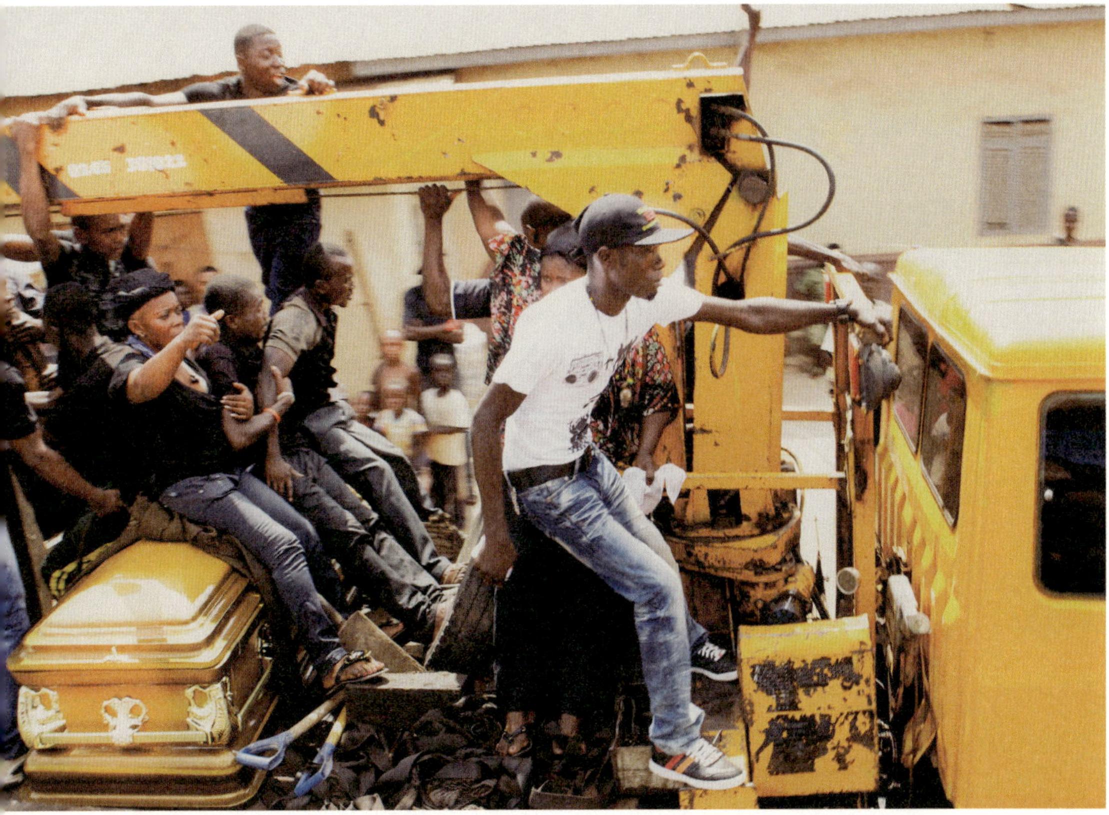

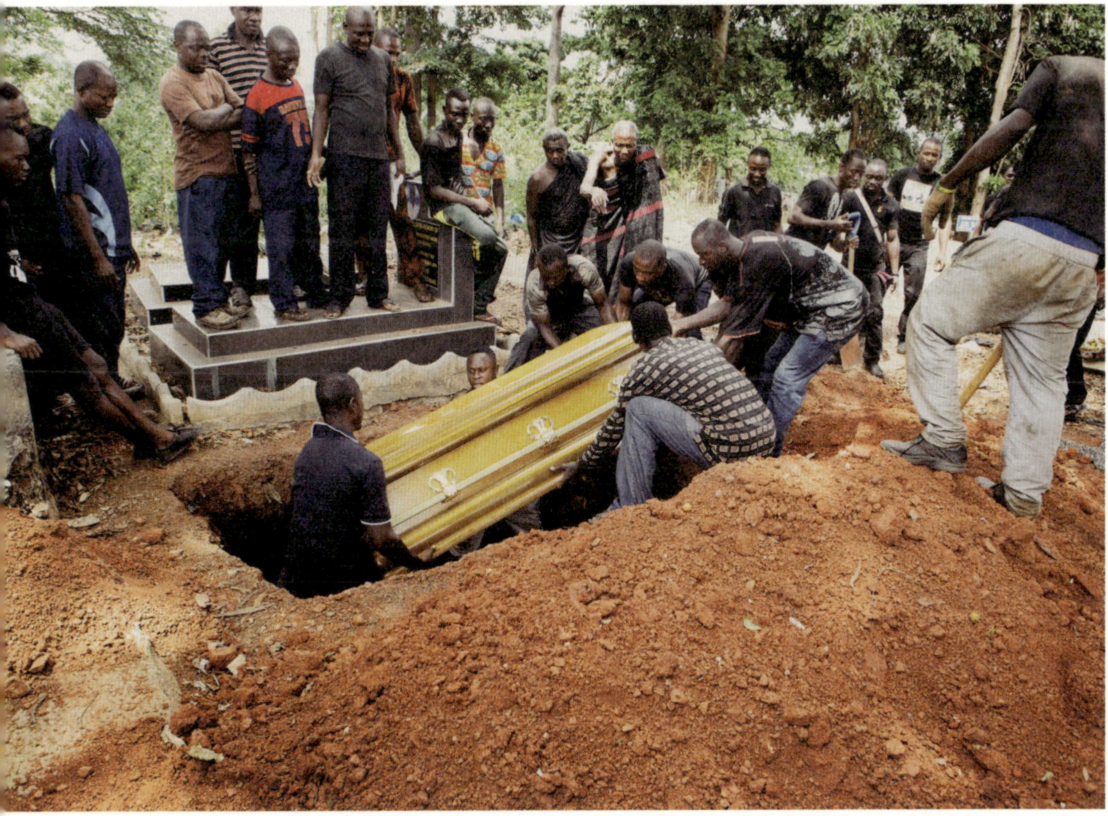

GH // 03.2013

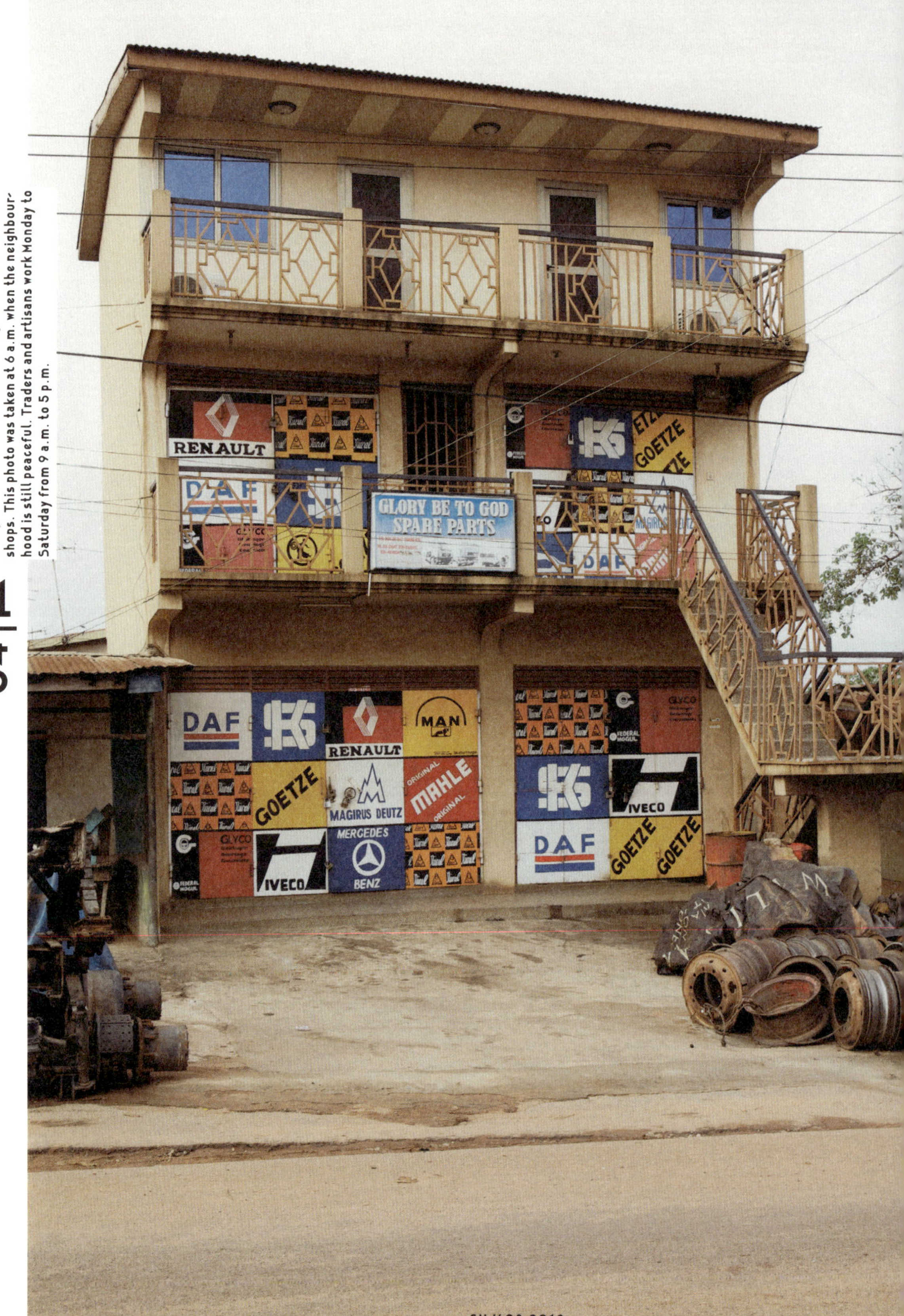

Wealthy car-part traders have built concrete warehouses along the main roads. These buildings are also used as shops. This photo was taken at 6 a.m. when the neighbourhood is still peaceful. Traders and artisans work Monday to Saturday from 9 a.m. to 5 p.m.

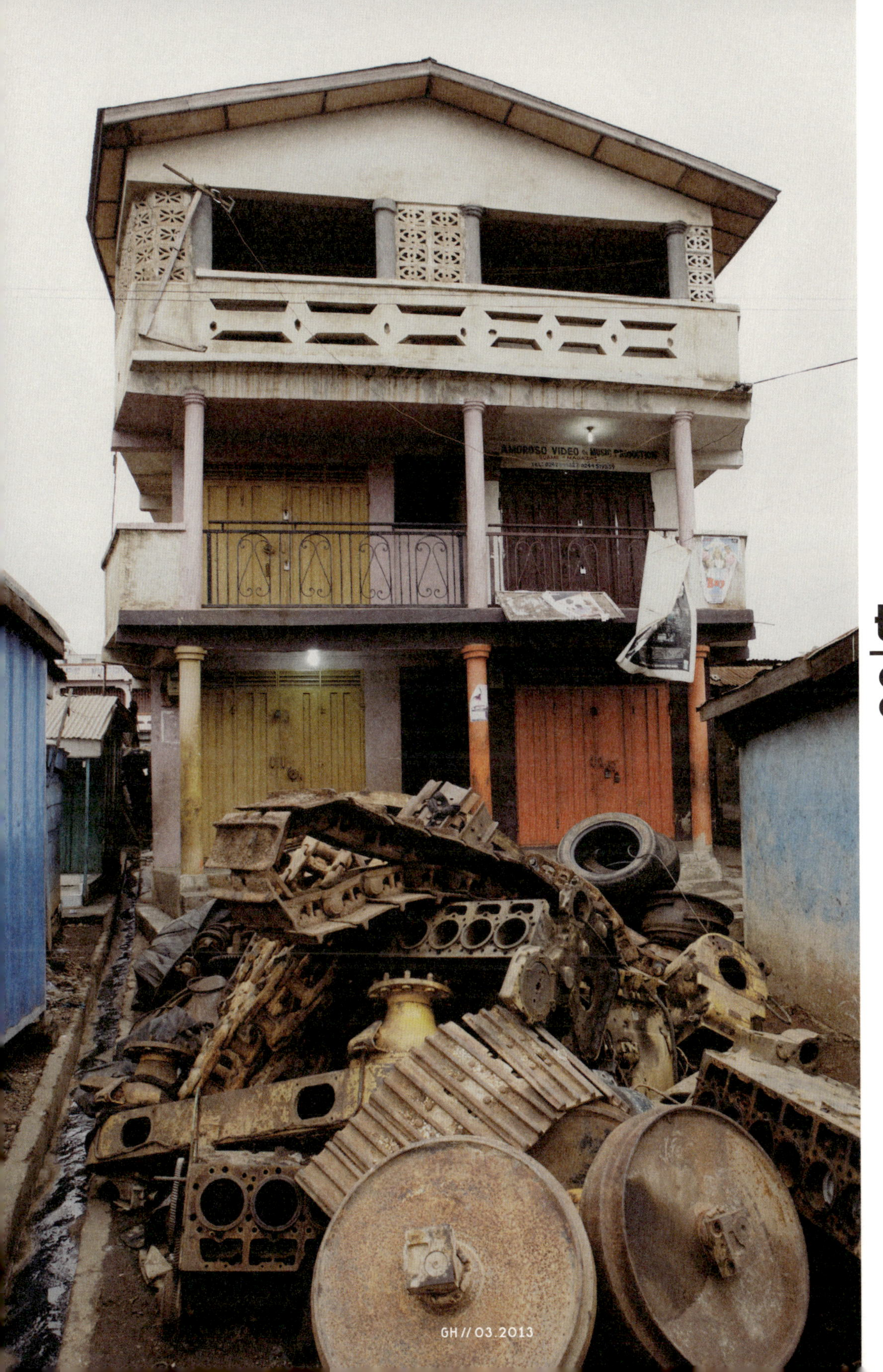

GH // 03.2013

Shops display their goods on the street. Smaller parts are brought out every morning, while larger parts are kept outside and concealed under a tarpaulin outside working hours.

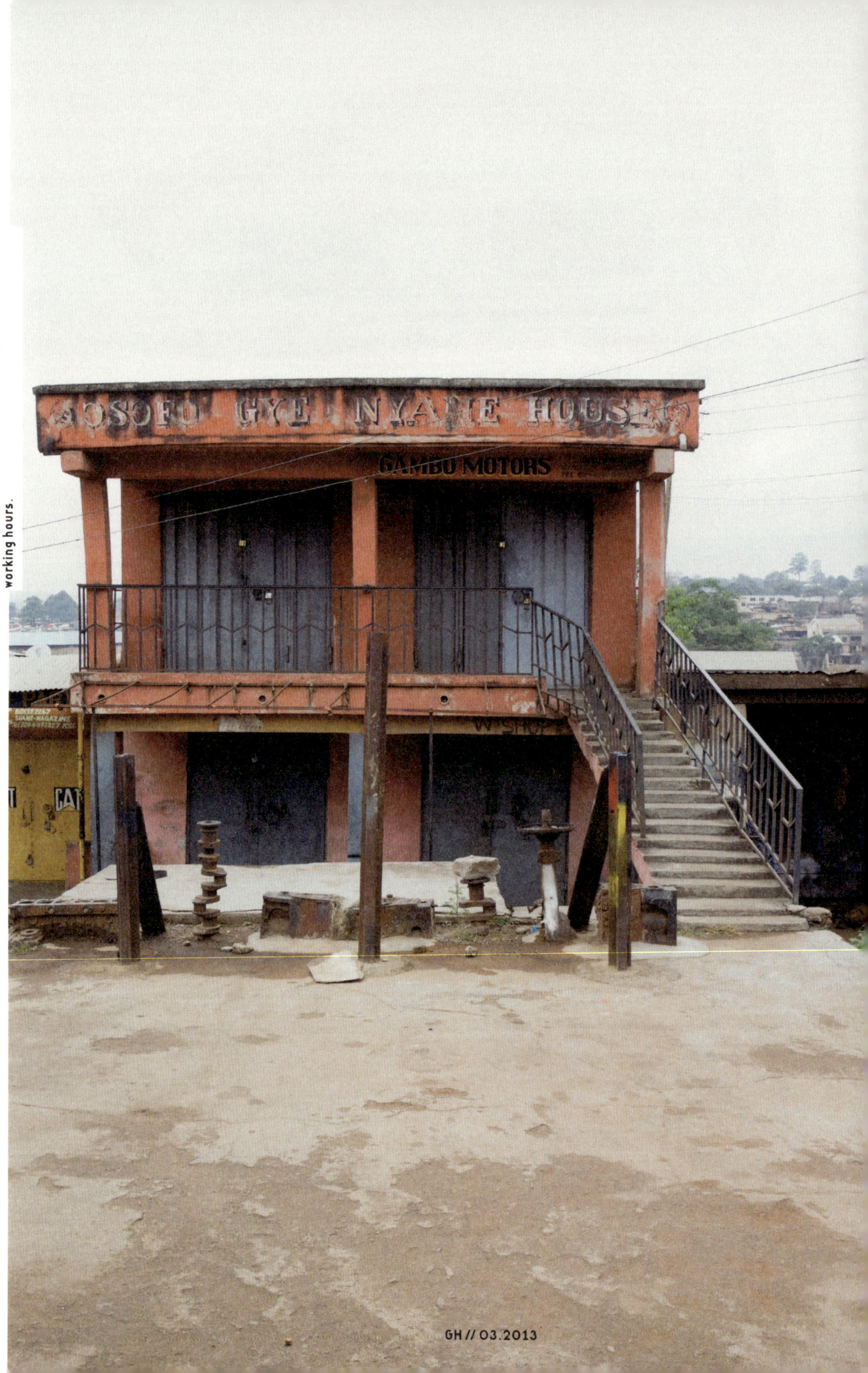

GH // 03.2013

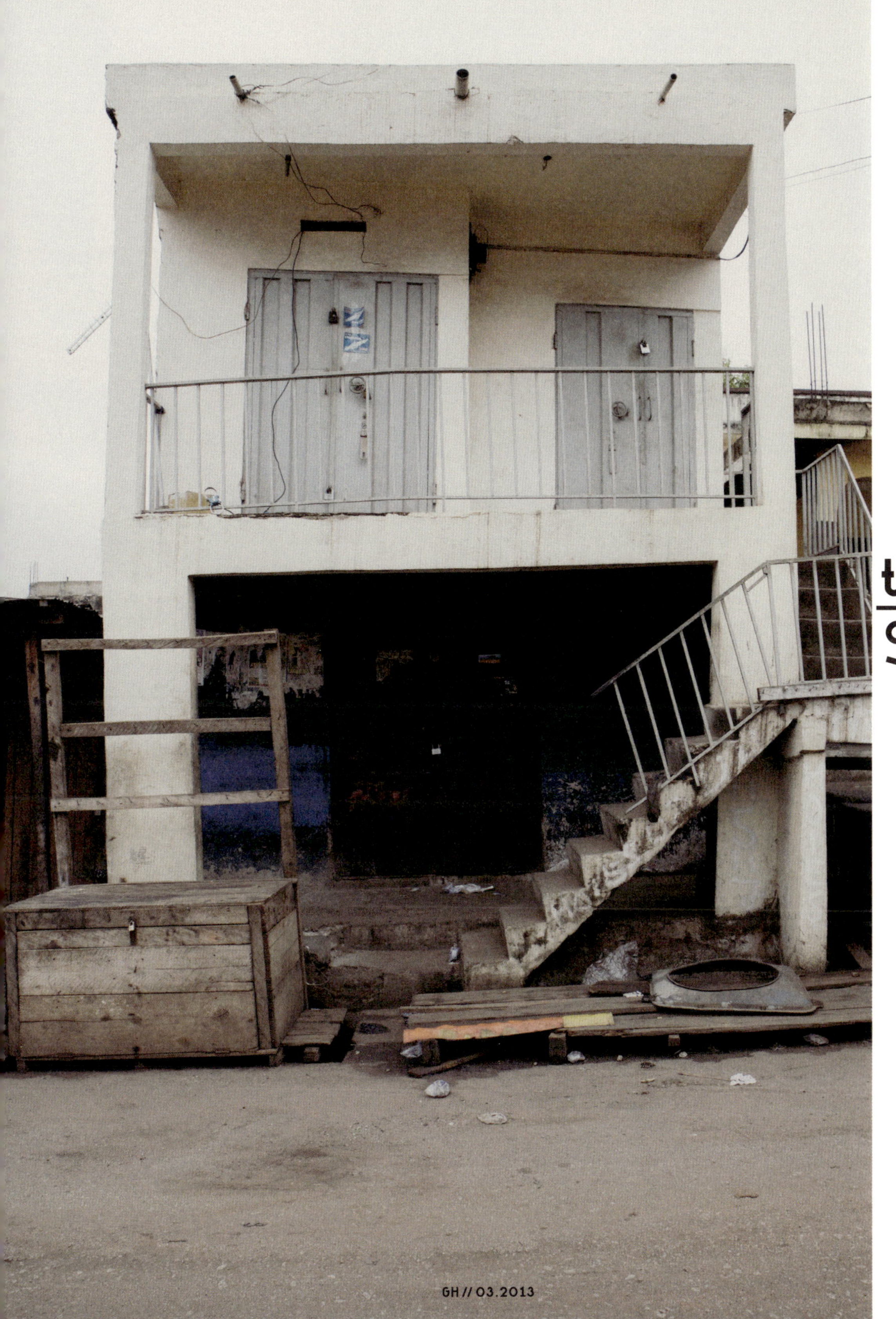

GH // 03.2013

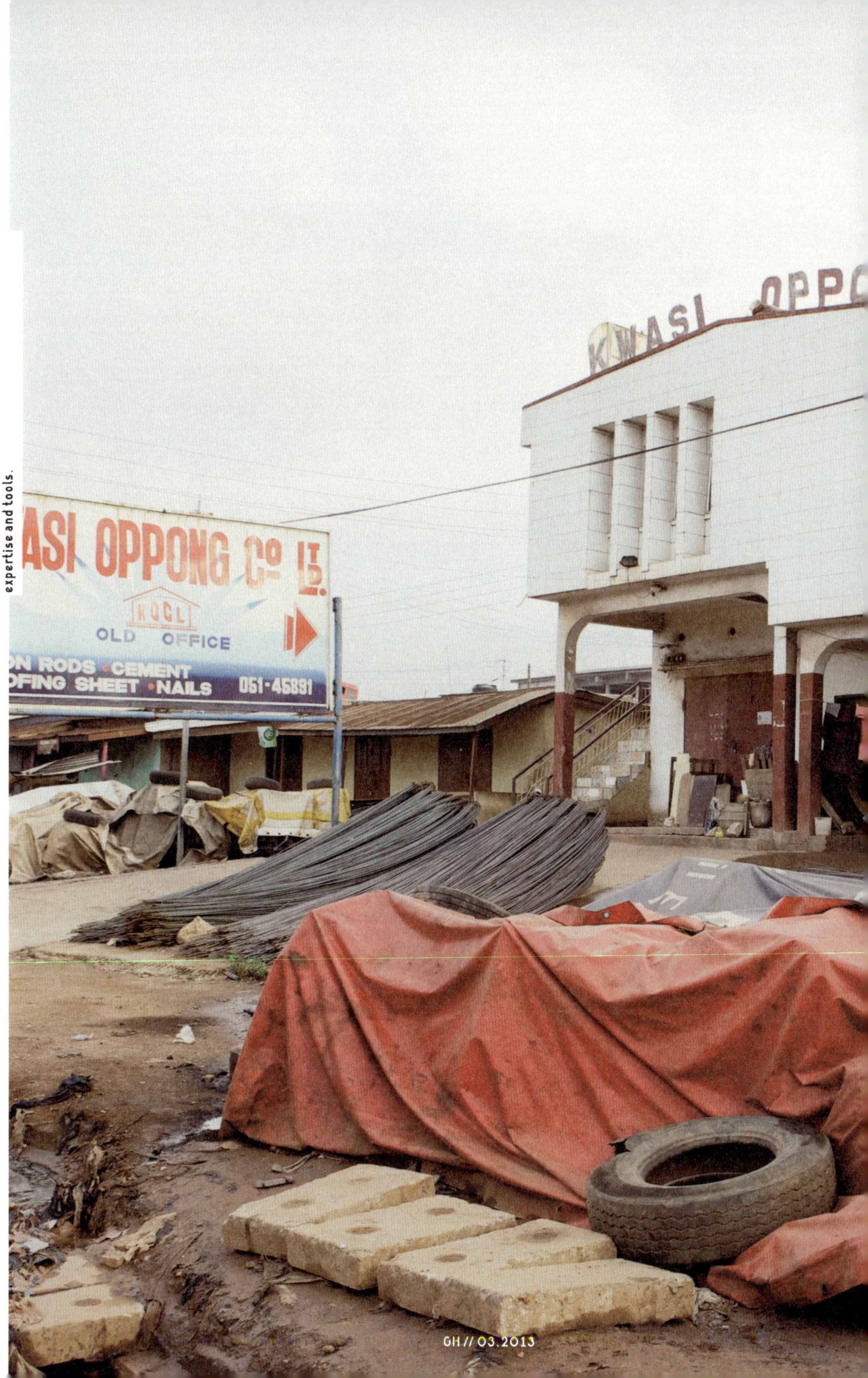

Suame Magazine is divided into clusters that function like villages. Every cluster is a unit where different workshops work closely together by using each other's expertise and tools.

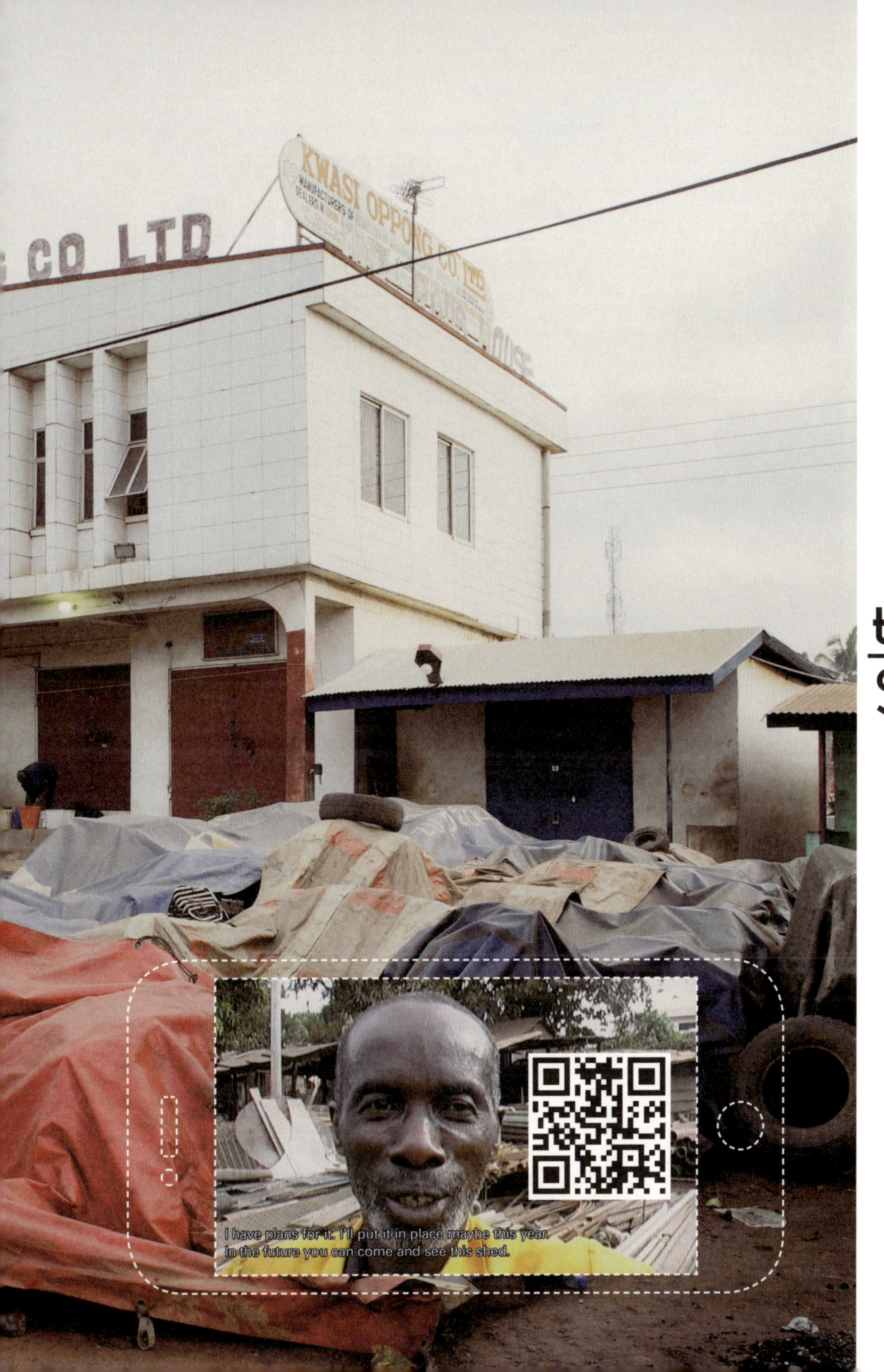
CO LTD
KWASI OPPONG CO LTD
MANUFACTURERS OF
DEALERS IN
I have plans for it. I'll put it in place maybe this year.
In the future you can come and see this shed.

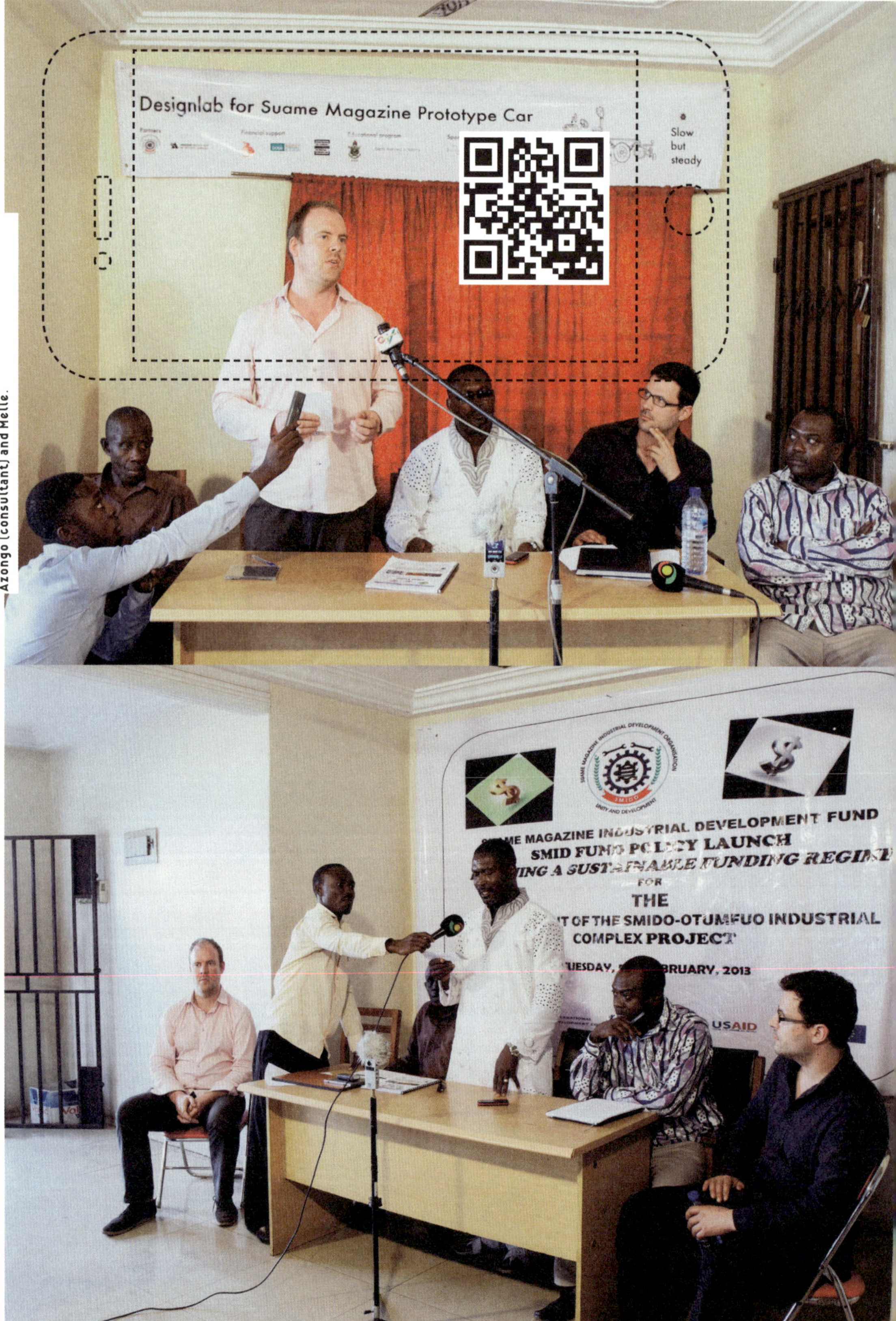

Press conference at the SMIDO headquarters.
BL: From left to right: Joost, reporter, Charles (SMIDO vice-president), George (SMIDO president), Azongo (consultant) and Melle.

GH // 02.2013

setting up shop

27 January 2013. When we left Accra the windows were still clean. Now, eight hours and 300 km further, they are covered in a thick layer of ochre-coloured dust. Our VIP bus with white fake-leather seats is on its way to Kumasi. The seats have all been tilted back into reclining position. This suggests great comfort, but in reality it means we slip off the shiny faux leather at every pothole in the road. We are a bit nervous about what awaits us; in fact, we don't know whether anything awaits us at all.

Joost is optimistic. Why wouldn't they turn up? We spoke to Azongo, the consultant, just yesterday. He told us he would not be able to make it, but that he would send a welcoming committee. Teun is not convinced. He is also worried, as his expensive lighting equipment is down in the luggage compartment. This will be crucial for his work as a photographer over the coming months. Every time the bus stops, which is quite often, Teun is glued to the window to make sure that no one takes off with his bags.

When you look out of the window, it is hard to tell whether we are driving through town or not. The roads are crammed with old vans that have been converted into taxis. Many of the trucks we pass look like zeppelins, lashed with ropes and tarpaulins to make sure everything stays in place. The cars spew black clouds over the ochre-yellow roads, leaving us in a permanent sandstorm. Along the road, an endless strip of market stalls. It feels like we are driving through a supermarket in motorised shopping trolleys. The lady in the seat in front of us is from Amsterdam and has been giving us tips and directions. She knows Ghana and is here on a family visit. She is a bit worried about us. Why are you going to Suame Magazine? It is a dirty industrial zone. Nothing but poor people, stench, lots of car wrecks and it is dangerous to boot. You have to be careful, this is Africa.

The bus station is a dusty open space, teeming with people and trotro buses (the local means of public transport in Kumasi). As soon as the bus comes to a standstill, a group of young men swoop down on the luggage compartment and start dragging out bags. Teun rushes down and shouts at them as he tries to pull his bags out of their hands. But they are not planning to let go. "Give me money, I carry for you!" Suddenly a man appears next to Teun who chases all the boys away with a single roar. Then he turns to us with a broad grin and says: "Hello and welcome!" More men join him, all dressed in ironed shirts and trousers. It is only then that we recognise Philip in the man who was just shouting so loudly. He represents Suame Magazine's electricians' guild. Soon after, he is joined by Dr Waco, Paha and Charles Taylor.

We last saw each other nine months ago when we came to Kumasi to find a local partner for our action research. At the time, everyone was wearing overalls, but today is Sunday and they have all just been to church so they are dressed to the nines. Three cars are waiting to accompany us. Joost notices that Dr Waco is driving a Mercedes, exactly the same model that he drives in the Netherlands. Not that Joost knows the first thing about car engineering; to him driving this kind of old-timer is all about the "cruising", the joy of rolling down the road like a ship at sea. Dr Waco is happy to have a Mercedes-enthusiast beside him. He proudly tells us that he has already kept this vehicle on the road for 20 years. But it is increasingly difficult to find spare parts. Does Joost also have such trouble finding parts for the gearbox? Joost hesitates. Should he already now admit that he barely knows how to open the bonnet?

According to good Ghanaian tradition, we first head to a restaurant. We are seated at a Coca-Cola table under a large awning. The waiters serve us large platters of fish. "Please eat!" says Dr Waco. The whole group looks on as we try to eat the fish with our hands. Charles Taylor gives us instructions. He is well into his seventies, but as the president of the Mechanics Association, he is used to bossing people around. He urges Melle to try the banku, which is the Ghanaian equivalent of chips and a favourite among the mechanics. It is made of plantain, cassava or other tubers that are first beaten into a mush. The chewing gum-like mass of dough is then left to ferment for a few days in a banana leaf to make banku. It is an excellent remedy against hunger as it continues to ferment in your stomach.

After the meal, the chairs are rearranged in a kind of law court set-up. Charles Taylor is the judge, with representatives on both sides beside him. Philip explains that this is when we are expected to announce our mission, the official welcome. Charles ceremoniously asks whether the head of mission can step forward. Joost and Melle look at each other. Who is the boss here? After 35 years of friendship, it does not take many words. Joost is the head of mission, Melle says solemnly. Joost gets up and uses the Coke table as a lectern.

Less than a year before, in April 2012, we had drawn up a memorandum of understanding, a list of agreements between the Suame Magazine Industrial Development Organization (SMIDO) and our Stichting Aardschap. That was when we had travelled down to Kumasi to visit the industrial zone, hoping to find a local party who would want to build a car with us.
Our first impressions had been rather overwhelming. We had gotten out of the taxi at the centrally located Post Office, a landmark in this neighbourhood where roads have no name and there are no facades to put street numbers on. Banks, churches and government buildings are the beacons by which you navigate through town. The Post Office area looks down over a sea of corrugated-iron sheets. An occasional plume of smoke rises up from the roofs; dirt roads run into the neighbourhood like riverbeds. Everywhere around us there were people fiddling under cars. The earth was black with motor oil; the buildings were red with dust. Engine parts, carcasses, whole truck cabins lined the narrow alleyways like walls.

Of course we got lost in no time. But obrunis (whites) are a rare sight in Suame Magazine and people soon gathered around us. Before we travelled to Ghana, we had done some online research and had found just one lead: the name of a local non-governmental organisation, SMIDO.

Who could take us to SMIDO? We wandered around for ages with our guides who kept having to ask passers-by for directions. Finally, we ended up at a four-storey concrete building. This was it. A torn banner that hung from a balcony read "SMID fund" and below that "SMIDO". We walked in with all our guides. There was an exchange in Twi with a man in a pristine white shirt who introduced himself as Reuben, SMIDO's English teacher. He was going to make a phone call and told us to take a seat on the plastic chairs that were scattered across the otherwise-empty space. The mechanics who had accompanied us were still hanging around.

Reuben instructed us to give them "social money" to thank them for bringing us here. Satisfied, they walked off with a crisp new 20-cedi bill (about €5). Reuben was excited and told us that the SMIDO president was on his way. The news that obrunis were visiting SMIDO spread through the neighbourhood like wildfire and soon the space was full of people who came to introduce themselves as members of SMIDO.
Then the big boss came in: George Amankwah. He eyed us from a distance while Reuben explained that we planned to build a car in Suame Magazine and were looking for a partner. George disappeared upstairs without a word. Reuben beckoned us. We were going to be formally received, but first the whole executive council had to be rounded up.
Finally, we were asked to come up. Around 30 people were crowded into a room and sitting in a circle. Three chairs had been prepared for us. George was sitting behind the only desk in the space. As soon as he started speaking, everyone was silent. George explained that SMIDO was originally established in 2006 as a training institute where mechanics could follow English classes and courses in car electronics. Then he took his time to present the

whole organisation to us: from the chairman, vice-president, financial officer, head of communications and representatives of all the neighbourhood's guilds to Reuben, the English teacher. SMIDO, George concluded his speech, now represents 5,000 entrepreneurs in Suame Magazine and is the umbrella organisation that unites all the guilds.

Over to you. Who are you? "What is your mission?" Joost took the floor. We were from Stichting Aardschap, he said, and had come to Ghana specially to research the resourcefulness, craftsmanship and talent for improvisation in Suame Magazine. In the West, we have lost our affinity with craftsmanship and this has made us more dependent. Our aim is to learn from Suame Magazine and re-find a degree of self-reliance. That is why we would like to build a car together to highlight the neighbourhood's qualities: a showcase car that we can then present to the world, to promote Suame Magazine.

The man sitting beside George, who had been staring at us blankly, suddenly perked up. His name was Azongo, a SMIDO consultant. He explained how Suame Magazine, and with it all of Ghana, were on the cusp of an industrial revolution. SMIDO was destined to become the organisation that would unite all the forces. Building a showcase car could become the symbol of the new era.

The room erupted in applause and all-round exclamations of "Joammm!", a Ghanaian expression of approval. George closed the meeting and summoned us to draw up a memorandum of understanding with Azongo. We were to be his guest for the rest of our stay. Without leaving much room for discussion, George sent a mechanic to pick up our luggage from the hotel and bring it to his villa.

In the following days, it became clear that we had come at the right moment. SMIDO had great ambitions, with plans to develop a new car district out of town. The idea of building a car appealed to them as it would allow them to put Suame Magazine in general and SMIDO's plans in particular in the media spotlight.

We concluded our first visit to Suame Magazine in April 2012 by drawing up a memorandum with SMIDO. We agreed on the following: we were going to build a showcase car that would display Suame Magazine's creativity and high level of workmanship to the world. When the car was ready, it would be taken on a promotional tour through Ghana and then be shipped to the Netherlands for an exhibition. SMIDO would provide mechanics and a workspace; we would take care of a construction budget and media coverage. And we would put SMIDO in touch with the Dutch private sector and government.
That was a less than a year ago. Back to the present. Joost concludes his speech at the Coke table. Now, a year after signing the memorandum, he says, Aardschap has raised the necessary funds and we have three months to build our showcase car. Charles Taylor nods as he takes in the words. Tomorrow there will be a press conference to present us to the Ghanaian public.

The following day everyone at the SMIDO head office is working hard to set up the press conference. Rows of chairs have been prepared and behind the press table there is a banner that reads "SMID fund". We thought that the press conference was going to be about our car project. When we ask Azongo what the SMID fund stands for, he explains that it is part of his master plan for the great leap forward. The idea is to combine a pension fund, an insurance and a savings bank into a single formula that will offer poor artisans a chance to build a more stable existence. To finance all of this, SMIDO wants to invest in a new plot of land north of Kumasi. This is where the new Suame Magazine will arise. The New Land will be a Western-style industrial estate, with clean streets and good facilities for factories; it will be safe and, above all, prosperous. Only SMIDO members will be allowed to establish themselves there. By paying a monthly contribution, they will become co-investors in the SMID fund.

"But today we are presenting your car project," he says. "Don't worry." A little dismayed, we take our seats behind the press table. We feel like white mascots of Azongo's industrial revolution. Luckily there is also a separate banner for our car construction project. "Designlab for Suame Magazine Prototype Car" it reads.

The space gradually fills up with journalists, but also with inquisitive mechanics from the neighbourhood, who are chased out of the building as soon as Charles Taylor walks in. "This is only for official press," he hisses to anyone who will listen. Most mechanics wander off, but keep hanging around by the entrance. It is not clear what we are waiting for exactly. We have been sitting here for hours. When George comes in everyone jumps up. He is wearing a traditional white Muslim outfit and dark glasses which he keeps on for the duration of the presentation. He sits down at the press table, and orders Joost and Melle to sit down to his left and right. Teun is assigned the role of European press chief and is told to set up his impressive camera equipment in front of the press table.

Debora, one of the few female executive council members and an automotive painter in everyday life, opens the programme with a poem in Twi. She is wearing a gala dress. Then George takes the floor. Nearly an hour passes, during which he and Azongo explain the plans for the SMID fund in great detail. The audience is restless. Journalists walk in and out. Halfway through, someone decides to make a sound recording of the presentation and tries to sneak a microphone through the audience, but the wire keeps getting stuck behind chair legs. Someone is on the phone and outside the hammering, cutting and shouting continue unabated. When the presentation is finally finished, the floor is opened to questions. No one raises a hand, which annoys Charles Taylor. "Members of the press, please ask questions!" he shouts. Then someone timidly raises a hand. "When are you going to present the car project?" "After the break," George snaps. No one dares to ask anything else.

After the break, the SMID fund banner has been replaced by the much smaller banner for our project. Azongo chairs this part of the press conference. He explains that, in the framework of the SMID fund, SMIDO has drawn on its international network to create a joint venture. SMIDO wants to develop Ghana's auto industry and that is why it has invited Stichting Aardschap to conduct a first study. "I now pass the floor to the head of mission, Mister Justice."

Joost gets up and addresses the press. In the West, we no longer know how to be self-reliant, he says, that is why we want to study how artisans in Suame Magazine go about their work. He explains that producing a car is a form of action research to penetrate the neighbourhood's social dynamic. The result will be a showcase car which will demonstrate the neighbourhood's resourcefulness and craftsmanship to the general public in Ghana and abroad. No one seems to mind that Joost's description of the project contradicts SMIDO's story in virtually every respect. A barrage of questions follows. When will the car be ready? How many will be produced? What kind of car will it be? What will it cost in the shop? How much money is being invested from Europe? We suddenly realise that what we see as an experiment or study is being translated as the first step towards a new industry here.

After the press conference, Azongo distributes a sheet to the journalists with the text of the newspaper article as SMIDO would like it published. Over the following days, the car project is a trending topic on local radio stations, in newspapers and on TV.
Mechanics from the neighbourhood contact us to ask if they can join. But more importantly, we get a phone call from Professor Yesuenyeagbe A.K. Fiagbe of the Kwame Nkrumah University of Science Technology (KNUST) in Kumasi. We need a workplace for the project. We do not have the money to rent a work space and SMIDO obviously doesn't either. But the KNUST has a large workshop in the middle of the neighbourhood. It was established in the 1970s in cooperation with the Massachusetts Institute of Technology (MIT) in the United States as a kind of vocational training institute. It is known as the ITTU workshop, which stands for Intermediate Technology Transfer Unit. However, the students hardly go there because they see Suame Magazine as a ghetto. The ITTU workshop is only open when representatives from MIT come for their annual visit with their own students. The rest of the year, the institute's staff does odd jobs in the neighbourhood to make some extra cash.

We had already met Fiagbe on the university campus back in 2012. He had kept us waiting for ages in a bare concrete space where students have to report for detention. The building dates back to the Cold War era, when the Soviet Union and the United States were competing for the favour of all the countries around the world. This campus was Kumasi's gift from the Americans. It is made up of a series of windowless high-rise flats. As soon as you step inside, the heat kills off any brain activity. We sat down among the students on the detention benches and slowly wilted away. Finally, the professor was free to see us. His office was the size of a broom cupboard with a wall-to-wall executive desk crammed inside. An air-conditioner blocked the window and with it any daylight. Fiagbe is a wiry man and he seemed even smaller behind his enormous desk. He first lectured us: Africa does not need Westerners. Then a second lecture: the people of Suame Magazine are not to be trusted. They steal your ideas and rip you off. He said any form of cooperation would be a non-starter. After having listened to Fiagbe, we tried a different tactic and told him that we could involve Dutch training institutes in a form of cooperation. He did not seem particularly keen on this either.

But one year on things are different. The media coverage that we have received from the very first day of our 2013 visit has drawn the attention of the university board. Fiagbe is suddenly a lot friendlier and invites us to drop by. We had contacted the KNUST art academy while we were back in the Netherlands and now Castro, the academy's director, pulls some strings for us at the university. Within a couple of days everything is set: we can use the university workshop in Suame Magazine.

MEMORANDUM OF UNDERSTANDING

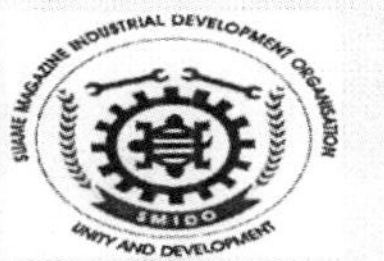

BETWEEN

SUAME MAGAZINE INDUSTRIAL DEVELOPMENT ORGANIZATION (SMIDO)

e-mail:smido06@yahoo.com

AND

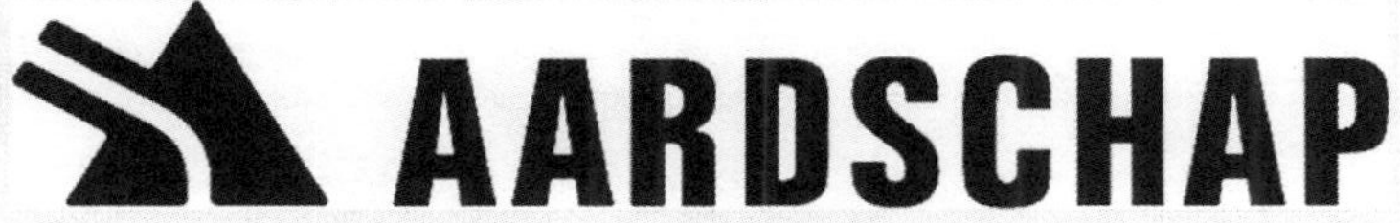

REPRESENTED BY

(Bram Esser,Melle Smets and Joost van Onna)

Stichting Aardschap for the joint construction of a car.
Signed on 3 April 2012.

THIS MEMORANDUM OF UNDERSTANDING is duly signed this **_3rd__ day of April, 2012** between the Suame Magazine Industrial Development Organization (SMIDO), acting per its President, George Asamoah Amankwa for technical and technology assistance **and AARDSCHAP FOUNDATION** represented by Melle Smets, Bram esser and Joost Van Onna, (hereinafter referred to as a **'Partner'**) authorized to transact a special purpose project business on behalf of SMIDO and as a partnership endeavour.

WITNESSES as follows:

- The parties have pledged to cooperate with each other and committed themselves to work towards the successful execution of a project to achieve the following objectives:
- Build a car as shared partnership initiative and run a documentary about Suame Magazine in the period of September---November 2012;
- Mobilize funding for the project in the Netherlands and other interested parties;
- Use (part of) these funds to build the car with the companies of Suame Magazine (buying their products and services)and hereby investing in Suame Magazine;
- Create exposure and publicity for Suame Magazine and SMIDO nationally and internationally
- Through expositions, lectures, media coverage, scientific articles etc.
- To make a publicity and exhibition tour with the car through Ghana and hereby creating exposure Of Suame Magazine and SMIDO;
- Contact interested Ghanaian Universities, NGO's and companies to cooperate with and/or invest In SMIDO and Suame Magazine;
- Contact interested Dutch companies, NGO's and investment banks to cooperate with and/or Invest in SMIDO and Suame Magazine;
- Create multimedia publications (website,films on the internet etc.) for the companies in Suame Magazine involved in building the car with the aim to generate publicity and attract a broader customer base For Suame Magazine;
- Contact interested Dutch (technical) universities with the aim to start an annual

2

- Notification letter must be typed, signed by the discontinuing party. It shall state the date on which the agreement is to terminate and the reasons for the termination.
- All outstanding services due either party must be fully executed before discontinuity can be enforced.

ARTICLE -9-BREACH

The following statutory conditions shall be the only bases under which this agreement can be abrogated by any of the parties:

- Poor and unsatisfactory execution of obligations under this agreement.
- Conducts and behaviours that are outside of this agreement by either of the parties but considered inimical to the brand image or reputation of the other party. This conducts and behaviours include but not limited to this following:

a. Theft
b. Bribery conducts
c. Funding or supporting illegal practices and organizations

ARTICLE -10-ARBITRATION

I. All disputes arising out of or in connection with the present agreement shall be finally settled under the Rules of Arbitration in accordance with the Arbitration Act, 1960 (Act 38) by one or more arbitrators appointed in accordance with the said rules.

II. The governing law of the contract shall be the substantive law of the Ghana Contract Act, 1960 (Act 25)

ARTICLE -11-MODIFICATION

This agreement may not be changed or modified, nor may any provision hereof be waived, except by an agreement in writing signed by the party against whom enforcement of the change or modification is asserted.

AGREEMENT COMPLETE

This agreement constitutes the entire understanding between the parties. All representations and undertaking, whether oral or written, have been merged herein.

....

FOR SMIDO

Signed.............................

Name: Mr. George Asamoah Amankwa

Title: President

Date: 3rd April, 2012

WITNESSED BY

Signed.............................

Name: Wormenor Albert Cophie

Title: Chairman, Sofoline Mechanics/SMIDO

Date: 3rd April,2012

FOR AARDSCHAP FOUNDATION

Sign.............................

Name: Melle Smets

Title: Project Leader

Date: 3rd April, 2012

WITNESSED BY

Signed.............................

Name: Bram Esser

Title: Project Member

Date: 3rd April,2012

Memorandum of Understanding between SMIDO and Stichting Aardschap for the joint construction of a car. Signed on 3 April 2012.

the construction of the Turtle 1. SMIDO attracts the first media coverage in the Daily Graphic on 24 October 2012.

NO. 18980. www.graphic.com.gh WEDNESDAY, OCTOBER 24, 2012.

Suame Magazine to start assembling cars

Story: Kwame Asare Boadu, Kumasi

THE Suame Magazine Industrial Development Organisation (SMIDO) and its external partners, Aaardschap Foundation of the Netherlands, have secured funding from the Netherlands Architectural Fund to manufacture a car at the Suame Magazine in Kumasi.

Two Dutch-based universities in Amsterdam and Rotterdam (Rietveld Academie and De Koning Academie) are currently designing the car.

A consultant to the SMIDO, Mr Nyaaba-Aweeba Azongo, told the *Daily Graphic* in Kumasi yesterday that the project was the outcome of a partnership brokered between the SMIDO and Aaardschap Foundation in April this year to build a car as a shared partnership initiative.

He indicated that the team of technicians from the Dutch universities under the leadership of Melle Smets, the project leader, would be in Ghana in January 2013 to work on the final design and subsequent production with the mechanics of Suame Magazine.

"By the arrangements, by the end of 2013, the car would be ready for exhibition," Mr Azongo said.

The SMIDO, he disclosed, was currently working on a workshop space to accommodate the plant for the manufacturing of the car and the team that would arrive in January 2013 for the project.

The Netherlands team, the consultant said, would take six to eight weeks to complete the preparatory work in Kumasi to pave the way for the exhibition and media documentary with both local and international media.

According to Mr Azongo, the SMIDO had approached the Kwame Nkrumah University of Science and Technology to collaborate with the SMIDO and its partners to ensure that the final product would bring the Suame Magazine engineering skills into the mainstream of high-profile engineering institutions to set the basis for more such partnership initiatives.

The Suame Magazine, with a working population of over 200,000, is recognised as the largest artisan-engineering cluster in sub-Saharan Africa.

Mr Azongo indicated that the partnership agreement between the SMIDO and the external partners would also result in an exchange programme between mechanics from the Suame Magazine and automotive technicians in Holland.

The partnership will also run a documentary on the car and Suame Magazine as a major part of the policy to infuse modern technology into their external partnership.

Mr Azongo said there had been more interest from newspapers and television stations in the Netherlands to document the building of the car and show the Suame Magazine to the world, and expressed the hope that the Ghanaian media would equally take keen interest in the major undertaking.

An art museum in the Hague in The Netherlands has also shown keen interest in doing an exposition about the car and the Suame Magazine in summer (the period June to August) of 2013.

He said the external partners had good contacts with the Dutch Embassy in Ghana, which is supporting the initiative.

Daily Graphic

WEDNESDAY, OCTOBER 24, 2012

THIS PARTNERSHIP IS ENCOURAGING

Ghana has been touted as a lower middle-income country since 2007. Unfortunately, however, its people do not live that accolade, as every conceivable item is imported, from toothpick to used clothing, used cars, used lorry tyres and used cooking utensils, compelling some social commentators to refer to Ghanaians as people clothed in other people's rags.

This is a sad commentary, but that is the reality on our streets, in our markets, offices, communities and homes. The paradox of our situation today is that about four decades ago, Ghana used to be a net exporter of many items that it imports today, such as rice, maize, palm oil and electricity.

Our first President, Dr Kwame Nkrumah, as part of his government's import substitution policy, established many factories throughout the country to process raw materials into finished products for local consumption and for export. His government also encouraged the private sector to establish many businesses, although it was considered a socialist regime.

The Accra North Industrial Area, which today boasts warehouses for imported rice and other items, used to be home to many factories that employed thousands of skilled and unskilled labour.

The Ghana Industrial Holding Company (GIHOC) was established by President Nkrumah to produce many items for local consumption and for export, as well as give employment to many people.

During the National Redemption Council (NRC) regime of Colonel Ignatius Kutu Acheampong, the government introduced many interventionist policies to address the economic challenges facing the country. Notable among those policies was the Operation Feed Yourself programme in which every available space was cultivated for the production of all kinds of food crops. That programme was so popular with the people that some students even abandoned the lecture halls to work on sugar cane and other plantations.

Also in the 1970s, all kinds of motor assembling plants were established to assemble all types of cars. Some local companies were able to put together vehicles such as Boafo to help traders and other business operators to carry their goods to and from the marketing centres.

Along the line, however, the unbridled liberalisation in the 1980s led to the neglect of all these productive processes for the importation of items that, ordinarily, we could produce locally.

It is against this background that we welcome the collaboration between the Suame Magazine Industrial Development Organisation (SMIDO) and its external partners, the Aaardschap Foundation of The Netherlands, to assemble cars at the Suame Magazine in Kumasi.

The DAILY GRAPHIC is aware of the capacity of the Suame Magazine and the skills of the artisans there to fabricate all kinds of engine parts to assemble vehicles. All that they need is encouragement and motivation by banks and the government with credit and other forms of support to realise their full potential.

Ghana abounds in human and material resources which, if well tapped by the government and its development partners, can move the country to a middle-income status in no time, at which point the resources could be used to create wealth, employment and prosperity for all.

The DAILY GRAPHIC calls on the government and the banks to identify potential growth poles in the country and nurture them for the development of the country.

The time to act is now and the latest collaboration between SMIDO and The Netherlands firm should be encouraged for the mutual benefit of the partners and Ghanaians.

In the past, Ghana enjoyed periods of strong export performance. SMIDO's leaders are betting on a new golden age that will start from the industrial cluster Suame Magazine. Our cooperation is part of this effort

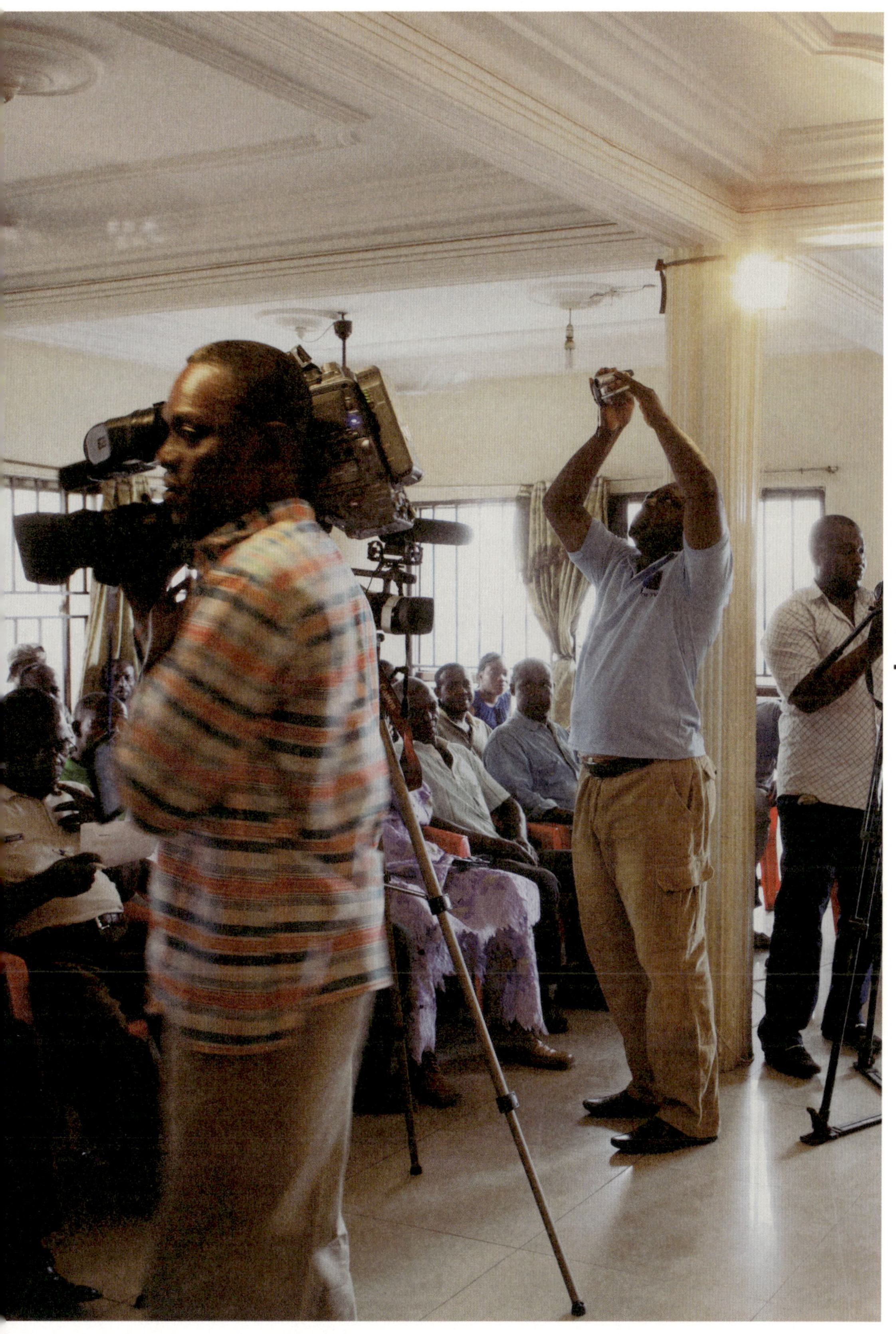

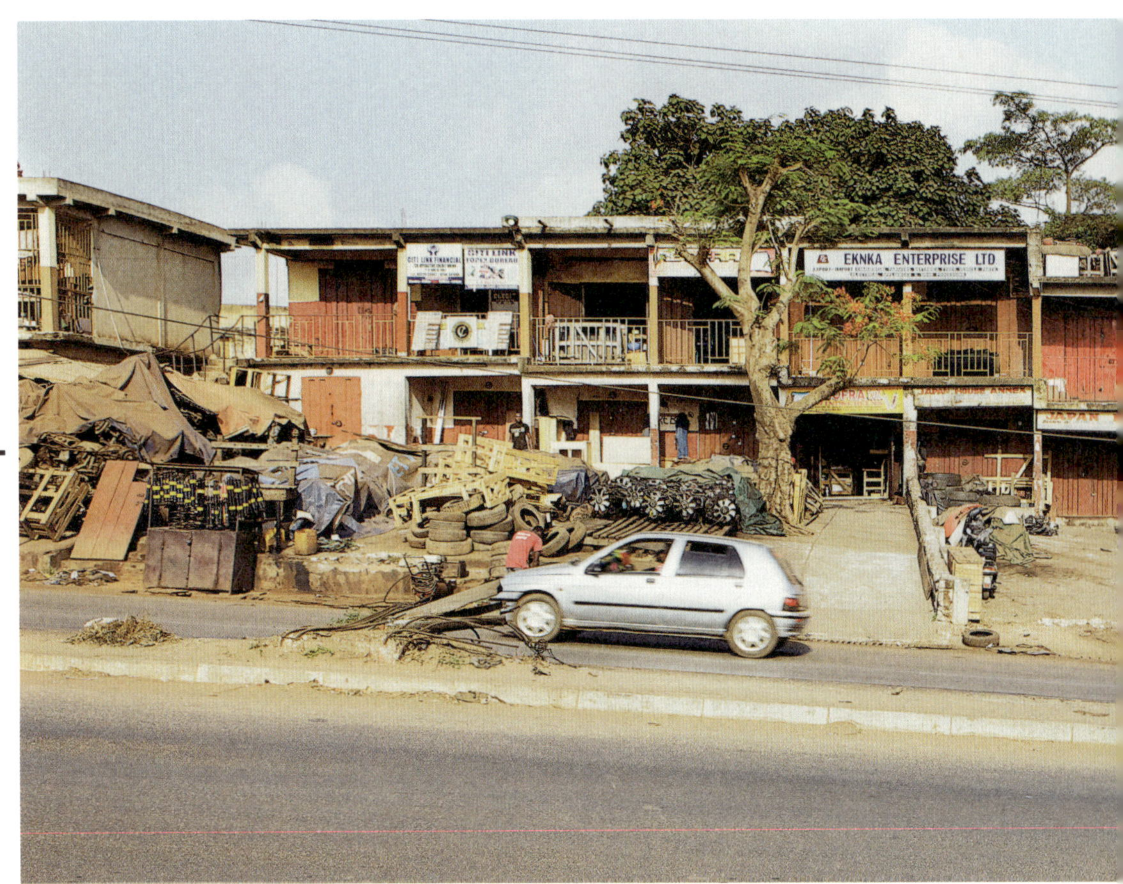

GH // AJ-14 / AT-14 // 02.2013

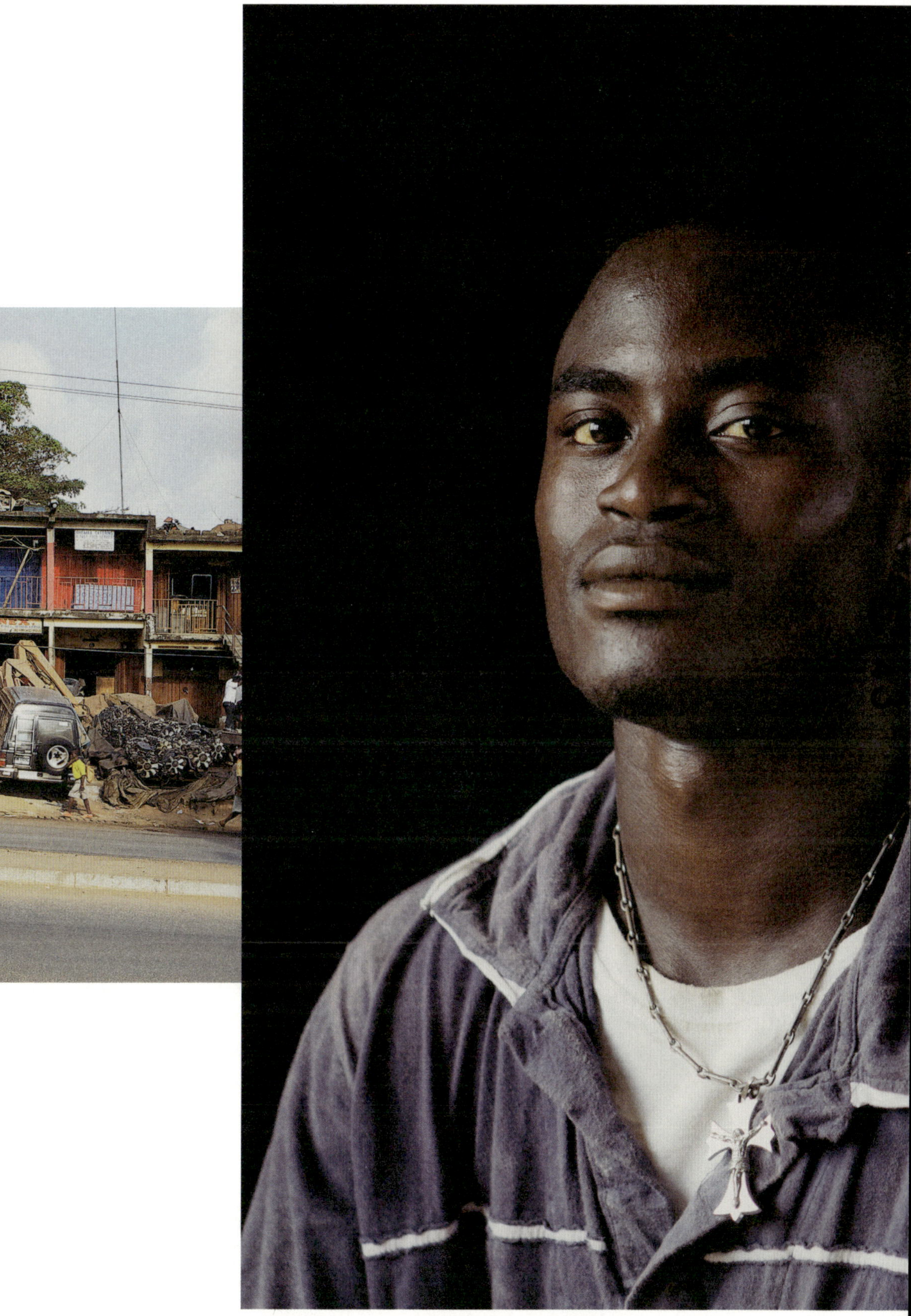

Atta Aghyemah (apprentice painter)

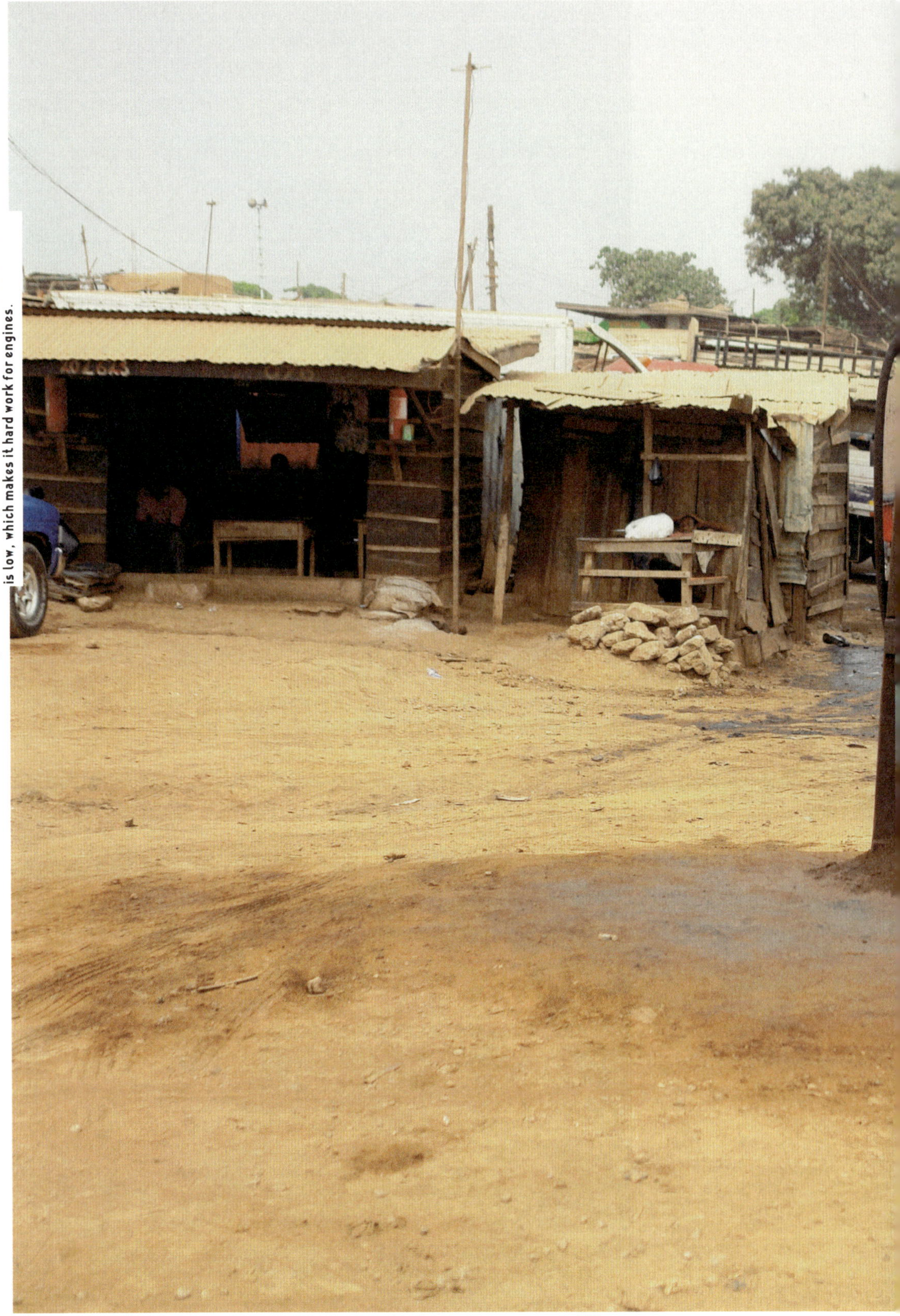

Filling station New Magazine. Petrol is imported and transported overland by truck. The further the petrol has to be transported, the more it is diluted. The octane level is low, which makes it hard work for engines.

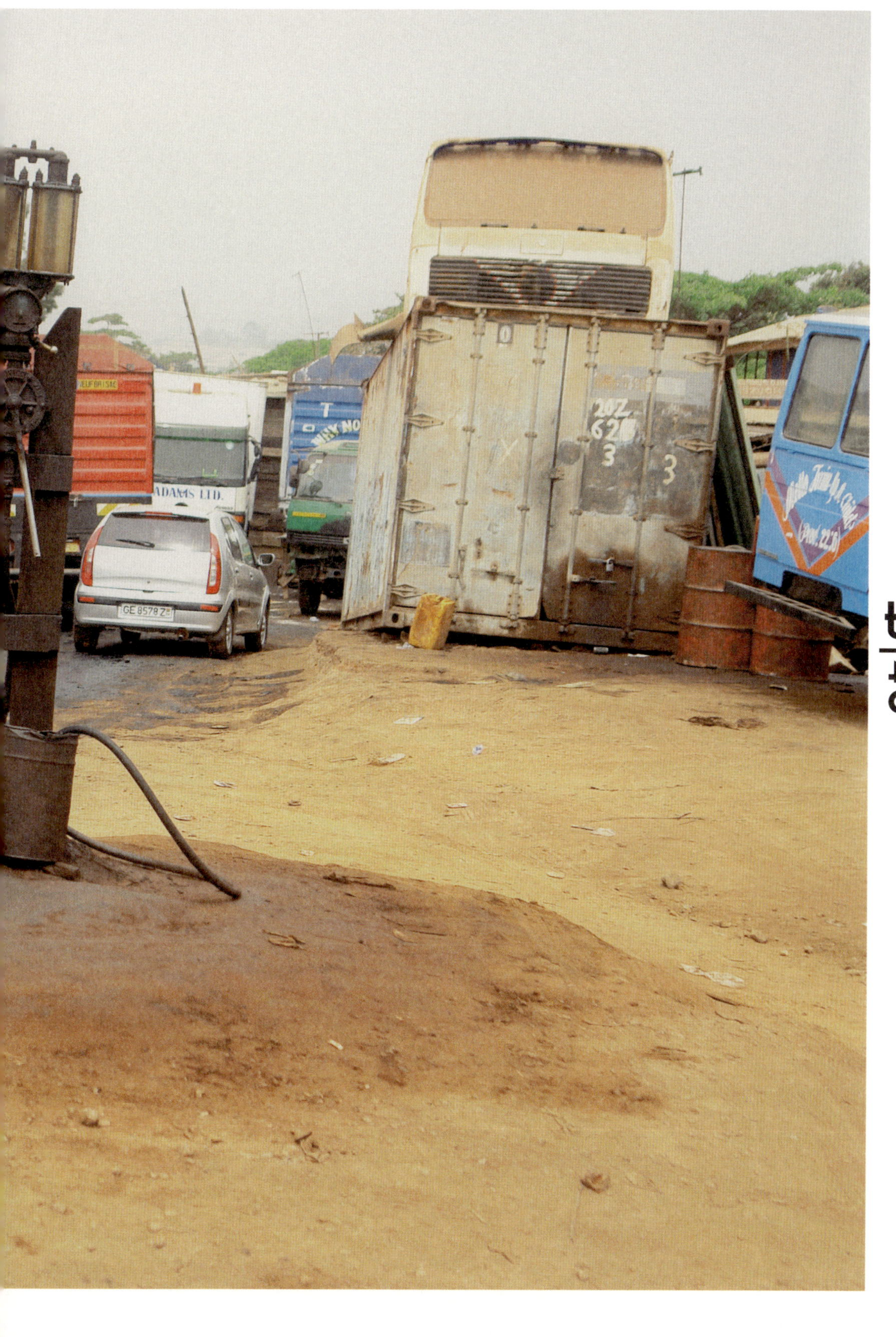
ADAMS LTD.
GE 8578 Z

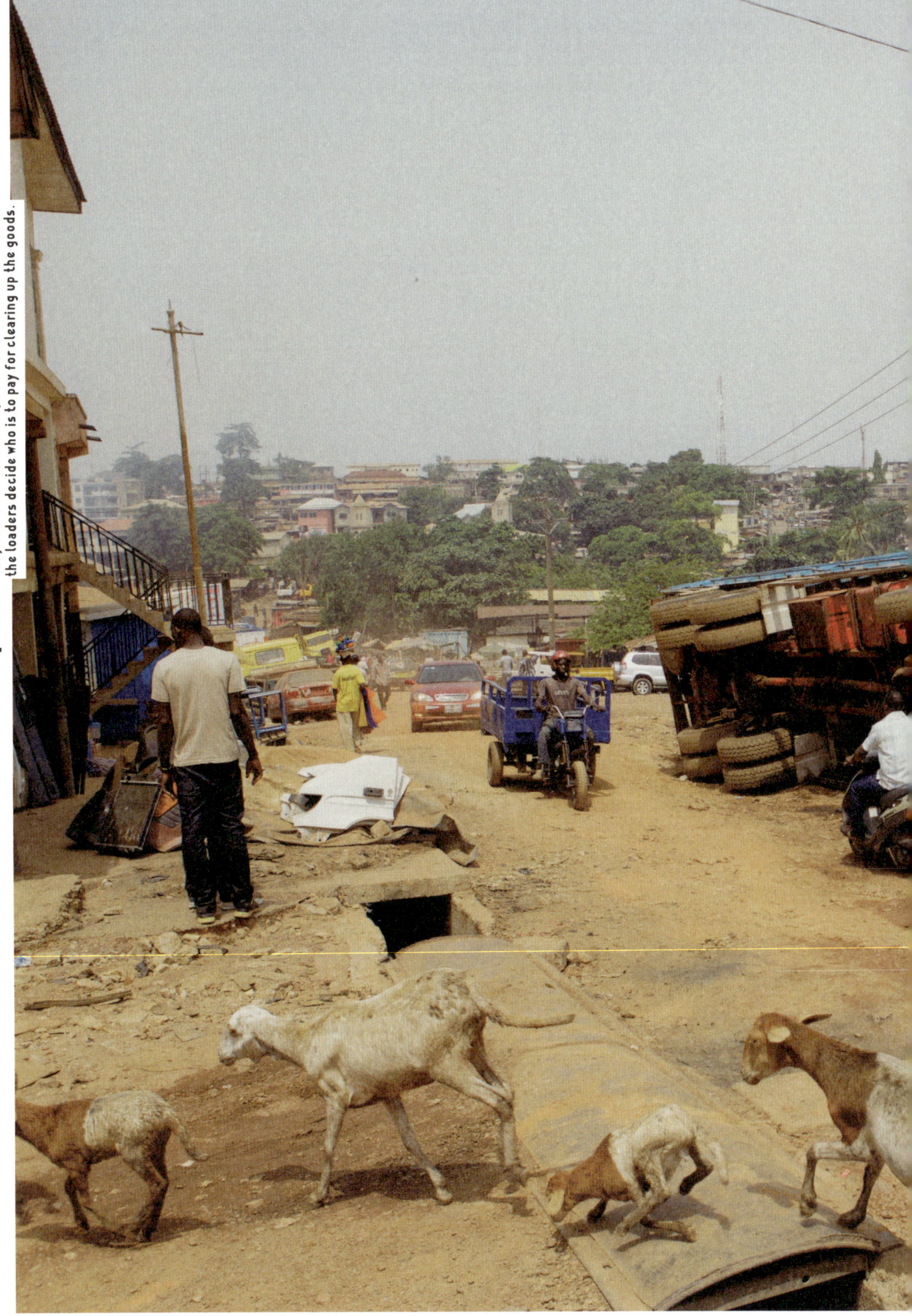

High petrol prices make transport expensive. As a result, trucks are overloaded with cargo and regularly capsize. They are then left on the spot until the truck's owner and the loaders decide who is to pay for clearing up the goods.

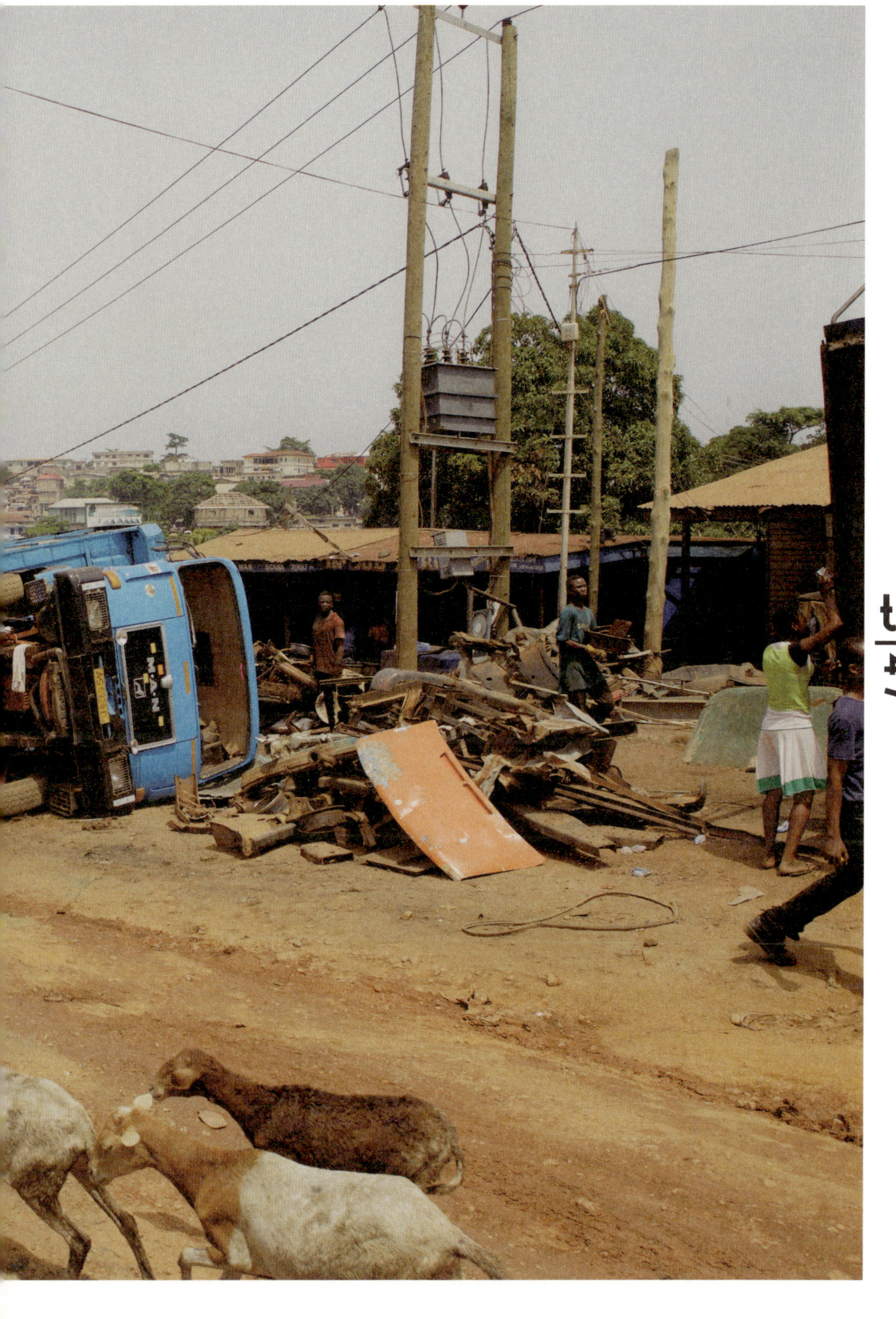
MAN

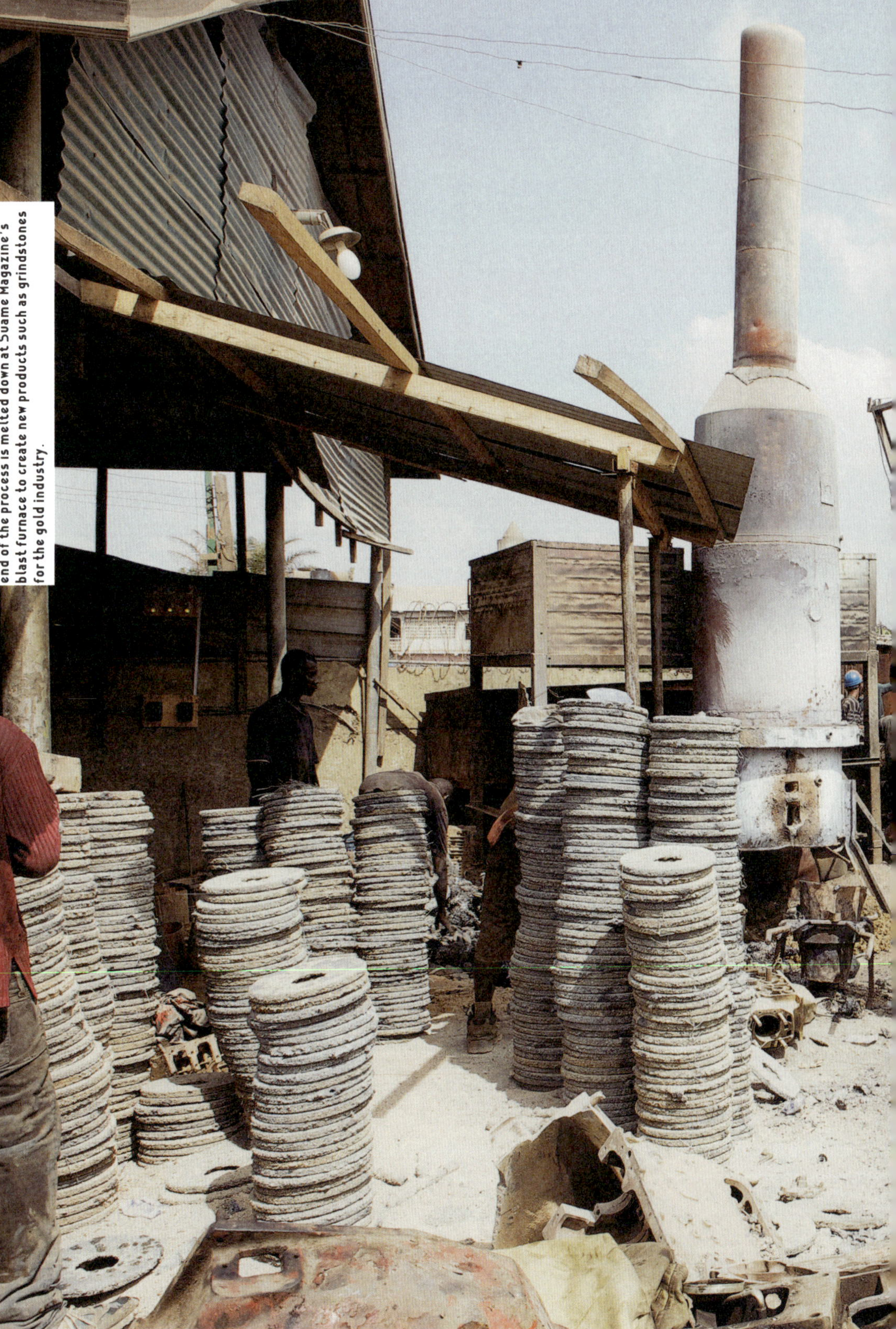

Our first attempt to understand Suame Magazine was through the metaphor of the informal car production plant. Every workshop is specialised and all workshops together form an assembly line. What is left over at the end of the process is melted down at Suame Magazine's blast furnace to create new products such as grindstones for the gold industry.

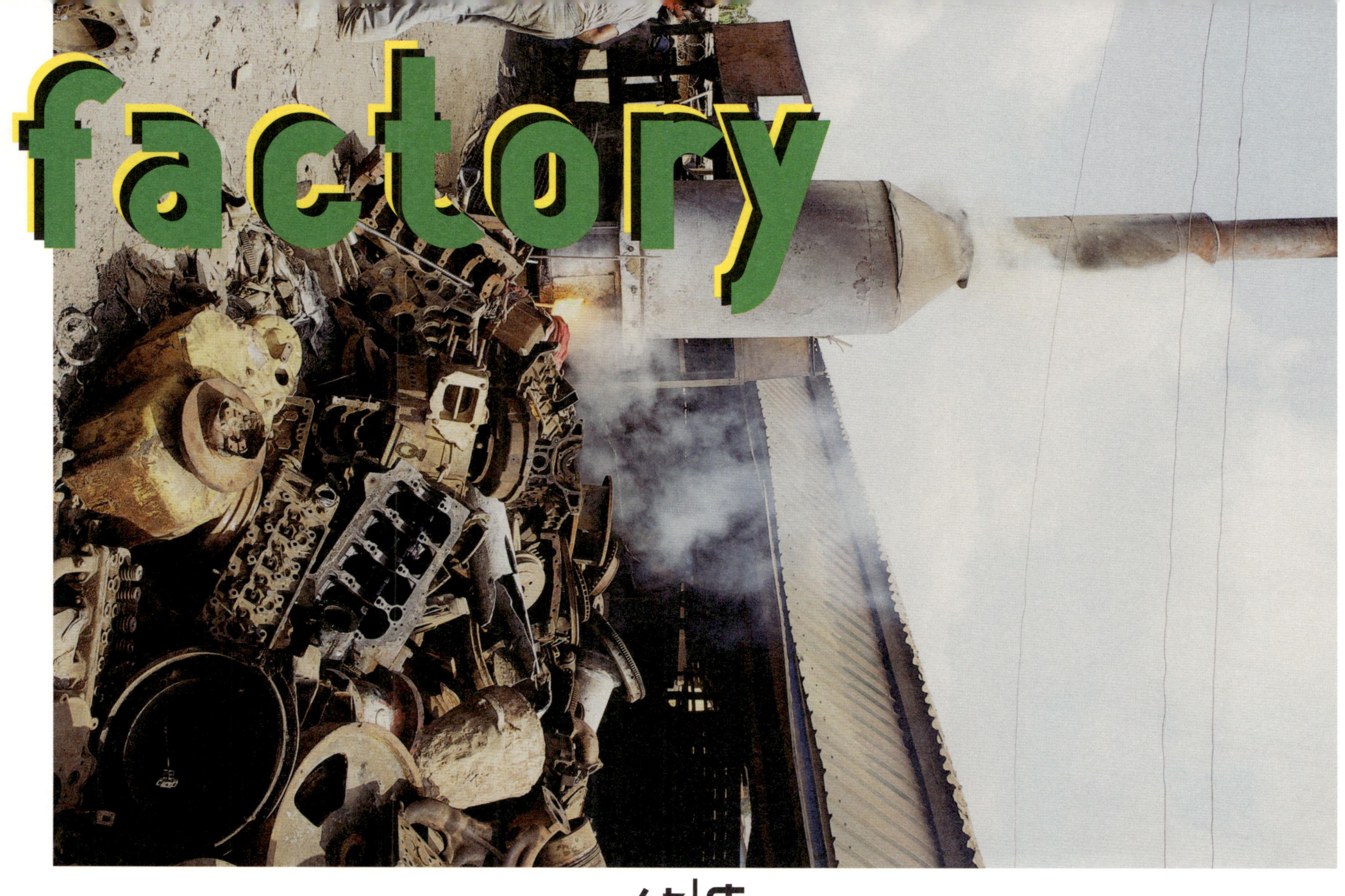
factory

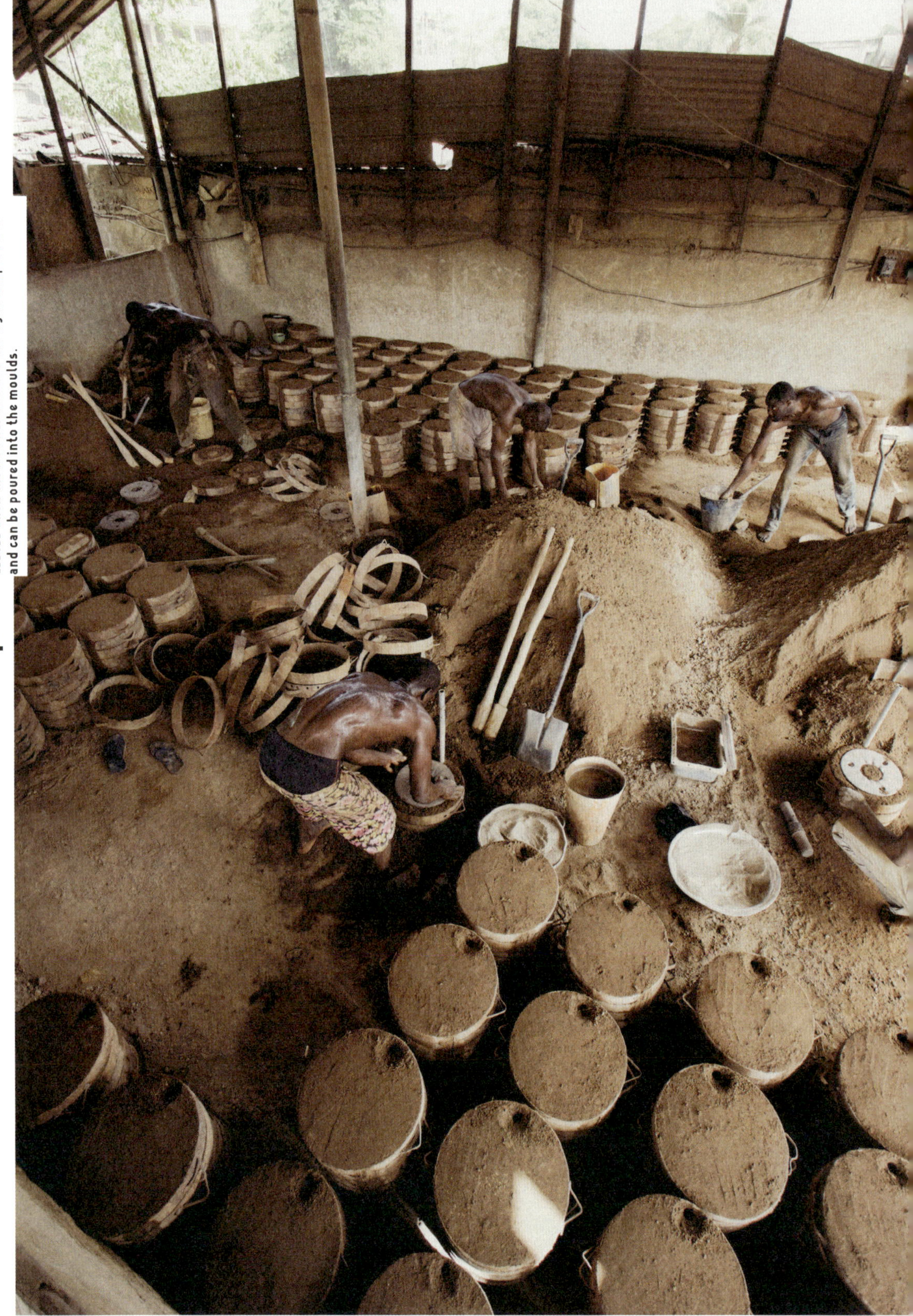

The smelters do not measure the temperatures in the handmade blast furnaces. They use their experience to assess when the iron has reached the right temperature and can be poured into the moulds.

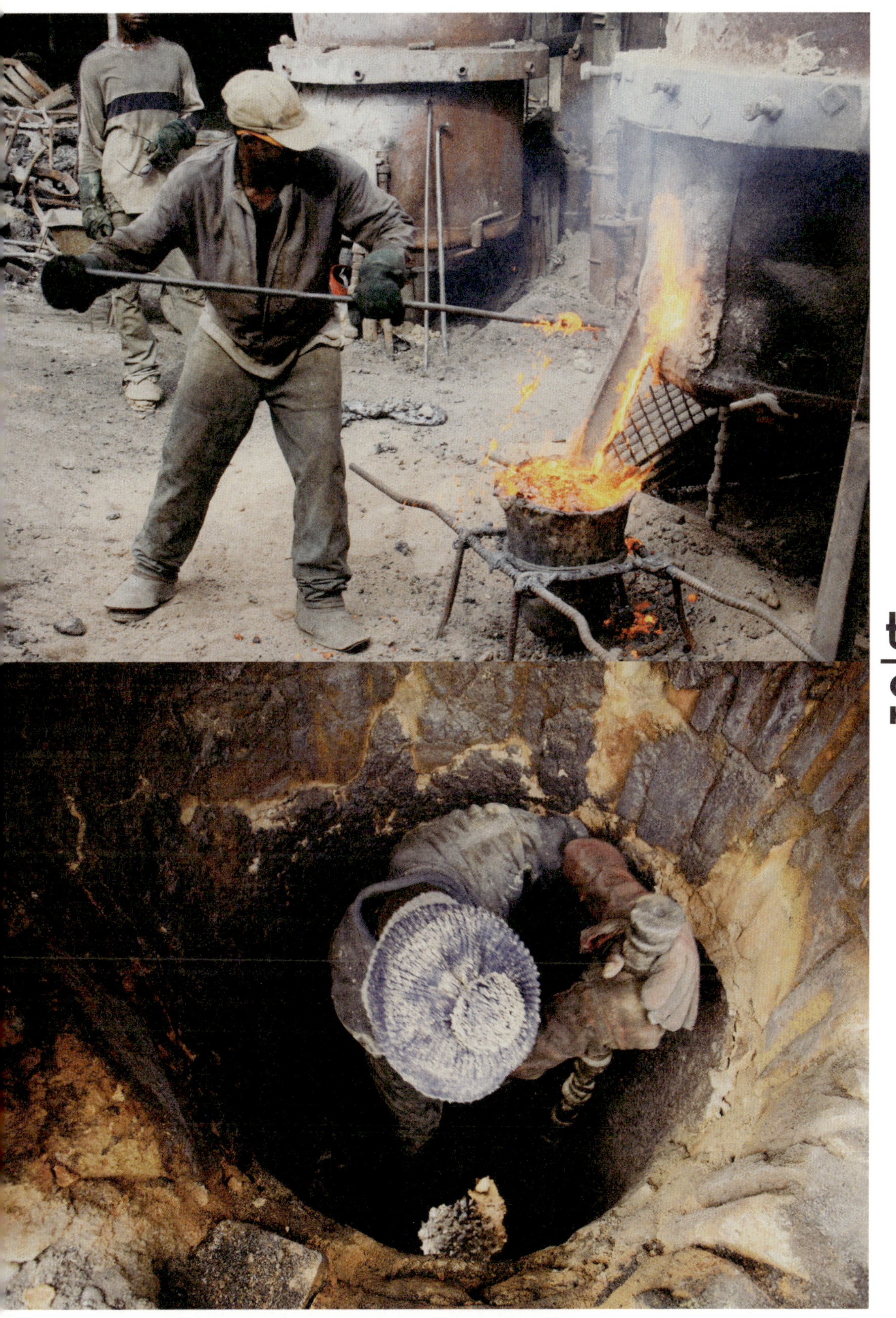

GH // 03.2012
GH // 04.2015

The informal car production plant has many canteens and changing rooms where the workers can relax and freshen up.

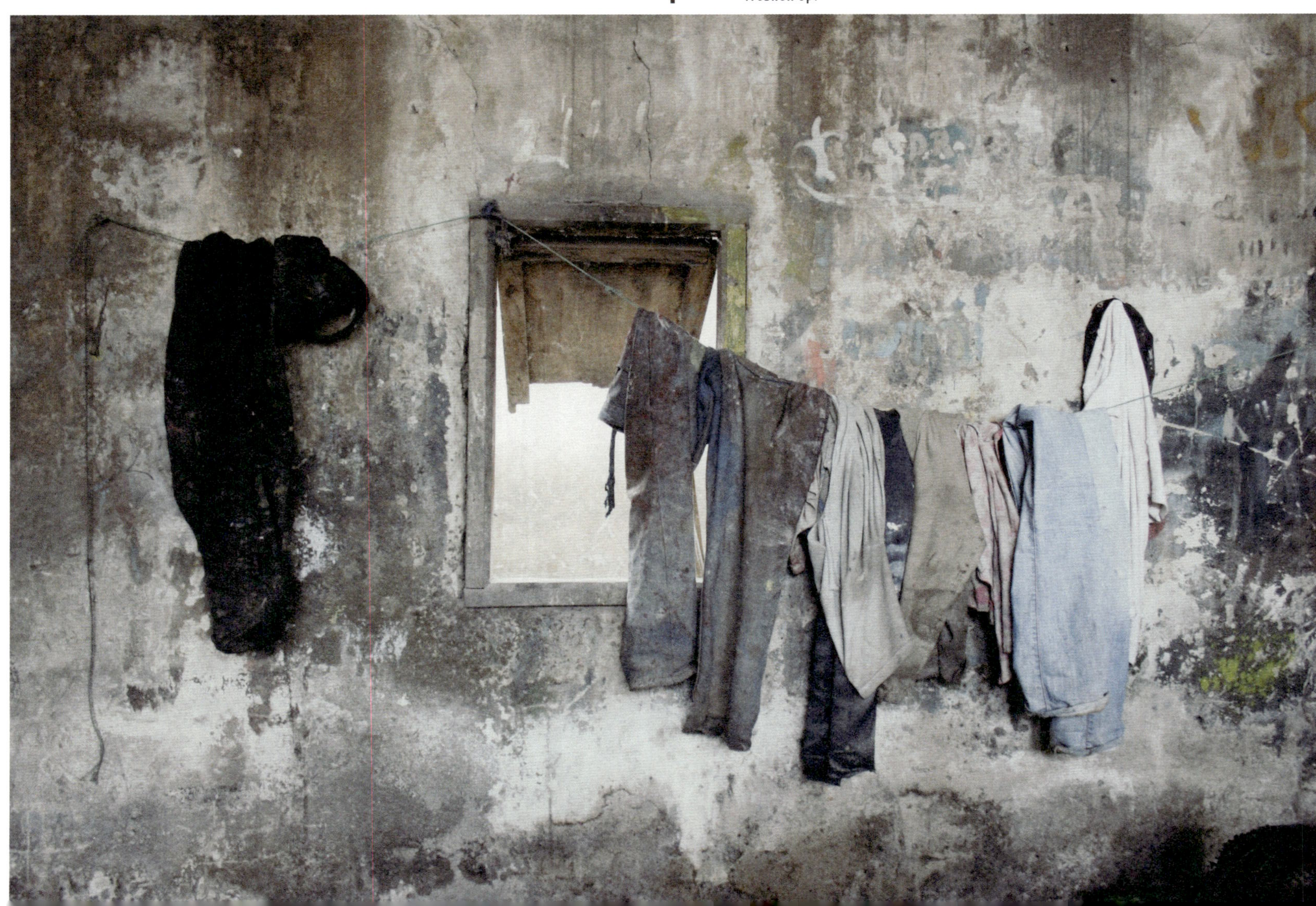

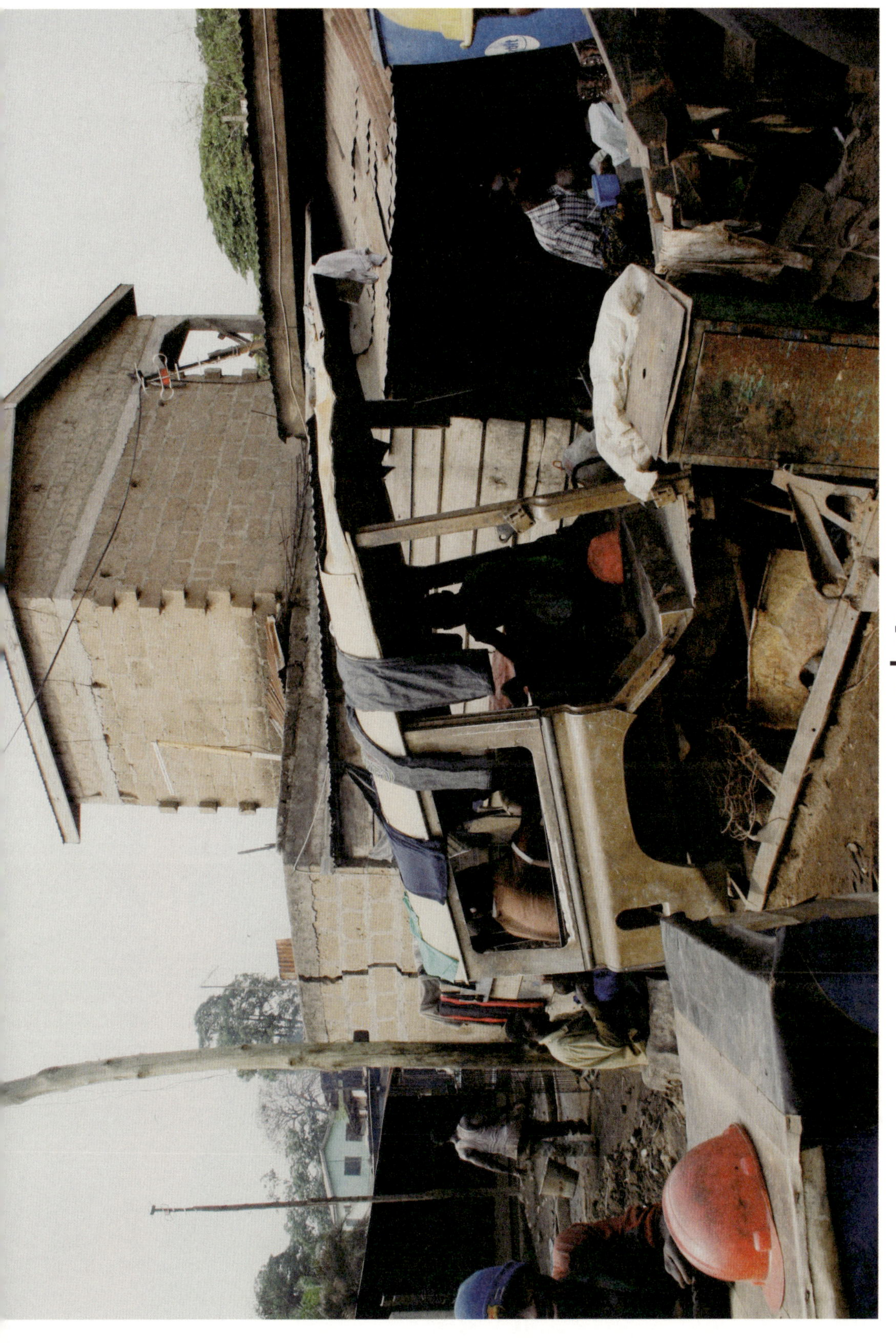

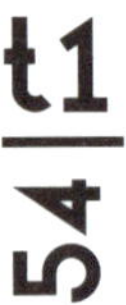

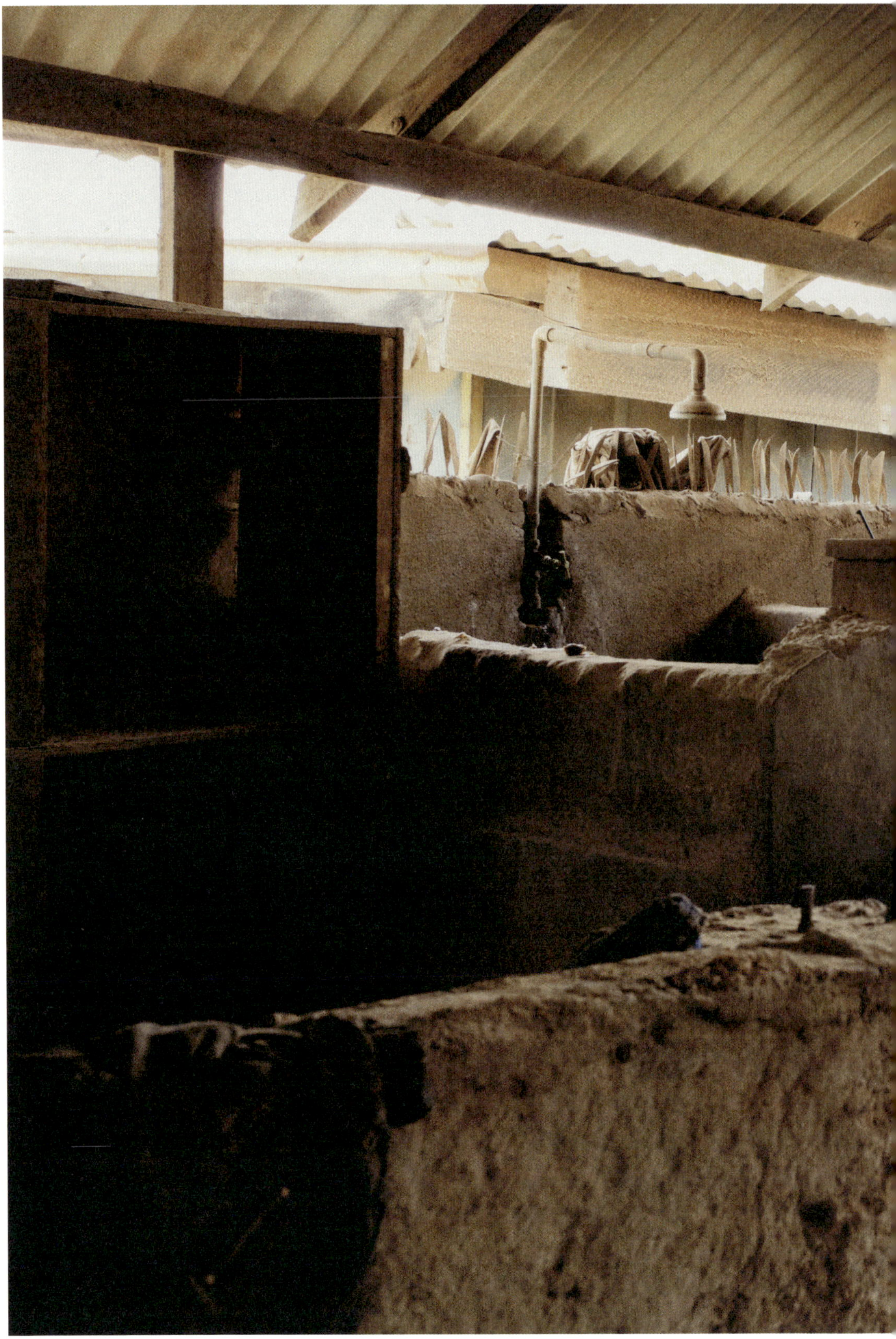

Showers at the Abu-Dia Company, one of the blast furnace companies.

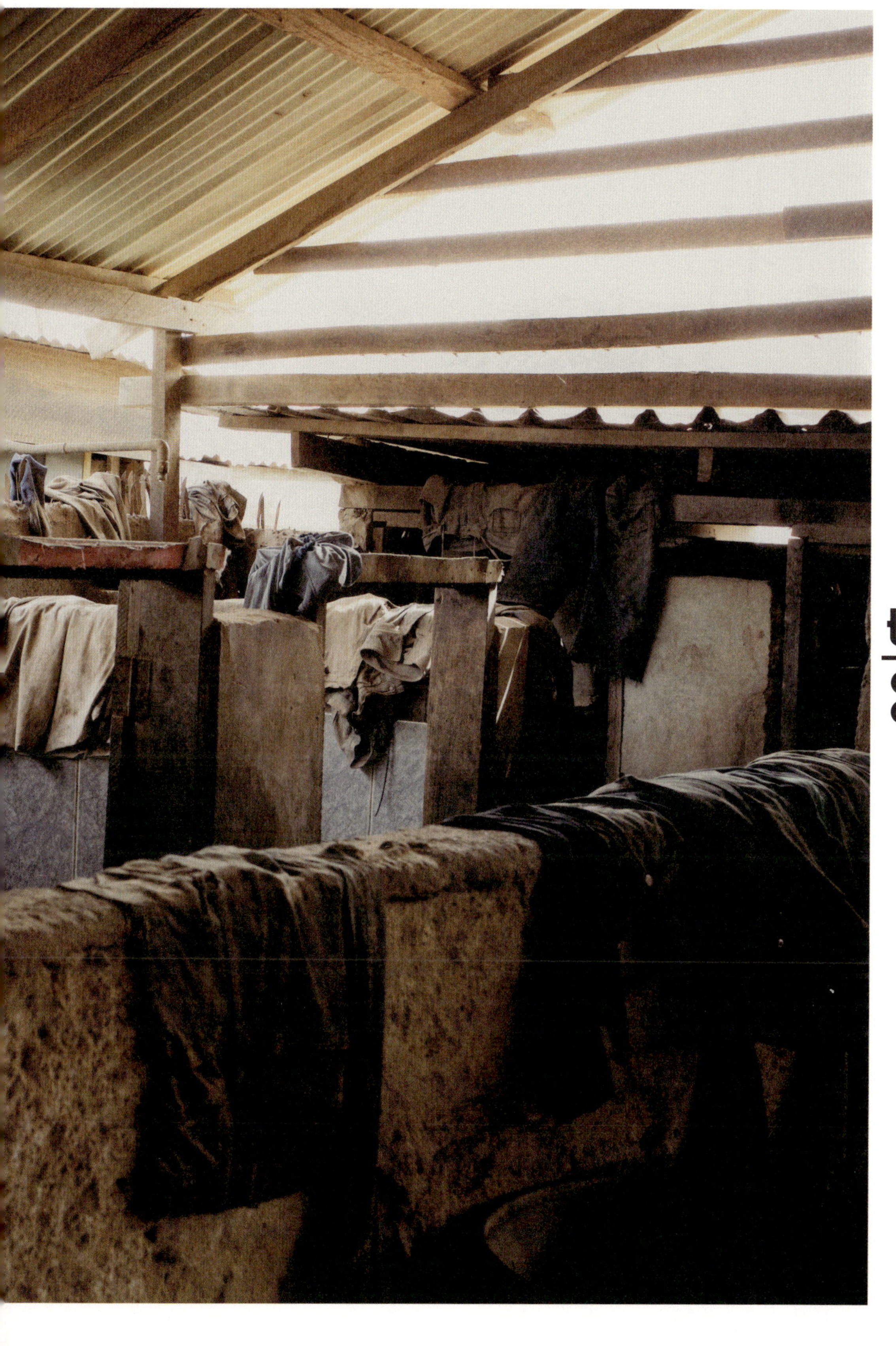

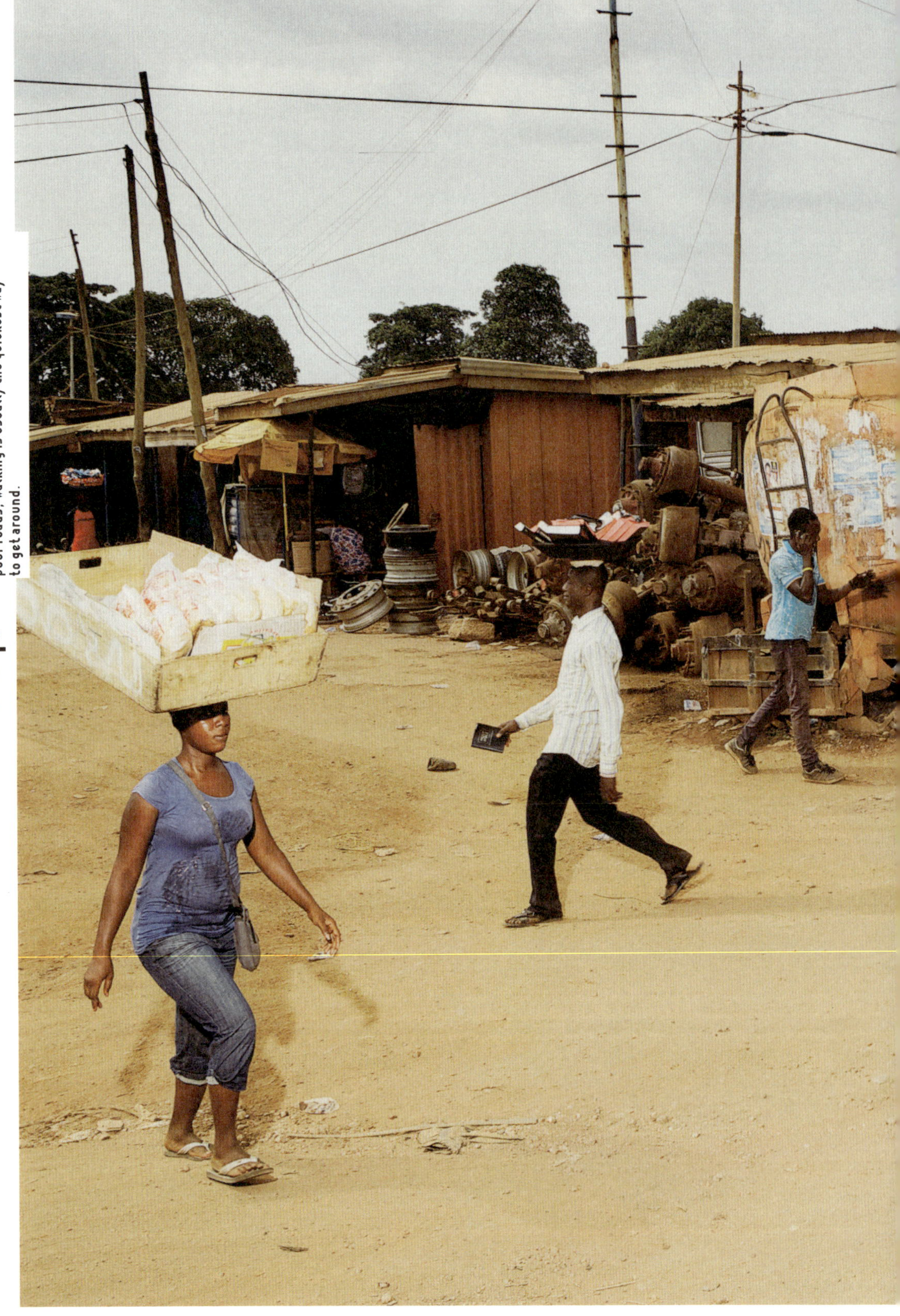

As the roads are often blocked because of traffic congestion, overturned lorries, accidents and poor roads, walking is usually the quickest way to get around.

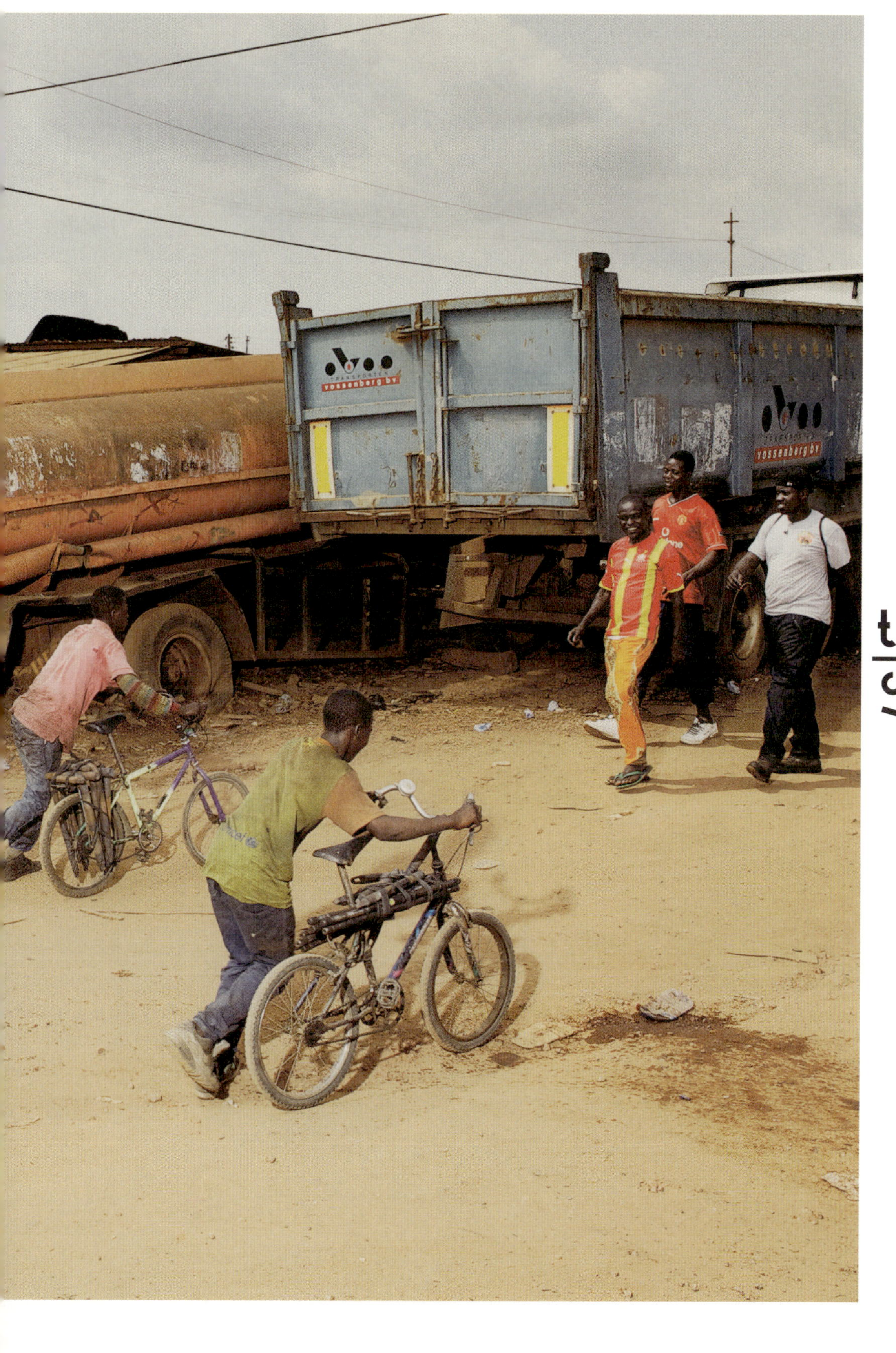
vossenberg bv
vossenberg bv

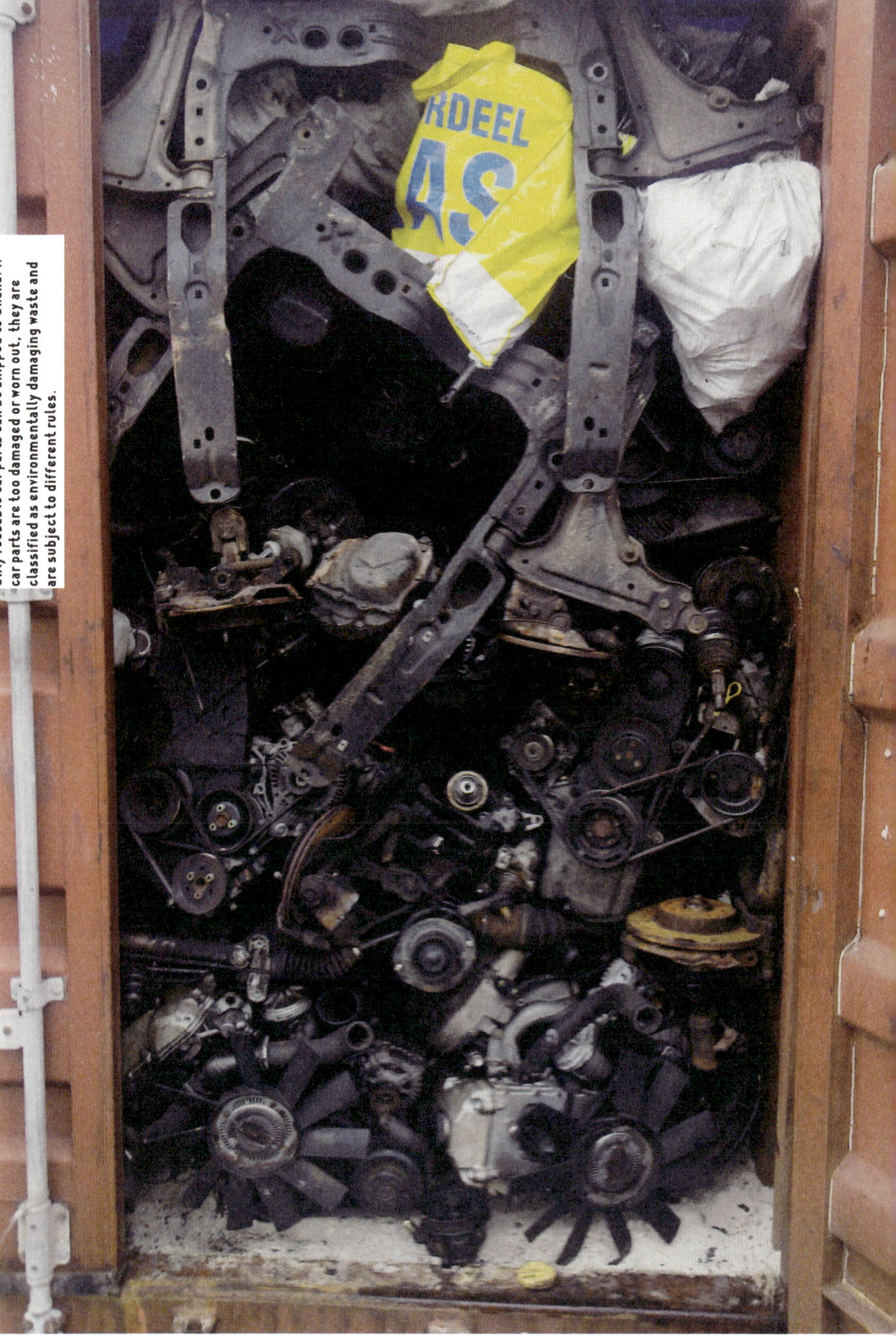

A customs officer and an Environmental Protection Agency officer check a container with car parts that is being sent to Ghana from the port of Rotterdam. Only reusable car parts can be shipped to Ghana. If car parts are too damaged or worn out, they are classified as environmentally damaging waste and are subject to different rules.

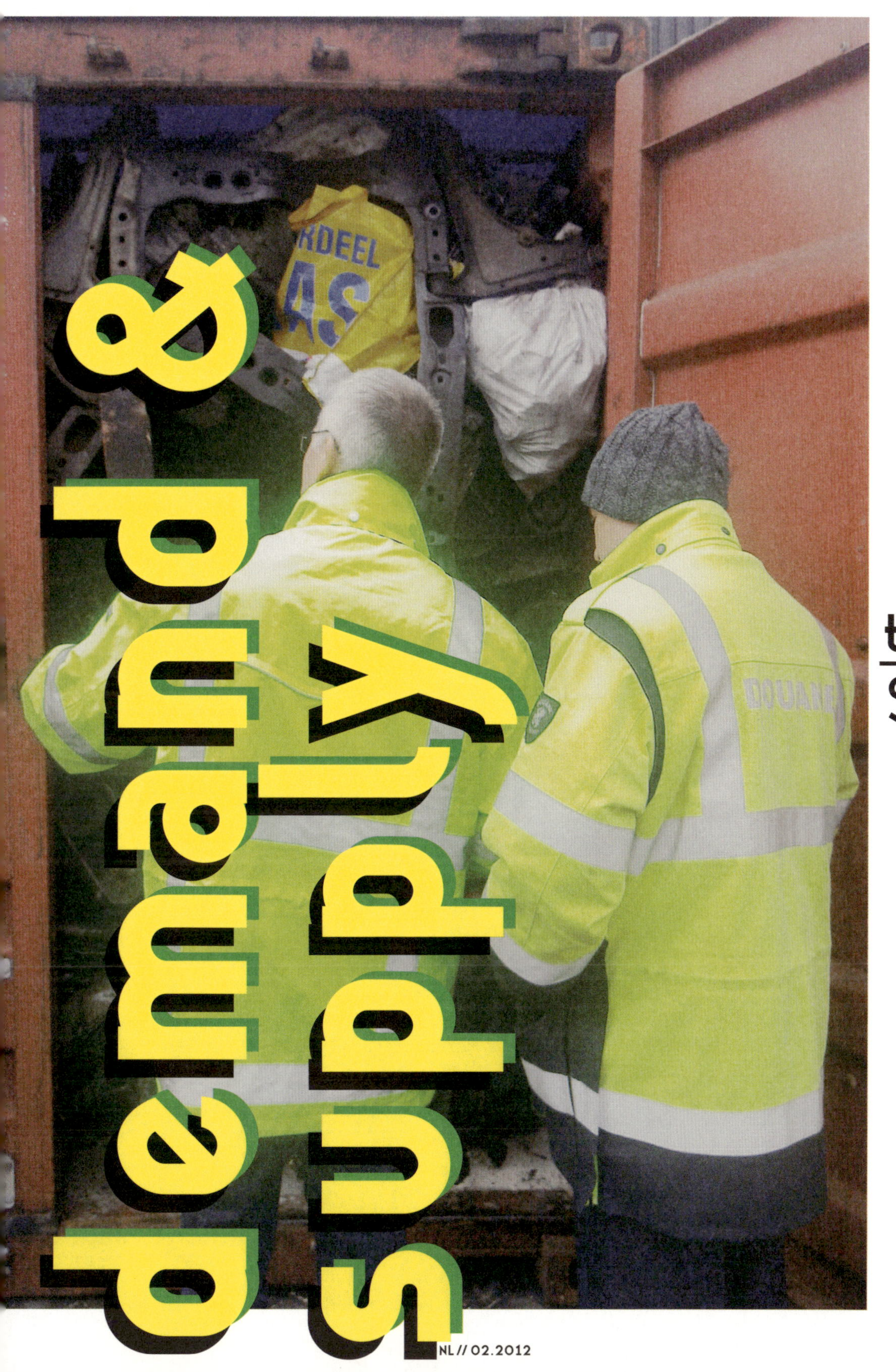
demand &
supply
t1|59
NL // 02.2012

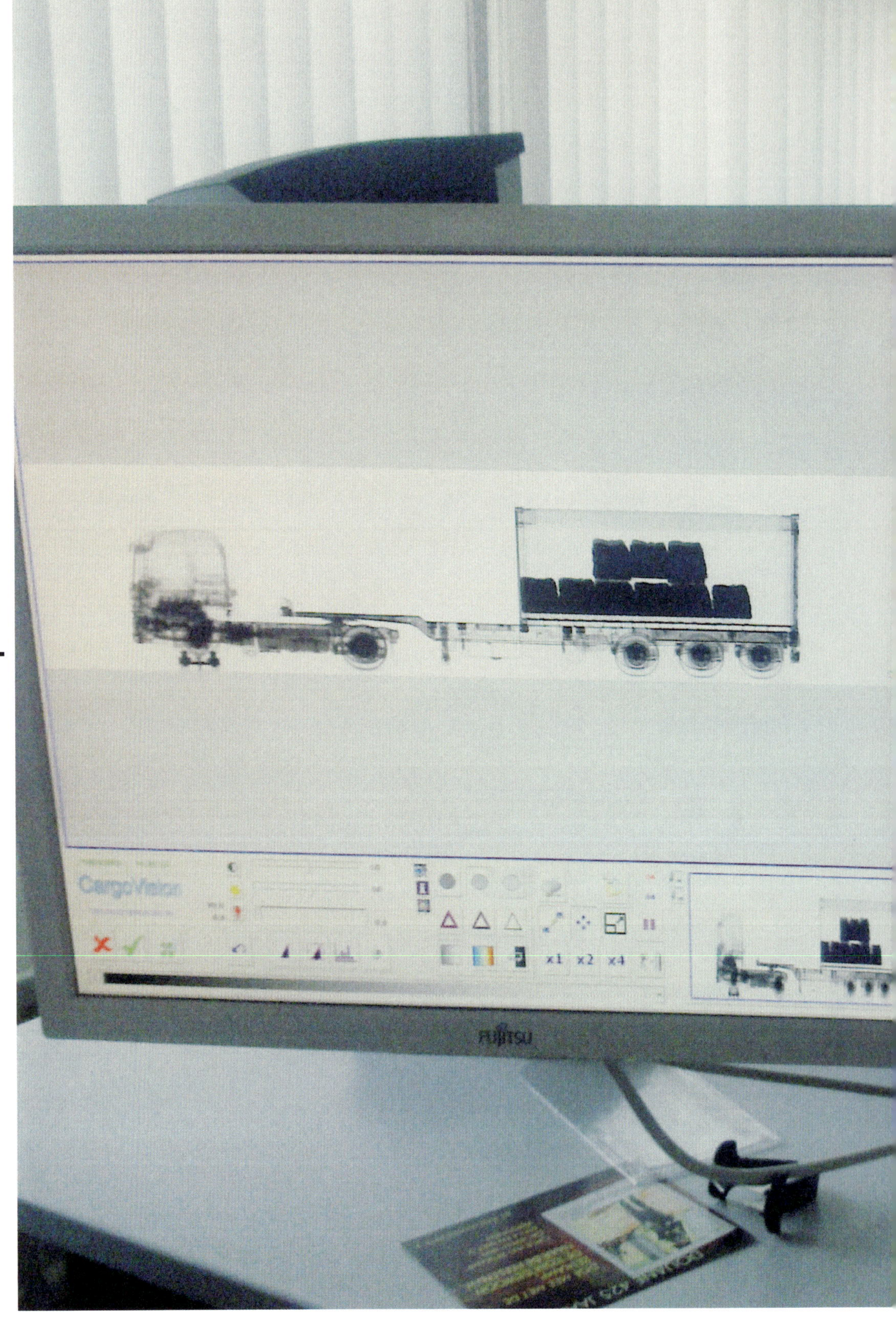

Scan of truck, customs office Maasvlakte, port of Rotterdam.

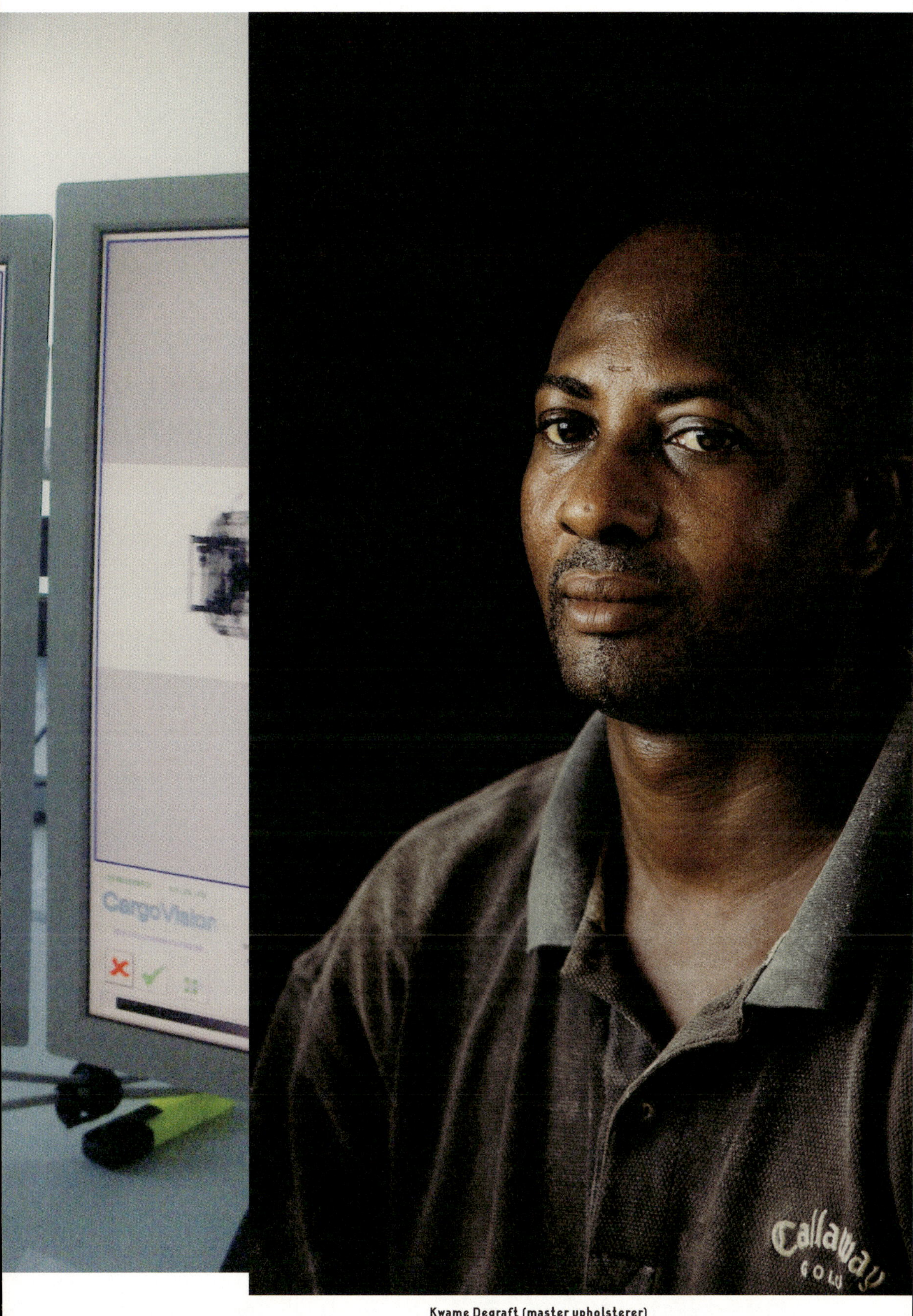

Kwame Degraft (master upholsterer)

Every day, Suame Magazine receives new shipments of used car parts through global supply lines. The dealers have their overseas contacts and keep phoning through orders until the container is full and ready to be shipped. The buyers come to collect their orders in Suame Magazine.

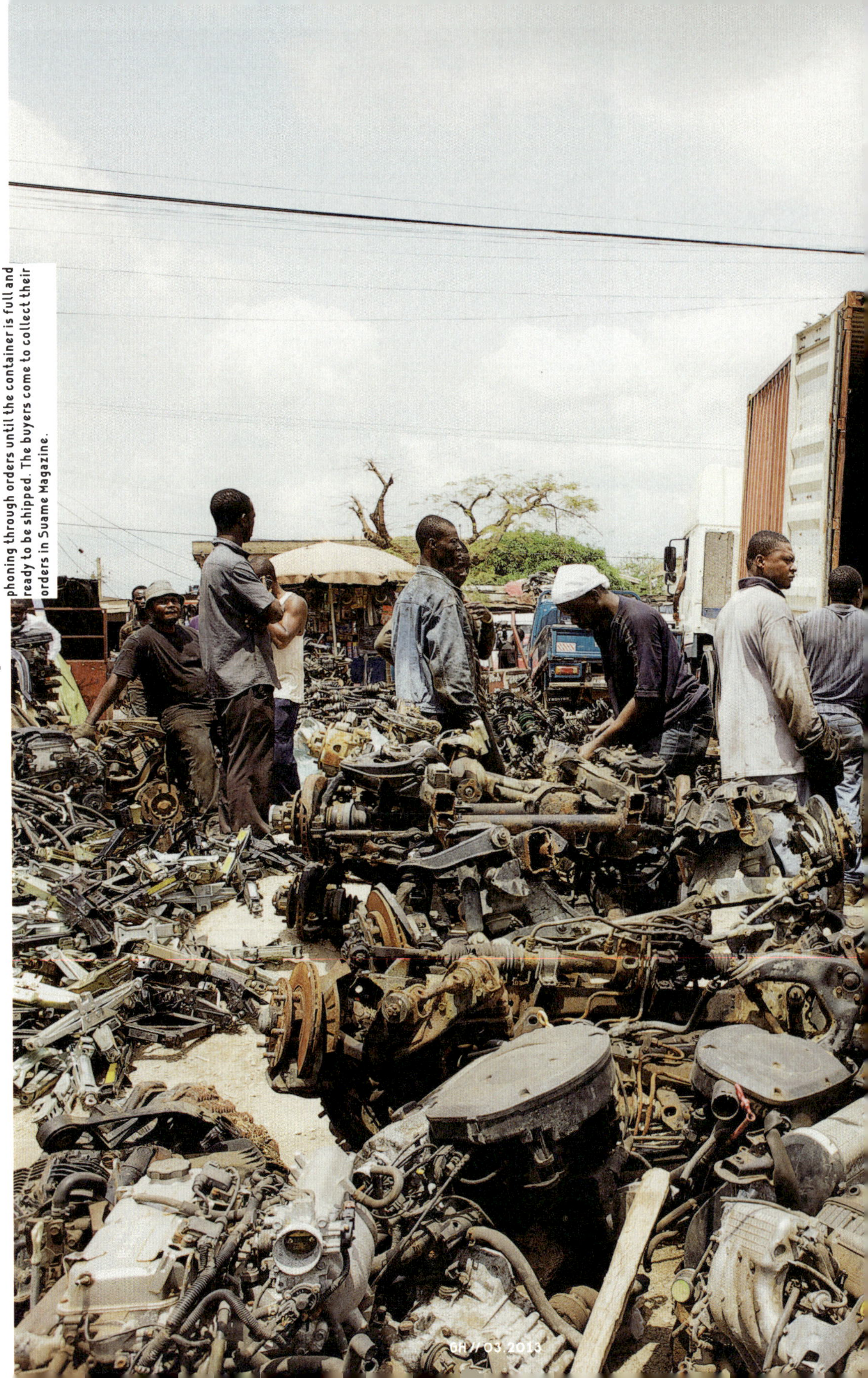

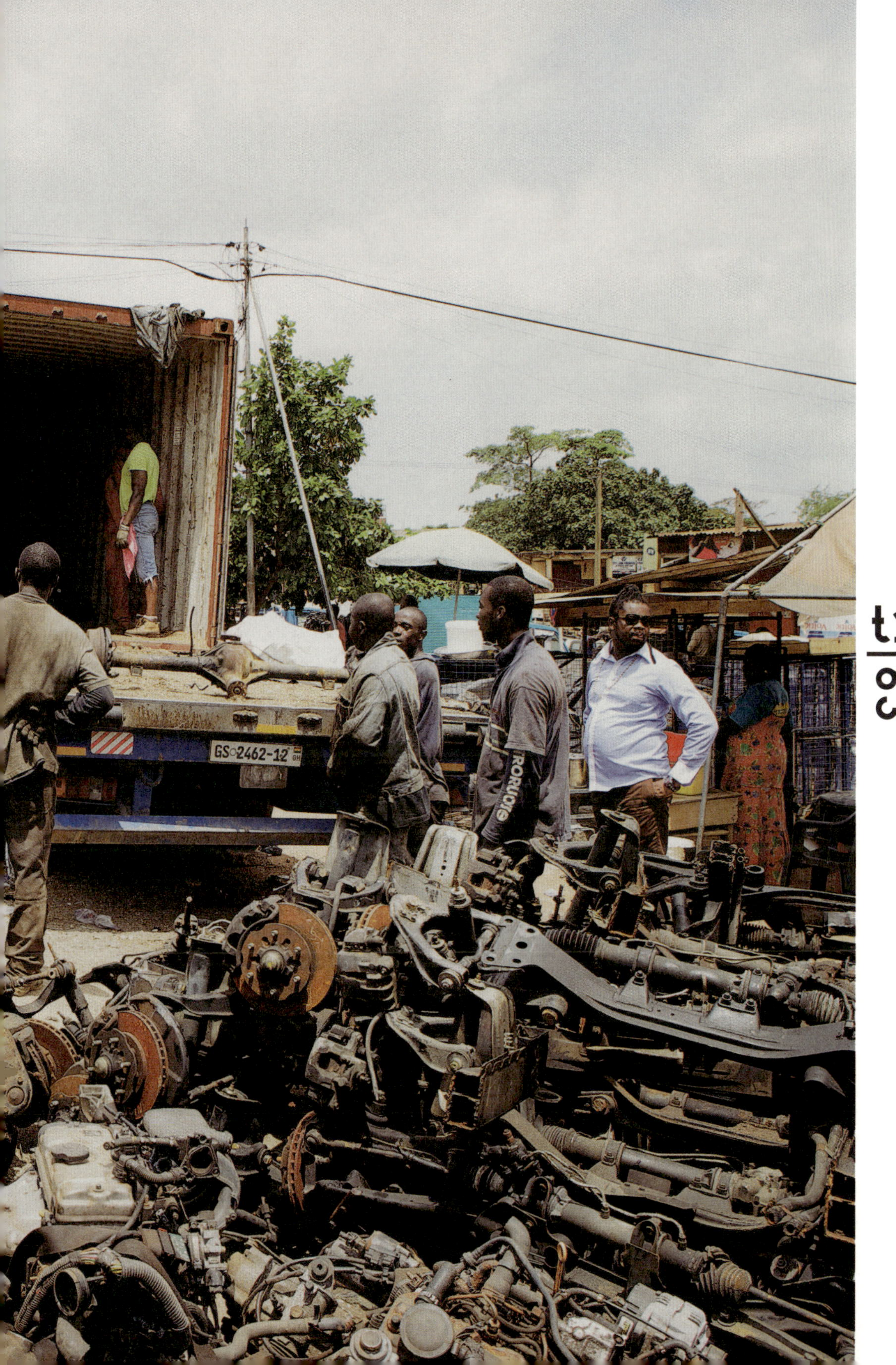
GS 2462-12

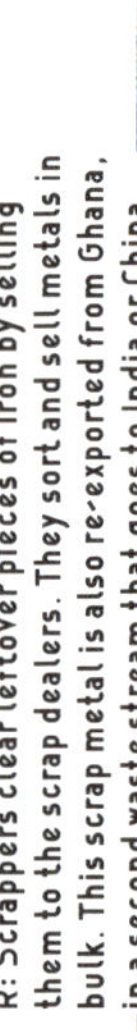
R: Scrappers clear leftover pieces of iron by selling them to the scrap dealers. They sort and sell metals in bulk. This scrap metal is also re-exported from Ghana, in a second waste stream that goes to India or China.

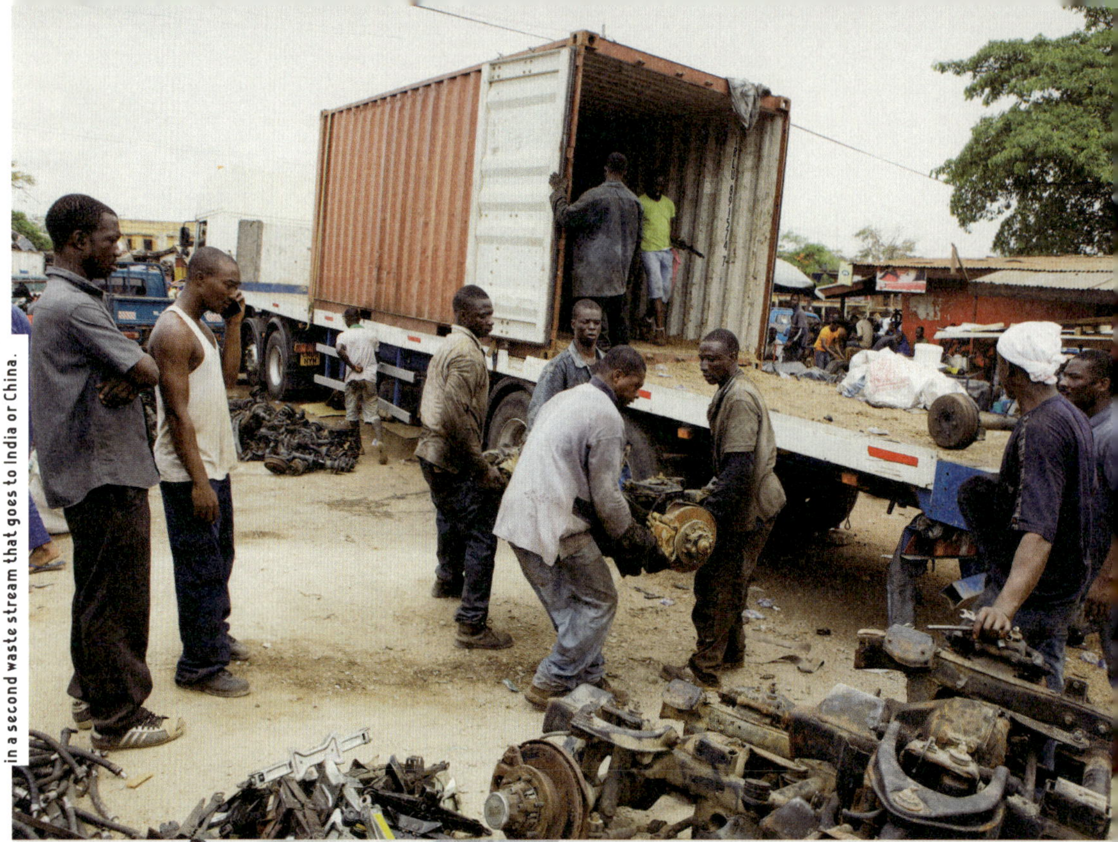

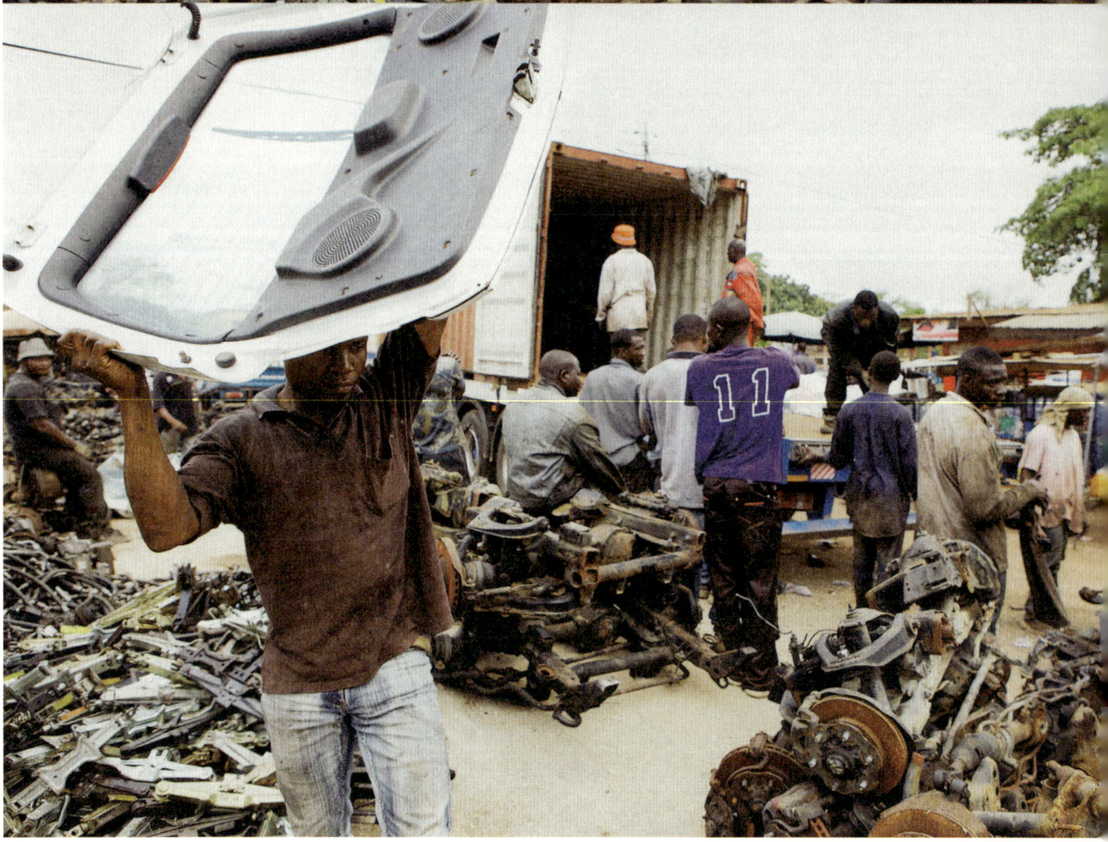

GH // 03.2013

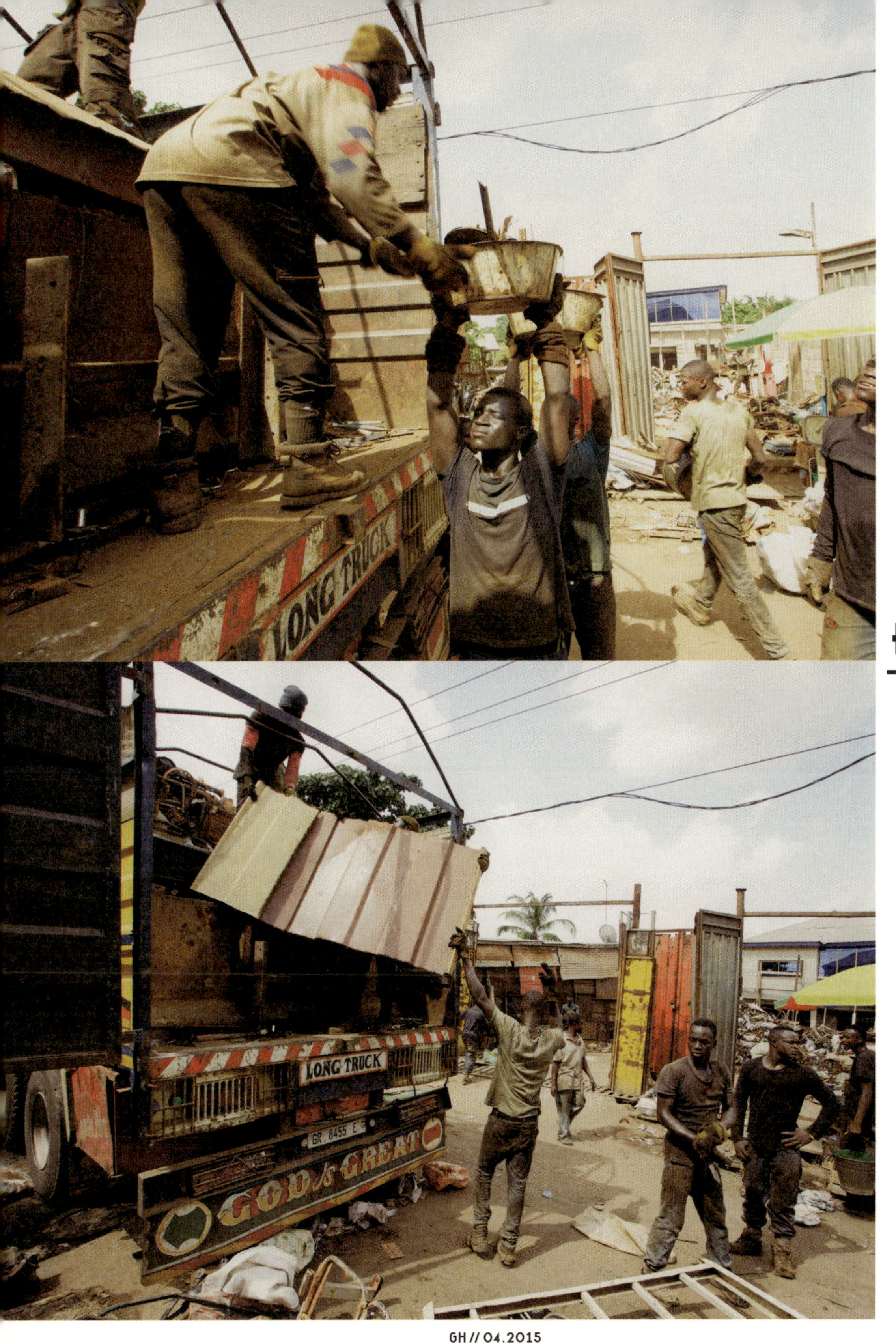

GH // 04.2015

GH // 04.2015

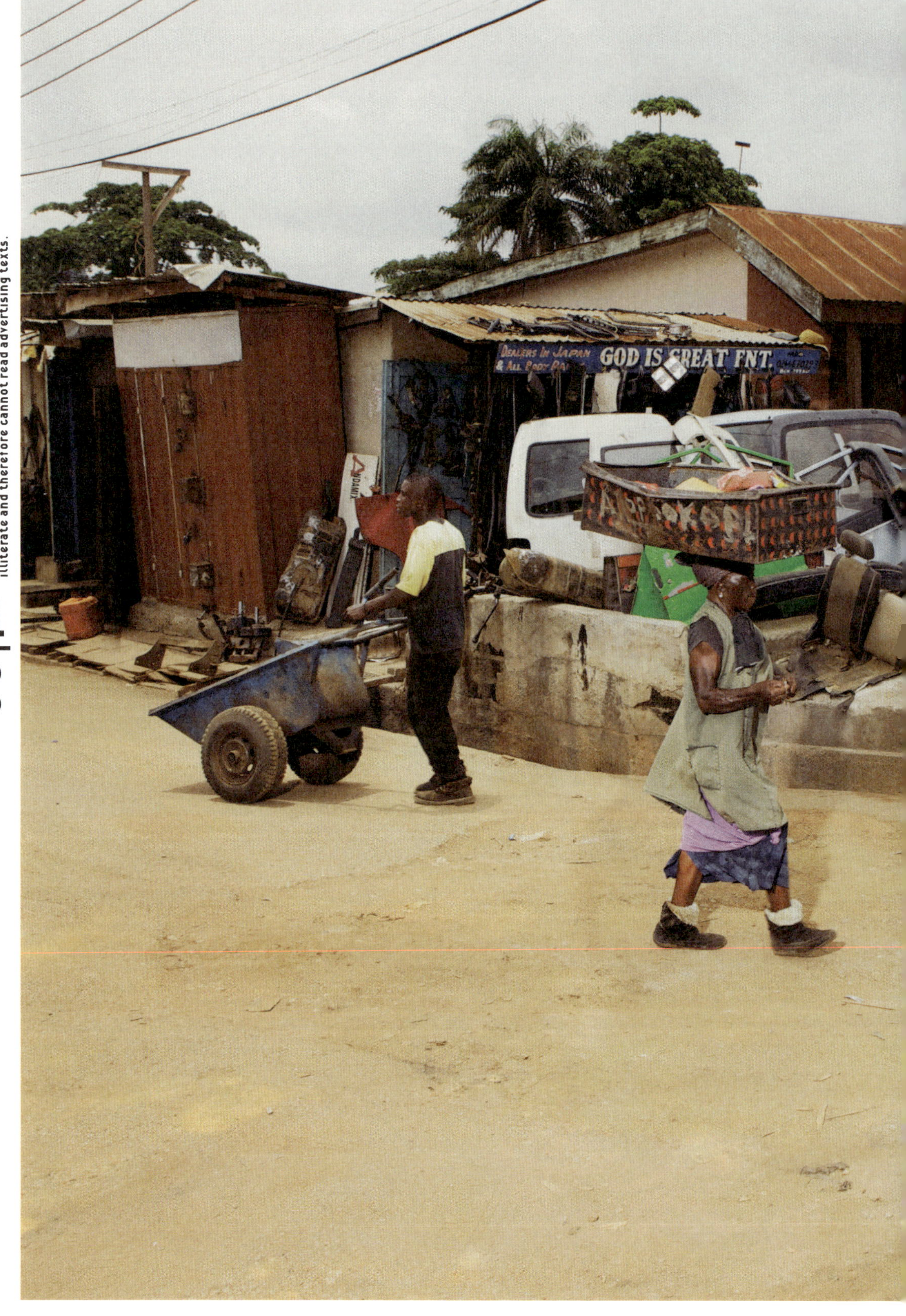

Most workshops have no signs as their clients are usually from the cluster. Furthermore, most workers are illiterate and therefore cannot read advertising texts.

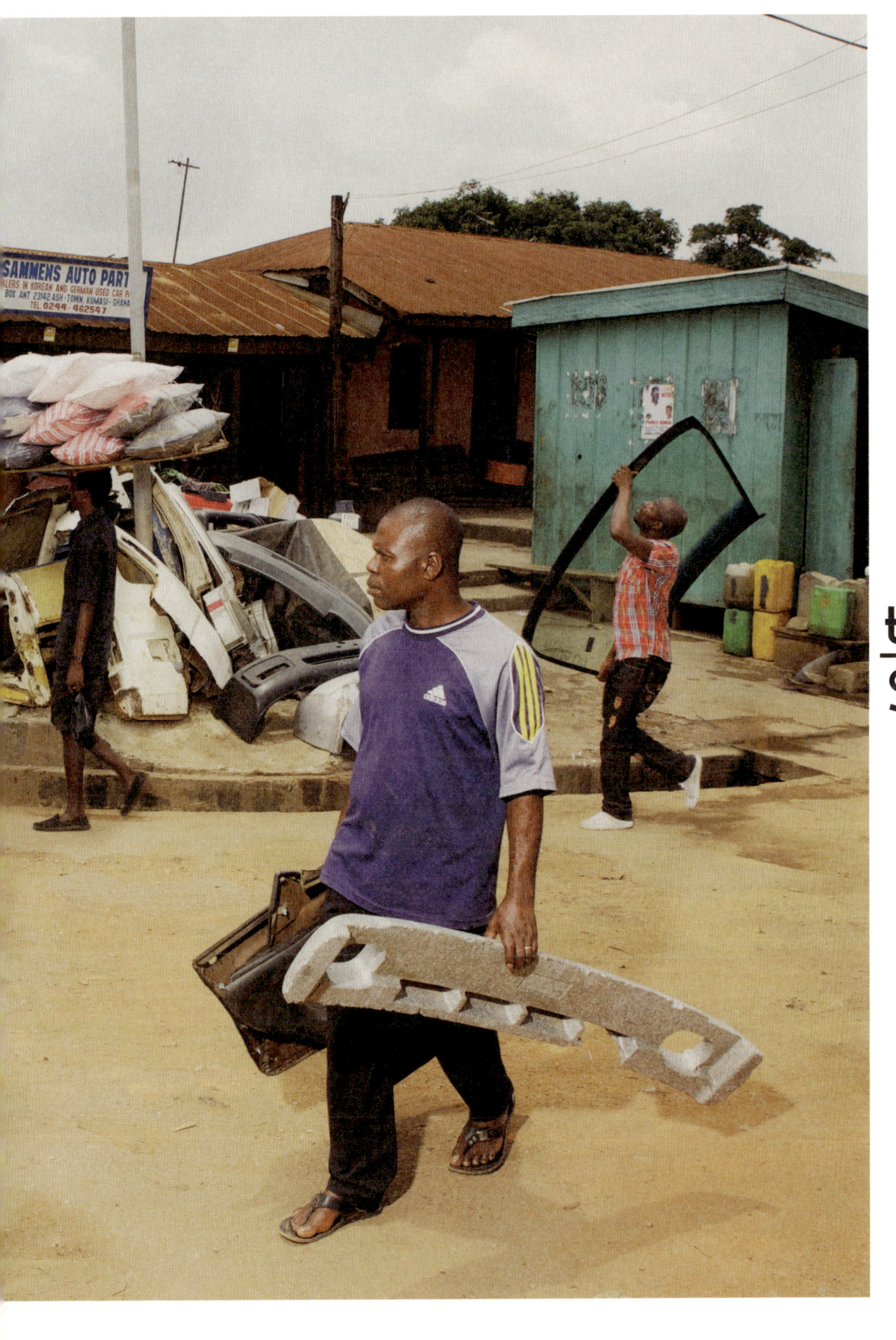
SAMMENS AUTO PART
LERS IN KOREAN AND GERMAN USED CAR P
BOX ANT 23142 ASH-TOWN KUMASI-GHANA
TEL. 0244-462547

The Suame Magazine car parts warehouse consists of highly specialised shops. Most focus on a single product or brand.

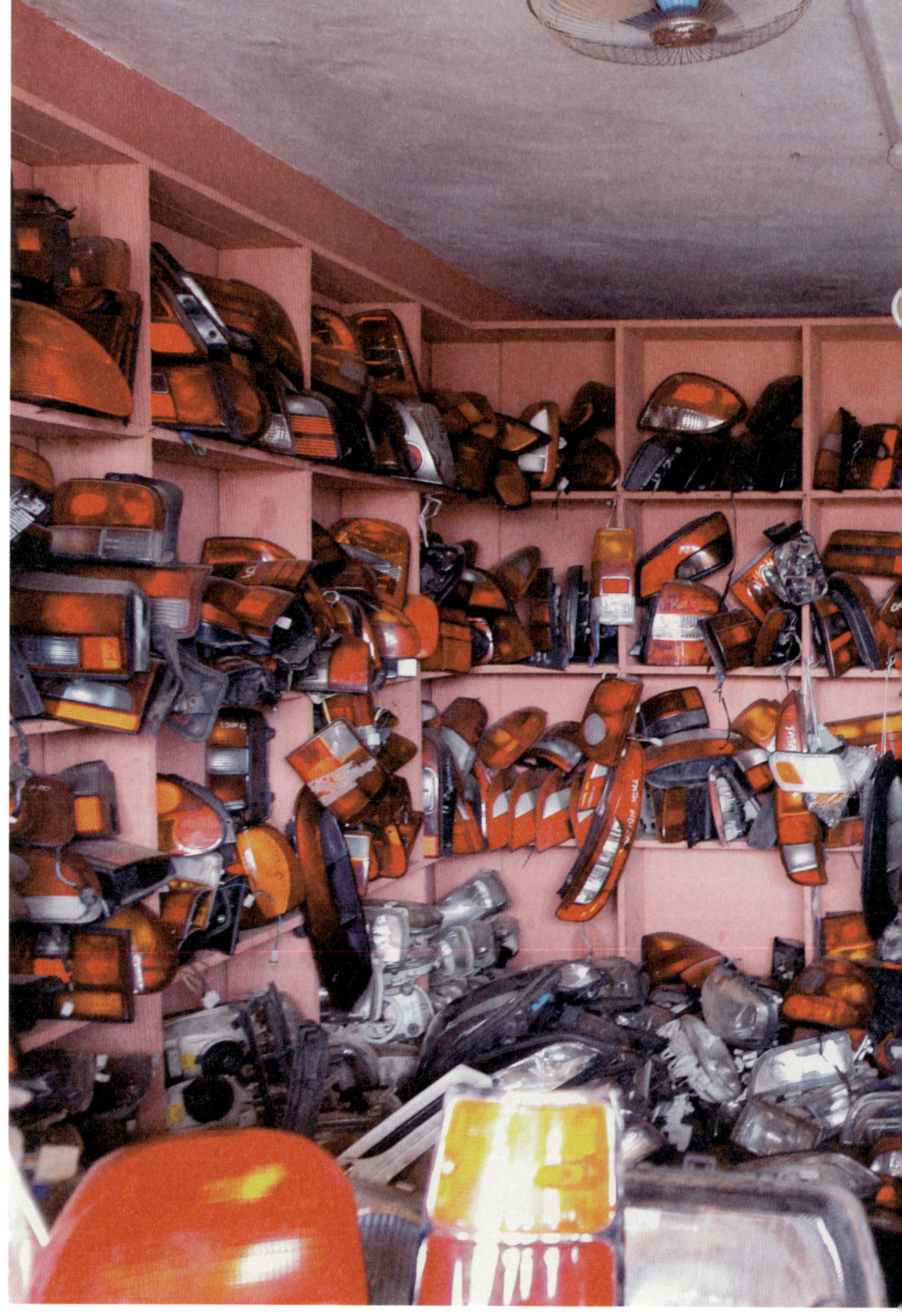

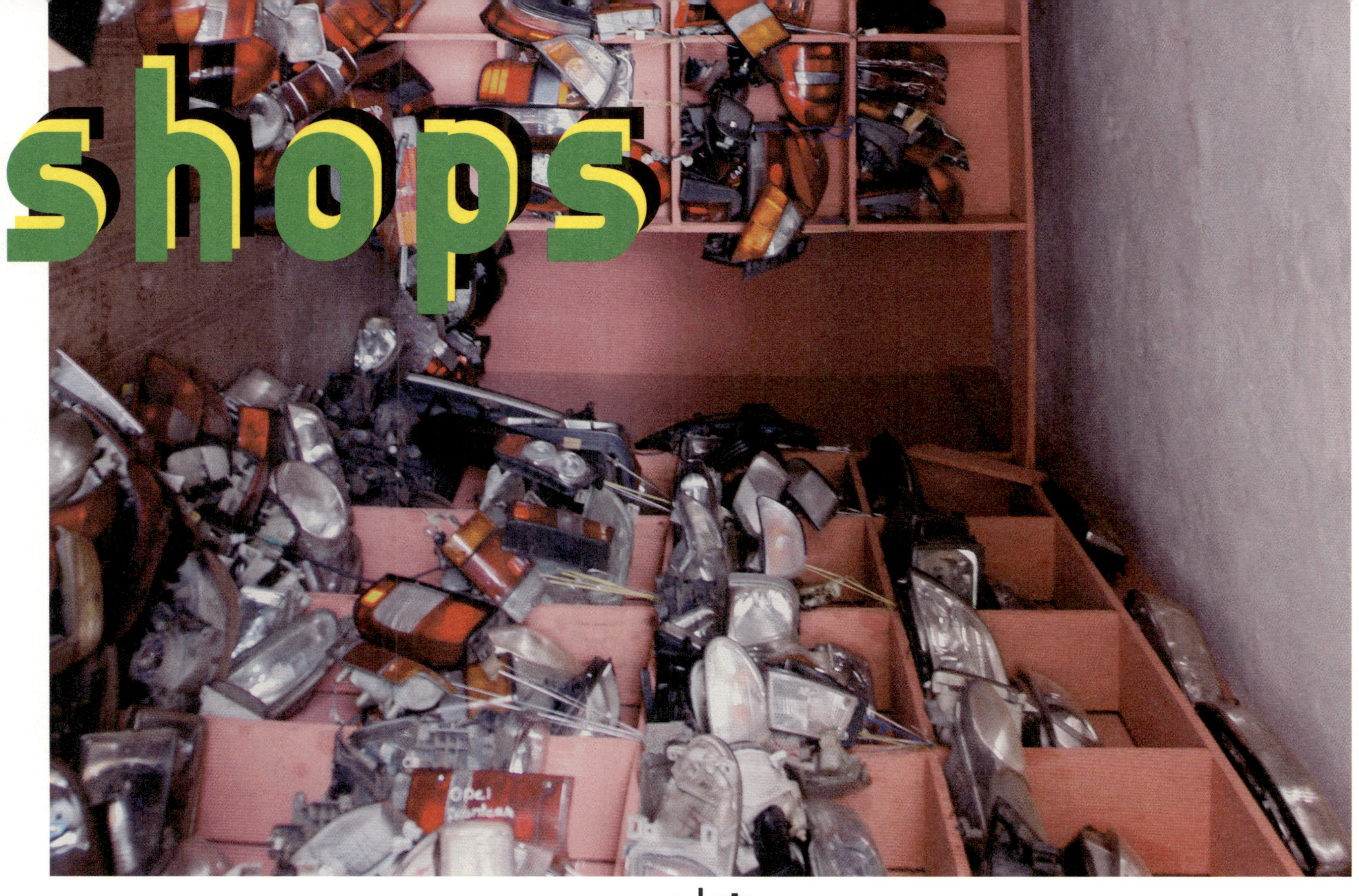

shops

L: Tommy Pipe House's shop supplied a composite exhaust system for the Turtle 1: a Mitsubishi muffler and a Mazda silencer.
R: The Catholic welder got his nickname because in addition to his welding work, he hears confessions and produces machines to press hosts.

MIS-194 / MAZ-457 // GH // AO-11 // 03.2013

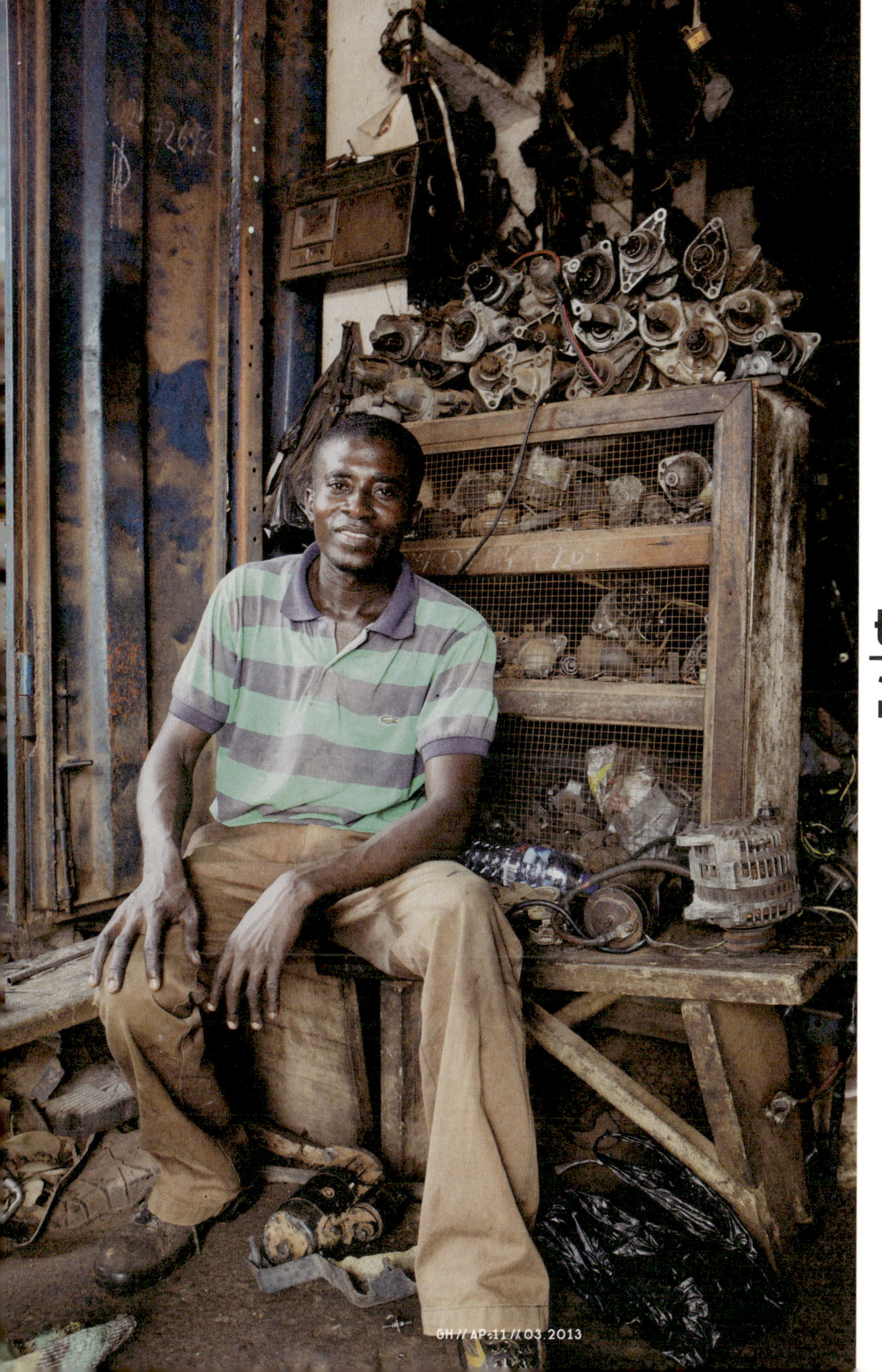

GH // AP-11 // 03.2013

TL: Japan Motor House, where the Turtle 1's chassis was bought.
TR: Nana Agyed Poku & Sons where we bought a Toyota steering port. Rare and hard to find.
BL: The front axle was bought at Enkasa Enterprise. A puzzle: it had to fit with the ladder chassis, the SsangYong engine and the power steering system.
BR: Boakye Yiadom Enterprise provided the Turtle's leaf springs. A speciality of Suame, perfectly suited to Ghana's poor roads and easy to repair. They can also bear heavy loads.

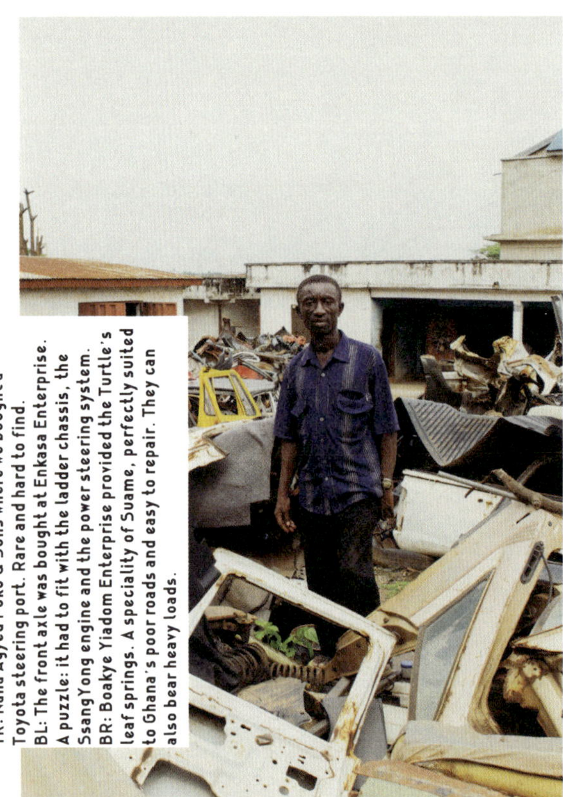

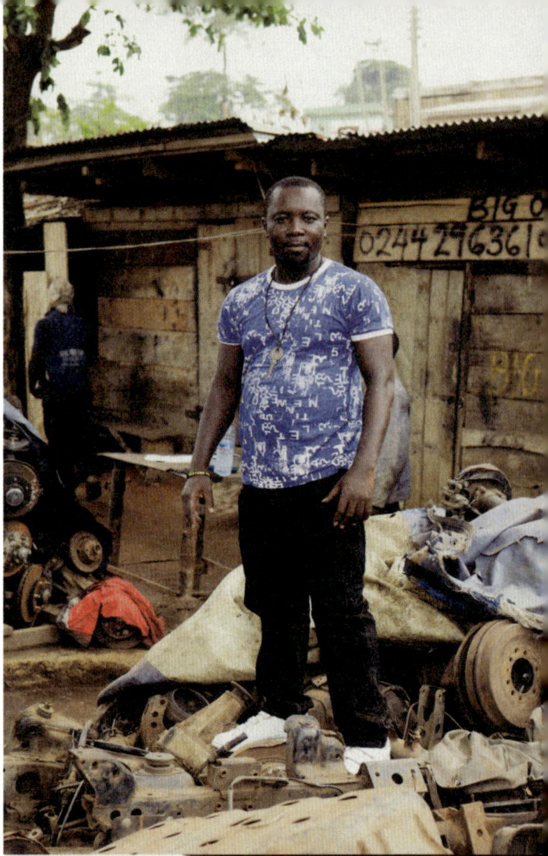

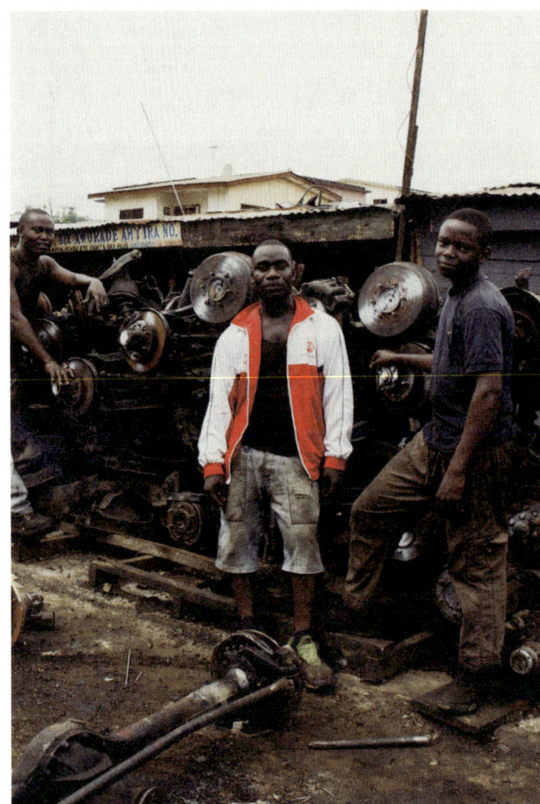

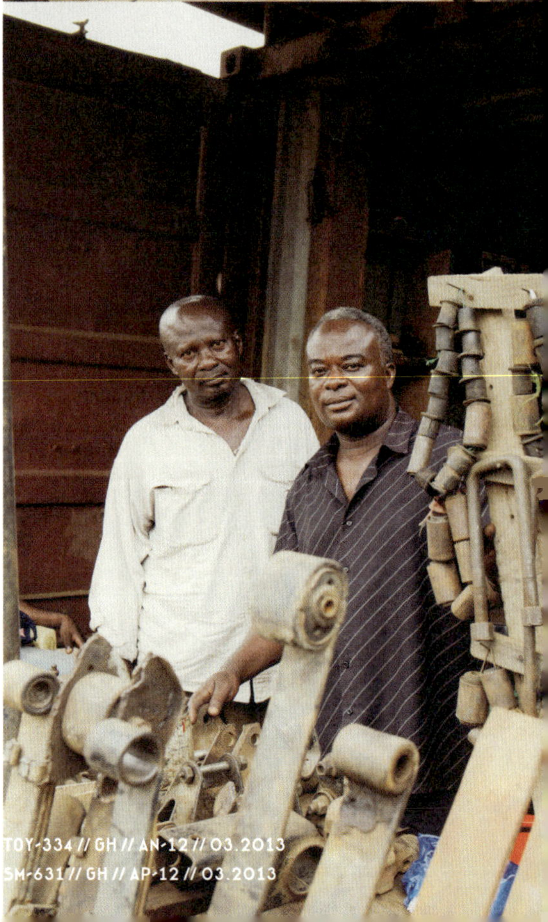

TOY-351 // GH // AT-13 // 03.2013
NIS-402 // GH // AR-13 // 03.2013

TOY-334 // GH // AN-12 // 03.2013
SM-631 // GH // AP-12 // 03.2013

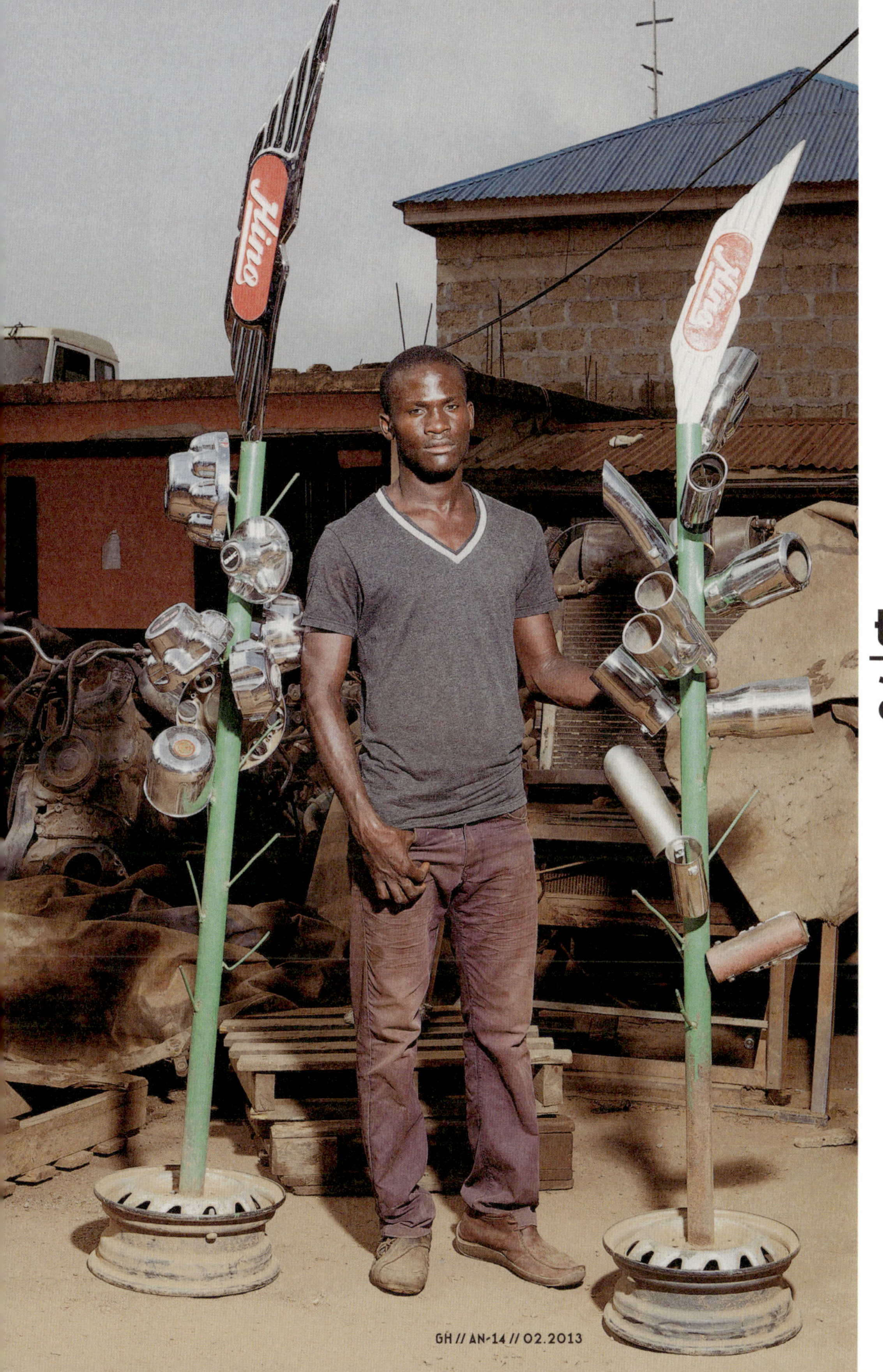

GH // AN-14 // 02.2013

L: Master Iddrisu's Rubber Company Business Center made all the Turtle's rubber parts.
TL: Manko Sons Enterprises, where we bought the accelerator.
TR: Alviant Rims & Tyres shop.
BL: Rose Wiring Electrics, where we bought the electric wiring. Every country has its own wiring system.
BR: The Big Sasruku Enterprise supplied the petrol tank, though they did not own it. Traders pay "affair people social money" to find the right parts.

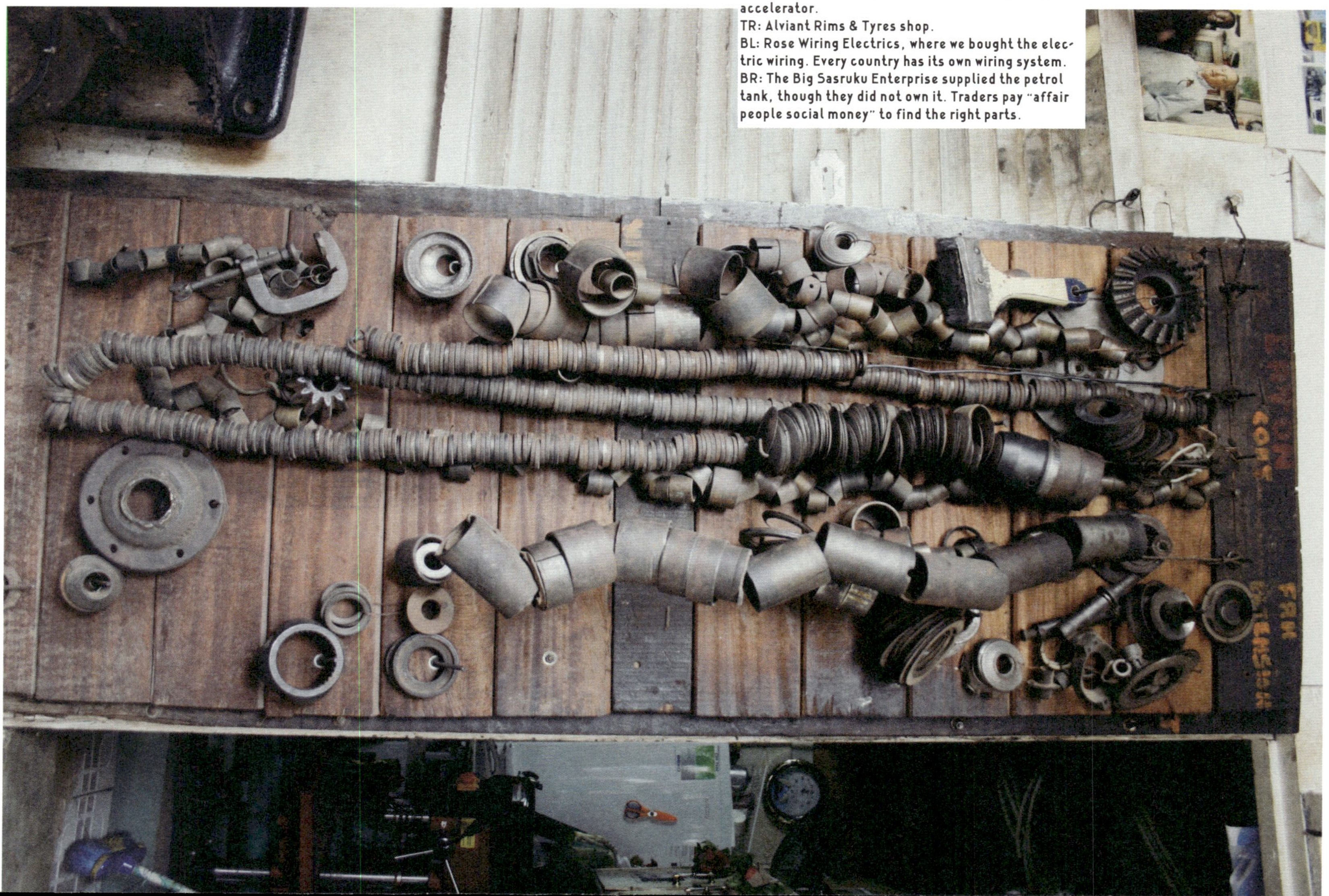

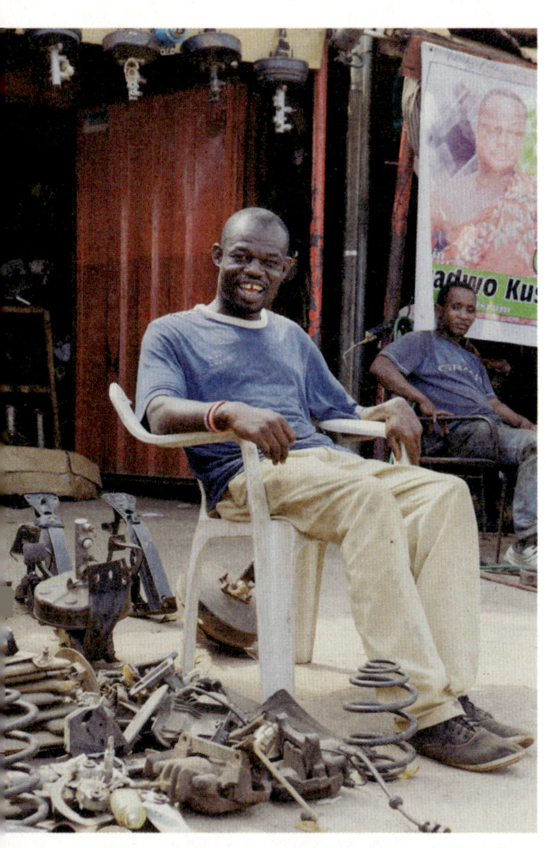

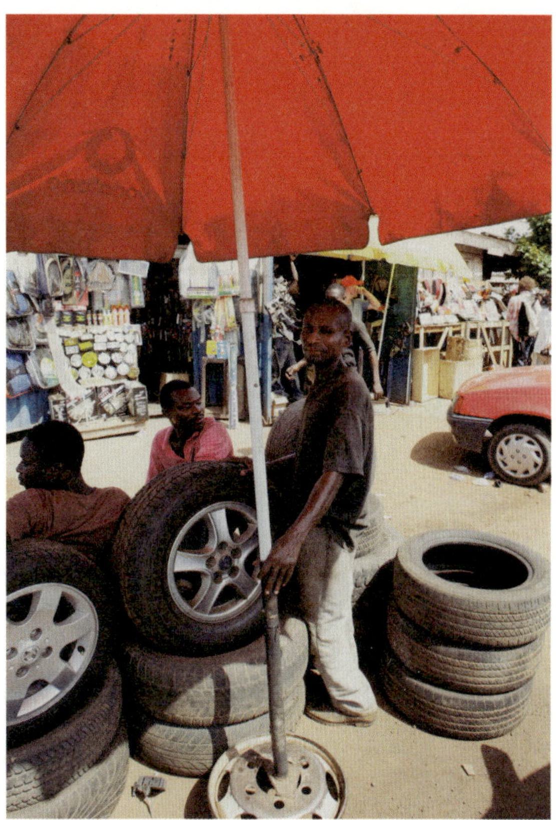

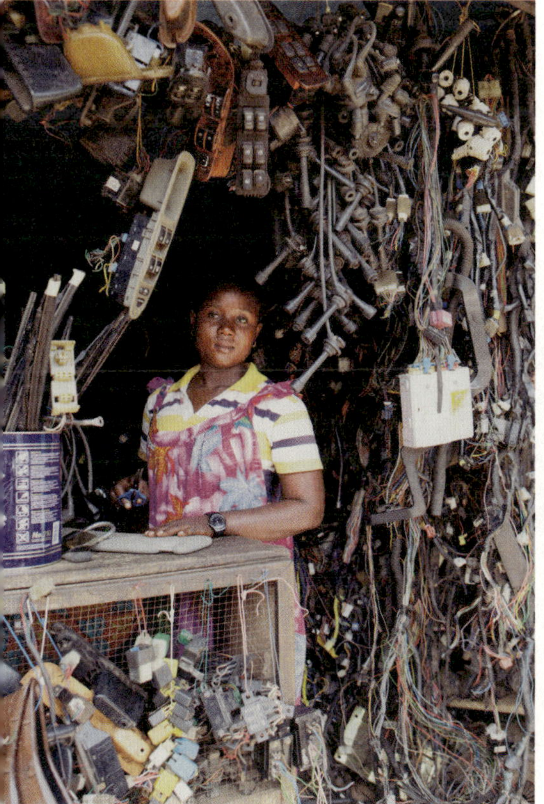

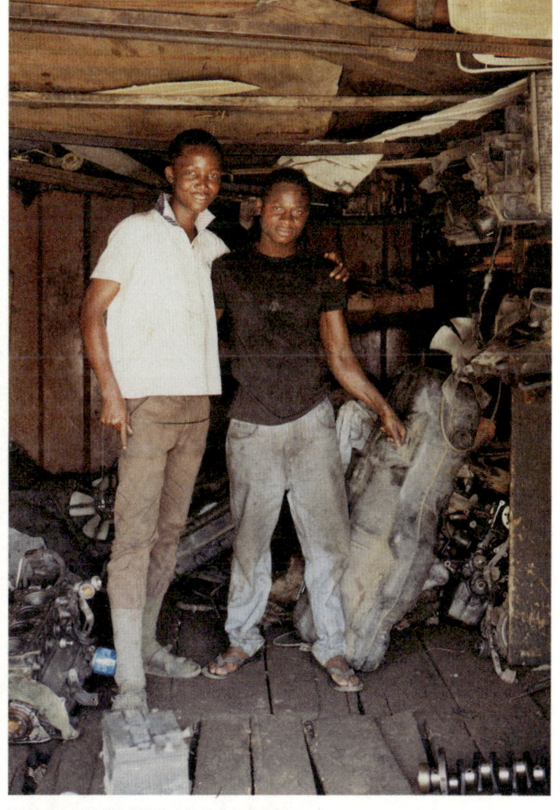

S-315 // GH // AM-14 // 03.2013
MW-312 // GH // 03.2013

TOY-396 // GH // AN-13 // 03.2013
MAZ-876 // GH // AO-13 //03.2013

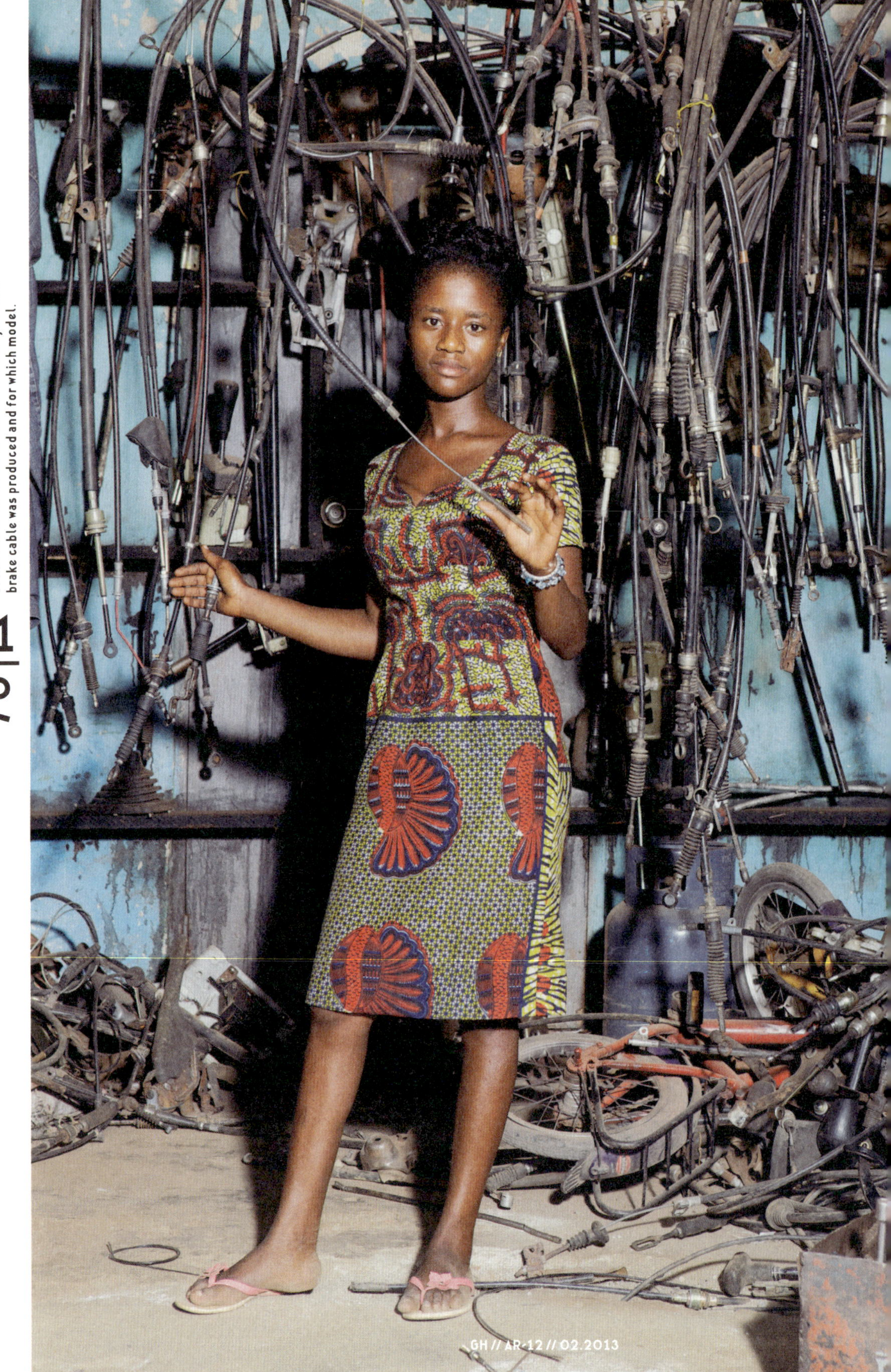

L: Salesmen become specialists at an early age. This brake-cable saleswoman can tell in which year this brake cable was produced and for which model.

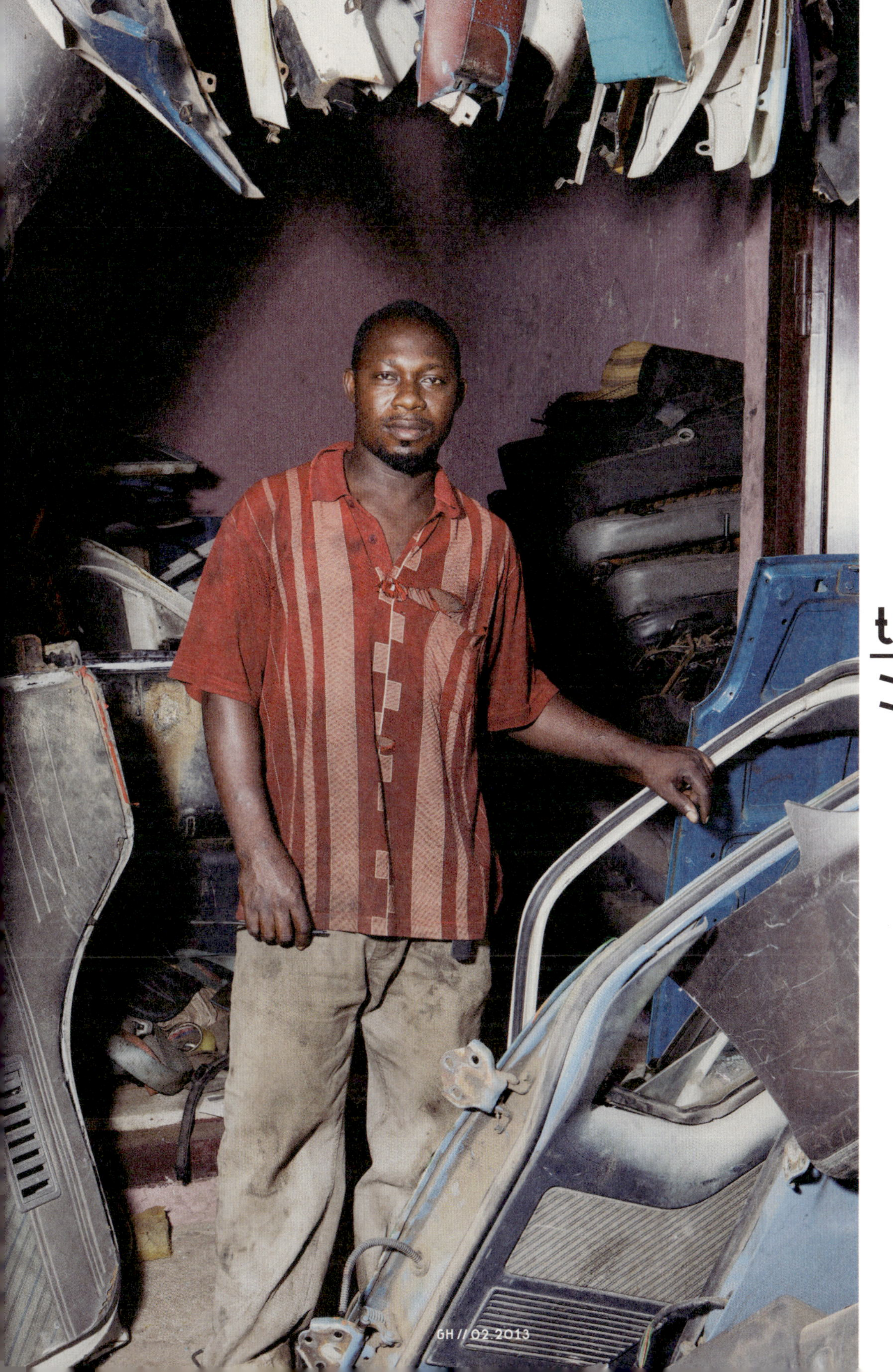

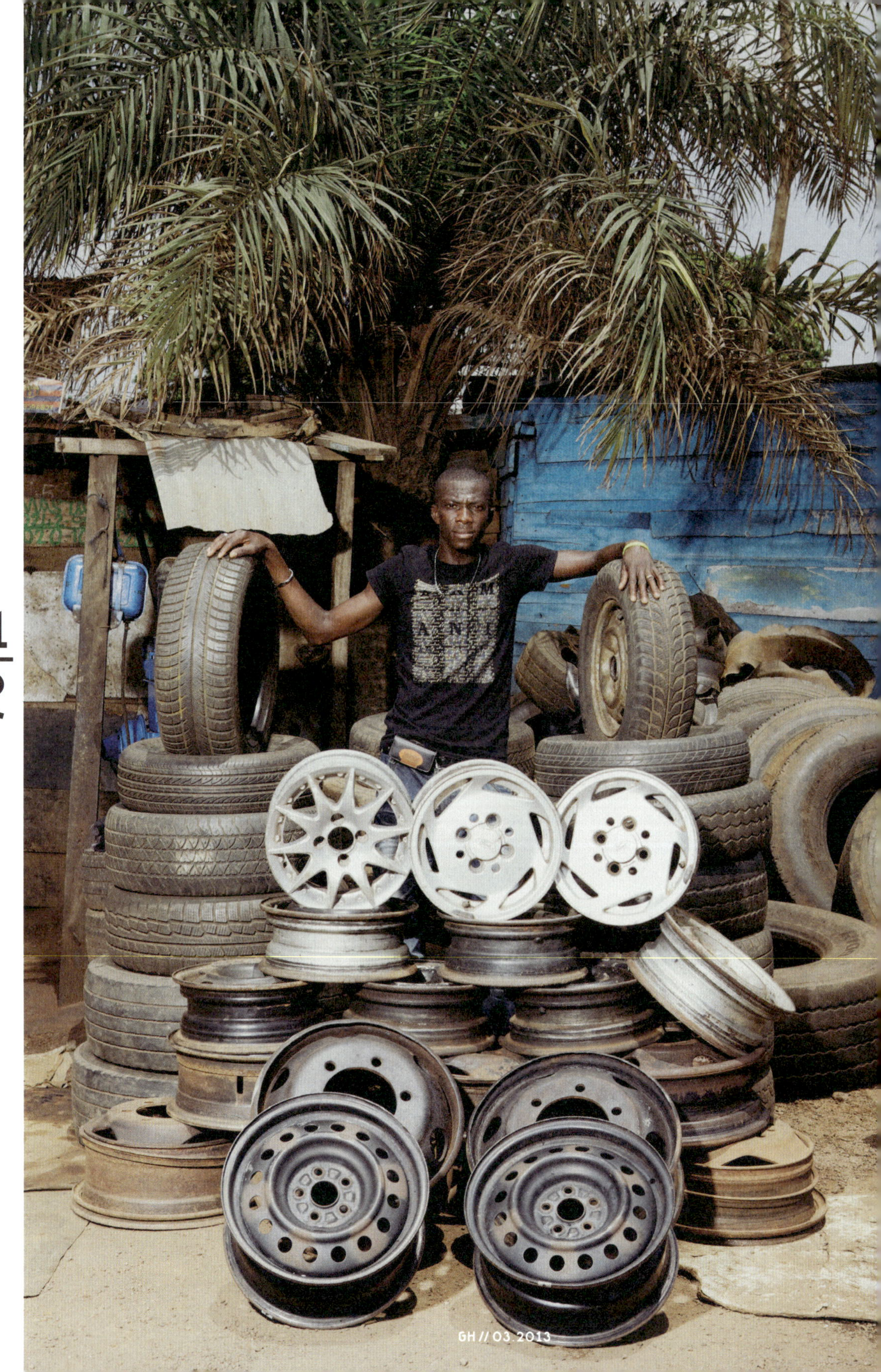

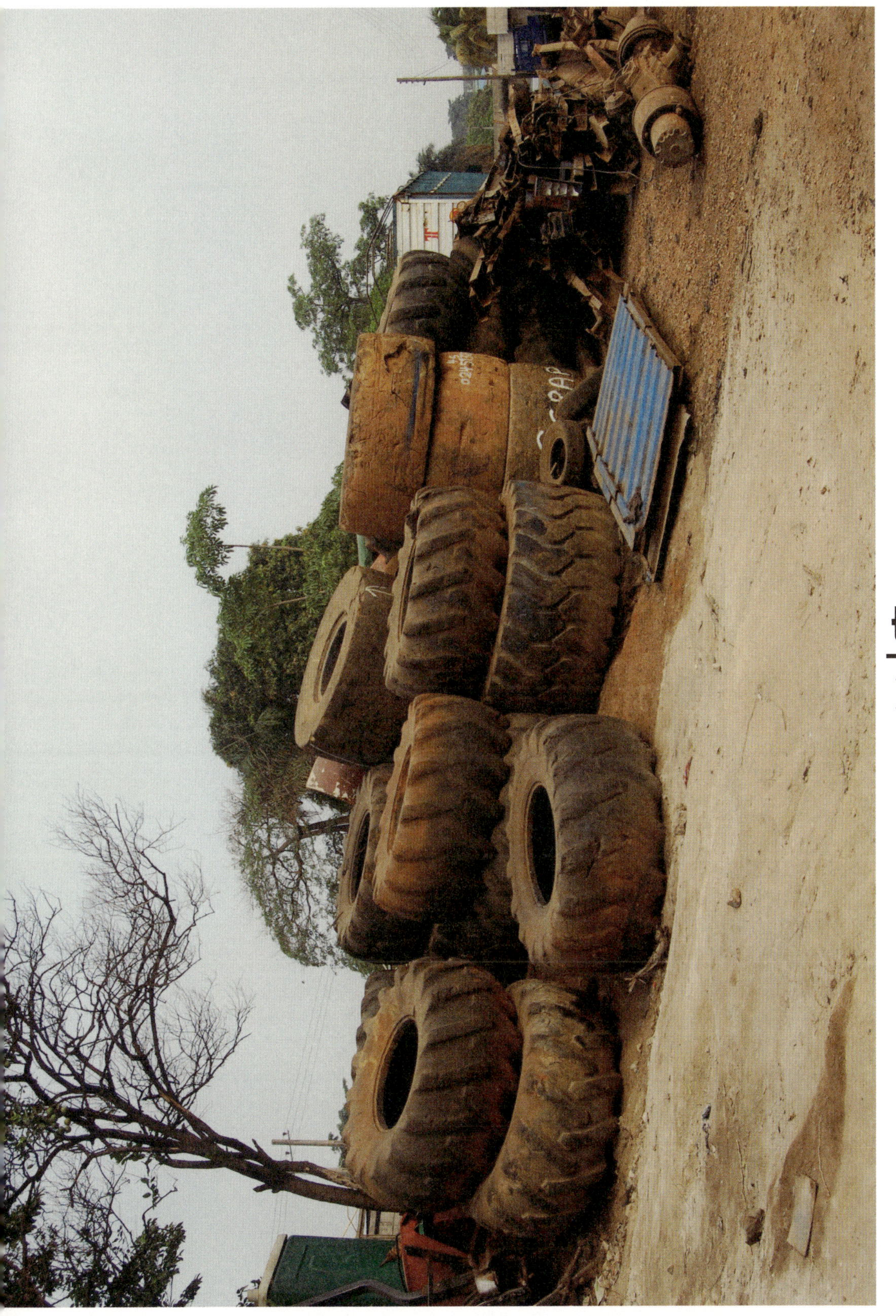

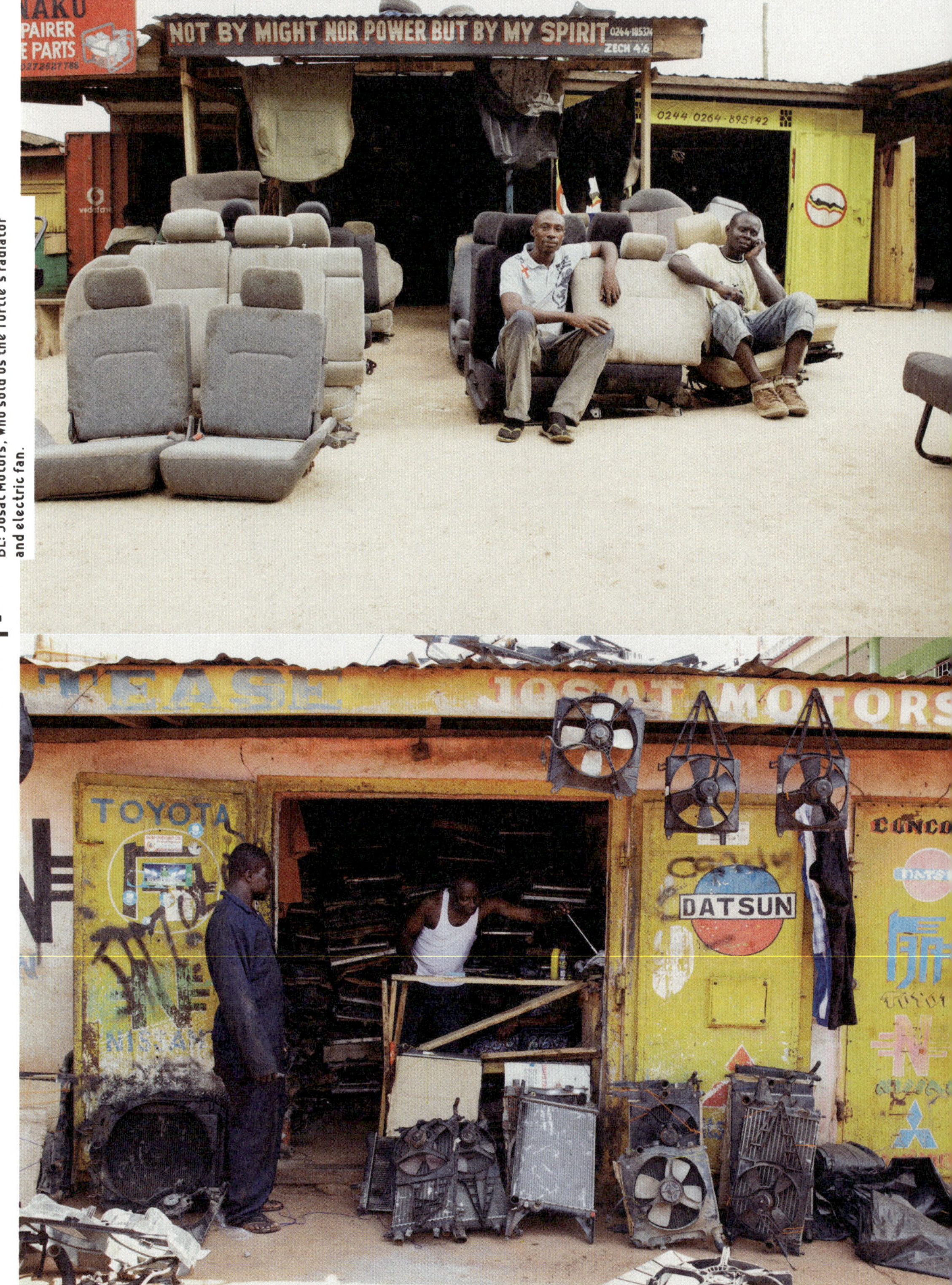

TL: Not By Might Nor Power But By My Spirit, car seat dealer.
BL: Josat Motors, who sold us the Turtle's radiator and electric fan.

MER-456 // GH // AL-13 // 03.2013
OPE-400 / FOR-256 // GH // AN-14 // 03.2013

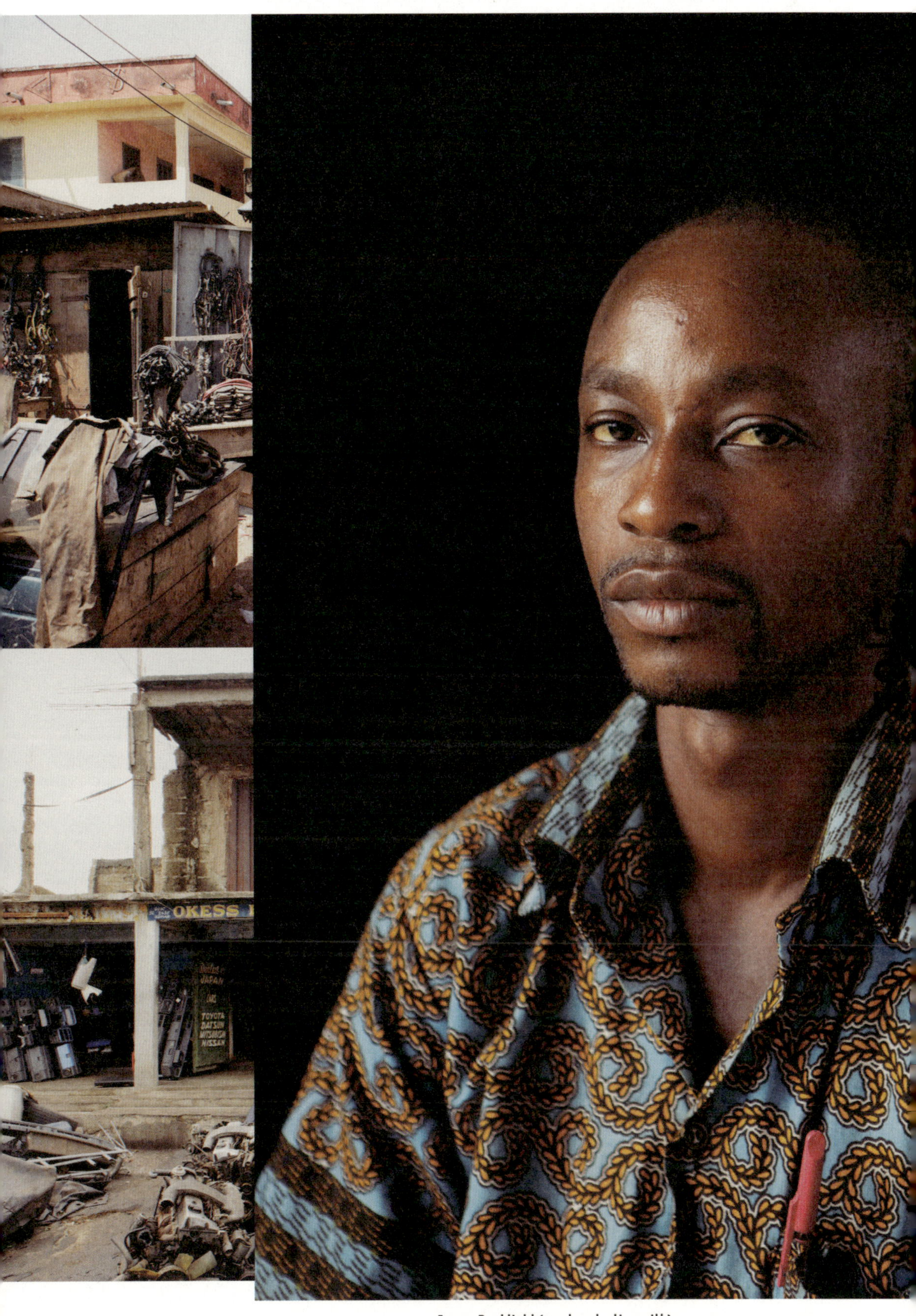

James Backlight (master plastic smith)

L: Drive shaft dealer. The drive shaft connects the rear drive to the gear box. As this part revolves quickly and is subject to many forces, it is important to buy a well-balanced axle.
R: Engine carriers. Once bought these musclemen lift the motor into the Suame Taxi.

GH // 03.2013

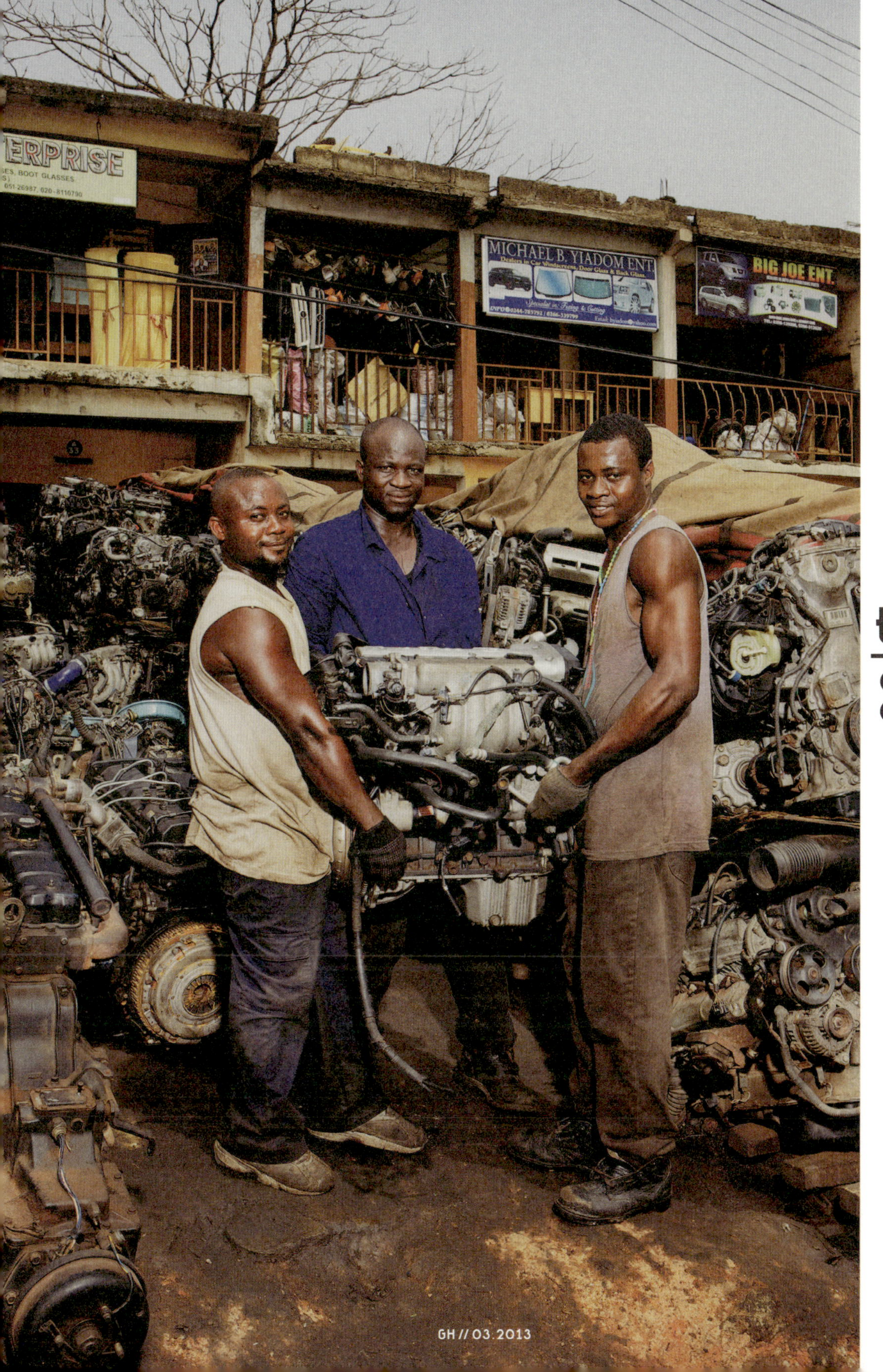
ERPRISE
MICHAEL B. YIADOM ENT.
BIG JOE ENT.

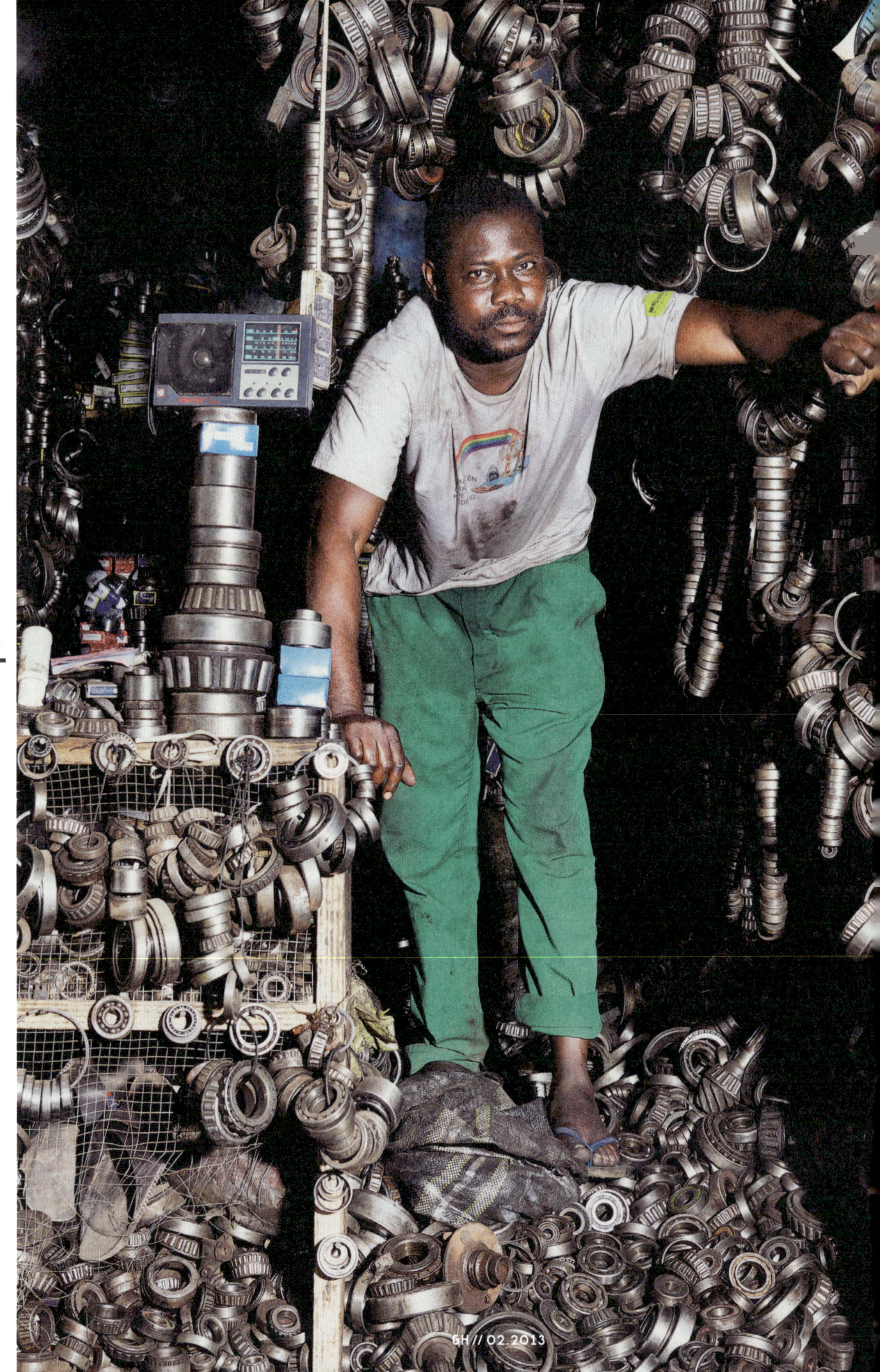

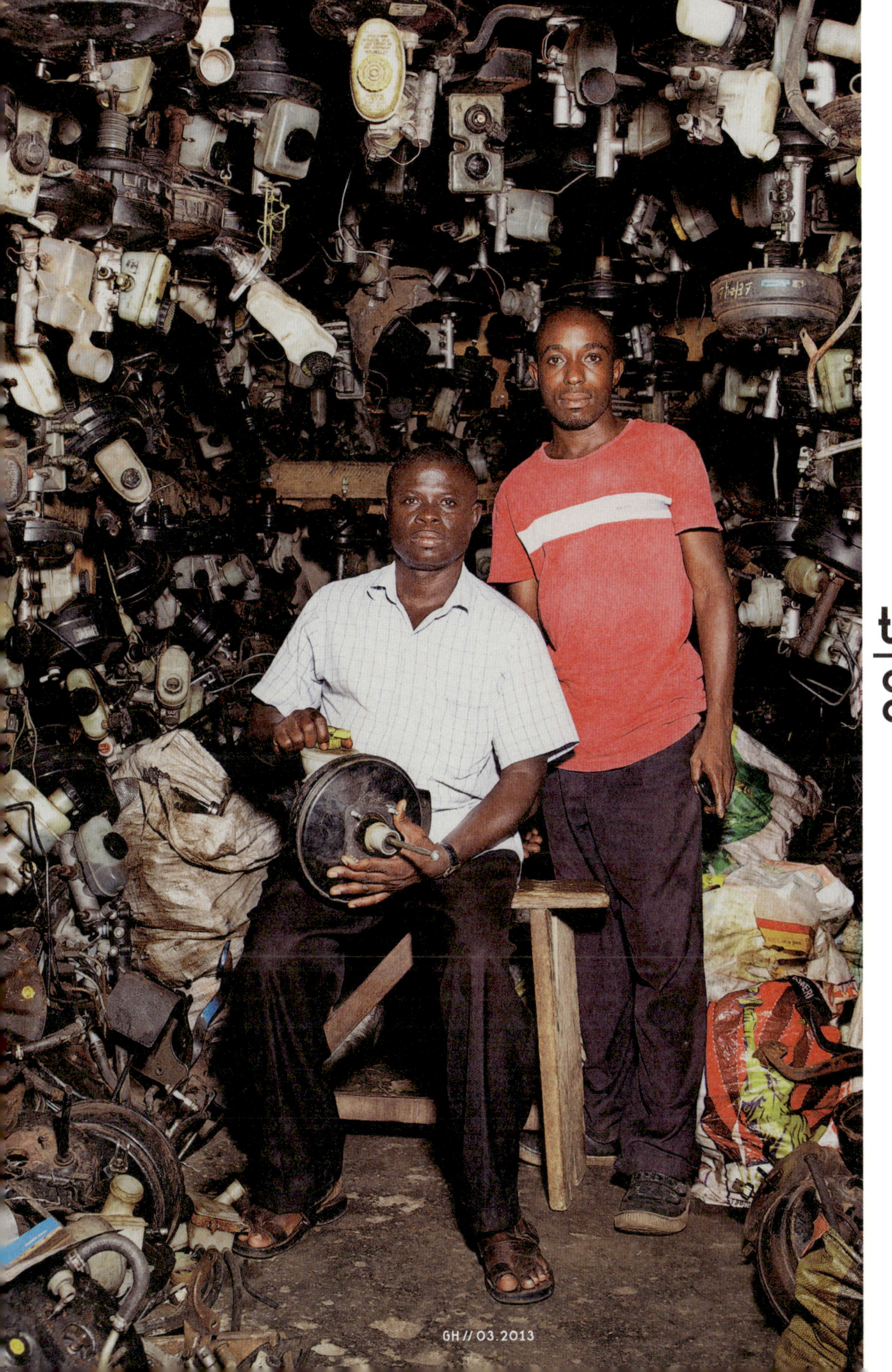

GH // 03.2013

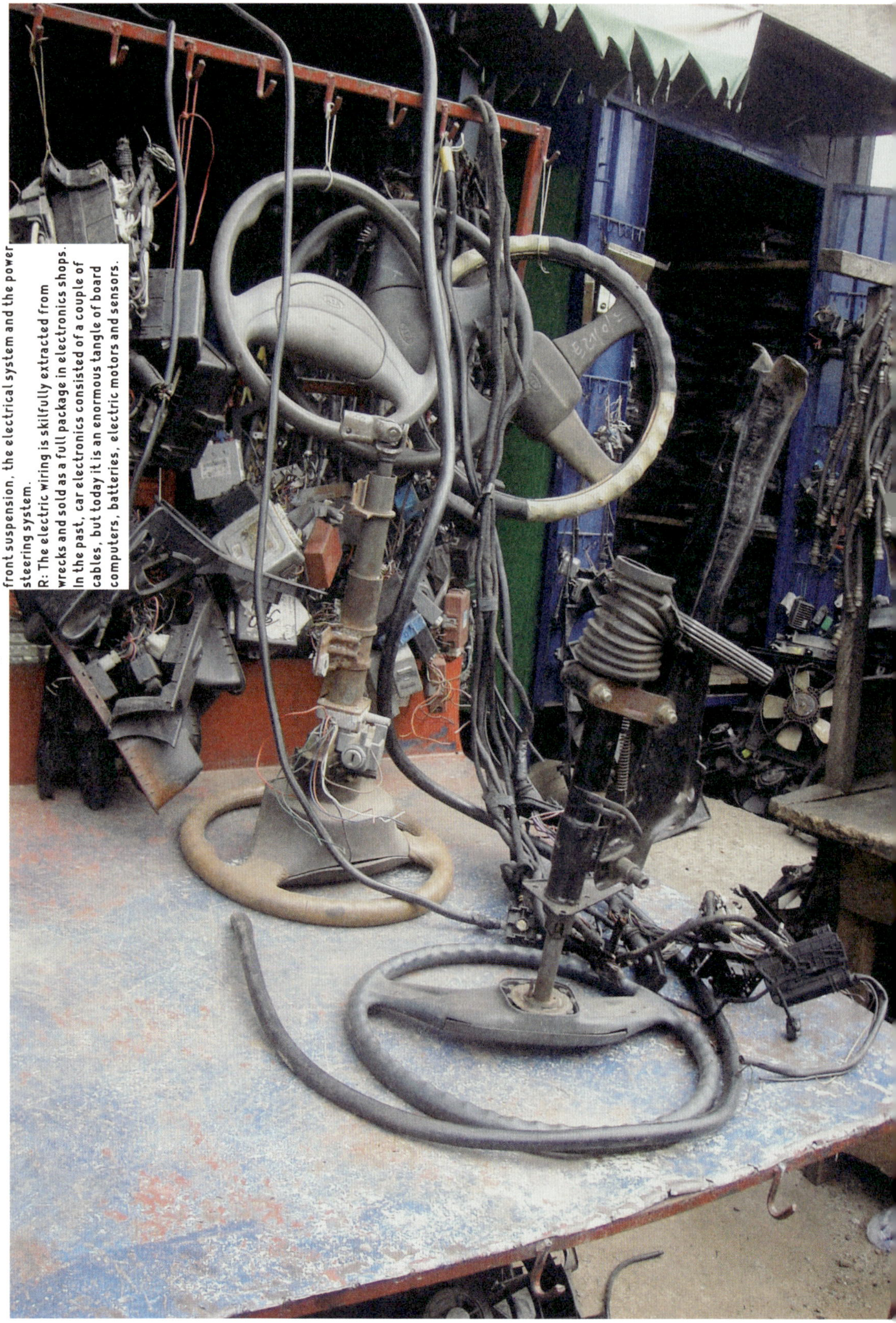

L: The steering column is like a neck: the car's whole nervous system runs through it. It is practically impossible to find a steering column that fits with the front suspension, the electrical system and the power steering system.

R: The electric wiring is skilfully extracted from wrecks and sold as a full package in electronics shops. In the past, car electronics consisted of a couple of cables, but today it is an enormous tangle of board computers, batteries, electric motors and sensors.

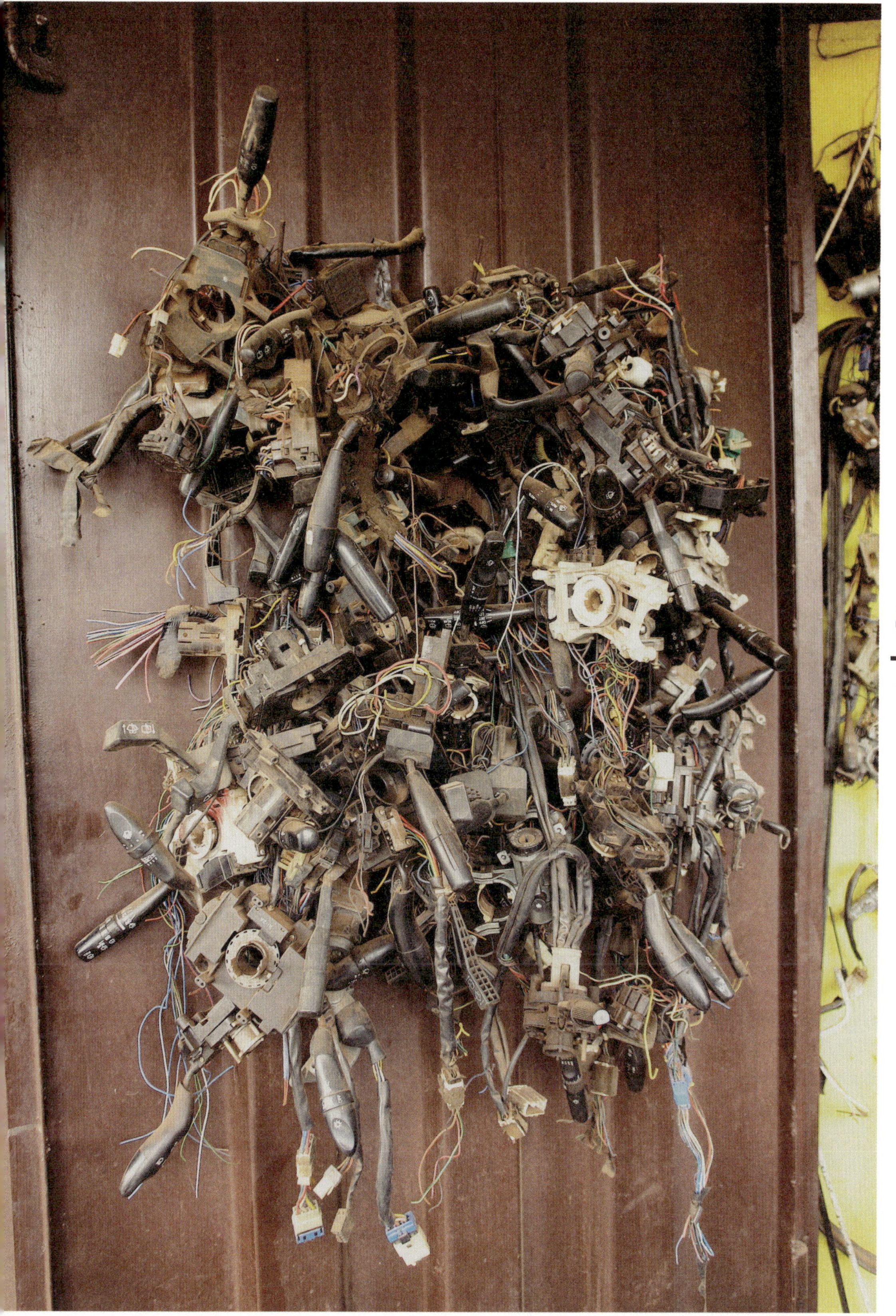

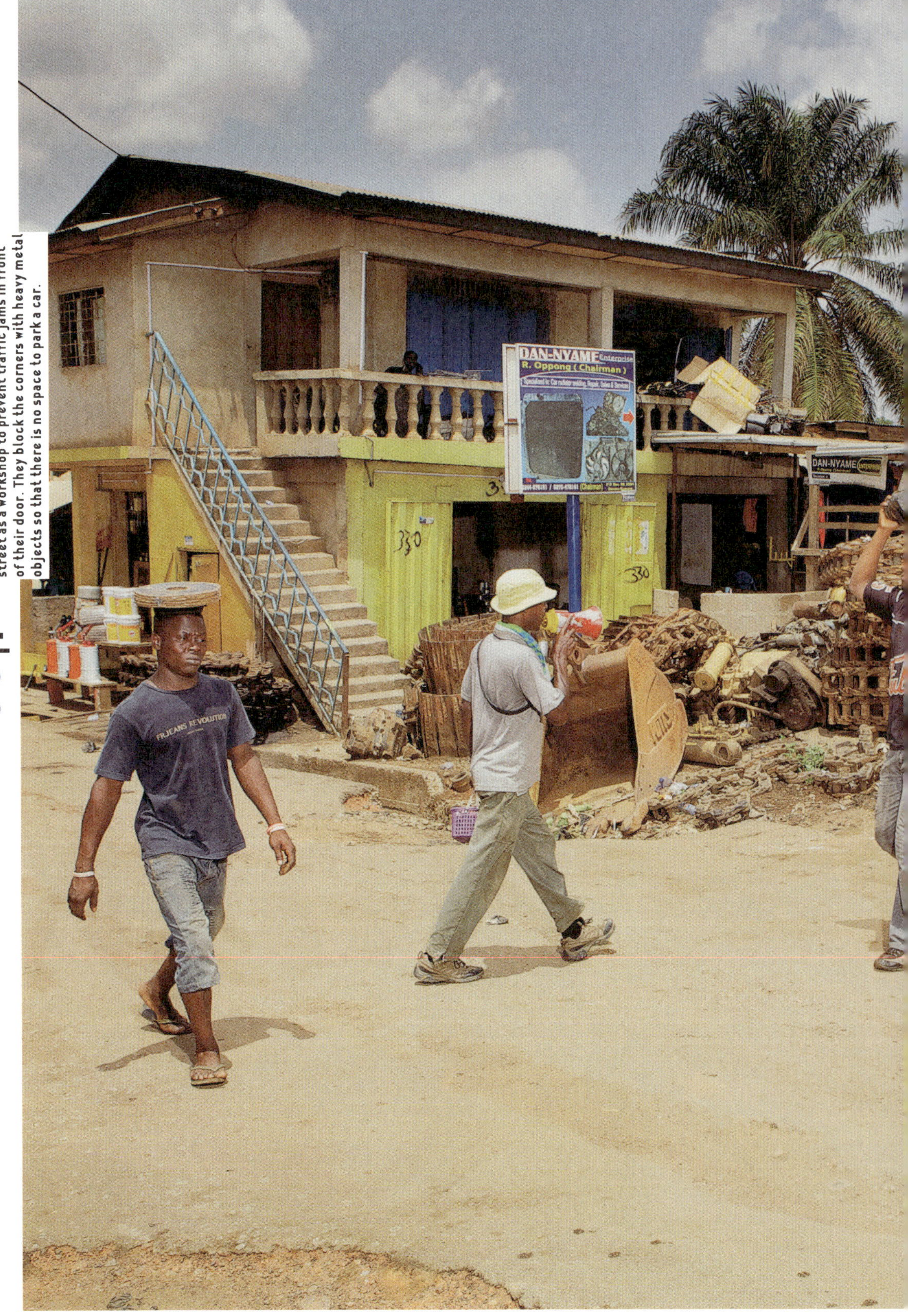

Intersections constantly get blocked with traffic. Shopkeepers try to stop mechanics from using the street as a workshop to prevent traffic jams in front of their door. They block the corners with heavy metal objects so that there is no space to park a car.

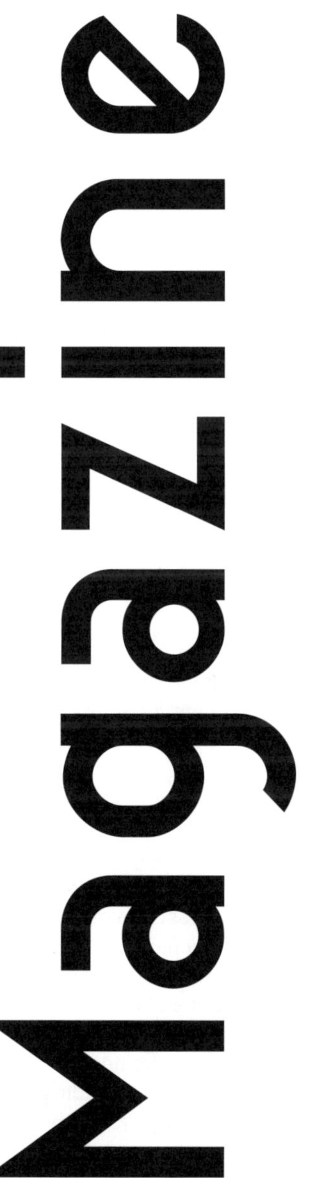

You can walk right into Suame, but in many respects it is still a closed world. To outsiders Suame appears chaotic – full of noise, congested roads and tough guys. Some see it as a ghetto, a place of poverty, oil and noise. It is a world with its own customs and language, but also a place where people work, eat, have fun and sometimes also live; where children grow up and where people go to church and to the mosque.[1]

One thing is for sure: cars are the binding factor between the tens of thousands of workshops. This is where repairs are carried out and car parts are traded. While you can also buy new parts like batteries, windshield wipers and motor oil here, it is mostly third-, fourth- and fifth-hand parts from Europe, North America and Asia. This is the back end of mobility, the lowest point in the auto industry.

Our plan is to learn by doing. But so far we have not really gotten anywhere. We have students from the KNUST University departments of mechanical engineering and arts and even a group of students from the Rietveld Academy in Amsterdam. Then there are about 30 mechanics and artisans from the neighbourhood who have come to help, mainly because they are curious to see what is going on. We hold a workshop and send out three mixed groups to conduct research; one to explore mechanical composition, one for the body work and one for the interior. The groups wander around the neighbourhood for hours. But what are we actually looking for?

The students follow us obediently through this strange neighbourhood where they would otherwise never set foot. They carry Bibles with them and occasionally sit down to read a passage. Reluctantly, they translate the questions we ask the workmen, who in turn do not understand why we want to know what they are doing. This is an industrial area where people communicate by trading, building and repairing, not by chatting.

The mechanics also do not understand all this wandering around the neighbourhood in the blazing heat. You must be mad to walk around like this in this climate. "Where you want to go? What you need?" Legitimate questions to which we have no answers. Professor Fiagbe had warned us in advance that it is not enough to bring artisans and students together in a workshop. The mechanics quit after the first day and most of the students do not come back either.

1 See for interesting reading on the subject: Wenningsted-Torgard, R., P. Schulz Schovsbo, B. Ballisager & J. Wegener Bonde. 2013. Suame Magazine. Light Industrial Living. Retrieved from: https://dl.dropboxusercontent.com/u/11586293/Suame%20 Magazine.pdf

Dr Waco urges us to get started. “Mr. Melles what are we doing? Let us start. We need a ladder chassis. I know where to buy this for a good price.” This is going to be our first lesson in car building. Modern passenger cars do not have a chassis; they have a monocoque body that is pressed into shape so that it can support itself. The problem is that if you saw a hole in it, it loses its solidity. It is like a piece of IKEA furniture: there is only one way of putting it together and it can only be done once. This means we have to rely on pick-ups and jeeps, which have a separate chassis. The chassis is the skeleton of the car and strong skeletons are popular in Ghana.

We trudge along behind Dr Waco. He knows exactly where to go. The large importers are located on the edge of the neighbourhood on the Offinso Road, a busy thoroughfare to northern Ghana. That is how we end up at Japan Motor House, a large plot filled with towering piles of rusting parts. Dr Waco looks around patiently. His eyes slowly scan the scrap, while we look on in confusion, not quite sure what we should be looking out for. To us, it all looks like old junk. Dr Waco kneels down and starts tugging at a piece of tubing that is wedged below a pile of frames. “This is what we need,” he says firmly. “This is a Toyota Land Cruiser. Very good quality.” By now the owner has been alerted, his staff have told him that he has customers. White customers. We shake hands and tell him where we are from. Incredulously he listens as we explain that we want to build a local car.

The chassis that Dr Waco is interested in seems firmly stuck at the bottom of the pile. We are told that if we manage to extract it, we have to buy it. When we enquire about the price, Dr Waco shoots us an angry look. He shakes his head disapprovingly when the owner quotes an astronomical sum equivalent to €300. Far too much, we will carry on looking. The owner shrugs and makes no effort to convince us.

There are many other shops around Japan Motor House that sell engine blocks, axles and cabins. Toyota parts are clearly popular, but also in short supply. If we pay ahead, we can place an order. The dealer will ask his overseas contacts to look out for the right chassis. But who knows whether it will be shipped with the next cargo.

It could take weeks. If we want to start tomorrow, we will have to pay the full price at Japan Motor House, especially now that we have been foolish enough to ask the price straight away. Dr Waco explains that this is totally the wrong approach. You should start by enquiring about something else, preferably more expensive, like a pristine undercarriage. When the dealer quotes a price, you make it clear that it is miles above your budget. Then you ask about a slightly lower-quality chassis that is a lot cheaper. That is how you work your way down, until you arrive at the part you wanted all along. Now that we have put our cards on the table, we will have to pay the full price. It is an expensive lesson.

Soon the chassis is on proud display in our workshop. The rust has been concealed under a thick layer of black tectyl. It looks as good as new. The next step is the engine block. When Dr Waco says that it should also be a Toyota, we object: we would like to create a composite car, made with parts from different brands. Dr Waco doesn’t really get it, but eventually resigns himself.

It turns out that a good engine block is just as hard to find as a chassis. Again we follow Dr Waco through the neighbourhood. We see hundreds of engine blocks piled up in rows along the road. Every engine looks the same to us and we stop to look at each pile. Dr Waco patiently explains that a Land Cruiser chassis requires a heavier engine, like the one in pick-ups and small trucks. The engine also has to be entirely mechanical, not totally worn out, preferably a diesel and with a not-too-large cylinder capacity. We spend days poking around at dealerships. At first we are still cheerful because each trader says he can fulfil our wishes. “Tomorrow I have new shipment. I can get you this motor in other shop, come with me.” Sometimes Dr Waco’s face lights up when he sees an engine block and he calls over the engine starter who turns it on for 5 cedis (just over €1). The engine is oiled, a small can of petrol with a hose is held up, the battery makes the starter turn and the block starts up. The buyer listens carefully for any untoward rattling or banging. But none of the engine blocks meet Dr Waco’s standards.

Days go by. The focus of our search shifts to dealers who carry European brands. Dr Waco knows them all personally. Some of them go to the church where he is a minister and they clearly have a lot of respect for him. We test several engines and find two that are suitable. But both are incomplete and we need to find a matching gearbox, which means we again have to go to other shops. The puzzle seems endless. Gearboxes are a fragile link. Most are in tatters. We have been at it for a week now and most dealers recognise us. Elaborate greetings are exchanged at every visit. Dr Waco has a very particular negotiating style. Dressed in his immaculate white coat, he exudes a natural air of authority and wisdom. He often calls people out on their faith in the Lord during the negotiations, after which he announces that we are building this car for a good cause. He is trying to force the dealers to drop their prices, but this does not always work. “Why should I give you a discount if you have two obrunis with you?" is a frequently asked question.

On a Monday morning, Dr Waco has good news. On Sunday after church, he managed to convince a dealer to sell us a SsangYong engine block at a reasonable price. It may not be a real Mercedes, but it is a good copy from Taiwan. When we get to the dealer's, we see that at least half of the approximately 100 engine blocks that were there earlier in the week have been sold, which means he has a turnover of around €40,000 a week. Once the deal is closed, the owner tells us he often travels to Europe on business. This sounds familiar: we have seen how West-Africans in Essen (Nigerians) and Amsterdam (Ghanaians) make sure that West-Africa in general and Suame in particular do not run out of car parts. Dutch customs officials have showed us how containers-full of rusty rear axles, leaking engines and damaged brake discs were being shipped out of the port of Rotterdam. When the containers arrive in Tema, the largest port in Ghana, the contents are displayed on a large platform in the port and the customs officers calculate the import tariff.

Now that we finally have the engine, the mechanics can get to work. Our puzzle is solved for the time being. The dozens of shops around our workshop sell bolts, ball bearings, rubbers, brake cables and shock absorbers in all sizes. The chassis is fitted to the engine block in no time. Two delivery boys are sent to fetch the necessary tools and materials; workshops do not have their own supplies as things only get stolen. Instead, the small neighbourhood shops serve as a kind of material "bank" where people can buy and borrow the necessary items.

There are two types of shops: those with second-hand parts and those with Chinese parts. The Chinese parts are cheaper. The market is flooded with them, but if you want to fix your car properly, you know to stay away from them because they are of poor quality. The second-hand material comes from rich countries. The quality is much higher, but so is the price.

The different components are gathered one by one and the car slowly starts to take shape. Thanks to our daily incursions into the neighbourhood, we soon get to know our way around. The KNUST workshop lies in Old Suame, an area where roads and sanitation were built in the 1990s. Now the roads are full of holes again. A small river, the Nkradam, runs down the bottom of the valley and collects all the wastewater and refuse that flow downhill. In the rainy season this stream becomes a churning river. The World Bank has financed a dam on the river but it has burst in several places following the growth of Suame Magazine. The people living and working behind the dam are the poorest of the poor, mostly Muslims who have migrated from the north. Across the river lies New Suame.
The British once built a cemetery here in 19th-century Romantic style, with neat rows of graves surrounded by a landscaped park. But today you quickly get lost here in a maze of parked trucks, workshops and mud pools. Sometimes you stumble over an old tombstone dating back to the colonial period in the area where the cemetery used to be.

We are told to stay out of New Suame. It is the territory of The Garages, an organisation that represents the auto industry across Ghana. They are eyeing SMIDO's car project with suspicion and are doing their very best to throw a spanner in the works. So we stay on our side of the river, where things are already complicated enough. Suame Magazine covers an area of about six square kilometres in total. It is impossible to know your way around all of it, as the neighbourhood is growing like a living labyrinth. Roads become overgrown, new paths are created around car wrecks that have been left to rust away; new loads of car wrecks form temporary walls that shrink and grow every day.

We soon learn that every cluster is centred around a forge, which makes sense as most mechanics use the forge fire in their work. Suame Magazine developed gradually on the site of the British arms depot – known as the Magazine – that was located on the outskirts of Kumasi at the beginning of the 20th century. This was where local artisans repaired coaches, weapons and later also cars. Sir John Maxwell, the colonial commanding officer at the time, designated an area where specialised mechanics could create a cluster of workshops.

The main thoroughfares are lined with shops, which have put their goods on prominent display outside. There is an incredible degree of specialisation: one shop may have only ball bearings, or brake cables, or exhaust pipes, or welding equipment, or steering columns, or only nuts and bolts.
The wealthiest shopkeepers deal in large machinery: they have piled up tracked vehicles, tractors, bulldozers and whole trucks in front of their shops. This is also how they make sure that mechanics do not set up workshops there.

Our novelty factor wears off within a few weeks. Even children no longer run away from the white ghost figures that are wandering through their neighbourhood. On the contrary, they have discovered that if they fetch us fruit and water, we can be a good source of income. At first we were just obrunis, but now we have names. Justice for Joost, Mr. Melles for Melle and Tony Spark for Teun Vonk. As social relationships are so important, we get to know more and more people, like John Damptey, the Suame narrator. The old man has a battery shop around the corner and is the local historian. We like dropping by to listen to his colourful stories.

In the 1930s, Kumasi became a trading centre with more and more companies dealing in cacao, palm oil, rubber, hardwood and coffee. The growing vehicle fleet was maintained and repaired in the Magazine, attracting mechanics from across Ghana. In the 1950s, Ghana became a front-runner of innovation in Africa thanks to its Pan-African politics. The British and the Germans, former colonial powers, built car assembly lines in Ghana. The British firm Morris even shipped a whole car production plant out to Ghana, while the German Mercedes built a plant with a training centre in Accra. This is where Dr Waco trained to be a mechanic. After the fall of President Nkrumah in 1966, there was a rise in nationalism. Factories started going bankrupt because inexperienced people were put in directors' posts and soon car manufacturing withered away. Import duties on cars increased sharply and Ghana became dependent on recycling. The only importers of cars were European adventurers who drove old cars to Ghana and sold them for good money to buy their plane tickets home.

It was not until the 1960s that the name Suame was added to Magazine. The auto industry had continued to grow rapidly and had swallowed the village of Suame, which was soon overrun with workshops. The repairs cluster rapidly became an industrial zone that served all of sub-Saharan Africa, not just for maintenance but also for the supply of machinery to the gold-mining industry and agriculture.

John Damptey's stories are a little more heroic than what we describe here. He tells us stories from different sources and none of them quite match. But there is no space for discussion with Damptey: he is Suame Magazine's narrator and an eyewitness to 100 years of history, though he looks about 60.

On 19 February we manage to get hold of a Nissan Patrol rear axle. Unfortunately, it does not match the Toyota front axle. Dr Waco is deeply engrossed in the construction drawing he carries around in his head. How can we solve this puzzle? Our naïve idea of trying out something completely new is turning into quite a challenge. The chassis of the Toyota Land Cruiser determines the rest of the structure. Our dream of working with parts from different cars is making the mechanics' task almost impossible.
This is the third time we have bought a rear axle that does not fit. The two previous times we managed to bring the axles back and only had to pay a bit of social money, a kind of compensation for not purchasing the parts. But now that this axle does not fit, we have to go back to the same shop for a second time.
Dr Waco is clearly not amused. We have visited just about every axle dealer in the neighbourhood and it is too risky to wait for new supply. But this one has to be returned and he sends one of the local kids off to order a taxi. The axle would easily fit into his car, but he does not want to get his Mercedes dirty. Presently the Magazine taxi drives into the yard: once upon a time it was a Toyota Corolla, but now all that remains is the driver's seat. The rest of the interior has been stripped to maximise the cargo space. We send two messenger boys ahead to help unload the axle and collect the money.

Christ the King Enterprise is just around the corner from our workshop. The boys come back with 200 of the original 500 cedis we paid (€50 instead of €125). The dealer told them we had kept the axle for too long and sent them off. He says he could have sold the axle to someone else. We want to get our money back, but Philip stops us. So far Philip has mainly been sitting in the shade and keeping his overalls nice and clean, but now he suddenly intervenes. "No you cannot do this. You wait." In the days that follow, Philip sends different boys to the shop to ask for the money. When we still have no luck on the third day, Philip decides to go himself. He says we have to come along. When we get there, we notice that the rear axle is lying in front of the shop and has not been piled up with the rest of the merchandise, a clear sign that the negotiations are not over yet. Suddenly Philip is not so friendly anymore. He angrily addresses the owner and unleashes a rapid-fire barrage of words, excitedly gesturing towards the axle, us and the shop. The owner is initially unmoved, until Philip appears to ask for money. Then the man starts to shout. Philip charges off and we scuttle off after him. Back in the workshop, he is seething at the dealer's attitude. He must reimburse the money, he says, especially because he is a member of SMIDO. "This man, aaarghhh," he says, shaking his head. "We will punish him. I call Charles Taylor." Charles who borrowed his nickname from the infamous Liberian dictator, got his reputation as a tough guy as a young man already. He was the one who stood up to The Garages when they tried to take power in Suame Magazine. With his men he chased those Accra guys out of the neighbourhood. Now that we have an insubordinate shopkeeper on our hands, it is his job to step in. Later that afternoon, a boy brings all the rest of the money back – down to the very last penny. Later we hear that Charles dropped by with his gang of heavies to settle the score.

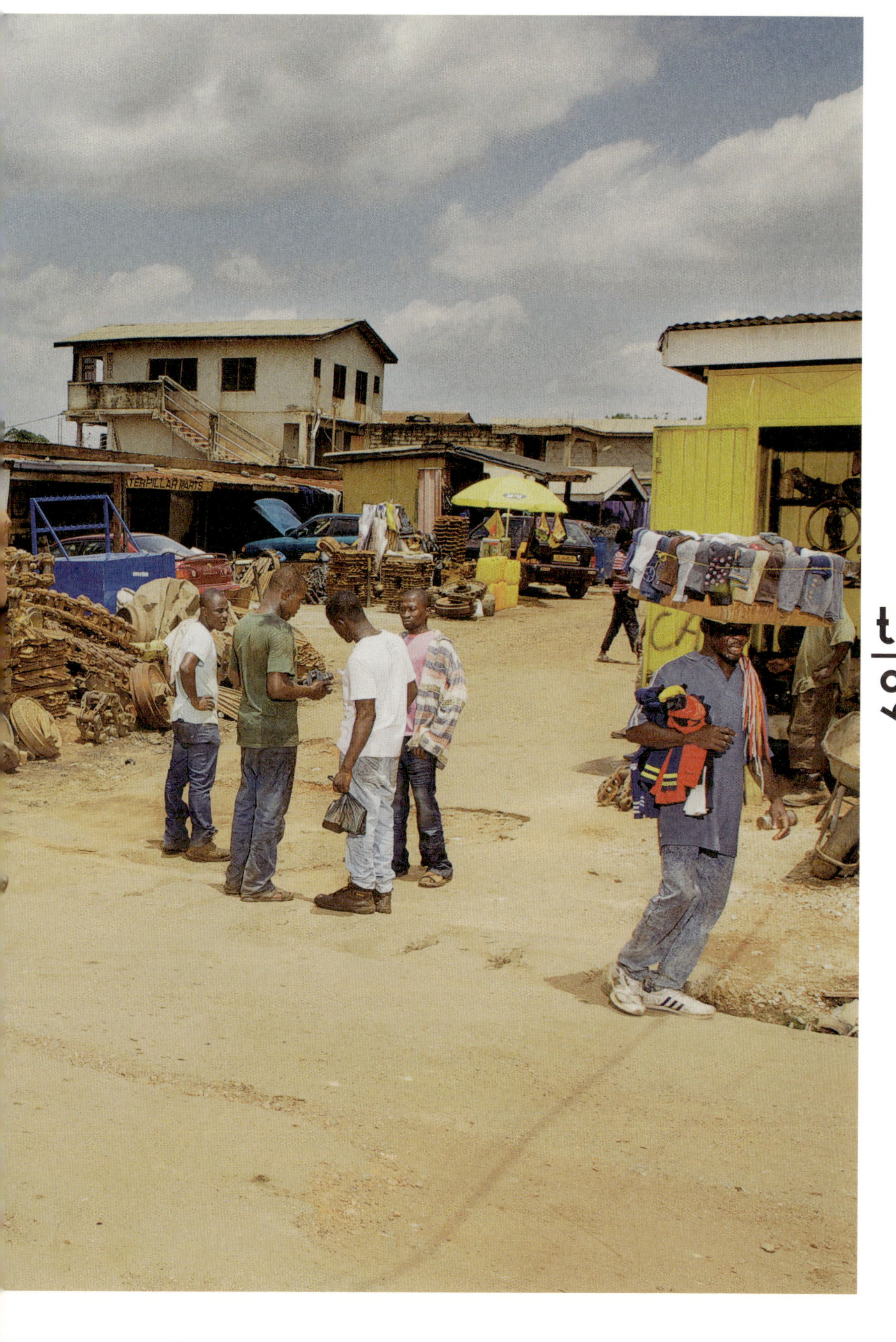
TERPILLAR PARTS

L: The ladder chassis is mainly used in pick-up trucks and trucks. These cars are popular in Suame Magazine because it is easy to reuse the chassis.

R: Modern cars are lighter in order to be more economical. The shape of the body gives enough stability to make a separate chassis redundant. Wrecks are often gradually picked apart. When the car has been completely stripped and if the body is damaged, it becomes scrap metal. Such cadavers are strewn across Suame Magazine, waiting to be melted down. Alternatively, the carcasses are left there for years until the owner has saved enough money to get them repaired.

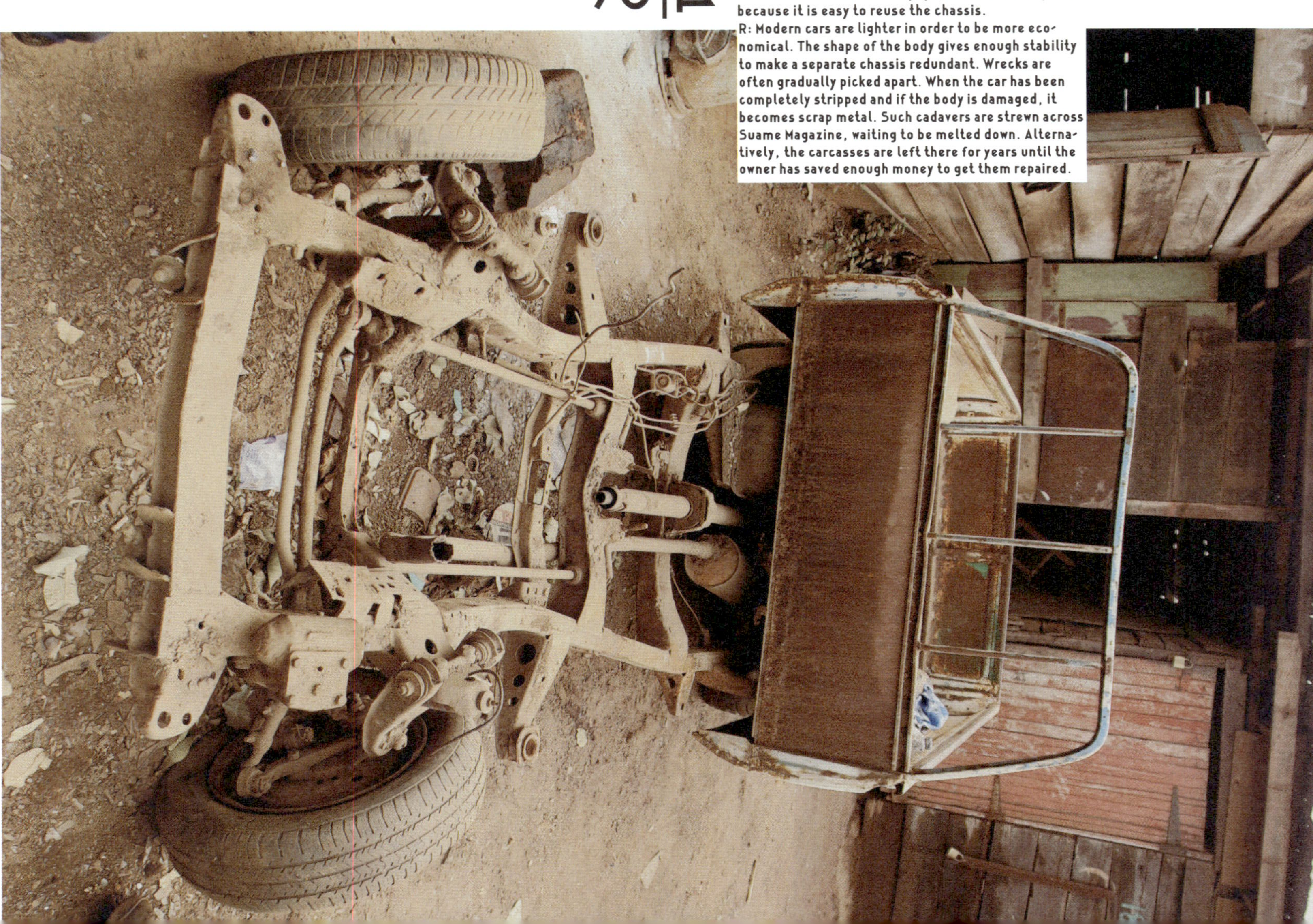

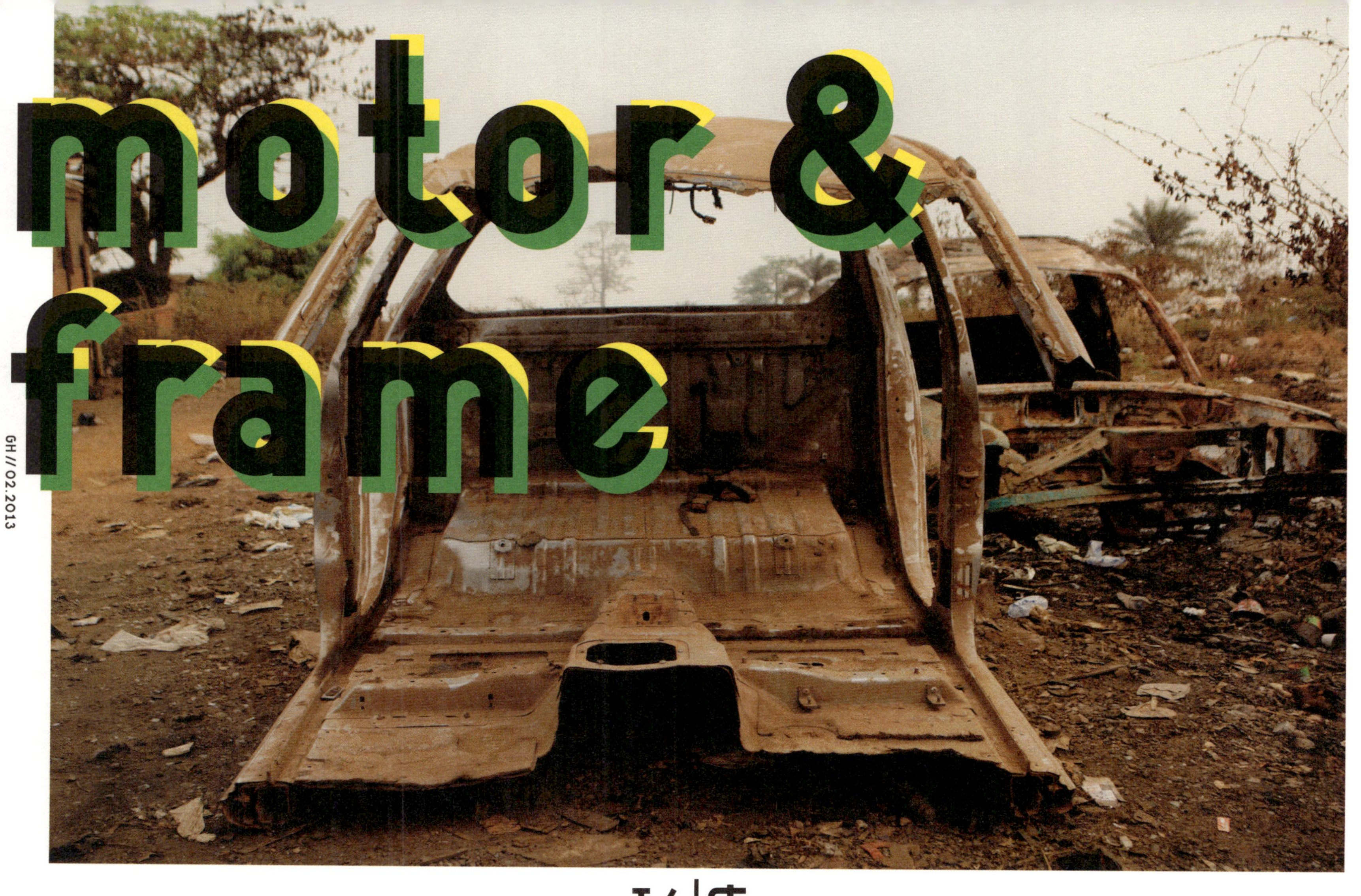

GH // 02.2013

t1 | 91

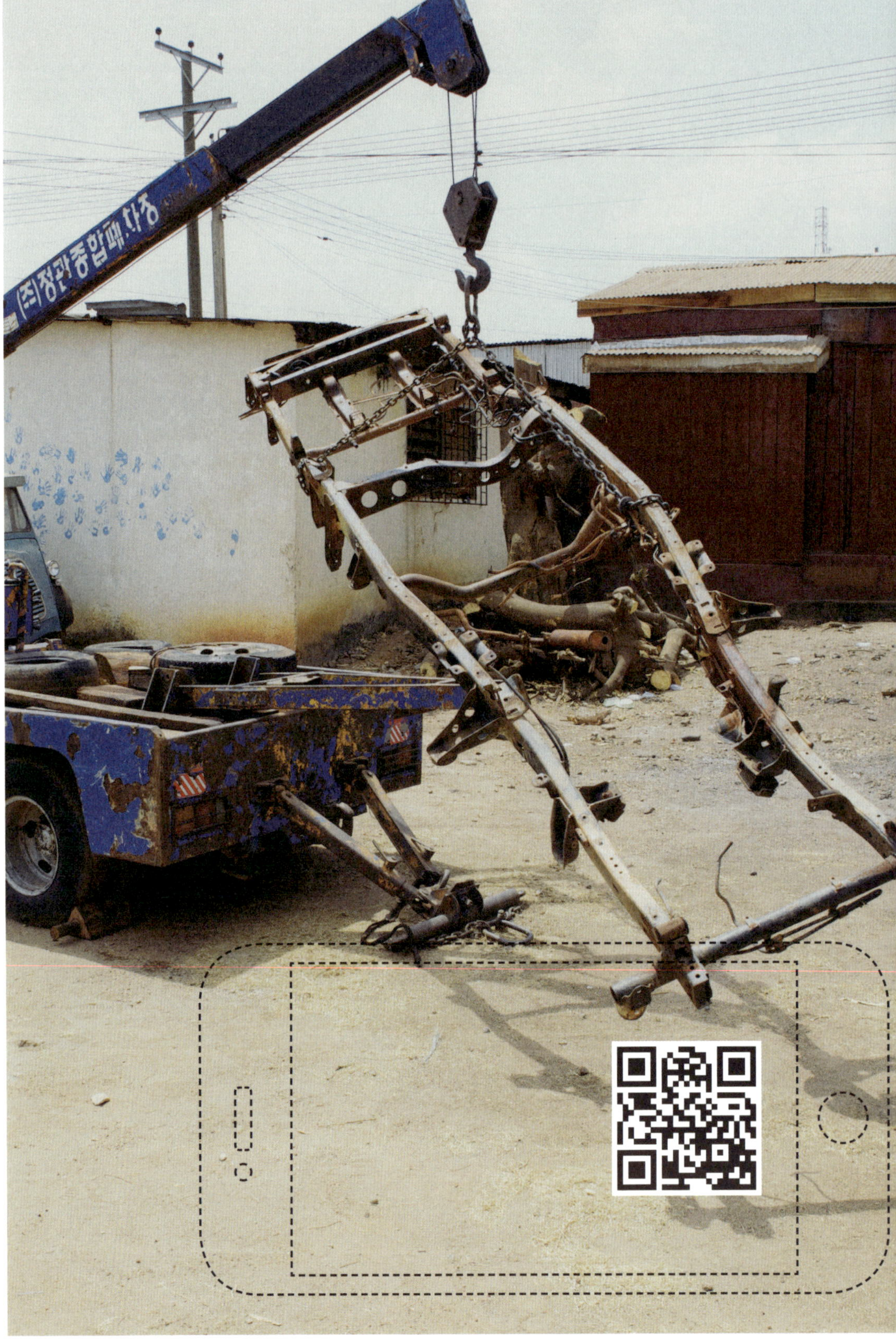

92 | t1

A Toyota Land Cruiser 2 chassis becomes the Turtle 1's undercarriage.

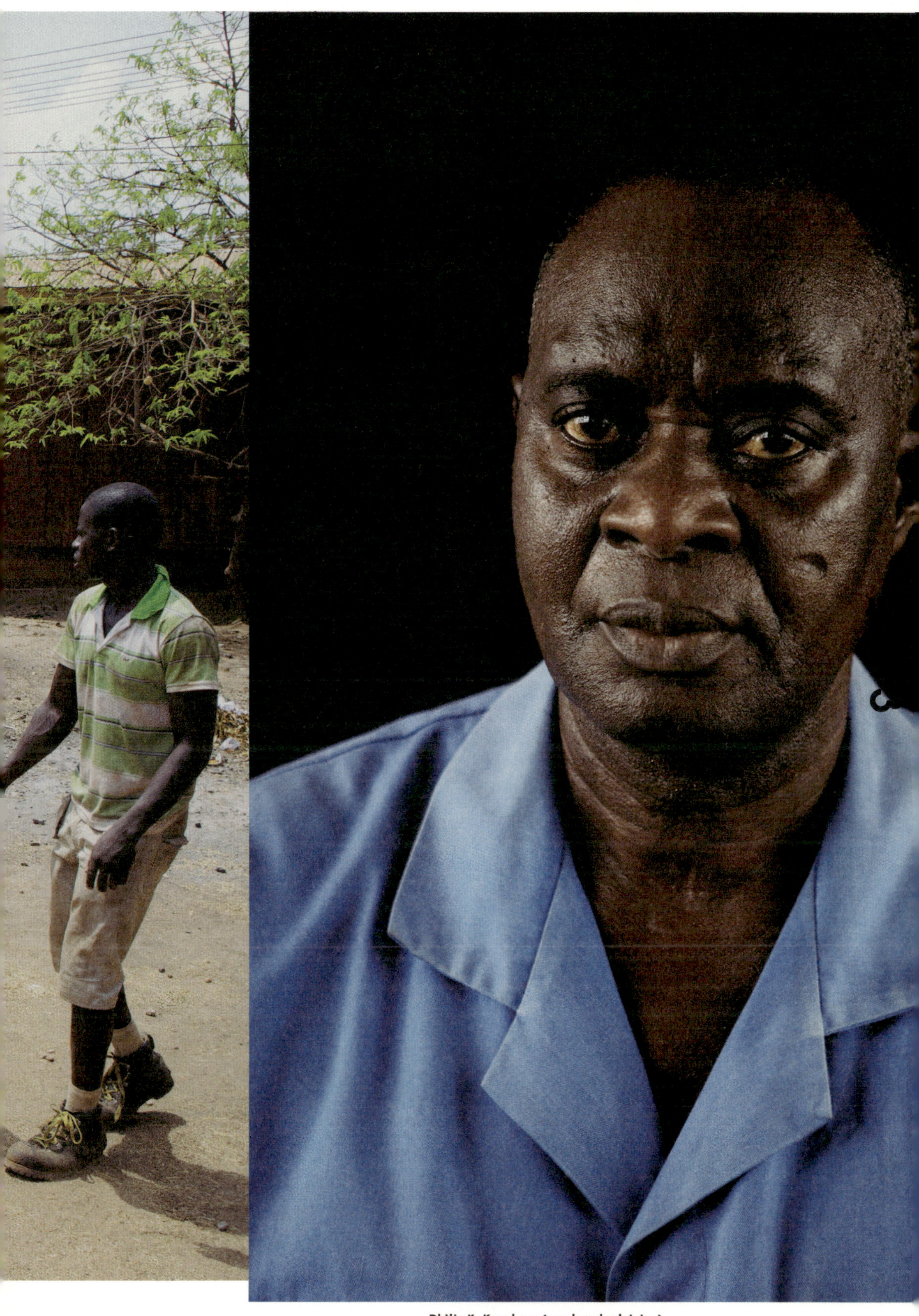

Philip K. Kwarteng (master electrician)

The Turtle 1's chassis.

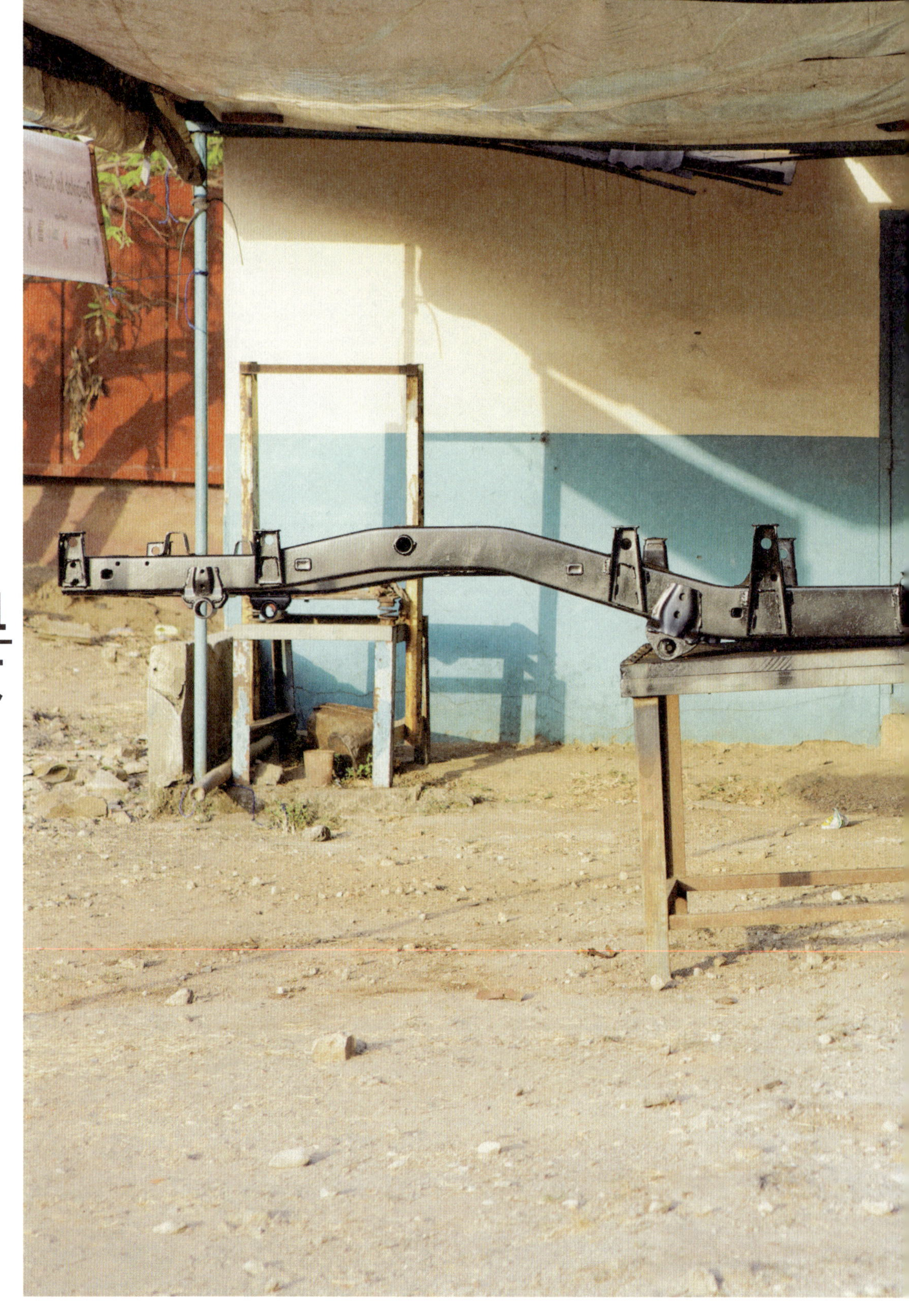

TOY-351 // GH // AP-12 // 02.2013

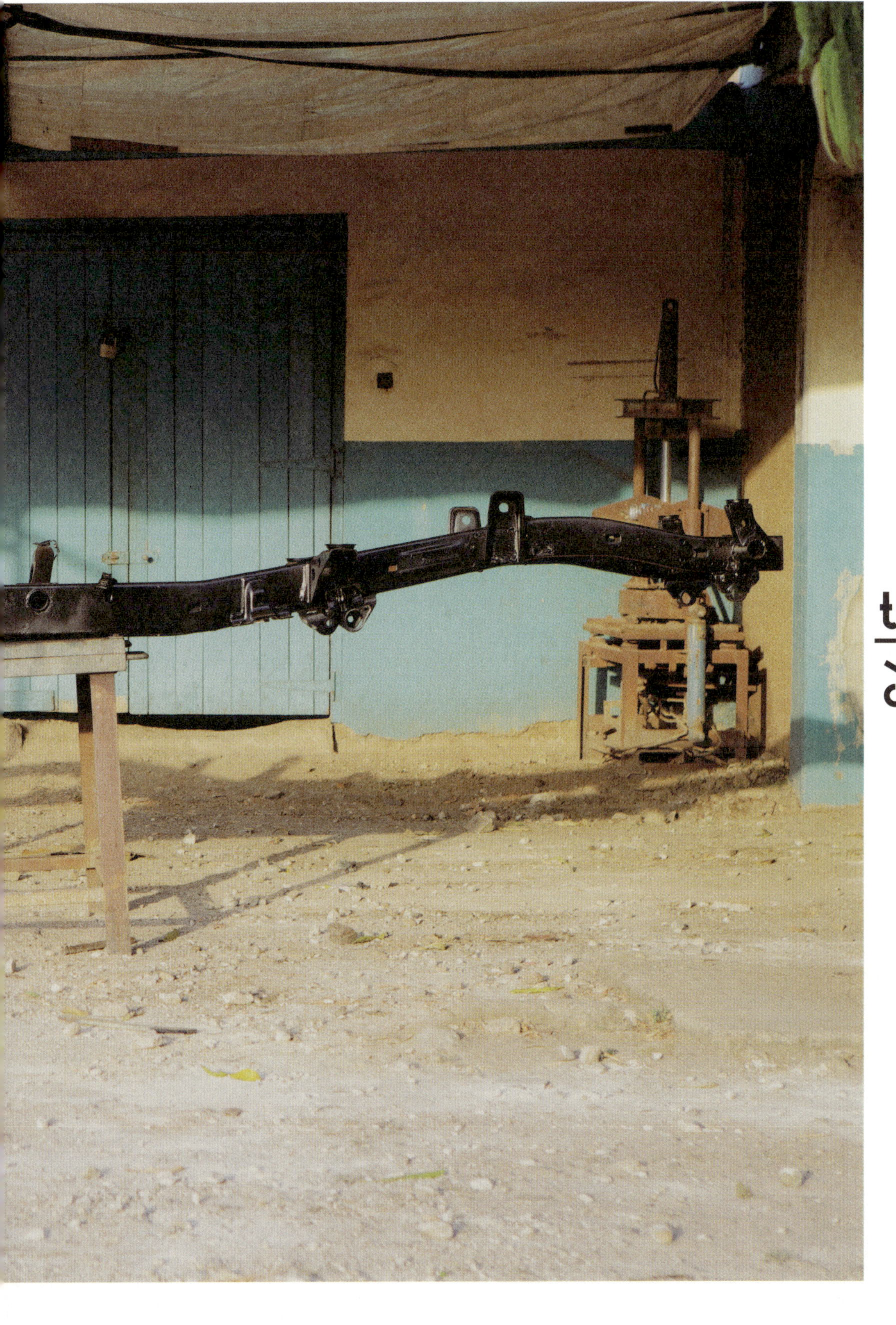

t1|95

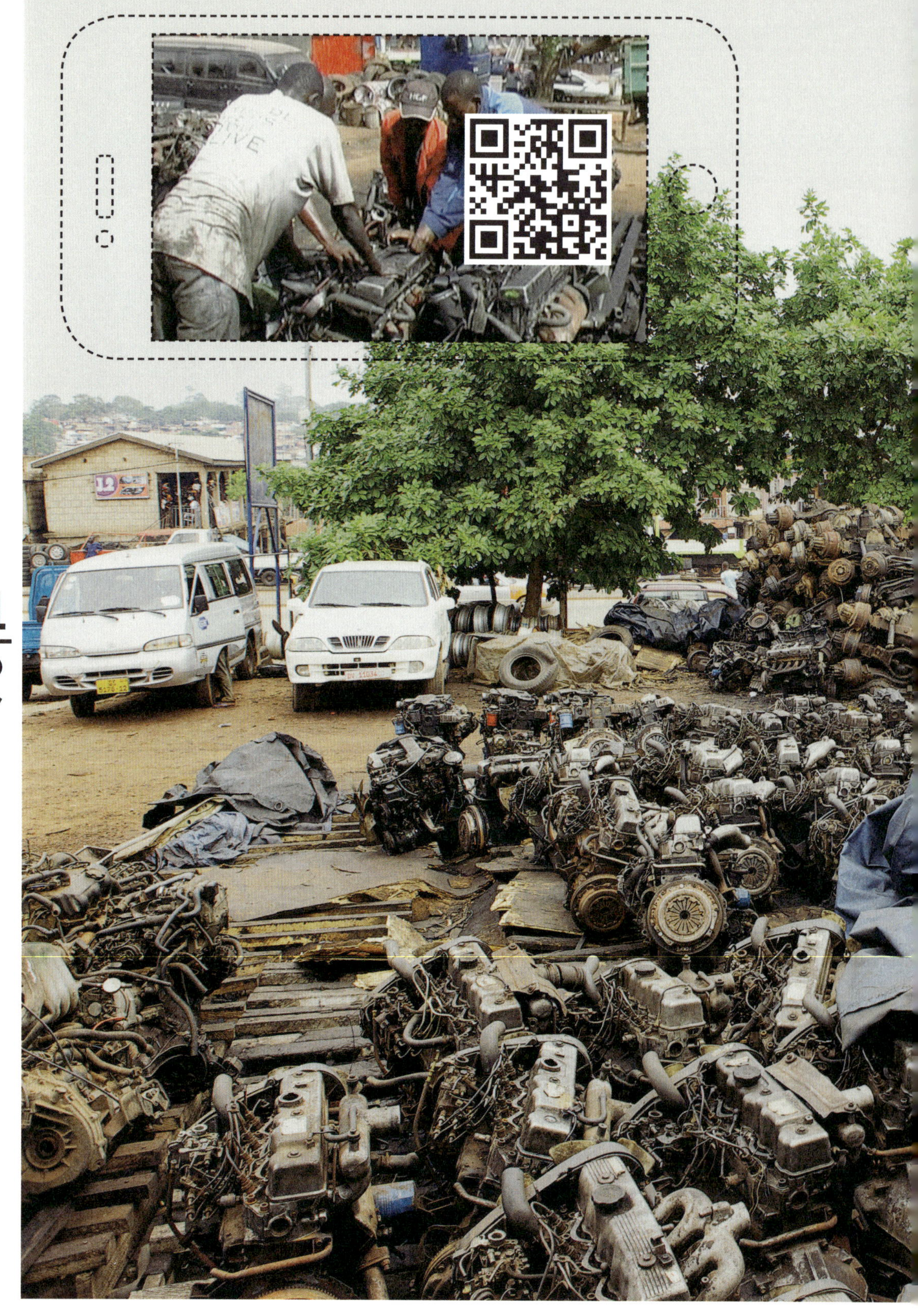

Ukess Enterprise, where we bought the Turtle's engine.

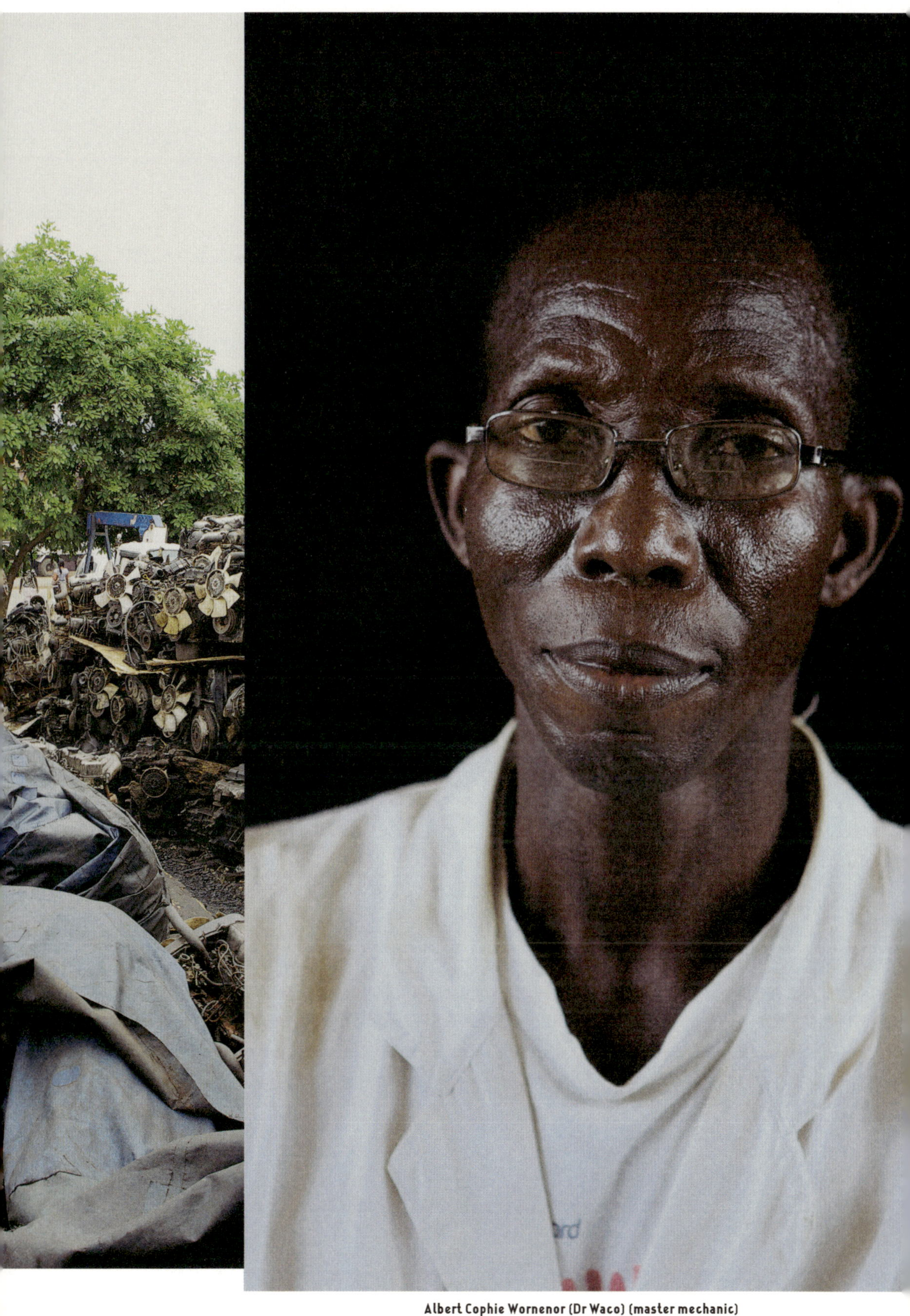

Albert Cophie Wornenor (Dr Waco) (master mechanic)

The KNUST University has a large workshop in the middle of the neighbourhood. It was established in the 1970s in cooperation with the Massachusetts Institute of Technology (MIT) in the United States as a kind of vocational training institute. It is known as the ITTU (Intermediate Technology Transfer Unit) workshop. We were allowed to set up our own workshop in its yard.

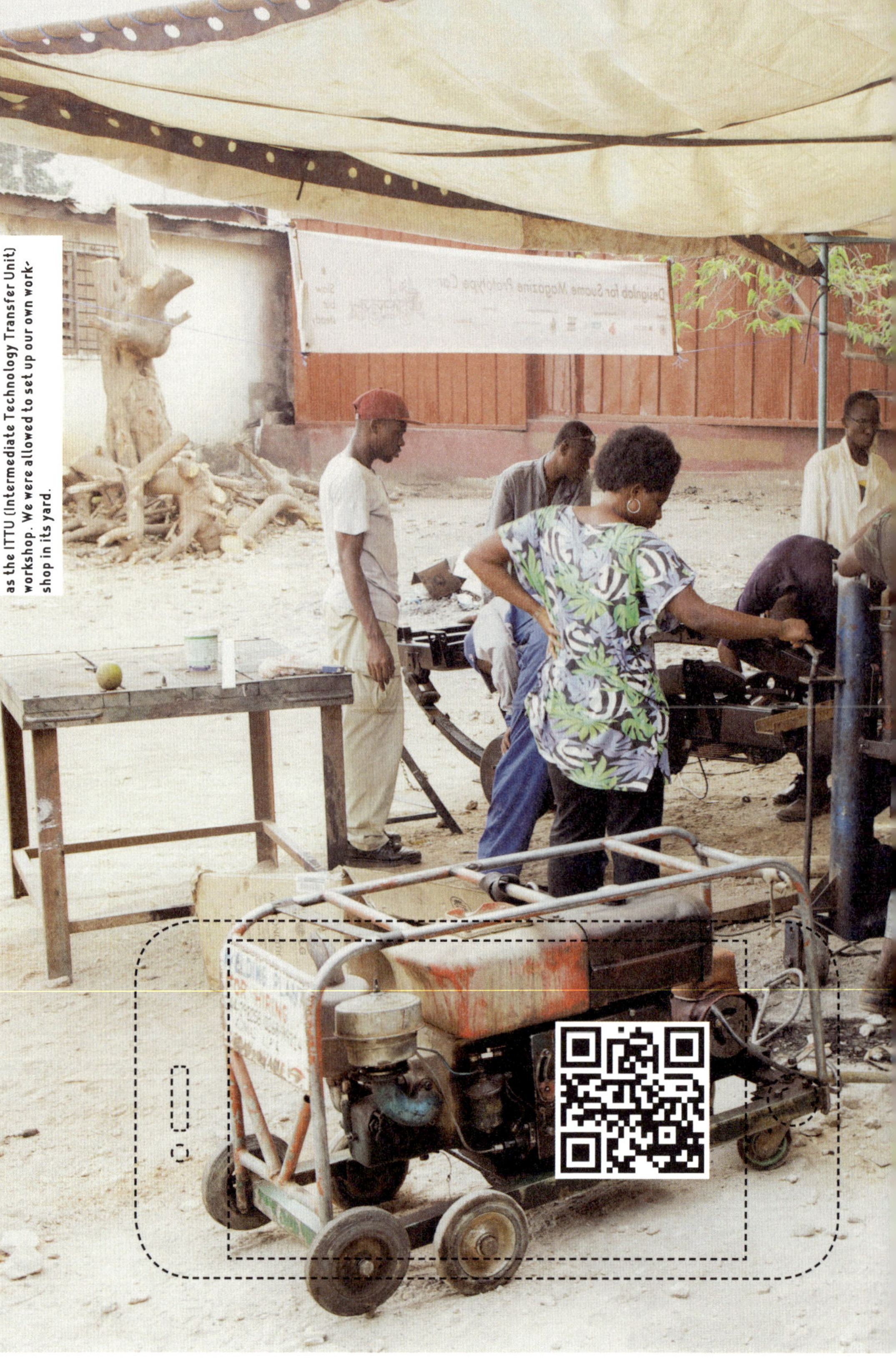

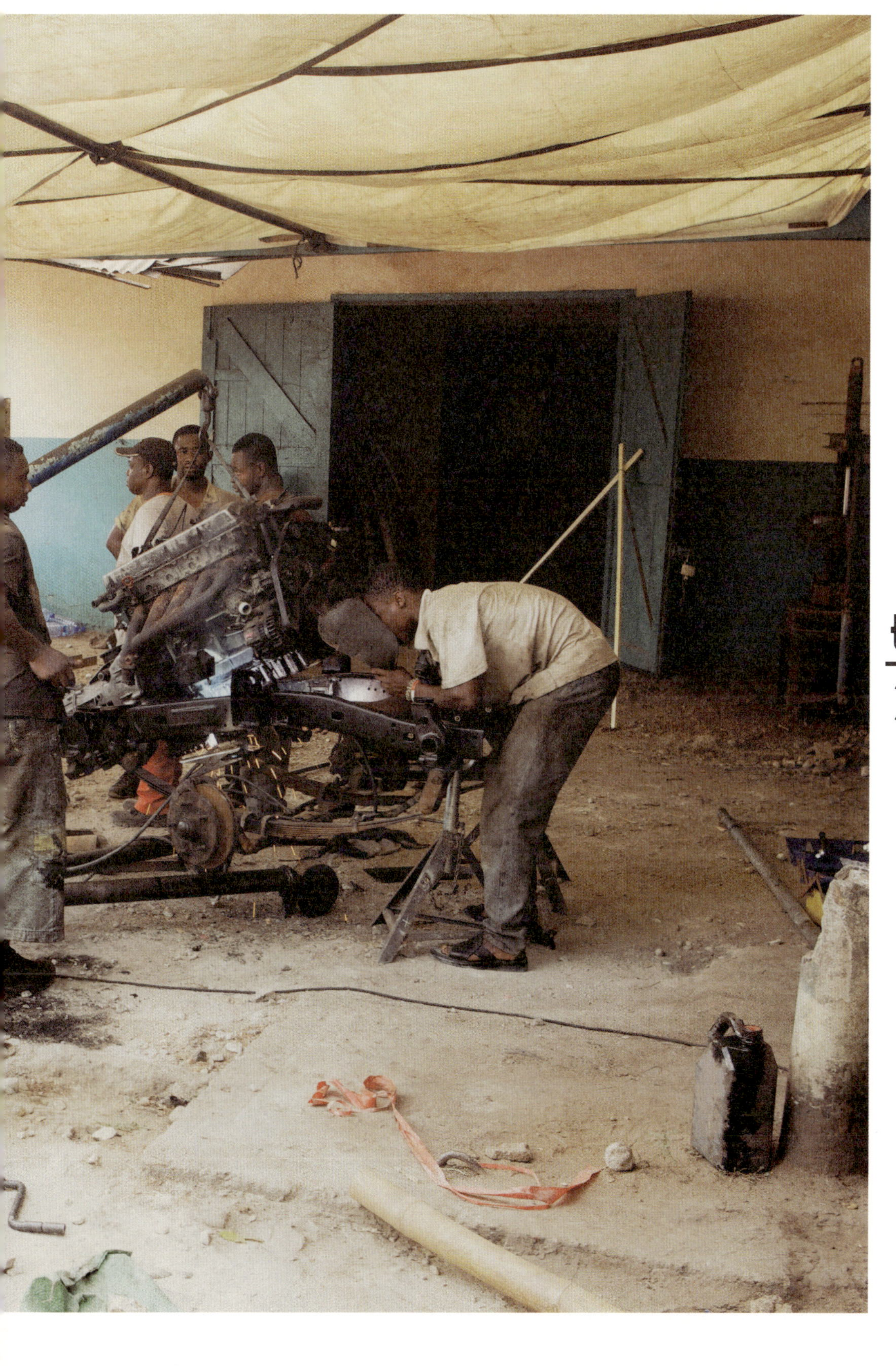

R: Each cluster is centred around a forge. The forges are always bustling, as many of the surrounding workshops use the fire there for their work. The walls of the forge serve as the neighbourhood's Yellow Pages. This is where you can find the phone number of any specialist you may need.

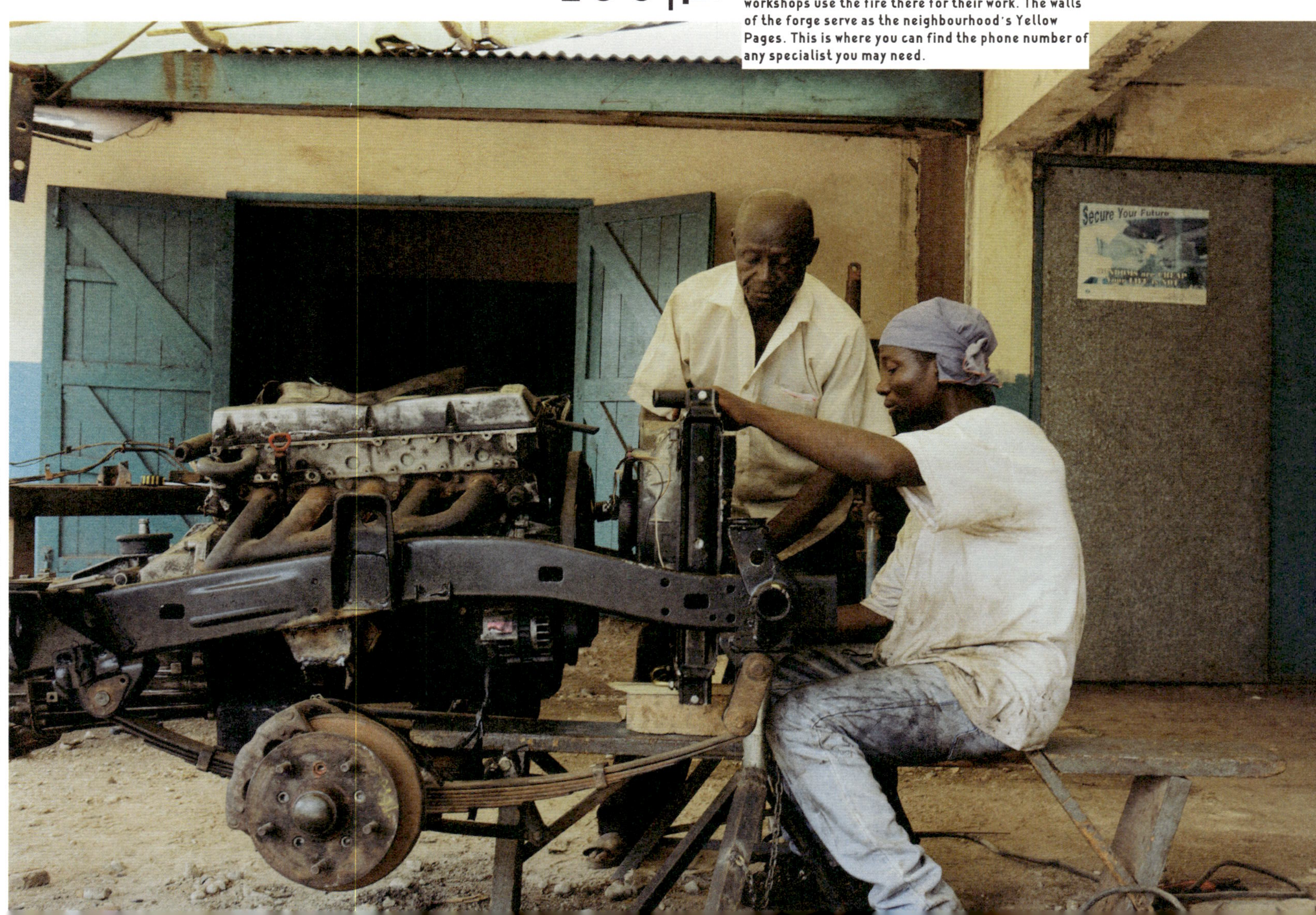

TOY-351 / SSY-285 GH / FOR-256 / NIS-402 / SM-631 // AP-12 // 02.2013

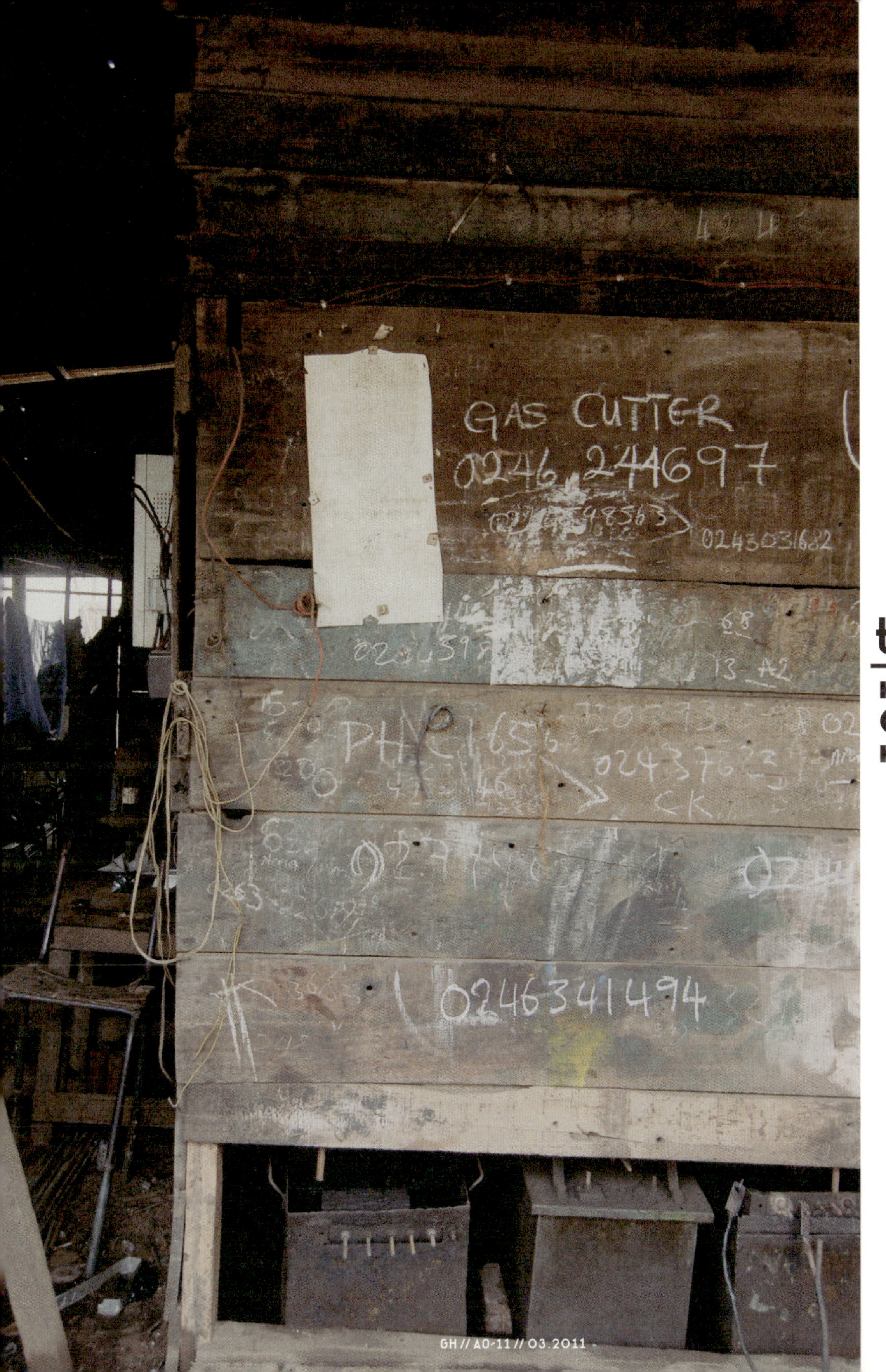

GH // A0-11 // 03.2011

L: The engine seat, the place where the engine leans on the chassis, was moved three times as we kept trying out new gear boxes. All these adjustments have compromised the solidity of the welding joints.

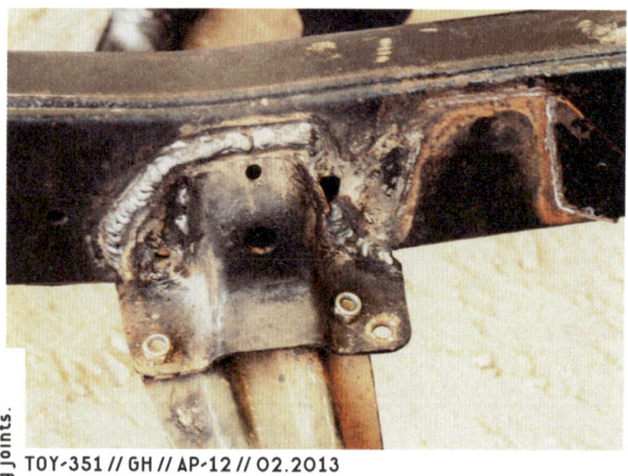

TOY-351 // GH // AP-12 // 02.2013

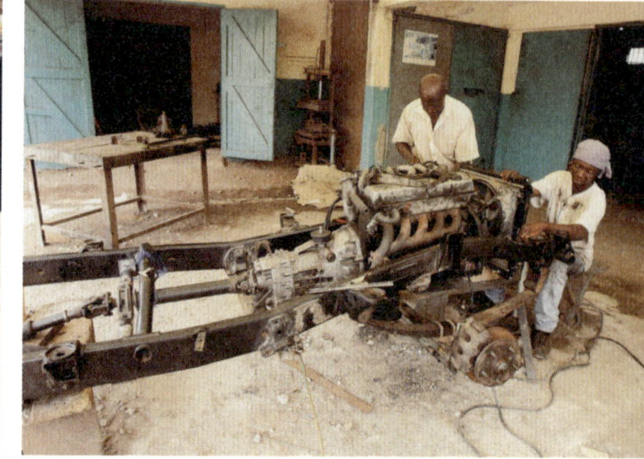

TOY-351 / SSY-285 // GH // AP-12 // 02.2013

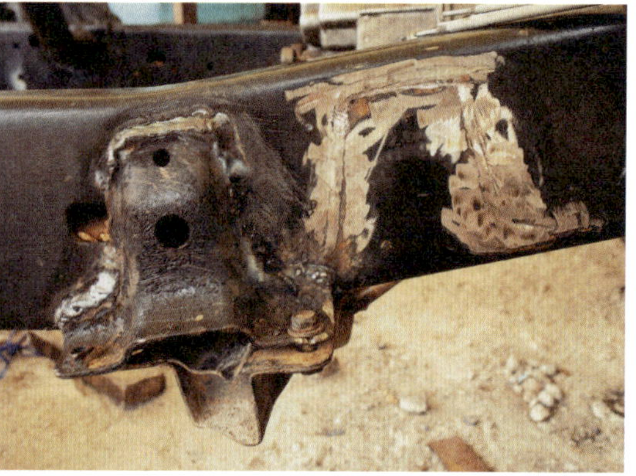

TOY-351 // GH // AP-12 // 02.2013

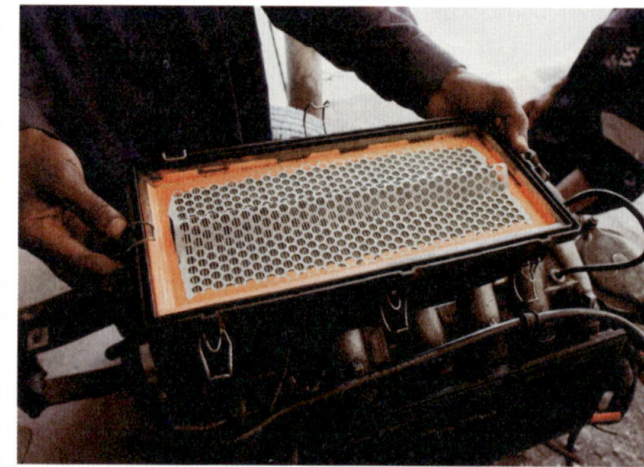

SSY-285 // GH // AP-12 // 03.2013

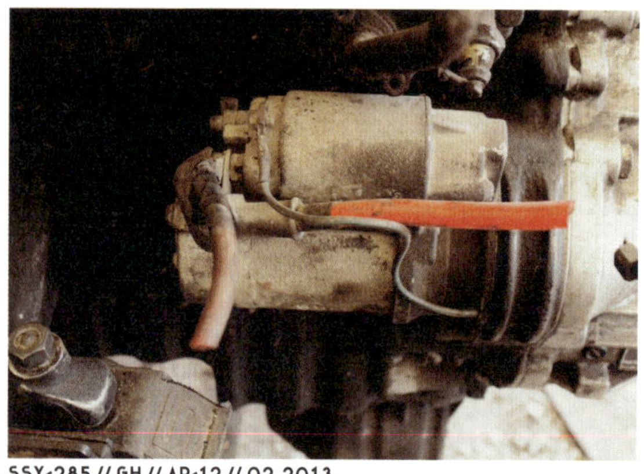

SSY-285 // GH // AP-12 // 02.2013

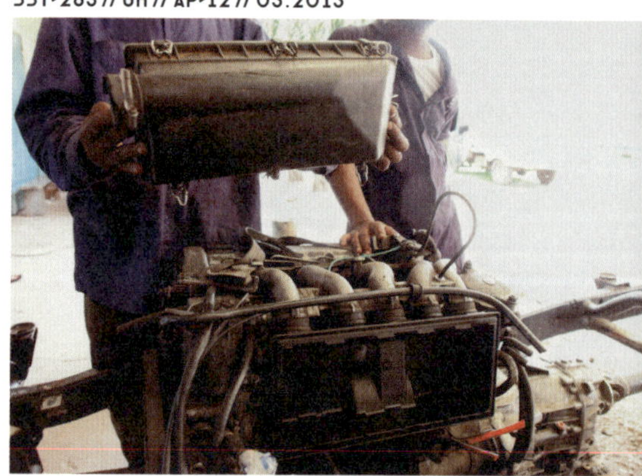

SSY-285 // GH // AP-12 // 03.2013

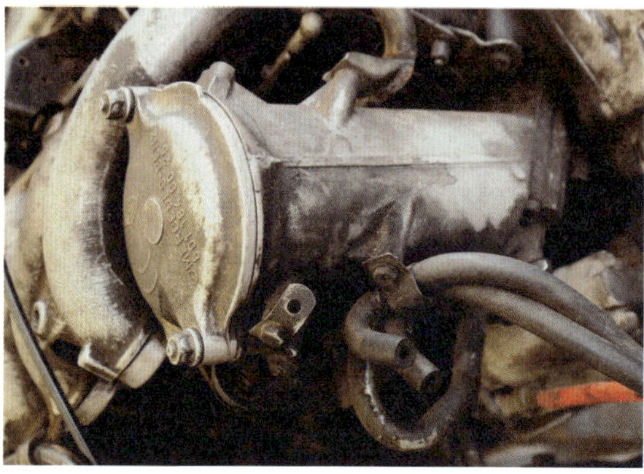

SSY-285 // GH // AP-12 // 02.2013

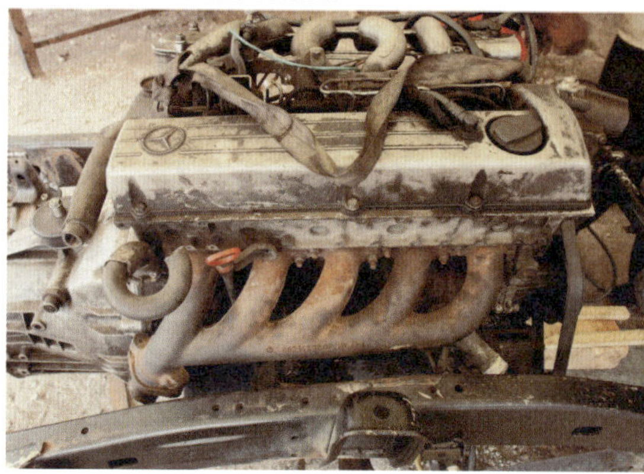

SSY-285 // GH // AP-12 // 02.2013

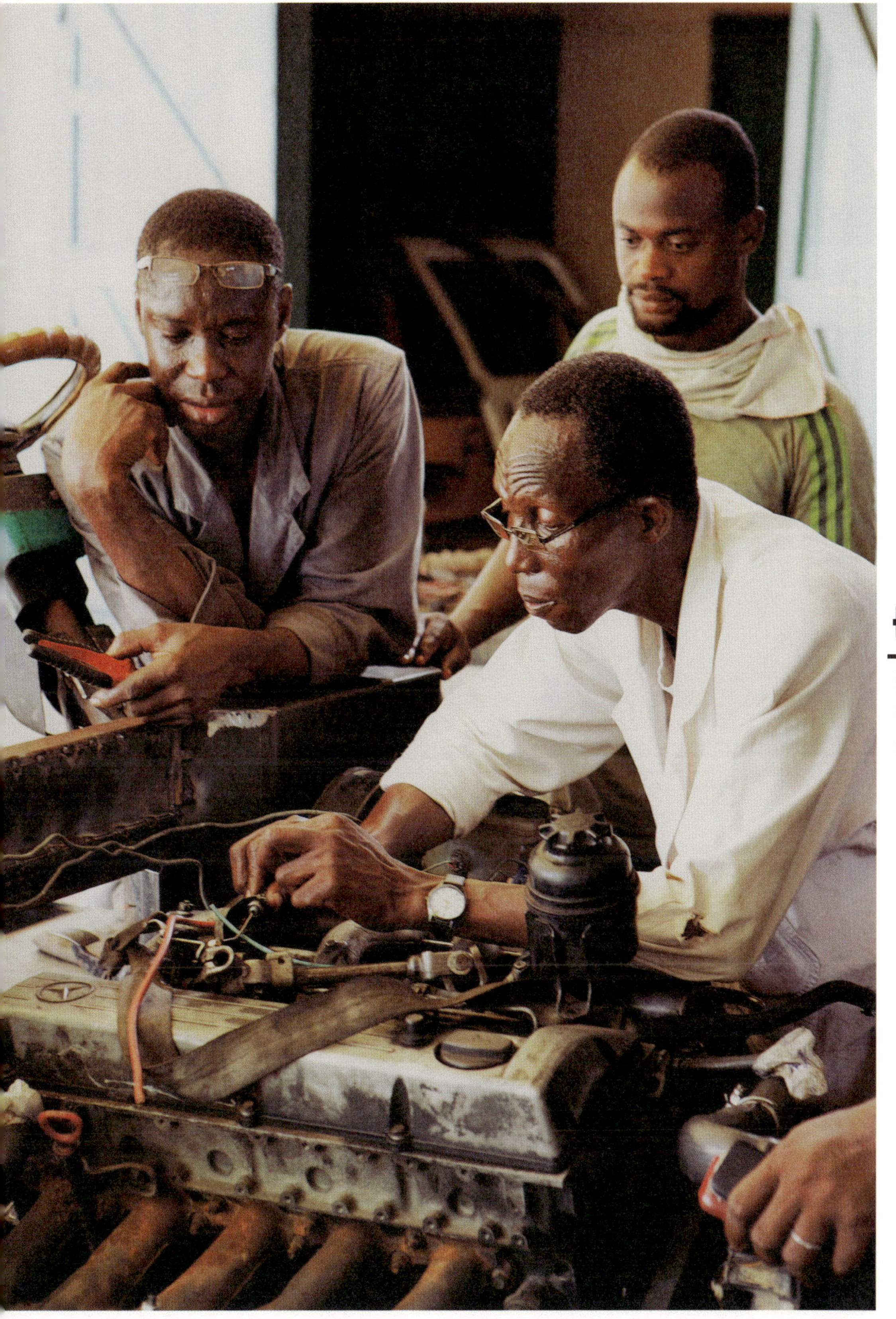

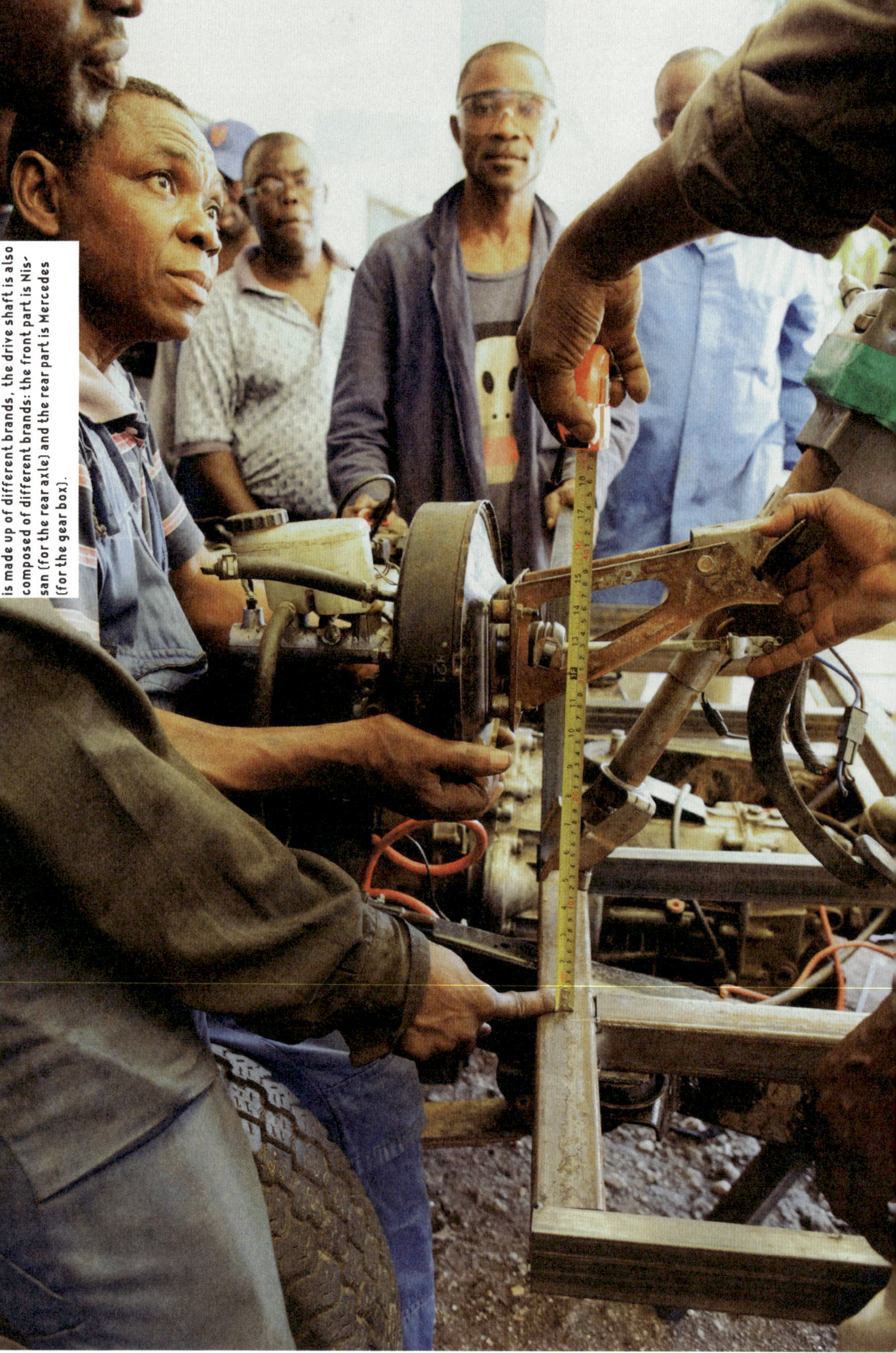

R: The drive shaft is the rod from the gear box that steers the rear drive. This rod has to be perfectly aligned. In Suame Magazine this balancing is done with the naked eye on a pre-war lathe. As the Turtle 1 is made up of different brands, the drive shaft is also composed of different brands: the front part is Nissan (for the rear axle) and the rear part is Mercedes (for the gear box).

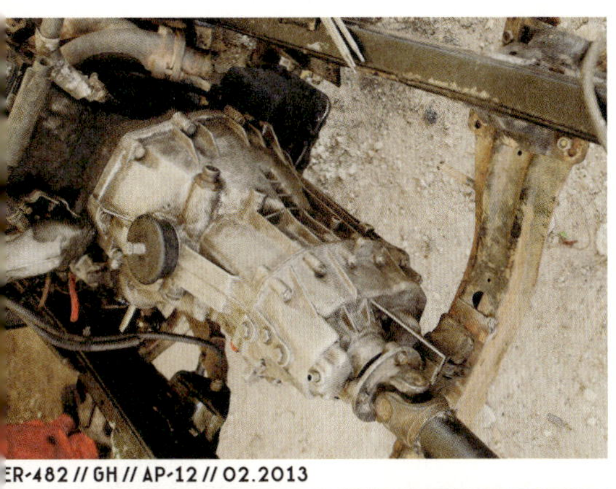

ER-482 // GH // AP-12 // 02.2013

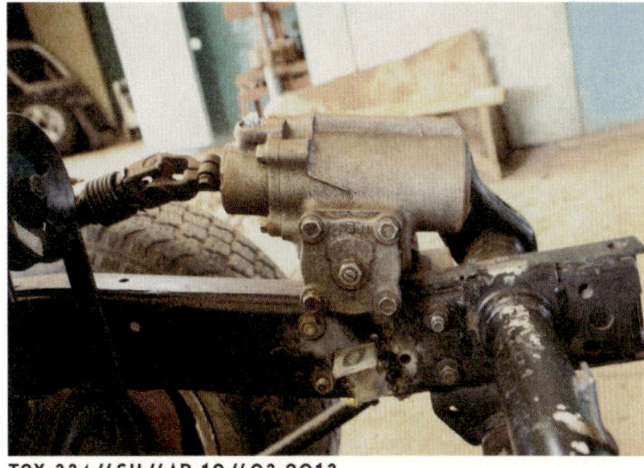

TOY-334 // GH // AP-12 // 03.2013

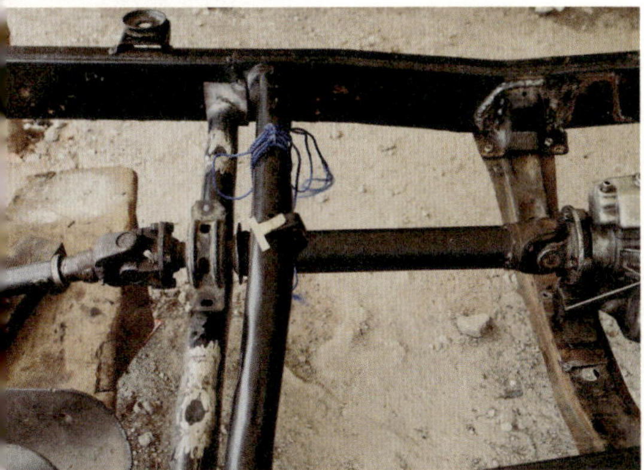

S-167 / MER-325 // GH // AP-12 // 02.2013

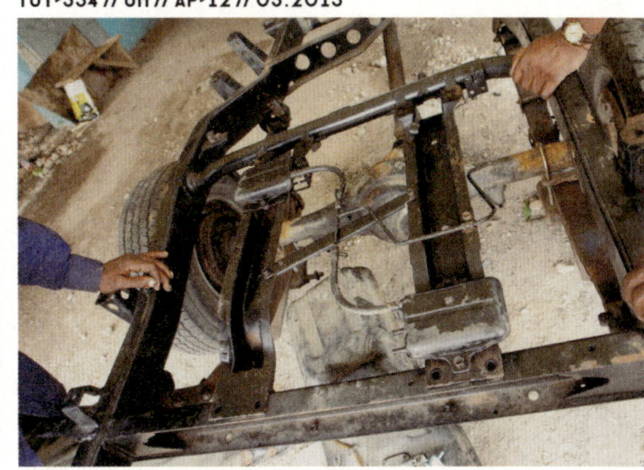

TOY-351 // GH // AP-12 // 03.2013

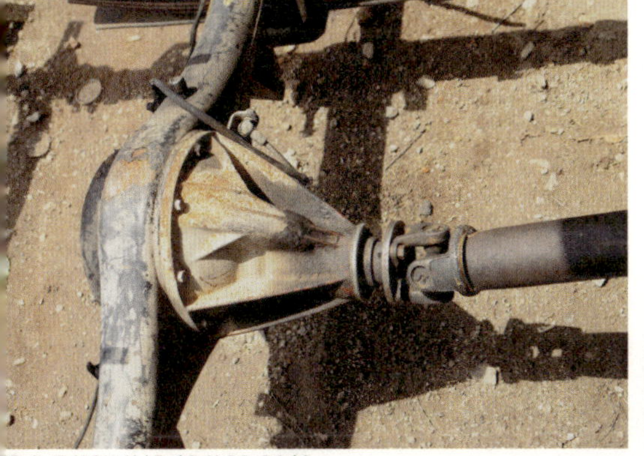

S-245 // GH // AP-12 // 02.2013

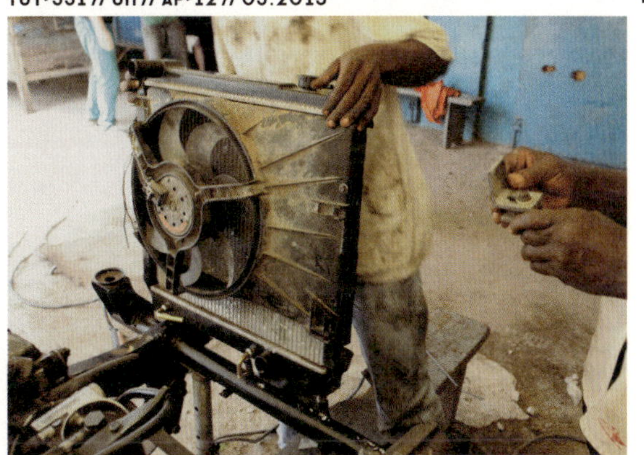

FOR-256 // GH // AP-12 // 02.2013

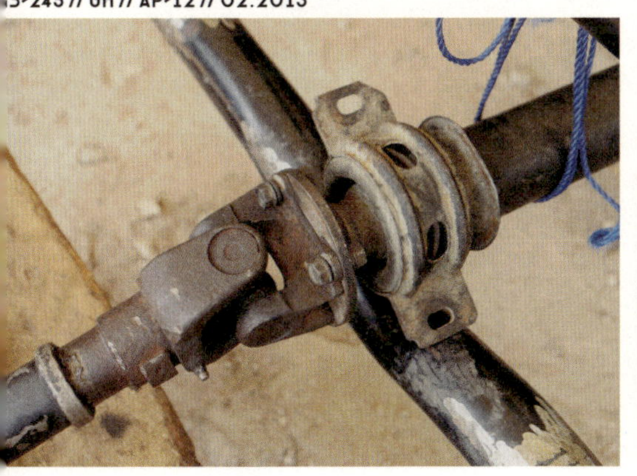

M-822 // GH // AP-12 // 02.2013

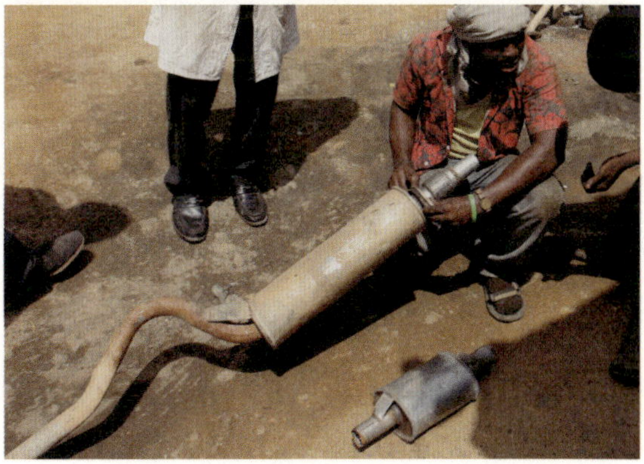

MIS-194 // GH // AP-12 // 03.2013

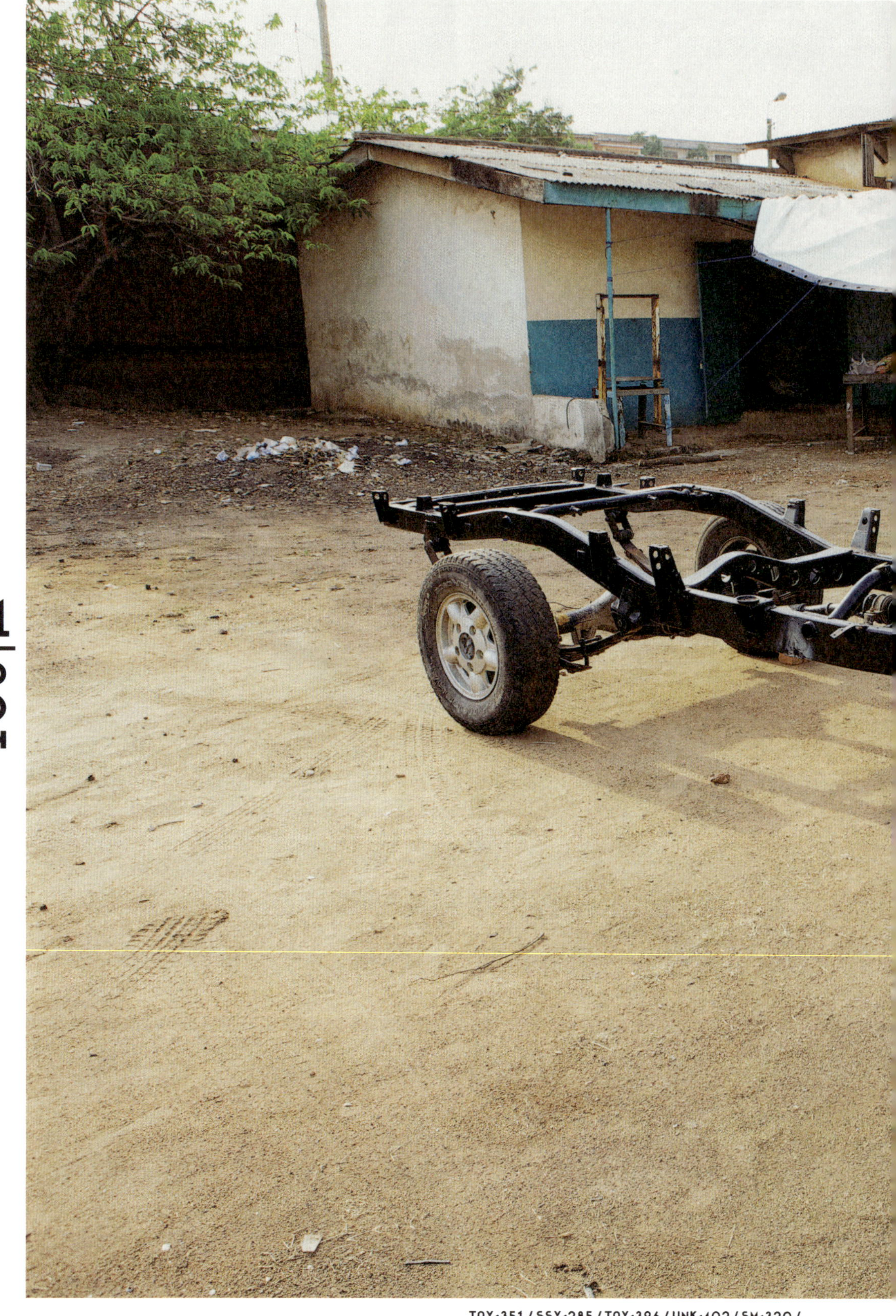

TOY-351 / SSY-285 / TOY-396 / UNK-402 / SM-320 / NIS-402 / NIS-245 // GH // AP-12 // 02.2013

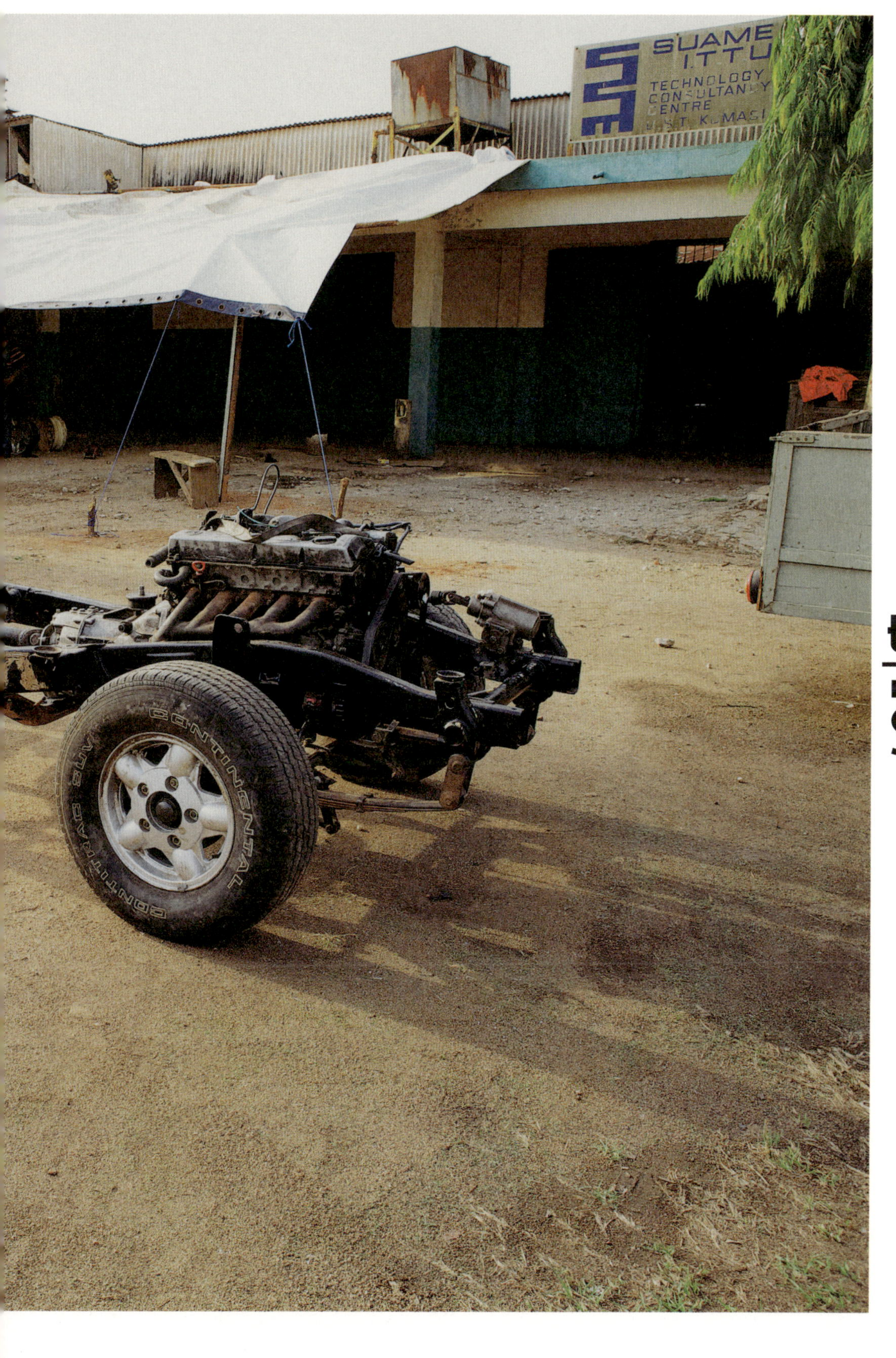
SUAME
I.T.T.U
TECHNOLOGY
CENTRE
CONTINENTAL

The pedals are too close to the bedplate, so that it is impossible to step on the brake properly. Instead of adjusting the floor, the pedals are sawn and re-assembled into a new shape.

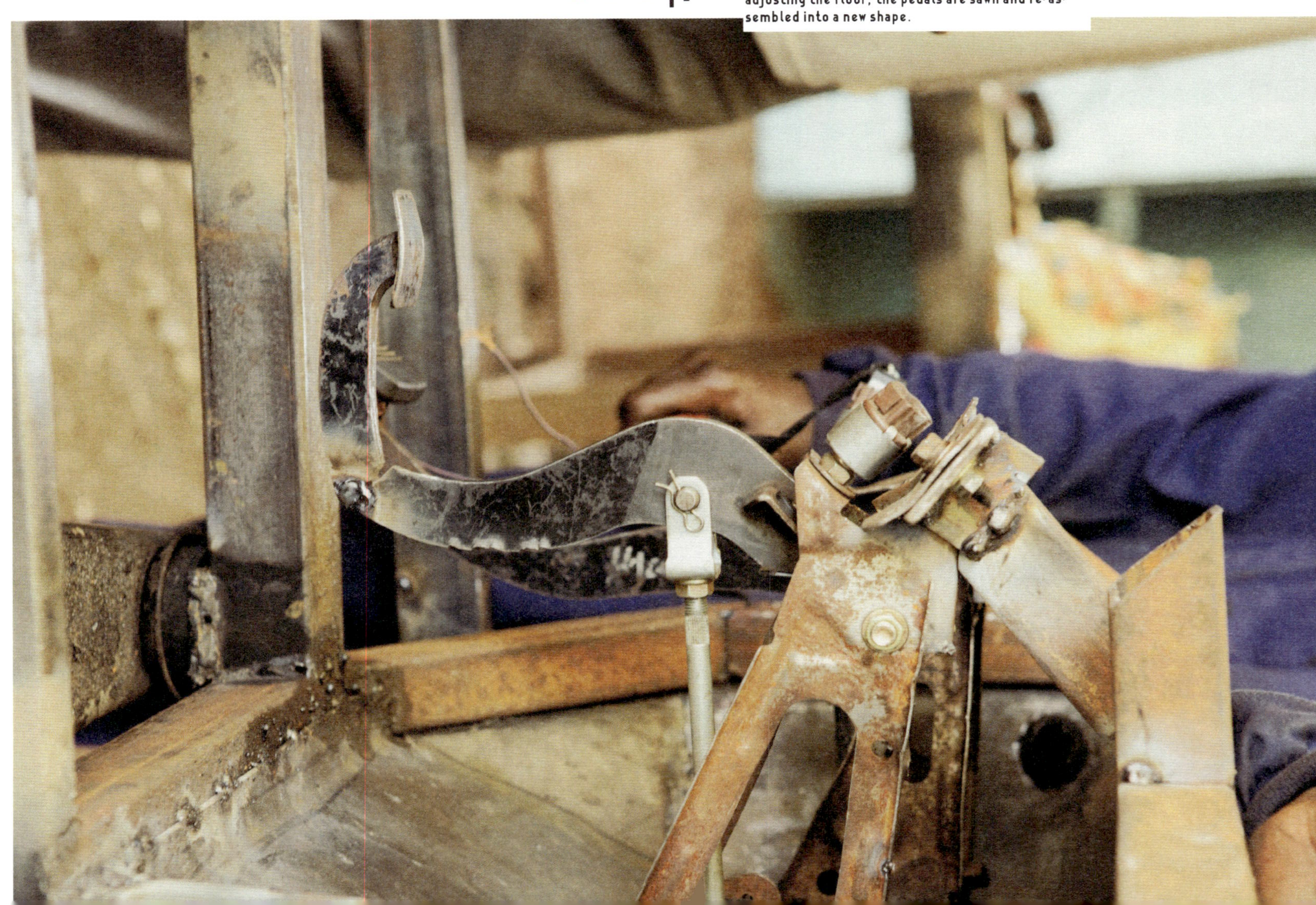

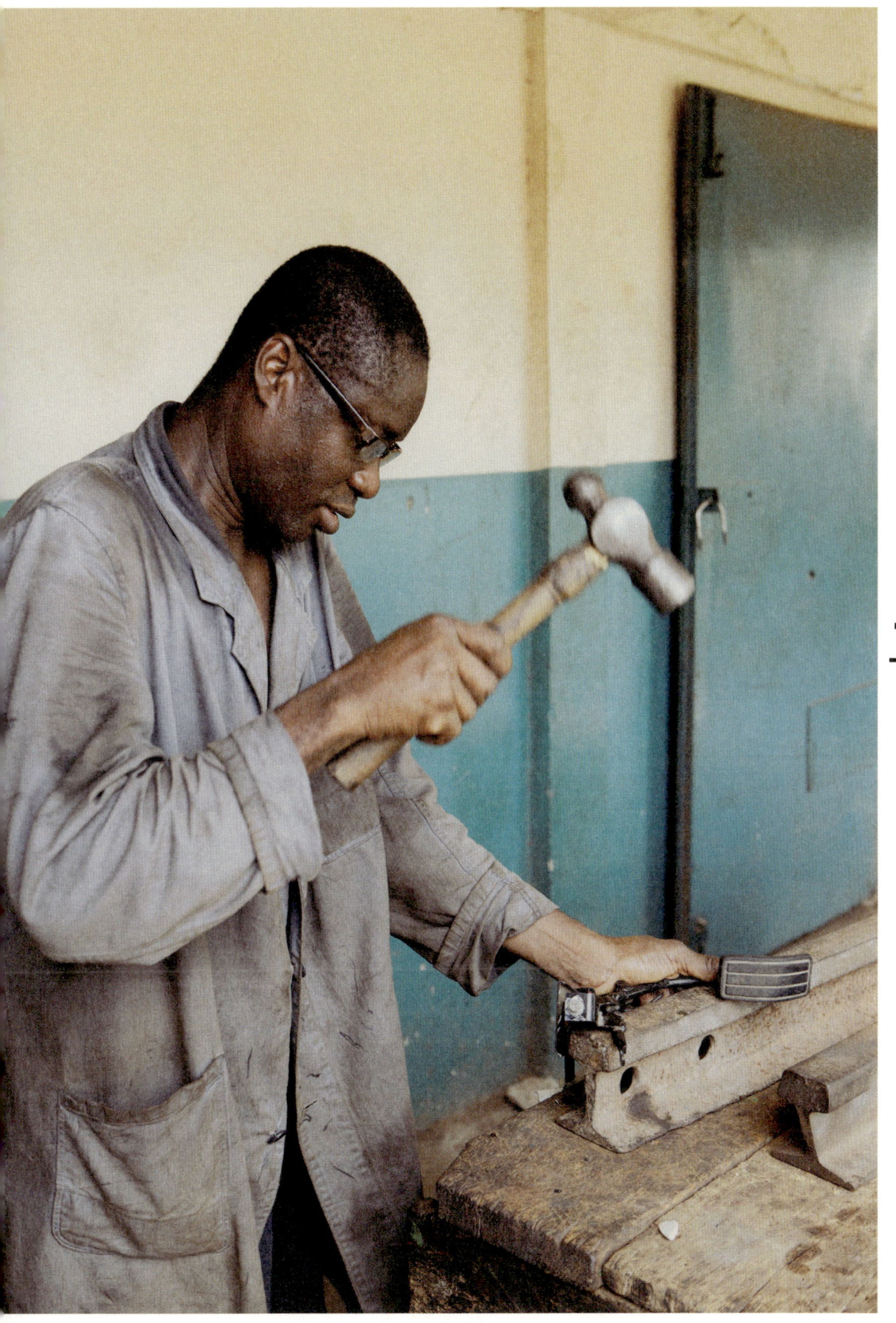

TOY-313 // GH // AP-12 // 03.2013

110 | t1

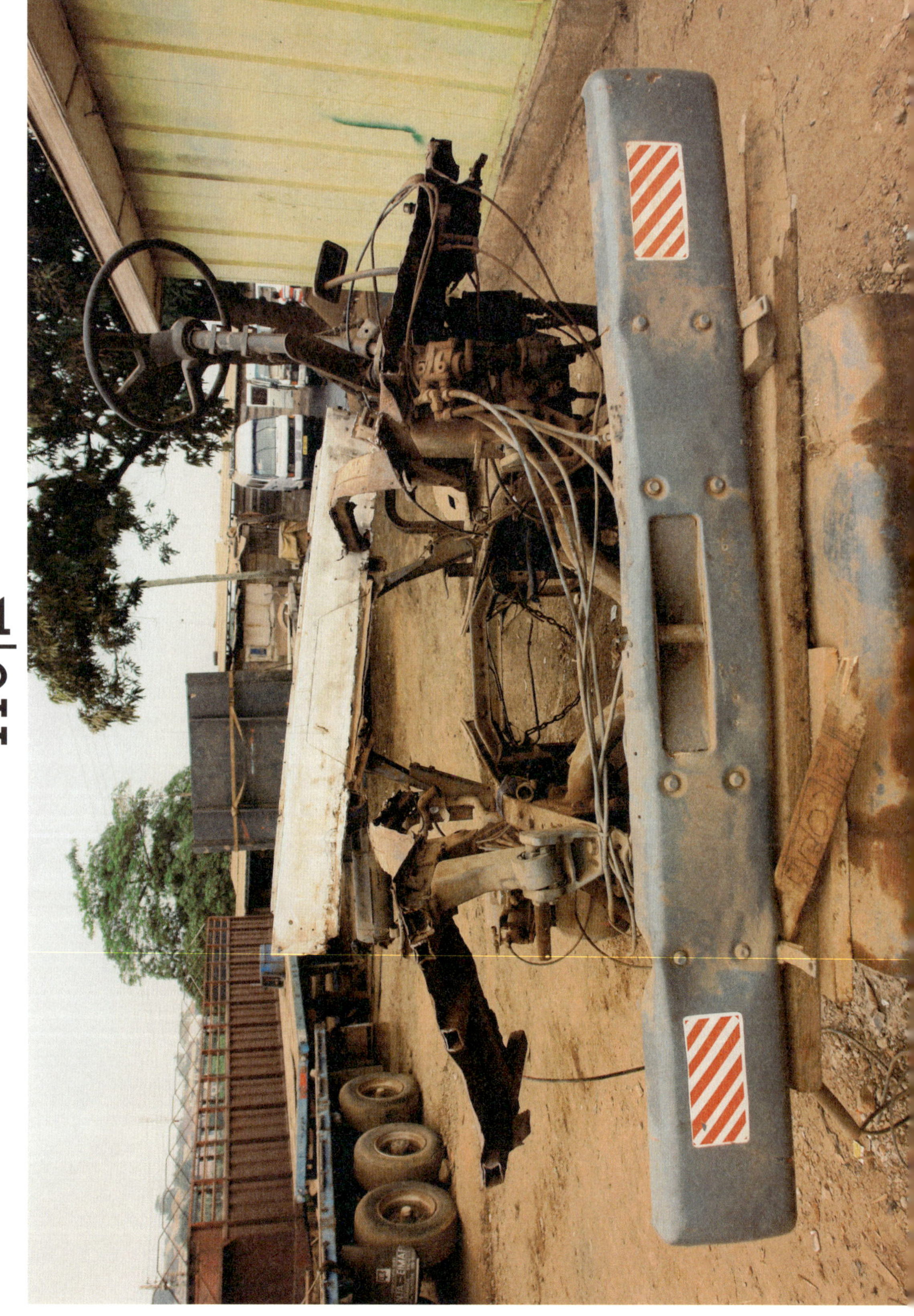

GH // 02.2013

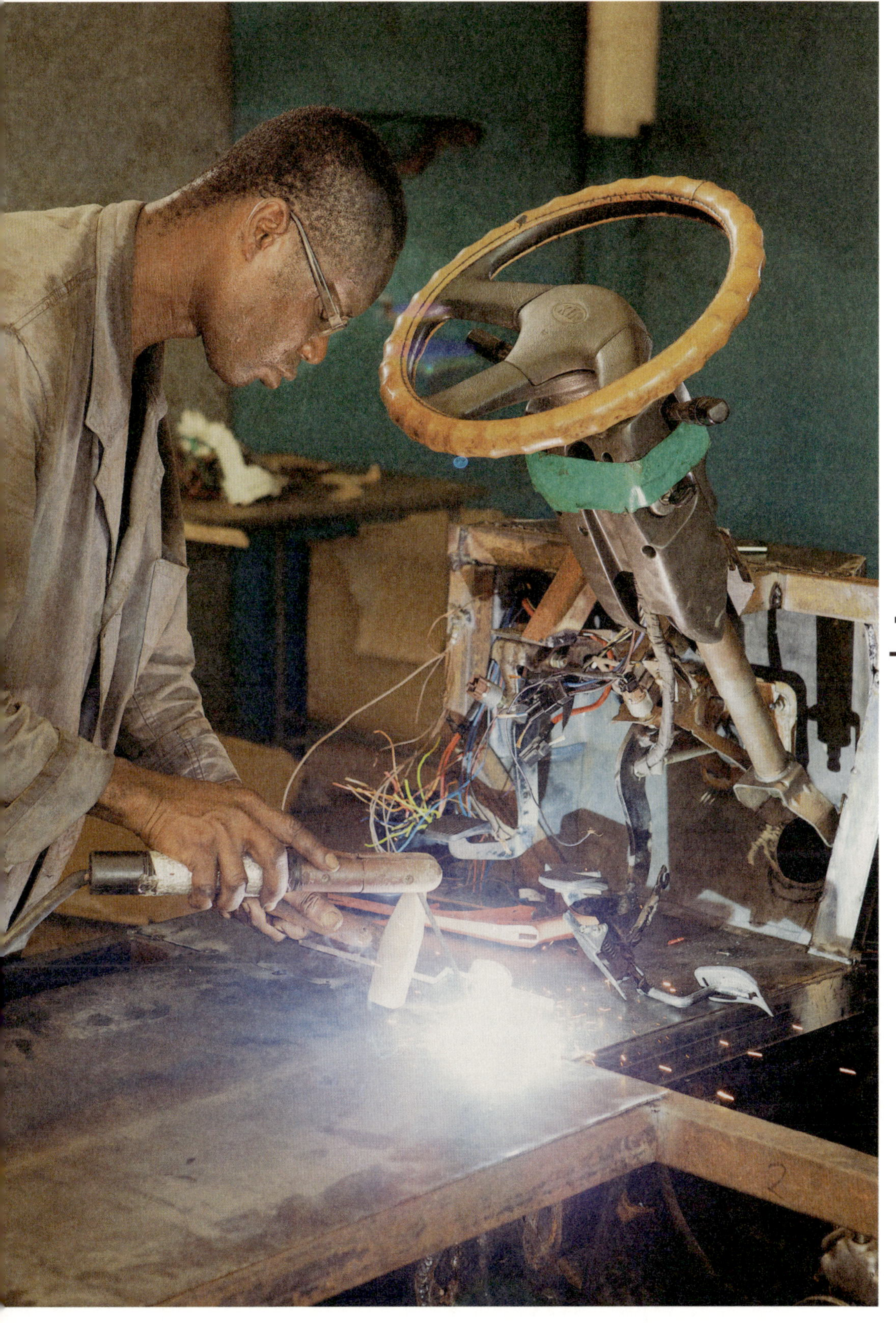

Masters usually head their own workshop, with the senior apprentices and apprentices below them. All those ranks are mixed up in our workshop and the masters have to work together to find a solution. During discussions between the masters everyone's opinion is heard until there is a consensus as to how to resolve a problem. They call this "sharing ideas".

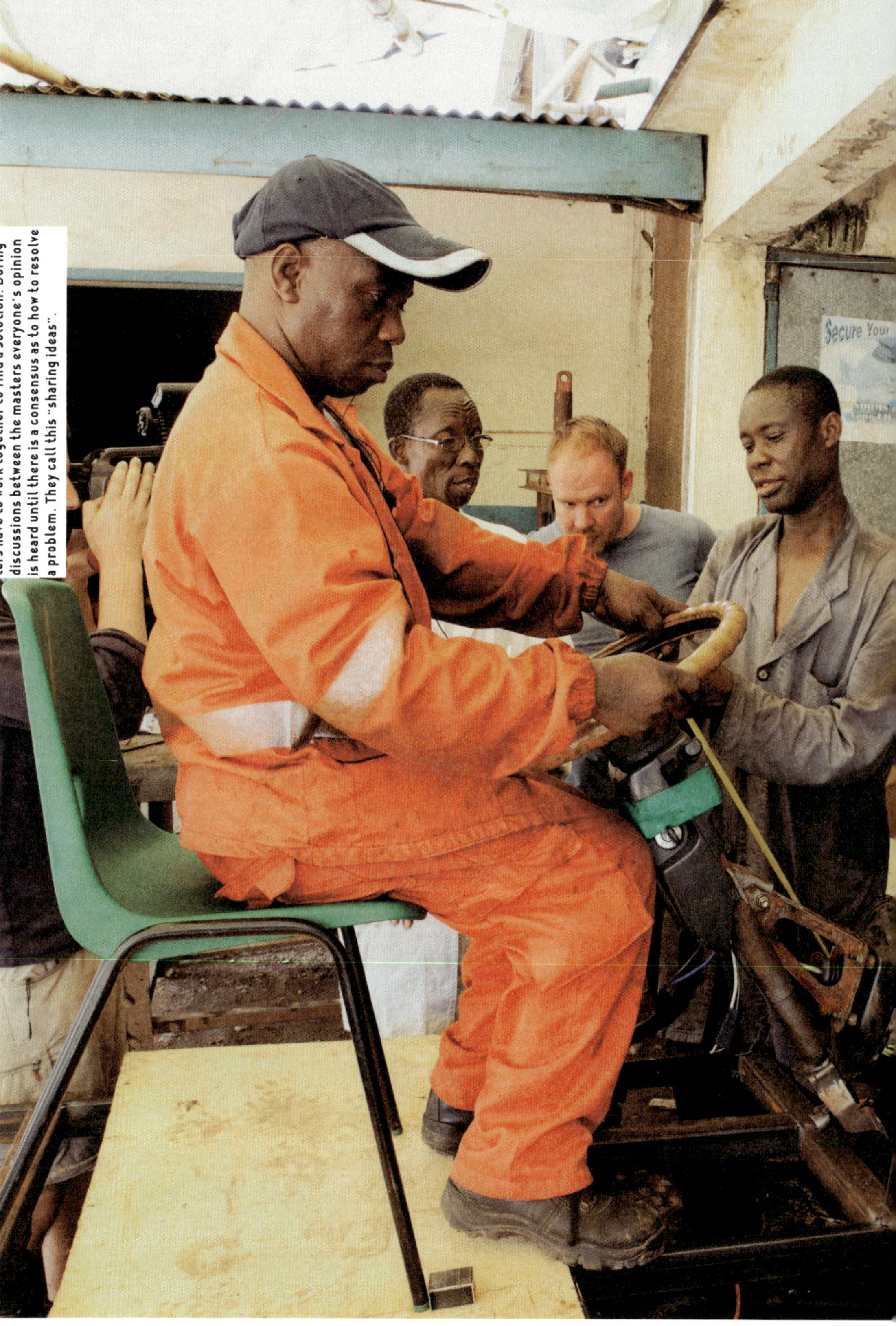

KIA-424 / TOY-334 // GH // AP-12 // 03.2013

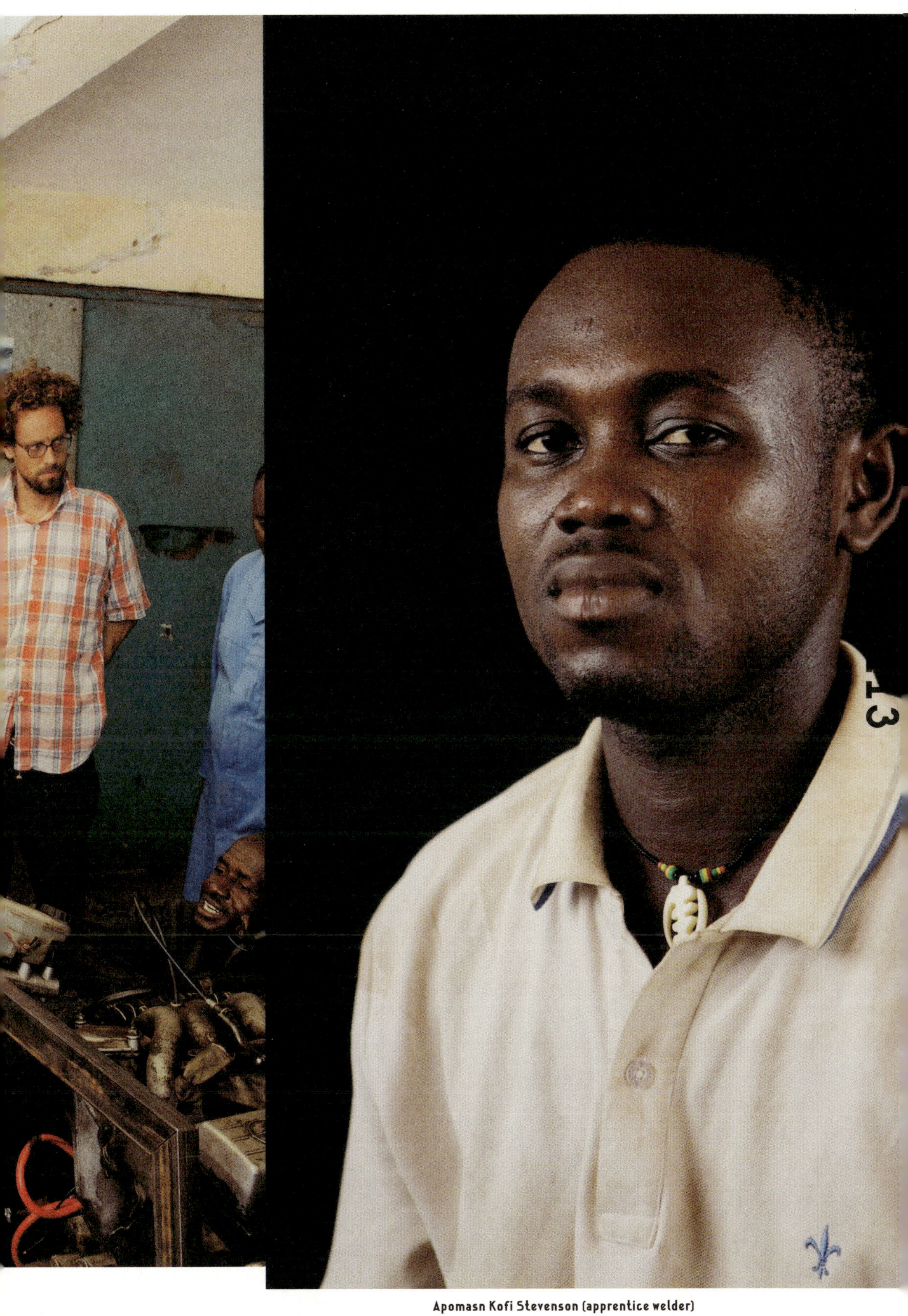

Apomasn Kofi Stevenson (apprentice welder)

L: First test drive, 9 March 2013.
R: Christopher Adusei's Mercedes

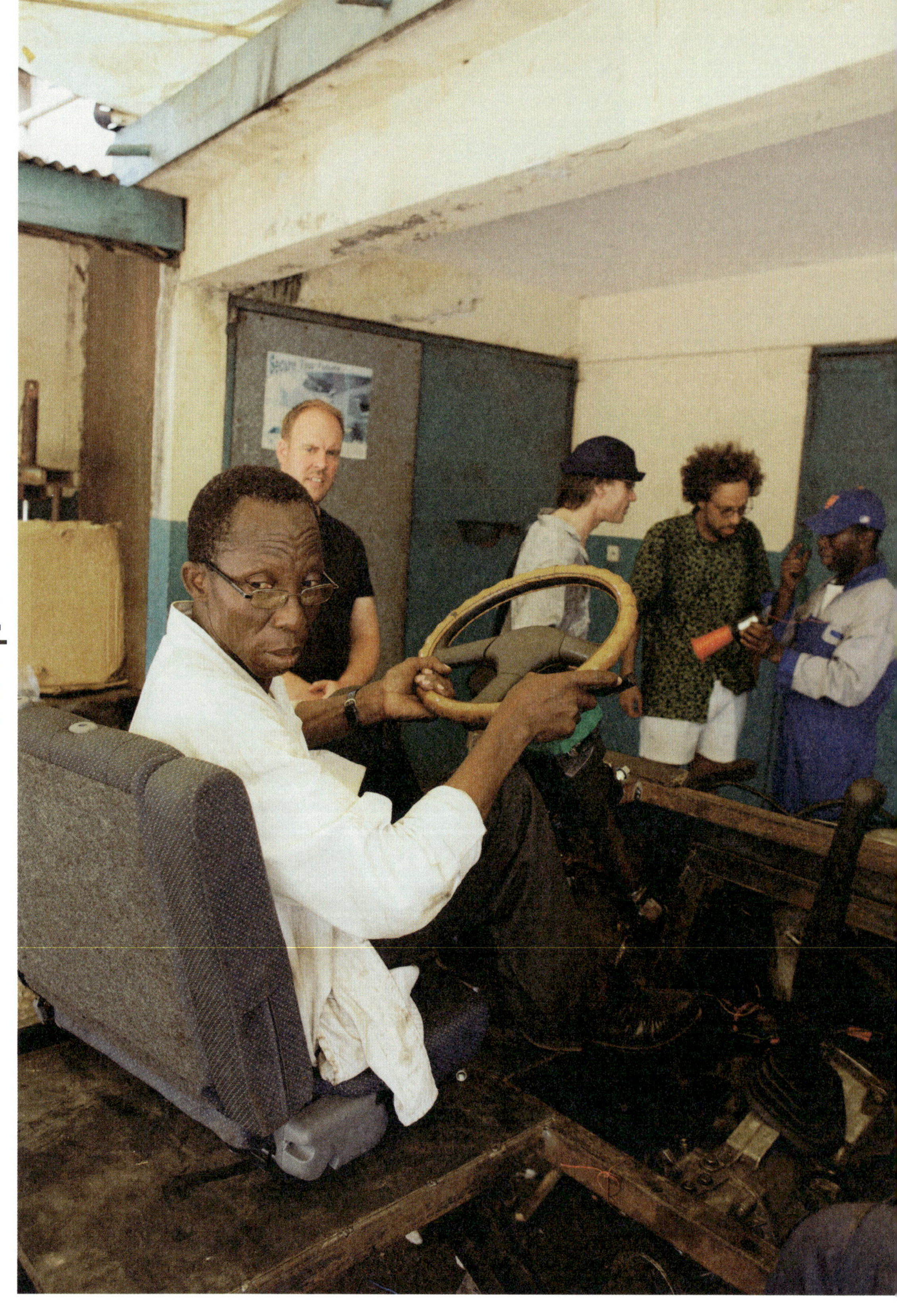

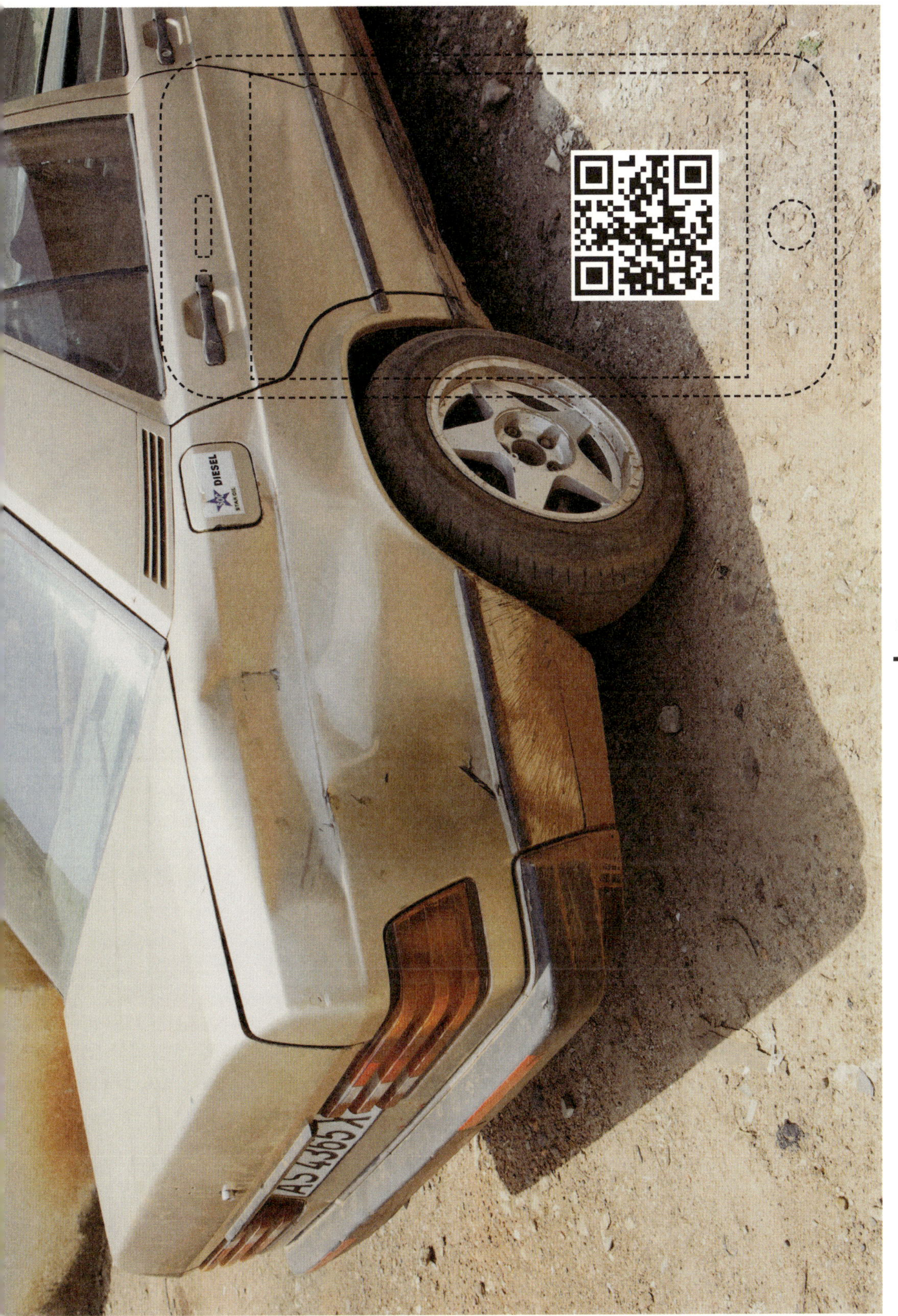

t1 | 115

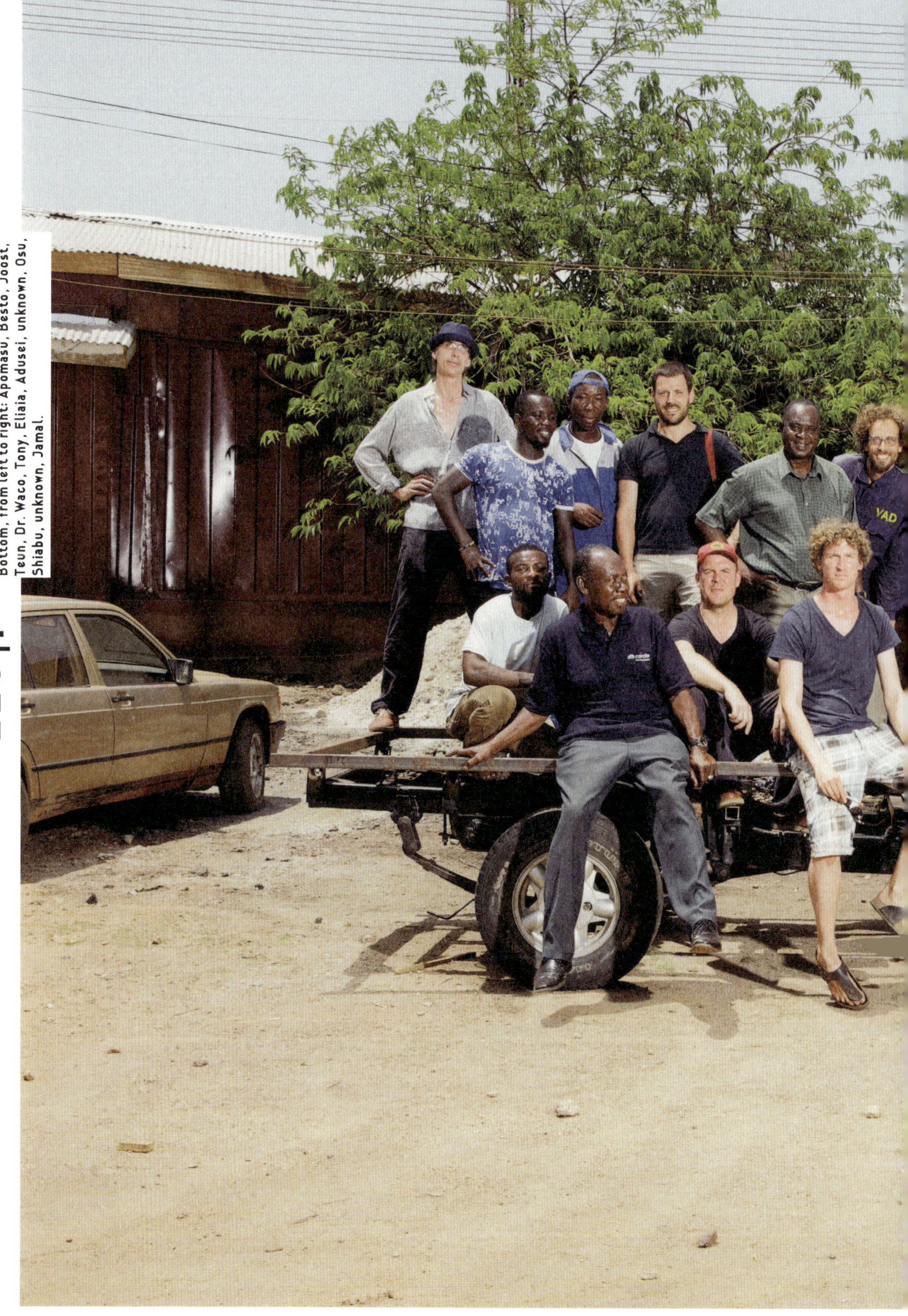

Top, from left to right: Tijs, salesman Totyota steering port, Lamus, Melle, Philip, Bram. Bottom, from left to right: Apomasu, Besto, Joost, Teun, Dr. Waco, Tony, Eliaia, Adusei, unknown, Osu, Shiabu, unknown, Jamal.

UNK-402 / TOY-351 / SSY-285 / SM-315 / NIS-402/ NIS-245 // GH // AP-12 // 03.2013

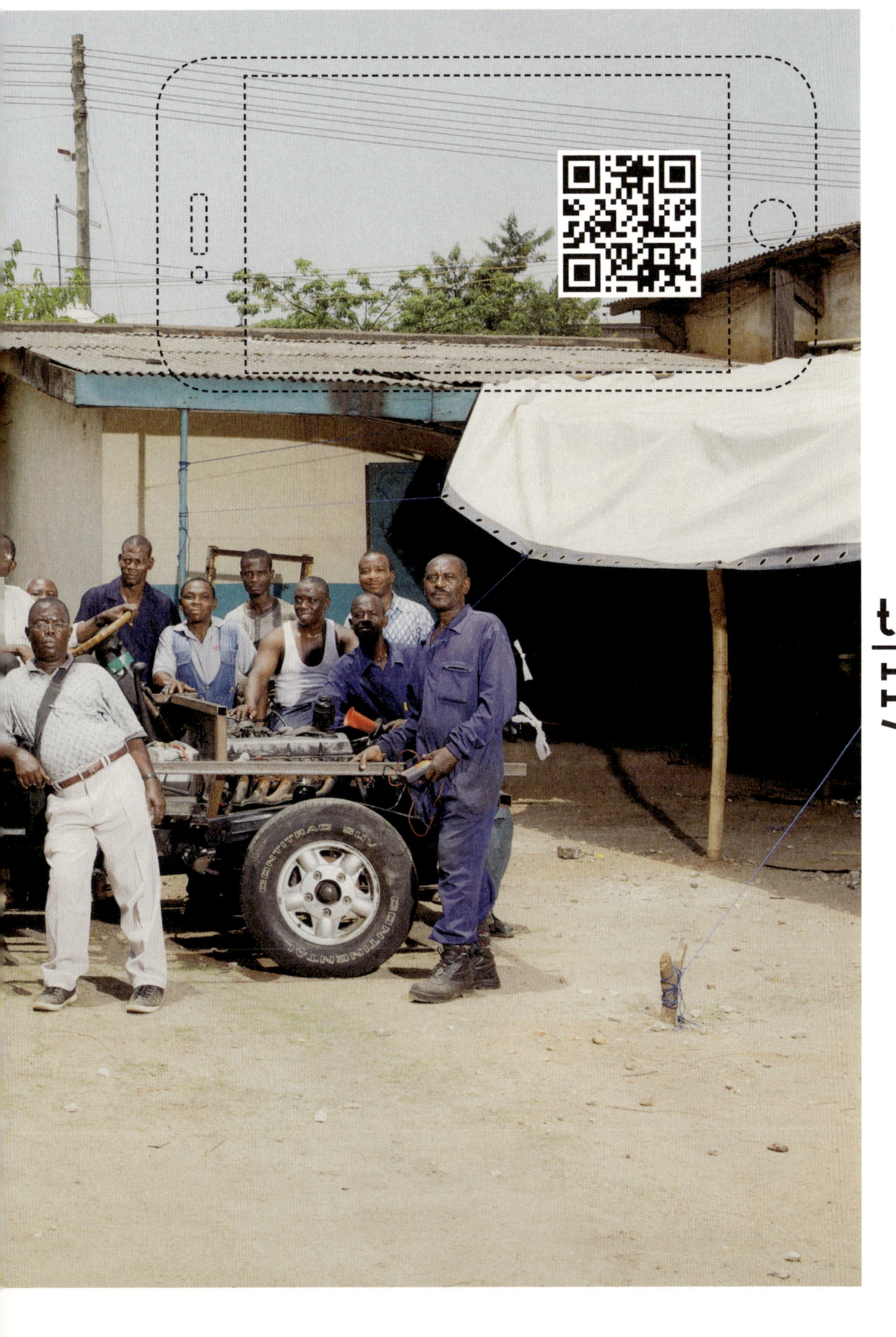
CONTITRAC SUV
CONTINENTAL

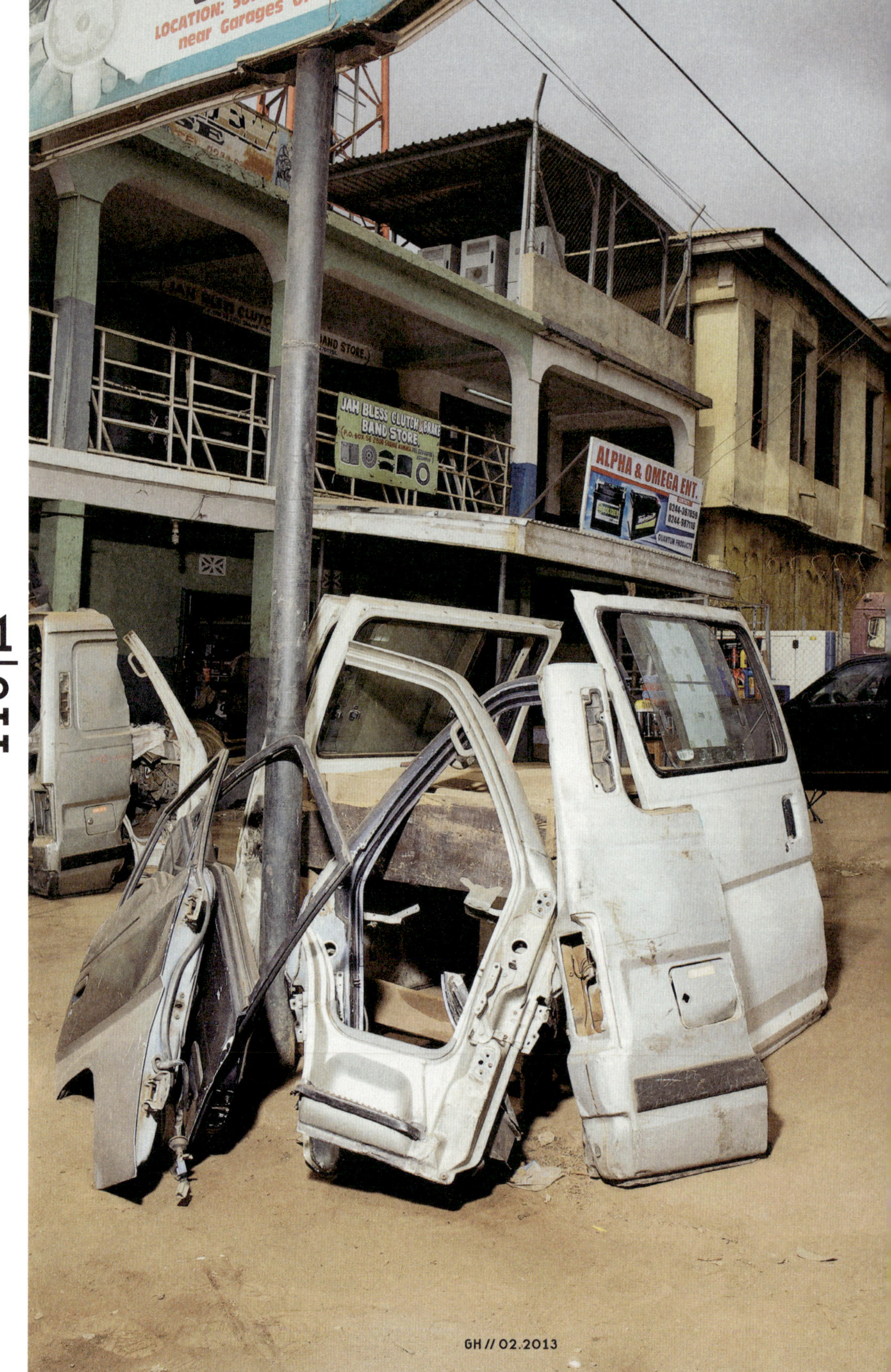

LOCATION:
near Garages
JAH BLESS CLUTCH & BRAKE
BAND STORE
ALPHA & OMEGA ENT.
QUANTUM PRODUCTS

GH // 02.2013

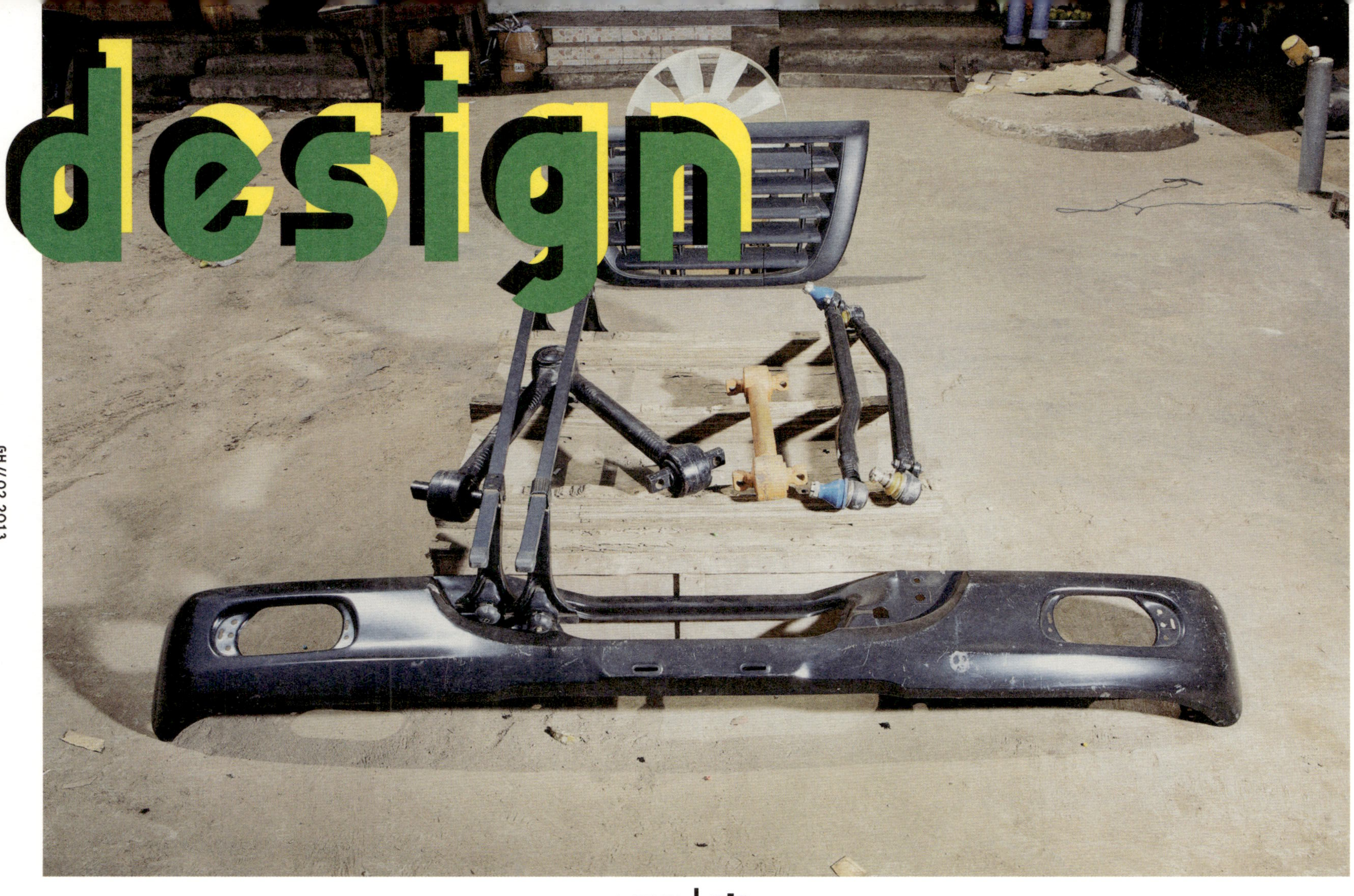

t1 | 119

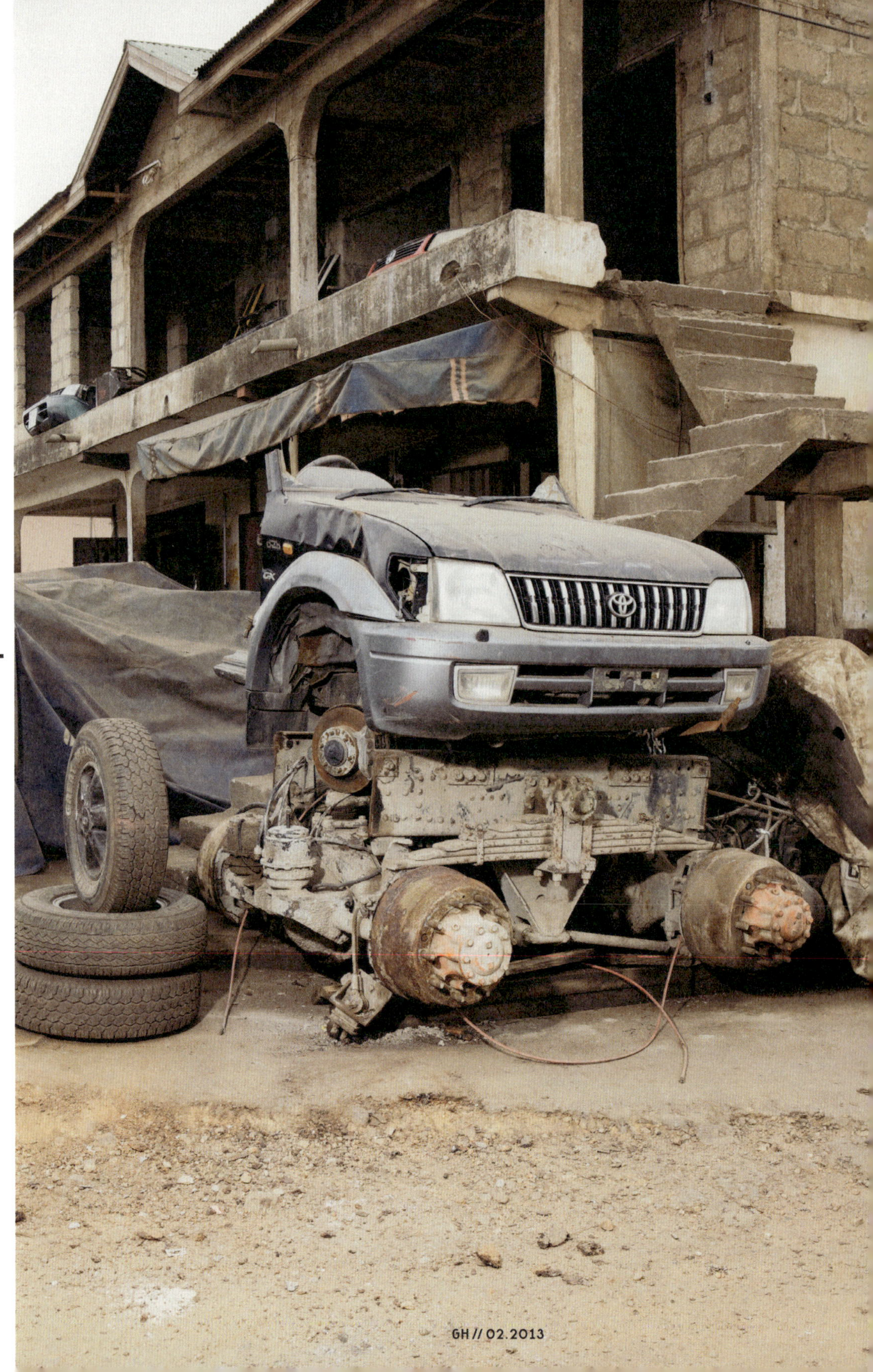

GH // 02.2013

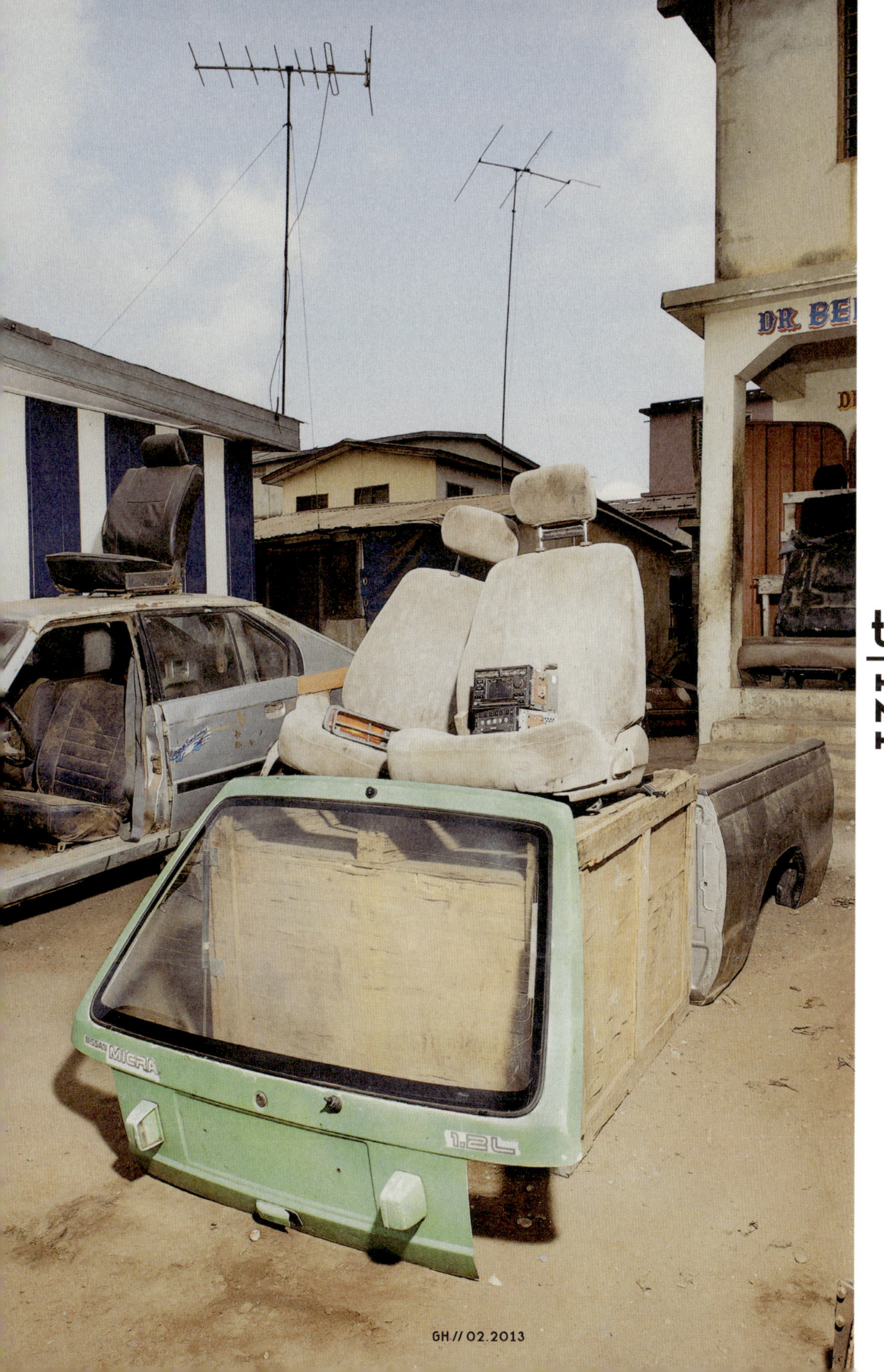

GH // 02.2013

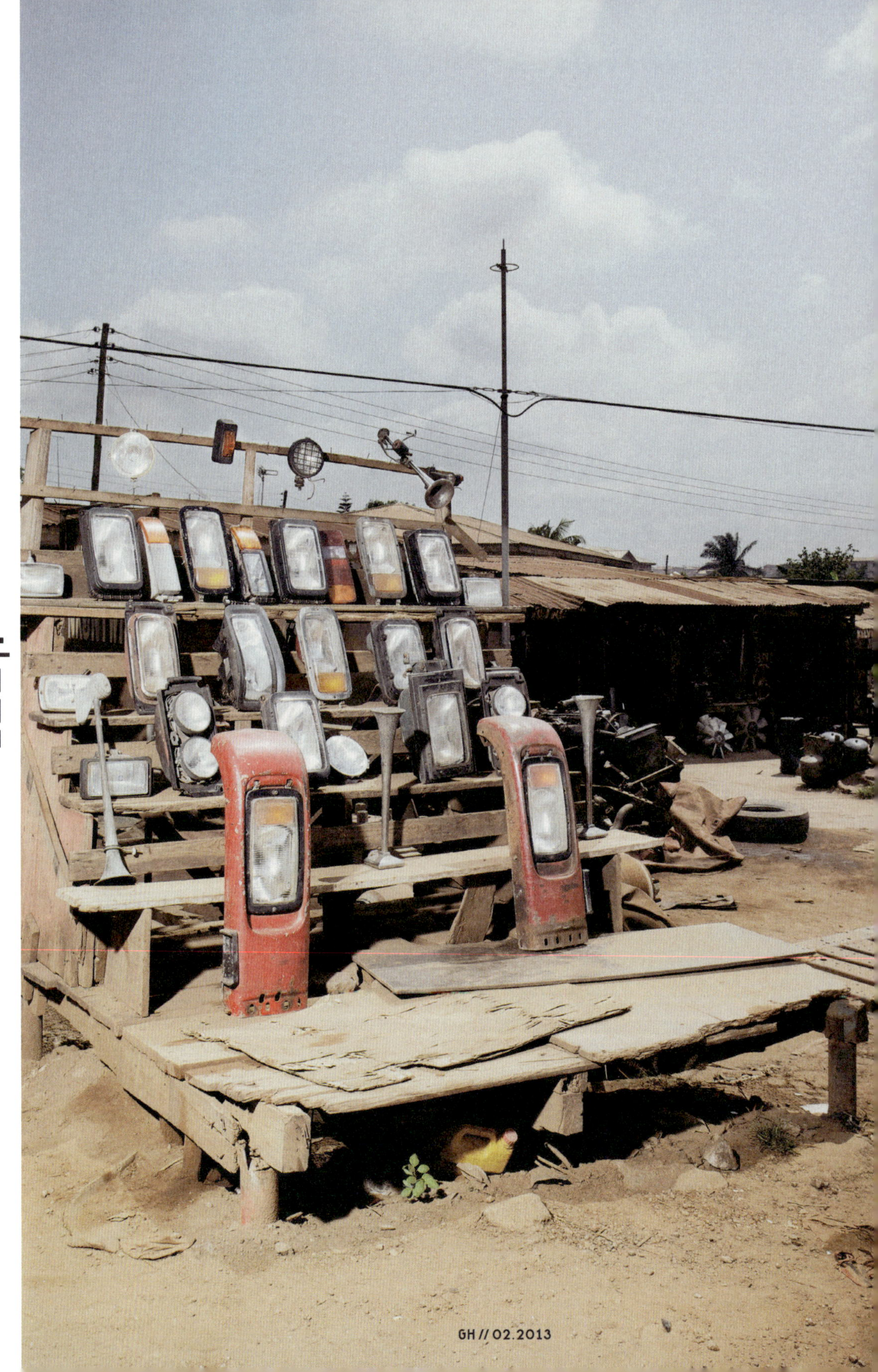

GH // 02.2013

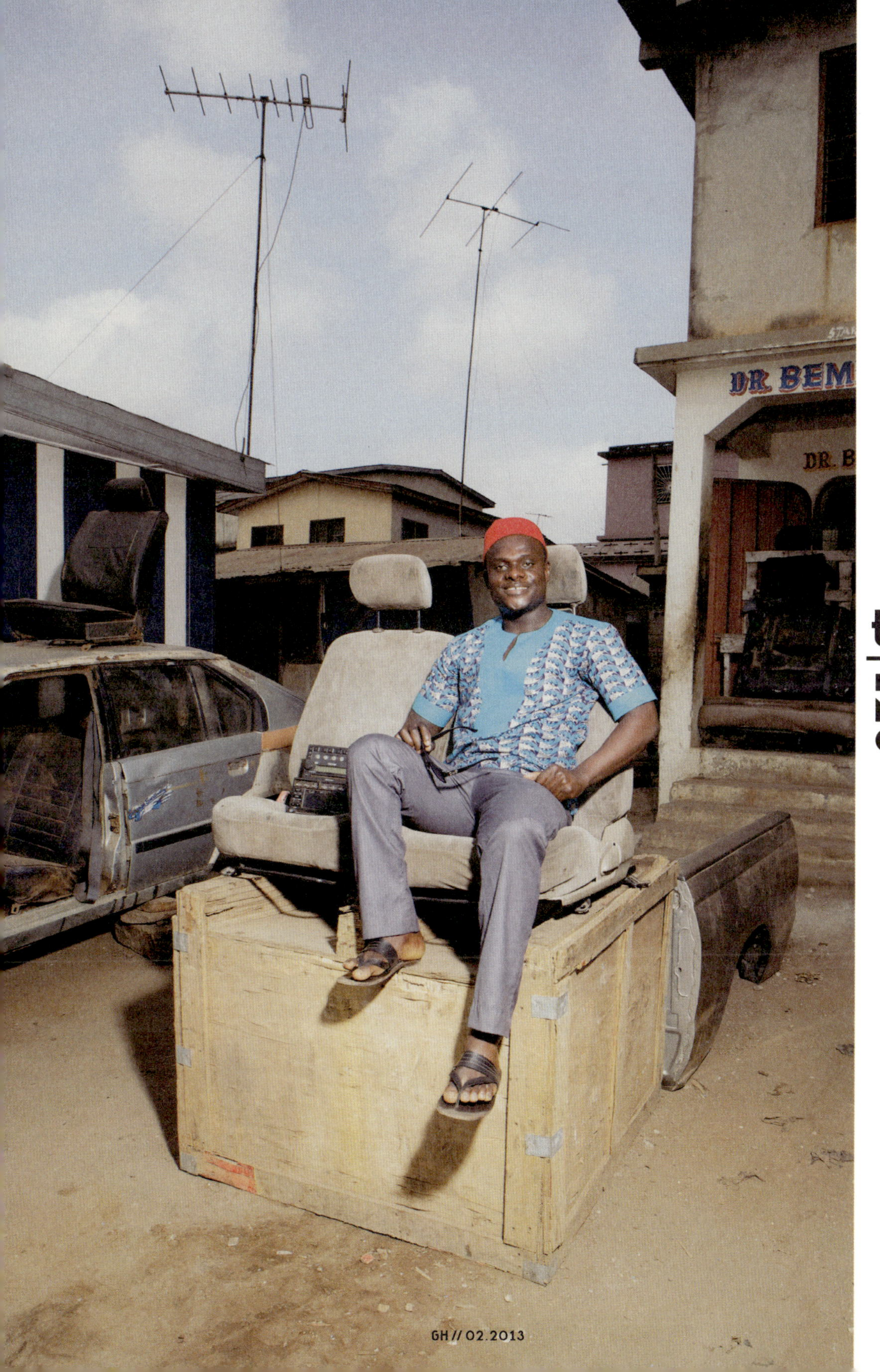
DR. BEM
DR. B

Collecting the Petuo at the KNUST University. The Petuo is an adapted Morris. It was the most common car in Ghana in the 1950s. Custom-finishing took place in Ghana. We transported the Petuo to our workshop to use it as an inspiration for the Turtle 1. From left to right: tow truck apprentice, tow truck driver, Dr. Waco, Joost, Osu, Philip, Lamus, Adusei, KNUST employee, Desmond, KNUST employee, KNUST employee, Melle, Fiagbe

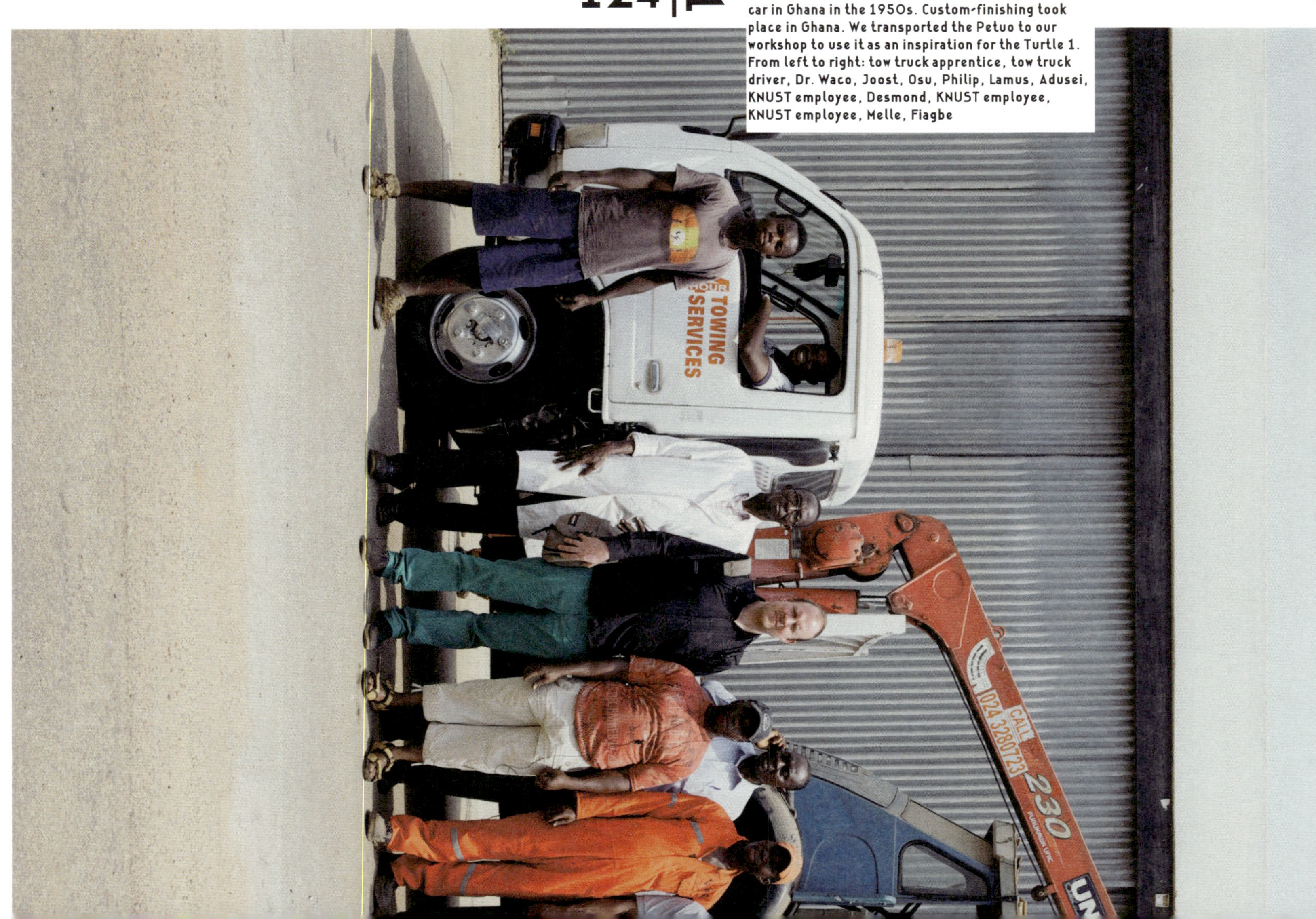

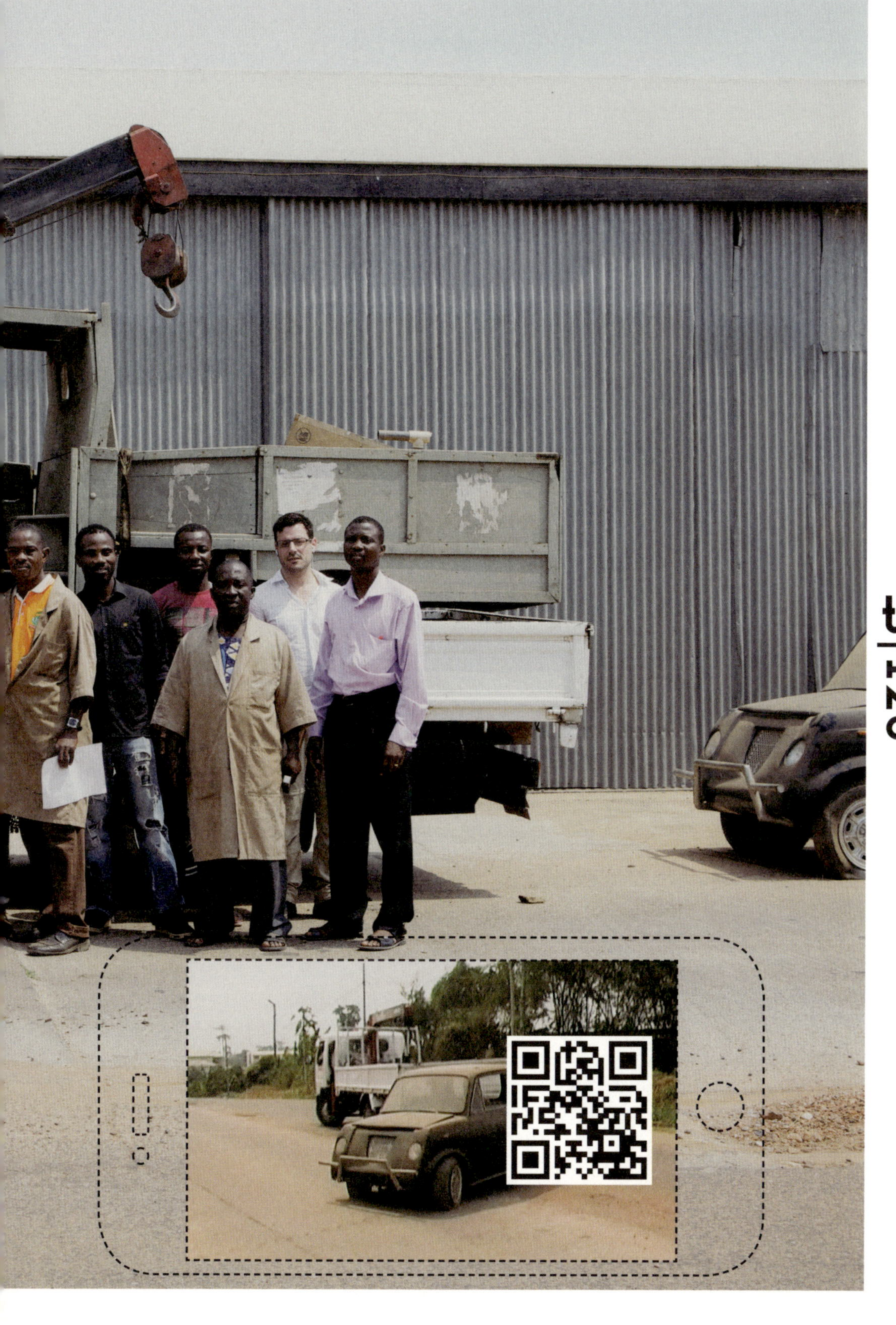

L: Pinboard displaying work produced during the Rietveld Academy and KNUST University design workshop.
R: The restoration of the Petuo, which had stood idle for 40 years.

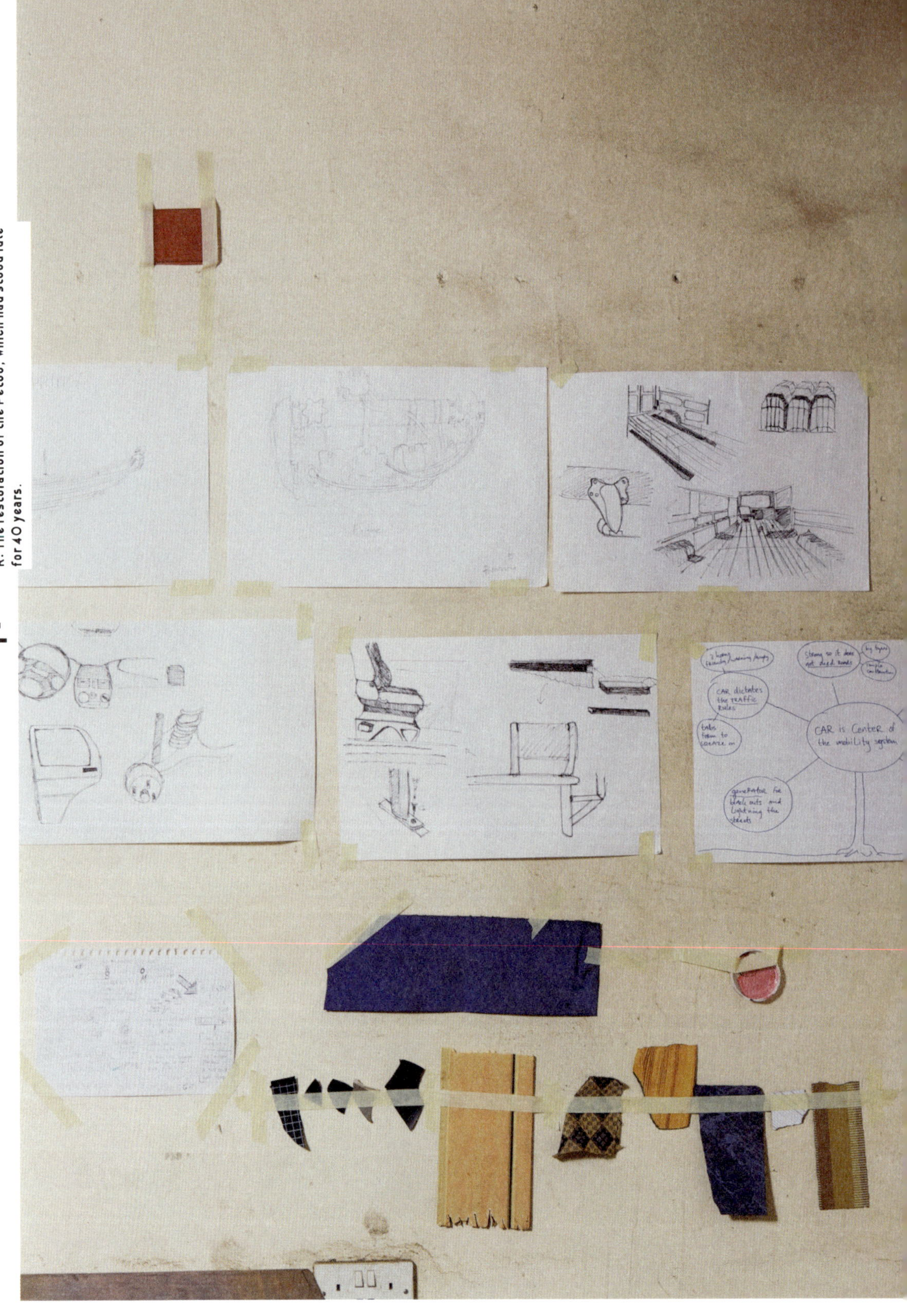

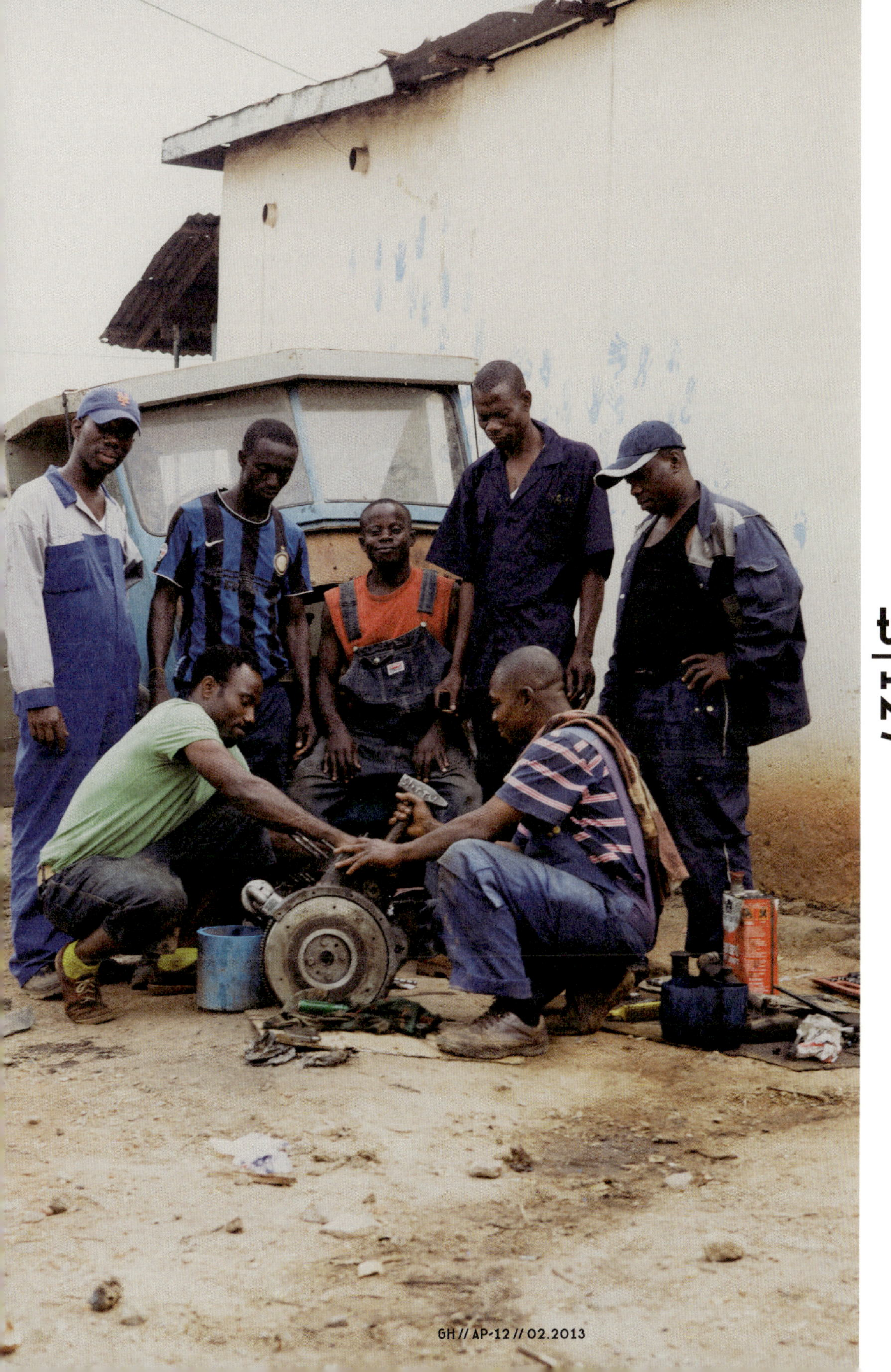

GH // AP-12 // 02.2013

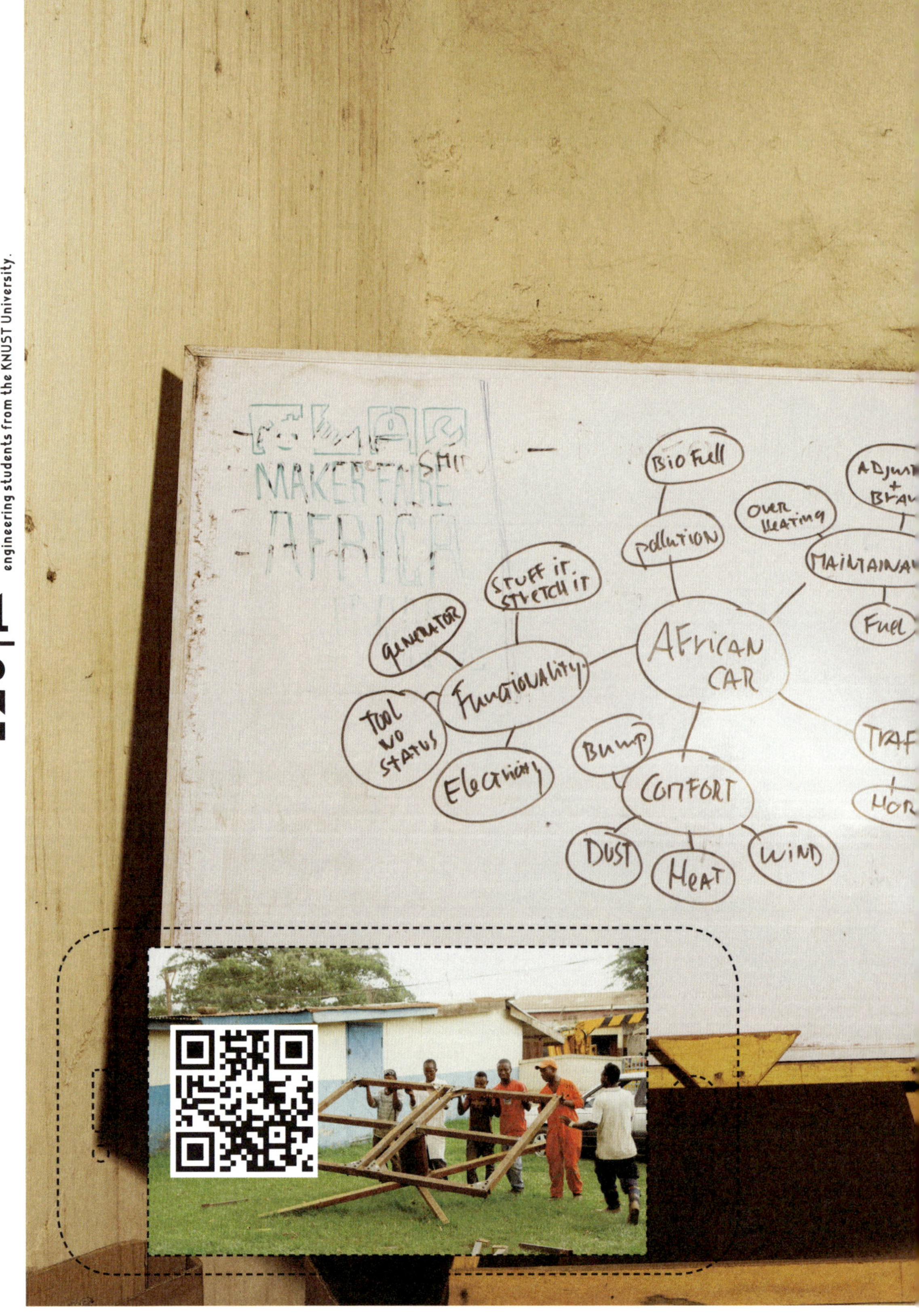

Diagram outlining the requirements of an African car, which was drawn up during a workshop with mechanical engineering students from the KNUST University.

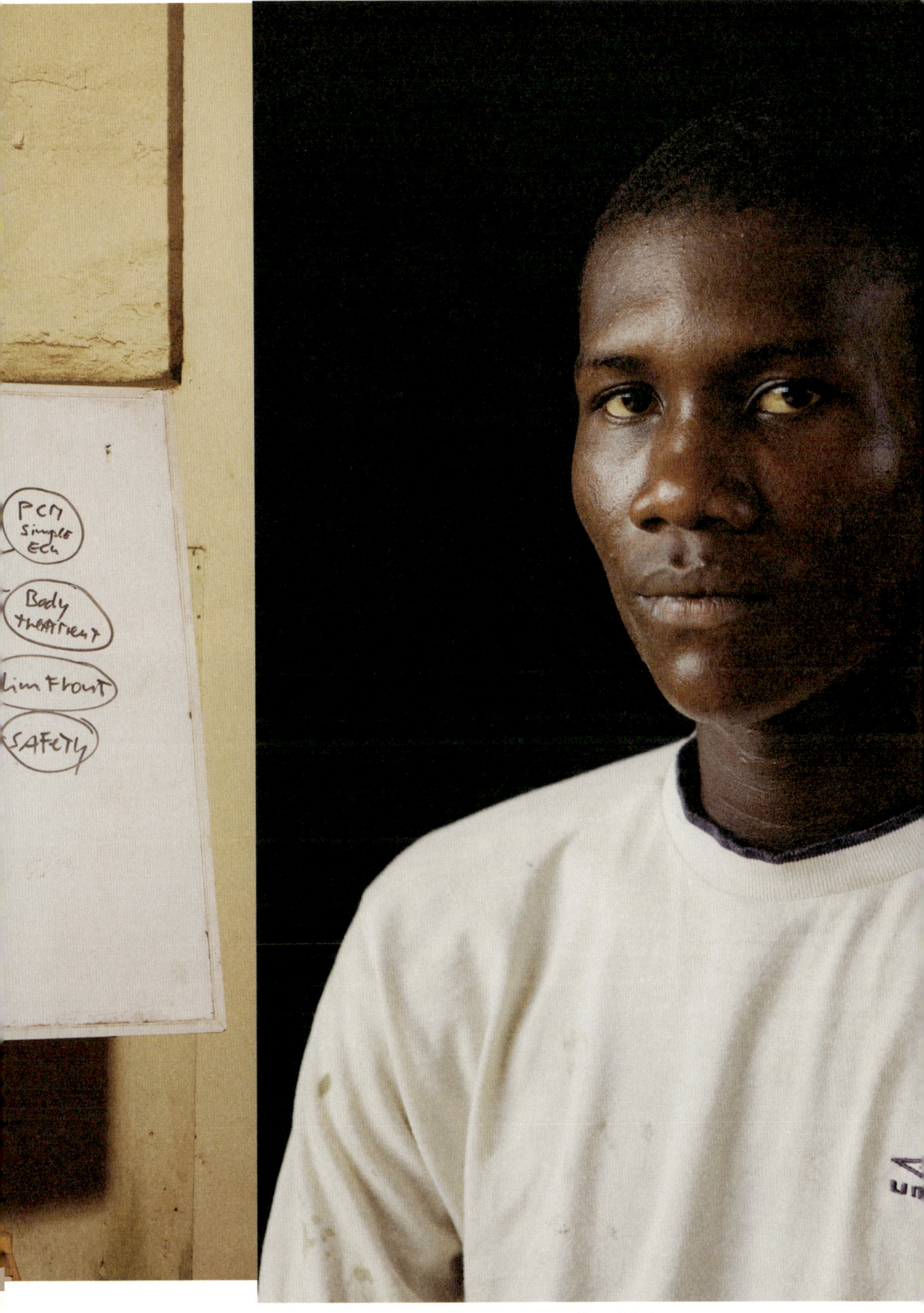

Thomas Owusu (apprentice painter)

L: Students develop different designs based on the techniques they have discovered in the cluster. James designed a Low-Tech Air Conditioning system made of baked clay (top left).
R: Cynthia Hathaway, Bob Vos, Stein van Kervel and Lukas Wolzak discover the double-roof technique that is used in Land Rovers to reduce the heat in the cabin. This technique was also applied in the Turtle 1.

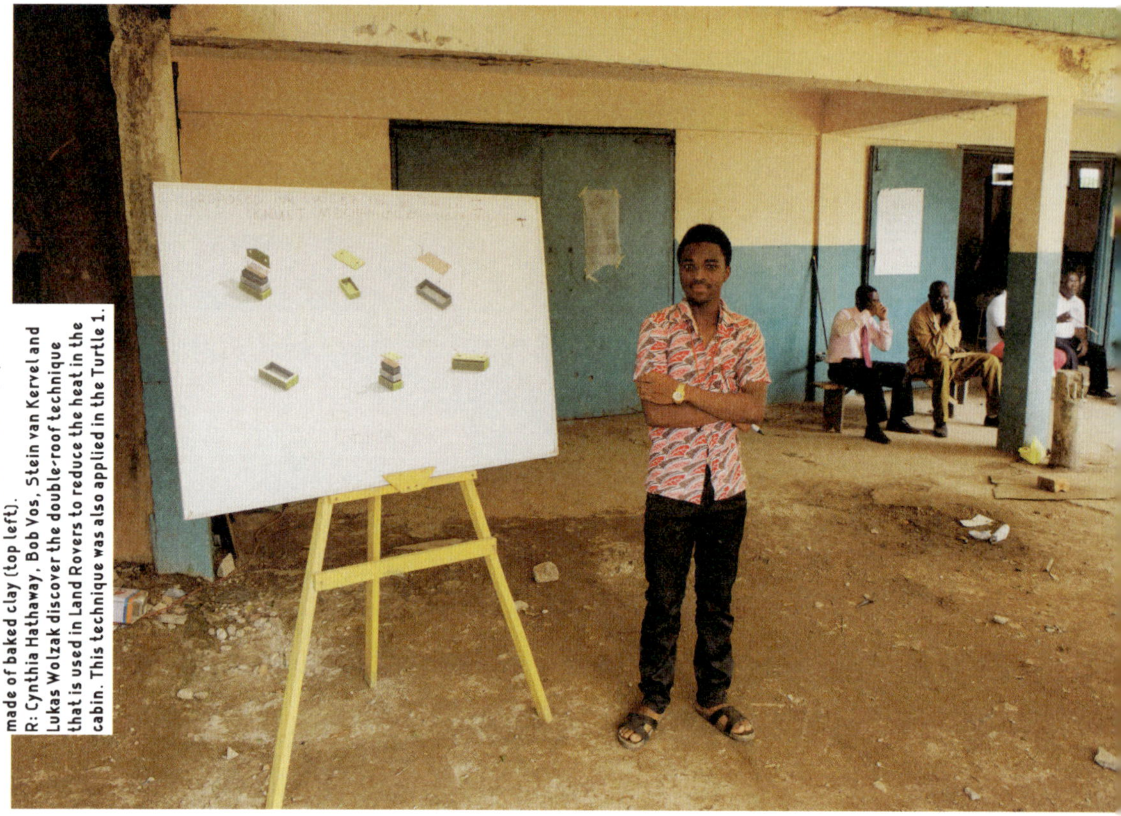

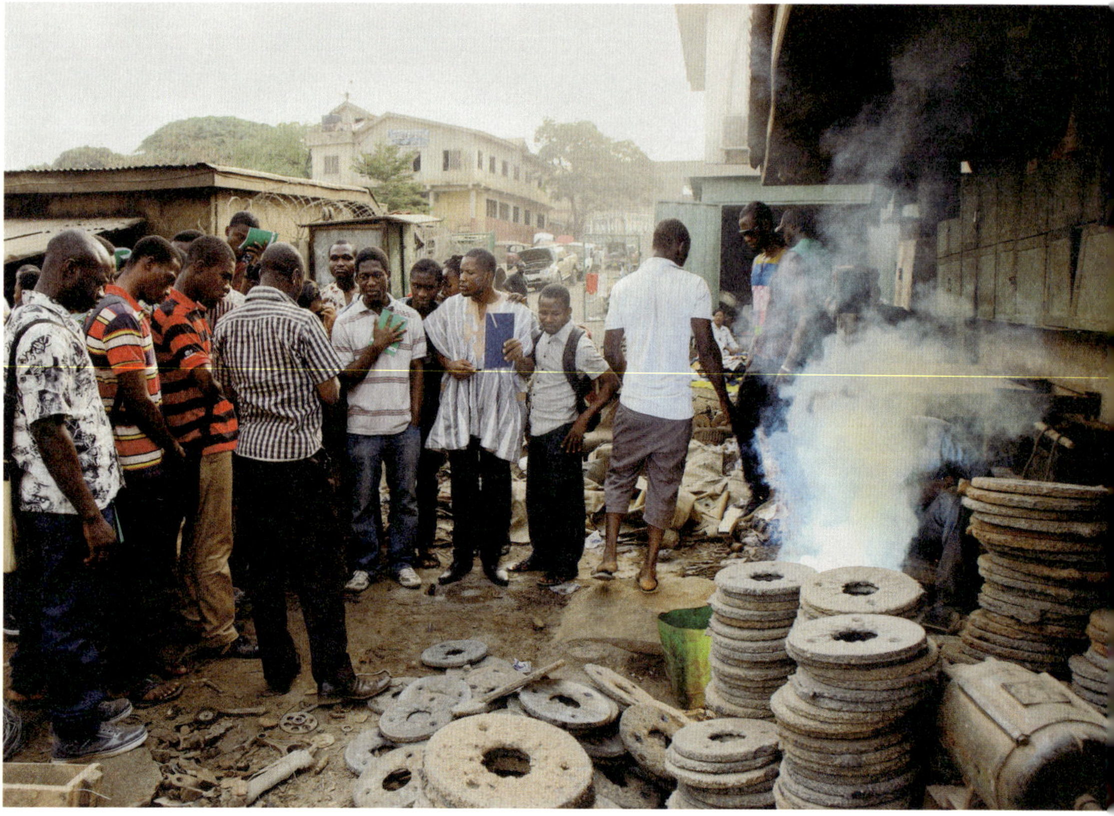

GH // AP-12 // 04.2013
GH // 02.2013

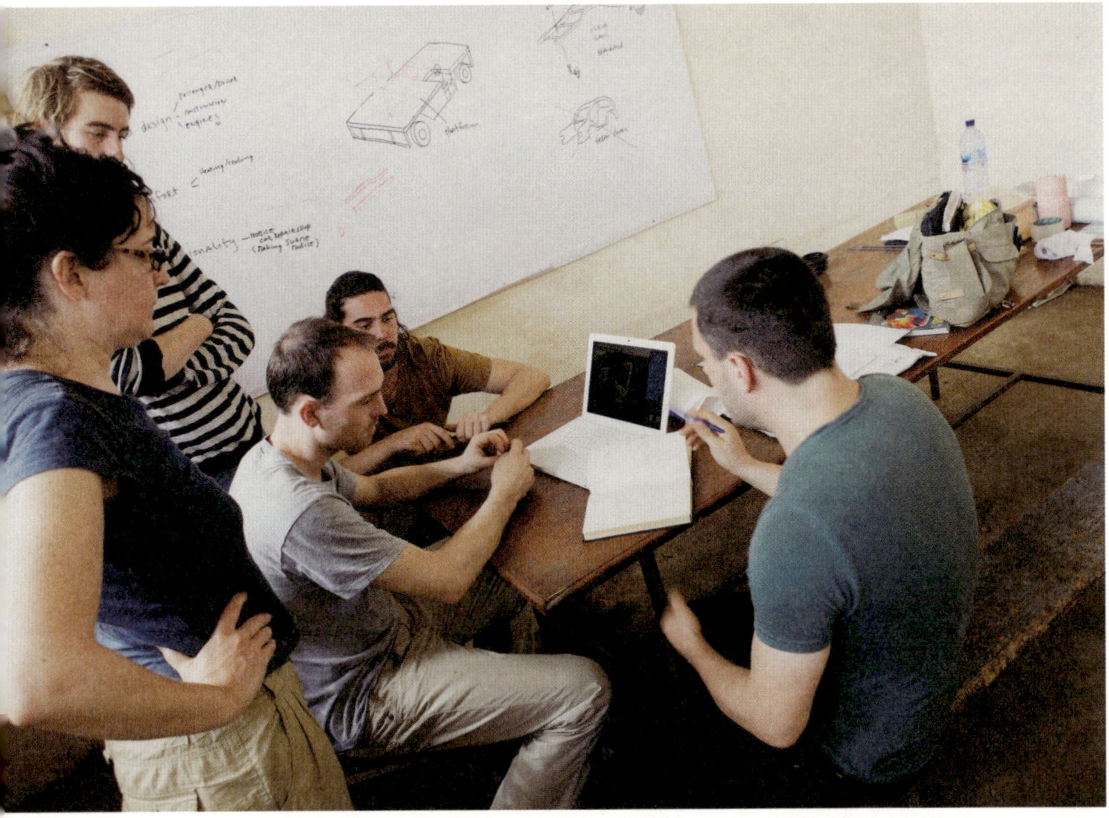

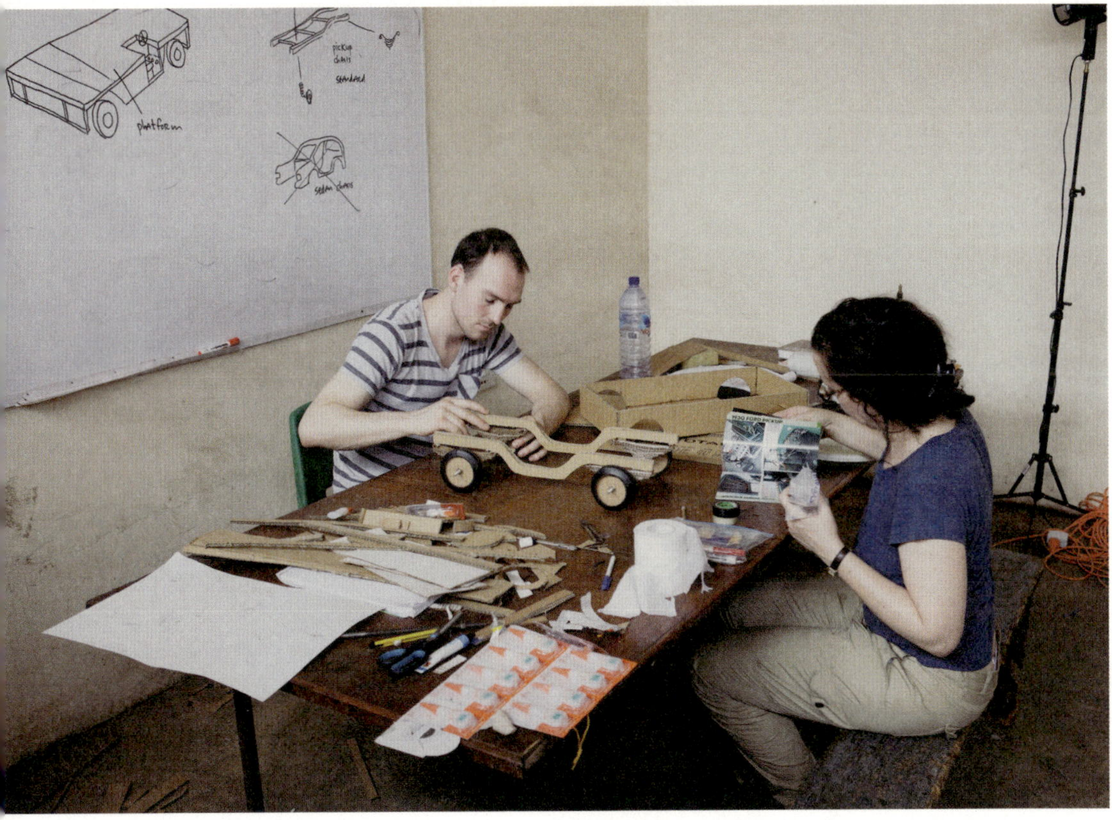

GH // AP-12 // 02.2013

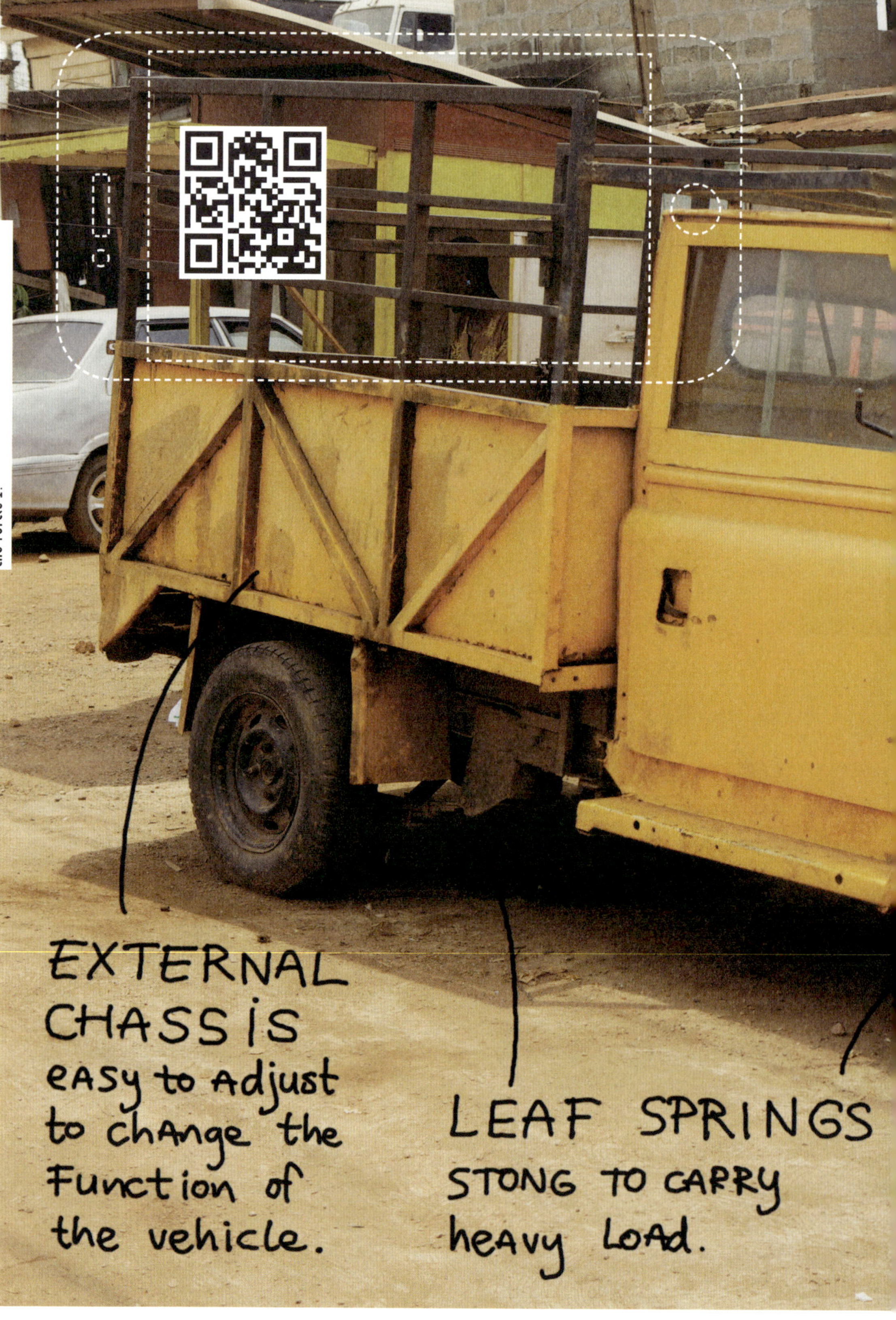

The Buafo car ("I will help you carry" in Twi), built in 1974 in Suame Magazine. The Buafo proved to be a perfect point of departure for the design of the Turtle 1.

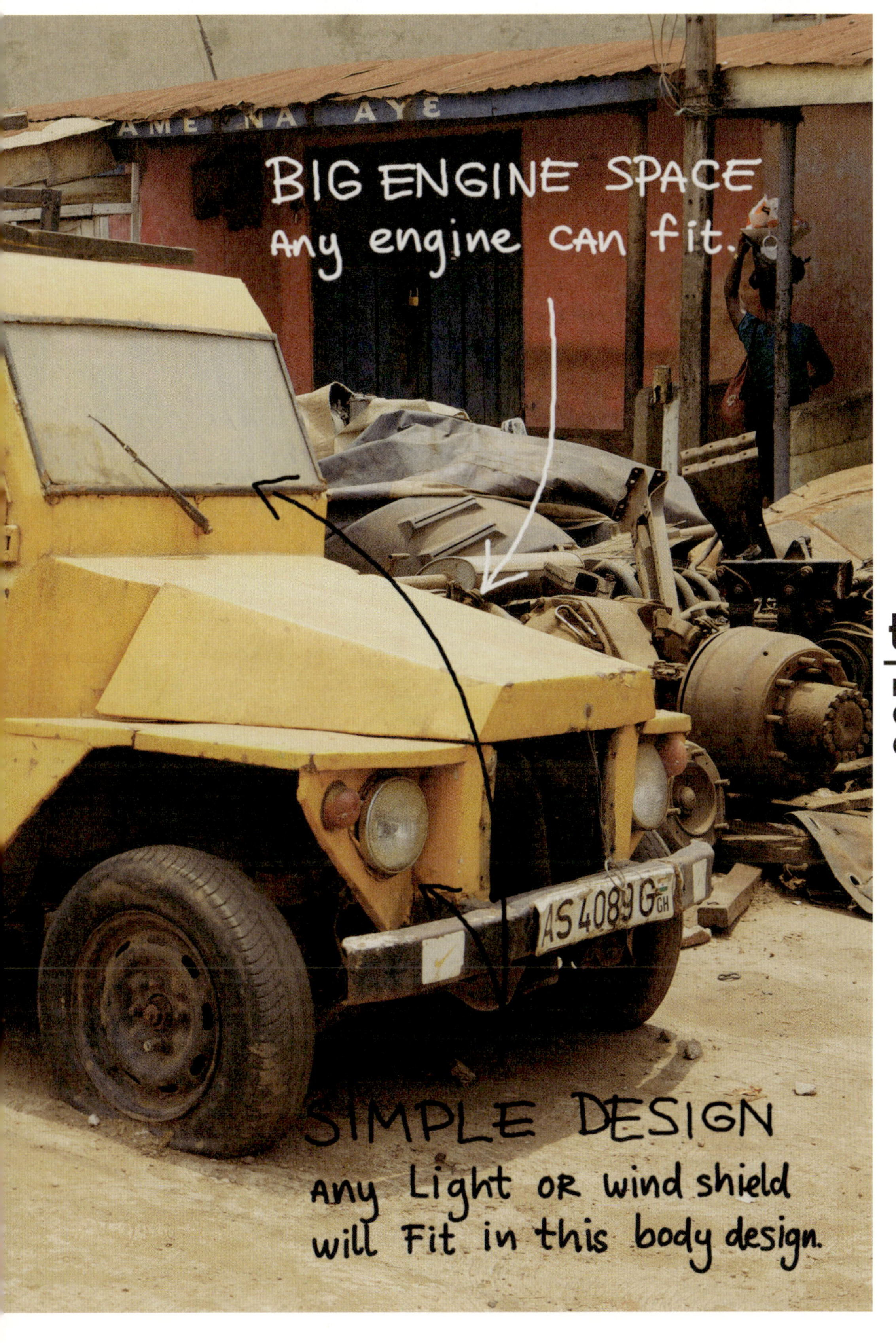
BIG ENGINE SPACE
Any engine can fit.
AS 4089 G GH
SIMPLE DESIGN
Any Light or wind shield
will Fit in this body design.

Design sketches by Melle Smets for the Turtle. The first design idea for the Turtle was a driving platform (bottom left) that a buyer could adjust to his specific needs. Later designs show multiple bodywork options.

GH // AP-12 // 02.2013
GH // AP-12 // 02.2013
GH // AP-12 // 02.2013
GH // AP-12 // 02.2013

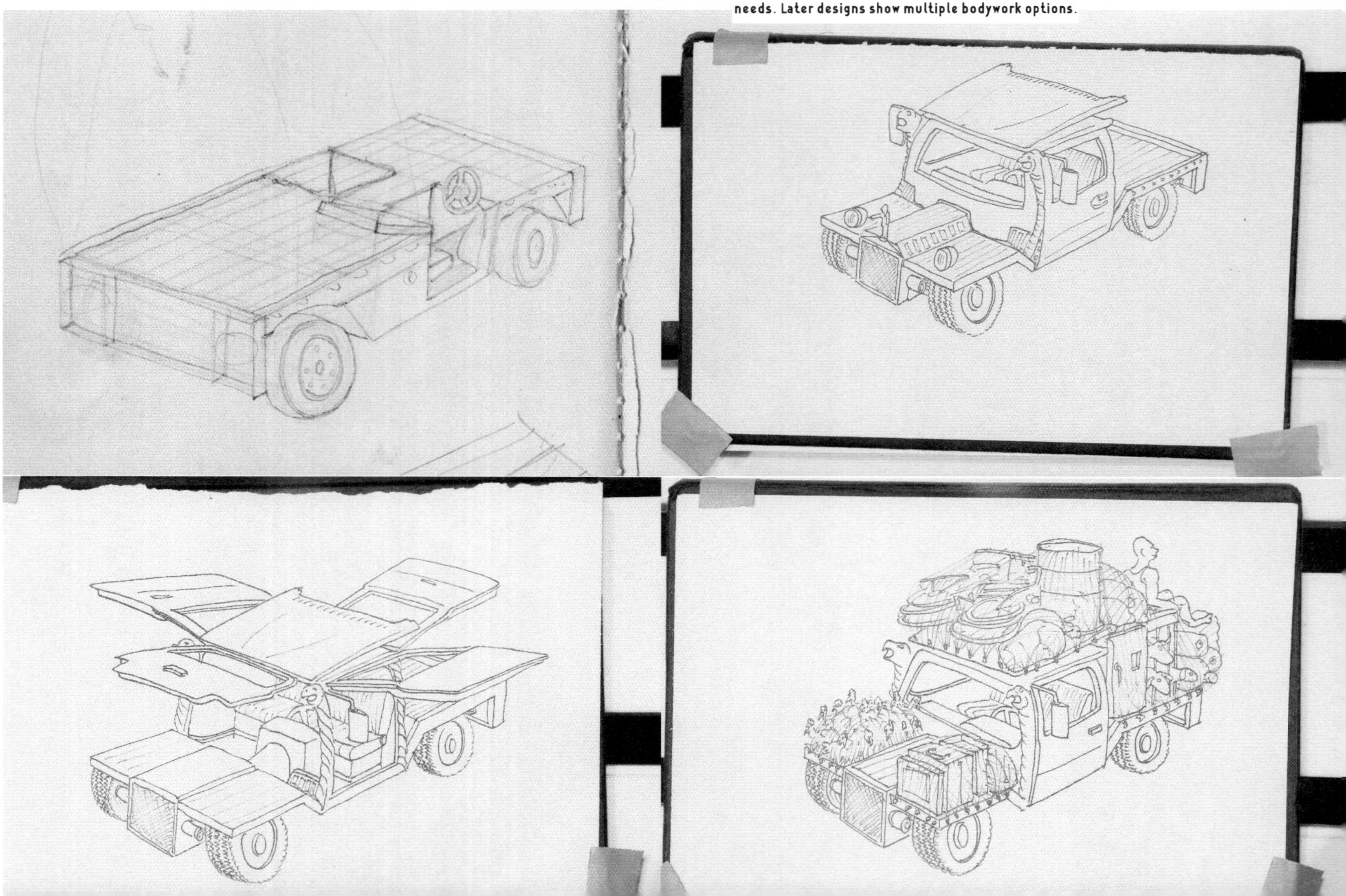

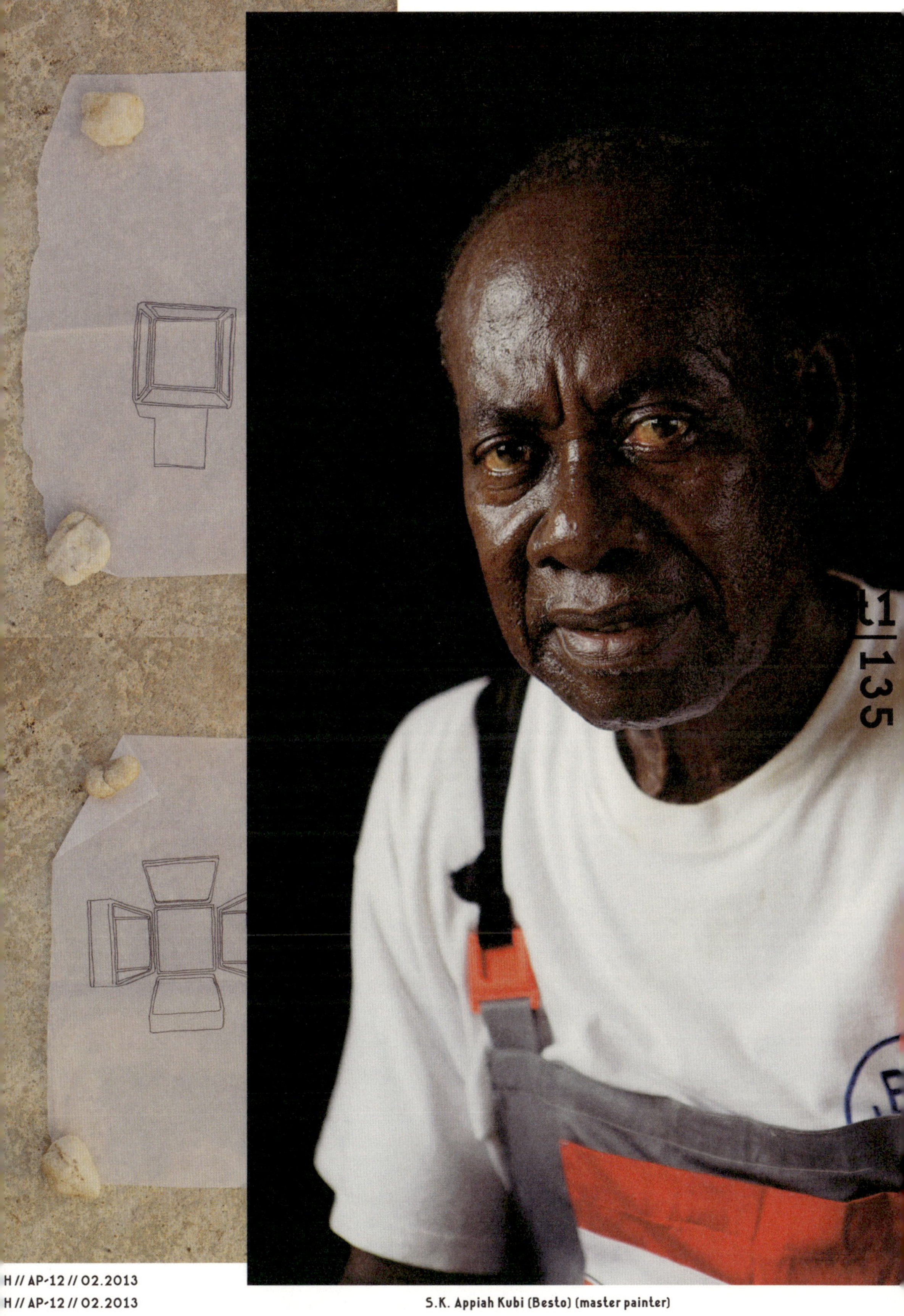

H // AP-12 // 02.2013
H // AP-12 // 02.2013

S.K. Appiah Kubi (Besto) (master painter)

Building the 1:1 wooden test model of the Turtle 1.

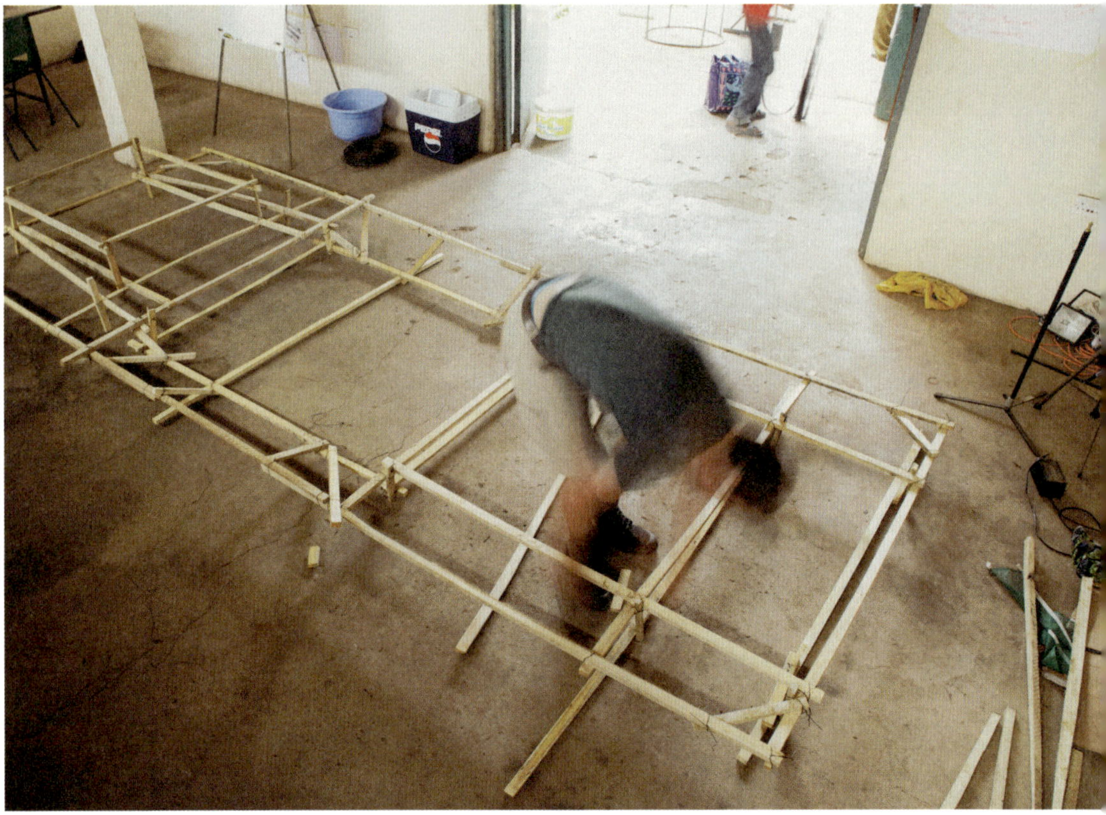

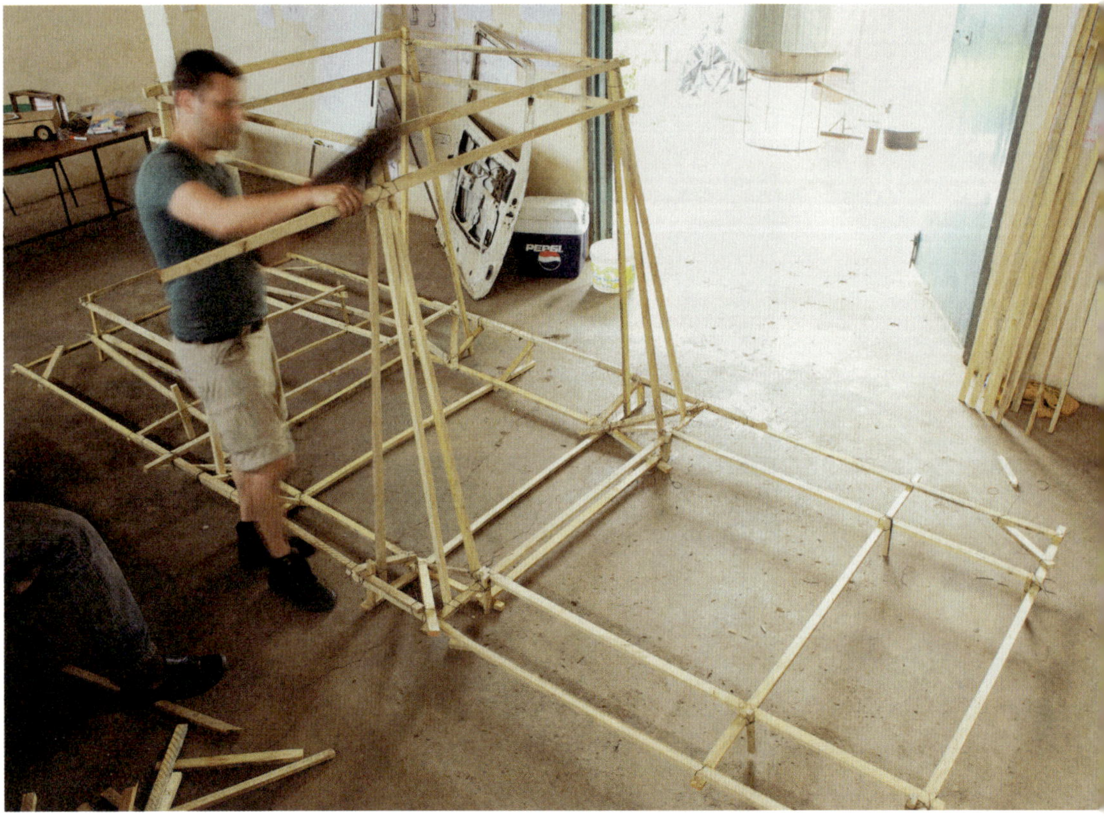

GH // AP-12 // 02.2013

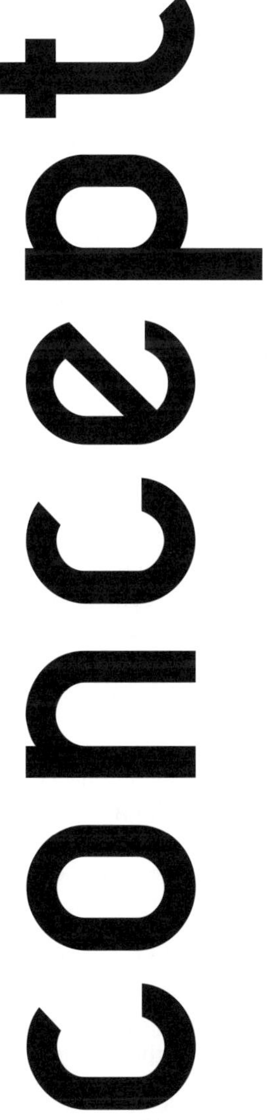

Back in the workshop, the car is taking shape. Every day, parts are fitted, adjusted and added – a fuel tank, a better brake disc – or removed. Meanwhile, the students of the KNUST University and the Rietveld Academy have displayed their sketches, drawings and models in a classroom next to the workshop. They have spent the last two weeks working with teacher Cynthia Hathaway to develop ideas for the Turtle's design. They were asked to analyse the landscape, potential clients, available materials, Ghana's infrastructure and the opportunities in Suame. Our idea was to design a car based on the local conditions, without any preconceived ideas. We wanted to abandon the Western model of linear thinking and instead work according to Suame Magazine practice: no detailed planning, no technical drawings, no measuring sticks. The students have made diagrams mapping the requirements of an African car. As the roads are so bad, the car has to be able to make its own path. The tropical climate is merciless, so the car must protect man and machine against the heat. The lack of materials means that the car must be easy to repair. And as every car has many owners, the model has to be adaptable for different uses.

We are pleased with the results, but the SMIDO members seem nonplussed. "Words with circles", says Osu when he looks at our white board. Osu was born and raised in Suame Magazine. He has been a mechanic for as long as he can remember. His hands are like those of a Playmobil figure, shaped to fit exactly around the tools. His workshop is right on the other side of New Suame. In his area, there is not much work because of the constant electricity cuts. Osu is happy at the prospect of months of "chop money", money for food. But he is not impressed with our endless discussions and theorising on a white board. "Why you do this? You are wasting your time." Osu wants to know what the car is going to look like and not in which conceptual framework it fits.

There is a rolling chassis in the workshop by now. Using parts from 15 different car brands, the mechanics have managed to create a working car. The first test drive is the cause of much hilarity. The engine had been working for a week, but Dr Waco and Philip had refused to let anyone drive the car. They kept finding new problems that had to be resolved. Placing the electric wiring was quite a job. Many car parts today have chips and if they cannot talk to each other, they do not cooperate. Philip had been fiddling with it for days together with three helpers. But now the time had finally come and all the mechanics came to look at the first test drive. We have already described how that went – the skeleton car suddenly leapt backwards and crashed into a parked Mercedes.

Still, the chassis is ready. Now we have to develop a design for the body. We remember John Damptey's story, about how there had once been a car construction industry in Ghana. We ask the older members of the SMIDO team. Most of them drop by the workshop at some point during the day, not to work but to provide a running commentary from a little bench in the shade. Besto is there every day and always has an answer to everything. Besto is not his real name but an abbreviation of The Best Sprayer in Suame Magazine. Besto is the best. Or at least he once was. Now he is worn out and has trouble walking. Since he found out that Melle went to an art academy, he seizes every opportunity to draw attention to his own artistic calling, as a painter of cars. "We have the magic eye," he says as he pulls down his lower eyelid so that it looks like his bloodshot eye is about to fall out.

When we ask Besto whether it is true that there was once a car construction industry in Ghana, he perks up. "Please you sit. You mean the Buafo." And he is silent for a moment as if he has just uttered a magic spell. "This car was built here in Suame Magazine back in the 1970s. Many many many, you can find them everywhere." We would love to see a Buafo and Besto sends a couple of boys out to find one. Philip looks on and chuckles; later he tells us that there never actually was a production line. You won't find that car here, he says, but at the KNUST University. Philip sometimes goes there to teach. We decide to go there straight away to have a look. Melle insists on bringing the historical car back to the workshop. At least it is a concrete object and hopefully we can use its history as an example. We take the tow truck with us to transport the car. On the way to the university, Philip calls his friend on campus who makes sure we are allowed past the entrance gates.

We find the old car in the corner of a warehouse. It looks a bit like a little Vespa truck with a wooden cargo bed and a small cabin. The car has been there for years and they do not mind if we take it with us. The university staff say it is beyond repair. But our team is about to teach those theorists a lesson. The old wreck is hoisted up and taken to our workshop.

Within a day the whole car has been taken apart and the components are carted off to other workplaces, while the engine block is thoroughly cleaned with Coca-Cola and OMO washing-powder. Soon the whole neighbourhood knows that a Buafo is being restored. The older mechanics are especially interested. They know the Buafo from way back when, but this car is no Buafo, they can tell straight away. This is the Anwona Petuo, or 'owl'. The car's name is inspired on its large headlights and split windshield. It is a Morris, a model that the British put on the market in the 1950s. At the time it was the most common car in the country. The cars were custom-finished Ghana and could therefore be tailored to clients' wishes. It was an incredibly popular model. As neighbours flock to the workshop, all sorts of stories come to the surface and someone remarks that there is a Buafo driving around the neighbourhood after all. Its owner has a workshop not far from ours.

When the whole group walks into his yard, the Buafo owner doesn't know what has hit him. Everyone gathers around a yellow wreck, an angular pick-up truck with windows that have not been washed in 40 years. "This is the Buafo," Osu says admiringly. The mechanics open up the bonnet and start negotiating with the owner. With a worried air, Dr Waco asked us whether we really intend to take the car with us. When we tell him that we only want to analyse the car, he gives us a blank look. What on earth does that mean? We ask Waco to tell us what makes this car special. Little does he know that his answer is going to determine the design of our showcase car. He rapidly fires off a list: "Heavy springs, front and back, big bonnet space to put any kind of engine in, simple ladder chassis so the body is adjustable, flat bodywork so you can easily replace it with wood or iron sheets. Simple, slow but steady," he concludes. Melle finally knows what to draw. We leave the Buafo with its owner.

The next day we present the design of the showcase car at the weekly board meeting of the SMIDO executive council. Melle spent all evening drawing to show different versions of the design. It has turned into a cross between an SUV and a pick-up truck: farmers can use it to bring their crops from the field to the market in town, but it can also be a market stall because the side doors can be folded up to make an awning. As cars are still important status symbols for Ghanaians, there is also a luxury version.

The SMIDO board members love the drawings. They are clearly relieved that the obrunis have finally delivered the goods and shown a picture. George laughs loudest and holds the luxury version high above his head. "This one is sold!" Besto says that the drawings should be kept in the safe to make sure that the design is not stolen. Azongo ignores Besto and tells everyone to sit down. The mechanics have done their job. Dr Waco, which team will get to work now? Waco has clearly not thought about this yet. "By the grace of God, we will find the right people." Azongo is not satisfied with this answer and turns to the executive council. “We have to find the most talented welders and bodyworkers to make the best of this great design. Who can we ask?” They all look at their flip-flops because everyone knows that once you accept the job, you are stuck with it. Azongo knows this game all too well. He first starts praising Waco as the successful experienced leader of this project and then shoves the full responsibility onto his plate. There is no time to lose; Waco has just a few days to find the right people. George closes the meeting with a prayer. Instead of water, we celebrate with a Coke to conclude the meeting.

As experienced masters, Philip and Waco have been an example to many mechanics. They have trained many boys and in the following days they ask everyone in their network to come by. Mechanics of all ages turn up and it is impressive to see how respectfully they treat both men. But convincing them to take part is a different matter. There are plenty of amateurs, but the really skilled masters have their own workshops to run. SMIDO members have volunteered to participate in the Turtle project, but we do not have much of a budget to pay workers outside the SMIDO cluster. We cannot pay more than an average fee, though no one really believes this as soon as they see that white men are involved in the project.

We decide to build a full-size wooden frame of our design so that everyone can see what it will be like. This proves to be a useful exercise as the proportions require great precision. The frame has been put together with small bits of wire so that everyone can adjust the model, which they do not hesitate to do. After a week, everyone has had their turn and there is consensus on the final shape. Philip and Dr Waco have managed to put together their team for the next phase: the assembly.

BONESHAKER

The African car is the road. It can make it's way through rough terrain. The Turtle is a real Boneshaker.

The mechanics of Suame Magazine are experts in transforming regular cars into boneshakers, robust all-terrain vehicles that can cope with the numerous and large potholes in Ghana's roads.

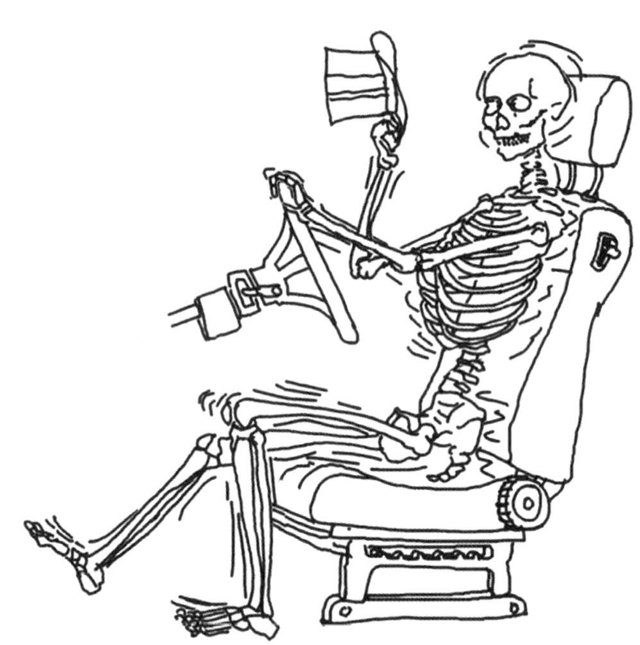

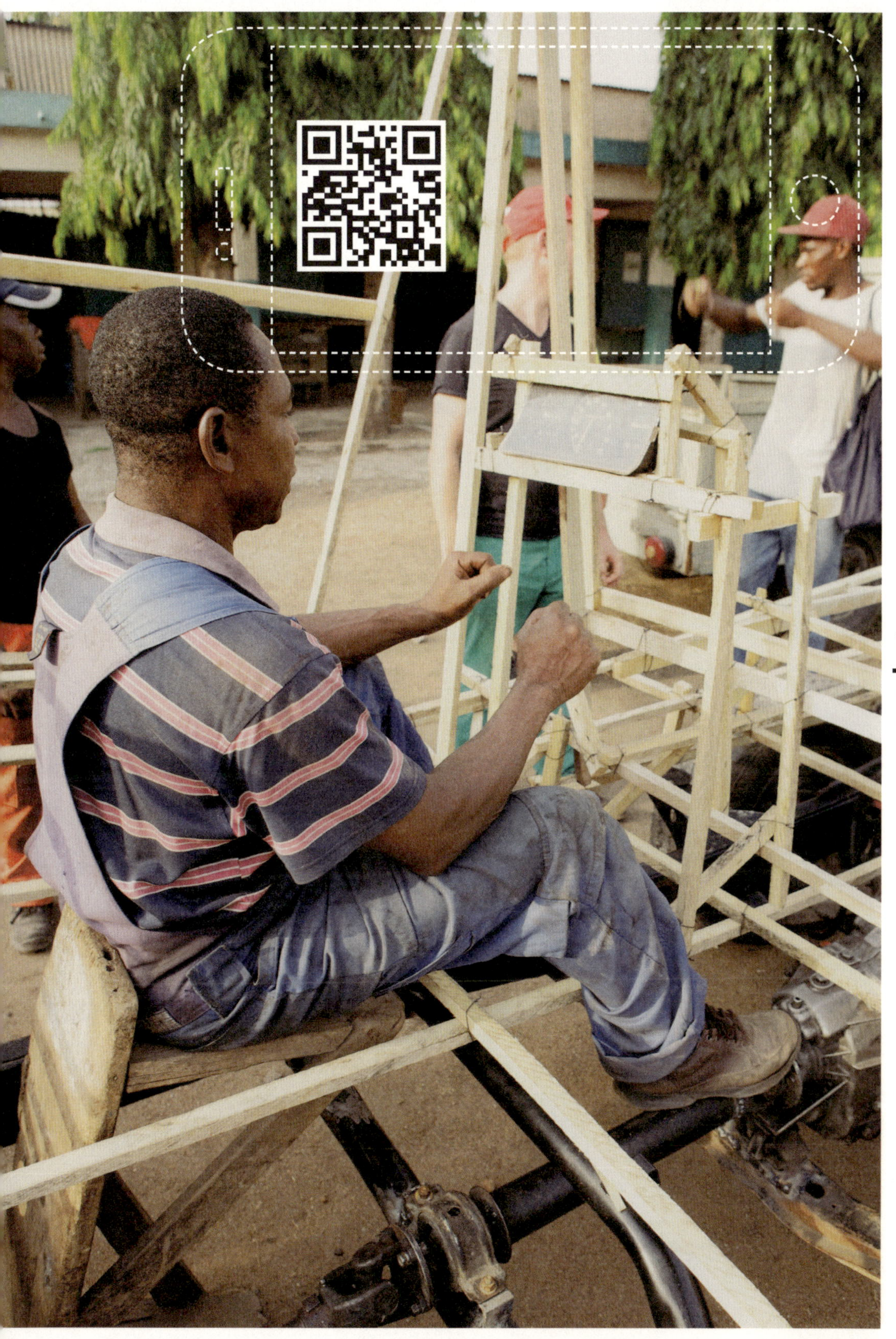

Design study into the reuse of old car doors.

GH // AP-12 // 02.2013

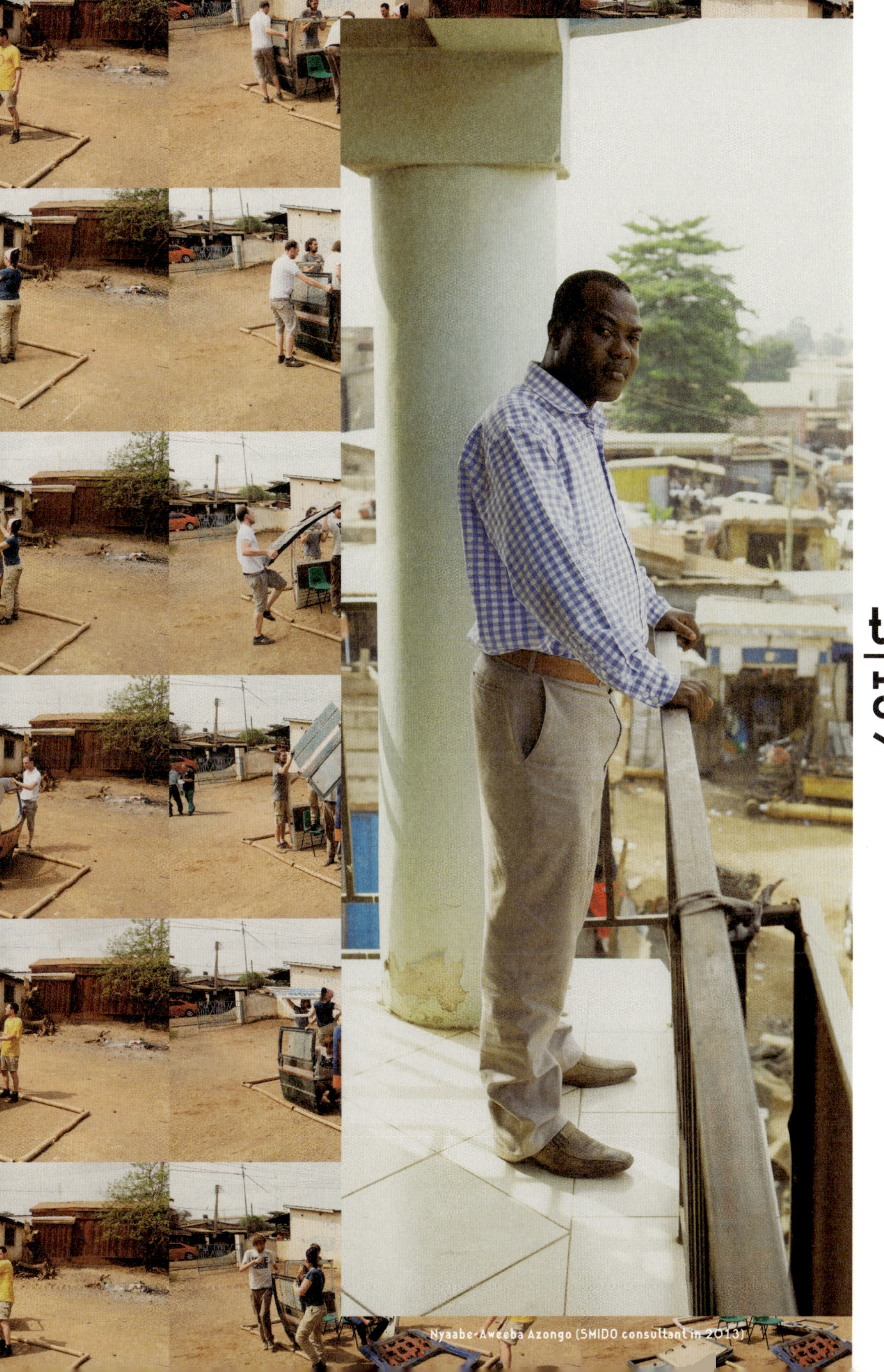

Nyaabe-Aweeba Azongo (SMIDO consultant in 2013)

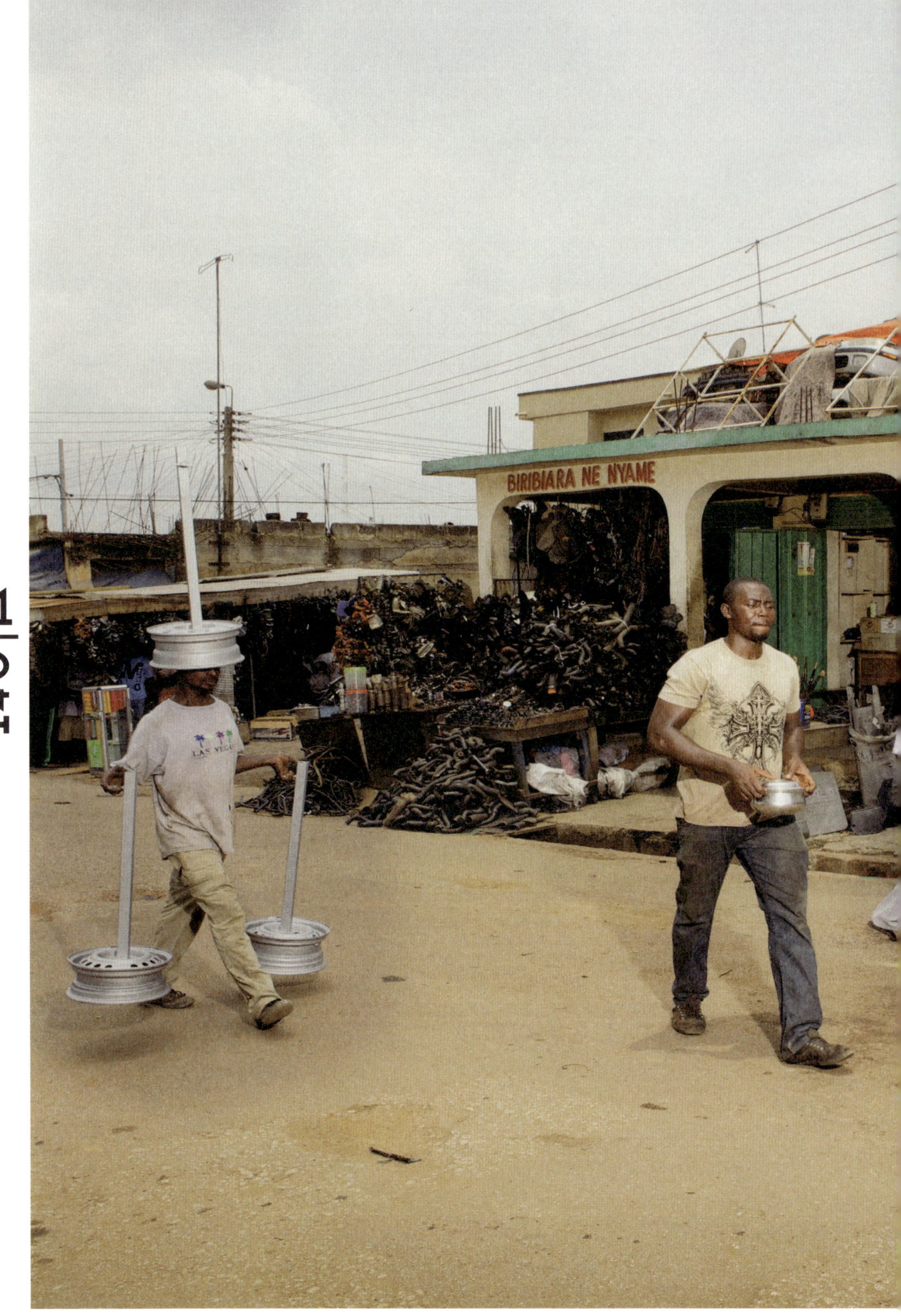
BIRIBIARA NE NYAME
LAS VEGAS

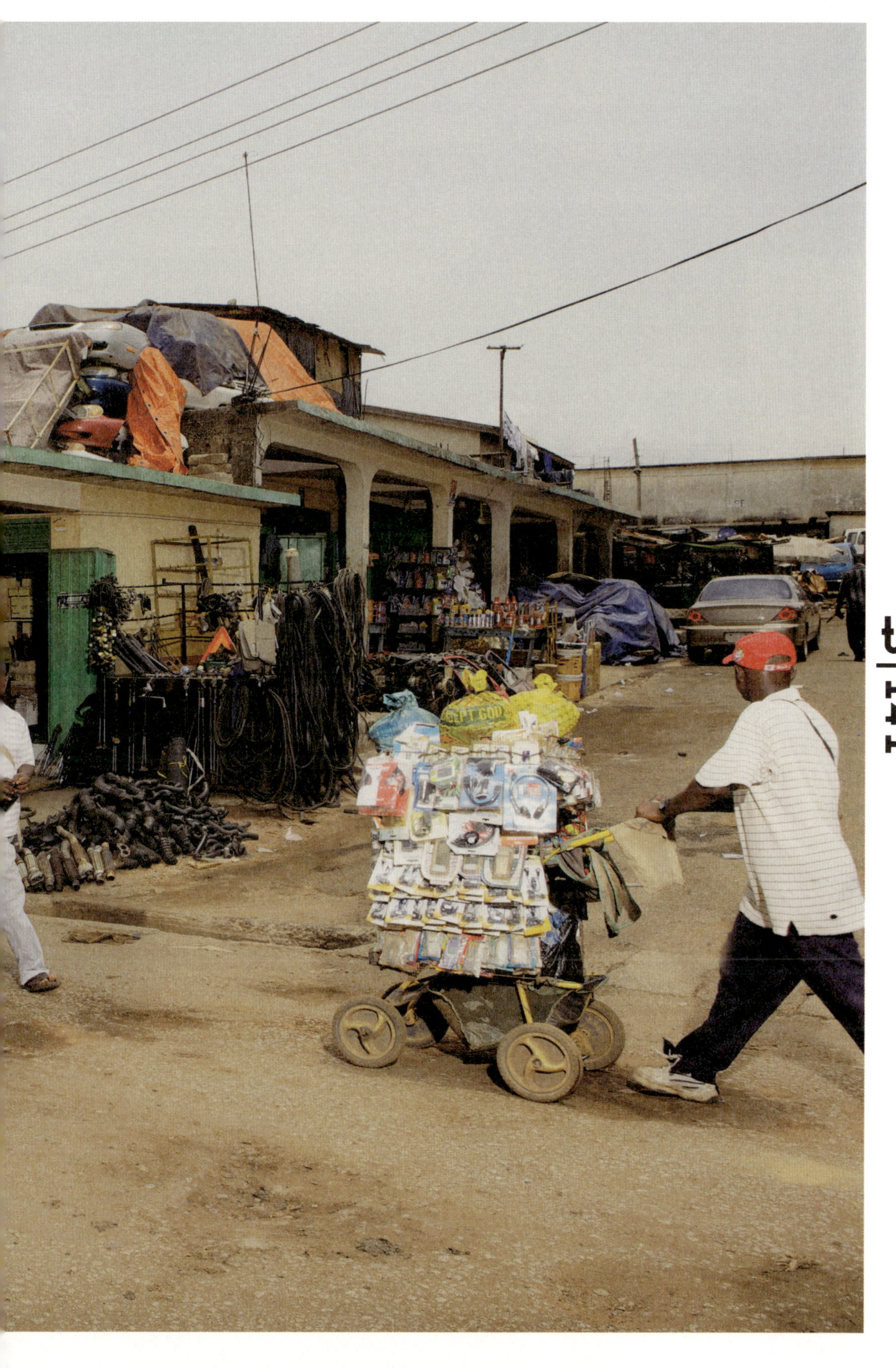

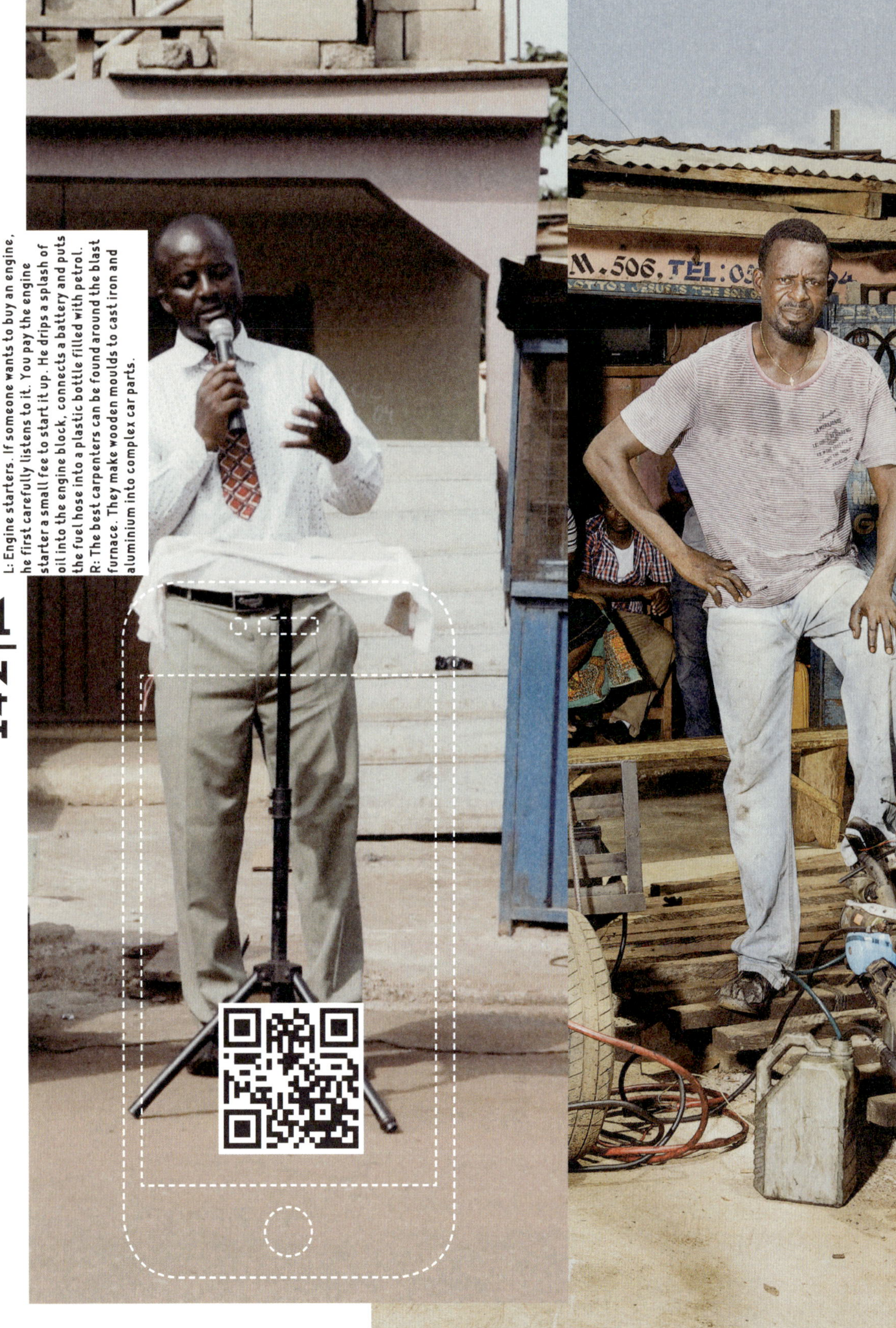

L: Street preachers are often artisans who preach for a few hours before they open their shop.
L: Engine starters. If someone wants to buy an engine, he first carefully listens to it. You pay the engine starter a small fee to start it up. He drips a splash of oil into the engine block, connects a battery and puts the fuel hose into a plastic bottle filled with petrol.
R: The best carpenters can be found around the blast furnace. They make wooden moulds to cast iron and aluminium into complex car parts.

GH // 02.2013

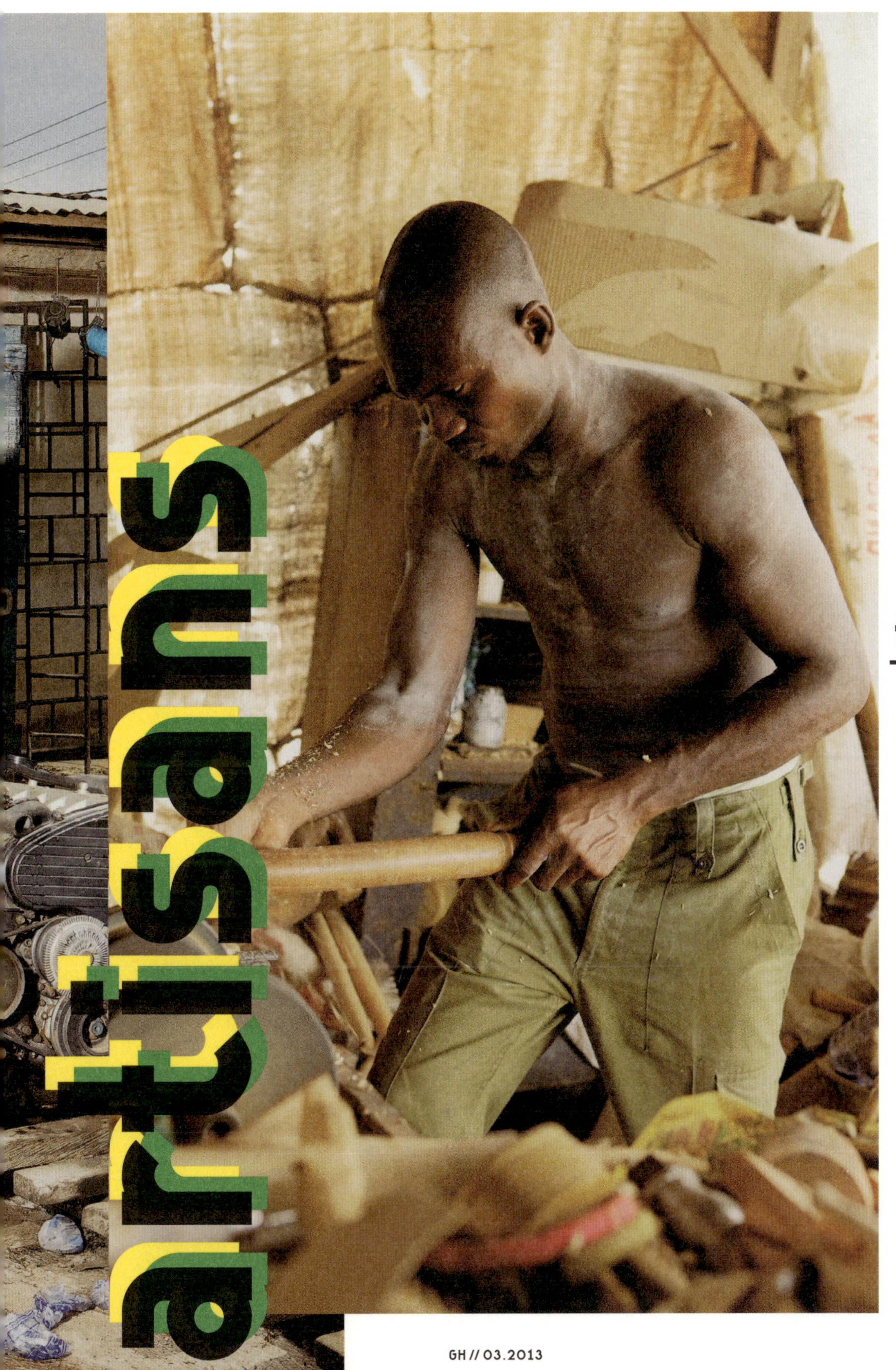

GH // 03.2013

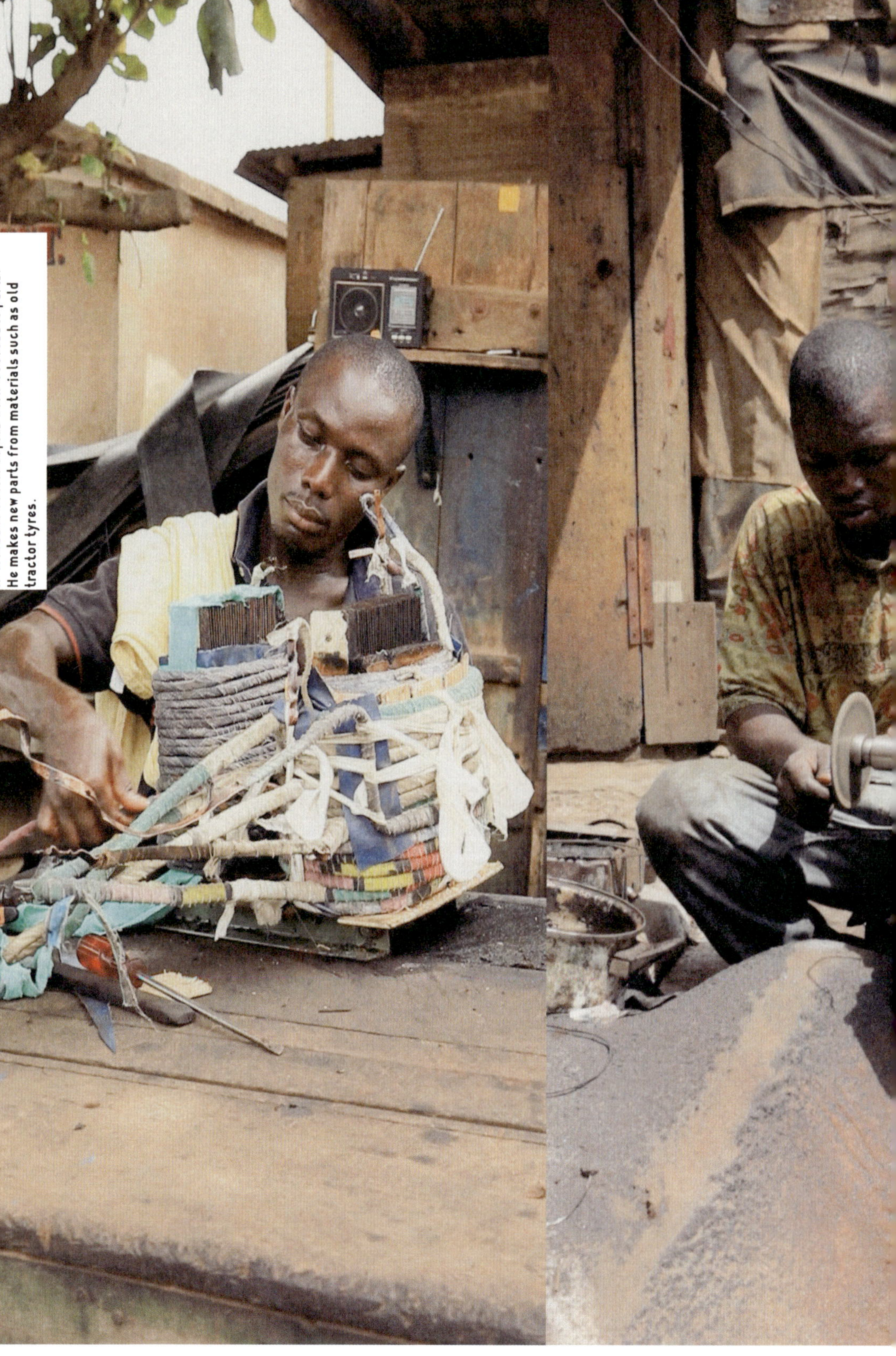

L: All sorts of machinery including welding machines are produced in Suame.
M: A tool which deburrs iron objects and smooths them down.
R: A rubber cutter copies worn-out rubber parts. He makes new parts from materials such as old tractor tyres.

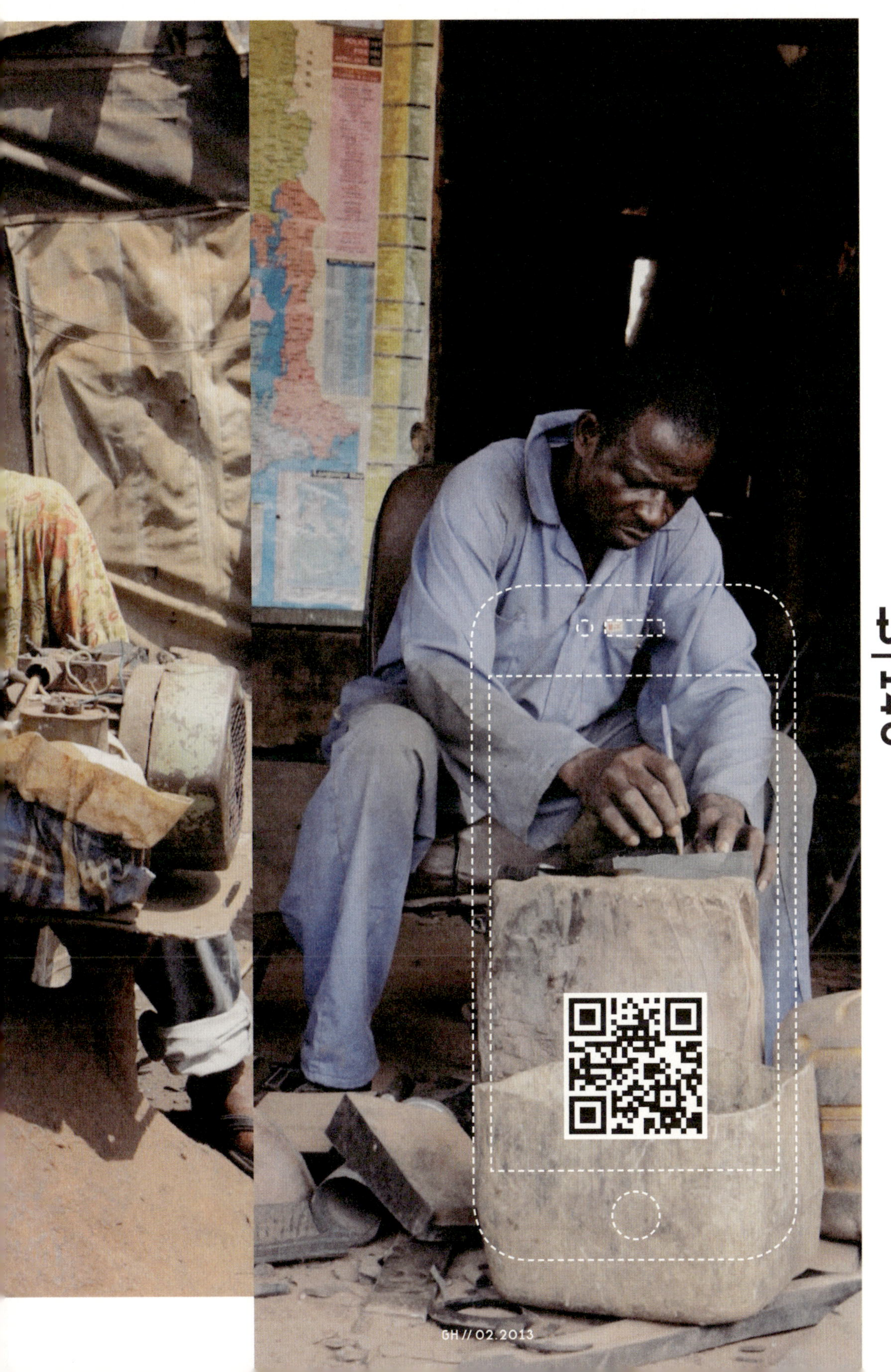
GH // 02.2013

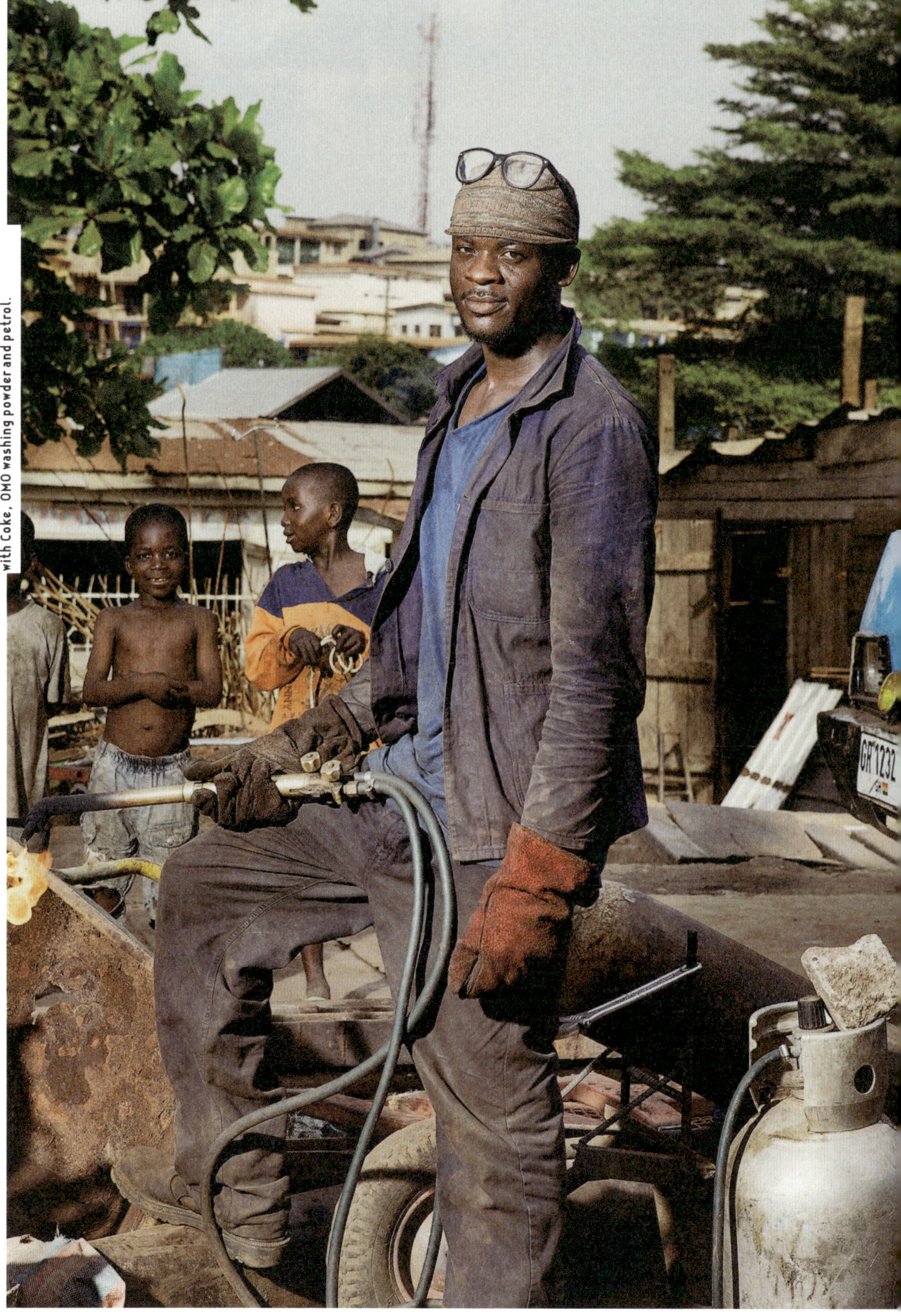

L: Gas cutters are itinerant traders who are called upon to burn through heavy pieces of iron.
R: A revision mechanic cleans clogged engine parts with Coke, OMO washing powder and petrol.

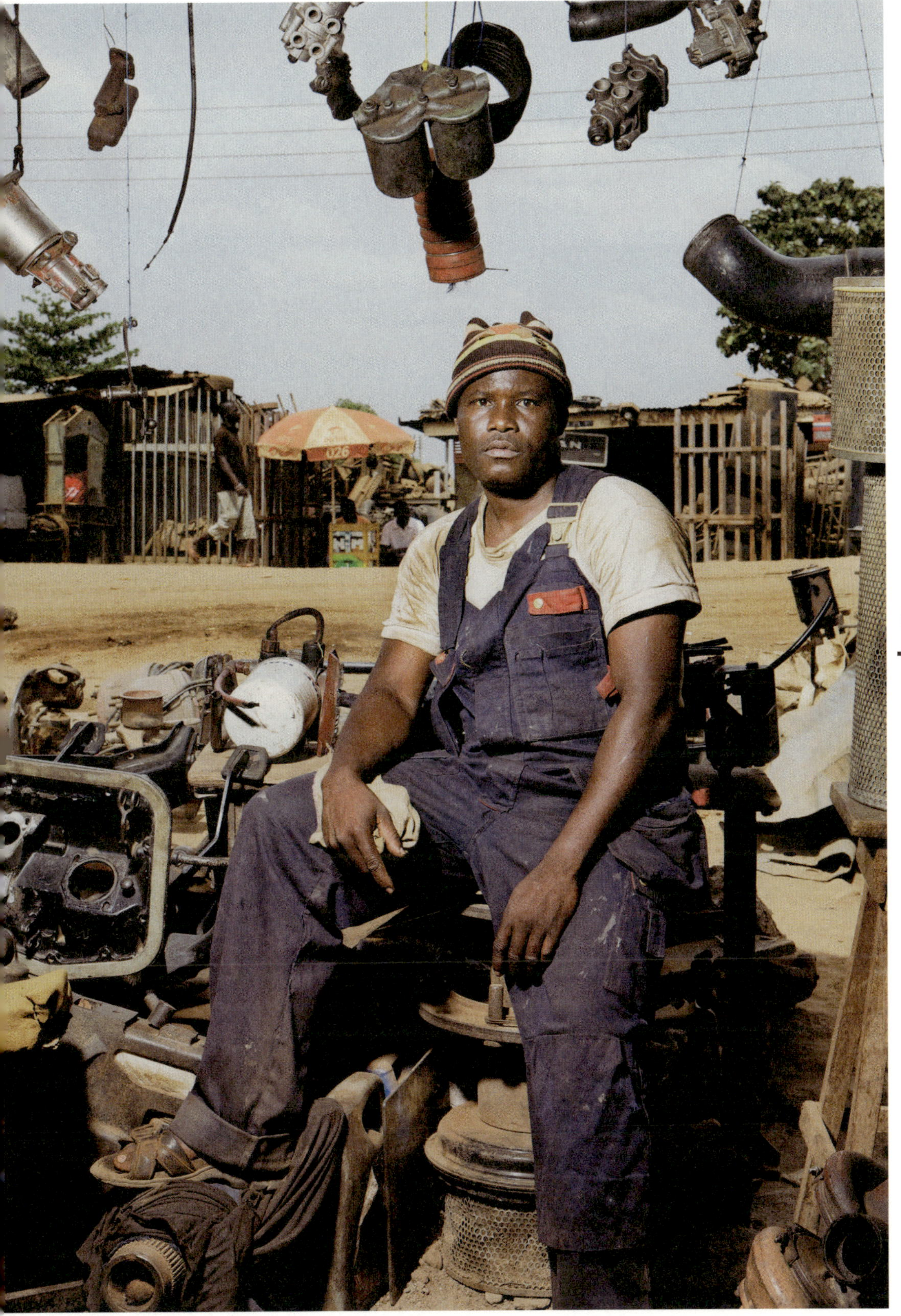

L: A rim welder repairs damaged worn-out rims.
L: The blacksmith hammers iron into any shape.
R: An engine buster shatters engine blocks so that they can be melted down in the blast furnace.
R: The radiator man welds radiators together to increase the engine's cooling capacity and adapt it for the Ghanaian climate.

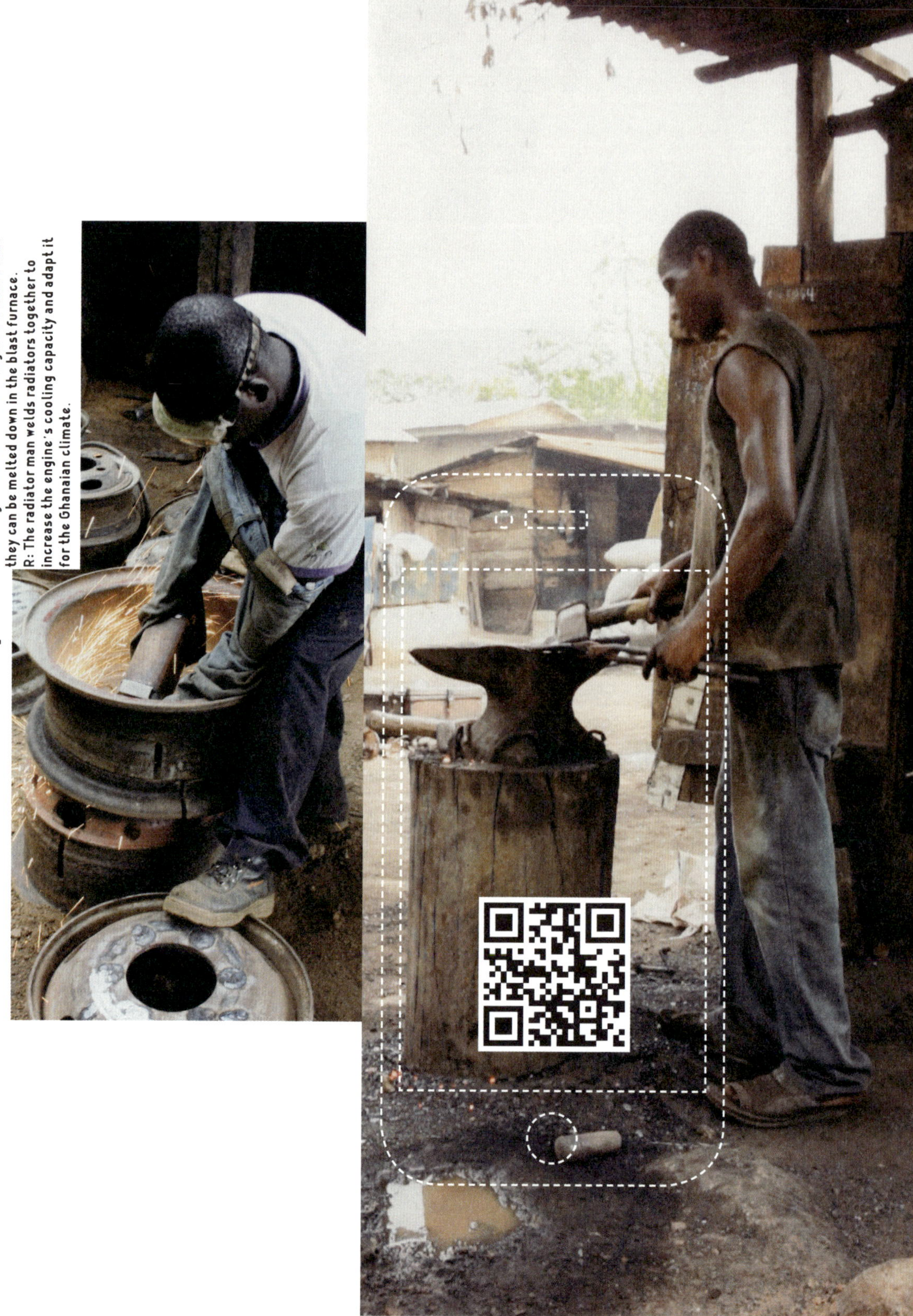

GH // 04.2012

GH // 03.2012

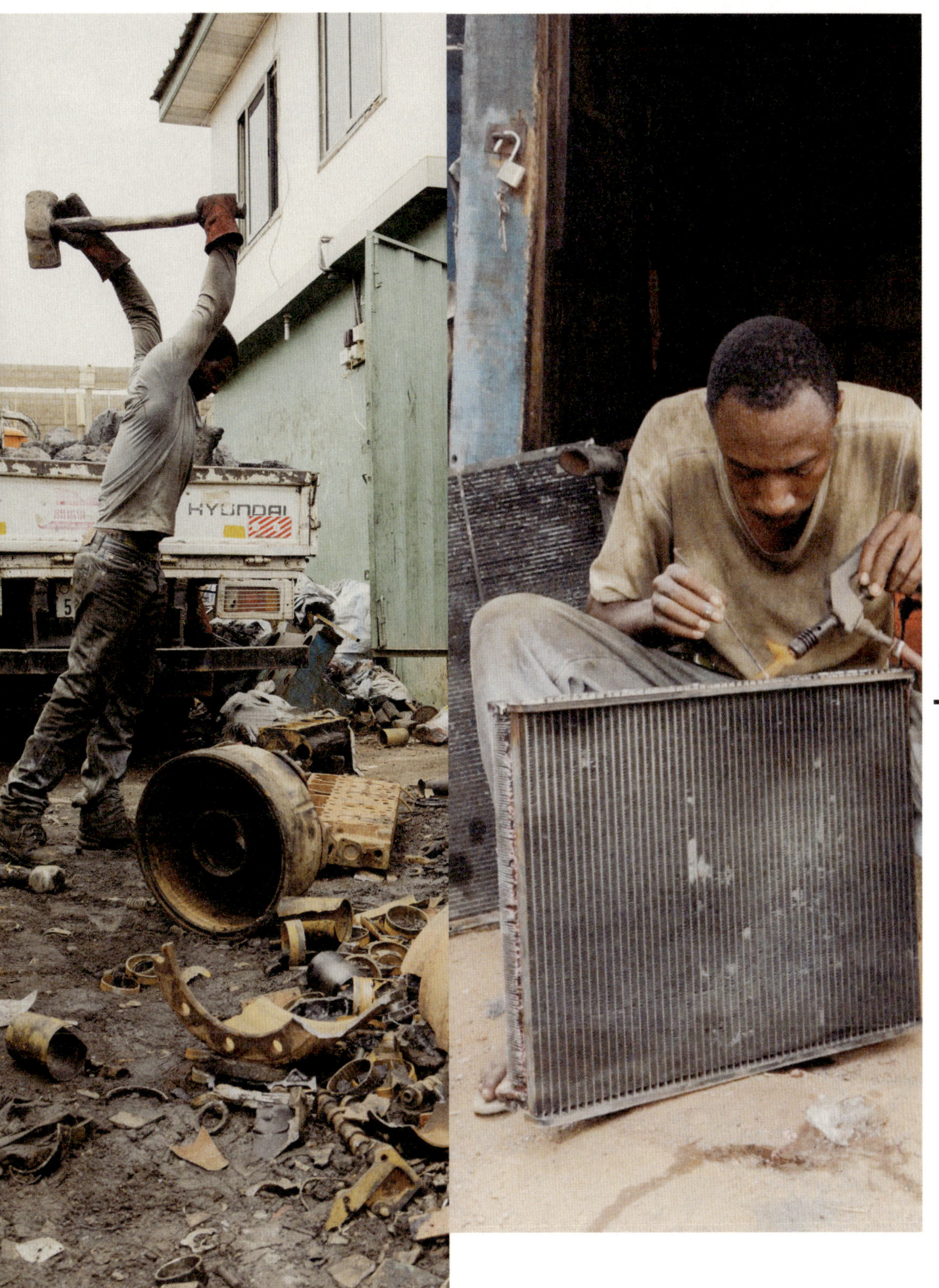

GH // 03.2012

L: The plastic smith repairs everything that is made of plastic in a car, from the bumper to the dashboard, mirrors and lights.
L: Suame attracts people from across West Africa. The wizards from Niger are known for their magical powers.
R: The column drill man drills holes in thick iron that cannot be penetrated with a hammer.
R: An aluminium caster at work.

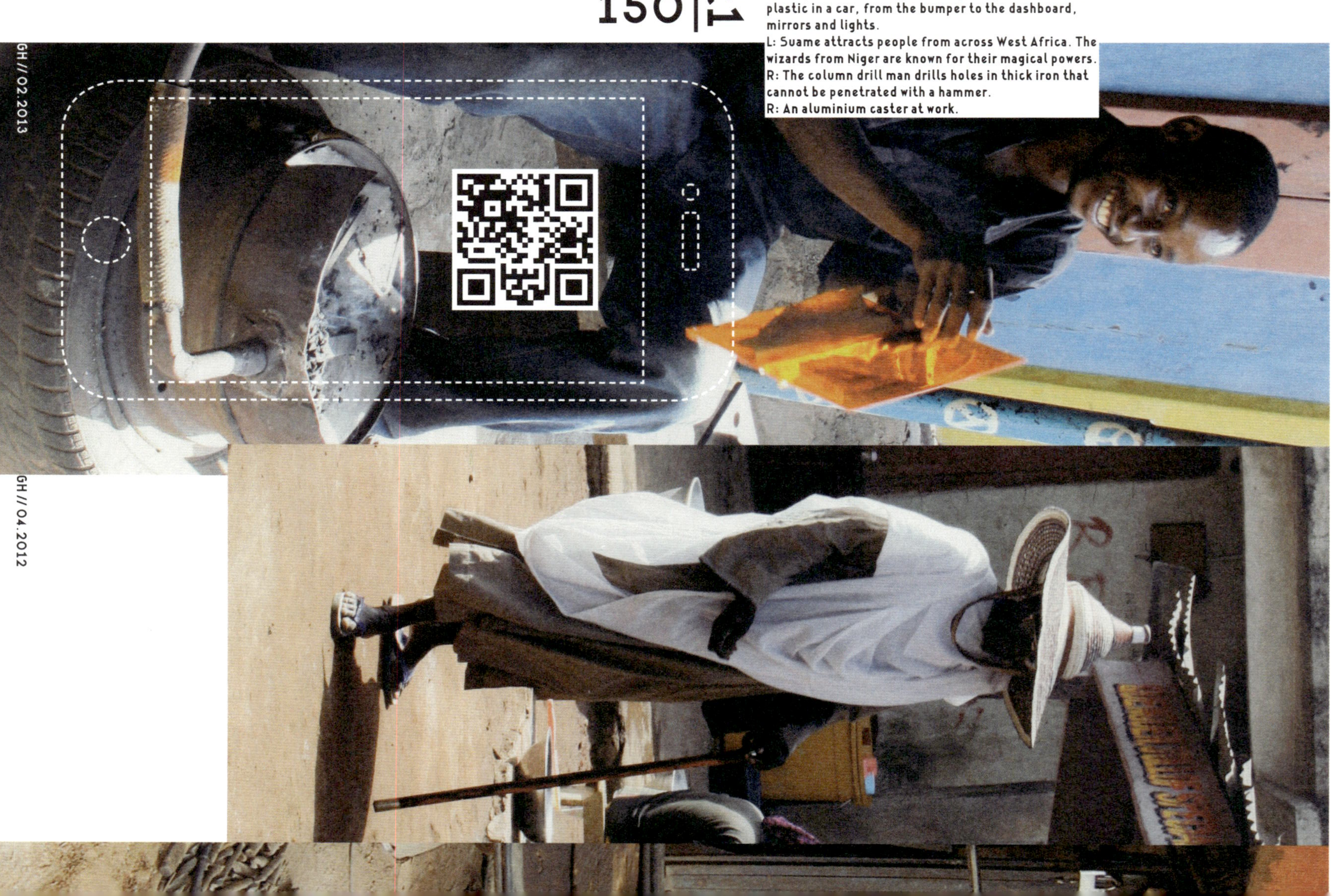

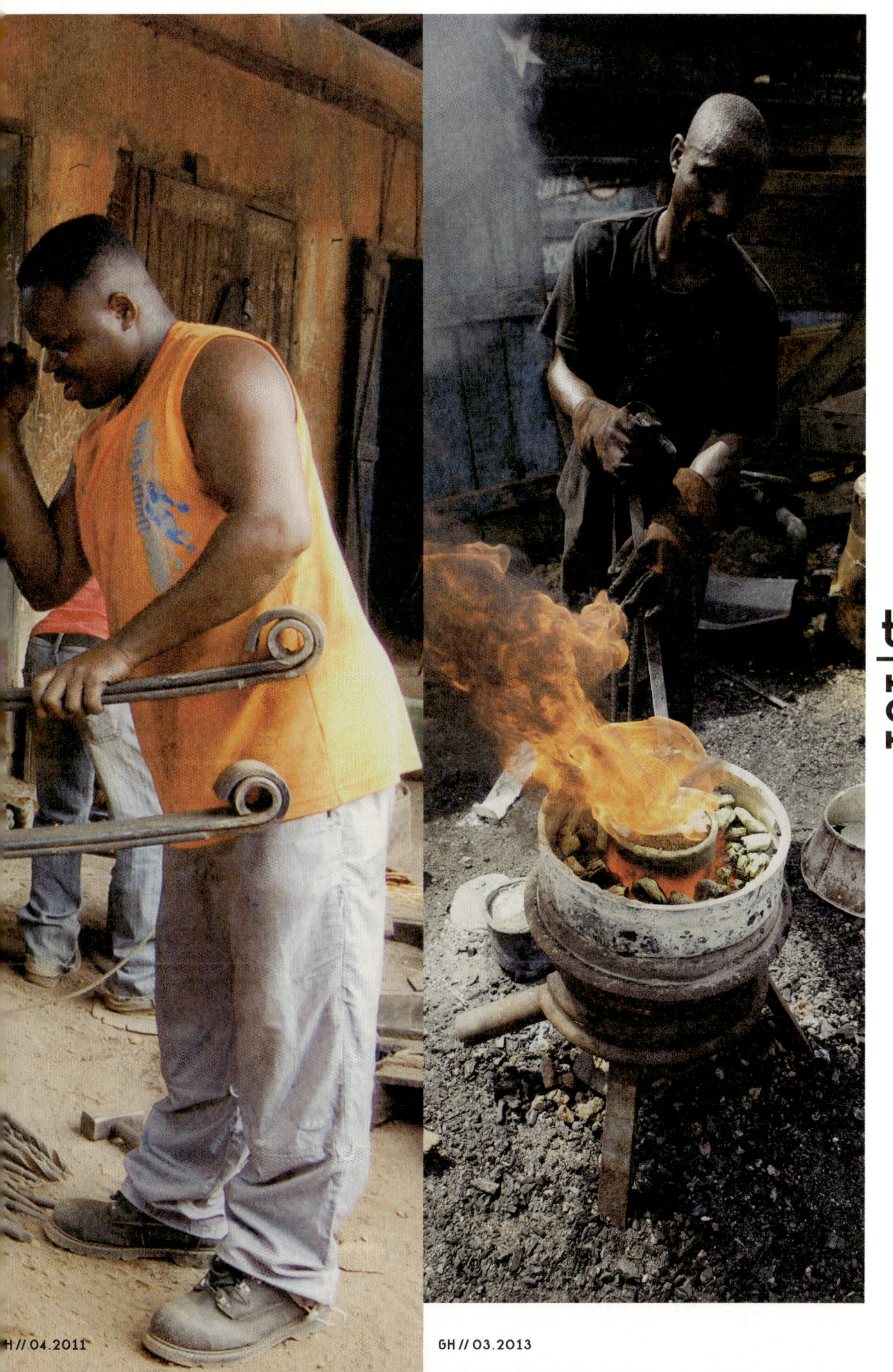

H // 04.2011

GH // 03.2013

The master-apprentice system is the social backbone of Suame. Young men get lodging, work and food from their master and the master pays his apprentices daily "chop money" (money for food). The apprentices are absorbed into the community of Suame artisans through their work.

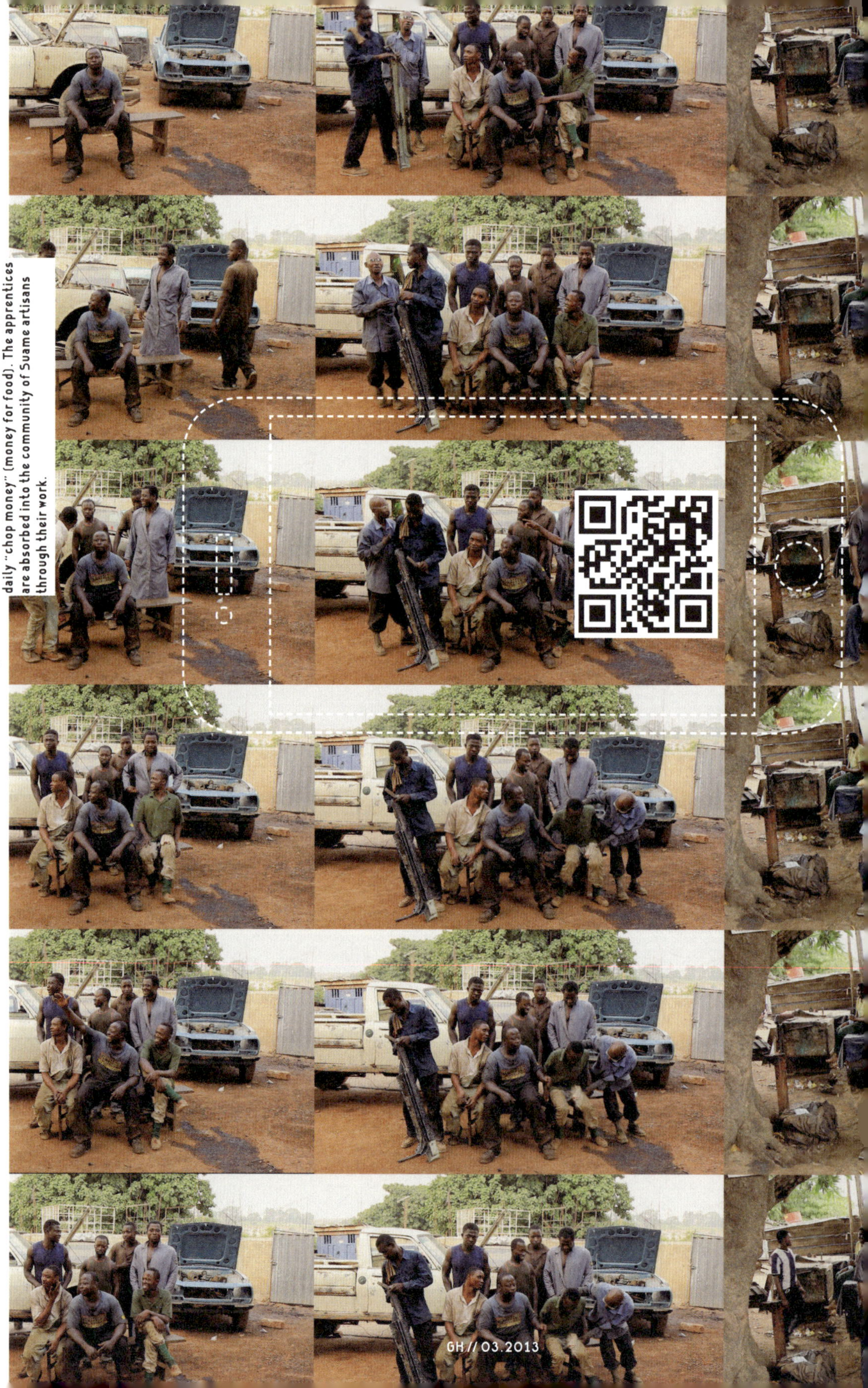

GH // 03.2013

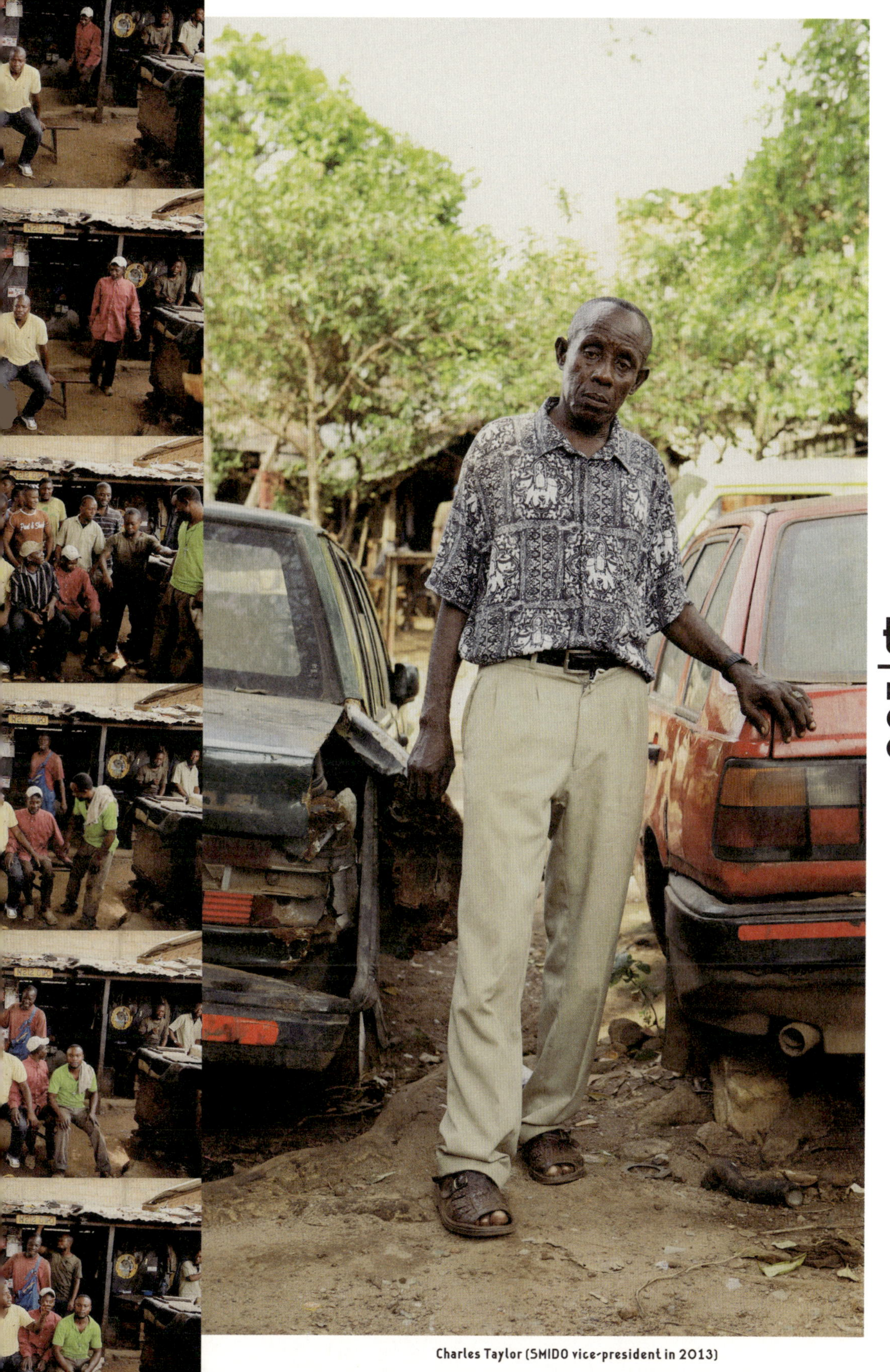

Charles Taylor (SMIDO vice-president in 2013)

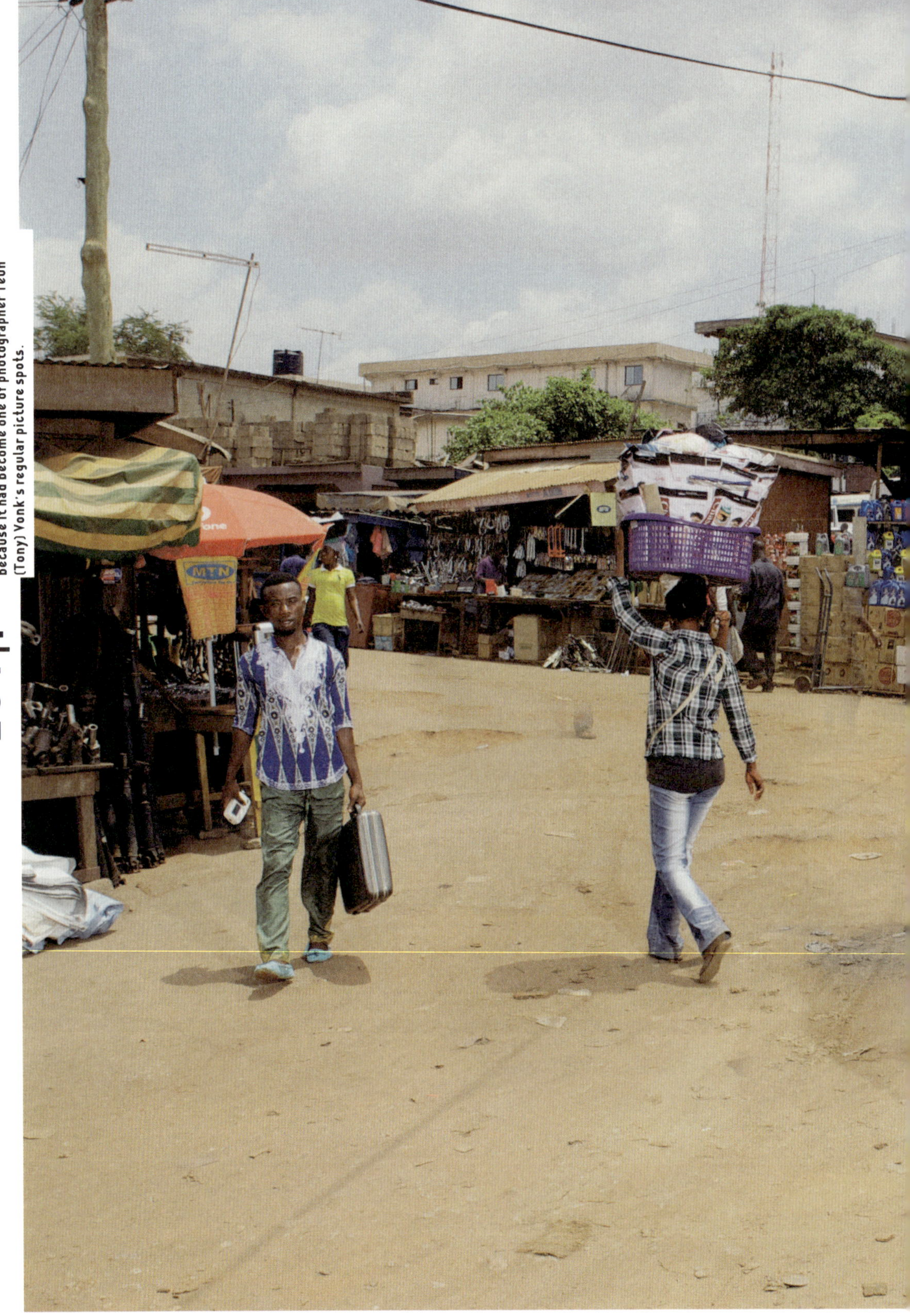

The intersection around the corner from the Turtle workshop acquired the nickname Tony's Corner because it had become one of photographer Teun (Tony) Vonk's regular picture spots.

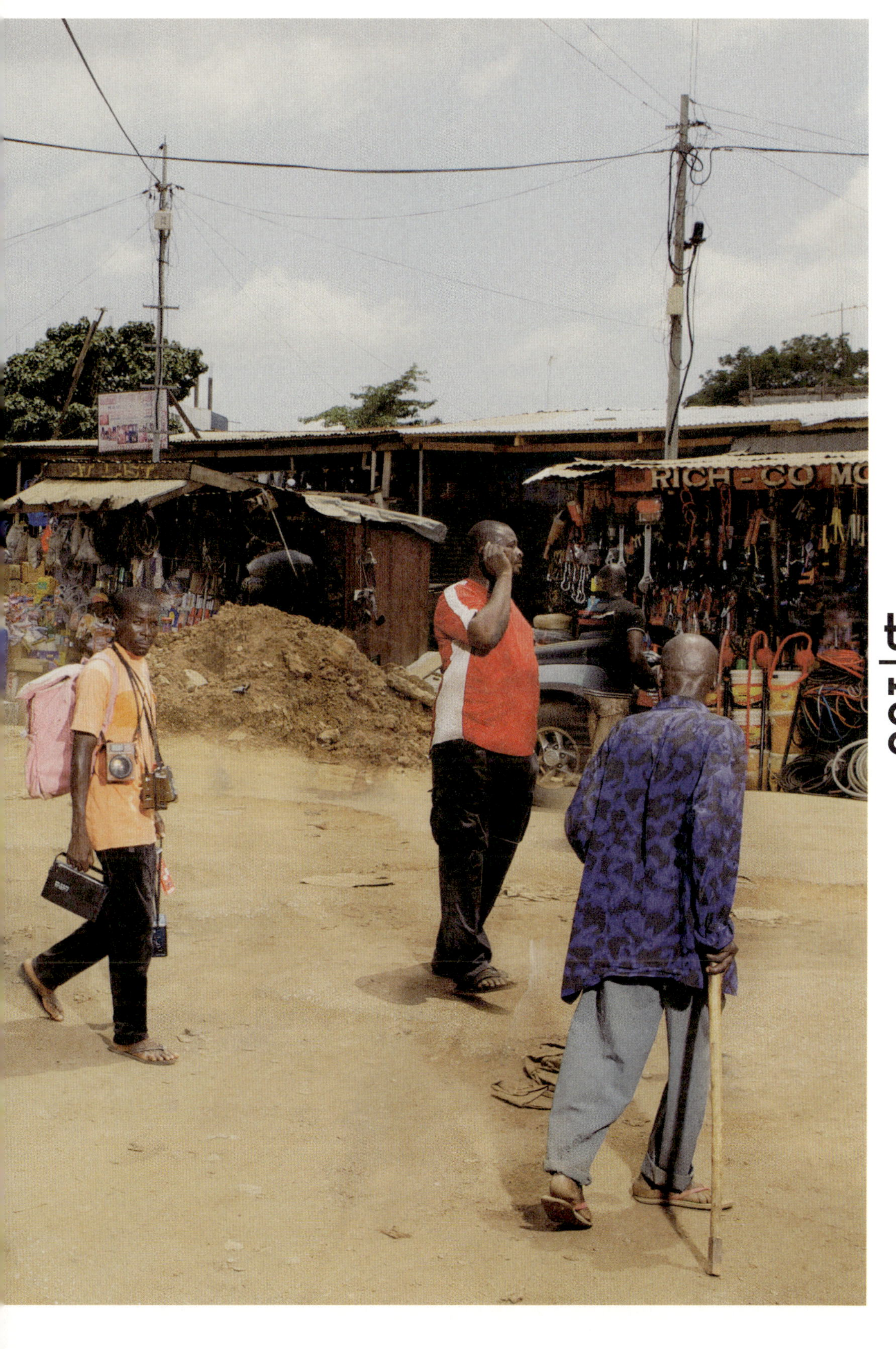
RICH-CO MO

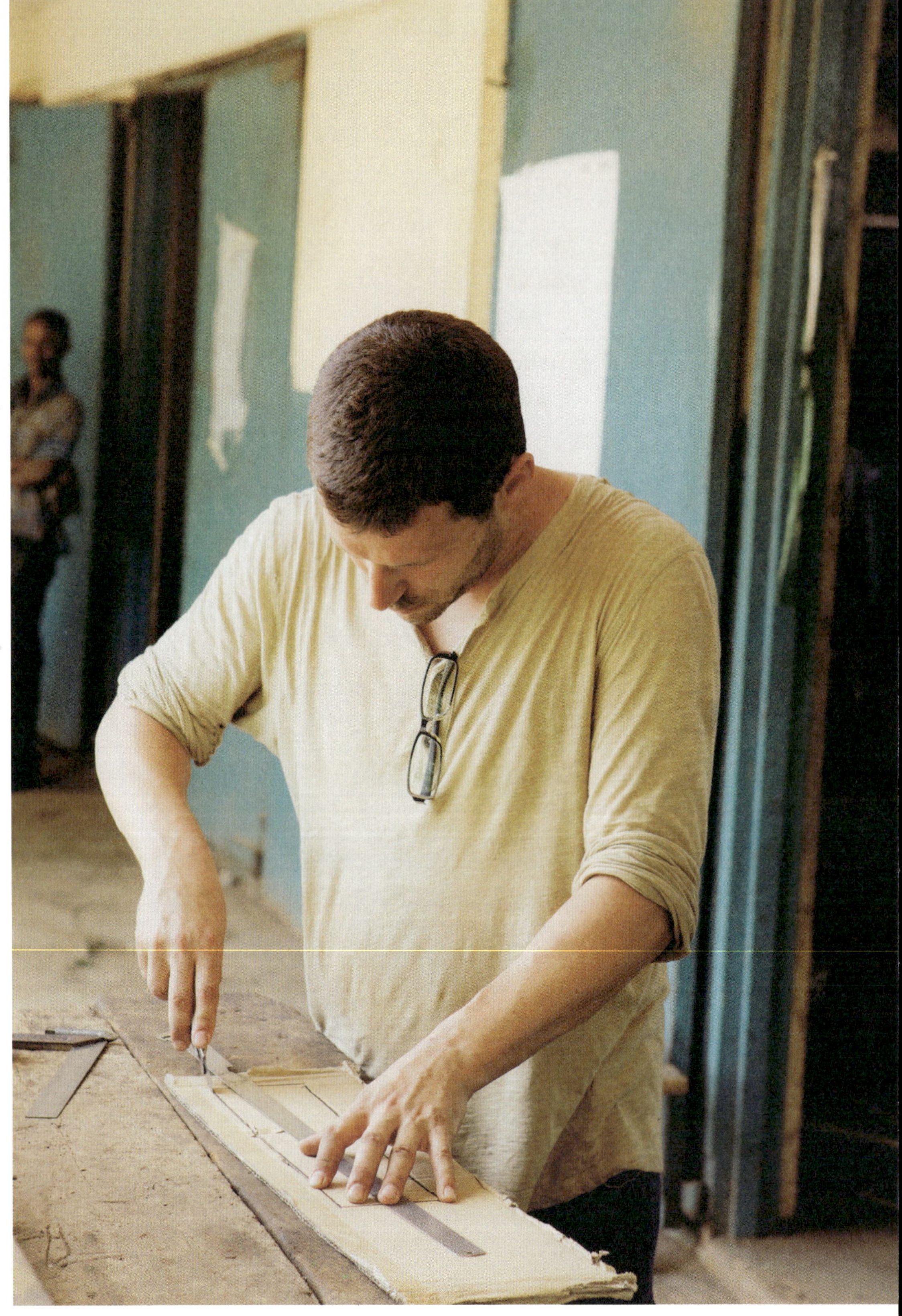

L: Melle cuts a 1:1 cardboard model.
R: Woodcutters will replicate the model of the dashboard in Ghanaian tropical hardwood.

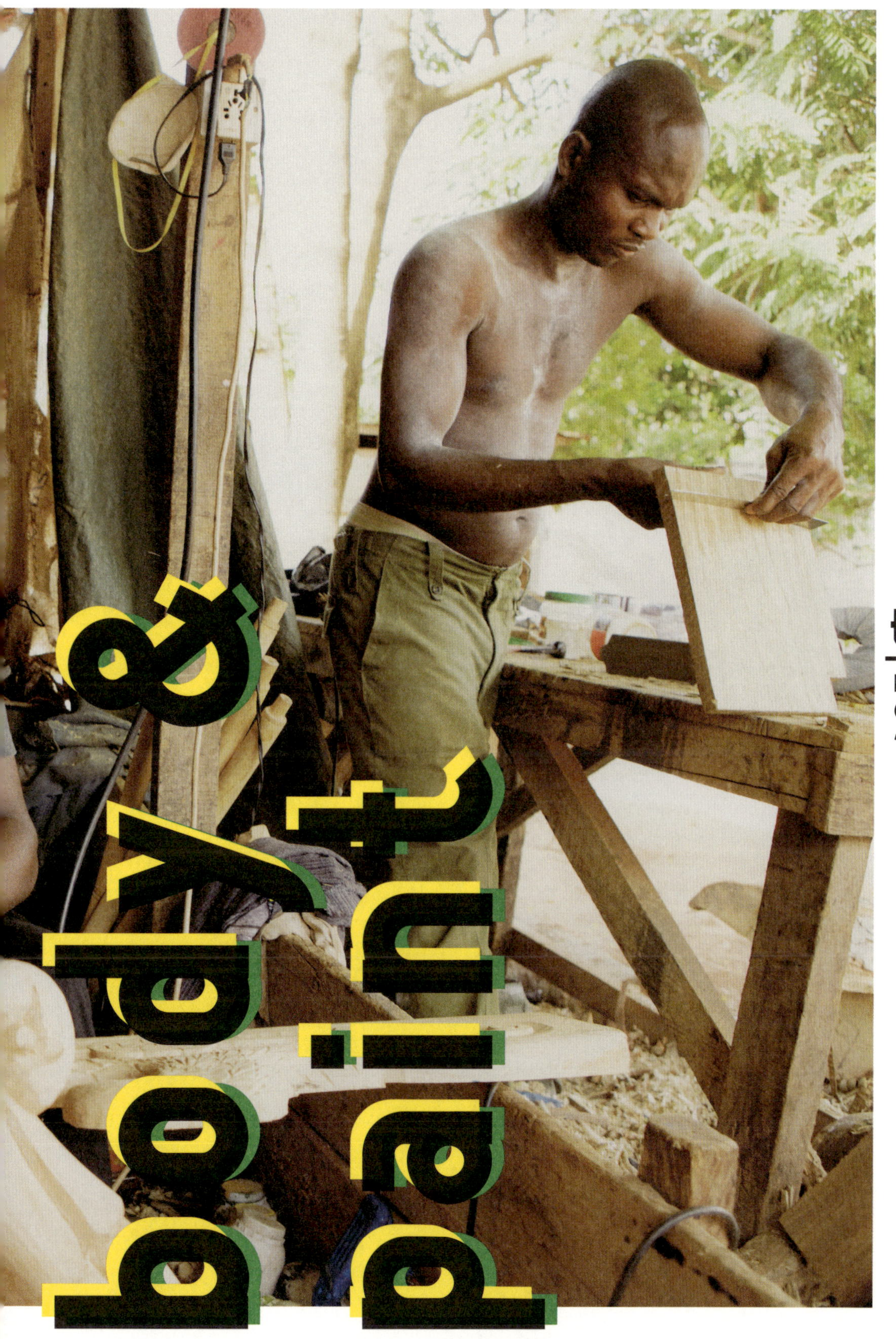

t1 | 157

GH // AP-12 // 03.2013

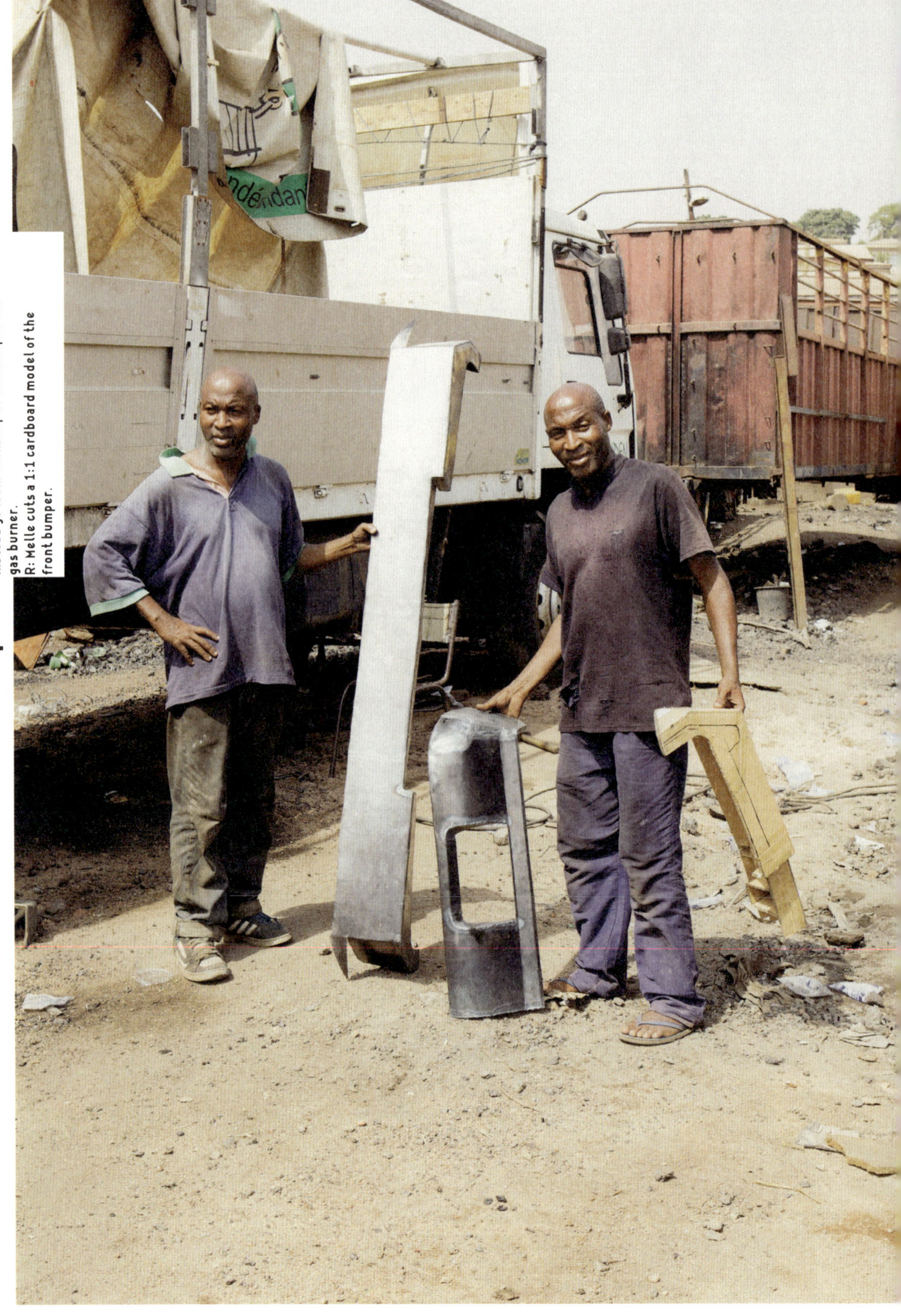

L: The bumpers of the Turtle 1 are made by twin brothers who have no workshop of their own but instead go from workshop to workshop with a gas burner.
R: Melle cuts a 1:1 cardboard model of the front bumper.

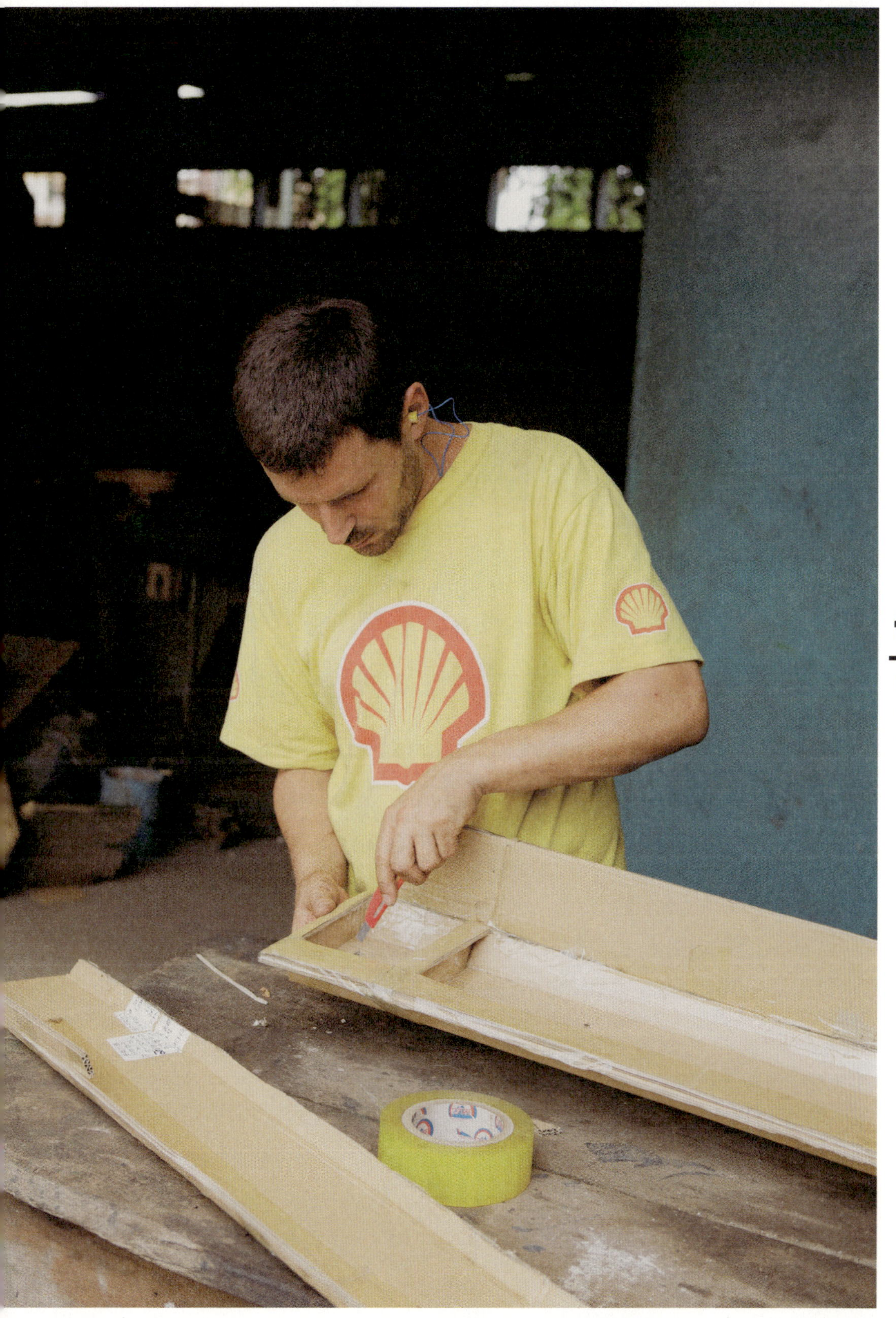

Planning board for the Turtle 1's assembly.

GENERAL PLAN

- GRinding Priming	Appi[illegible] Deb[illegible]	1st paint
- electrics	Philiph	connecti[illegible] electric devi[illegible]
TEST 3		TEST
- Dashboard panel	philiph	to buy:
X Locks & handles	Sul. & Abdul	- Rubbers doors
- electric devices	philiph	- wooden floor
- Dashboard wood	Mofi ATA	- Hook
		- mirrors
X seats welding	via WACU	- ceiling ca[illegible]
- Lights	James	- doorhandles
X air shafts	FABRIEK	- statue
		- POOK
	Appiaih phillip LAmouse	TEST
- windscreen	George melle	- FINAL [illegible]
- paint	SULO George	

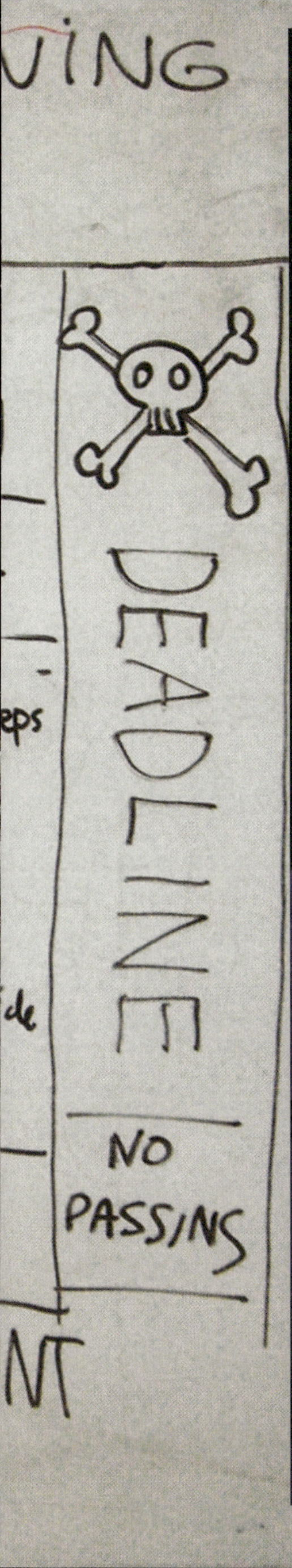

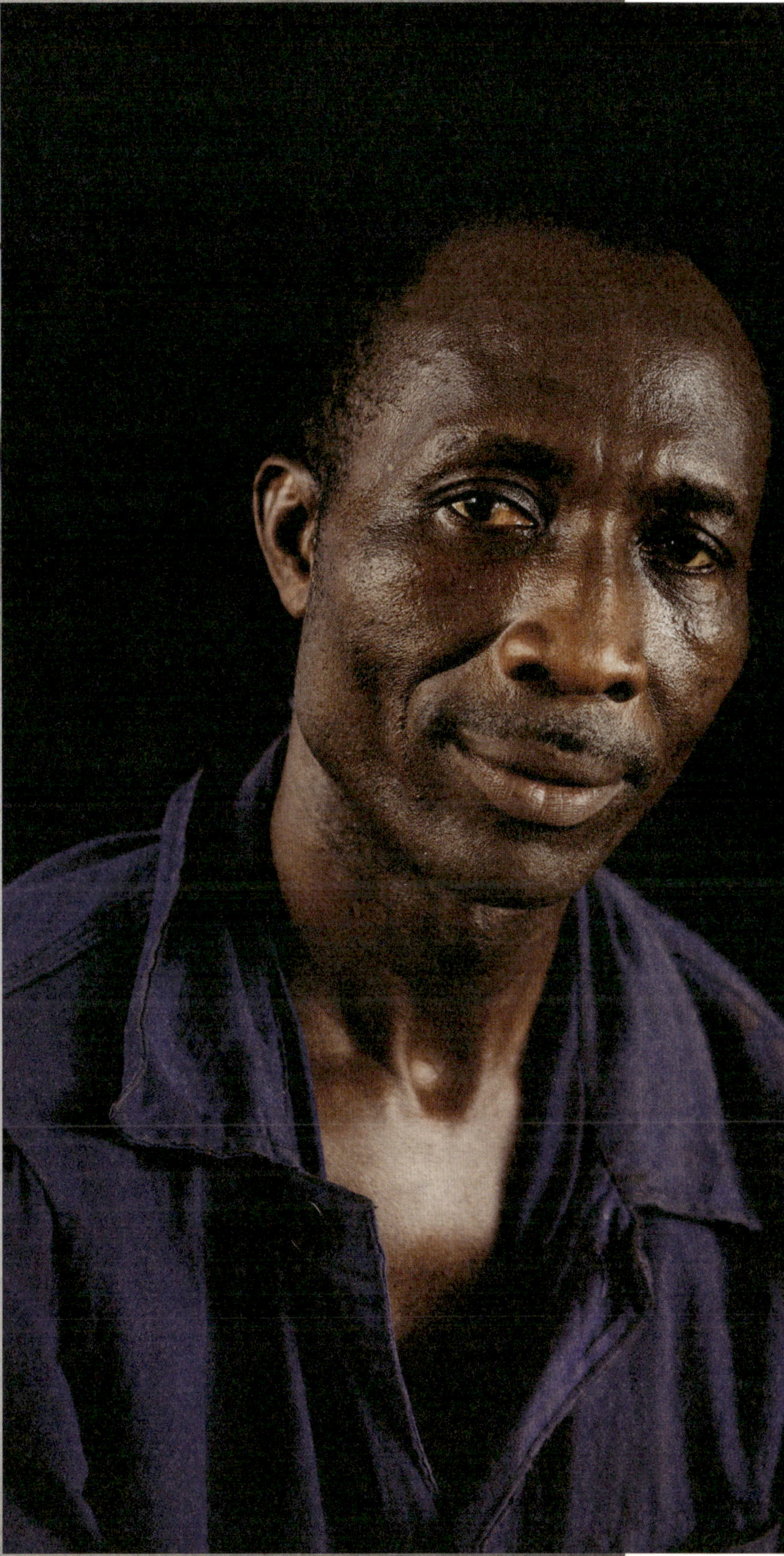

Ofori Charles Antipem (ITTU employee)

L: The use of car parts from different brands complicates the installation of the electrical circuit. The car parts only listen to their own electronic system and it is difficult to close the circuit.

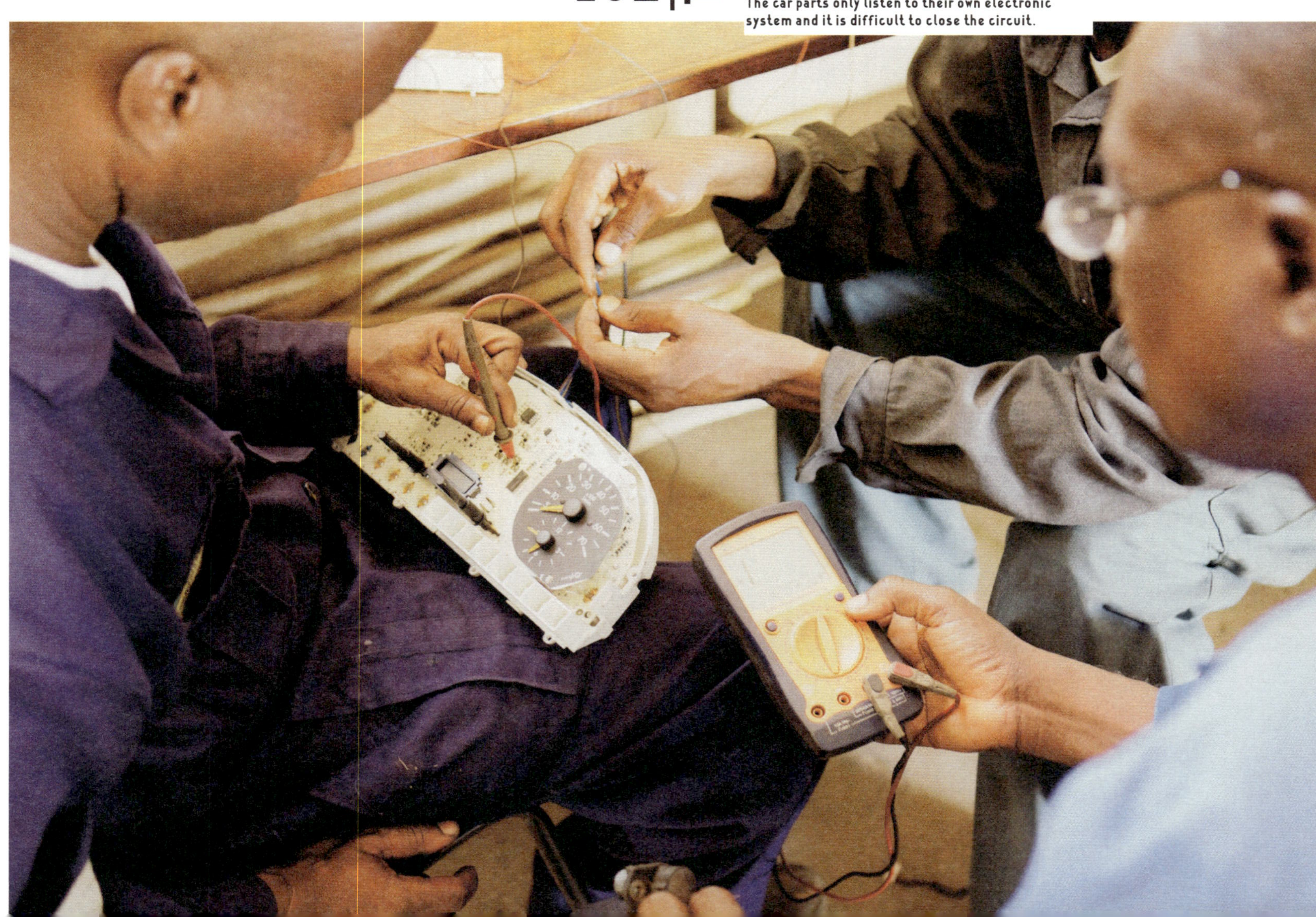

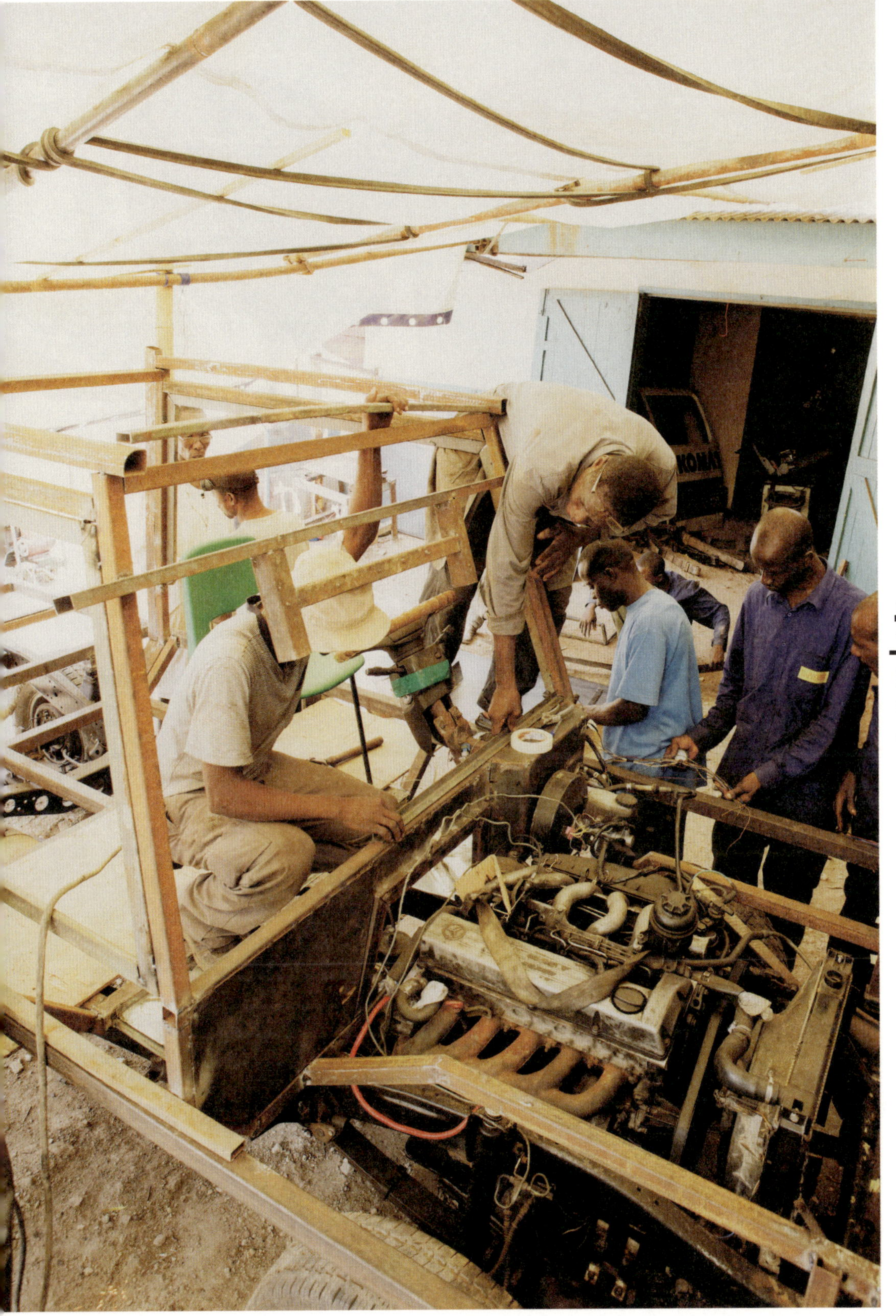

SM-385 / SSY-285 / SM-315 // GH // AP-12 // 03.2013

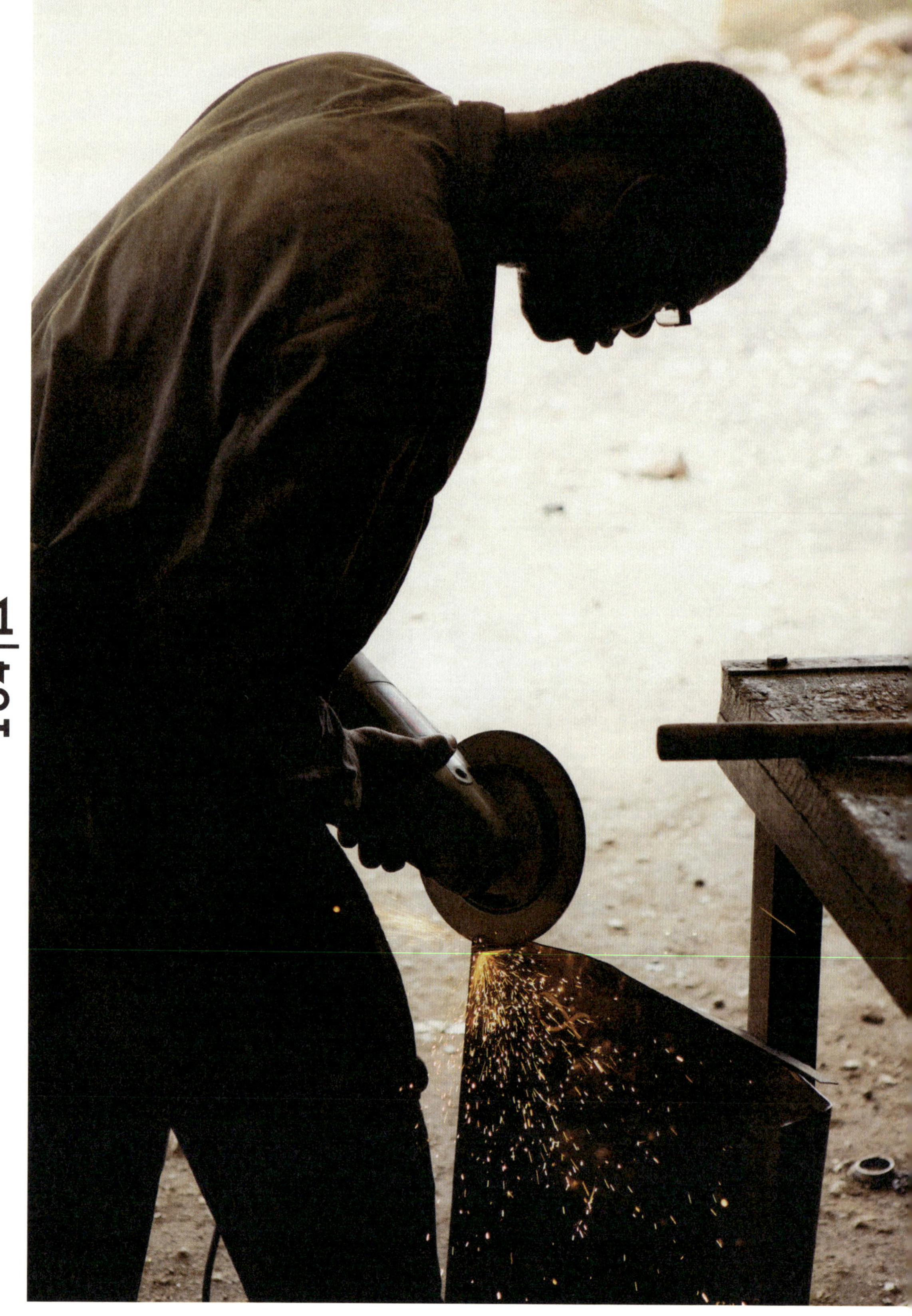

SM-502 // GH // AP-12 // 03.2013

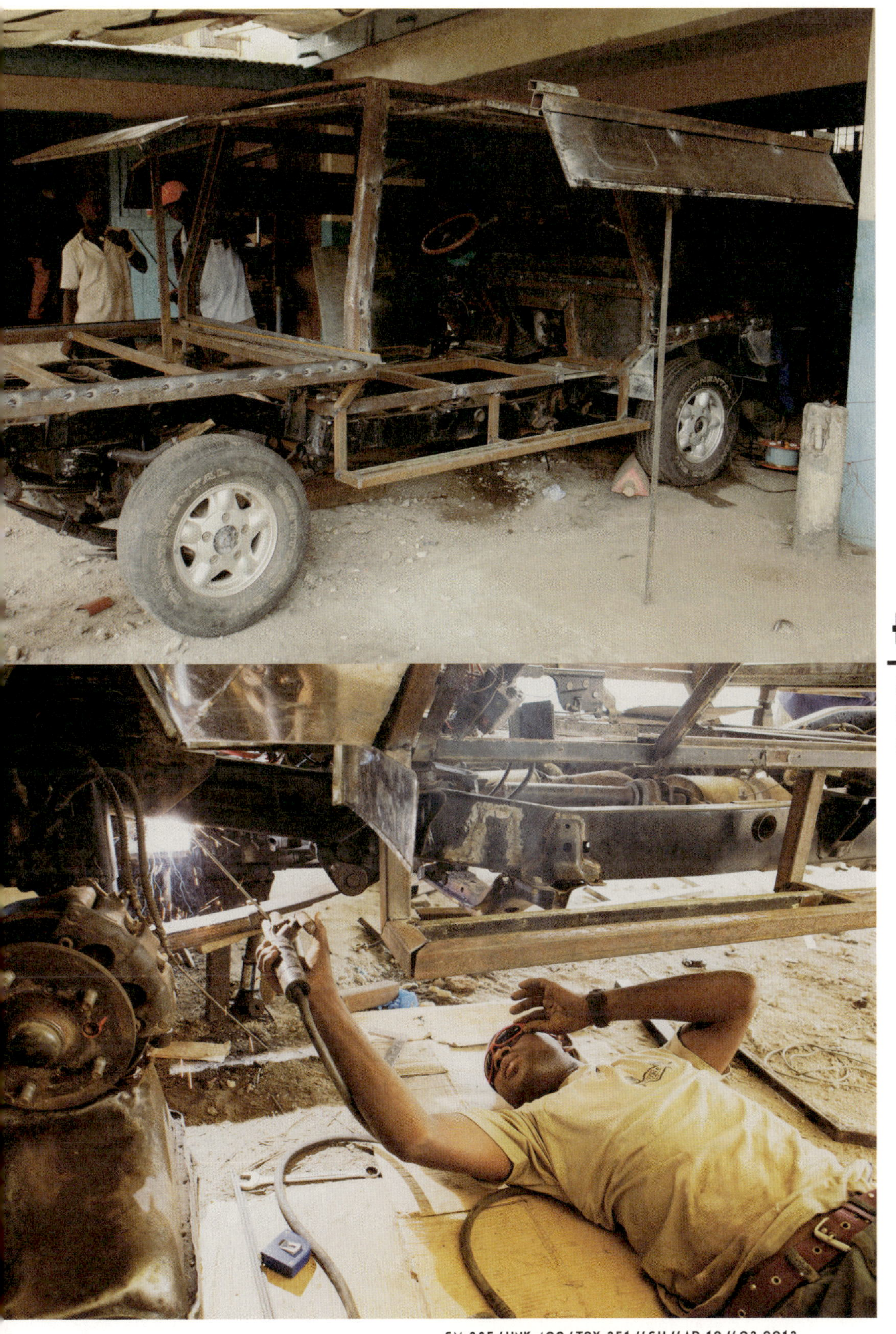

SM-385 / UNK-402 / TOY-351 // GH // AP-12 // 03.2013
SM-385 / TOY-351 // GH // AP-12 // 03.2013

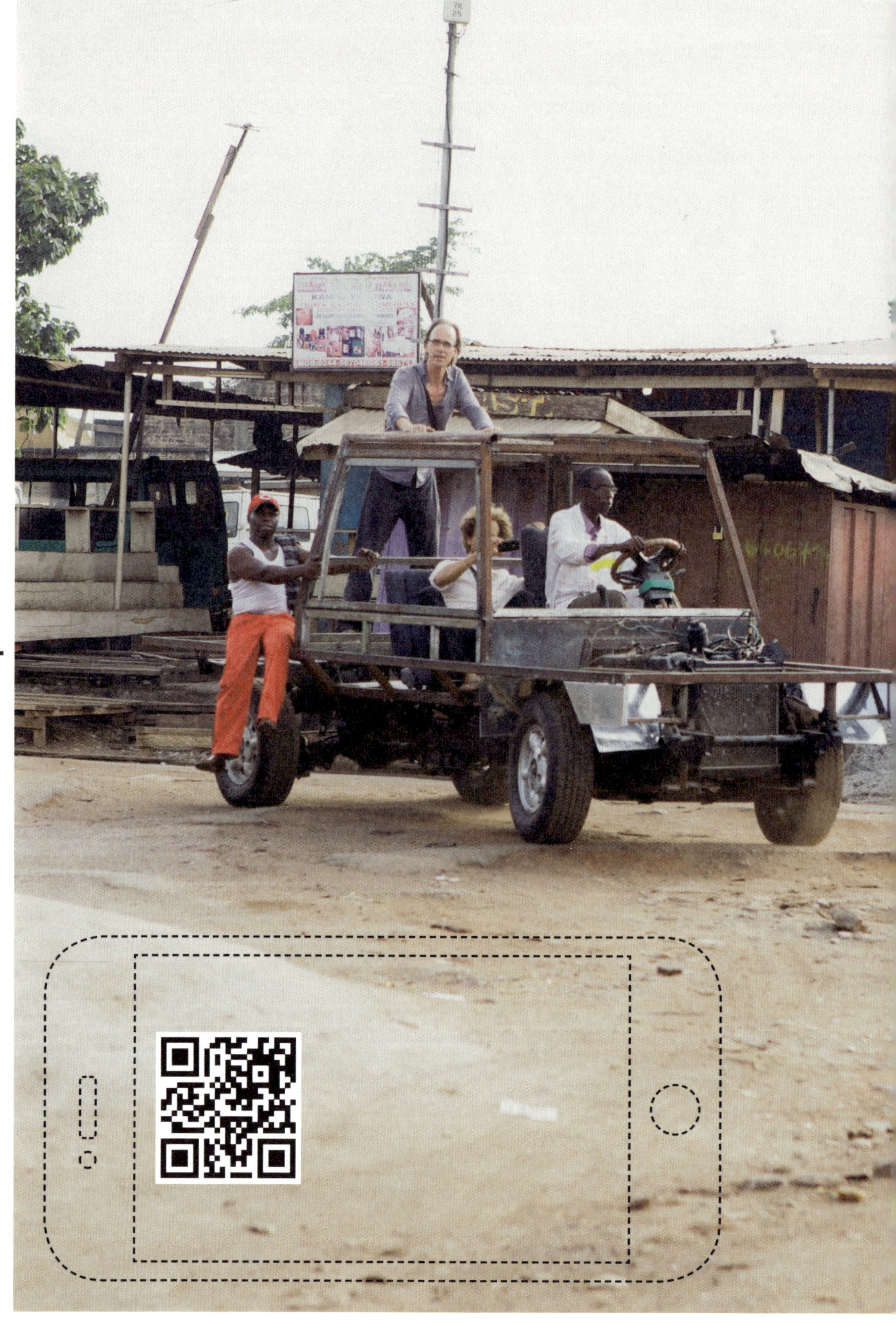

L: Second test drive through Suame Magazine, 17 March 2013.

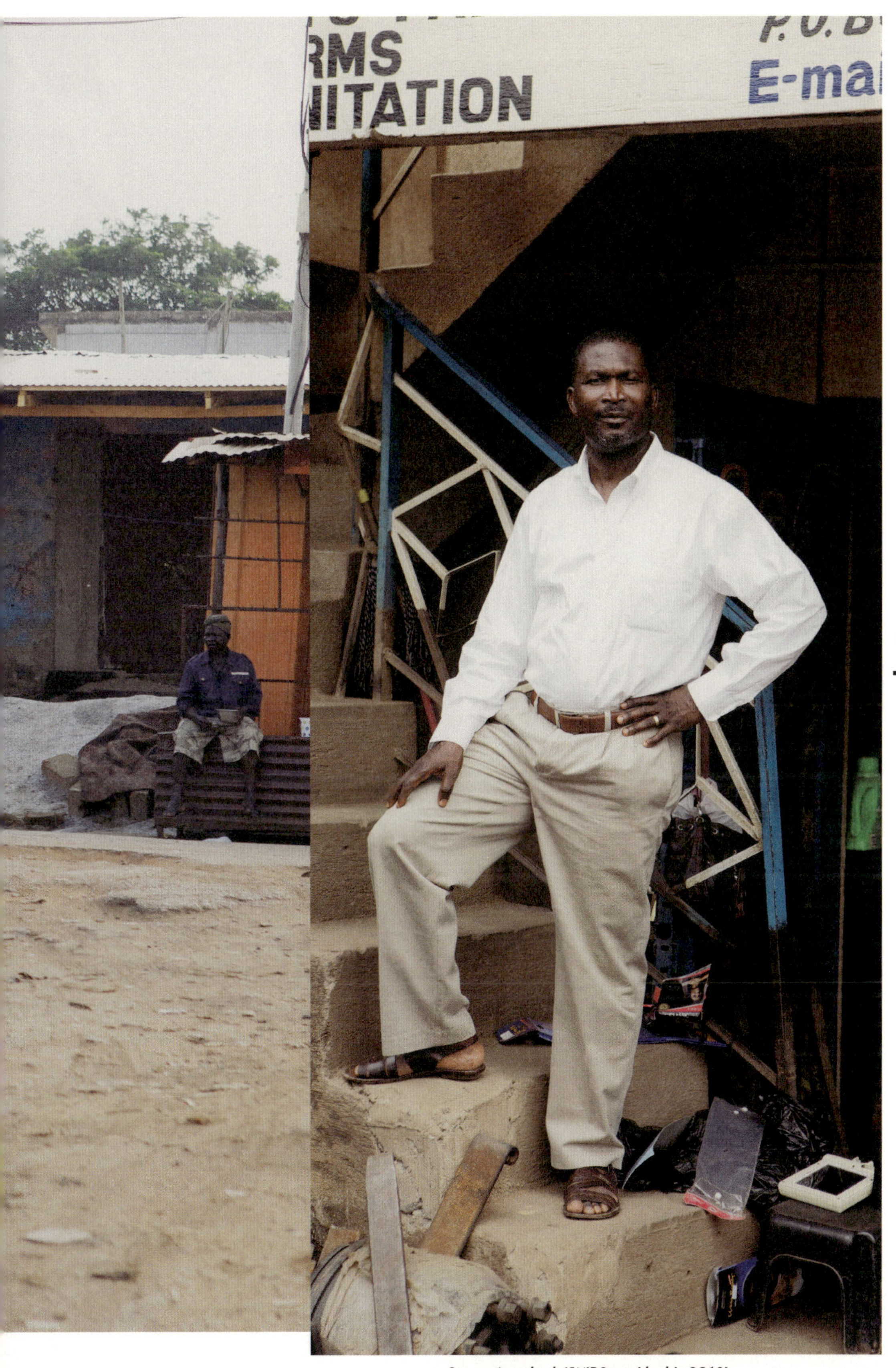

George Amankwah (SMIDO president in 2013)

L: The lining for Turtle 1 was done by Atta Joseph Arthur.
R: During the daily 'lights off', Suame is left without power. There is nothing to it but to wait it out.

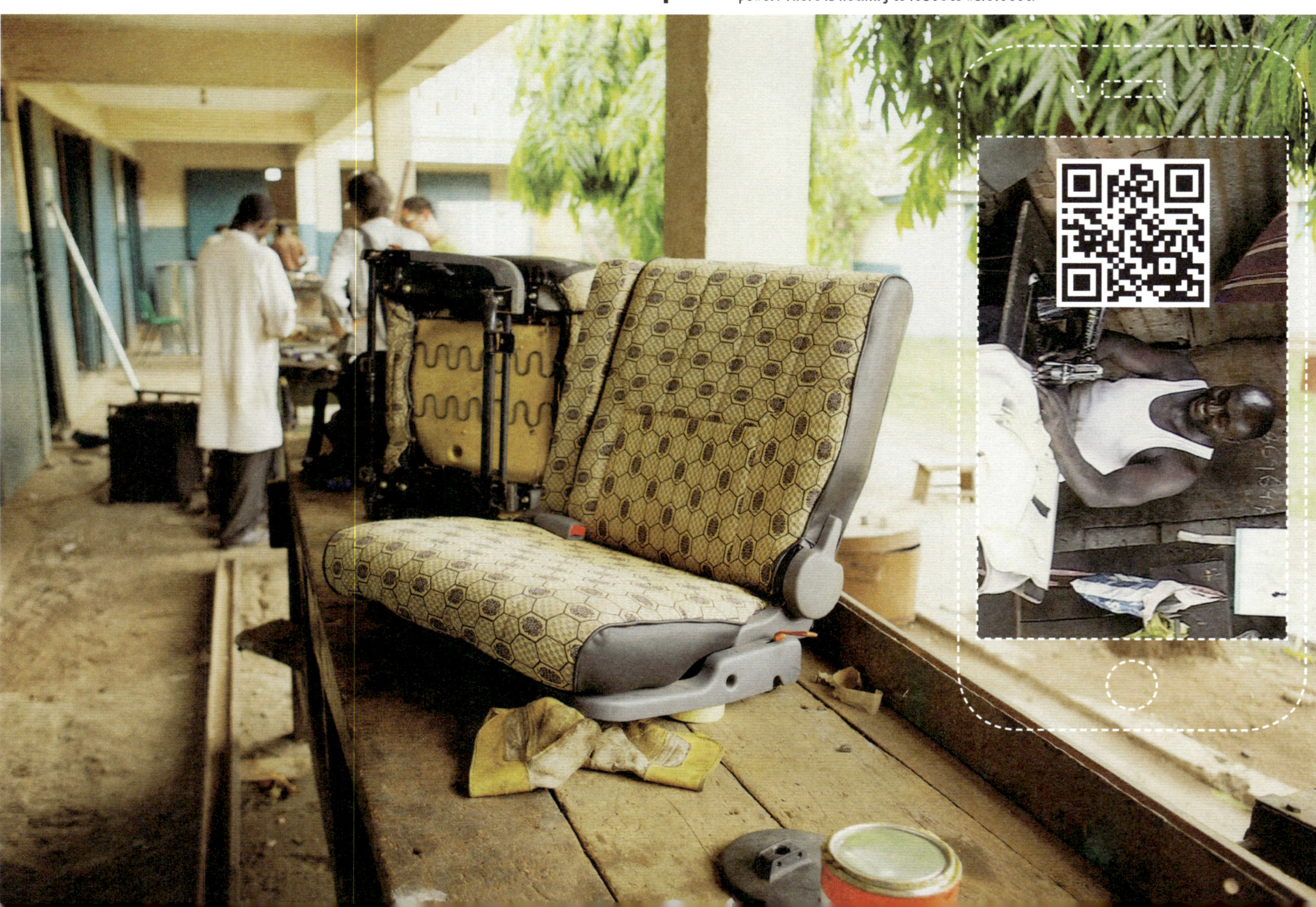

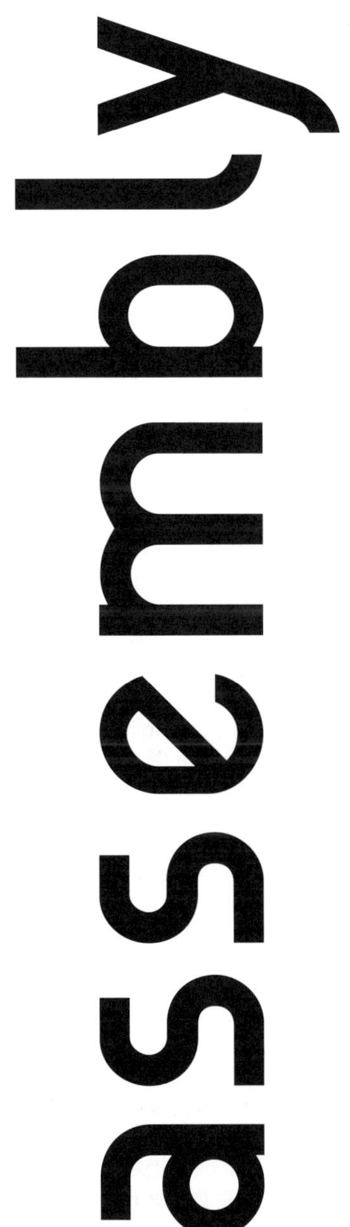

Suame is an oasis of tranquillity in the early morning. When we cycle to the workshop at 8 a.m., the streets are empty. All the rear axles, engine blocks and car parts in front of the shops have been covered up with old tarpaulins. A thin mist that smells of burnt plastic hovers over the area. In Suame, the day starts with the burning of leftover garbage. Organic waste is consumed by dogs and insects during the night; whatever is left over in the morning is thrown into the fire. In half an hour, Suame will wake up. Even though there are no collective labour agreements in place, the inhabitants of Suame stick to a strict nine-to-five schedule.

The gate of our workshop on the ITTU site is still locked. As always, Osu is the first to arrive. He is dragging something heavy behind him. As he draws near, we see it is a rolling suitcase minus the wheels, though this detail does not seem to bother him. "What are you carrying?" Melle asks. "I bring my toolbox." In true Suame style, this formerly rolling suitcase is filled with tools.

Osu has become our partner in crime over the past weeks, the person we can rely on most and our guide in this unfamiliar world. As obrunis, we only pick up on a very small part of the social dynamics around us. When there is an argument, we turn to Osu; his weathered face says it all.

At nine o'clock on the dot, Daniel and Abdul walk in. They are highly skilled sheet metal workers who we have "leased" from workshops in the neighbourhood. We had to negotiate at length with their masters before they would lend us their best men. Abdul and Daniel have their own tools with them: a hammer and a couple of chisels. Anything else they need they find in the discarded bits of material lying around: a piece of wood becomes a workbench and a ruler, old nails become pencils. With a hammer and chisel, they shape the doors, the bedplate and the bonnet, effortlessly hammering symmetrical crosses, tapered strips and perfect circles into the metal sheeting.

They are happy to have escaped their master's workshop for a while. The work there – restoring wrecks to their original state – is boring. Abdul and Daniel were both born and raised in Suame Magazine's master-apprentice system – not learning for work but learning through work. They hardly talk and instead give each other directions through hand gestures and by making drawings in the sand.

For the coming hours we will in any case have to resort to sign language if we want to make ourselves understood. The corner priest, also the owner of the ball bearings shop, starts his day by delivering a fiery sermon – when the power is on that is. He turns the volume of his sound system to the very maximum, making the sound so crackly that his words can hardly be made out. Initially we were irritated by these kind of noisy types who seemed to be on every street corner. But our irritation threshold has shifted considerably by now. For the past week, a deranged man has been standing in front of our house at 3 a.m. every night screaming his lungs out. Everyone in the neighbourhood wakes up but no one steps in. "He is a priest of some kind," the neighbours tell us. In this country where religion is omnipresent, that basically means he can do whatever he likes.

During the course of the day the small benches in the shade of the workshop fill up with elderly mechanics who provide a running commentary of the building process. Besto's voice can even be made out over the screaming of the corner priest. In the first weeks, only the mechanics were at work, but by now the workshop has become a hive of activity. Besides the mechanics, there are sheet metal workers, welders, electricians and painters at work.

Lunchtime is an important part of the day. Rice with chicken, peanut soup with fufu, or peanut butter sandwiches – a leftover from the British colonial period. At lunchtime, the work team temporarily doubles in size, only to shrink back to the actual construction team after lunch. We have had to accept this, even though the loyal workers find it unfair that there are people who only drop by to get a free lunch. We try to look on the bright side: it is a chance to smooth over conflicts, get to know new people and listen to stories.

There is a clear hierarchy in the workshops of Suame. The master is the boss, then there are the senior apprentice and below them the apprentices. All those ranks are mixed up in our workshop. Different masters work on the car at the same time. SMIDO has appointed Dr Waco as the head technician; he is expected to manage everyone. At the beginning of the project he explained how to build a car. First the mechanics, then the electrics, then the welding of the cabin, then the paintwork and finally the finishing of the interior, the lighting and the mounting of mirrors, cooling system etc. That is how Dr Waco learnt to do it back in the day in the Mercedes factory and that is how we are going to do it.

But six weeks on there is not much left of the schedule he outlined. The technical side of the car is a constant source of problems. Today they are yet again taking out the engine block. The suspension was not properly welded and now it is already getting rusty. The handmade welding machine only has one setting. The welding wire is cheap Chinese produce and the spark that fly off it keep setting the car's electric wiring on fire, which means that the electricians keep having to repair it. Meanwhile the painters carry on, cheerfully covering up the patches of paint that have just been damaged by the welders.

It is going to be a tough job for Melle in the coming period. Joost has returned to the Netherlands because of other work obligations and will only be back in four weeks. Dr Waco and Philip have stopped coming every day as they have their own workplaces to run and a lot of work to catch up on. It is down to Mr. Melles to manage the building process.

Every Monday during the executive council meeting at the SMIDO office, Melle makes urgent requests for extra workers. We have just one welder and that is no enough to finish the whole structure. After weeks of nagging, a new worker arrives from Accra: Sami. He claims to be an inventor and to have developed a car that can drive without petrol or electricity, a perpetuum mobile. He is now seeking funding to get his car produced. He used to work in Suame Magazine but says it is too dirty and chaotic. Sami is a hard worker, exactly what we need. He studies the drawings that are on display in the workshop in great detail. "I like the flying doors, very original design. We can build it, no problem." Once he has changed out o his Hawaii shirt into overalls, we get to work. There is no need for a tape measure: Sami holds up the metal bars and Melle calls out when he has the right angle. Within a few hours the frame is welded. Sulomon, the master who was originally assigned to the job, turns up in the afternoon. He was visiting his ailing mother in hospital. He is indignant and shakes his head disapprovingly as he walks around the car. "What is this?" Melle answers that we have little time and that any help is welcome. "But I can do it, don't worry." Luckily Melle gets support from the old boys on the bench. They scold Sulomon, who listens impassively but is clearly offended.

After lunch, Sulomon and Sami both get to work. Sulomon works on the frame and Sami is going to focus on the flying doors. But first we have to find more metal. Sulomon disappears off to the scrap market with two helpers. Ten minutes later one of the boys comes back and says that Melle has to come along. Sulomon is standing by a gigantic heap of metal that looks like a tower crane that has been crumpled up by a giant. "Look, we need to buy this now! This angle iron has round corners, very rare!" It is a piece of luck: we can extract enough lengths for the whole car body from this crane wreck. We ave already wasted a lot of time looking for suitable ieces of metal, which then had to be welded together order to get the right length. And all those welding ints only weakened the structure.

turns out that Sami really is an inventor; he is full of .ever solutions. We need strong gas springs to keep e swing doors up. While they do exist, our chances f finding them here are virtually nil. Sami draws an genious system in the sand that allows the door to e folded open in two halves so that the springs do ot need to be so strong.

he following day, Dr Waco drops in briefly. Sami has elded one of the flying doors and is just hanging it to its frame. Dr Waco promptly tells Sami to stop at and make regular doors. Dr Waco is not into ashy extras – and so far he has always been proven ght. We have come to realise that after more than 00 years of car development, there is a certain logic building a car. There is simply no denying that the chetypical car, with an engine in front, a cabin and boot in the back, is very functional. And when you ave to build it out of random objects like we do, you on't have much choice.

ut once you have the basic structure, there is still e finishing and that is a different story. Sami oes over to Melle and says that he should talk to r Waco. Dr Waco is adamant that flying doors are uite impossible. 'these doors are too heavy. It is angerous and you can hit your head." To illustrate his oint, he walks up to the car and theatrically knocks s head against the open door, which is indeed angerously positioned at eye height. "How do you ant to open the door in a parking lot? Mr. Melles, this annot work." Everyone has stopped working. Melle as to admit that he had overlooked these practical etails and, with all the workers looking on, gives in to r Waco. Now it is Sami's turn to explode. Melle has stand up for his design, otherwise Sami is getting e bus back to Accra tonight. Melle suddenly realises at he is no longer the outsider researching Suame agazine, but that he is part of a team and therefore as to act the part. The car will have flying doors, ome what may. This is unacceptable to Dr Waco who orms off to his Mercedes. He does not come back r a whole week.

o far we managed to keep the peace through haring ideas', the exchange of ideas among equals ntil there was a broad-based solution. But now at the car is taking shape, the different ideas often ad to conflict. As a master and teacher, Dr Waco is sed to getting his way. But now that he has to take l these opinions into account, he no longer gets round to what he is good at: building cars. Process management does not form part of the master-apprentice system. And Melle starts to realise that being in charge of equals is awkward for Dr Waco. After this project ends, he will have to continue working with the other masters, while we will return to the Netherlands.

As Dr Waco has stopped coming, other masters also stay away. Every morning, Melle starts the day with a round of phone calls: "Where are you? Are you coming? Why not?" Everyone remains courteous and promises to return to work soon, but meanwhile not much is happening in the workshop. The only ones who are steadily working on are Daniel and Abdul and the painters. The painters keep on plastering, only to then sand the plaster off again. It is obviously pointless, but it is impossible to send them home. The daily guarantee of chop money is too tempting.

One early morning, Osu and Sami are the first to arrive at the workshop. There is commotion around the power generator. Two boys are pulling on one end of it and Osu on the other. The owner wants it back. Melle says that we are renting the power generator and that he wants to speak to their master. They clear off. Osu tells Melle that SMIDO has not paid the rent for two weeks. This explains a lot: now that there is "lights off" (power cuts) every day, power generators are great moneymakers as they are the only source of electricity across Kumasi.

The boys from the rental shop come by every day to crank up the machine. It is a dangerous job, because when the engine fires, the handle gets an enormous wallop. If you do not let go in time, it can dislocate your shoulder. The cranking up is kind of a service, but it is also a way of getting bad payers to cough up the daily rent first. Each in turn, we try to get the generator going, without luck. We have no choice but to go and see the owner. Sami goes off and comes back after half an hour. We first have to pay.

This is one of the many extra expenses that ends up on our plate. SMIDO had promised to provide an infrastructure of electricity, tools and staff, which they did for the first few weeks, but now all three are lacking. We slowly discover that SMIDO is putting its members under pressure to work on this project as volunteers. But it has become clear that most artisans cannot afford to work just for chop money and we therefore have a considerable number of people on our payroll by now. We have also invested in safety equipment like helmets, gloves, ear and eye protectors, because no one else has. We pay for lunch every day, because otherwise nobody eats. And now we are also paying for the power generator. We are coming to realise that it is a game in which everyone is constantly passing the buck, until we are the only ones left. Too often, we are the ones who foot the bill, because we are on a tight schedule and do not want to waste time.

So far we always preferred to give in, in order to keep the project moving forward. But that doesn't work anymore. Melle decides to stand his ground and even, if necessary, waste a day. He says he has no money. Osu and Sami give him a stunned look. They know he is lying. "Call Dr Waco. He represents SMIDO," says Melle. But neither Osu nor Sami feel like it. So Melle picks up the phone himself to announce that the electricity man needs to be paid. They bicker for a bit and when it becomes clear that Melle is not willing to spend one more penny, Dr Waco says he is on his way.

It is nearly afternoon by the time he arrives. By now Philip has also been warned. The three of them pay a visit to the master who rents out the power generator. The workshop is little more than a wooden shed with a padlock. The master is behind the shed, working hard to piece together a new generator. These machines are made after a 50-year-old Chinese model and are shipped to Ghana as a DIY kit. When the master sees us he does not stop to greet us but carries on doggedly fiddling with his generator. We look on for a little while and then there is a long conversation in Twi between Philip, Dr Waco and the generator man. Finally, they appear to arrive at a consensus. Dr Waco reports back cheerfully: tomorrow we will receive a new generator on loan. Today it is still being used in a goldmine to fuel the water pumps. "But we have a generator," Melle says impatiently. 'that one has to go to the repairman," Dr Waco mumbles. "I will call George," says Melle. But the three masters all seem to think that is a bad idea. 'oK, let's see other rentals. No problem," Philip says, and he drags us out into the street, in search of another rental place. There are lengthy negotiations at the next shop. When the deal is done, Waco and Philip look over at Melle. The man has to be paid. Melle refuses. 'this is a SMIDO problem." We give each other sheepish looks over the generator. This is the first time that Melle has not pulled out his wallet. They phone another shop, where we can rent a generator for half the price. But when we finally find the place, the generator has already been let out to someone else. Meanwhile Dr Waco is working his phone. After a few calls it looks like he has finally found one. It is a generator without wheels, which means we need a vehicle. Melle chuckles and suggests using Dr Waco's Mercedes. That is out of the question. Melle does not wait around and starts walking back to the workshop where everyone is hanging around aimlessly. No power means no welding work. The generator that SMIDO had rented has been picked up by now. Osu is annoyed and asks why Melle is making such a point o[f] this. "How about you ask Dr Waco," Melle snaps back.

What are we actually trying to prove? We have less than three weeks left before the boat leaves for the Netherlands. Do we insist on delivering a finished car by then? Or is the process enough, and is it all right if the whole thing is a failure? Melle phones Joost to give him the weekly update. If we keep muddling along at this pace, the project will never be finished. That would obviously be embarrassing for everyone involved. The only way to get the car finished in time is if all the workshops in our cluster join in. It is finally time to put our idea of Suame Magazine as an open-air car assembly line into practice.

The white board in the classroom next to our worksho[p] becomes the planning board for the car's assembly. The first column lists the various tasks, the next column shows the names of the workers who are to do the job and the last column states the date by which the task must be completed. Philip walks in just before lunch. He carefully studies the schedule and then erases all the dates in the right-hand column with his handkerchief. "If you show this to the workers they come back on the end date you write. Don't ever tell them." When Melle shows Dr Waco the schedule later that same day and sums up all the tasks, Dr Waco nods all the way through. Melle then counts out the number of days we have left and sets its off against the size of the team. The conclusion is that we are seriously running out of time, but Dr Waco seems unfazed. "Let's make more time," he suggests. But th[e] boat leaves in three weeks, we have to go home and we have run out of money. The only solution is to get subcontractors in. Dr Waco shakes his head. "Don't worry, we can do it," he says. "But how?" Melle asks. Dr Waco tries to reassure him. He has already asked everyone to come more regularly. And they have all promised they would. That is also a form of truth here if someone said it, it is true.

We still need a lot of parts, and many of them have to be made to measure. A dashboard, the mirrors, the air cooling, bumpers, a grille, a loading platform, seats, lighting, mudflaps and upholstery. The perfect opportunity to create an assembly line. Melle first visits James Backlight. He has just opened his own workshop after having been an apprentice for seven years. He is a plastic smith now and can repair all the plastic parts in a car. With a small coal fire and a few bits of metal, he models and repairs dashboards, broken levers, handles, but also entire bumpers, light fittings and roof windows. James rents a lean-to behind a shop. He keeps all sorts of coloured pieces of plastic in a wooden cupboard against the wall. As a plastic smith, James has the advantage of operatin[g] a niche, and he only needed a small investment to pen his own workshop. But when he hears that we ant him to make all the car's light fittings, he gets bit nervous and shows melle a nearby shop, where ey sell all the lights you could ever want, but brand ew from the box. But we don't want new lights on ur car; we want handmade lights. It is after all a howcase car that is meant to highlight the quality craftsmanship in Suame.

he bumpers are made by twin brothers who have no orkshop of their own. Instead they go from workshop workshop with a gas burner. One of the reasons e choose the mobile Brazing Workshop is that the MIDO team does not want to bring other workshops to the building process. Melle has taken the initiative finding a brazing workshop himself, but the twins eliver shoddy work: the bumpers are 20 cm too long nd made of poor-quality iron. Besto sends them away nd brings the job to a good shop around the corner. hey do the work perfectly and for half of the price.

he cooling system in the roof is being made by company that handmakes fridges and freezers. he best carpenters can be found around the blast urnace in Old Suame. They make wooden moulds hat are used to cast iron and aluminium into complex ar parts. Murphy Martey is the best known of the lot nd he is willing to make the whole interior and the argo bed out of hardwood. The neighbourhood's est upholsterer is tasked with upholstering the eats with an African print. But when we look at his election of fabrics it turns out that he mainly has rey, white and beige tones, and no colourful African rints. He explains that clients want their refurbished ar to look like it has just rolled out of the factory, hat is to say with authentic Japanese, German or merican patterns. He will have to go to the market look for an African print for us. Over the course of week, we work our way down the list and subcontract ll the tasks.

o far, SMIDO members have done well off the anufacturing process, as they have been getting rst pick of all the jobs. Everyone has been taking heir time, because rushing through the job would nly mean finishing it sooner. Now that we have tarted working with people from outside the SMIDO etwork, there is competition. When the upholsterer omes by to measure the cabin, he is chased away. tta, who usually sits quietly in a corner, says that e will be doing this job and no one else. Atta is one f the older members and also an upholsterer. He as been coming to the workshop faithfully every day ince we started, taking his seat among the elders on he little bench and observing the work process from here. Atta had his own workshop with apprentices, until he went off to Benin one day to work on a job for three months. When he came back he found that his workshop had been completely looted. His former apprentices had set up shop for themselves and Atta noticed that several neighbours had pinched his tools. Since then he has had to depend on people's goodwill and generosity. The car project provides him with food and some pay. By trying to bring in a non-SMIDO member to do the interior, we have clearly crossed the line. In no uncertain terms, Osu tells Melle that he has to give the job to Atta. Atta is a senior master and a member of the executive council. You have to keep the elders on your side. This is not about efficiency or the best quality. The community comes first. Atta gets the job and we immediately set out to buy the material so that he can get to work.

Our decision to ignore Philip and Waco's advice to stick with the SMIDO gang makes tensions rise. So far George and Azongo have stayed out of the process, but now that we have gone off on our own and started finding new contacts in the neighbourhood, they are getting a bit nervous. We have not attended the weekly executive council meeting for weeks because it usually means wasting a whole day as no one arrives on time. But today at ten o"clock sharp, Melle receives a personal phone call from George asking where he is. A little anxious, Melle walks over to the SMIDO building. For once the entire team is assembled there. After the prayer, George turns to Melle. 'obruni, what is the name of the car?" George can give the most deadly looks when he wants to. As he puts it: "I have a talent for a certain kind of anger." Melle does not quite understand the reason for his sharp tone. But George does explain why they need to think of a name. Azongo has caught the attention of a national TV channel. Next week we will be on "Live Breaking News". And the car definitely needs to have a name on TV.

Luckily we had already spent a lot of time fantasising about this. Dr Waco's slogan "slow but steady", the history of the Ghanaian Petuo (owl) and our realisation that an African car is never really finished but continues constantly evolving can all be nicely brought together in a single animal: the turtle. It is a symbol that is also incorporated in the SMIDO logo. A turtle is not fast, but it is stable and strong. It grows slowly but it can reach a great age. Furthermore, the idea of an animal name fits in with the international tradition of animal car names such as the Jaguar, Mustang, Impala and Beetle.

George is not impressed. "Why not lion or panther?" But luckily Melle gets support from the team. Dr Waco takes the floor first and says that the Turtle will never be fast, considering the old materials we are working with. The Turtle is the perfect car for farmers in Ghana. They need a strong car that will last them a lifetime. The members now all grow enthusiastic and finally George closes the meeting. Turtle 1 is the name. Melle can go because there is SMIDO business to discuss.

But two hours later, he is called back. By now Azongo has arrived. Of course as a spin doctor he wants this story to show SMIDO in a positive light in the media. 'turtle 1 is OK but the first name will be SMATI." When SMIDO was established, the first initiative was to set up the Suame Magazine Automatics Technical Institute (SMATI), a training institute where mechanics could follow English classes and courses in car electronics. But Azongo has more ambitious plans. The Turtle can be SMATI's first product and more products will follow. So SMATI Turtle 1 it is.

The news that national television is coming to Suame Magazine spreads through the neighbourhood like wildfire. That same afternoon Melle receives a phone call from Azongo asking whether he can receive a delegation from the Ashanti royal family the next morning. The chiefs of King Otumfuo Tutu II are coming to inspect the car to see whether it is good enough to present to His Royal Highness at the palace.

The next morning, the workshop is bustling with people who have come to help make the car presentable. Even George is there, running the show. That afternoon a group of men in traditional dress alight from a convoy of SUVs. We are lined up military style in order of importance. Melle gets to stand in front, next to Waco. George is standing up front and addresses the delegation. They solemnly inspect the car. They do not seem to mind that part of the engine block is missing. We are told to come and present the Turtle at court next week. Melle is hugely relieved: now SMIDO's reputation is at stake and with it George's personal honour. It is the ultimate form of what Ghanaians call "putting pressure".

This is it: today the car is going to the palace. For once, Melle skips his morning ritual. Instead of phoning the whole team personally, today he just waits. The Turtle's rear axle collapsed during the last test drive and has been taken away for reparation. The seats have still not been mounted and are piled up in the sand. The gas springs of the flying doors were quickly painted over yesterday, so now the doors cannot be left open. The car's maximum speed is 30 km/h and there is so much play in the steering system that even at low speed the car starts swaying over the road.

Around ten o"clock nearly the whole SMIDO team has arrived at the workshop. There was no way of convincing the construction team that we had to get started at the crack of dawn if we wanted to be at the palace with a roadworthy Turtle by 10 a.m. on the dot. Now everyone is working feverishly and the atmosphere is tense. This past week a lot of time has been spent on the Turtle's appearance. Besto found the perfect lacquer, an ochre-yellow metallic that turns to gold in the sun. But a heavy downpour during the spray-painting ruined the paint job and the lacquer is now full of sand and water marks.

Around two o"clock, the hottest time of day, the whole workshop is full of people from the neighbourhood. Three policemen on motorbikes are standing guard around the Turtle, which is now ready for departure. People are singing and making jokes. Dr Waco gives the signal for departure by starting the engine. The policemen turn on their flashing lights and everyone scampers off as the motorbikes charge into the crowd. It looks like a liberation parade through the neighbourhood. The mechanics shout "Ghana car, Ghana car". The motor police are clearly well versed in the art of intimidation: lurching wildly across the road, they free up all the streets through the city. Anyone who does not get out of the way in time gets a good dent kicked into his car. Dr Waco is sweating heavily and is trying with all his might to keep the Turtle on the road, while in the back the mechanics are merrily singing and waving at onlookers.

The palace gates swing open. The Turtle stays behind in the royal parking lot while the delegation goes in to greet the king. We are not alone. Hundreds of people have come to the palace today.

Even at this royal level, being on time is apparently unimportant. We hang around for a bit, but suddenly we are called up by the king's narrator. According to tradition, Otumfuo only addresses his people indirectly. The narrator serves as a kind of mouth-piece. We are standing in the middle of the hall that is packed with men in traditional dress. The king is sitting on a stage in their midst, wearing an array of gold necklaces. A male choir standing behind the king accompanies the narrator in song. Bellowing at the top of his voice, George tells the audience about SMIDO's greatness and the glorious future that awaits Suame Magazine. When he is finished, we shuffle back to the parking lot.

Back outside we wander around for a bit and then there is suddenly great commotion as all the men in traditional dress stream into the parking lot. A parasol sticks out over the crowd. The king has decided to interrupt the audience to come and see the Turtle with his own eyes. Melle is standing at the back next to Azongo and looks on as Otumfuo Tutu II climbs ehind the wheel. Teun elbows his way through the orde of Ghanaian journalists to get a photo through e window. 'this is it. We now have what we need, picture of the king in the Turtle," says Azongo. he following morning there is long article in the aily Graphic, but no photo. Azongo is furious and hones the paper. They will publish the article again morrow, but this time with a photo. He who pays the per calls the tune.

few days later Joost is back. He narrowly missed e palace visit, but he is happy to be back in Suame agazine. He is full of energy to help get the job done. elle can do with that optimism. He has lost a lot of eight by now as a result of excessive sweating and diet of rice and fruit. Aunt Vicky, our cook, does her ery best to take good care of us but healthy food is re in Suame.

hen we arrive at the Turtle, Joost proudly slaps veryone on the back. He knows that there are ountless problems hidden below the surface, but it a real car! And it works! "Are you ready for a test rive?" he asks Dr Waco. Thinking back nervously the trip to the palace, Waco says: "sure, maybe morrow, I have to make some adjustments before." elle is sceptical. Since the visit to the king no further ork has been done. We have exactly a week before e boat leaves for the Netherlands. The drive from umasi to the port of Tema is about 300 km over dirt oads. How will we get the car ready for that? Once gain, we need a miracle.

he workshop is teeming with people. The Turtle has be prepared for a new test drive. There is a rumour oing around that the king wants to come to Suame agazine to have a drive in the Turtle. The pressure is n again. This time our test drive goes way out of town. fter months of rooting around in the oil-drenched arth, we are surprised by the greenness. The whole ore team has come along. The mechanics are being ested to the limit, especially now that we have learnt hat the king, a car buff, wants to drive the Turtle. eople look up in astonishment as they see us come y. Osu and Philip are sitting in the back, listening for ny irregularities. The Turtle is running like a dream! r Waco honks in every village we pass through. He is learly in a better mood, after having toiled away for wo days to resolve all the technical problems.

eun wants to take this opportunity to photograph e Turtle in natural surroundings. He has spent e last two months making video portraits of the orkmen in Suame. Together with his assistant tan he has been dragging his lighting equipment, ipods and batteries through the neighbourhood. veryone has gotten used to Tony Spark, the "Red Eye". He transforms workshops into true film sets and everyone in the neighbourhood crowds around to see what he is doing. Like a film director, he orders people about and tells them to act normally. That is how he got the nickname "Red Eye" – the Ghanaian expression for someone who is stressed. Now Teun is looking for the perfect green Ghanaian landscape. "Where is the green? Where is the green?" he calls out to Lamus who was born in this region. When we finally find a good spot and he can take photos, Teun gets a new nickname: Tony "Where is the Green Red Eye". Everyone is laughing and there is great relief all round. We made it.

The smouldering heaps of rubbish have been cleared. The pavement outside the shops have been tidied up. The wrecks that block the roads have been pushed aside. The king is coming. For the first time in the three months we have been here, the team carried on working until late into the night to spray on the Turtle's final paint layer. We go straight to the paint shop where the Turtle is drying in the paint booth. This time SMIDO did not want to take any risks and made sure we would not end up with patches of dried sand in the paint. The Sunburst Orange Metallic paint glistens in the morning sun as we push the Turtle to the workshop. We are pushing because the gearbox is still missing. Once we get to the workshop dozens of people get to work and within an hour the whole car has been taken apart. According to the schedule we received, the king should have arrived by 11 o'clock. But everyone carries on working calmly past the deadline. We ask Azongo what is going on. He pulls an A4 out of his pocket and shows us the real programme. Instead of a list with programme components that will be worked through one by one, the different items are scattered across the page in a bubble diagram. "What comes first will be decided on the spot." As soon as they are ready, Azongo will phone the king's retinue.

More and more people start coming to the workshop in the early afternoon. Large party tents have been prepared that can accommodate hundreds of people. In the middle there is a decorated podium for the king with a wall of loudspeakers on both sides. When the cortege of armoured SUVs swerves into the street, soldiers form a cordon to keep people at a distance. Cheers erupt when the king gets out. He walks along the guard of honour of SMIDO members and shakes everyone's hand. Then he climbs into the Turtle and switches on the engine. The crowds prevent the car from going forwards or backwards.

After this symbolic test drive, he delivers a speech in which he says that it is important to work together, indirectly referring to the strained relationship

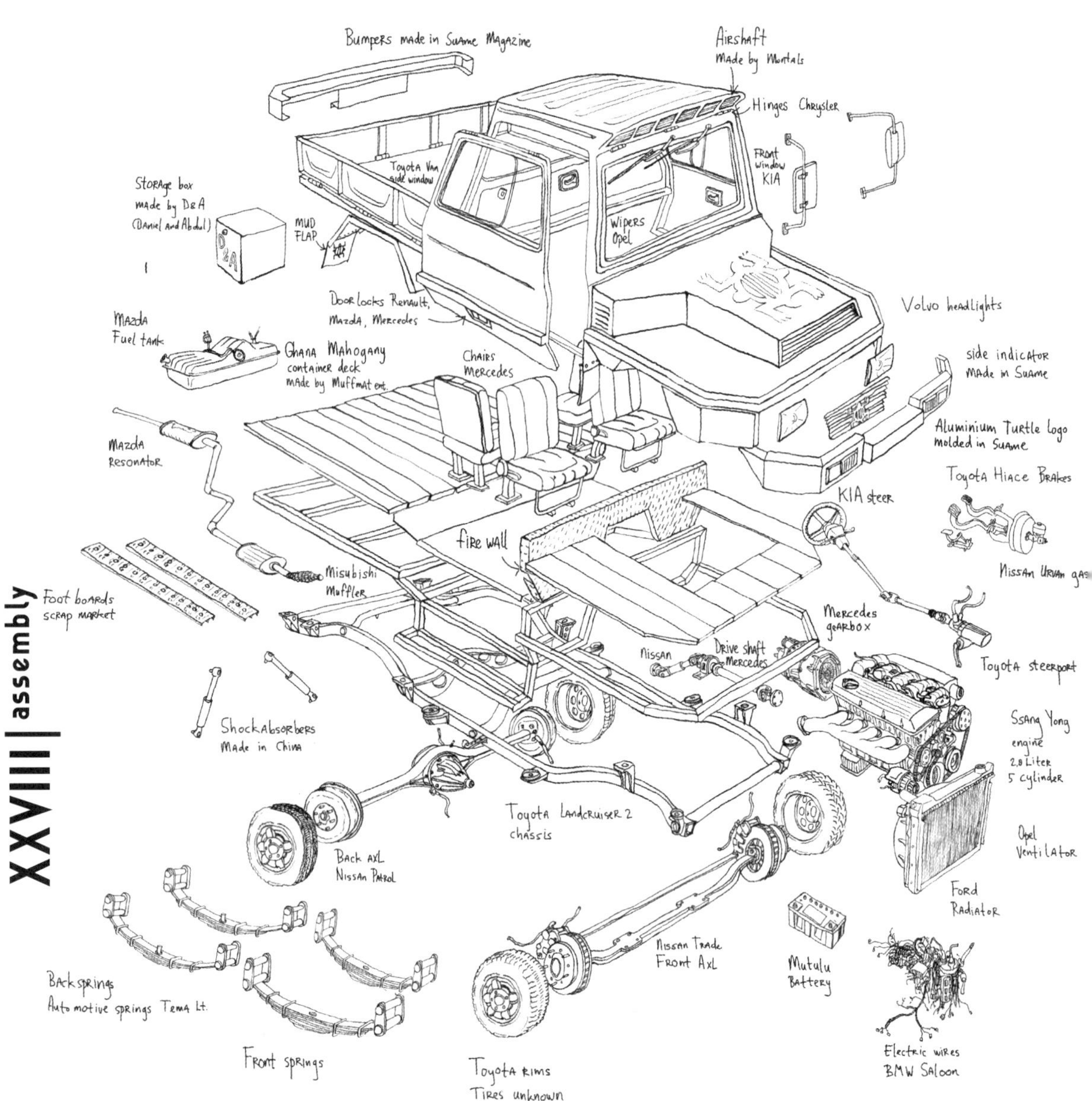

between the National Garages Association and SMIDO. The Turtle is living proof that everything is possible when there is unity, he says. If everyone contributes, a glorious future lies ahead for Suame Magazine.

When the royal delegation has left, the party really gets going. Unfortunately, we cannot stay for long. We have to get to Tema where the Turtle has to be cleared through customs before it is shipped to the Netherlands. We have to drive through the night to be there on time. As the festivities continue, hardly anyone notices that the guest of honour has left. We drive through the dark night in a small convoy without encountering any significant problems. We arrive at the port at nine in the morning.

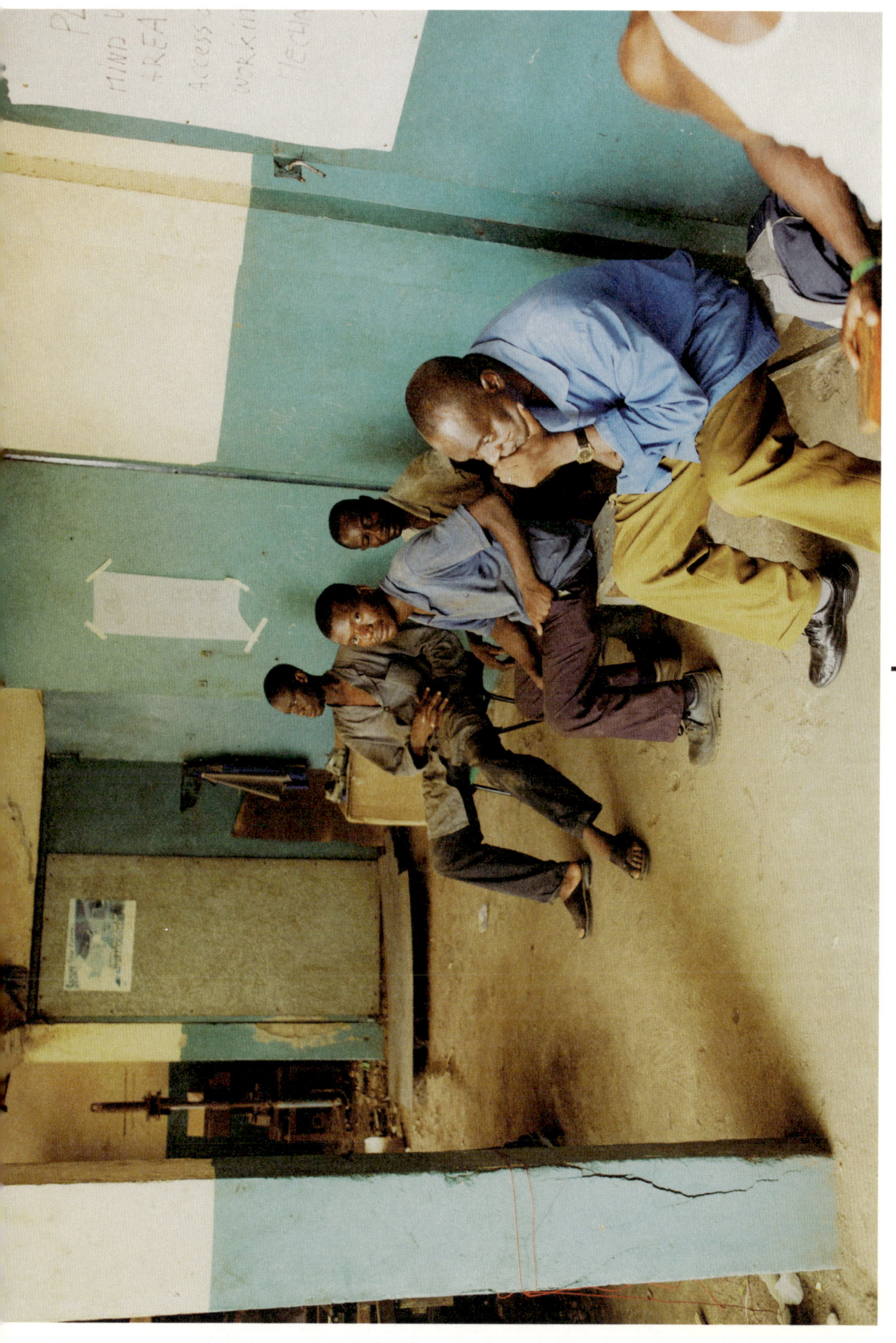

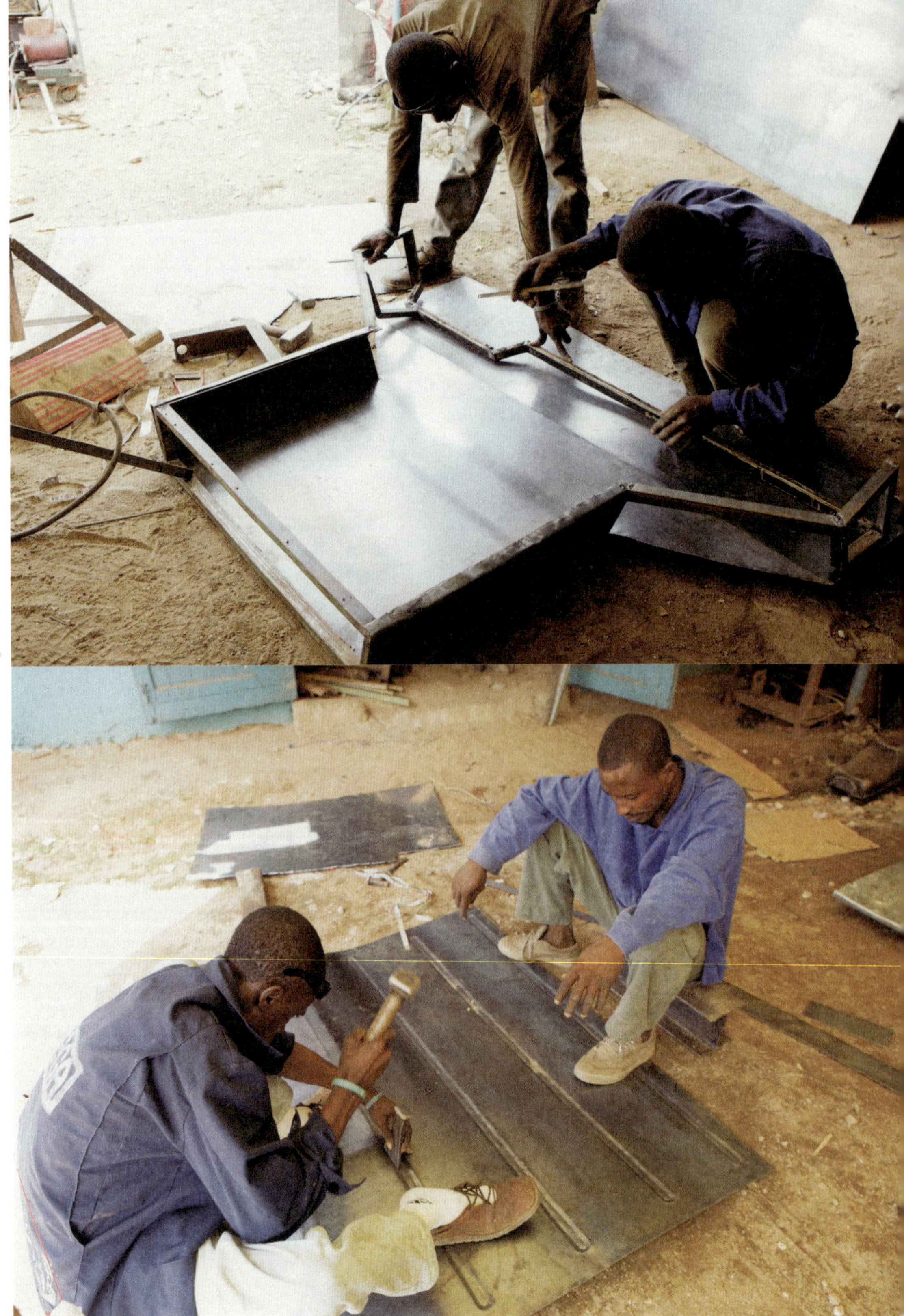

L: Daniel and Abdul at work. They effortlessly hammer symmetrical crosses, tapered strips and perfect circles into the metal sheeting.

SM-502 // GH // AP-12 // 03.2013
SM-502 // GH // AP-12 // 03.2013

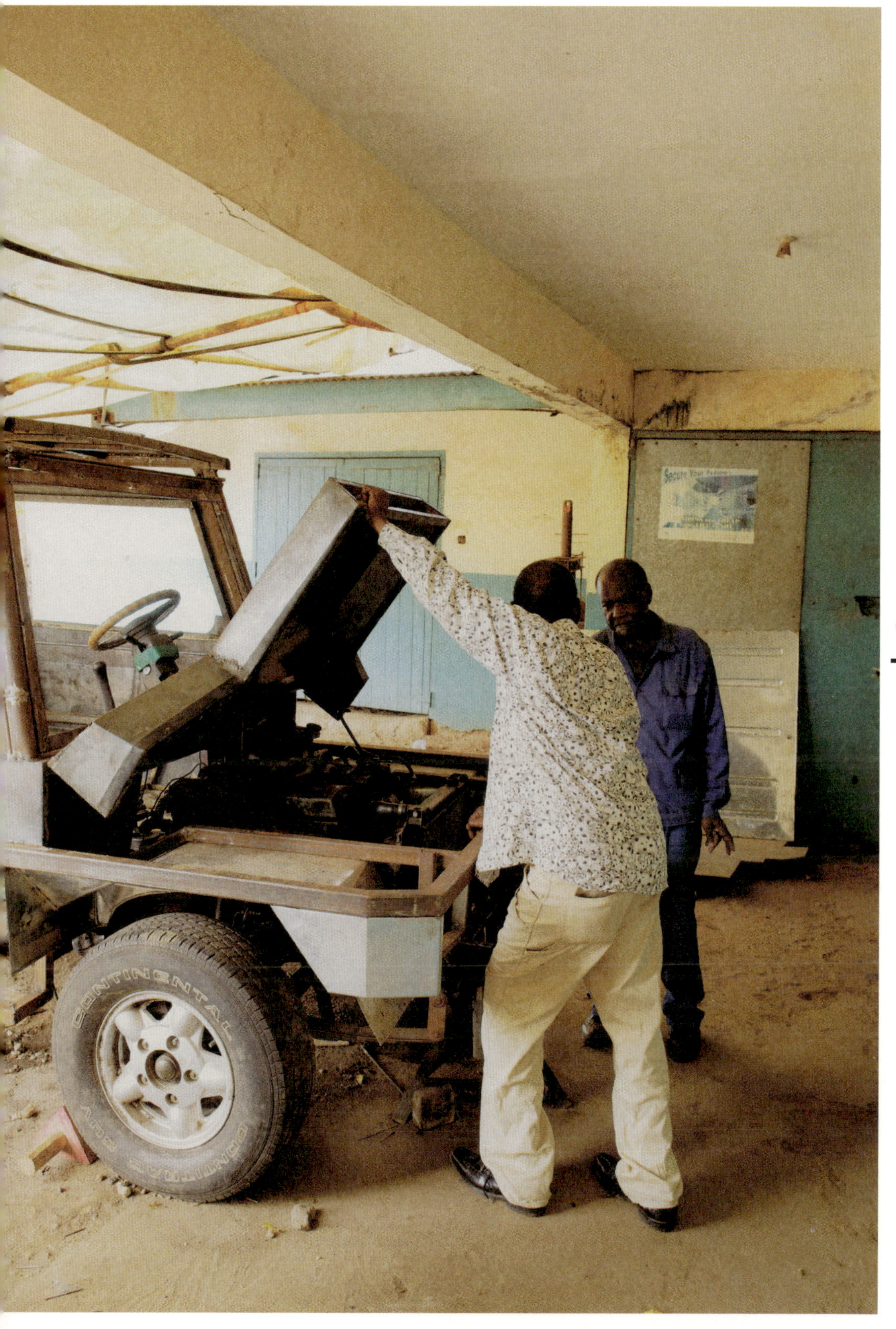

SSY-285 / SM-385 / SM-502 // GH // AP-12 // 03.2013

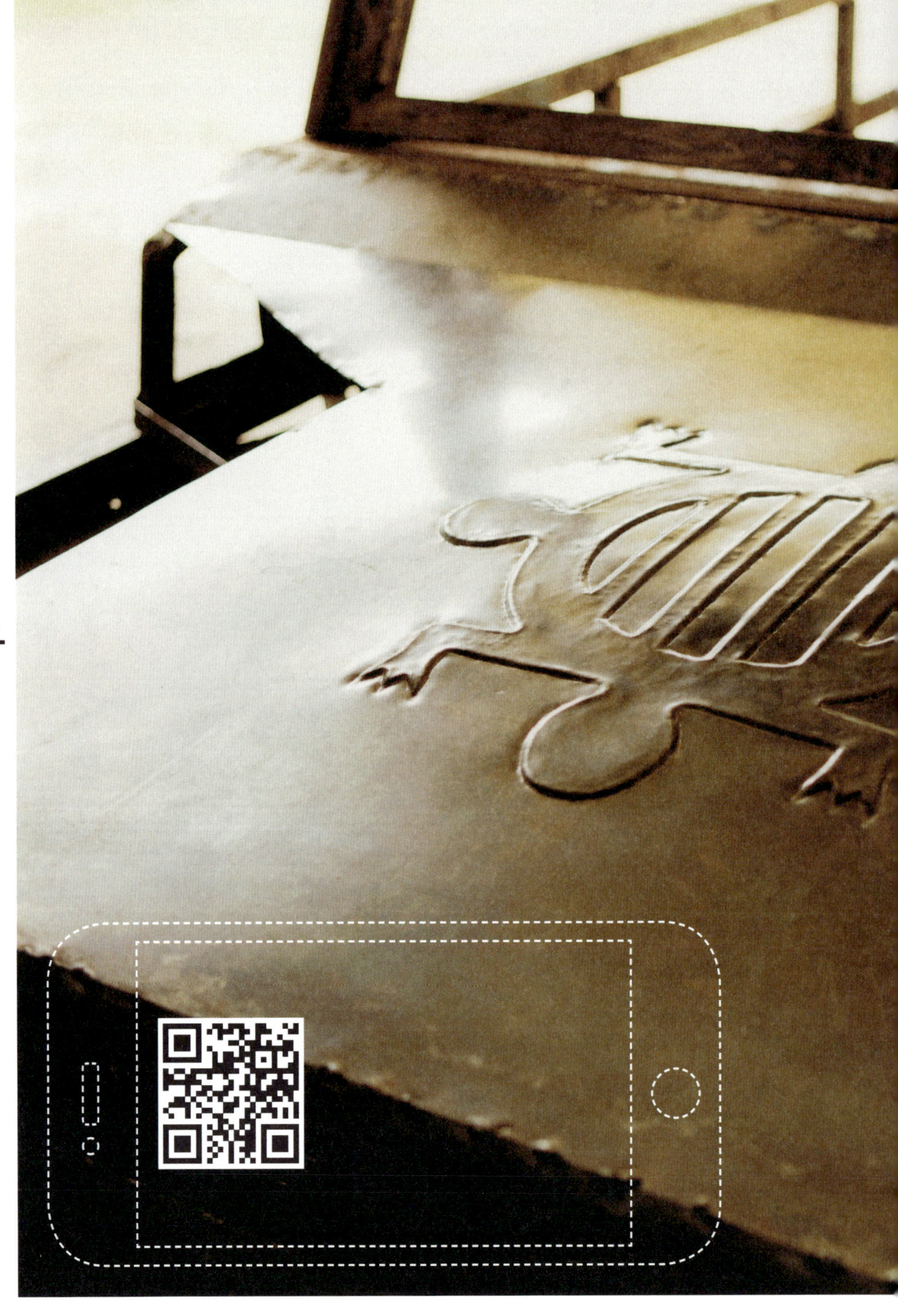

The logo of the Turtle is hammered into the bonnet.

SM-502 // GH // AP-12 // 03.2013

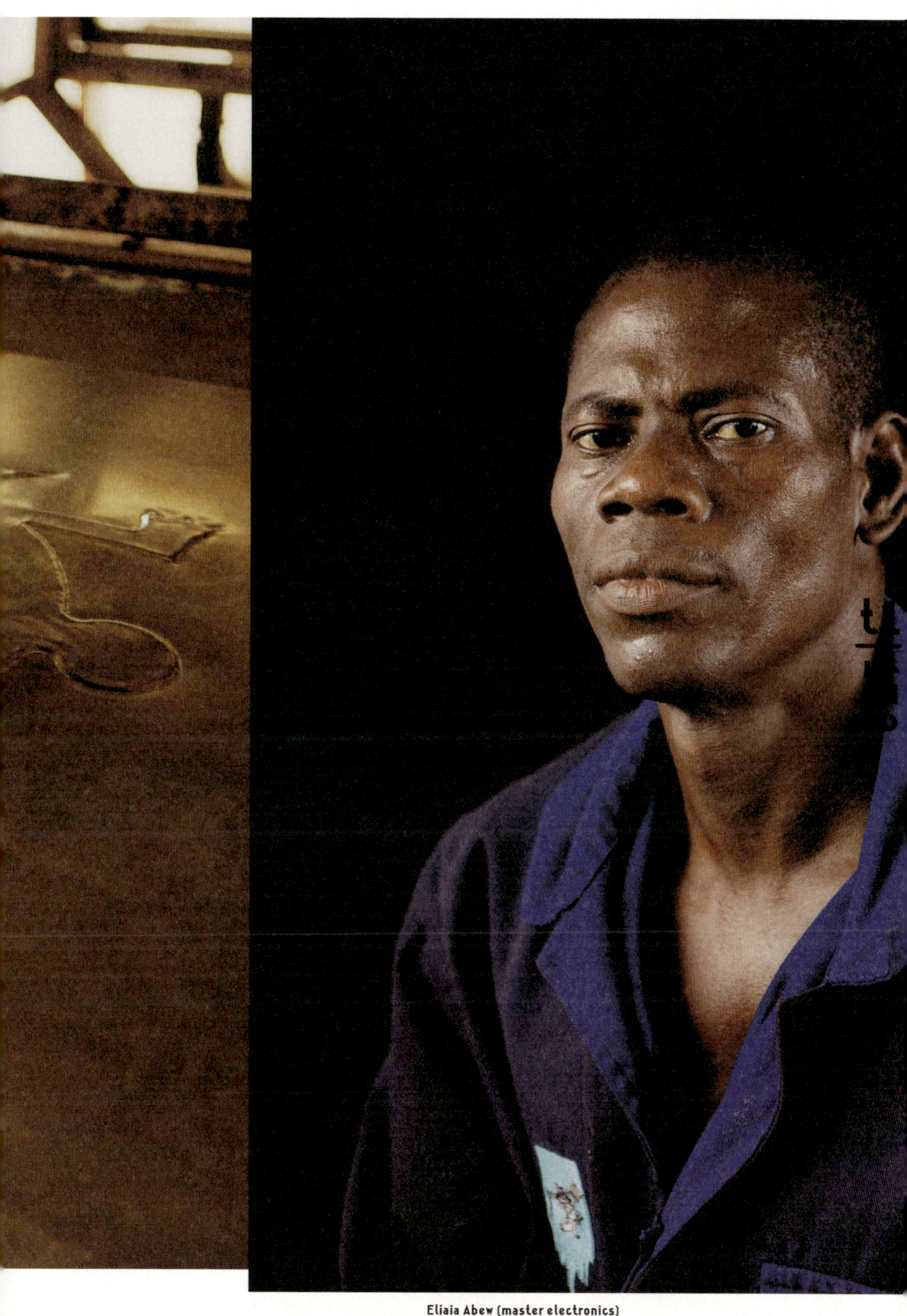

Eliaia Abew (master electronics)

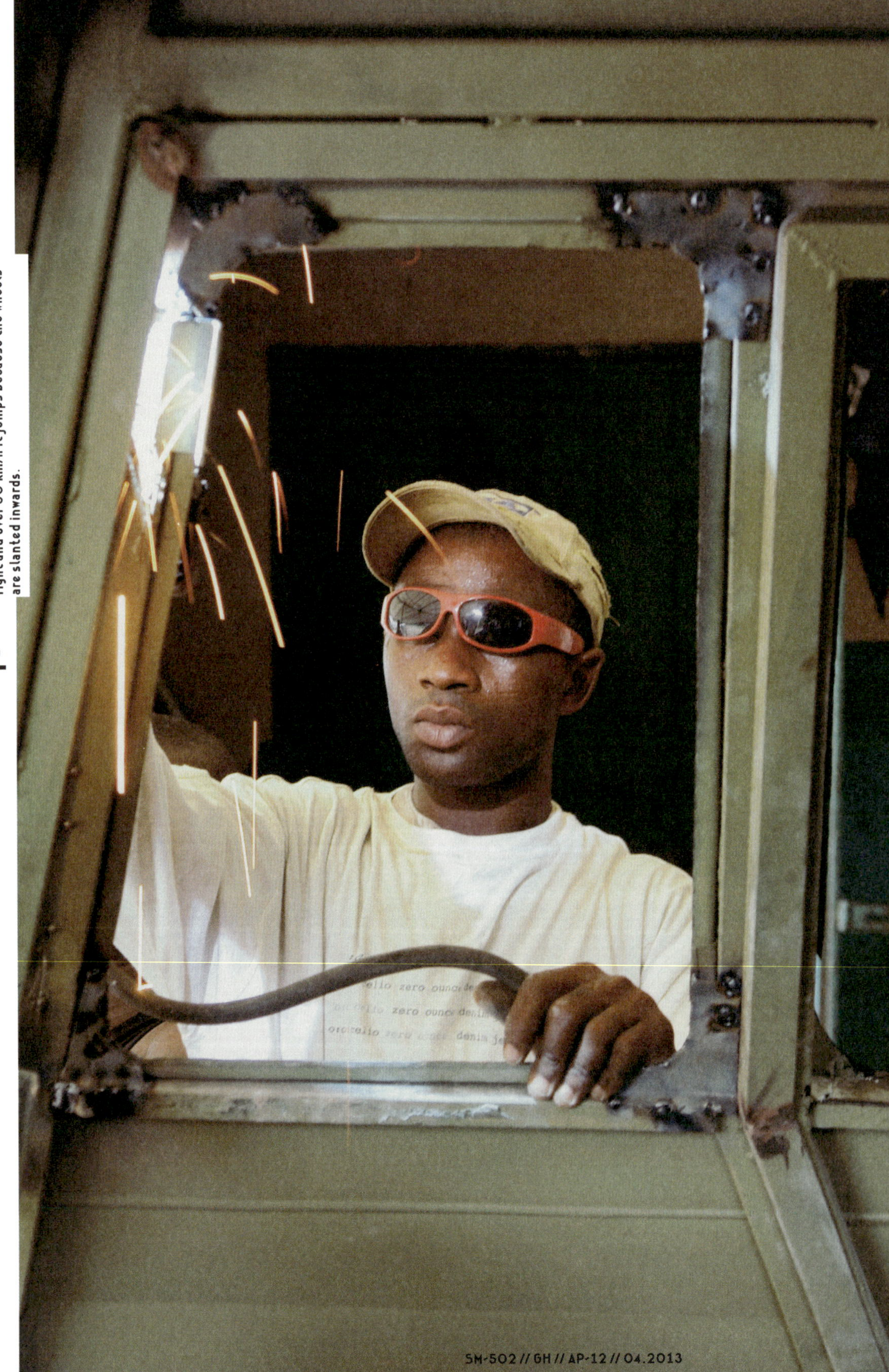

R: During the third test drive on 5 April 2013 the rear axle breaks down. The car also pulls strongly to the right and over 30 km/h it jumps because the wheels are slanted inwards.

SM-502 // GH // AP-12 // 04.2013

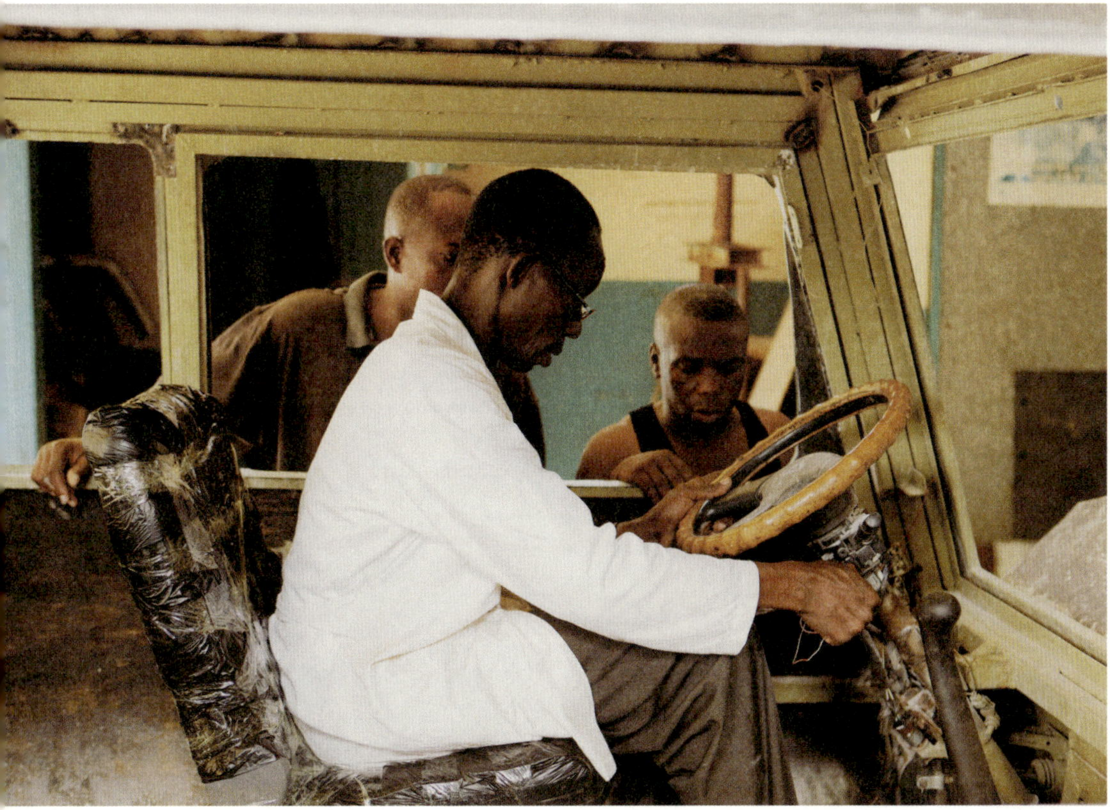

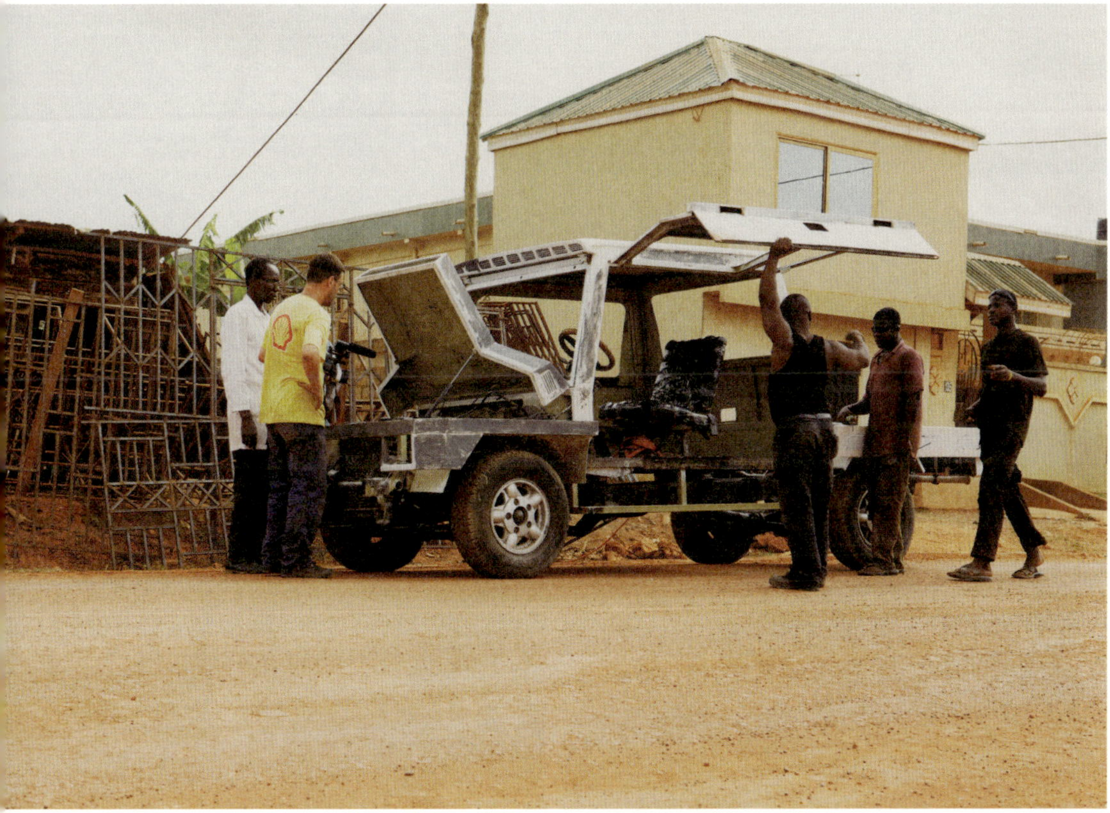

GH // AP-12 // 04.2013
SSY-285 / GH // AP-12 // 04.2013

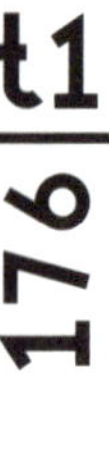

The mechanics, sheet metal workers, welders and painters are all working on the Turtle 1 at the same time. This leads to arguments, for example when a welder damages the painter's work because of sparks flying off the welding machine.

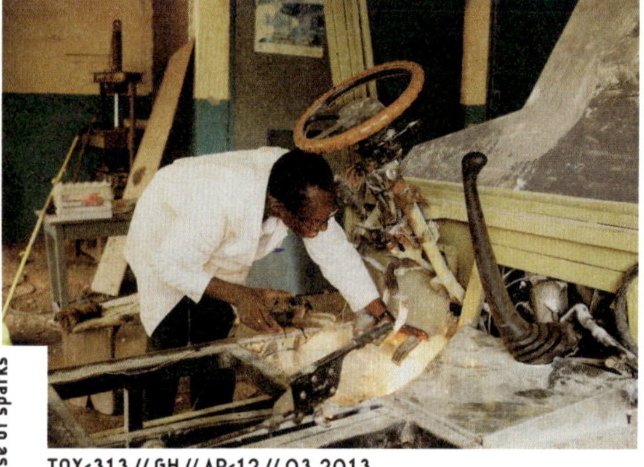

TOY-313 // GH // AP-12 // 03.2013

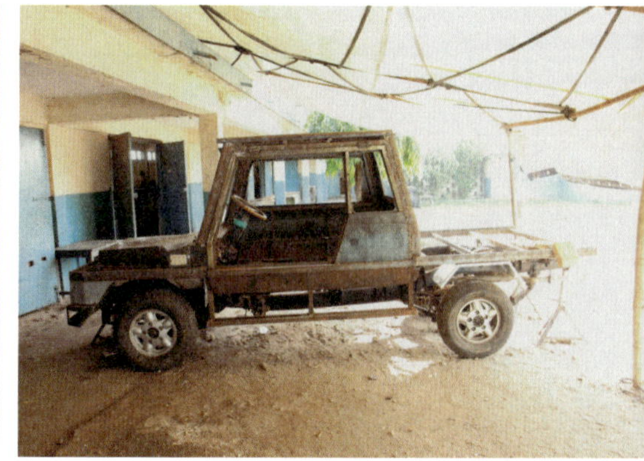

SM-385 / SM-502 // GH // AP-12 // 03.2013

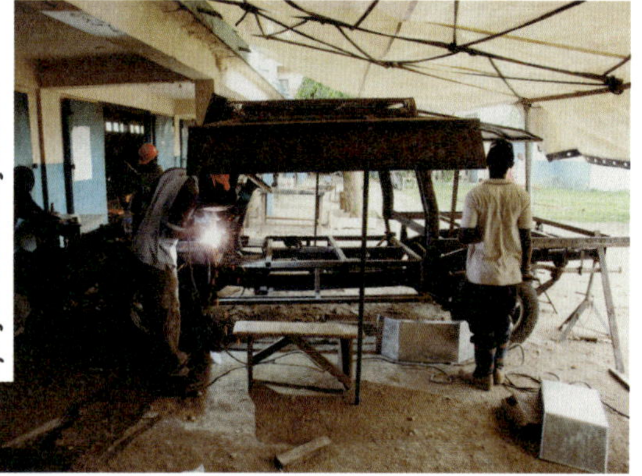

NIS-315 / TOY-313 // GH // AP-12 // 03.2013

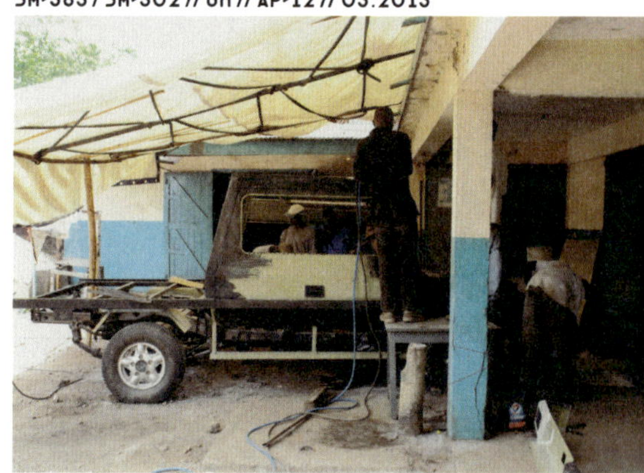

UNK-964 // GH // AP-12 // 04.2013

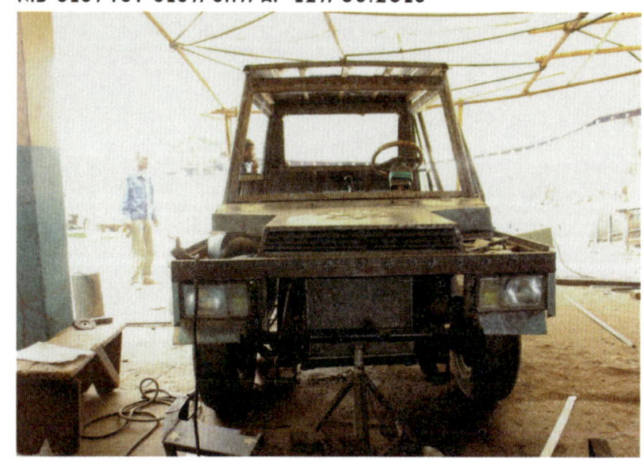

SM-385 / SM-502 // GH // AP-12 // 03.2013

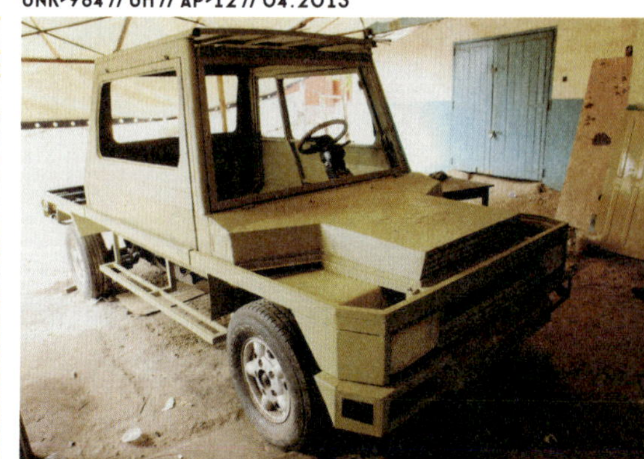

UNK-964 // GH // AP-12 // 03.2013

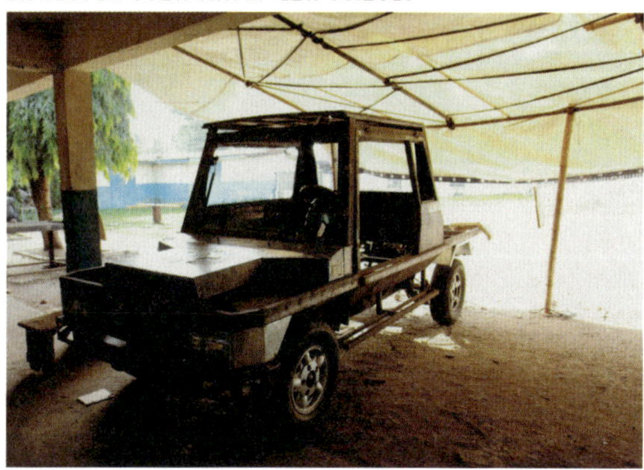

SM-385 / SM-502 // GH // AP-12 // 03.2013

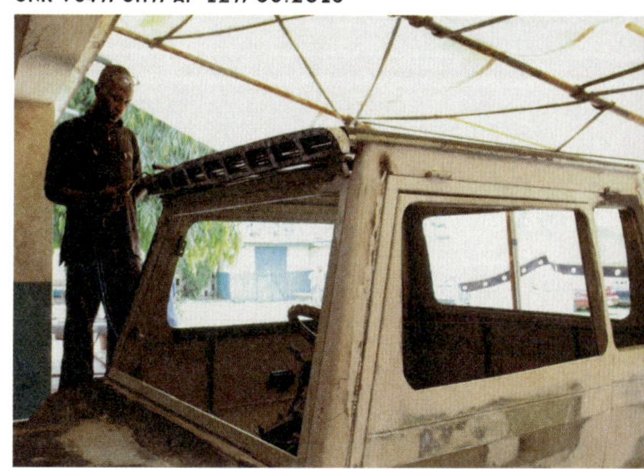

UNK-964 // GH // AP-12 // 04.2013

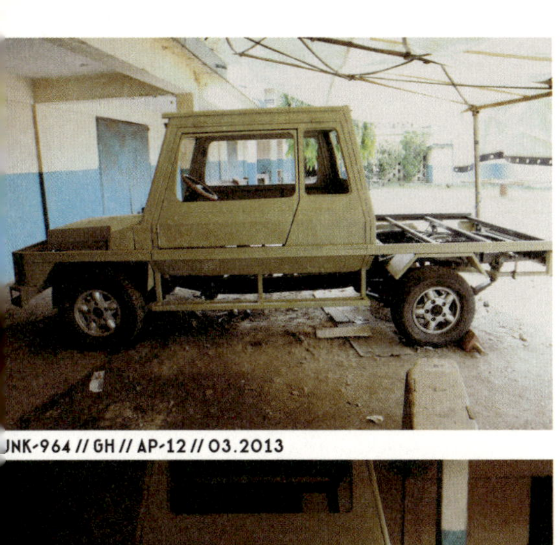

UNK-964 // GH // AP-12 // 03.2013

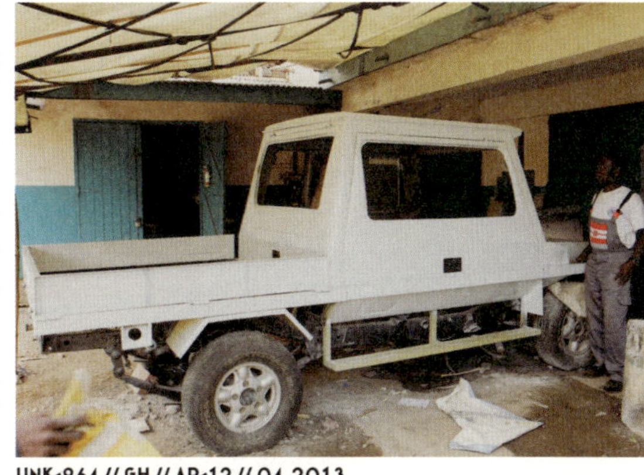

UNK-964 // GH // AP-12 // 04.2013

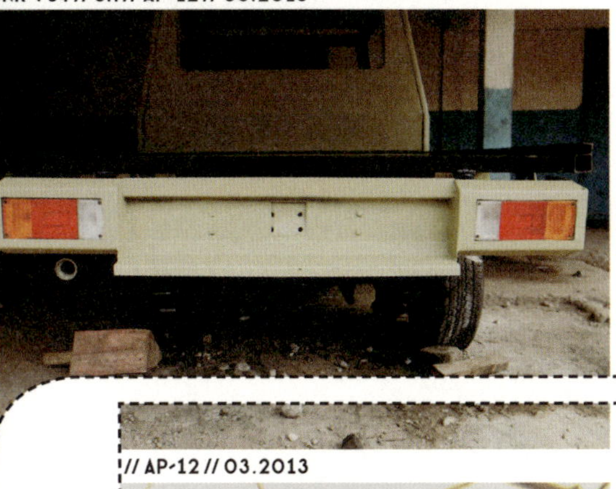

// AP-12 // 03.2013

UNK-964 // GH // AP-1

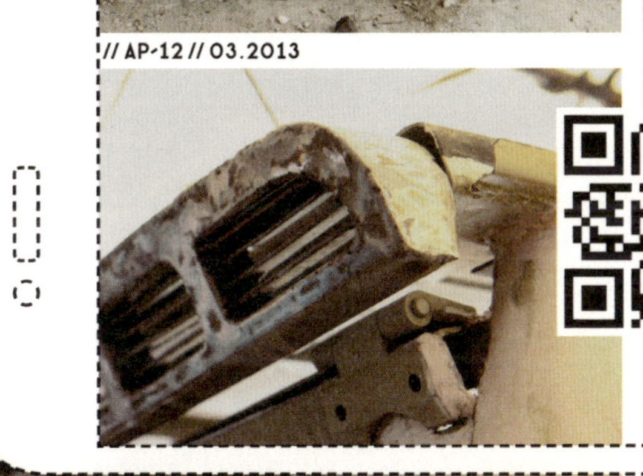

UNK-964 // GH // AP-12 // 04.2013

UNK-964 // GH // AP-12 // 04.2013

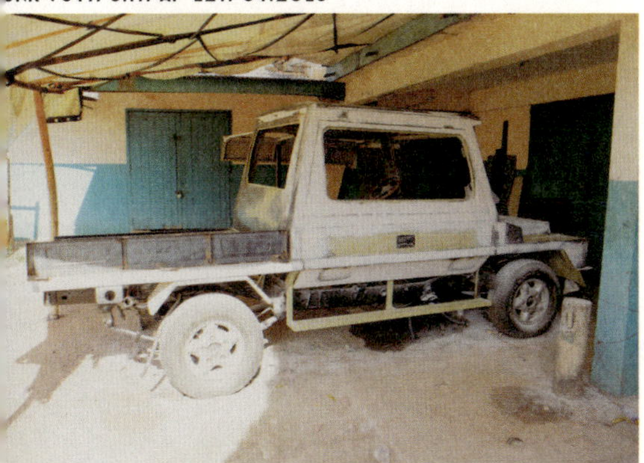

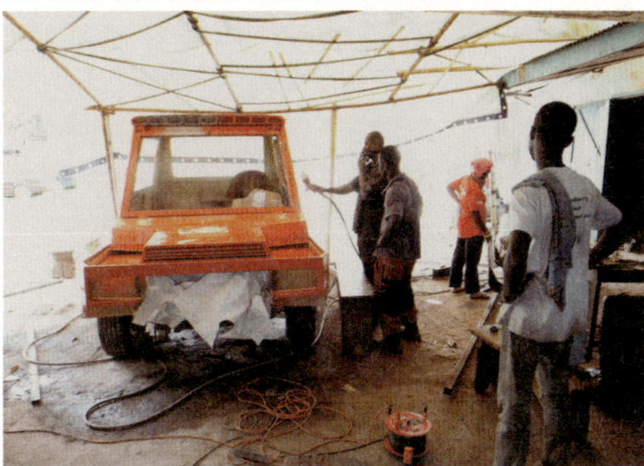

UNK-964 // GH // AP-12 // 04.2013

UNK-964 // GH // AP-12 // 04.2013

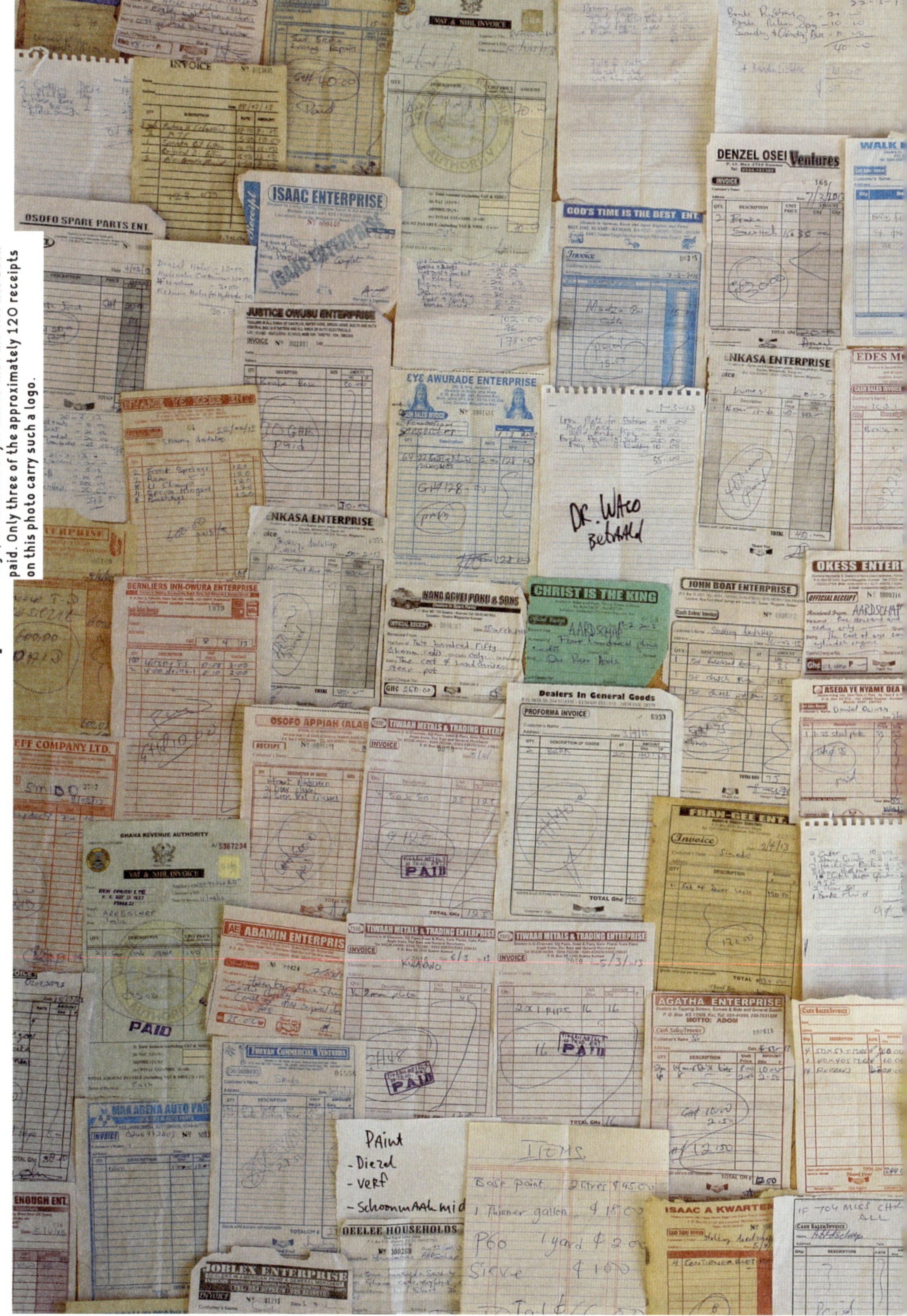

L: Receipts of the building process. The Ghanaian Tax Authority issues VAT receipts with a shiny golden logo, so that the buyer knows that the VAT has been paid. Only three of the approximately 120 receipts on this photo carry such a logo.

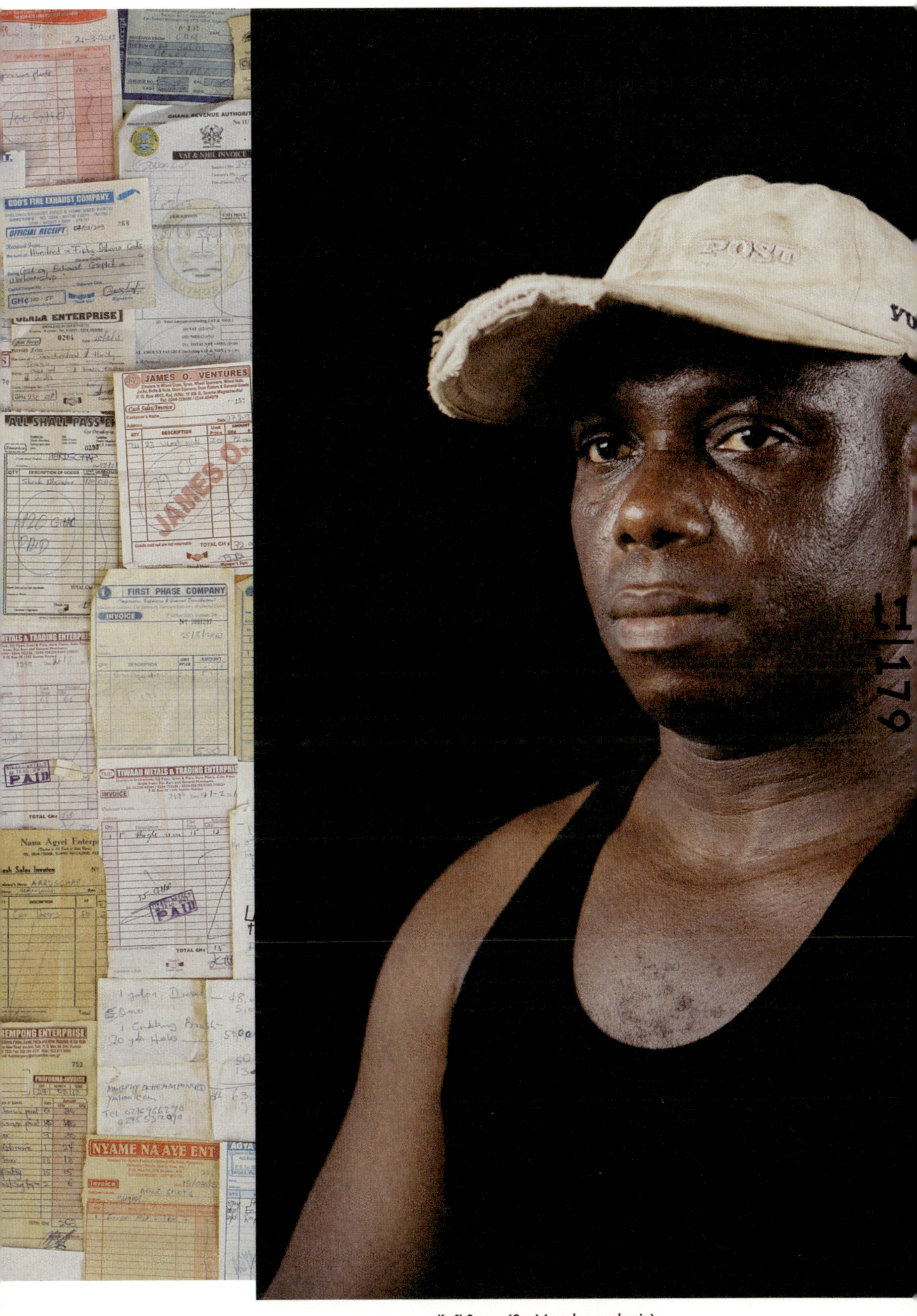

Kofi Owusu (Osu) (master mechanic)

180 | t1

Suame is an oasis of peace on Sunday – the perfect time to get behind the wheel ourselves.

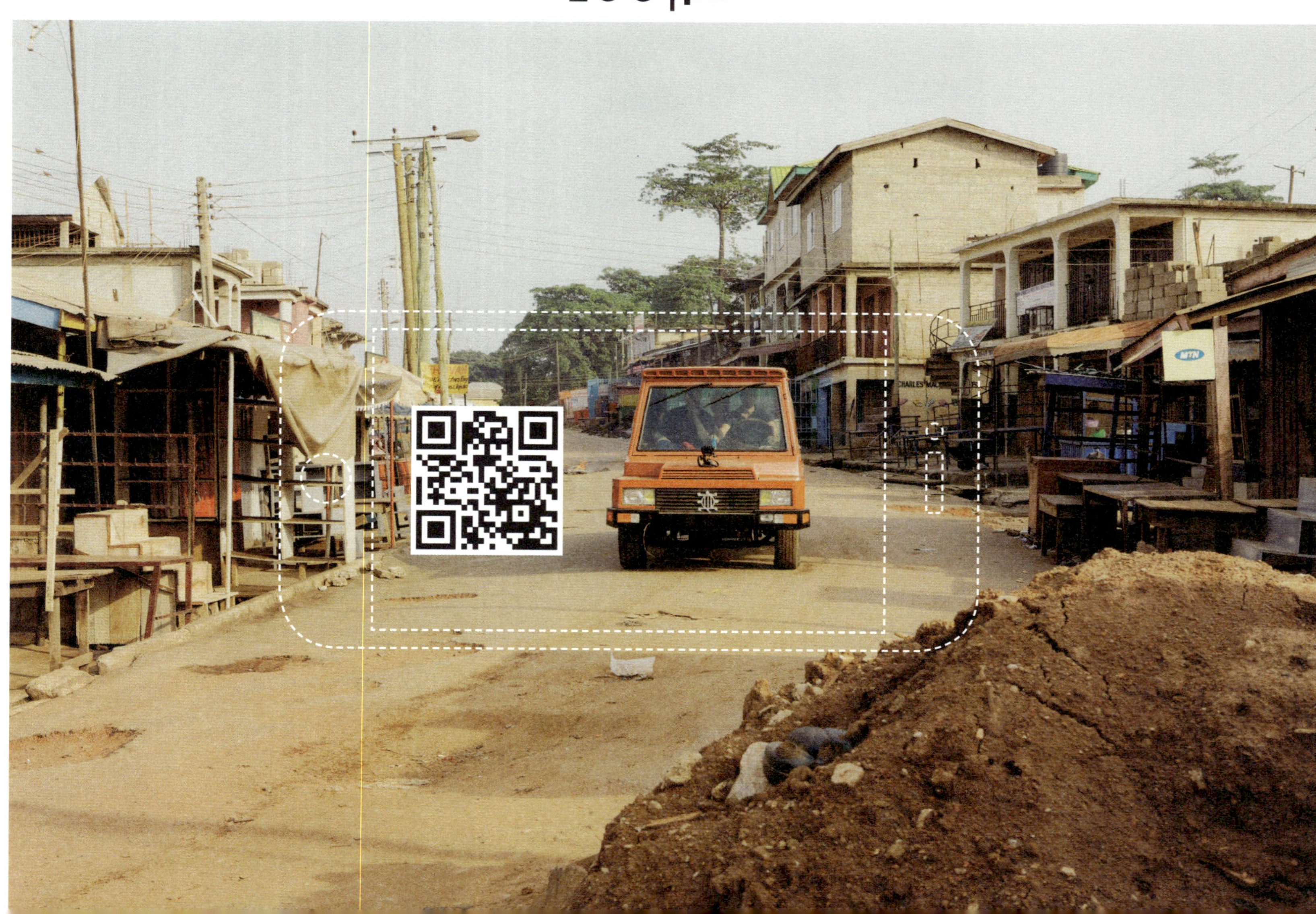

L: 10 April 2013, King Otumfuo Osei Tutu II breaks protocol and emerges from the palace to test the Turtle 1.

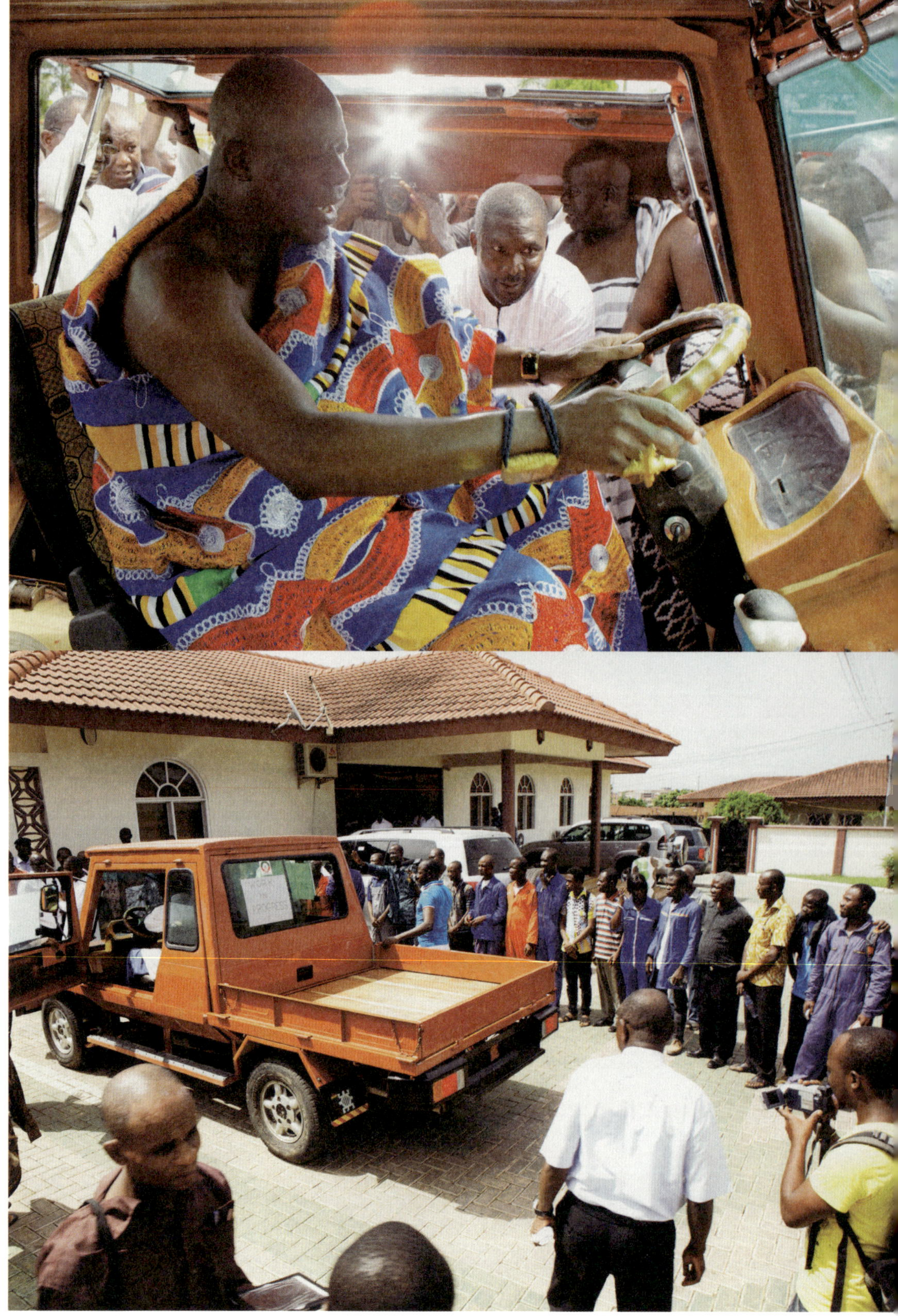

GH // 04.2013
GH // 04.2013

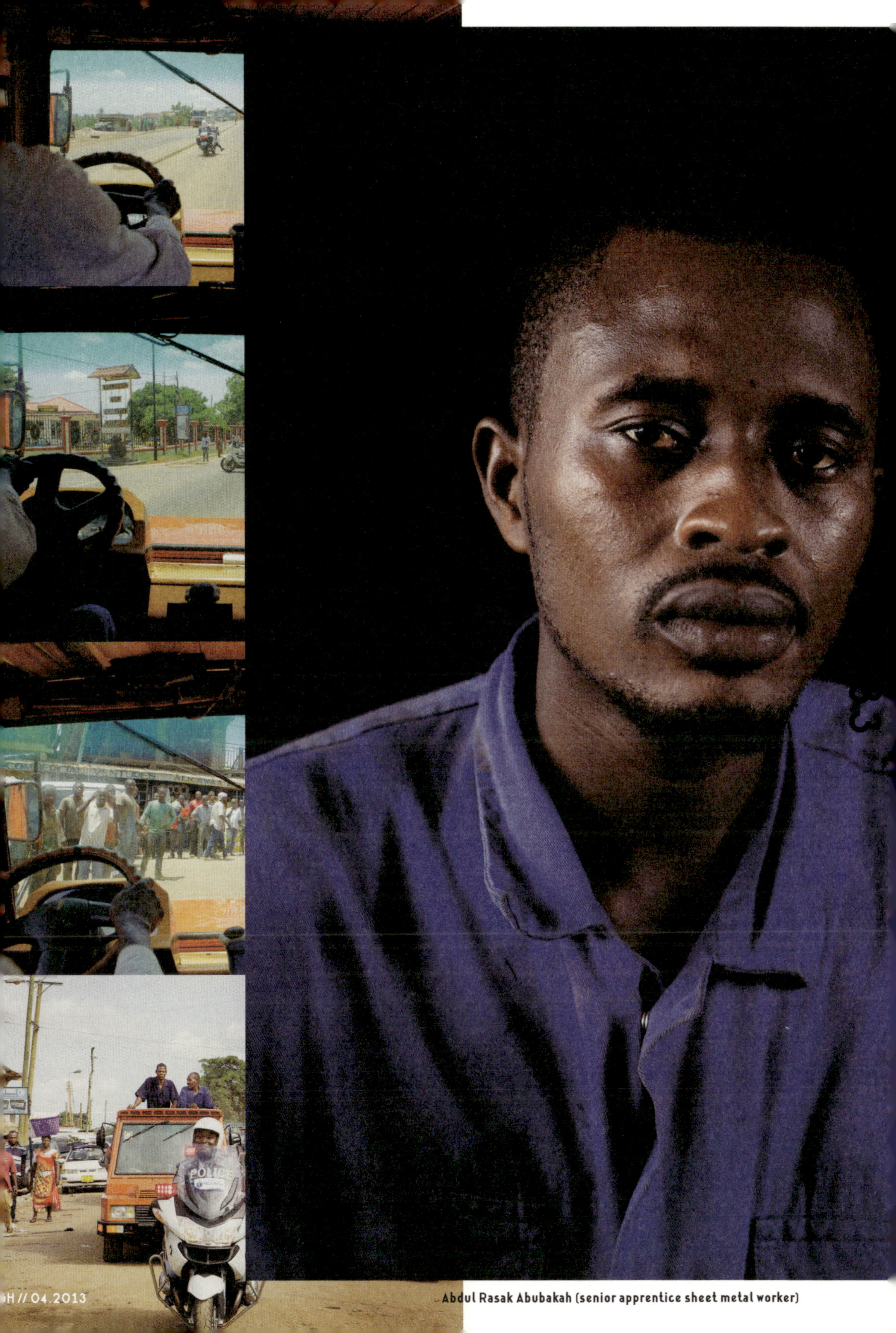

Abdul Rasak Abubakah (senior apprentice sheet metal worker)

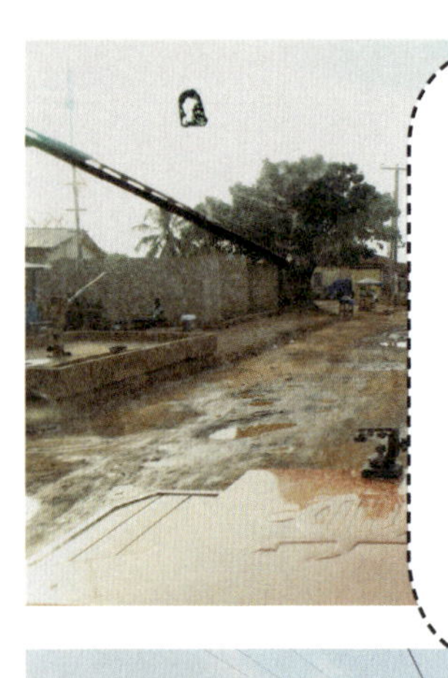

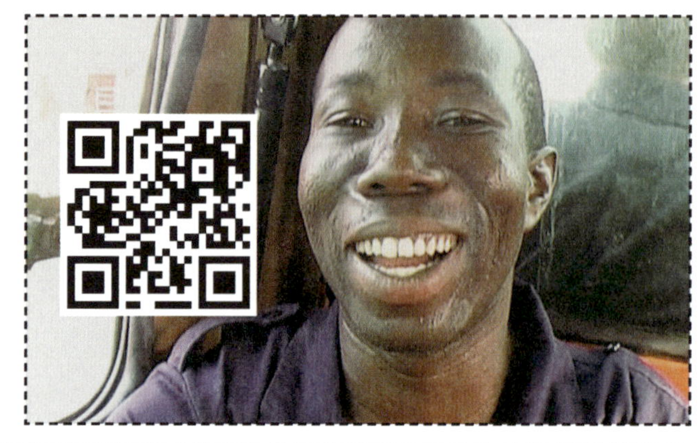

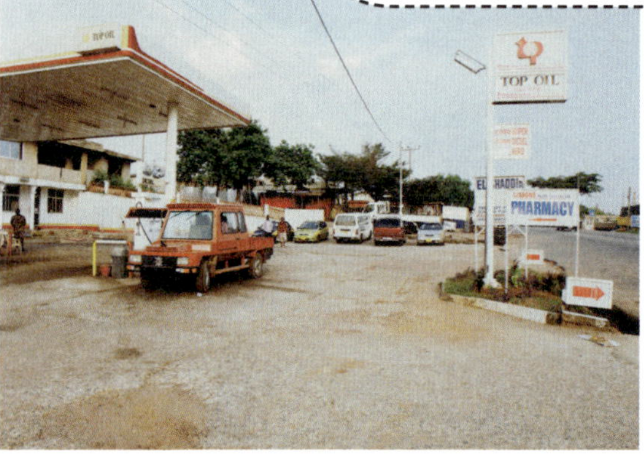
TOP OIL
PHARMACY

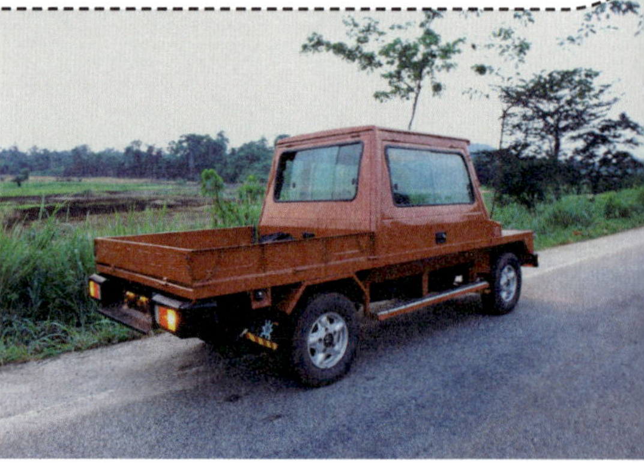

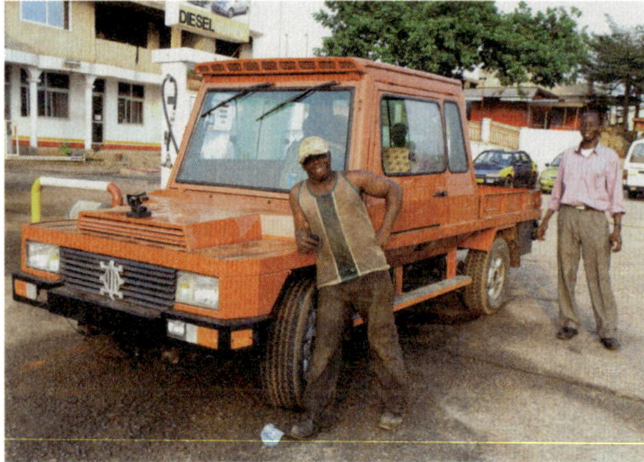
DIESEL

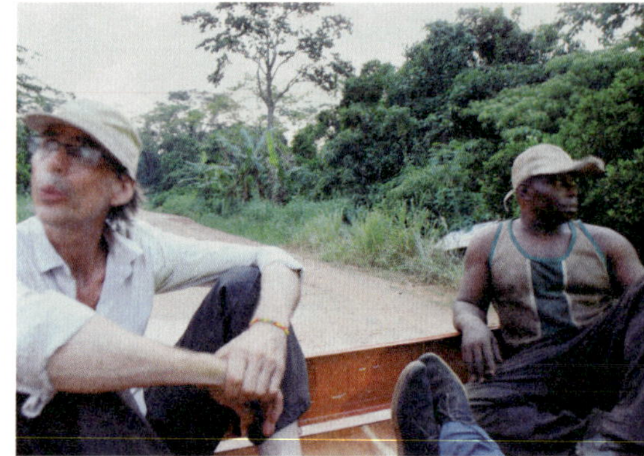

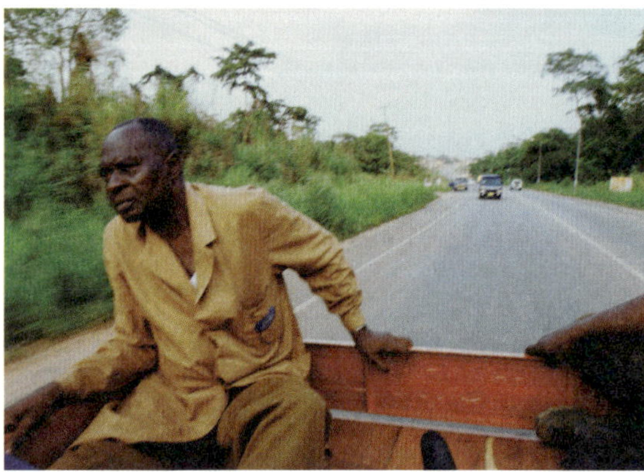

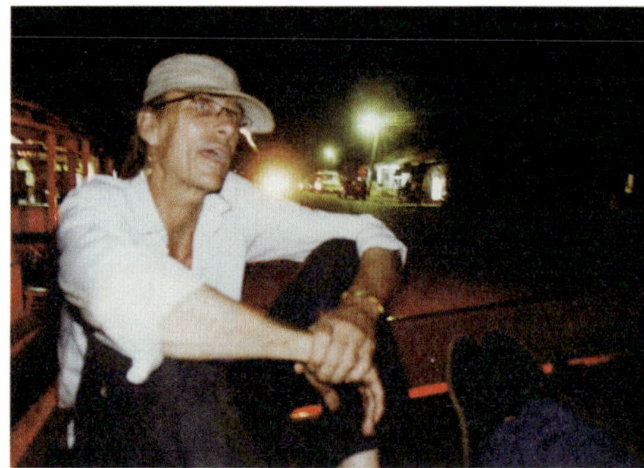

Daily Graphic

FRIDAY, APRIL 12, 2013

Suame artisans manufacture vehicle

Story: **Kwame Asare Boadu, Kumasi**

THE prototype of a vehicle built by artisans of Suame Magazine, in collaboration with their Dutch partners, Aardschap Foundation, will be displayed at an international exhibition in the Netherlands in May, 2013.

The exhibition, which is an initiative of the Dutch partners and would be covered by the international media, is to court international investor interest for the commercial production of the vehicle.

Named "Smati Turtle1", the vehicle was the outcome of years of systematic planning by the Suame Magazine Industrial Development Organisation (SMIDO), an umbrella non-governmental organisation and development institution for Suame Magazine.

SMATI is the acronym for Suame Magazine Automatics Technical Institute, an institutional engineering training concept for the artisanal engineering industry being pioneered by SMIDO.

The 'Turtle' is a robust reptile and an amphibian, which symbolises strength and the ability to withstand the African terrain.

SMIDO said the vehicle had some features of the old 'Boafo' vehicle, which was developed at the Suame Magazine in the 1970s.

According to SMIDO, the feat achieved by the artisans in producing the Boafo vehicle actually inspired the organisation and Aardschap Foundation to embark on the venture to produce the new vehicle.

On Wednesday, April 10, officials of SMIDO and the German partners presented the vehicle to the Asantehene, Otumfuo Osei Tutu II, for inspection at the Manhyia Palace.

The vehicle would be formally presented to the Ashanti Regional Minister, Mr Eric Opoku, for his inspection before a test drive to Accra for subsequent presentation to the Netherlands Ambassador to Ghana after which it would be shipped to Netherlands for international exhibition

Otumfuo Osei Tutu, who sat in the vehicle to experience the way it works, highly commended SMIDO for showcasing the engineering ingenuity of Suame Magazine, and called for a renewed national interest and support to develop Suame Magazine as a major national asset.

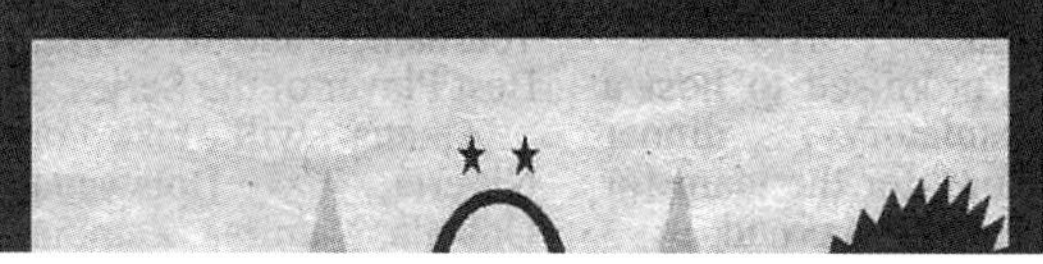

OTUMFUO's TOUR OF SUAME MAGAZINE PROGRAMME

Date: Wednesday, 17th April, 2013 *Event Venue: ITTU-Magazine*

Arrival @ITTU

SMIDO office

Babasika Mohamed Engineering-0244460904

Muntari Engineering

ABUDIA FOUNDRY LTD

Obeng Engineering-0244750990

Kankam Welding & Frication

OWUSU & SONS TANKER BUILDERS

Kwaku Dua Egineering

Kwame Asare Engineering

BACK TO ITTU

King Otumfuo Osei Tutu II's visit follows a carefully planned route that passes by all the important parties in Suame Magazine. We receive the programme pictured on the right. The real programme (left) leaves out the times and order of events.

OTUMFUO's TOUR OF SUAME MAGAZINE PROGRAMME

Date: Wednesday, 17th April, 2013

Event Venue: ITTU-Magazine

9.00 a.m	SPECIAL GUESTS AND ARTISAN LEADERS SEATED	
10:00 a.m	Arrival of Asantehene at the ITTU Grounds	Sarpong Boateng
10:30 a.m	Brief welcome, Introduction and Recap of programme	Sarpong Boateng
11.00am-1.00pm	Tour of Suame Magazine	Led by Executives
1.30 p.m	Inspection and Inauguration of SMATI Turtle at the ITTU-Suame Magazine	Dutch-Ghanaian project Team
2.00 p.m	Address /presentation of 50 copies of 'BUILDING prospects for posterity, the Economic Fate of Kumasi & Ashanti'.	president of SMIDO/Assisted by Consultant/Leaders of Suame Magazine
2.20.p.m	Special Address by the Asantehene	Otumfuo Osei Tutu II
2.30.pm	Close of programme	MC

MC: .Sarpong Boateng, Chairman of Mechanical Association
Opening Prayers and Vote Of Thanks-Pastor Kusi Boadum

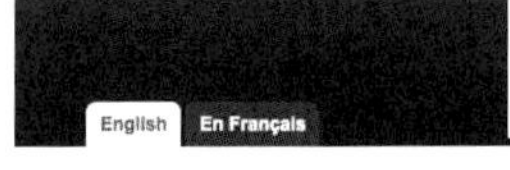

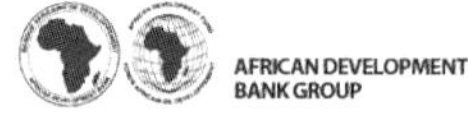

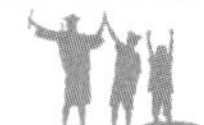

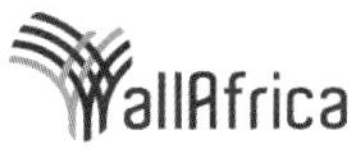

Ghana: Otumfuo Recommends Smido-Garages Collaboration

BY SEBASTIAN R. FREIKU, 19 APRIL 2013

Kumasi — OTUMFUO OSEI Tutu II, the Overlord of the Ashanti Kingdom, has called for collaborative efforts between the Ghana National Association of Garages (GNAG) and the Suame Magazine Industrial Development Organization (SMIDO) to further develop and promote the auto mechanical engineering industry in the Sub-Sahara Africa.

He said the proposed collaboration would be beneficial to the nation and the two bodies and their artisan members.

Otumfuo also called on the leadership of the two bodies to unite and ensure that their objective to make a positive impact in the artisanal engineering industry in the Sub-Saharan Africa and beyond is attained and sustained into the future.

The Ashanti King made the recommendation when he toured the Suame magazine on Wednesday during which he visited the headquarters of the Ghana National Association of Garages and SMIDO Secretariat in Kumasi.

The King's visit of the industrial hub was inspired by the manufacture of a prototype vehicle christened SMATI Turtle 1, built by local artisans in partnership with a Netherlands-based NGO, AARDSCHAP Foundation, using simple tools from a cluster of engineering workshops at the Suame Magazine, which he had the honour to inspect and test drive when it was presented to him last Week Wednesday at the Manhyia Palace.

Addressing artisans at the Suame Magazine industrial hub, the Asantehene commended them for their ingenuity and the great service being rendered to Mother Ghana as a result, and hoped master artisans would step up apprenticeship to impact their knowledge to JHS and SHS graduates, who for one or two reasons cannot further formal education.

He pledged his support for them assuring that he would always be at their beck and call. "Governments will come and go but I will be there for you as always", he said.

He called for a peaceful co-existence of the artisans who are into different auto mechanical engineering related areas and further advised them against acts of hooliganism and negative tendencies that impede the growth of their profession.

He reminded them of the fame Suame Magazine has gained in the whole wide world couple with the honour the hub has brought to Asante Kingdom, Ghana and the entire Black African continent and urged them to continue to look for ways of improving upon their capabilities in their respective fields.

1 2 › View All

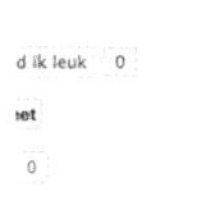

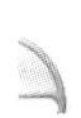

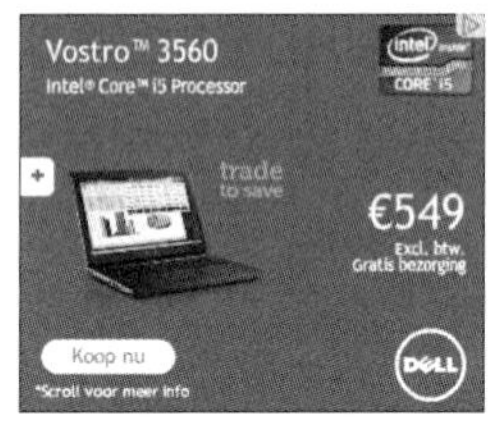

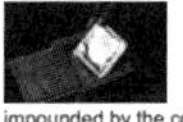

Ghana Seizes One Million Faulty Condoms
More than one Million condoms have been impounded by the country's Food ...

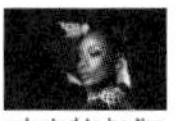

Ghanaian Star Efya to Perform in Kenya
Afro-eclectic songstress and actress Efya has been selected to be the ...

Ghanaian Musician Dedicates Song to Kenya
The reggae Maestro Rocky Dawuni will use a peace concert in Nairobi ...

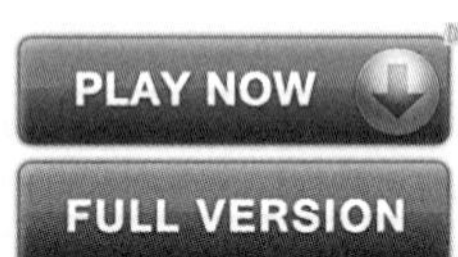

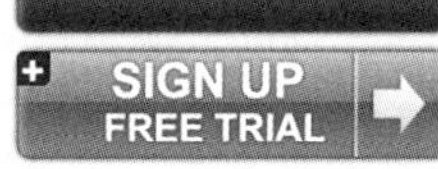

STORIES: Ghana »

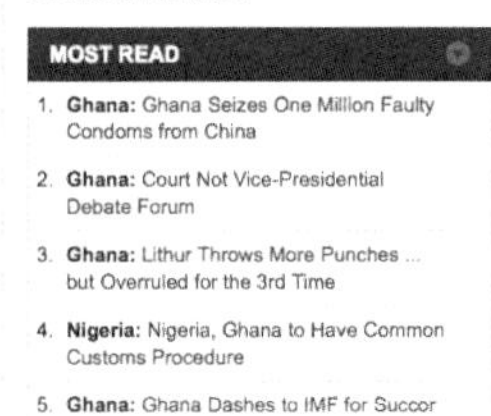

MOST READ

1. **Ghana:** Ghana Seizes One Million Faulty Condoms from China
2. **Ghana:** Court Not Vice-Presidential Debate Forum
3. **Ghana:** Lithur Throws More Punches ... but Overruled for the 3rd Time
4. **Nigeria:** Nigeria, Ghana to Have Common Customs Procedure
5. **Ghana:** Ghana Dashes to IMF for Succor
6. **West Africa:** Ecowas Parliament Seeks

After King Otumfuo Osei Tutu II calls for cooperation during his visit to Suame Magazine, a lively discussion ensues on Ghanaian blogs about the way forward.

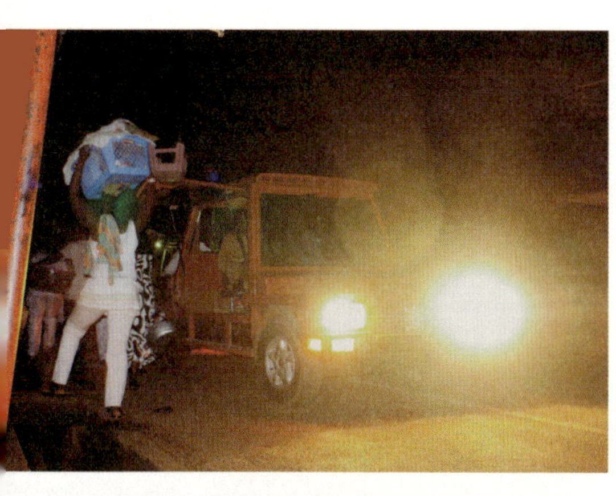

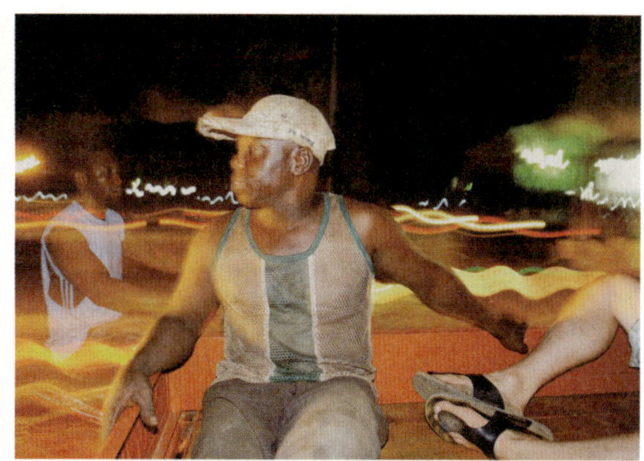

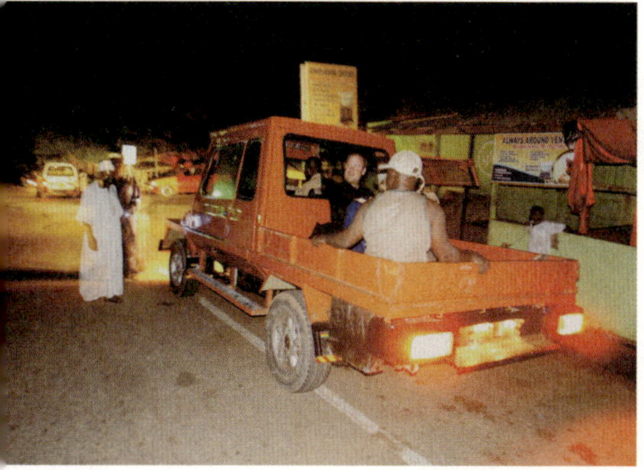

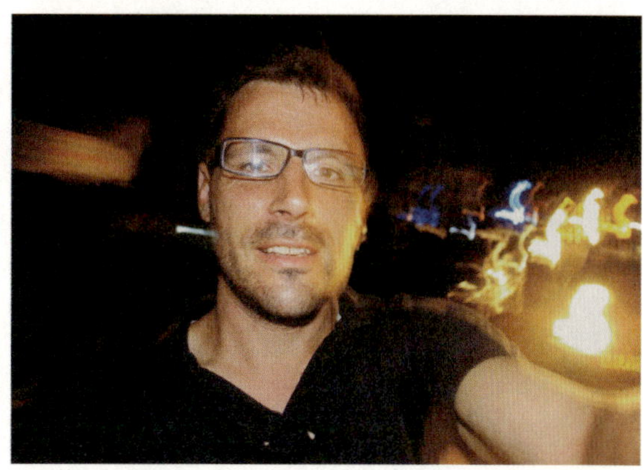

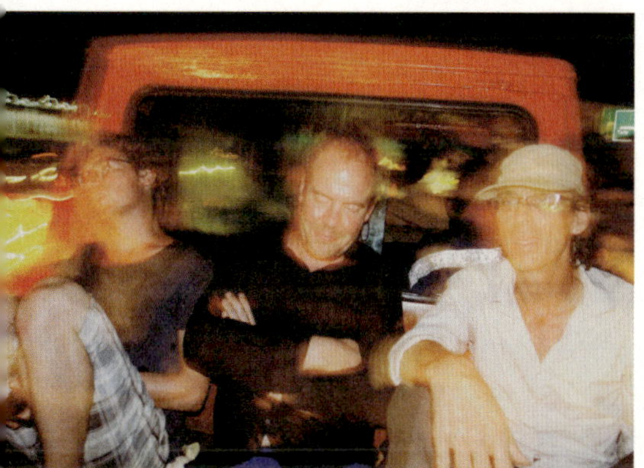

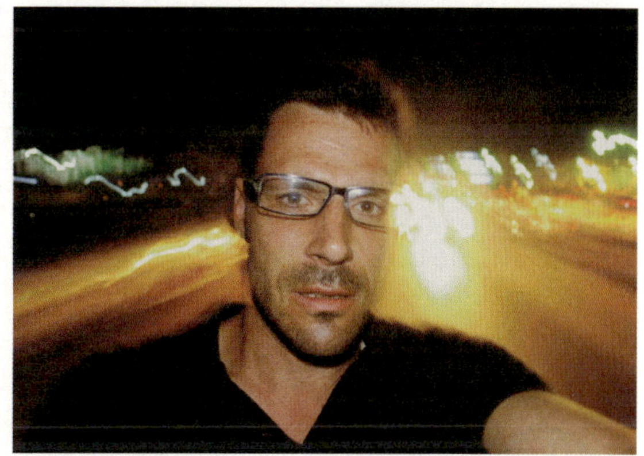

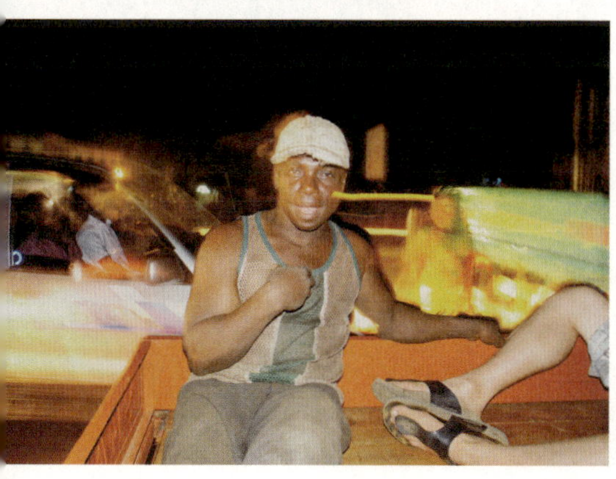

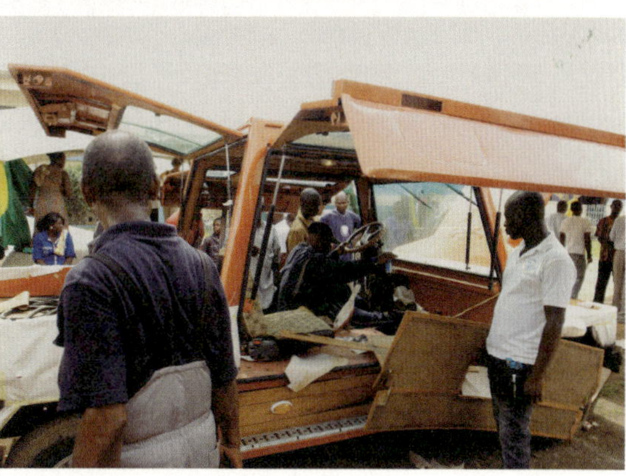

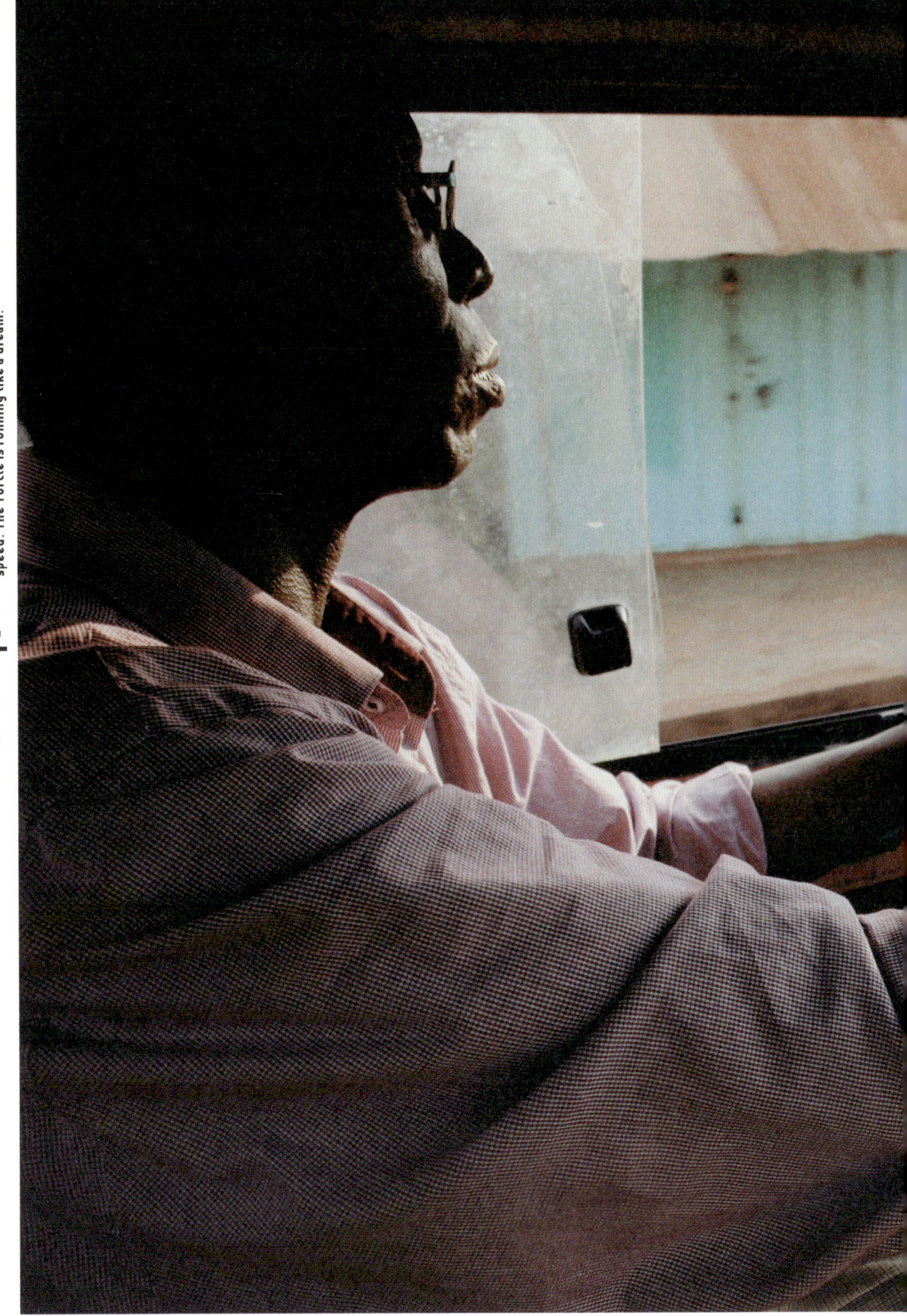

Fourth test drive, 14 April 2013. It is the first time that we drive out of town for a long test drive at high speed. The Turtle is running like a dream.

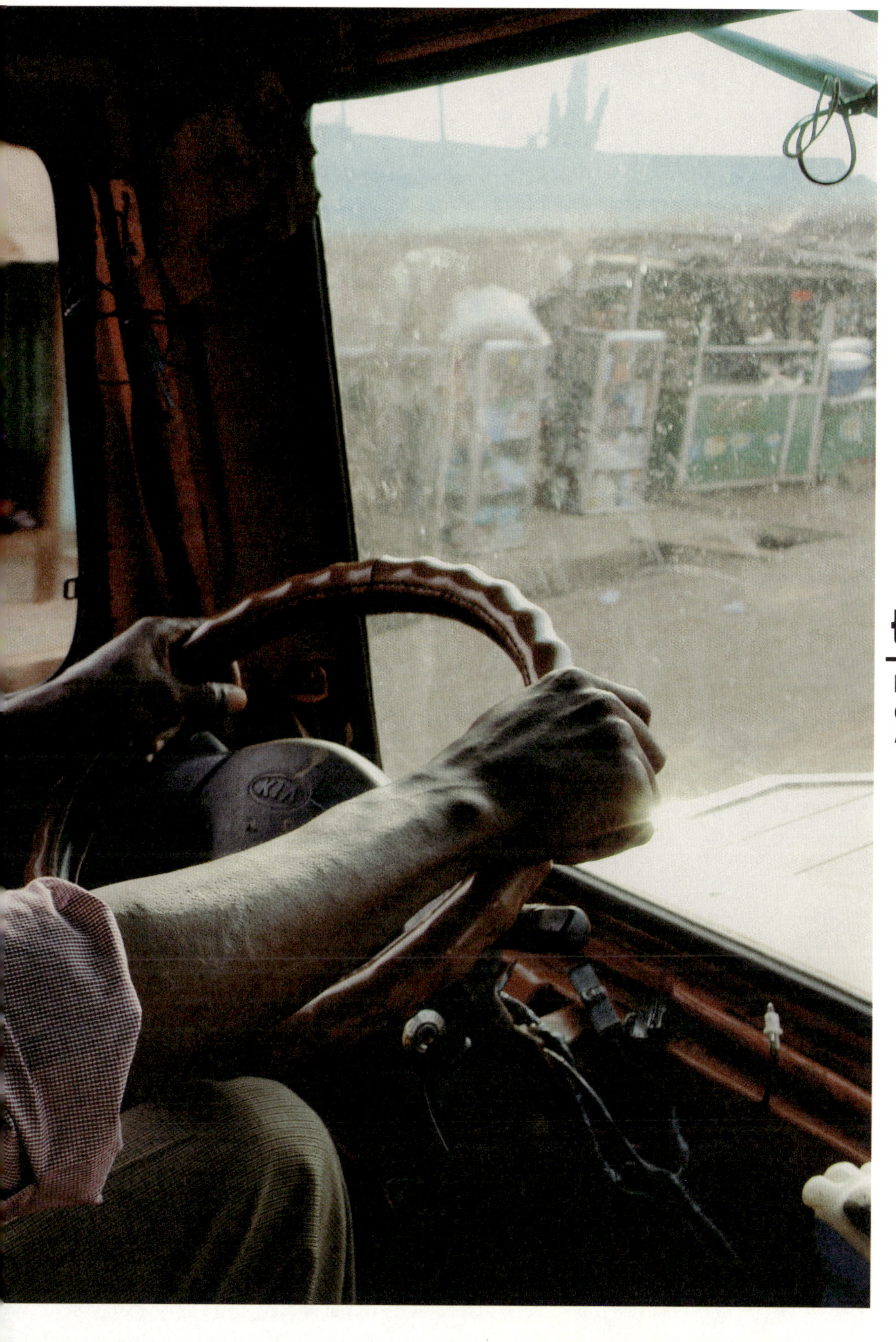
KIA

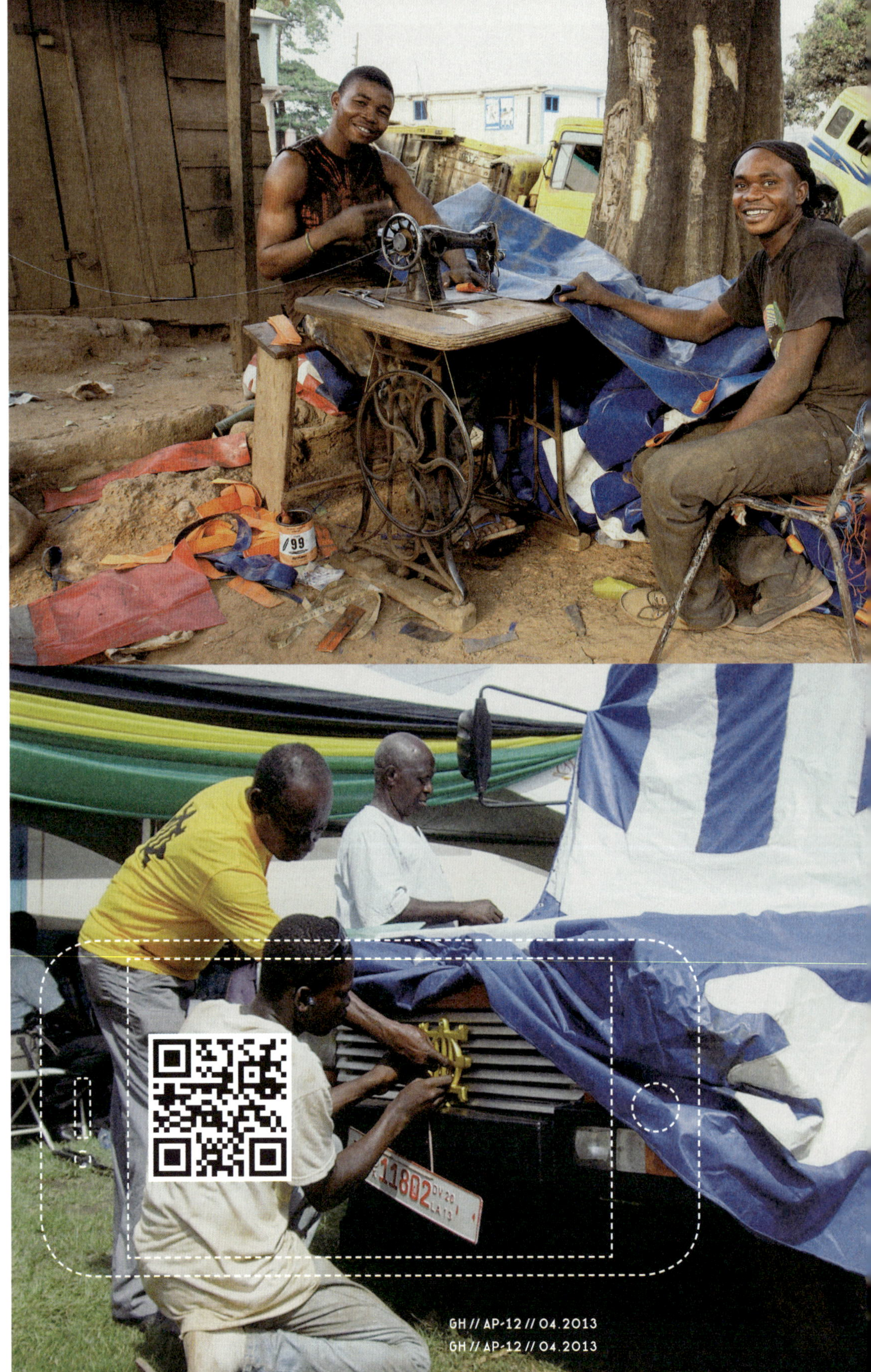

LT: Upholstery artisans make the covers of the Turtle 1.
LB: Mounting the golden Turtle logo just before the king's arrival.

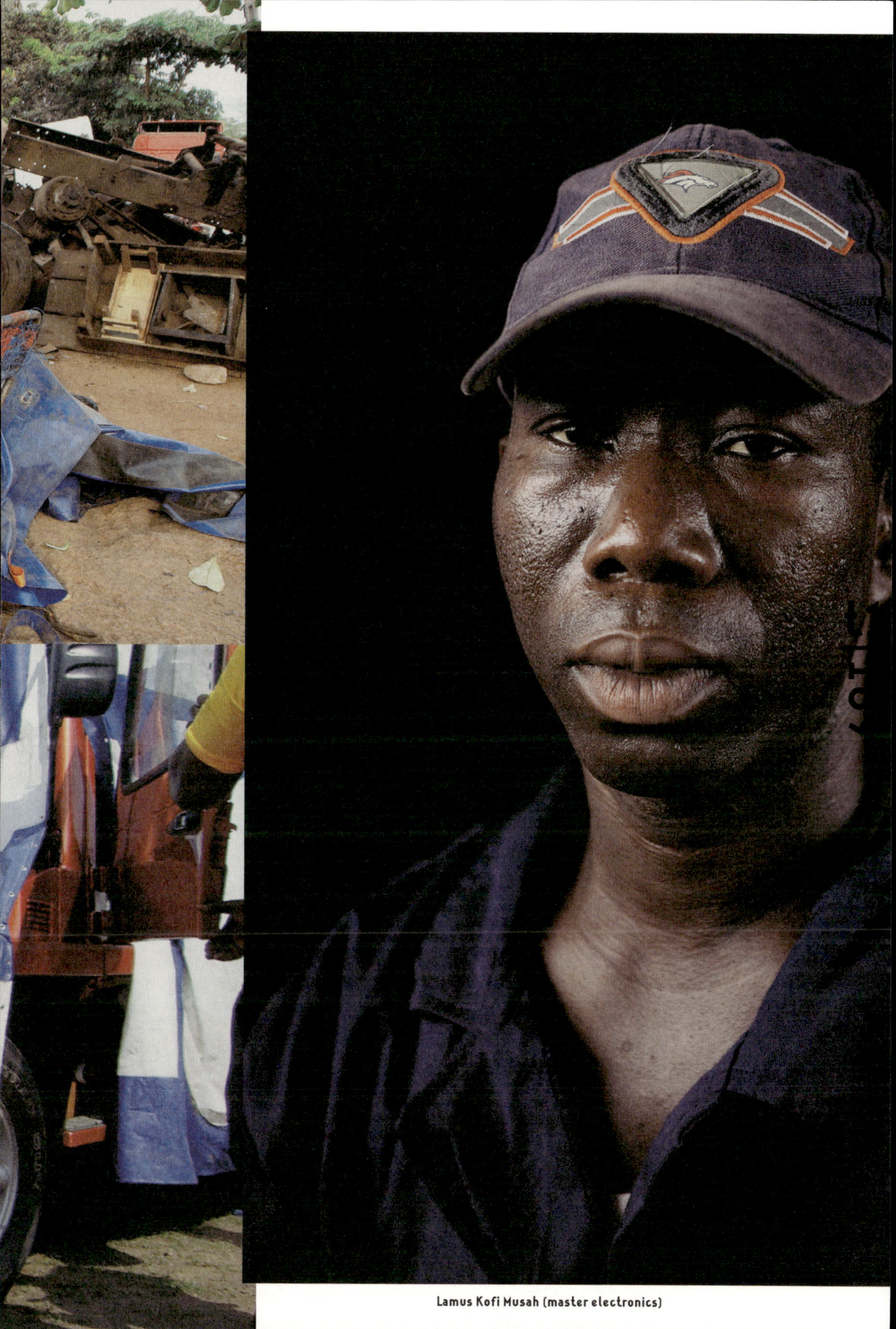

Lamus Kofi Musah (master electronics)

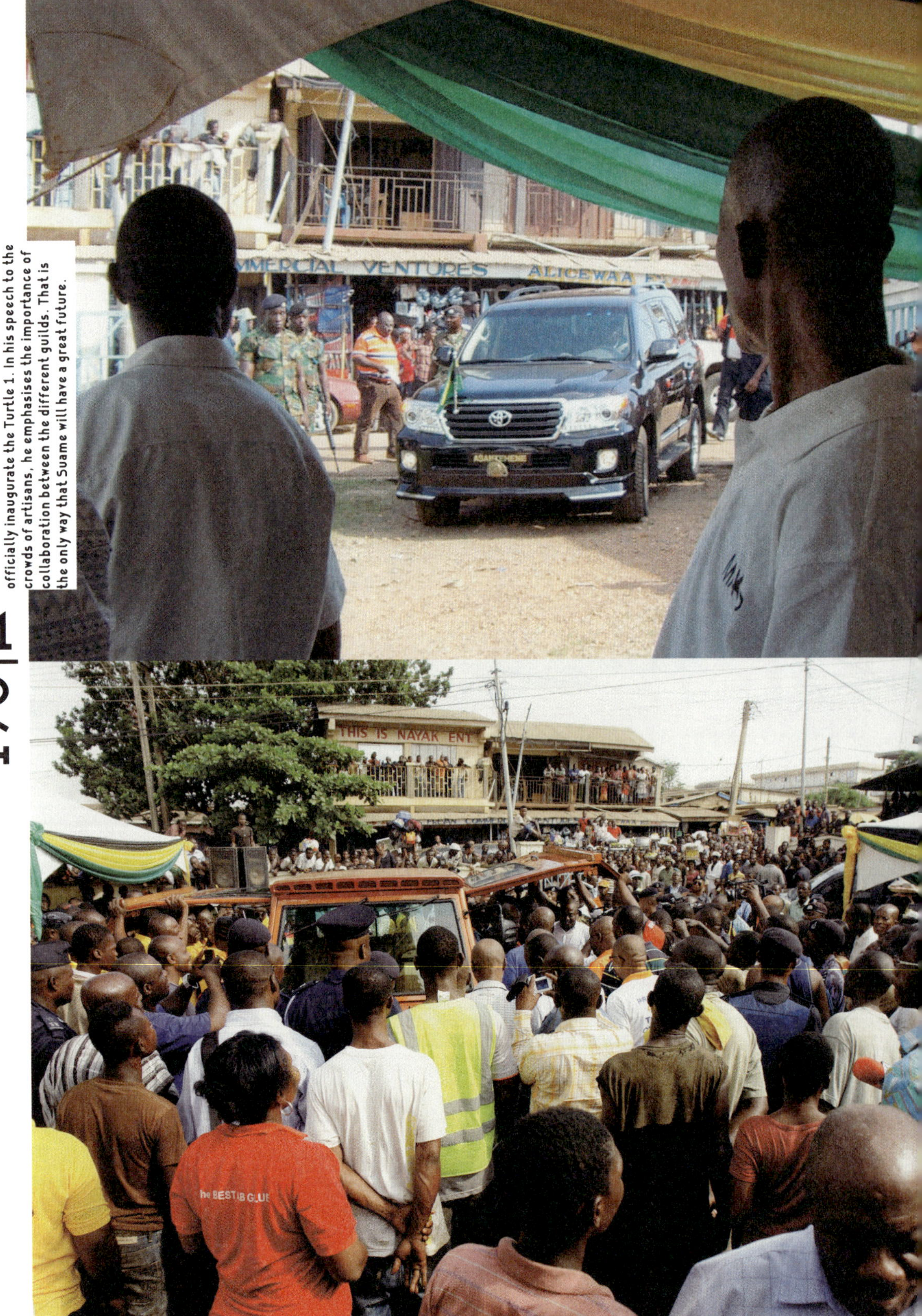

For the first time during his reign, King Otumfuo Osei Tutu II decides to visit Suame Magazine to officially inaugurate the Turtle 1. In his speech to the crowds of artisans, he emphasises the importance of collaboration between the different guilds. That is the only way that Suame will have a great future.

GH // AP-12 // 04.2013

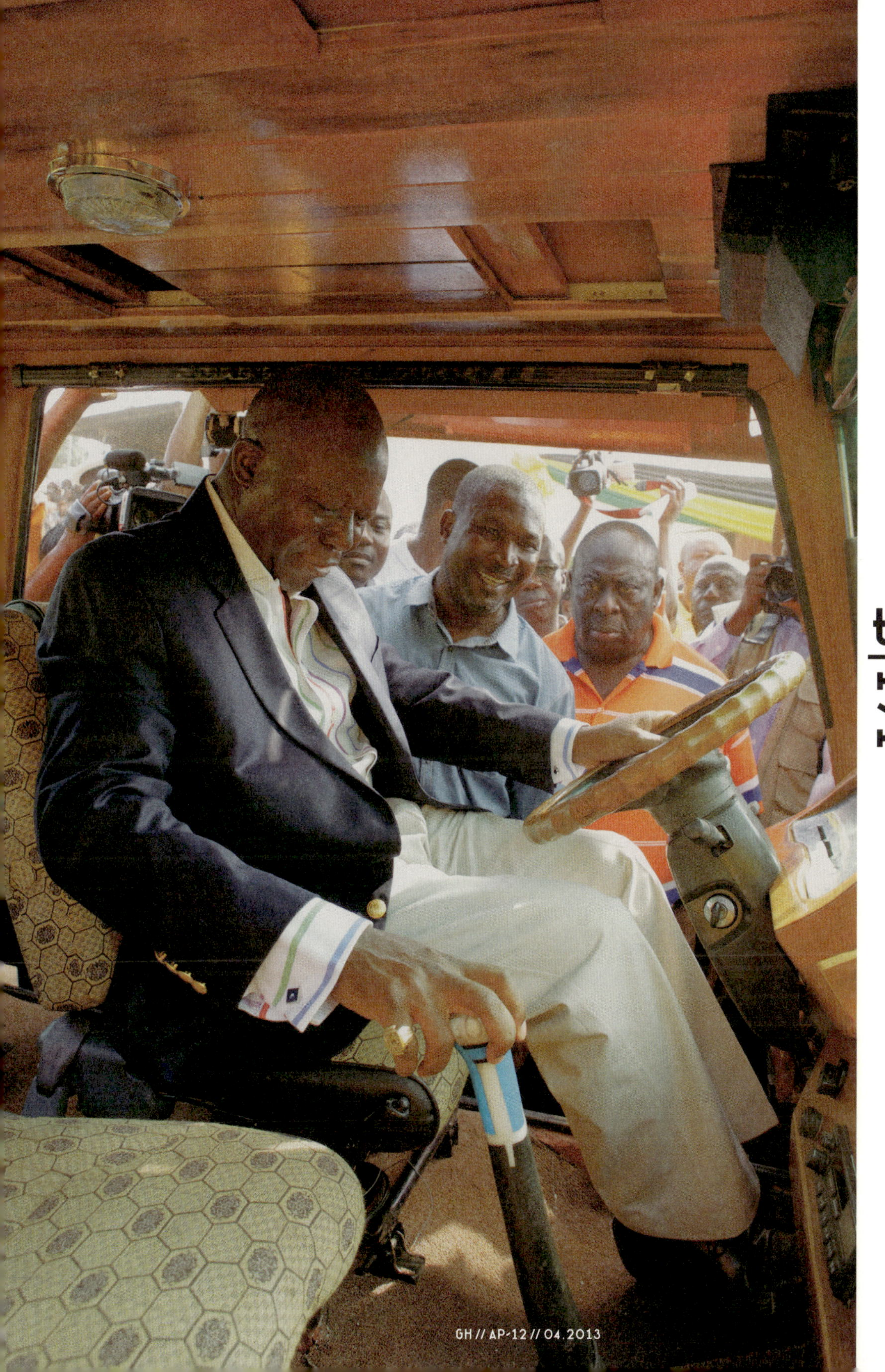
GH // AP-12 // 04.2013

We left Suame on the day that the king inaugurated the Turtle.
L: From left to right: (Top) Atta, unknown, Sulomon, Thomas, Debora, Abdul, Daniel, Melle, Shabu, Owusu, unknown, Sami. (Bottom) James, Atta, Francis, Jamal, Lamus, Adusei
R: From left to right: Atta, unknown, Ranford, Osu, mother of Ranford, Melle, unknown, Jef, Joost, Apiah, Aunt Vicky, unknown

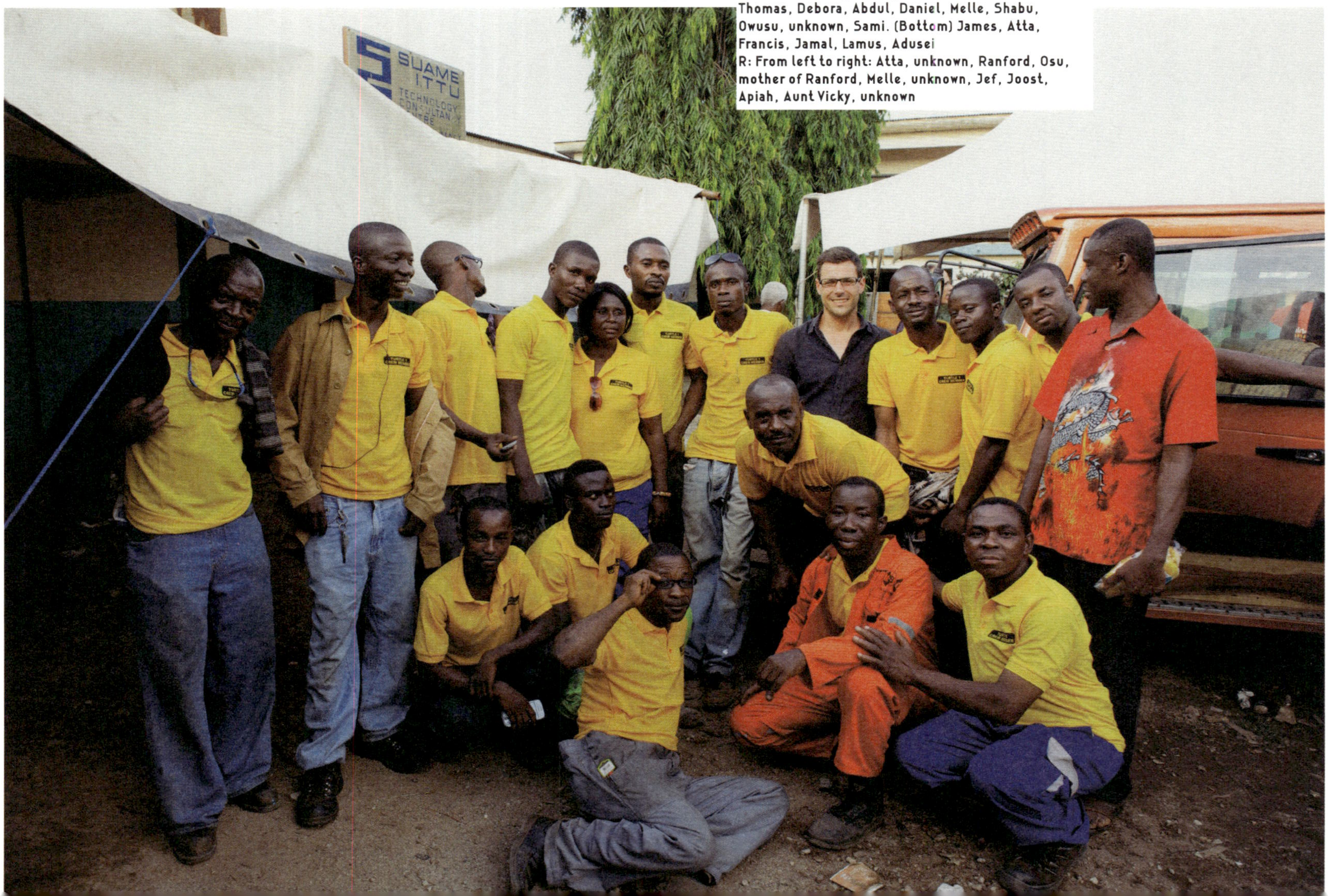

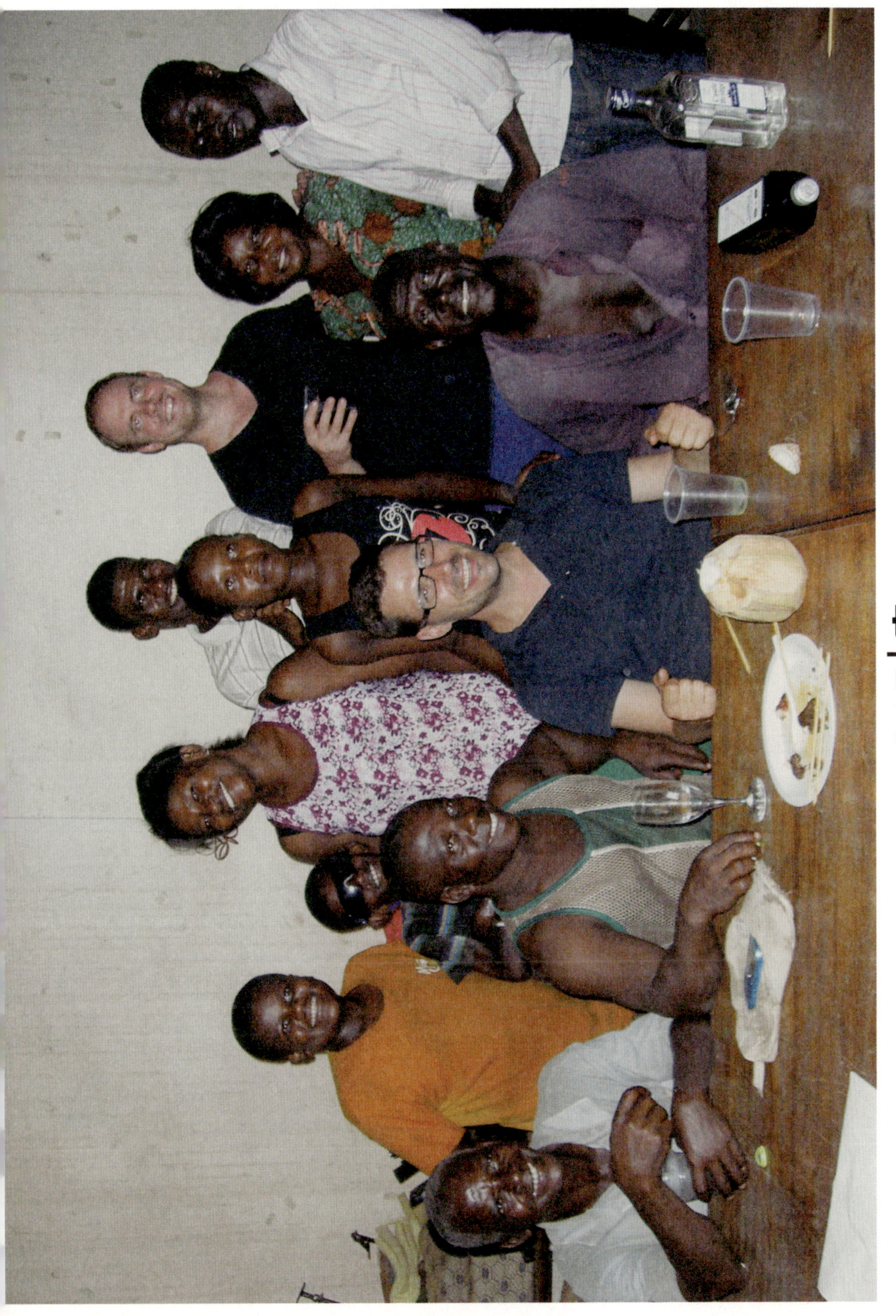

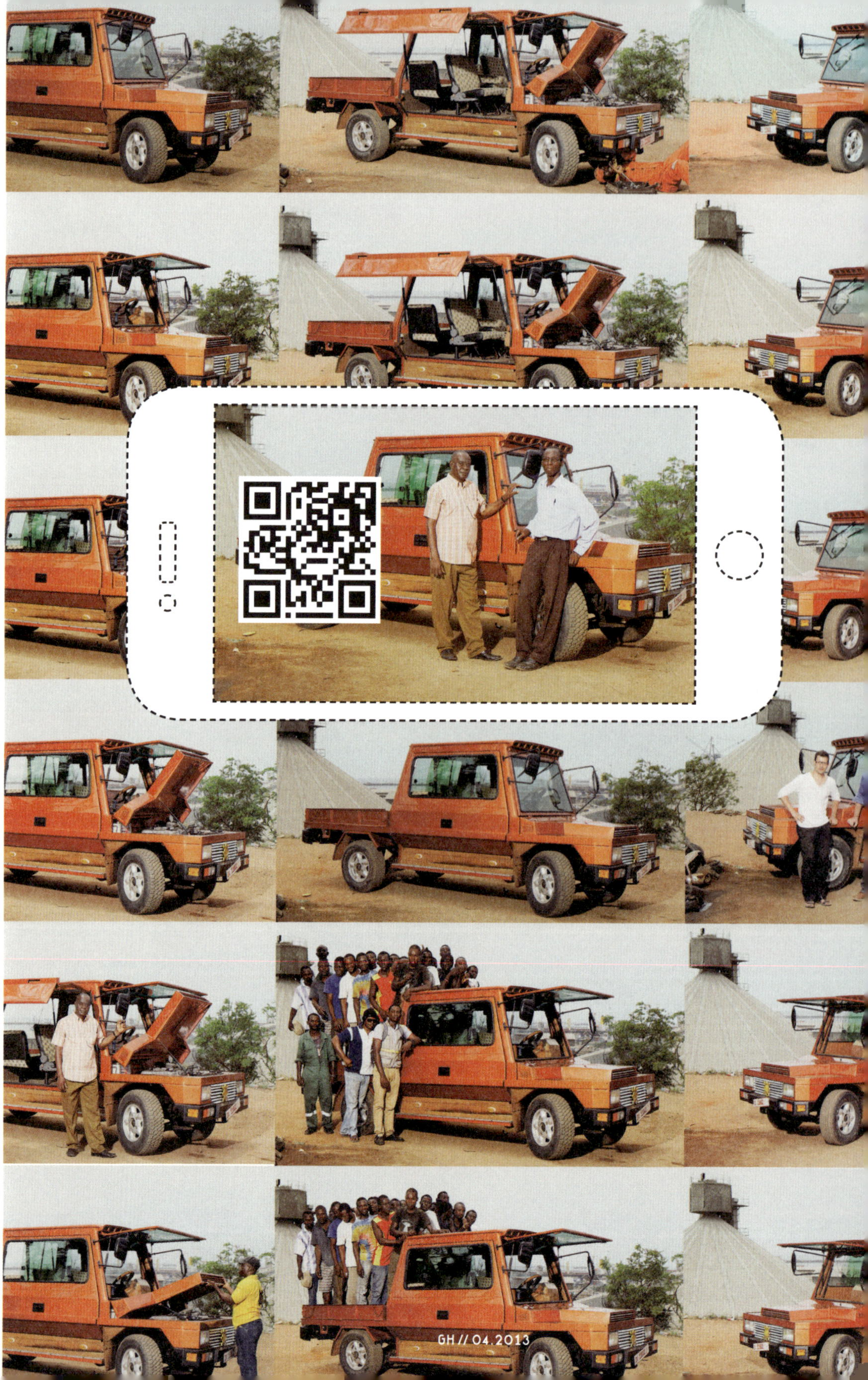

GH // 04.2013

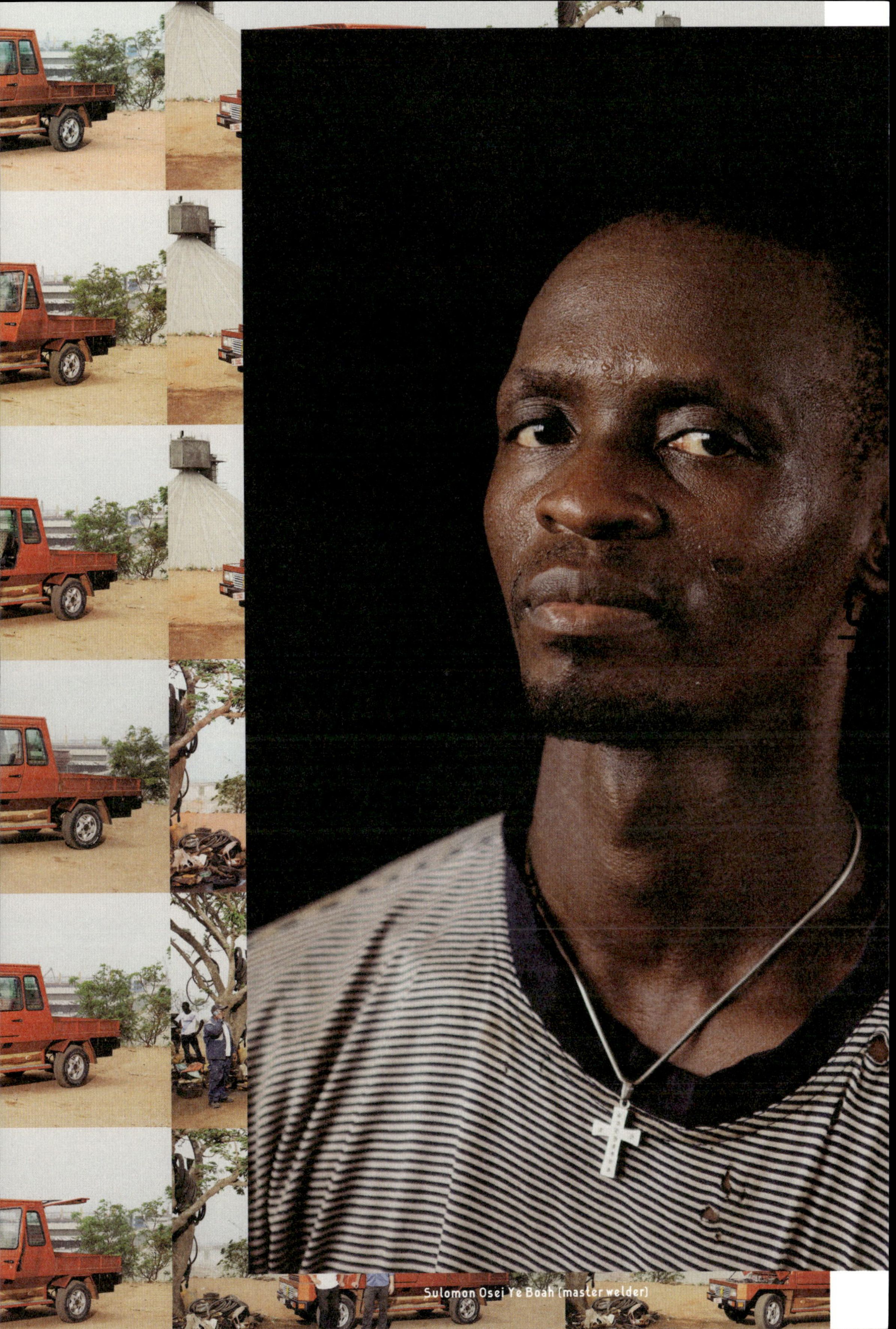

Sulomon Osei Ye Boah (master welder)

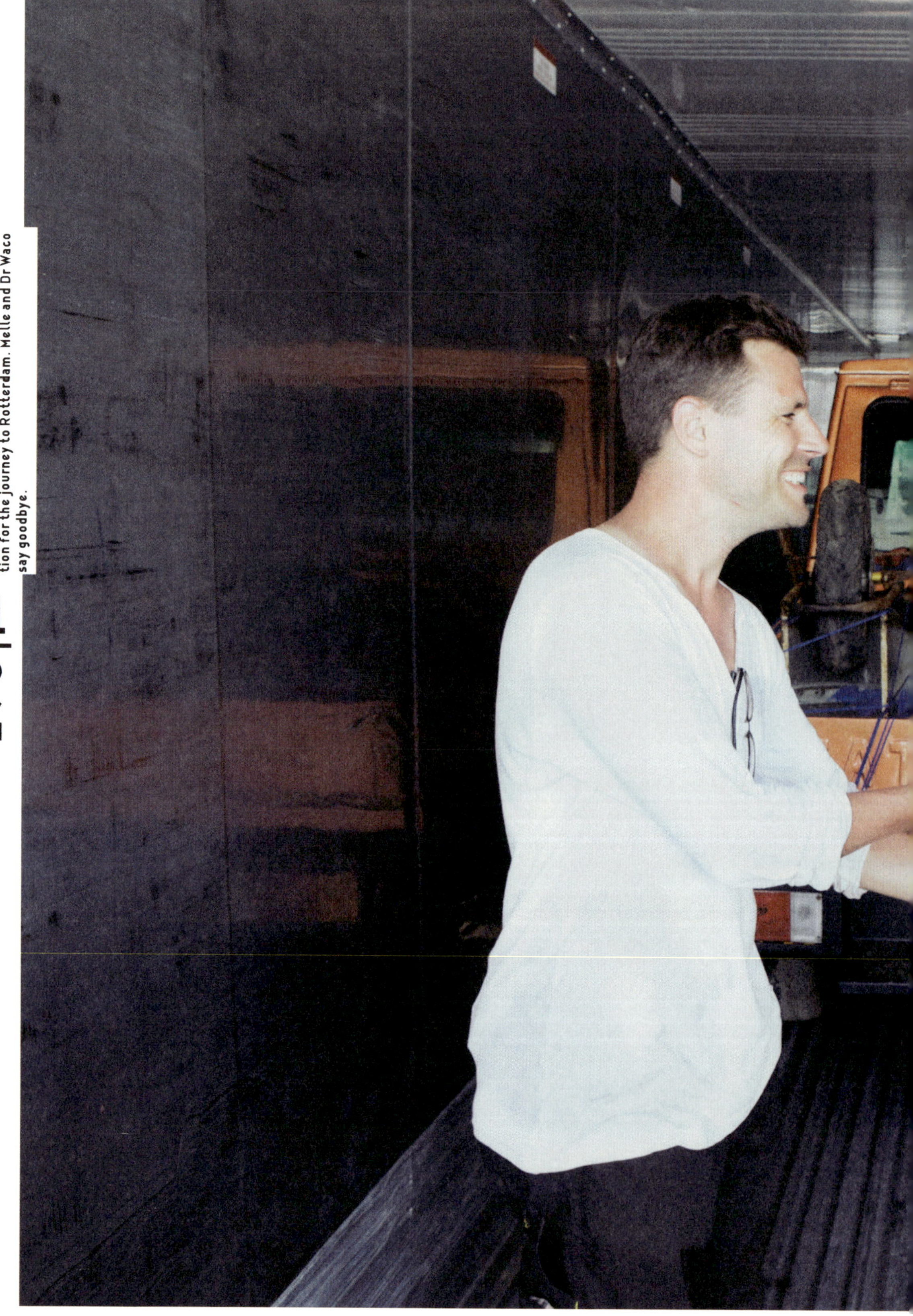

After the Ghanaian customs has cleared the Turtle, the car is strapped down in the container in preparation for the journey to Rotterdam. Melle and Dr Waco say goodbye.

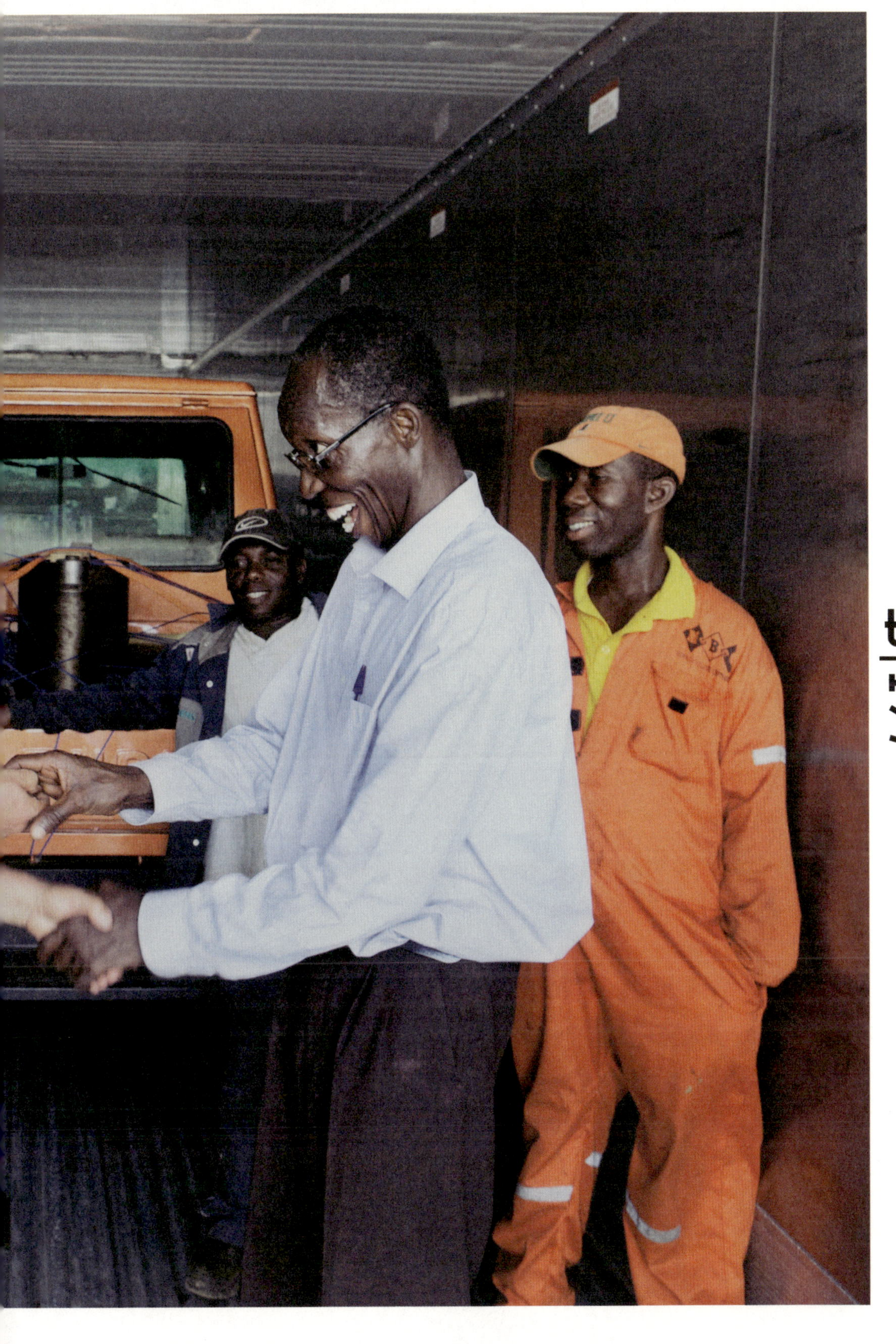

L: Dr. Waco in Kinderdijk, the Netherlands.

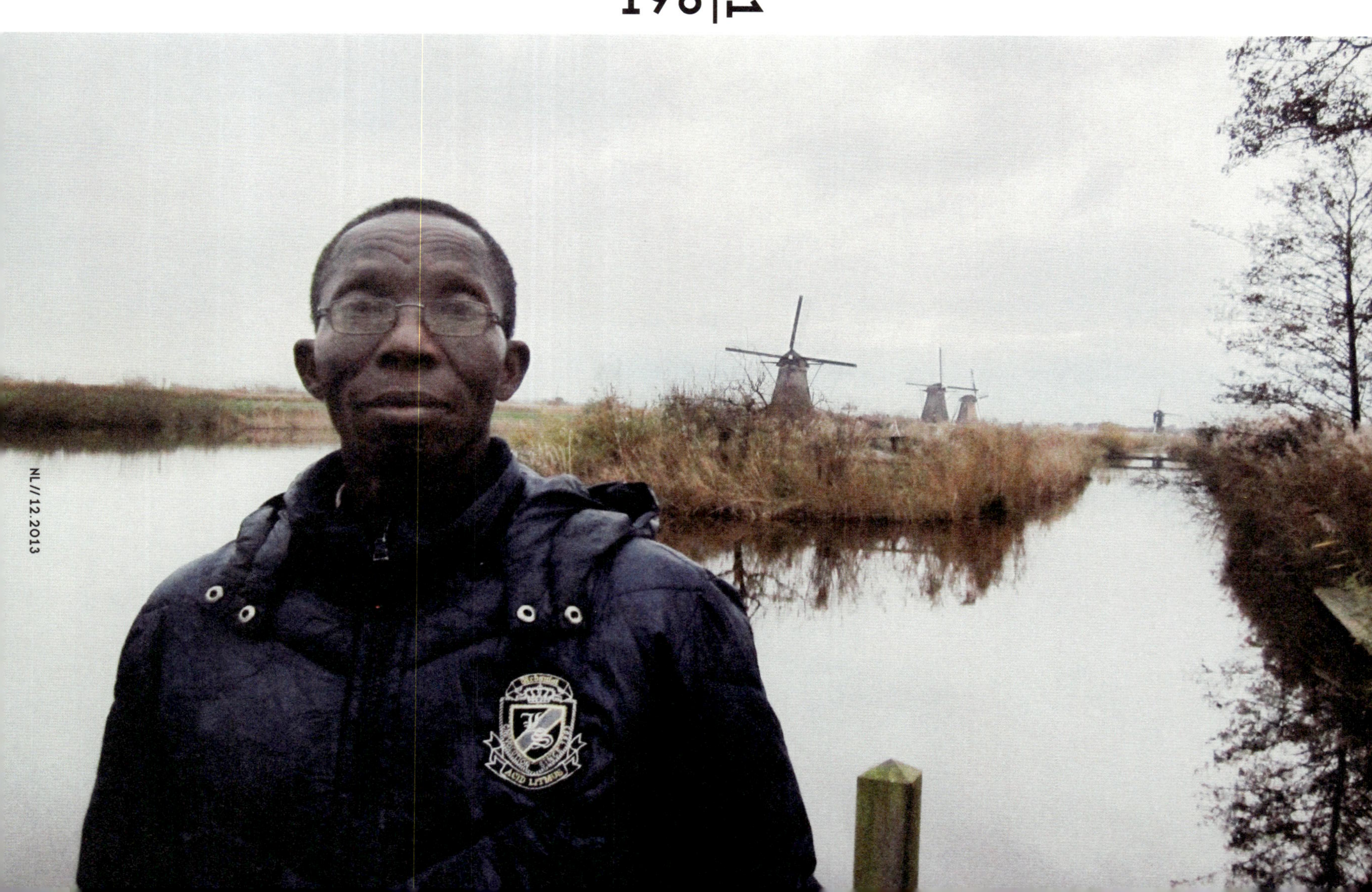

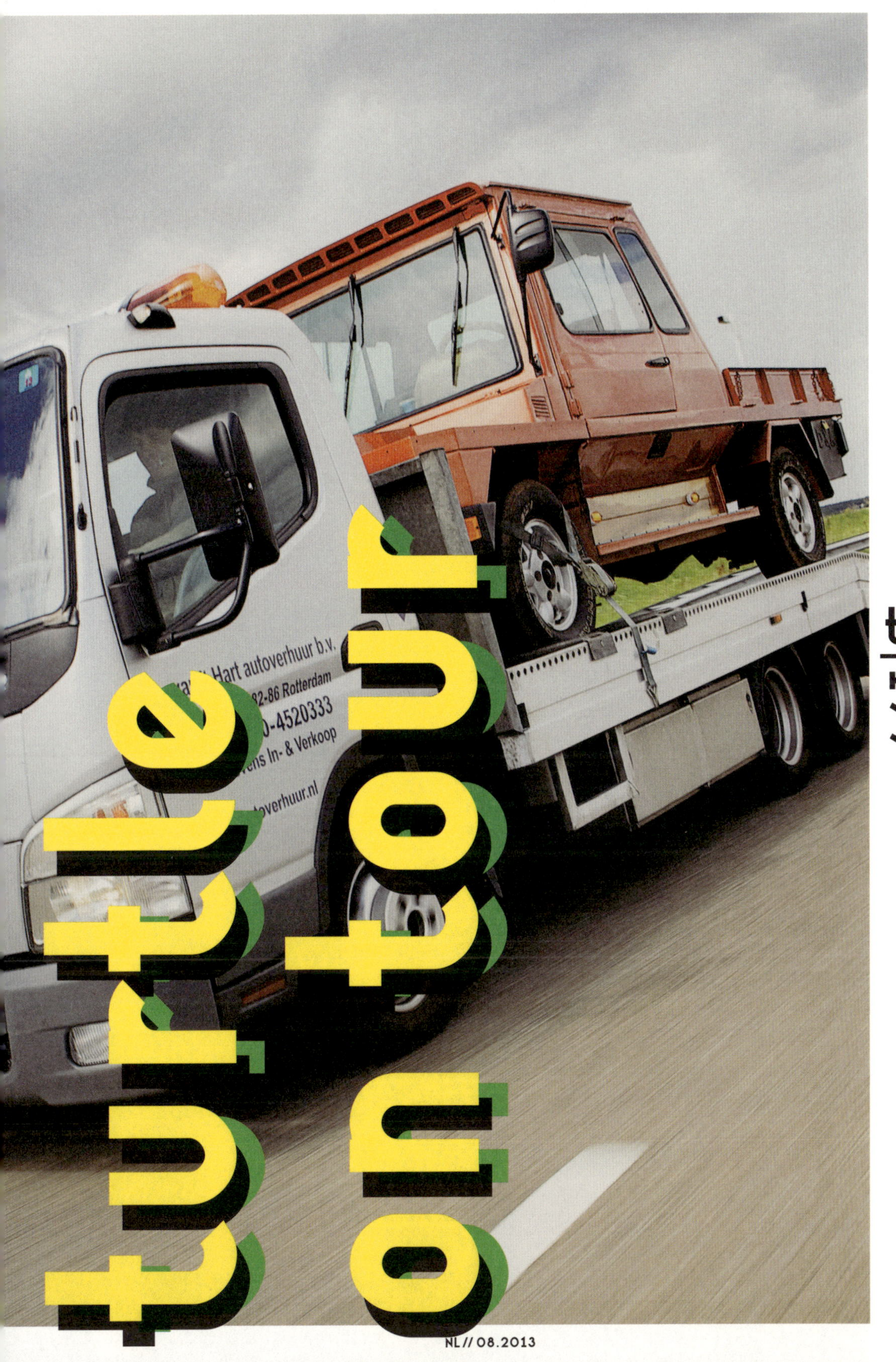

turtle
on tour
t1|199
NL// 08.2013

L: VOX Auto Mobil, the most popular tv car show in Germany, interview with Joost van Onna and Dr Waco about Turtle 1, 31 January, 2014
L: Pauw & Witteman, Dutch television show, interview Melle Smets 26 September 2013
R: A special Turtle-themed evening in Amsterdam's Paradiso presented by Marcia Luyten, 26 September 2013 (p 201)

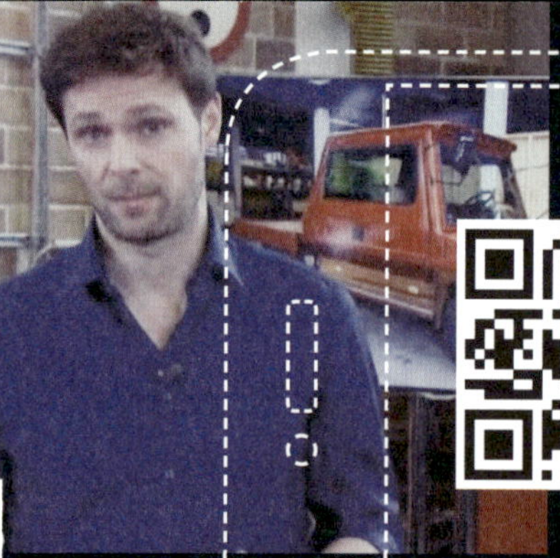

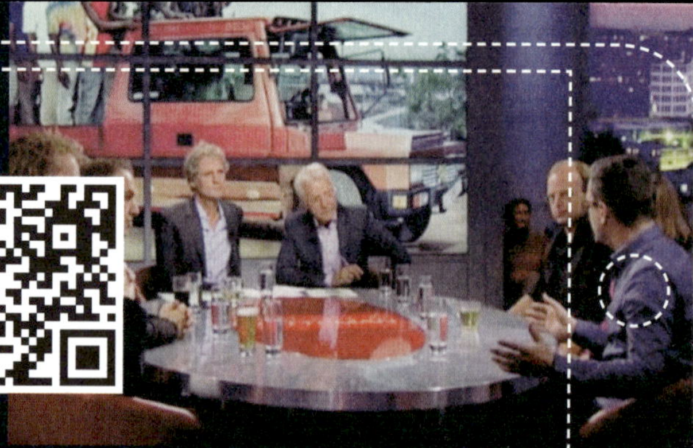

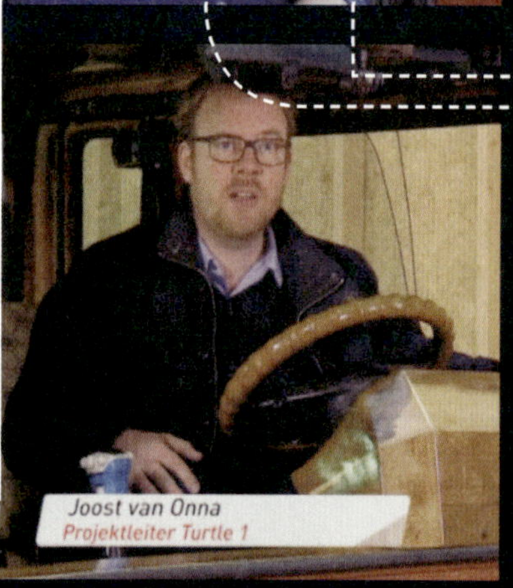

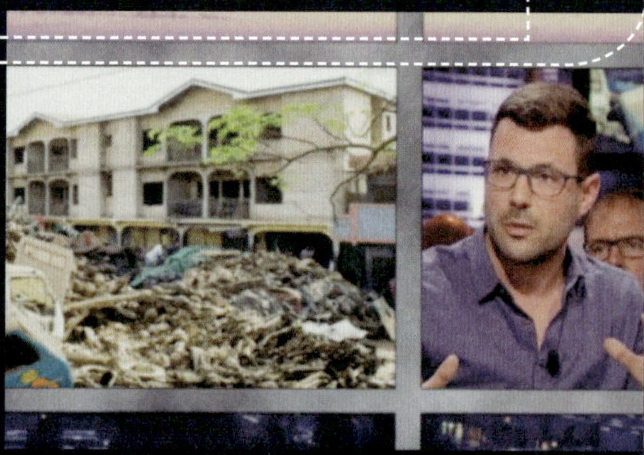

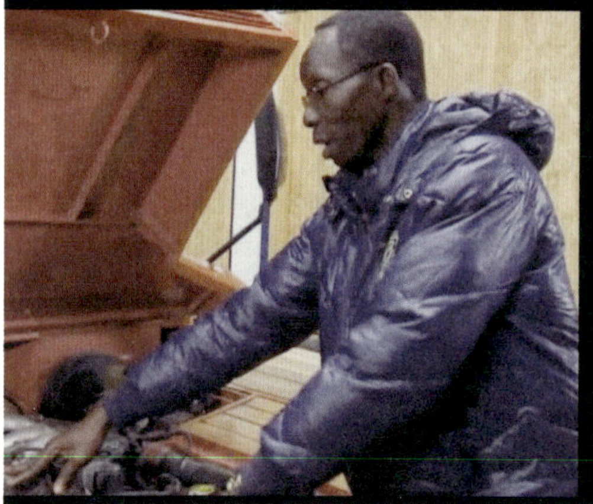

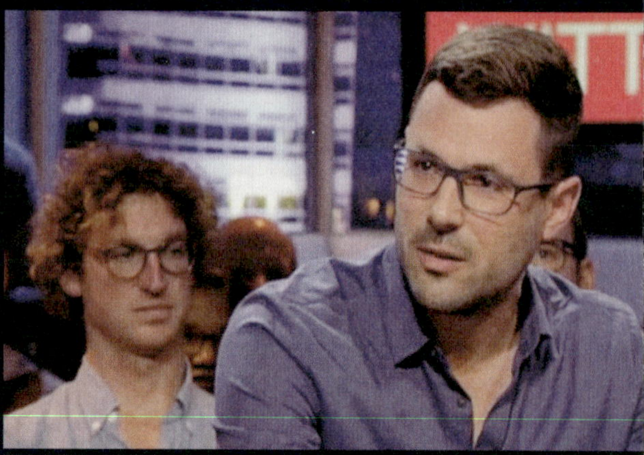

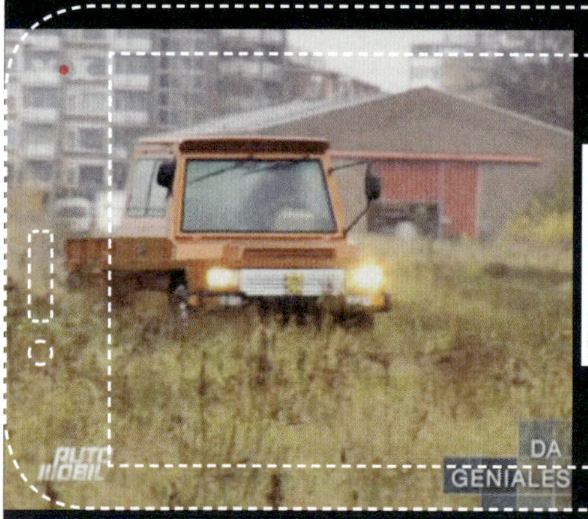

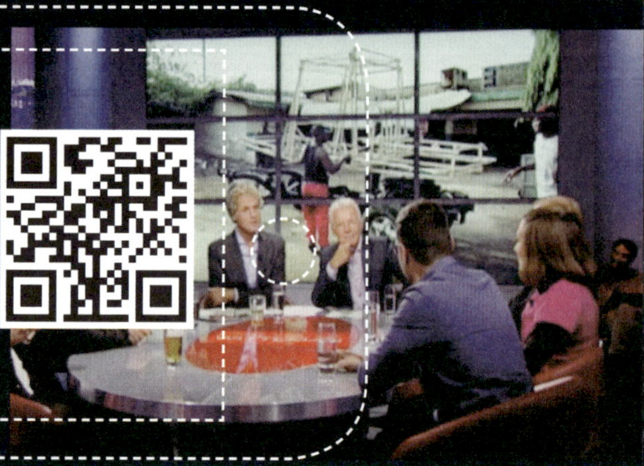

DE // 12.2013

NL // 09.2013

Strapped down in a container that is otherwise used to transport bananas, the Turtle got through the journey without any problems. But before we can take it onto the road, it has to be inspected by the Dutch Vehicle Authority (RDW) in Lelystad. A week after our visit to the RDW test centre, we anxiously read the test report. "We have serious questions about the vehicle's welding joints. We can imagine that user requirements in Africa are of a totally different order than here in the Netherlands and Europe. And we also understand that this vehicle was composed within a short timeframe, from many different parts and under conditions that we are not familiar with here. This is why we do not want to give you the impression that if the above points were adequately addressed, the car would get a Dutch licence plate; the fundamentals are simply too weak for that. As the vehicle has many defects and is therefore not considered safe to drive, we did not carry out any dynamic tests."

During the test, we had been surprised to find that the inspectors were mainly looking for the barcodes of the individual parts. This code allows them to verify whether a product is certified. But our windshield for instance was taken from a KIA truck and as the glass was too long, the glazier cut a piece off. Unfortunately, the part with the bar code has stayed behind in Ghana. The final conclusion after the inspection: this is not a car.

Meanwhile back in Ghana there are high hopes. Over the past weeks we have been phoning and emailing the SMIDO team on an almost daily basis. We translate the test report for SMIDO. On Monday afternoon we phone Dr Waco. He is in good spirits. "It is great that the Dutch government is now supporting the SMATI Turtle. Azongo will bring the good news to the media since they follow the developments closely." In the following weeks, we see more and more online news articles emphasising how the Dutch government is going to boost the Ghanaian auto industry.
In the autumn of 2013, a Dutch promotion tour follows, with a premiere at the Amsterdam pop venue Paradiso. Dutch publisher Fosfor publishes its first long read *Turtle 1, de auto uit Afrika* ('Turtle 1, the car from Africa'), written by journalist Tijs van den Boomen. Fosfor has provided free publicity in newspapers and magazines. Thanks to all the media attention, we manage to get a visa for Dr Waco, so that he can come to the motor show in Ahoy in Rotterdam. We have organised a place for the Turtle there. Our promotion tour is getting off to a good start. We even make it onto the evening talk show "Pauw & Witteman". We explain that the Turtle is an ongoing action research project, but soon a very different narrative takes hold. Is it aid to poor people?

Or is it in fact exploitation? Can you give people false hope? Is this serious research or simply self-promotion by a bunch of neo-colonials? As soon as Africa comes into the picture, people start passing moral judgements. Our starting point was our interest in a world – whether it is in Africa, America or Asia – where people have to resolve their problems without government support. But that idea is soon drowned out in this debate.
In November 2013, Dr Waco arrives at Schiphol. It is cold and he is almost unrecognisable in his thick winter coat. As we drive to the motor show in Ahoy, Dr Waco inspects Joost's Mercedes. It is the same as his. Something in the engine is rattling. "A mechanic has to have good ears, Mr. Justice!" Joost had never noticed the rattling.

At the show, the Turtle is displayed beside the icon of future mobility, the Tesla. It has been sawed in two so that you can see the battery. Tesla has hired good-looking girls and boys in shiny outfits to give the car a young vibe. We have Dr Waco in a thick winter coat and ourselves to answer the questions of the thousands of car buffs. Dr Waco soon gets into his role as a sales representative. Amidst all the splendour of the new car models, he sees only problems for his continent. "All these cars are like iPads on wheels. This is consumer waste." Then the Tesla team gets an unsolicited lecture: "Where are you going to charge those batteries when there is a 'lights off'?"
In the days after the show we have a busy schedule. We receive a German television crew; we visit the HAN Automotive (Hogeschool Arnhem Nijmegen) in Arnhem and we visit several scrapyards. But Dr Waco is most taken by a visit to the church in Delfshaven, Rotterdam, from where the Pilgrim Fathers departed for the New World. He knows the church from the bible lessons he attended as a child.

We also get the latest news from Ghana. A lot has happened since the Turtle's departure. After the king called for reconciliation between SMIDO and the Garages in his speech, tensions rose to an all-time high. Azongo saw an opportunity to reinvigorate his visionary plans for Suame Magazine and immediately wanted to go and negotiate with The Garages. But as the president, George categorically rejected any form of merger between the two organisations as it would compromise his leadership. When George discovered that Azongo had nevertheless engaged in negotiations, he sacked him.

Meanwhile all the media coverage of the Turtle had attracted a pension fund from Accra: United Pension Trustees (UPT). The fund sees Suame Magazine as a growth market, they would like to offer workers a pension. Their slogan is "Formalising the informal". UPT offered SMIDO a sum of $250,000 to buy new land out of town. This money was to be used as a down payment to the local chief and to make the first basic investments such as building a road, electricity, water and sanitation. The master plan that Azongo had developed years ago could now be financed. The idea is simple: turn a piece of jungle into an industrial area, a New Land. You earn back your investment by letting plots. It also means you can register every tenant, levy taxes and offer a pension. The building blocks of a formal world.

As SMIDO has no official legal form, George called in h bank to help transfer the funds. This raised suspicions among the executive council that he was in fact plannir to seize the land himself. So they met behind his back and dismissed him.
But once they had fired their president, the executive council was out on the street, as George was the owner of the SMIDO building. No offices, no SMATI training courses, no money and, as a result, no New Land. From that point on, UPT took over George's role The SMIDO executive council went on UPT's payroll. In exchange, UPT got access to the SMIDO rank and file to canvass new customers.

We are quite upset by Dr Waco's stories. He is devastated. "Our leaders are only thinking for their own good. They are obsessed with greed and power hunger." And then, without missing a beat, Dr Waco starts outlining his own vision of the future. With his large hands, he describes a huge workshop on the New Land, far removed from the crowds of Suame Magazine. He will manage the workshop personally. "If only we can have this, I promise you, we will build many Turtles. You can be the president of the Turtle factory!" All that is needed from our side is a budget to build the workshop itself, the machines and the investment in materials. After a week we say goodbye t Dr Waco and promise to develop an idea for the Turtle

We now finally have time to think about our experience Our experiment has taken on a life of its own, especial in Ghana. The Turtle has even become part of the muc larger dream of the New Land. Has our action researc worked? Which insights has it brought us and what changes has the project set in motion?

The building of the Turtle has taught us that the informal world is, paradoxically, a restrictive system – almost diametrically opposed to our romantic idea of freedom. In fact it is our formal system, with its rules and institutions, that offers a lot of freedom. It enables a society to channel and ritualise all sorts of elementar processes, so that there is time left for more complex things, like building an auto industry.
But how could we transform our insights about the

ınctioning of Suame into change? More concretely, ow would the construction of low-tech cars in Suame ver get off the ground? We soon concluded that a urtle 2 would only succeed if we kept it small. That ieant not going along with the large-scale factory that zongo and the UPT had envisioned in the New Land. hrough the exhibitions, shows and media coverage e had made contact with companies and industry rganisations. We also got talking to INOVAM, the aining centre for mechanics in the Netherlands. he institute developed a model to set up trainings or mechanics in Ghana. And we organised an expert ieeting with V2, an institute in Rotterdam that studies ie relationship between art and technology. People om industry, science and the government were ivited to contribute to the development of a plan for Turtle 2. Nyaabe Aweeba Azongo was the special uest of honour.

zongo presented his report "The Regional Investment ateway Project", in which he described Suame lagazine as the most promising industrial hub in Vest Africa.[1] But for that industrial hub to really take ff, processes will need to formalised considerably. Ve seemed to disagree on how this goal could be eached, though Azongo did not seem to think so. He aid the SMATI Turtle would attract foreign investors. ncouraged by Azongo and inspired by the expert ieeting, we expand our research. HAN Automotive is illing to put two student teams to work on a design for low-tech car, starting with a simple universal chassis. he design has to suit the conditions of West Africa nd Suame Magazine, meaning that the chassis needs fit with any engine block and that you must be able build it in a traditional forge.

or the last part of our research, we work with Xelvin, specialised agency that sends technicians out to ie four corners of the globe. Together with them e organise a second expert meeting during the utch Design Week in Eindhoven. Experts from the utomotive industry build on the ideas presented by ie HAN students. With their input we can perfect our lan for a Turtle 2.
ur point of departure is still the strength of Suame lagazine: the craftsmanship, the large number of pecialists, the cheap labour force, the convenient ocation in West Africa and the steady supply of sed parts from around the world. These are the igredients for establishing an assembly line for ow-tech cars. But then there are the problems, such s the poor infrastructure, an unreliable electricity rid, overpopulation, corruption and a lack of training acilities. Those problems cannot be resolved in the hort term, and we have taken that into account in ur plan. Our idea is to establish a practical training centre in Suame, in which the Technical University, the Polytechnic Colleges, the Vocational Automotive Training Center and SMATI will participate. Every training programme can supply a number of talented students to carry out part of the car construction process. This composite team will be expected to build a Turtle within six months. The end result, a working car, would also be their Master's project.

Students will thus take part in and learn about every stage of car construction. And perhaps more importantly, they will get to know the industrial cluster and learn how to use it. They will also learn about other aspects of the construction process such as safety, management, design and planning. The course will be supervised by masters from the neighbourhood and professors from the training centres.[2]

"This is a car." Genevieve pauses as she presses her finger down on a pile of forms. It is 20 April 2015 and we are sitting in the offices of the Supermaritime shipping company in Tema Harbour, Ghana, like schoolboys waiting to be scolded. We are surrounded by towering piles of files. Genevieve is a controller at the shipping company that exported the car in 2013. "You white people think you can do anything," she continues sternly. "This Turtle car is never exported from Ghana. There are no papers. And now you come to me saying it is not a car but iron on wheels?" Tweneboah Kodua Boakye, TK for short, a representative from UPT, is patiently listening as Genevieve gives us a dressing down. When she is finished, he starts talking. First he praises her dedication, then he mentions his influential network of parliamentarians and entrepreneurs, and he concludes with a mention of the king of Ghana, who is actually waiting for the Turtle's return. With a deep sigh, Genevieve picks up the phone and rings yet another customs officer.

After its Dutch tour, the Turtle had to return to its country of birth, this had always been the plan. But we have been in Tema for more than a week now to clear it through customs. Apparently the car was never officially exported and did not have the correct paperwork and so now we have to pay import tax. We show photos to prove it is a made-in-Ghana car. But there are no forms for Ghanaian cars. Genevieve is our last chance. She turns the case into a matter of honour. "If this is a Ghanaian car, it needs to be registered." Now a whole process is set in motion. It is the first time in the history of the Ghanaian customs that a Ghanaian car brand is registered. Thanks to TK's impressive network ans ability to put pressure, it is all resolved surprisingly quickly. The Turtle gets official papers and a licence plate and we can finally get going.
When we arrive in Kumasi late that night, we are

1 Nyaaba-Aweeba Azongo. 2013. The Regional Investment Gateway Project.

2 Stichting Aardschap. 2015. S.M.A.T.I. Turtle 1. Action Research. Ideas for a Local Car Manufacturing Industry in Suame.

received by several members of the SMIDO executive council. With no leadership, no headquarters and with an average age that is well above 60, the council looks helpless. UPT has clearly taken the upper hand. TK gets up and welcomes us on SMIDO's behalf. As it is getting late, we give a concise synopsis of our mission statement. We have two objectives. The first is to give the Turtle back to the artisans of Suame. The second is to discuss ideas for a Turtle 2. We propose to organise a conference with representatives from the local authorities, trade and industry and educational institutions.

The following morning, we wander into the neighbourhood. It feels a bit like coming home. People recognise us and we embrace each other like family. UPT has opened an office near the former Turtle workshop, and this is where we find the SMIDO team. A dozen young women are hanging around the UPT building, all wearing tight T-shirts with a SMID fund logo. They head into the neighbourhood with bank booklets and a flyer that reads "The Return of the Turtle". TK has disappointing news. The king is in the Maldives and cannot attend the handover of the Turtle. Instead, Chief Nana Owusu Appeasa II of the New Land will come to receive the car.
In our former workshop we set up an exhibition about the Turtle 2. The party tents are put up again, just like two years ago. This time no police escort, but a brass band that accompanies the Turtle from the main road to the handover point. To the sound of blaring trumpets, the Turtle parades down the road with a horde of people in tow. The chief is standing on the podium. A large wooden key covered in gold spray-paint has been made specially for the photo opportunity. The chief receives the key and the Turtle is officially home again.

Over the following days, we are dragged all across town, from the police commissioner to the dean of the KNUST University to the deputy mayor of Kumasi. We make group photos everywhere and TK actually manages to convince all the training institutes to participate in a conference about the future of the Turtle. UPT has hired a huge room in the most expensive conference venue in Kumasi. The tables are arranged in a U shape with golden chairs. In the middle, there is a screen and a flip chart. It is cold inside, we might as well be in a conference centre along the A2 motorway near Amsterdam. Every institute arrives with a whole delegation and soon the room is packed. UPT has flown in its managing-director to chair the meeting. After the prayer, there is a lengthy introduction: UPT is going to offer Suame Magazine a new horizon with the New Land. And the Europeans will support the project with their plans for a training centre.

After these hopeful words we first show how the Turtle was received in the Netherlands. There is great interes in the RWD test report and also great disappointment a its findings. When we conclude the presentation with a call for collaboration, everyone nods. But who will pick up the gauntlet?

Professor Fiagbe of KNUST University is the first to get up. Before a Turtle 2 can be built, he says, fundamenta research needs to be carried out. There needs to be a research budget for this and collaboration with Dutch universities. After Fiagbe, the director of the Polytechn Institute takes the floor. This is a unique meeting he says: never before have the various training programm come together in a single space. Then he says that the best place to develop a new Ghanaian model is their institute. With the right financial stimulus from the We they can shape the whole programme. The director has not even sat down before Mr. Krossman gets up. His ITTU workshop made the creation of the Turtle 1 possible. They have the network in Suame Magazine a the space for a project like this. But they do need new machines. If the Dutch partners can provide funding, the SMATI-Turtle workshop can be established. The lis keeps getting longer as we go around the table.

The basket of wishes is like an elephant in the conference room. Joost slowly gets up. We are please to see these first steps on the path to collaboration, he says. It is good to hear that all the parties have the ambition to get this project off the ground. We see the opportunities, but we also see that all the resources are already available. As long as – and Joost silently pushes the basket back into the room – as long as the is collaboration, in which case a Western investment w not be necessary. Interference by Dutch parties will or make the project more complicated.

At that point the meeting is interrupted. The chief of the New Land enters in traditional dress. The meeting is suspended and he starts delivering a long speech in Twi. He concludes with an old Ashanti saying: Agho-g nia-tji-ting-gru. Let's grow a village with strangers. Wh he finishes, there is some listless nodding and TK clos the conference by planning a follow-up meeting. Every institution will send a representative. During the closin lunch, Philip explains what the chief said: the "gratuity that was given as a down payment more than a year ag will expire if no action is undertaken now.
To date no follow-up meeting has taken place. Without investments from the West, most of those involved see to have given up on the dream. But not everyone: after we left Suame Magazine, Dr Waco took in the Turtle ar it is now safely stored under a cover in his workshop. W phone him regularly to see if there are any new plans. And there always are. "Slow but steady. Don't worry!"

printen | opslaan

Aanvraag afgifte Nederlands kentekenbewijs voor een personenauto of lichte bedrijfsauto ≤ 3500 kg aan de hand van een individuele toelating speciaal (ITS)

- *Dit formulier is tevens opdrachtformulier (dit formulier bestaat uit twee bladen en moet zo volledig mogelijk worden ingevuld). Met de ondertekening van dit formulier verzoekt de aanvrager de in behandelingname van de kentekenaanvraag voor het op dit formulier vermelde voertuig tegen het basistarief ITS. Indien aan de orde zullen eventuele bijkomende kosten voor de voertuigbeoordeling eerst aan de aanvrager worden voorgelegd.*
- *Dit aanvraagformulier moet duidelijk leesbaar worden ingevuld. Bijgevoegd moet worden een kopie van het buitenlands kentekenbewijs of bouwjaar verklaring of certificate of origin. Zo niet, dan wordt uw aanvraag niet in behandeling genomen.*
- *Het ingevulde en ondertekende formulier sturen naar: RDW, afdeling IKS, Postbus 777, 2700 AT Zoetermeer*
- *Adres aanvrager is factuuradres.*
- *Aankruisen wat van toepassing is.*

The form that the Dutch Vehicle Authority (RDW) uses to assess self-build projects is left blank. The individual parts cannot be traced to the original factory and safety standards cannot be assessed as key components were created by combining different brands.

Gegevens aanvrager

m ______ Voorletters ______

m ______ Huisnummer ______

en its ______

on ______

ax ______

E-mail adres ______

Gegevens voertuig

Voertuig betreft: [ ] Personenauto [X] Lichte bedrijfsauto (≤ 3500 kg)

Merk ______

Type ______

Identificatienummer ______ Bouwjaar [1] ______

Plaats identificatienummer ______

Max. massa voertuig ______ Laadvermogen lichte bedrijfsauto ______

Max. last as nummer 1 ______ Max. last as nummer 2 ______ Max. last as nummer 3 ______

Toegestane max. massa van het samenstel ______ Max. massa te trekken aanhangwagen geremd ______ Max. massa te trekken aanhangwagen ongeremd ______

Max. aanhangwagen gewicht gewenst? [ ] Ja [X] Nee

Koetswerk ______ deurs

[ ] Coupe [ ] Sedan [X] Open wagen (Pick Up) [ ] Gesloten wagen

[ ] Stationwagon [ ] Cabriolet [ ] Hatchback [ ] Combinatiewagen

[ ] Anders ______

Gegevens motor

Motorcode ______

Plaats motorcode ______

Merk ______

Type ______

Brandstof: [ ] Benzine [X] Diesel [ ] Anders ______

Cilinderinhoud ______ cm³ Aantal cilinders ______ Max. vermogen ______ kW bij ______ omw./min.

Gegevens remsysteem

- Bedrijfsreminrichting

Gescheiden systeem: ☒ Ja ☐ Nee

- Parkeerrem

Mechanisch op: ☒ Achterwielen

☐ Voorwielen

☐ Transmissie

- Remvloeistofniveaucontrole

Controle door middel van: ☒ Doorzichtig reservoir

☐ Niveausignalering

☐ Andere wijze ______

Afmetingen voertuig

Lengte ______ cm

Breedte ______ cm

Hoogte ______ cm

Wielbasis ______ cm

Banden

Maat ______

Loadindex ______

Snelheidssymbool ______

Snelheid voertuig

Max. snelheid ______ km/h (fabrieksopgave)

Op- of aanmerkingen

______

______

______

______

______

______

Ondertekening

Door ondertekening van dit formulier verklaart de aanvrager tevens akkoord te gaan met de voorwaarden geldend vo een ITS keuring bij de RDW

Datum ______

Plaats ______

Handtekening aanvrager ______

The first presentation of the Turtle Project in the Netherlands sparks sharp criticism with some of the public.
It became clear that for some the cooperation between
an artist and a scientist resulted in a hybrid project that
transgresses the boundaries of the respective disciplines.

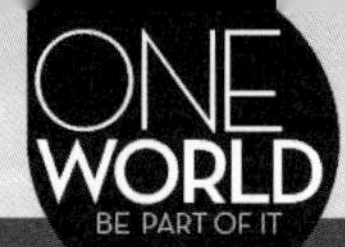

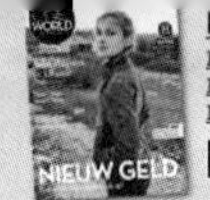

Deze maand in OneWorld

Daar buiten lijdt een schaap
Lieve Joris: "Ik heb een nieuwe familie
Dit geld maakt wél gelukkig

GRATIS ABONNEMENT | LEES DIGI

LEZEN KIJKEN WERKEN DOEN BLOGGEN MEEM

Home » Lezen » Opinie » Het sprookje van de Turtle 1

Het sprookje van de Turtle 1

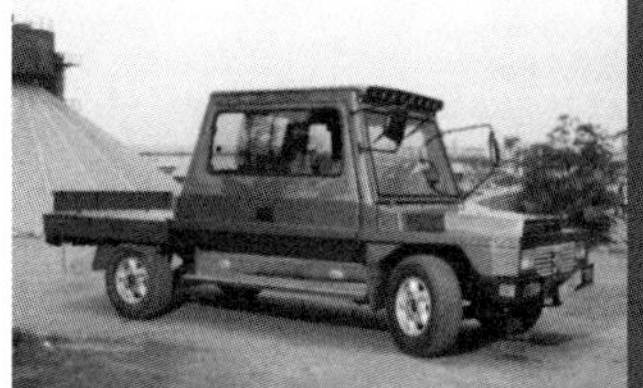

Datum:
21-10-2013

Auteur:
Harro Maat, Thomas Jaarsma en Dominic Glover

Bron:

33 | 6
Aanbevelen | Tweeten

Hij schitterde bij *Pauw en Witteman*, in Paradiso, bij *Fosfor* en in *OneWorld Magazine*: Turtle 1, 'de eerste Afrikaanse auto'. Maar zijn die benaming en faam wel terecht? Drie wetenschappers zetten vraagtekens bij het beeld dat is neergezet van de auto.

In het september nummer van OneWorld stond een verslag van Turtle 1. De Turtle is een auto gemaakt op initiatief van kunstenaar Melle Smets en onderzoeker Joost van Onna in het Suame Magazine, een wijk in Kumasi, de tweede stad van Ghana. Het project heeft veel aandacht gekregen in de media. De auto zelf wordt op verschillende plaatsen in Nederland tentoongesteld. Hieronder stellen we zeven vragen.

Uit de antwoorden blijkt dat het Turtle project een vertekend beeld geeft van het Suame Magazine. Daarmee bevestigt het een stereotype van 'wildernis' Afrika versus 'beschaving' Europa.

1. Is Suame Magazine een autofabriek?
In Suame Magazine worden auto's gerepareerd. Het is reparatie in de meest fundamentele vorm. In principe wordt alles vervangen en gemaakt, zolang de klant, de groeiende middenklasse van Ghana, betaalt. Doordat auto's soms geheel worden gestript en weer in elkaar gezet, lijkt het alsof een auto uit onderdelen wordt opgebouwd. Dat is ook de manier waarop de Turtle is gemaakt. Behalve de onconventionele vormgeving is er niets bijzonders aan de Turtle. De werkwijze is dagelijkse praktijk in Suame. De eerste indruk van Suame is een ontplofte autofabriek. Maar in werkelijkheid is het een industrieel complex opgebouwd uit honderden werkplaatsen en kleine bedrijven.

2. Is er in Ghana een gebrek aan creativiteit?
Met de Turtle wordt de suggestie gewekt dat Afrika zelf een auto-industrie kan opzetten. Het enige wat nodig is, zo lijkt het, is een injectie van Westerse creativiteit om een ontwerp van een auto te maken. Dat beeld is gretig opgepikt door de media. De suggestie van een potentiële auto-industrie in Ghana die met Westers initiatief tot leven kan worden gewekt spreekt tot de verbeelding. Maar er is in Ghana al een auto-industrie! Een industrie die zeer effectief de Ghanese middenklasse mobiliteit verschaft. De gedachte dat er een gebrek is aan kunstzinnige vormgevers en ontwerpers berust op een Westers idee van wat een auto-industrie is of zou moeten zijn.

3. Is een Afrikaanse auto een origineel idee?
Het Turtle project in deze vorm is een origineel plan. Maar het idee van een Afrikaanse auto is zeker niet nieuw. Wie 'africar' intypt op Wikipedia (de Engelse versie) kan lezen hoe dertig jaar geleden iets soortgelijks is geprobeerd. Afrika heeft (net als andere continenten) een geschiedenis van kansloze prestigeprojecten en serieuze initiatieven die het niet hebben gehaald. Ook op het gebied van het produceren van auto's. Smets en Onna stonden er in hun presentatie in Paradiso kort bij stil. Maar lessen zijn er niet getrokken uit dat verleden.

4. Is Suame gebaat bij een ontwerp van een nieuw type auto?
Kunstenaars en ontwerpers werken vanuit abstracte projecties. Precies wat je nodig hebt voor vernieuwende vormen. Ontwerpen moeten worden omgezet in materiële constructies. Dat is met de bouw van de Turtle met veel moeite gelukt. Hoewel lokale monteurs zijn ingeschakeld, heeft het maakproces van de Turtle geen enkele aansluiting met de werkelijkheid van Suame Magazine. De kennis en vakmanschap van de Ghanese monteurs is er op gericht om bestaande modellen te repareren. Dat is waar de klant voor betaalt.

5. Kunnen Ghanese monteurs iets leren van de Turtle?
In *OneWorld magazine* wordt gesproken over een deal: "Mister Melles zou de auto krijgen en Smido de technische kennis die voortvloeit uit het ontwerp en de bouw van de auto." Wat voor kennis eigenlijk? Afrika heeft talloze kunstenaars en ontwerpers. Maar kennis van ontwerpprincipes of een blueprint is niet wat ontbreekt of nodig is in Suame (zie vorige vraag). Voor het bouwen van de auto werd bestaande kennis en vakmanschap van de monteurs ingezet. Elders hebben we laten zien dat die vakkennis is gebaseerd op een geavanceerd 'leerlingstelsel'. In Nederland, zo is een veelgehoorde klacht, is een groot gebrek aan technisch geschoold en vakbekwaam personeel. De suggestie dat Nederland iets kan leren van Afrika is niet zo eenvoudig uit te leggen. Dat Afrika iets kan leren van ons is vanzelfsprekend, toch?

6. Wat is Smido voor organisatie?
Het Turtle team ging op zoek, zo legde Smets uit bij *Pauw en Witteman*, "naar een wereld waar niet allemaal van die structuren zijn waar wij hier zo aan gewend zijn." In Suame zijn allerlei sociale structuren. En waar sociale structuren zijn, zijn conflicterende belangen en verschillende meningen. Smido is een van de vakorganisaties. Maar er zijn er meer. In Suame wordt er, zoals overal, op open en minder open wijze gestreden om invloed en macht. Het heeft er alle schijn van dat de welwillende steun van Smido bij de bouw van de Turtle een politieke zet was. En een slimme politieke zet, want de koning én de nationale televisie van Ghana kwamen langs. Smido heeft handig de naïeve Hollanders voor het eigen karretje gespannen.

7. Moeten we naar de Turtle gaan kijken?
Het project en het verhaal erachter, zoals dat in de media naar voren is gebracht, leest als een jongensboek. Door de auto naar Nederland te verschepen is het een jongensboek dat met een goede stunt wordt verkocht. Als het lukt om daarmee mensen te interesseren voor Afrika, internationale relaties en ontwikkeling, is dat allemaal mooi meegenomen. Wij zijn er nog niet helemaal zeker van of dat werkelijk de bedoeling is van Smets en Onna. Ons advies: lees het verhaal en ga kijken naar de Turtle als je de kans krijgt. Kijk door de auto heen naar een wereld waar auto's anders functioneren dan wij gewend zijn. Een wereld ook die weinig kan leren van argeloze avonturiers. En vergeet niet wat kritische vragen te stellen.

Harro Maat (Wageningen Universiteit), Thomas Jaarsma (Open Universiteit) en Dominic Glover (Wageningen Universiteit).

Wil je weten hoeveel auto's er eigenlijk in alle landen rondrijden? Bekijk de OneWorld Data Atlas

MEER OPINIE

Vind ik leuk 33 | Tweeten 6 | +1 0 | Tip de redactie | Printen
Share 13

Reacties

James Everts | 24-10-2013

De hele Turtle 1 was een fake 'projekt' vanaf het begin. Toen de heer Smets in de week na de internationale publikatie (tot in Zuid Afrika) niet bereid of in staat bleek enkele vragen te beantwoorden omtrent de technische en ontwikkelings-aspekten van deze auto heeft een korte rondvraag bij relaties in Ghana snel duidelijk gemaakt dat veel Ghanezen het een belachelijk product vinden, waarmee ze niet willen worden geïdentificeerd. Het hele circus rondom de RDW keuring was een farce en het is onbegrijpelijk dat de Nederlandse Ambassade in Accra hierin is meegegaan. Een groepje ijdele naïevelingen die het wel interessant vonden op een podium te staan en internationale hulp te kunnen suggereren. Hopelijk wordt deze Nederlandse wanprestatie in Ghana snel vergeten.

MariekeDouma | 24-10-2013

Ja dit is een prachtig geschreven stuk. Ook op veel andere terreinen zijn dergelijke situaties terug te vinden. Mijn persoonlijke ervaringen hieromtrent : sport, visserij, landbouw en vluchtelingenwerk. Ik ben zeer blij dat hier aandacht aan wordt gegeven. Populaire projecten-ideeen-ontwerpen-technieken kunnen rare gevolgen krijgen, wanneer je je realiseert dat de context (en dus het gebruik) overal ter wereld anders is. Dit heeft overigens weinig te maken met zuiden-westen verhoudingen, maar eerder culturele verschillen. De meest essentiele vraag wordt vaak vergeten...... ".. wat willen jullie? waarom willen jullie dat?..." ..... Dit zou in mijn ogen een prachtig uitgangspunt zijn om techniek, programma's en overige externe interventies te ontwerpen.

Plaats je eigen reactie

Naam *

Email *

MEEDOGENLOOS.NL *insert gevatte ondertitel*

Home | Contact | Over meedogenloos.nl | Petities | PGP Petra

« Wanneer verdwijnt Ivo achter de tralies? Zwarte Piet »

Turtle 1: anatomie van een mislukt project

Door OpPinkPower | oktober 15, 2013 | Actueel

Door Sam Nemeth

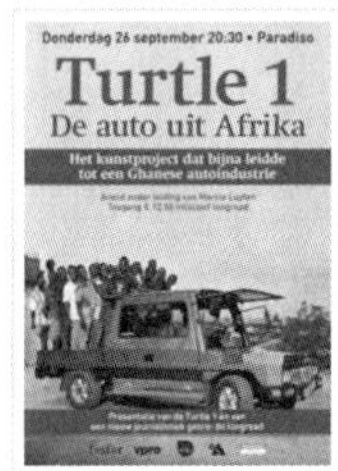

Het kunstproject Turtle 1 — De auto uit Afrika zette mij, en een aantal mensen met mij, aan het denken. Melle Smets maakte een auto, samen met Ghanezen, om de economie van het land aan te zwengelen, door aan de hand van dit prototype een autoindustrie te starten. Althans, dat was het verhaal daar, in Afrika, hier bracht Smets het toch vooral als een kunstproject.

Op het eerste gezicht een aardig idee: een Nederlandse kunstenaar, Melle Smets, geholpen door onderzoeker Joost van Onna, hebben een auto laten maken in een wijk in Ghana waar veel garages zitten. De opgegeven redenen: 'ik wilde weten hoe een auto werkt, in Europa kun je auto's alleen mbv computerprogrammeur repareren', waren niet opzienbarend, maar alla. Joost Conijn maakt ook zelf een vliegtuig en vliegt daarmee naar Afrika, heel legitiem.

Alleen was dit niet het verhaal waar ze de Afrikanen mee paaiden. Die dachten dat ze aan een echt model voor een Afrikaanse auto bouwden.

Het duo presenteerde de auto in Paradiso. Daar deden ze, overigens voor een overwegend blank publiek, er was niet één betrokken Afrikaan uitgenodigd, geholpen door bevriende filosoof Bram Esser en free lance journalist Tijs van den Boomen, het verhaal uit de doeken. In de vorm van een talkshow. Met amusementswaarde. Er werd met dédain over Ghanezen gesproken: die maakten er maar een bende van, en daar moesten zij dan een project mee zien te draaien. Dat al deze mensen voor niks meewerkten aan een prototype waarvan ze dachten dat het ze verder zou helpen maar uiteindelijk een kunstproject bleek, werd een voetnoot.

Wie de 'longread' -een uitgave van Fosfor- van Tijs van den Boomen erop naleest, komt tot de conclusie dat Smets met een web van lokale bazen heeft samengewerkt en daarbij voor de konsi koos die mot had met de lokale universiteit. Hierdoor konden ze vreemd genoeg wel van hun werkplaats gebruik maken, maar niet met studenten/docenten samenwerken. Het resultaat kan kort samengevat kan worden met: Afrikanen zijn onbetrouwbaar, we hebben gedaan wat we konden maar uiteindelijk is er een auto gemaakt die nauwelijks rijdt en de 'kennis' die met dit project is vergaard kon niet worden achtergelaten want Afrikanen schrijven nou eenmaal niks op. Dat er eventueel sprake kan zijn van een mislukt project, komt bij de makers niet op. Kunst kan niet mislukken.

De heren lieten trots zien hoe ze op de Ghanese nationale tv aankondigden dat deze auto zeker kans maakte om geëxporteerd te worden en de industrie in Ghana een boost kon geven. Ook in andere media -en de kunstenaar en onderzoeker gaven grif toe dat ze die gekocht hadden 'want zo gaat dat in Afrika'- deden ze uitspraken waarvan het waarheidsgehalte op zijn minst dubieus is. Zo beweerden ze op een nieuwssite dat de auto door de Nederlandse regering juichend was binnengehaald om de vernieuwende aspecten in het ontwerp.

Ook beweerden ze, zittend voor de auto -niet achtergelaten maar meegenomen, de Ghanezen met letterlijk lege handen achterlatend- dat ze geen technische tekeningen wilden maken. Zouden die Afrikanen toch niet snappen. En ze bleven er ook maar om zeuren. Begrepen onze manier van werken niet. Zij hadden moeten opschrijven wat ze zelf deden, wij niet. Informele economie hë .

Er was in Paradiso een meneer van de Rijksdienst voor het Wegverkeer die de auto niet eens op hun testcircuit wilde laten rijden, na tijdens een 'statische test' gecontateerd te hebben dat de remmen en stuurinrichting te onveilig waren.

Maar dus wel goed genoeg voor de Afrikanen, zeiden de heren, want dat gaat daar nou eenmaal zo. Die nemen het niet zo nauw.

Hoe het verder gaat, vroeg VPRO-interviewster Marcia Luyten, en de heren antwoordden dat ze op autobeurzen wilden gaan staan omdat er zo veel vernieuwende ideeën in het project zaten. Wel heel veel naïviteit om op een donderdagavond te verstouwen. Alsof er geen serieuze autoprojecten in Afrika ondernomen worden, er geen autoindustrie is in Afrika en er geen Afrikaanse auto-ontwerpers zijn en een kunstenaar uit Nederland, naar eigen zeggen gespeend van enige kennis van zaken, dit oplost. Het geheel ademde zo veel misplaatste bravoure en (ook mannelijk) chauvinisme dat ik erover op mijn website en Facebook postte. Dit leidde tot een uitgebreide discussie waarin ook door veel deelnemers geconcludeerd moest worden dat de heren de kluit belazerd hebben.

Nou wil ik ook nog wel aannemen dat dit met de beste bedoelingen gebeurd is, maar dat maakt het eigenlijk nog erger. Want dat zou betekenen dat er inmiddels een klimaat heerst waarin het normaal is om neerbuigend over buitenlanders te spreken en het ook heel vanzelfsprekend wordt gevonden om arme Afrikanen voor de gek te houden, met subtekst 'want zo zijn ze zelf ook'.

En het werd almaar erger. Op mijn Facebook pagina reageert initiatiefnemer van de Fosfor Longreads, Jeroen van Bergeijk, als volgt:

> *'Smets heeft drie maanden mijn zijn poten in de modder gestaan. Dan heeft iemand wel recht van spreken over hoe het er toe gaat in deze specifiek wijk. Meer heeft hij niet verteld. Zeker je kunt hem gebrek aan groter perspectief verwijten. Dat de Ghanezen het project alsmaar opblazen en groter maken (en keihard staan te liegen) dan kun je hem niet kwalijk nemen. Dit was een project waarin iedereen gelijkwaardig is ingestapt met hun eigen verwachtingen. De publicitaire waarde voor de wijk (Suame Magazine) is enorm geweest. Dus dat is er in ieder geval gewonnen. En ja het project is mislukt, als je kijkt naar de auto an sich. Daarom was die RDW meneer ook uitgenodigd. En we hadden graag een paar Ghanezen laten overkomen, maar dat konden wij, Smets en Paradiso niet bekostigen (los van alle praktische problemen)*

Resumerend: hij noemt het project zelf dus wel mislukt en geeft daar de Ghanezen de schuld van. Ik heb Ghanezen niet zien liegen, Melle Smets wel, controleerbaar, keihard. Dat de Ghanezen dan denken dat er echt iets gaat

Vinden

Search OK

Free Download

Meest recente berich

- 1 dag, 2 demonstraties
- Beatrice de Graaf en d kakelen als een kip zo
- „Half of jihad is media" politie aan online opru uitlokking doet
- 3 miljoen extra voor be plantjes in Brabant
- "All police are dogs" – politie in het verkeerde
- La Kramer versus Van
- Dear Future Generatio
- War On Weed
- What A Way To Go: Li of Empire
- Nieuwjaarswensen

Recente reacties

- Petra op The Netherlands: Administrative detention, chasing refugees and the case of the hunger strikers
- Debie op Nederland, politiestaat?
- Mathew Alias op The Netherlands: Administrative detention, chasing refugees and the case of the hunger strikers
- Petra op Geert Jan Heijstek, cybergoeroe
- Joost Fraissinet op Geert Jan Heijstek, cybergoeroe

Van de redactie

- Corporate Clout: The Influence of the World's Largest 100 Economic Entities
- De mythe van de groene economie
- How Israel, is a White Supremacist, Xenophobic, Apartheid State
- Human Rights violated in Holland. Once a Showcase of Tolerance. Now of Apartheid
- Monsanto, a half-century of health scandals
- New security system singles you out from the masses
- The Net Delusion: The Dark Side of Internet Freedom
- Why the Right to Water Is Under Attack
- World War 3.0

Tags

"sterf mensheid sterf" 30c3 acab beschaving cannabis corporatisme EPD EUSSR fopdemocratie Free Bradley Manning Free Chelsea Manning fuck zionism hongerstakers hypocriet hypocrisie It's not a crisis it's a scam it's the banks stupid! ivo

The spectre of the colonial past looms large during the presentation of the Turtle 1. Doesn't this project abuse our privileged position as rich Westerners? Blog mee-

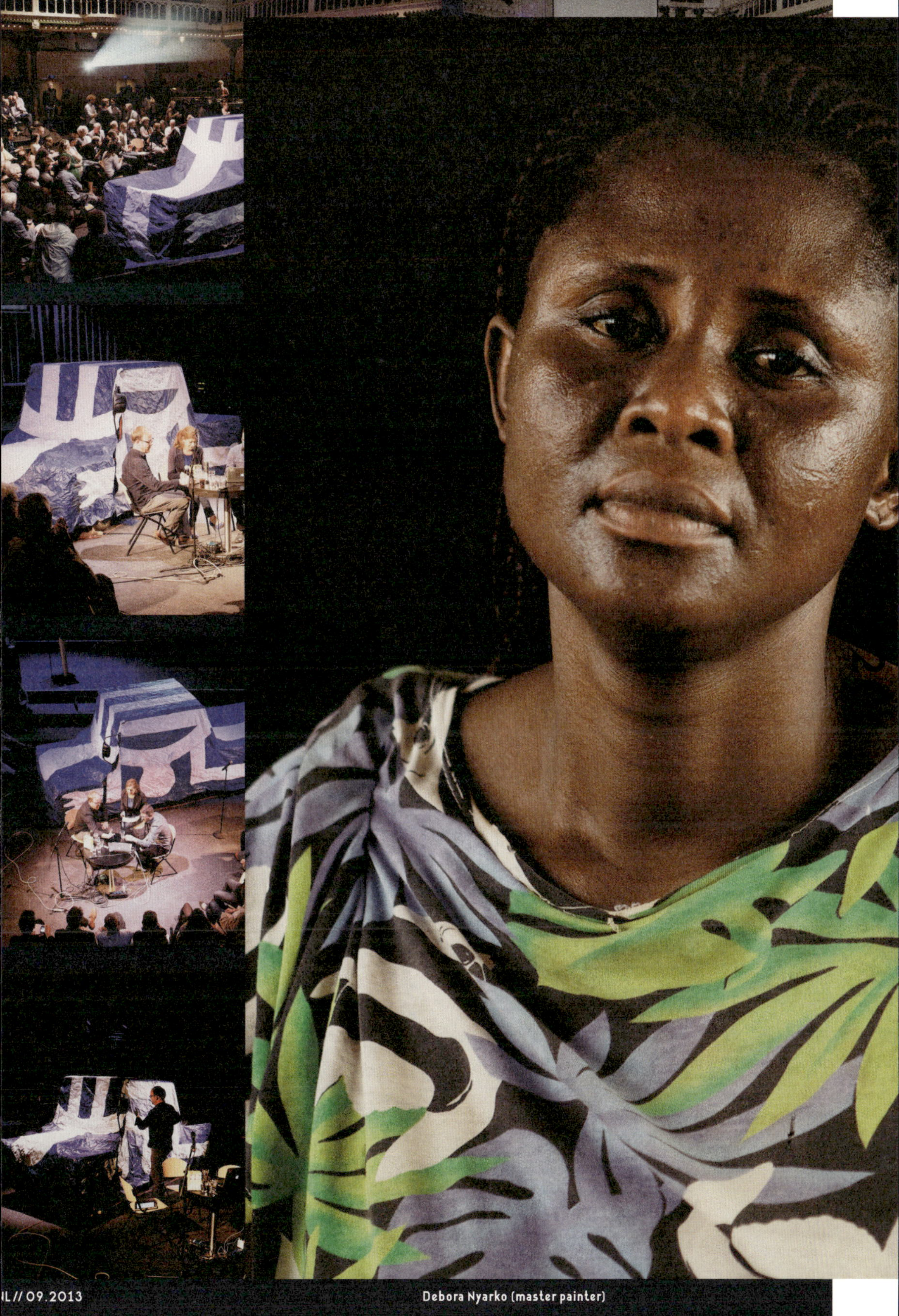

Debora Nyarko (master painter)

Inspector Ramon van Dijk of the Dutch Vehicle Authority (RDW) conducts static tests on the Turtle. Due to the large number of defects, the second phase – the dynamic test on the test track – cannot be carried out.

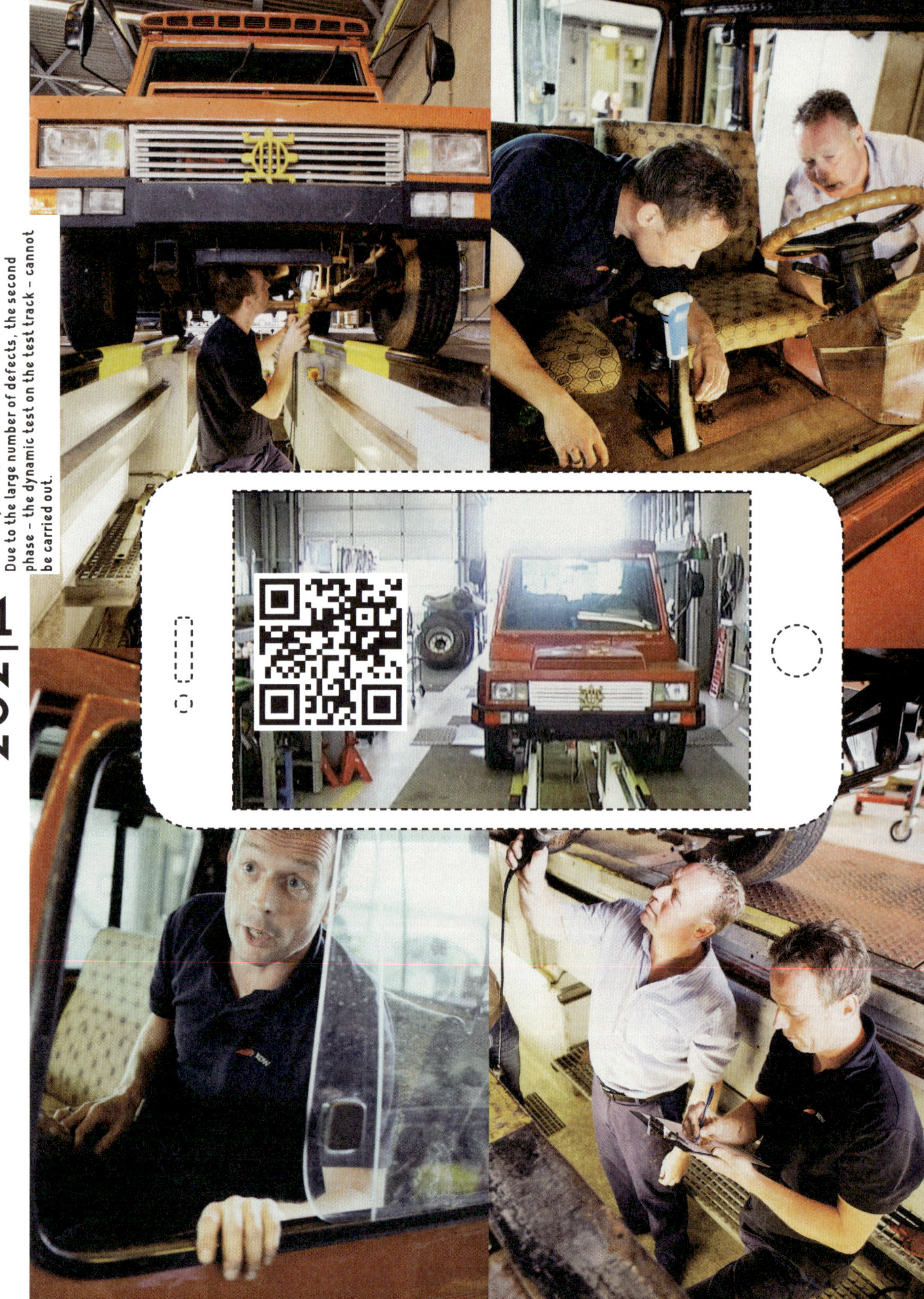

NL // 08.2013

NL // 08.2013

NL // 08.2013

NL // 08.2013

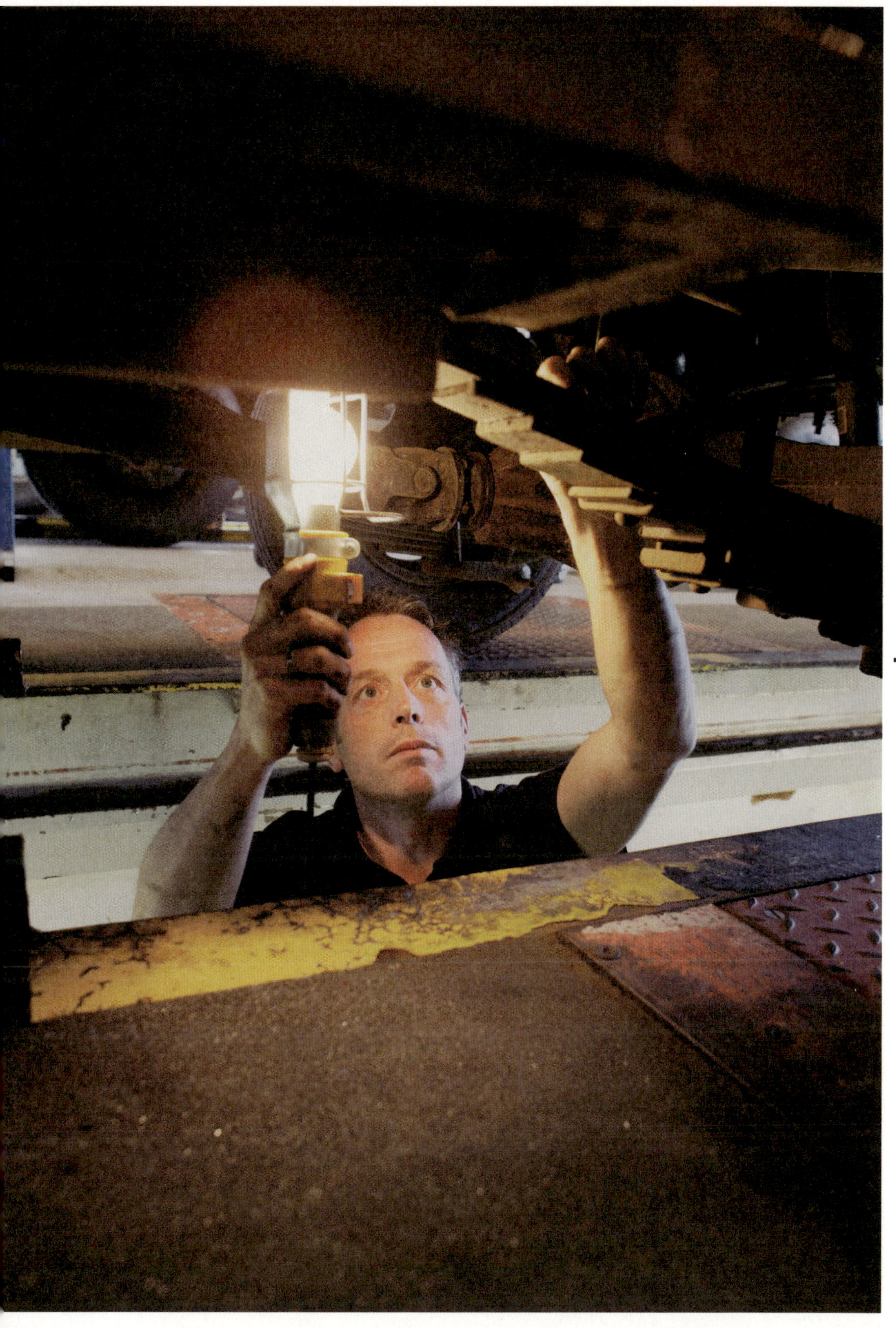

t1|203

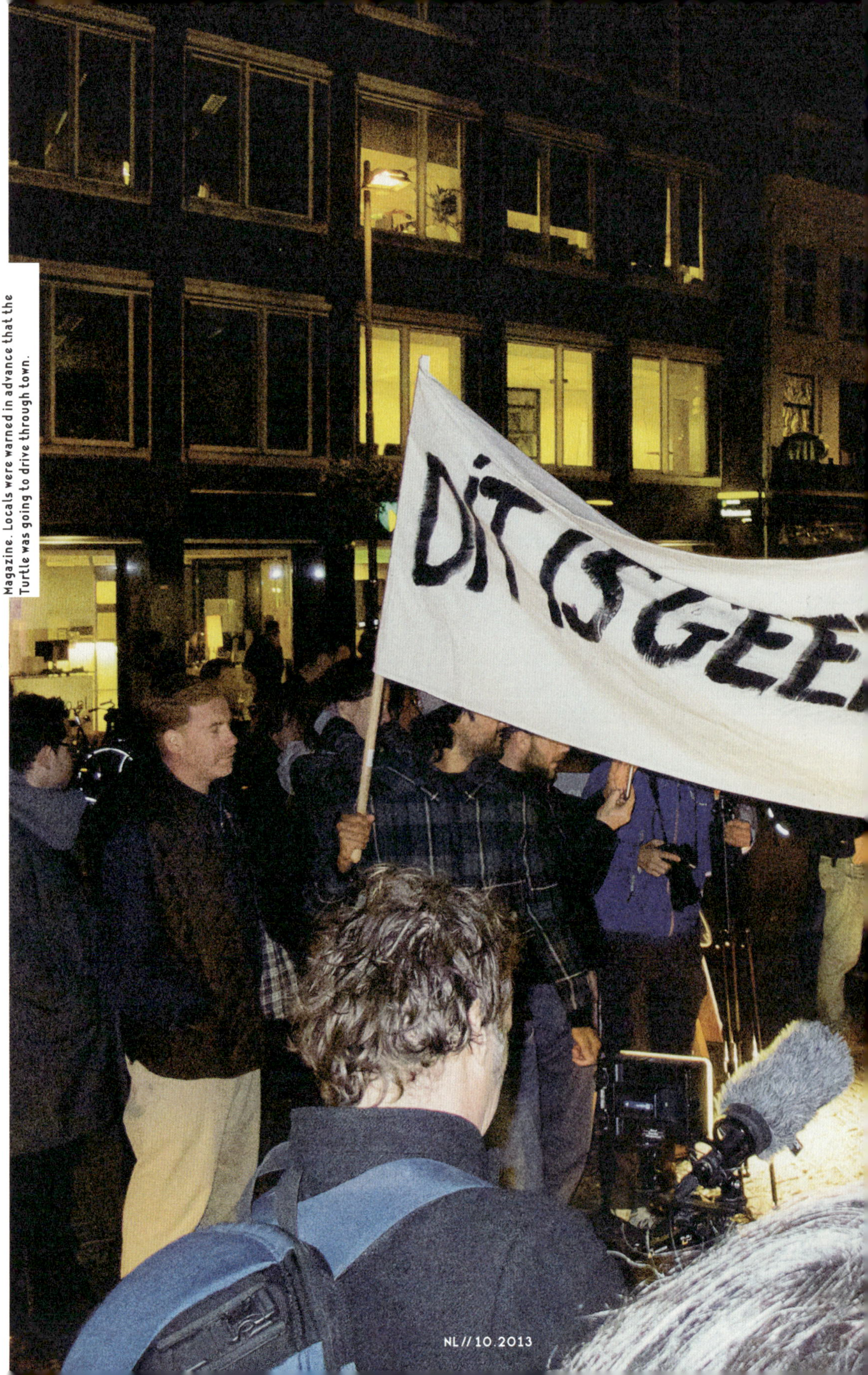

The Turtle participated in the IMPAKT festival on the Neude Square in Utrecht between 30 October and 3 November 2013, with evening lectures about Suame Magazine. Locals were warned in advance that the Turtle was going to drive through town.

NL// 10.2013

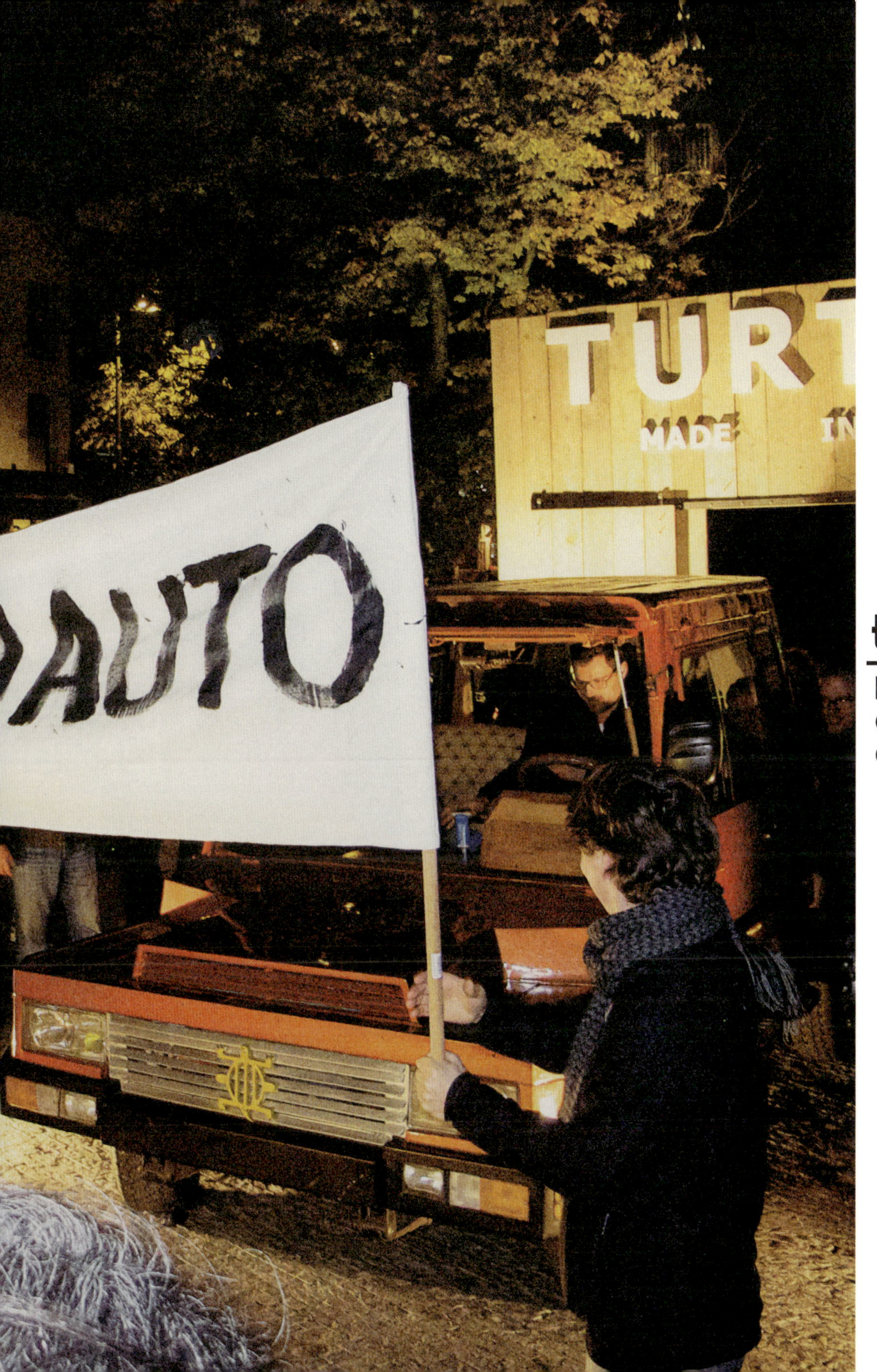
AUTO
MADE

206 | t1

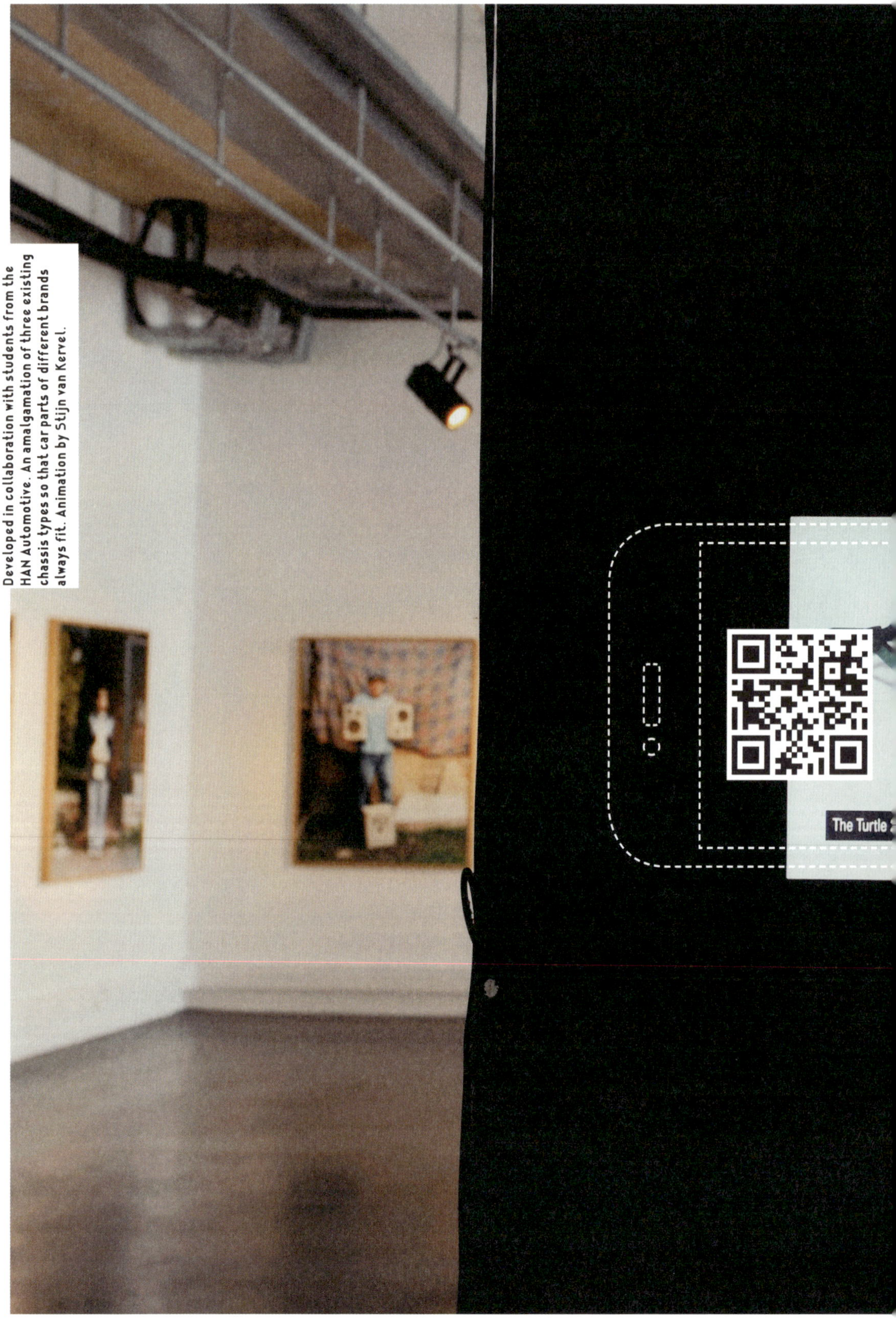

The Disnovation exhibition at the Accès(s) festival, Pau (France), 8 October – 6 December 2014.
Animation of the design of an One-Fits-All-Chassis. Developed in collaboration with students from the HAN Automotive. An amalgamation of three existing chassis types so that car parts of different brands always fit. Animation by Stijn van Kervel.

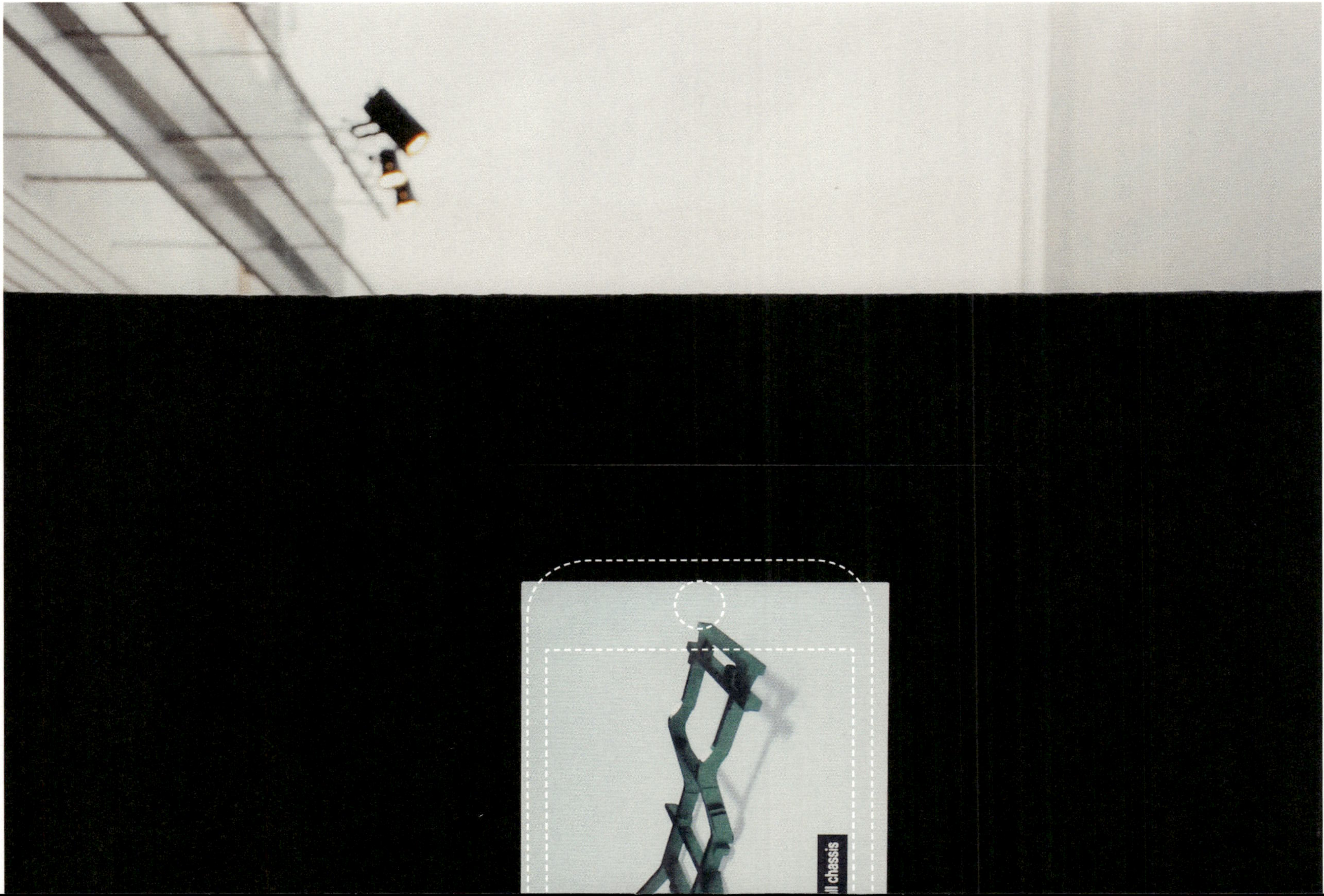

ll chassis

L: Progress Trap Exhibition at the DEAF Biennale, Het Nieuwe Instituut, Rotterdam, 21 May - 9 June 2014.
R: Turtle 1 at Art Rotterdam, February 2014.

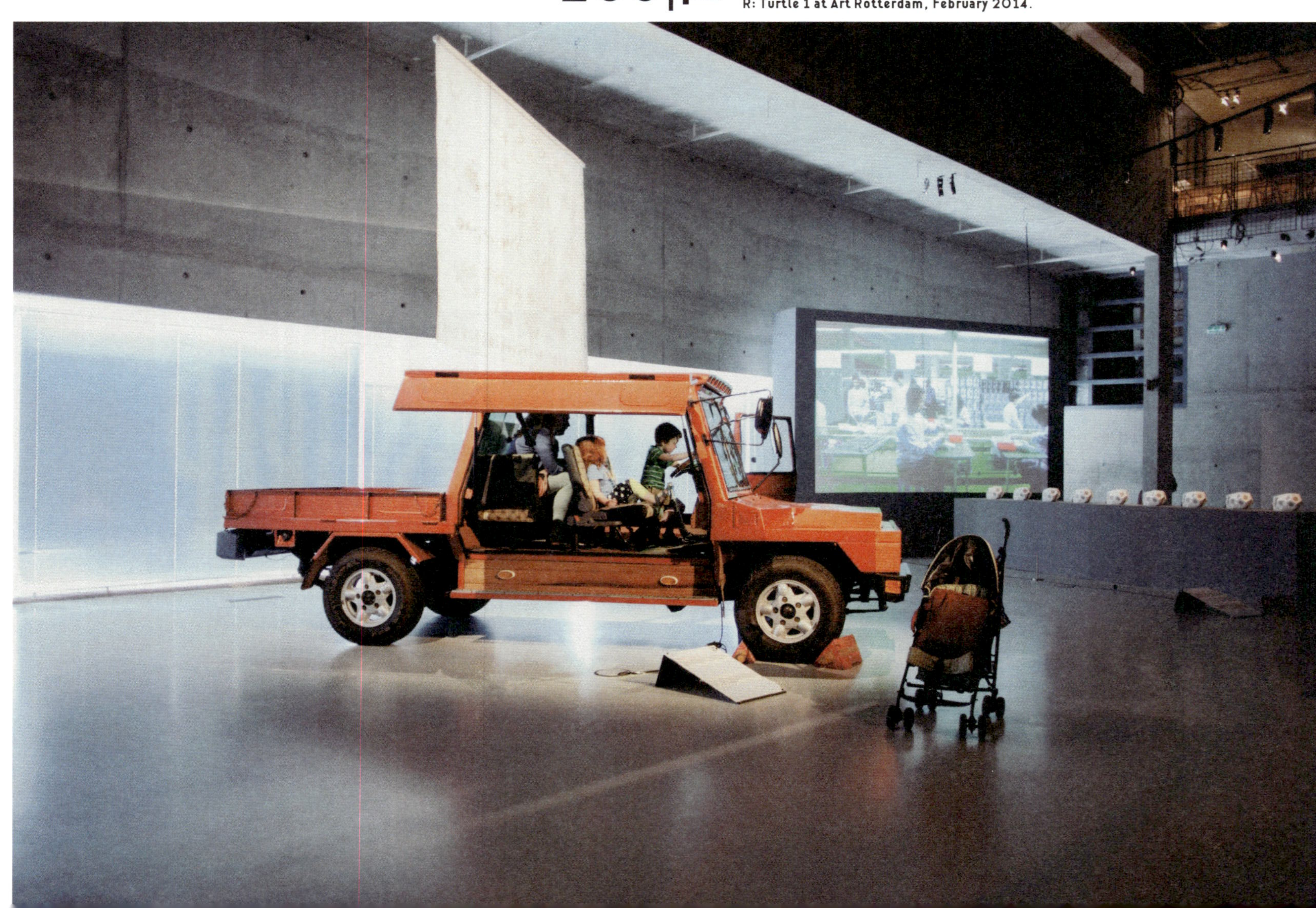

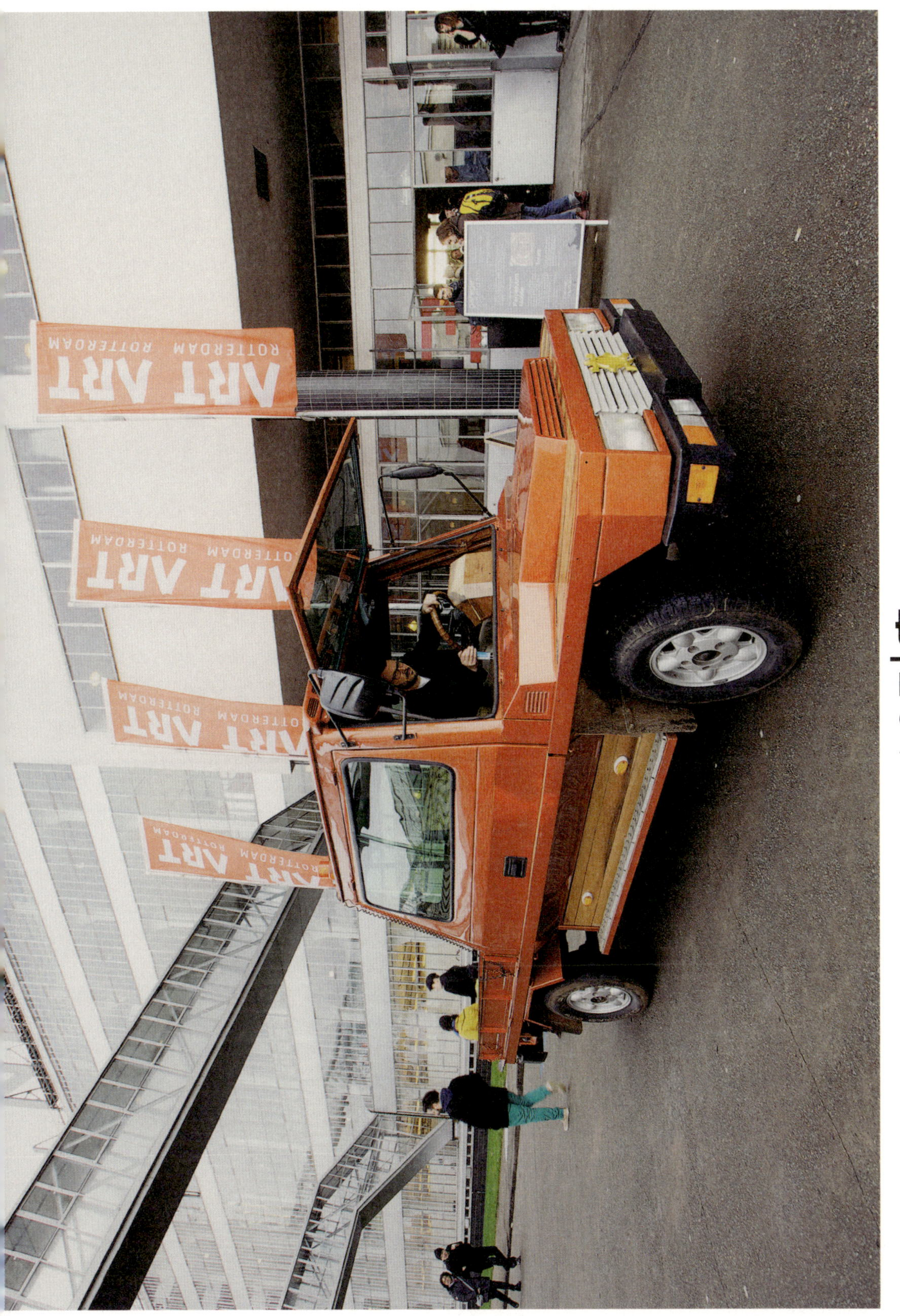

t1|209

210 | t1

The Turtle 1 on display next to the Tesla at the motor show in Ahoy Rotterdam. A low-tech versus a high-tech vision of the future.

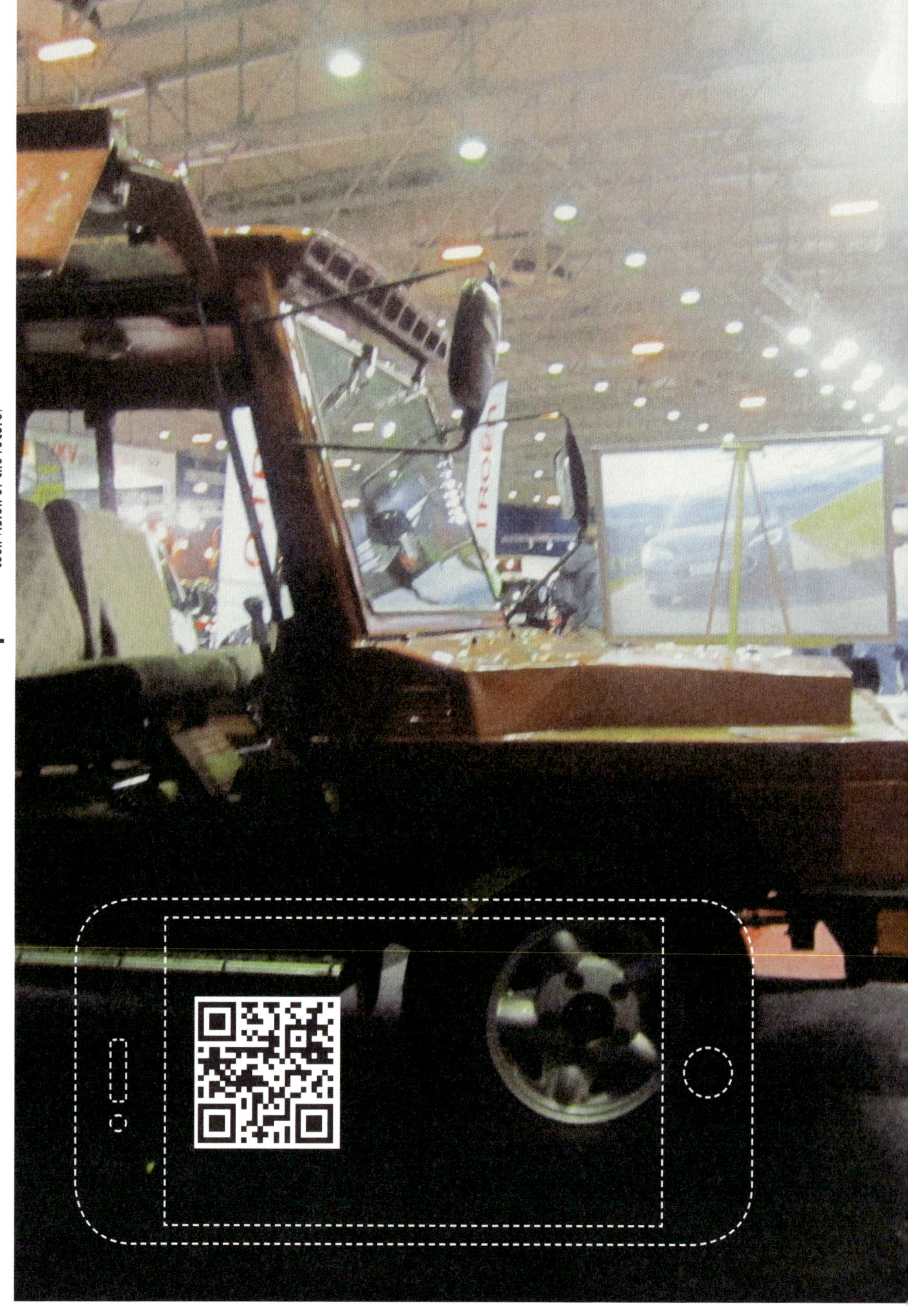

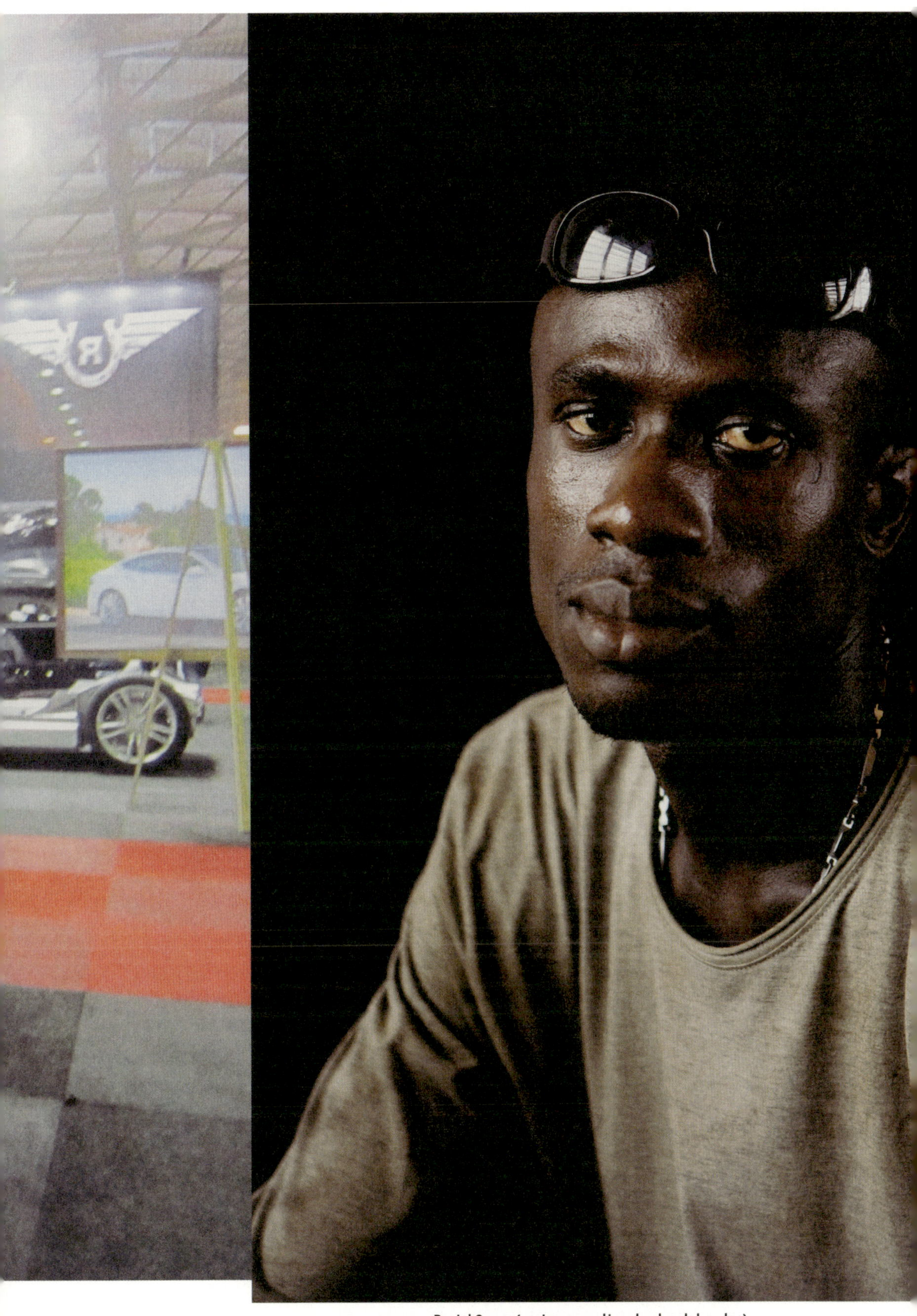

Daniel Owusu (senior apprentice sheet metal worker)

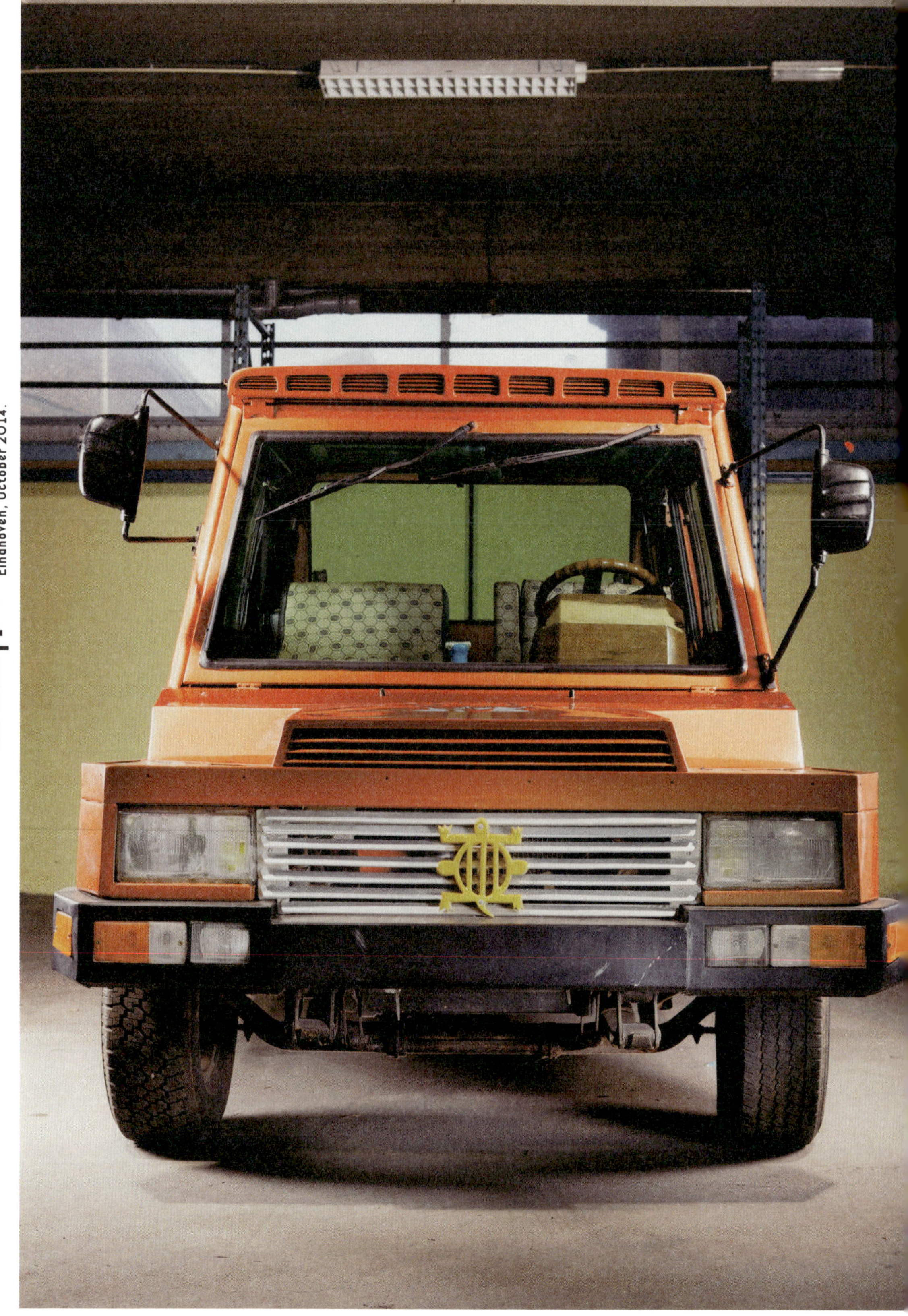

R: Together with Xelvin BV a workshop was organised with automotive experts at the Dutch Design Week, Eindhoven, October 2014.

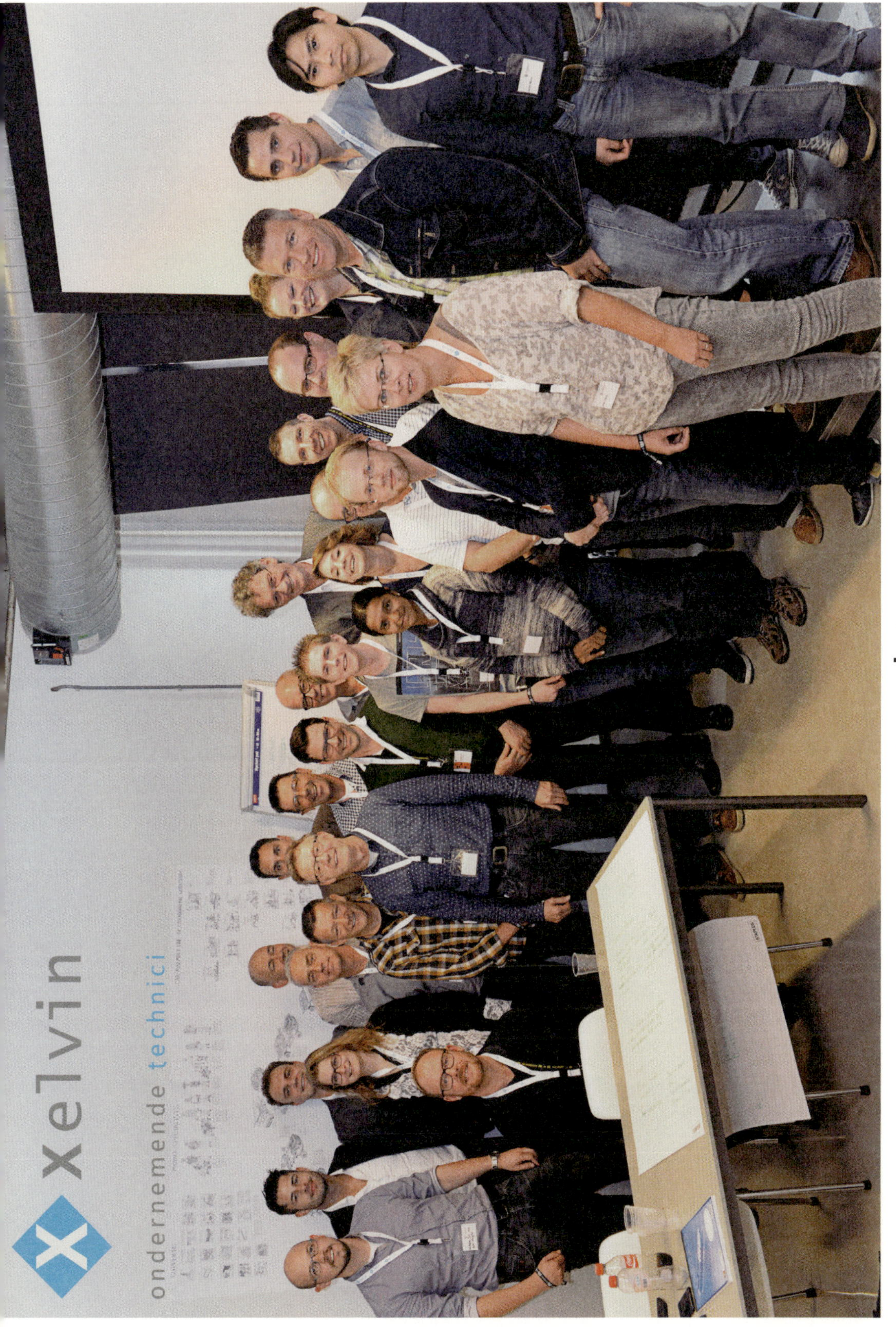

t1|213

L: Nyaabe-Aweeba Azongo is a special guest at the Turtle 2 expert meeting. V2_, Rotterdam, 7 March 2014. From left to right: Michelle, Joost, Azongo, Melle, Michel

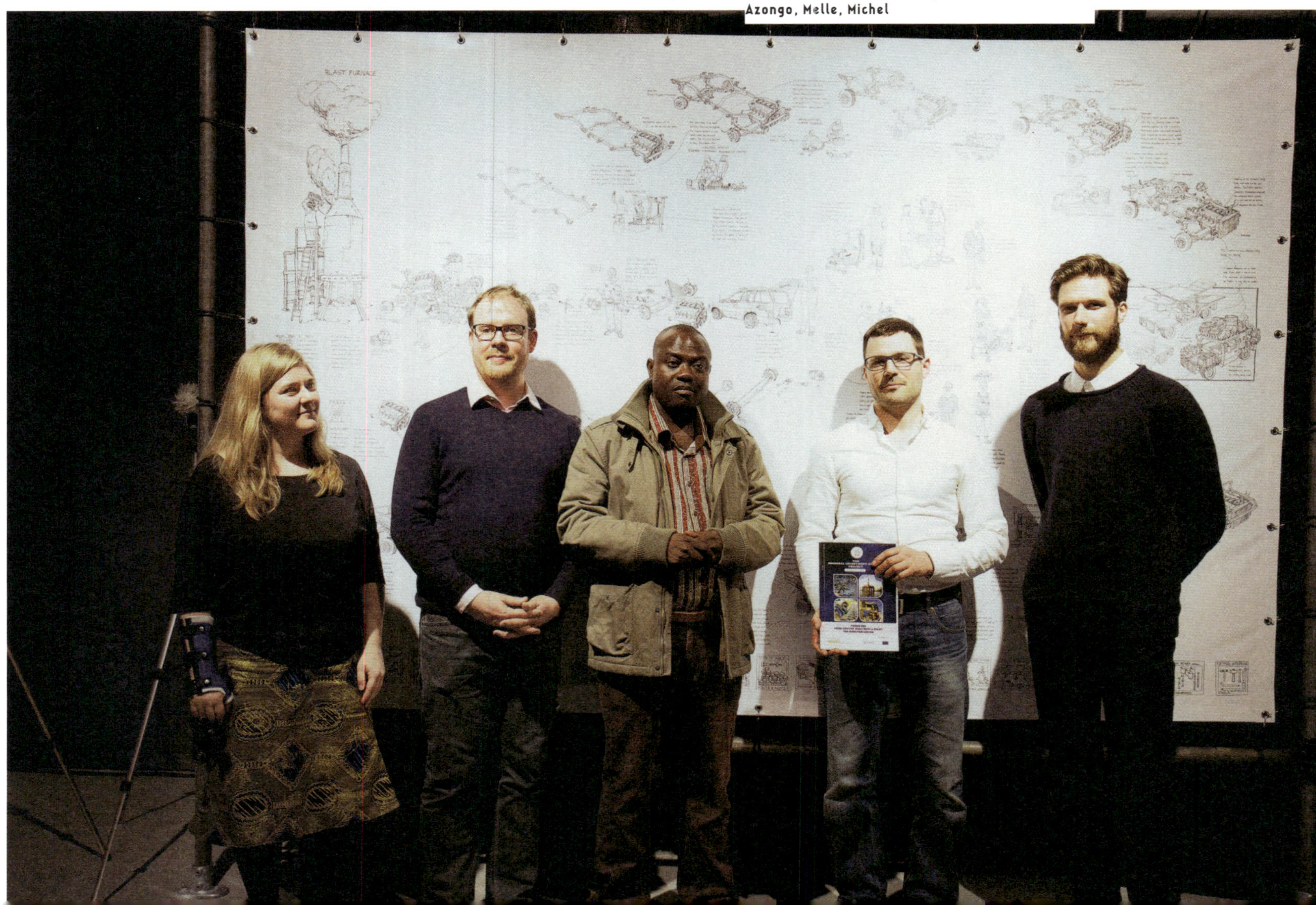

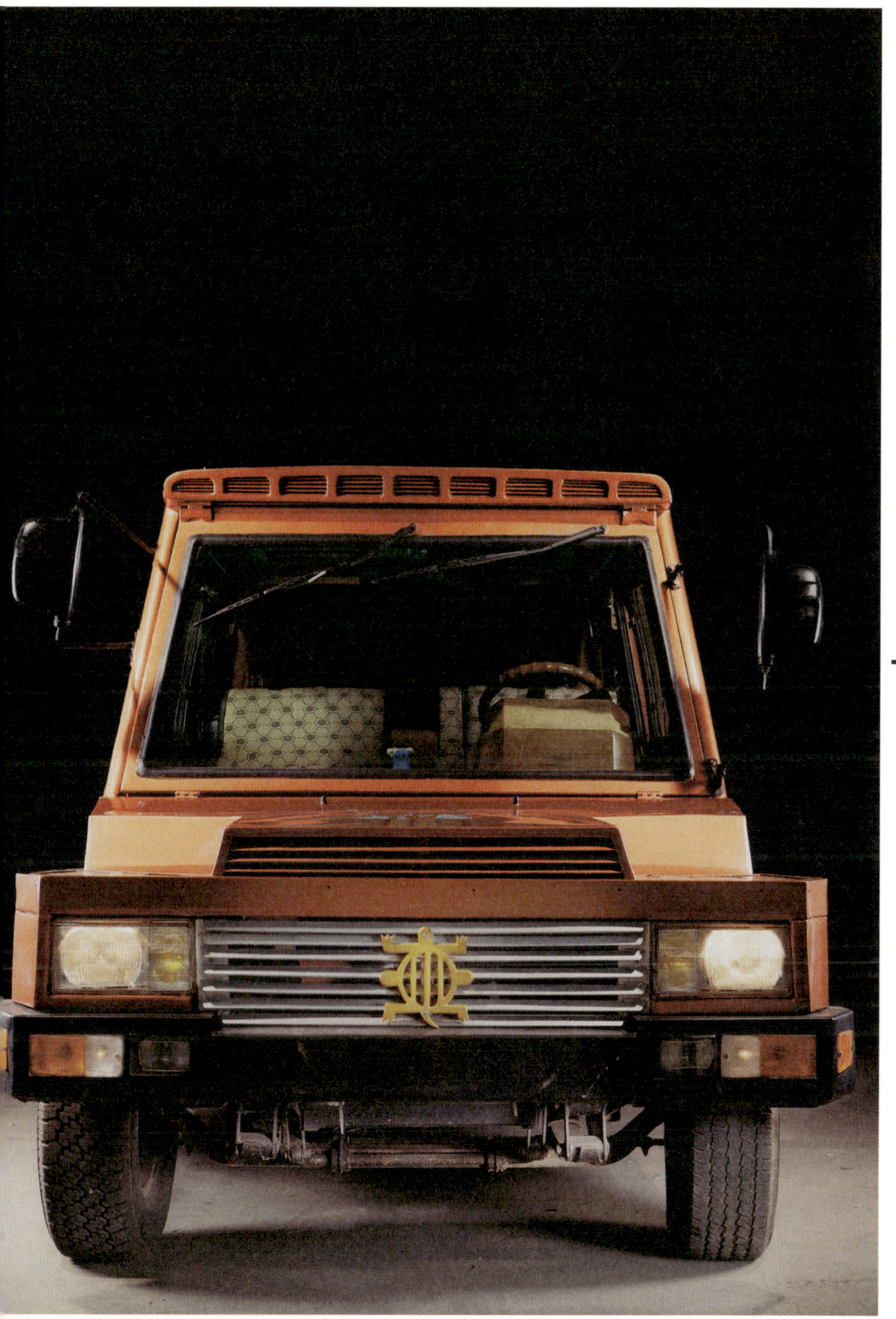

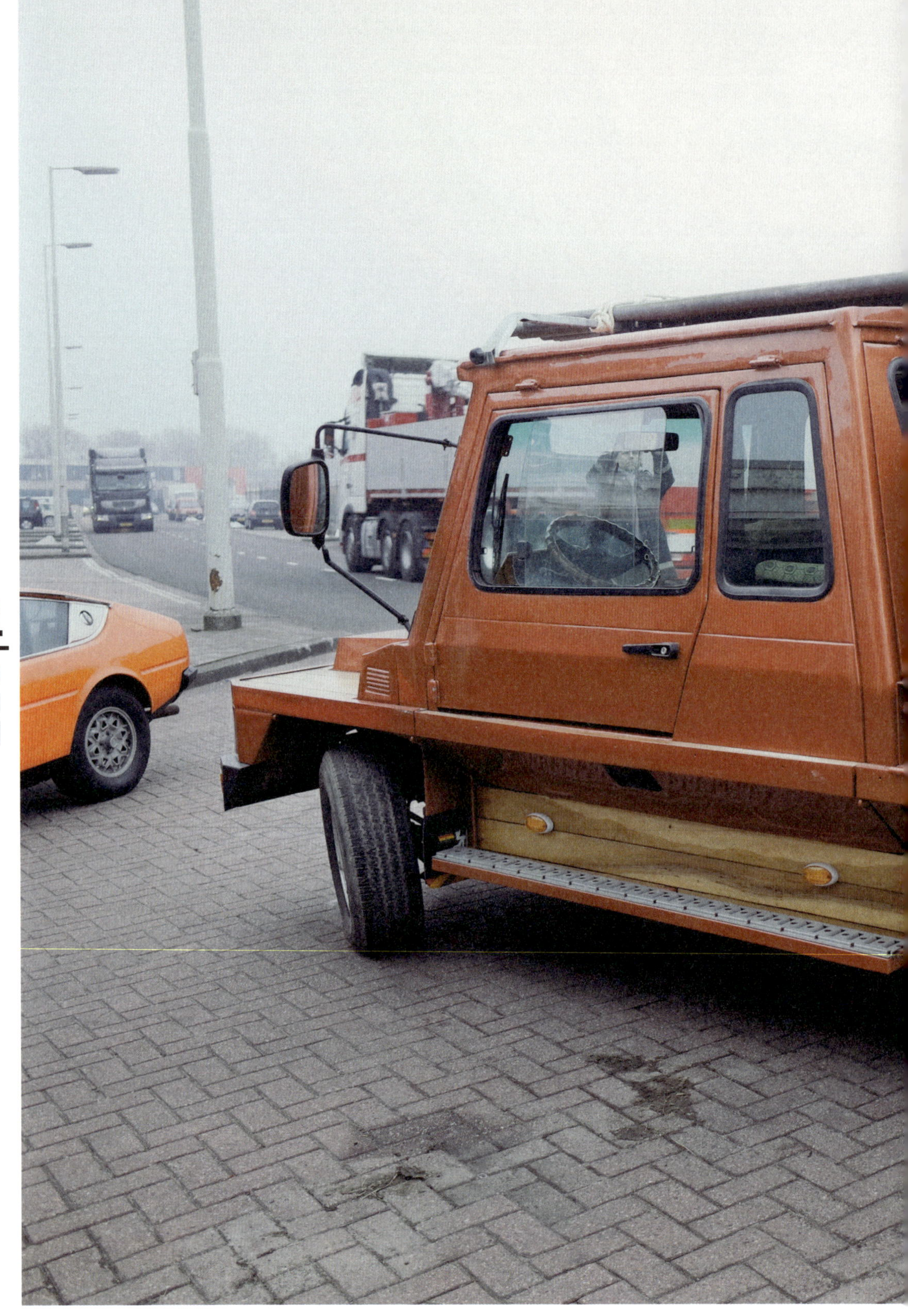

NL // 03.2015

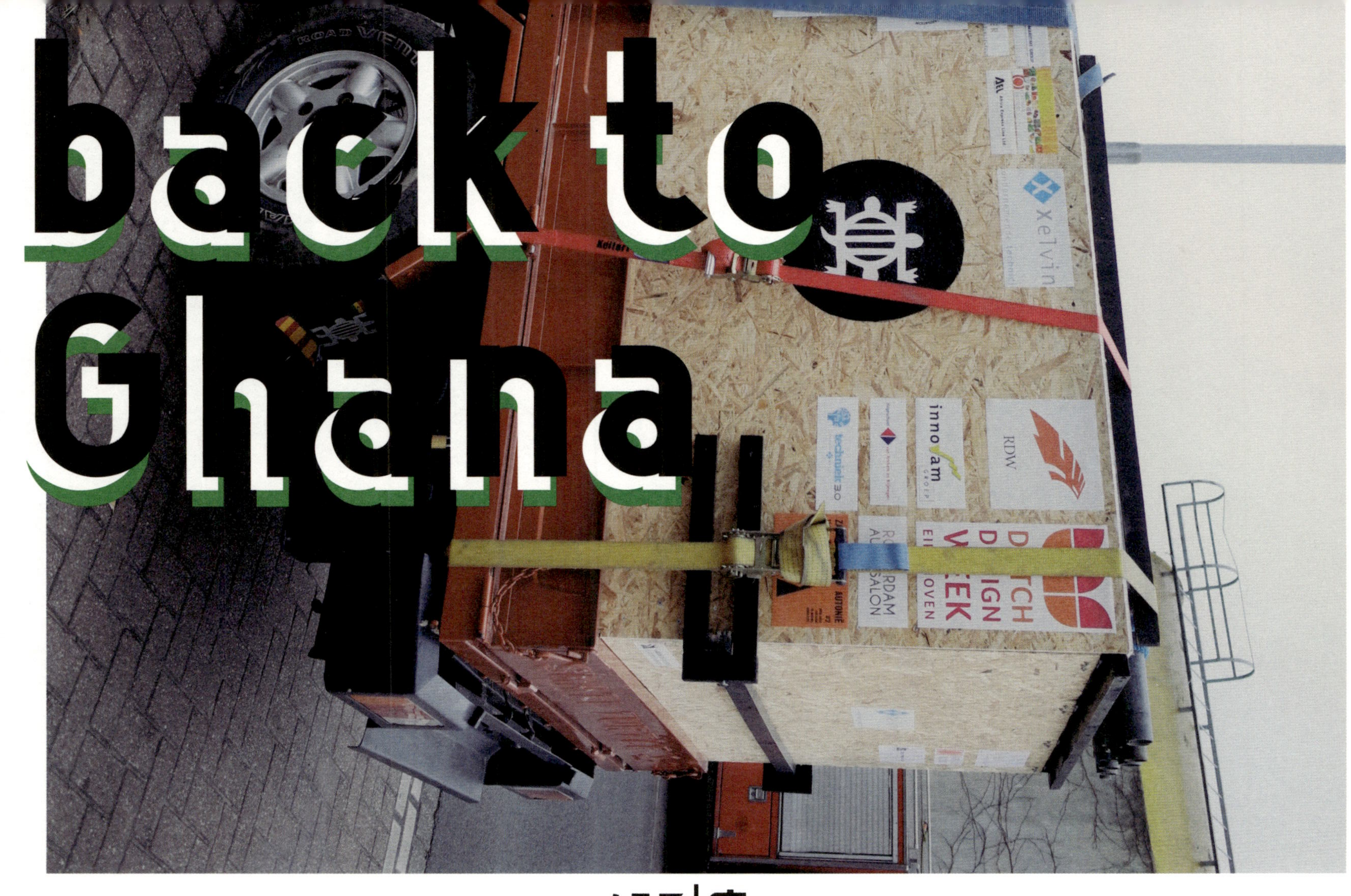

back to Ghana

t1|217

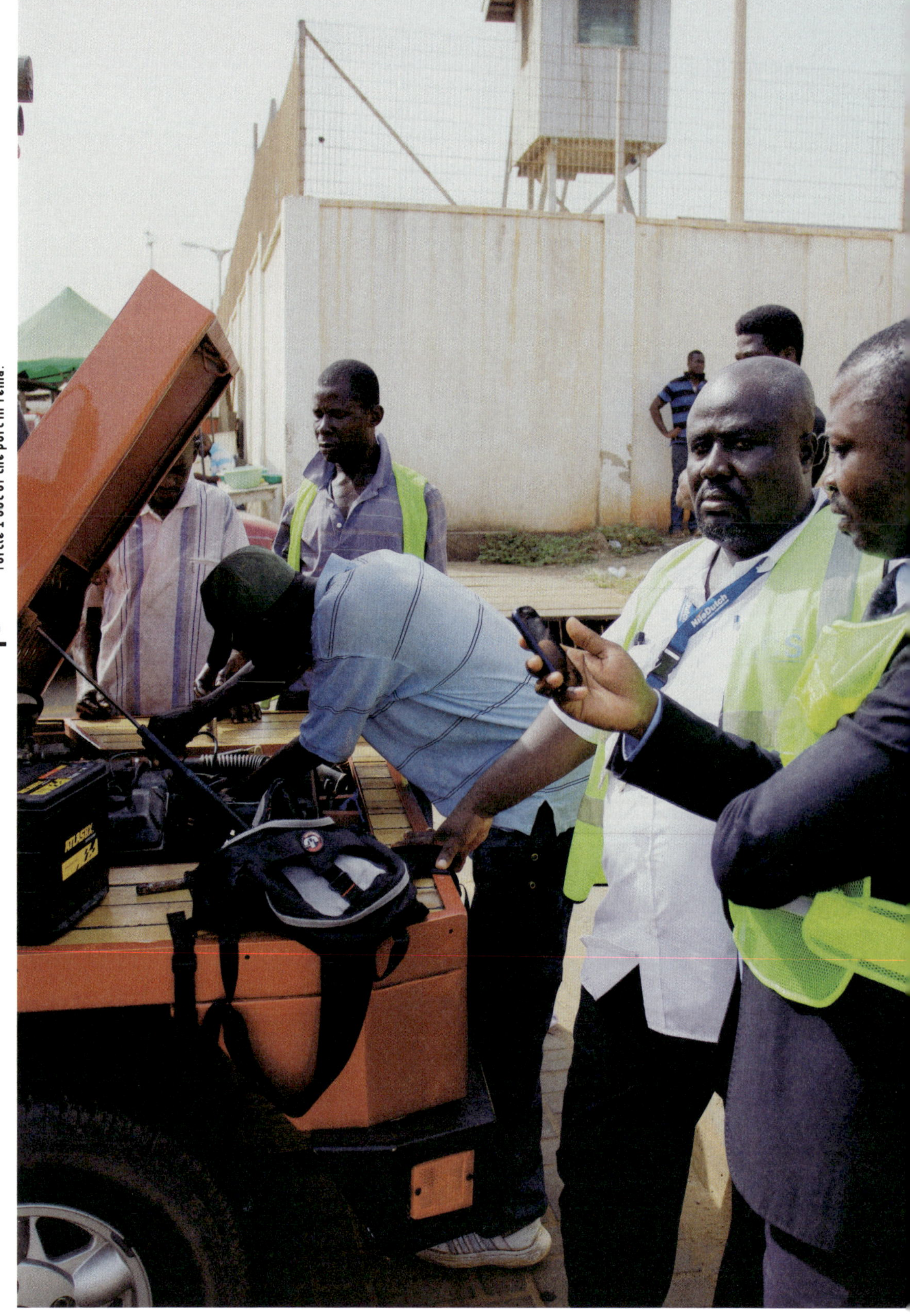

Tweneboah Kodua Boakye, a representative of the pension fund UPT, is putting pressure to get the Turtle 1 out of the port in Tema.

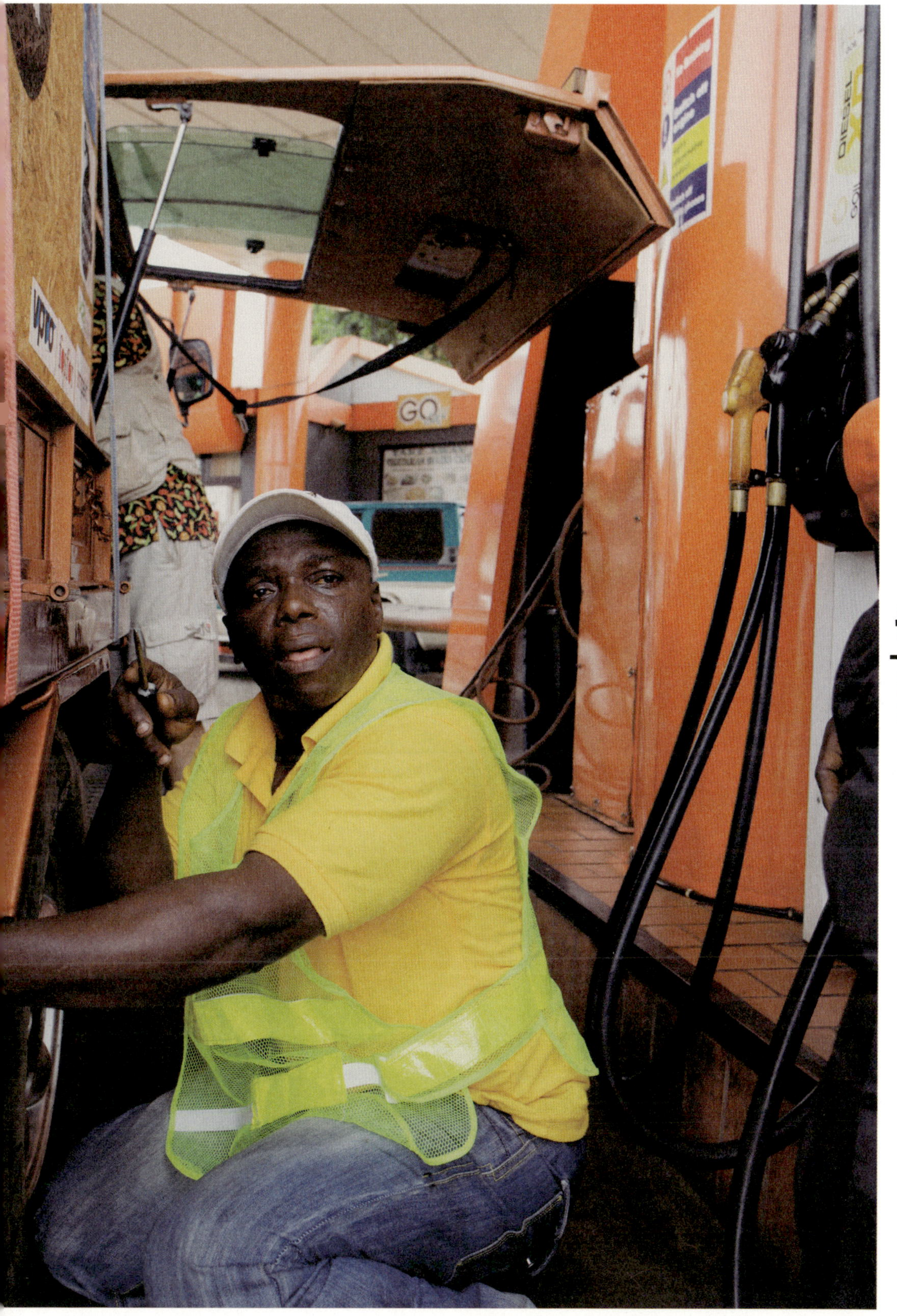

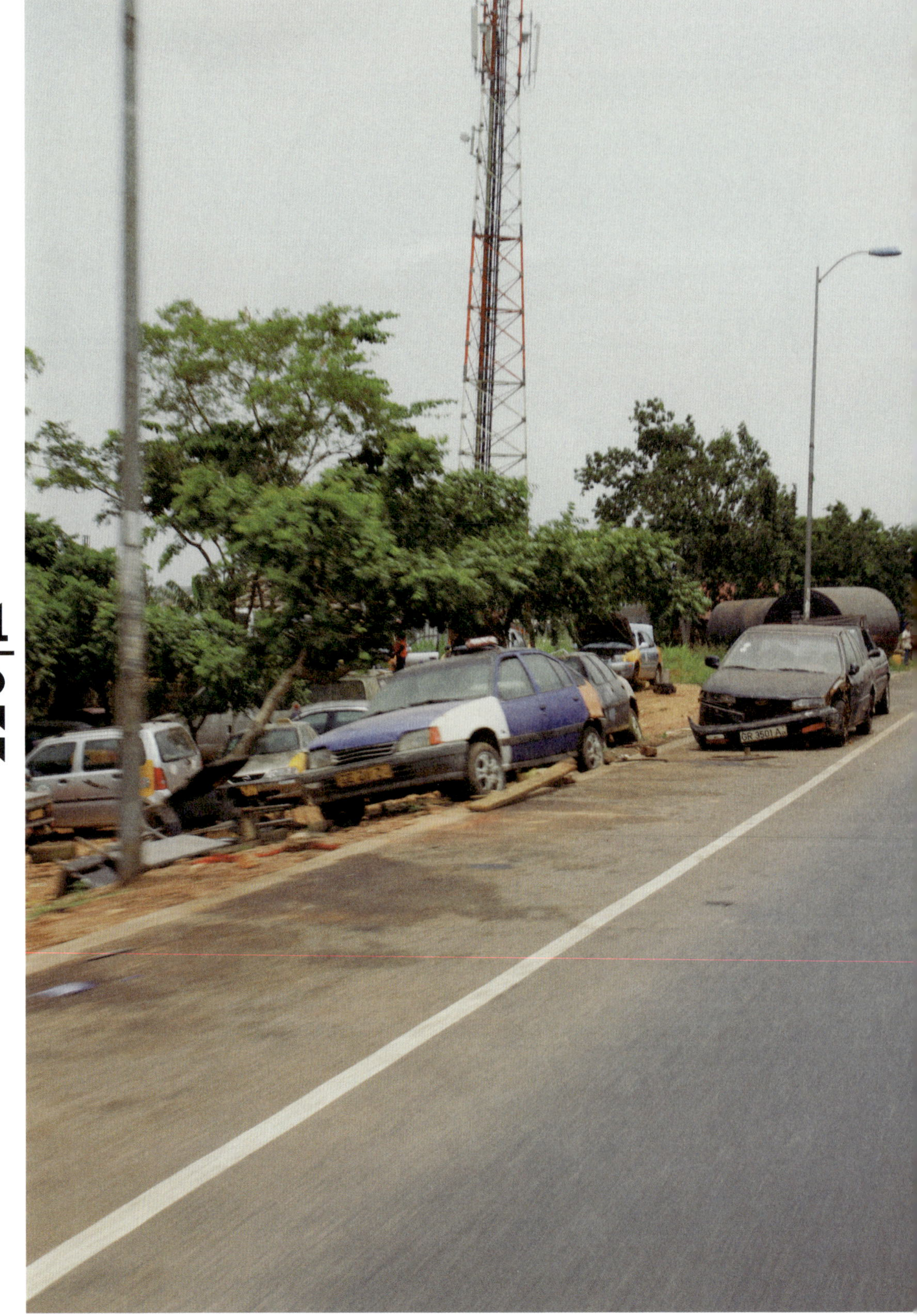

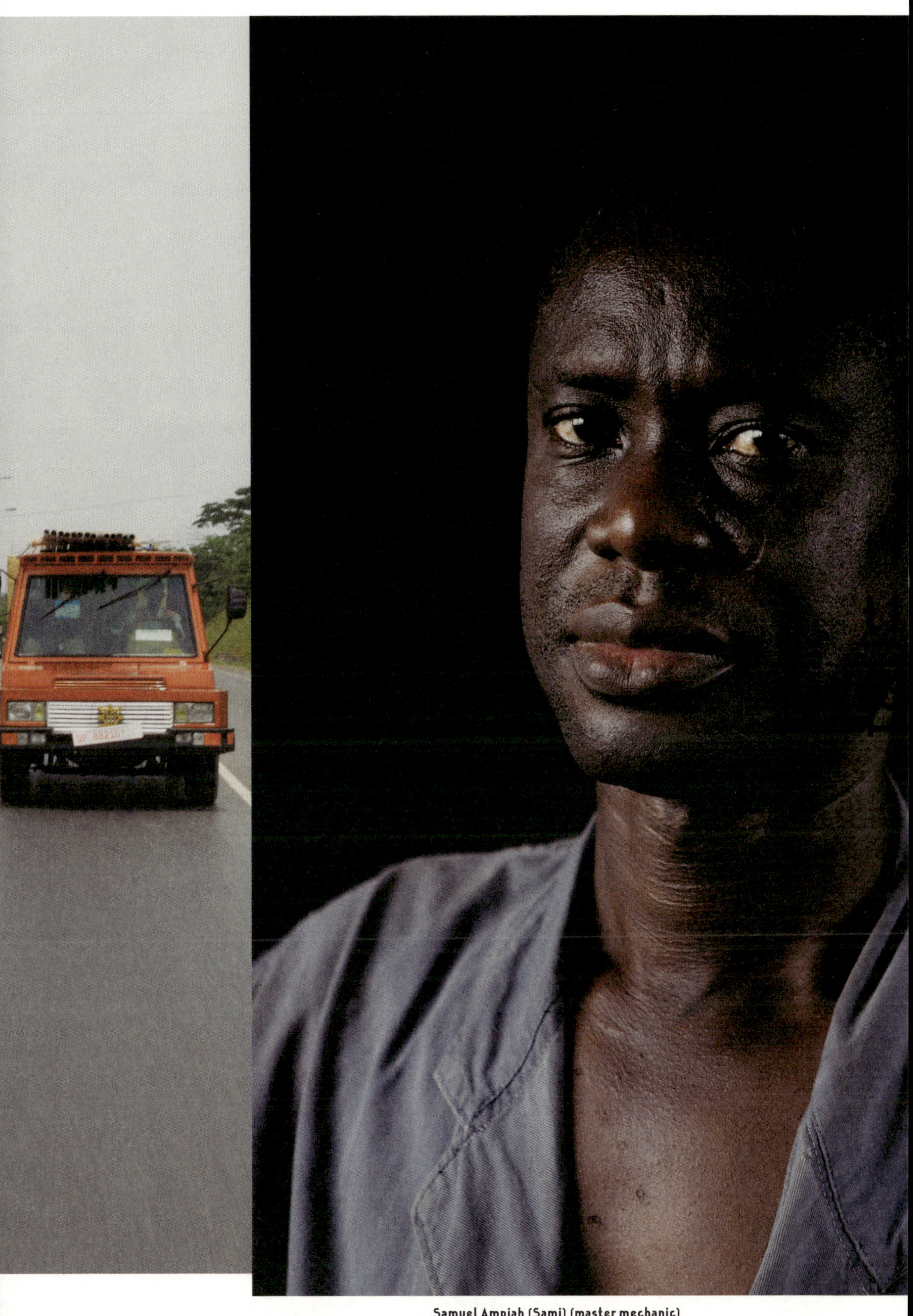

Samuel Ampiah (Sami) (master mechanic)

Because we lost time at the port, we had to make the 300-km journey to Kumasi in a single day. As the Turtle 1 cannot drive faster than 50 km/h, it took us more than 10 hours.

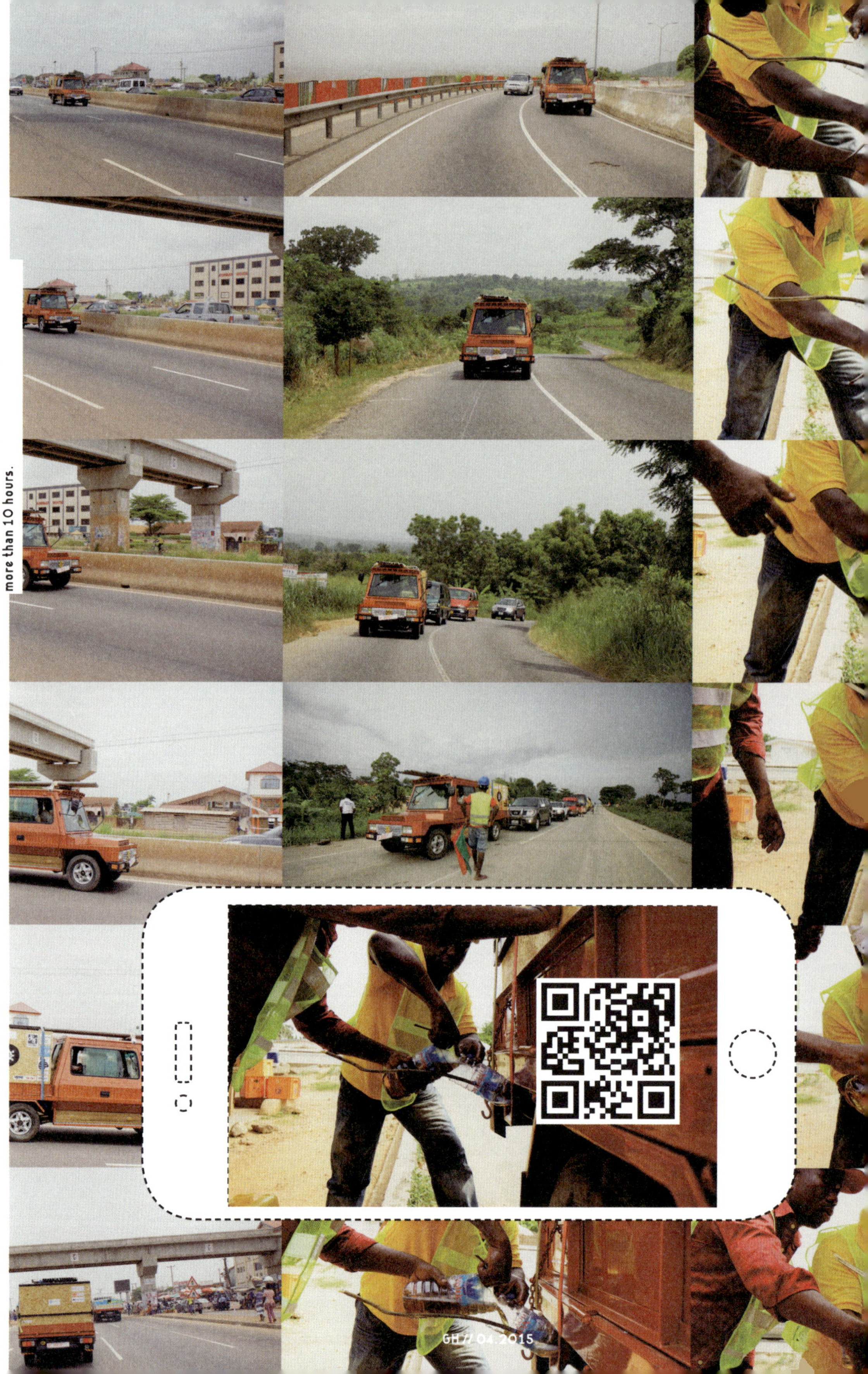

GH // 04.2015

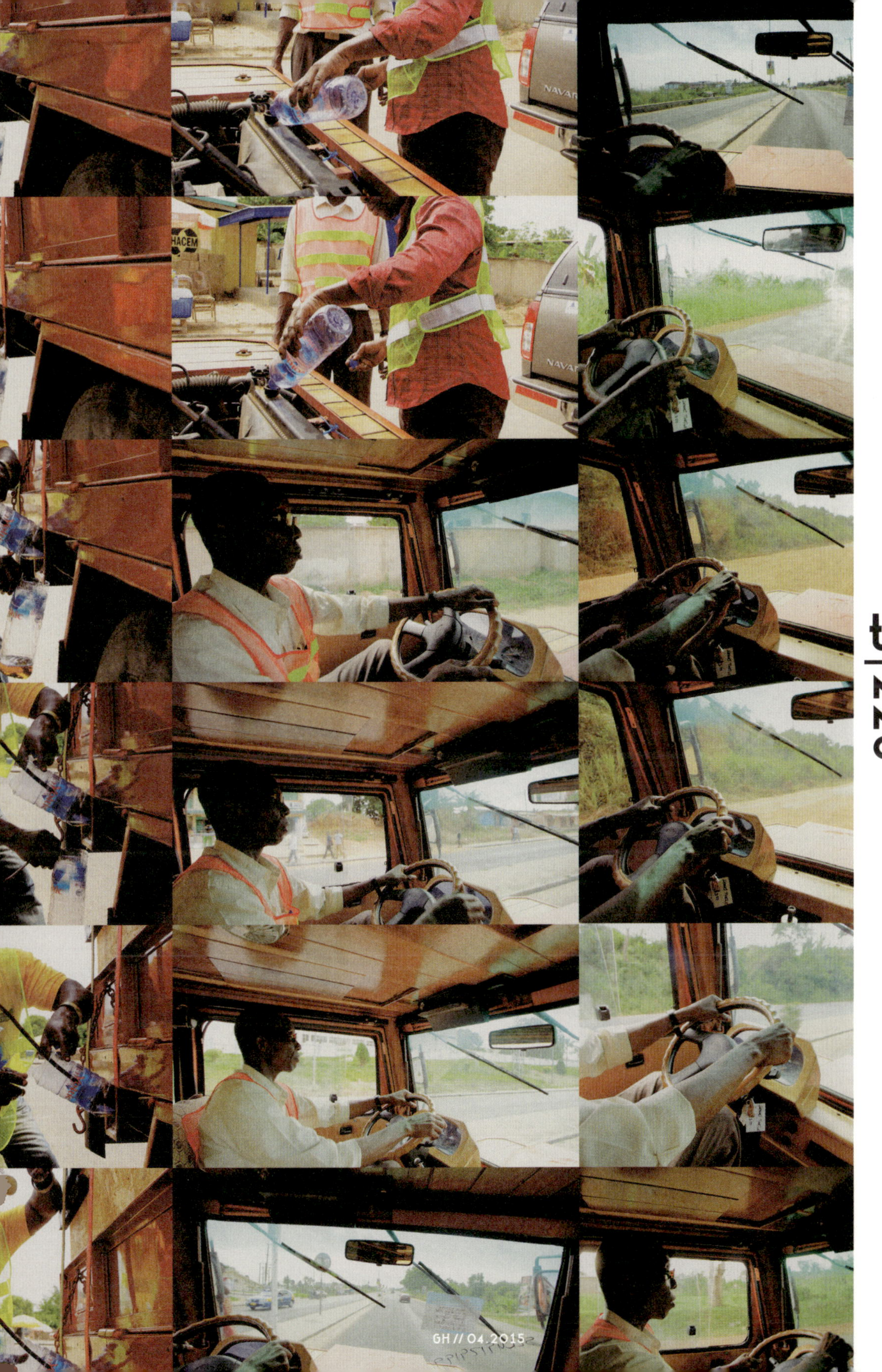
NAVAR
HACEM
NAVAR
GH // 04.2015

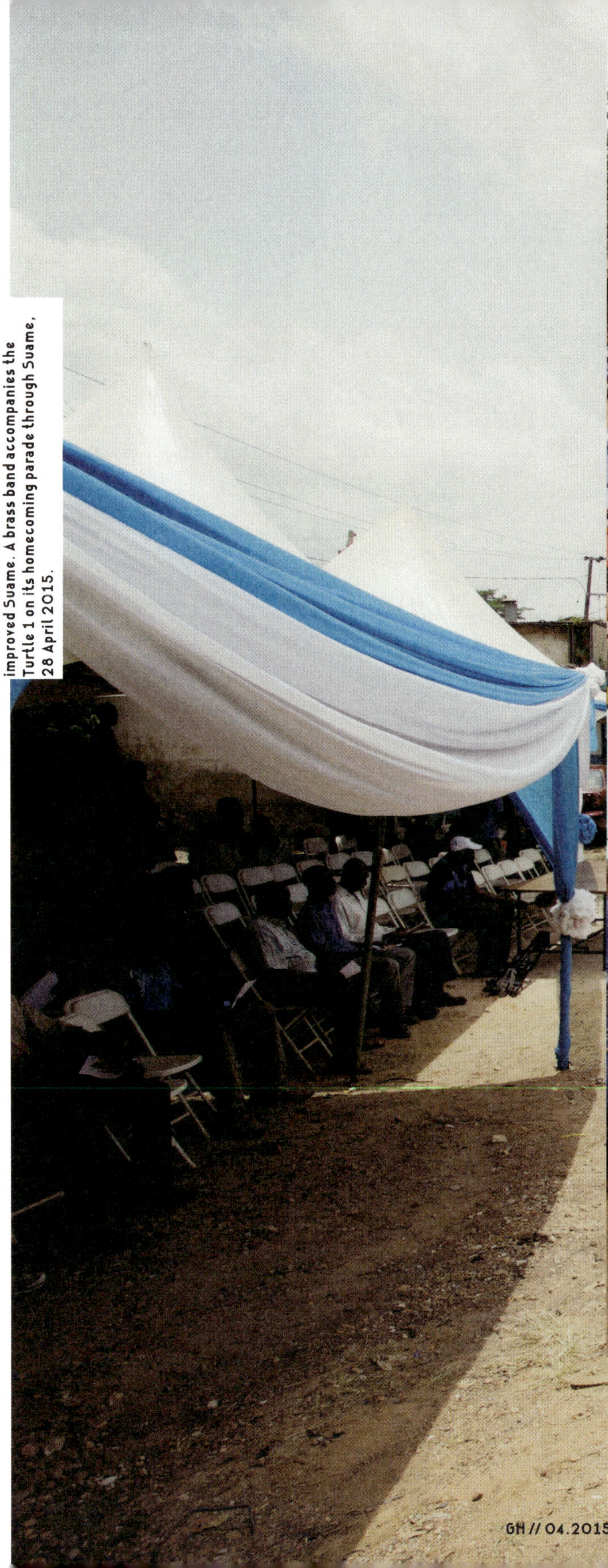

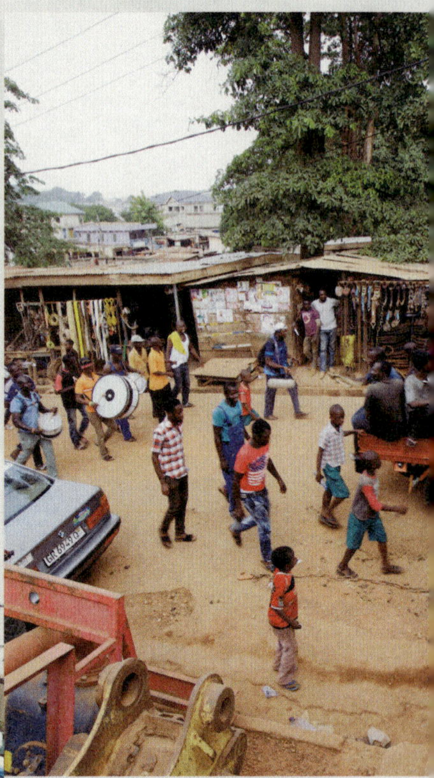

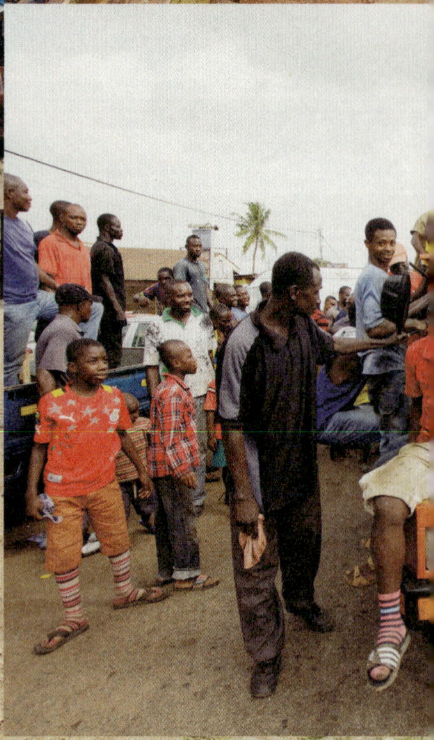

The official handover of the Turtle 1's key to the chief of the New Land Nana Owusu Appeasa II. The New Land is designated as the location of a new and improved Suame. A brass band accompanies the Turtle 1 on its homecoming parade through Suame, 28 April 2015.

GH // 04.2015

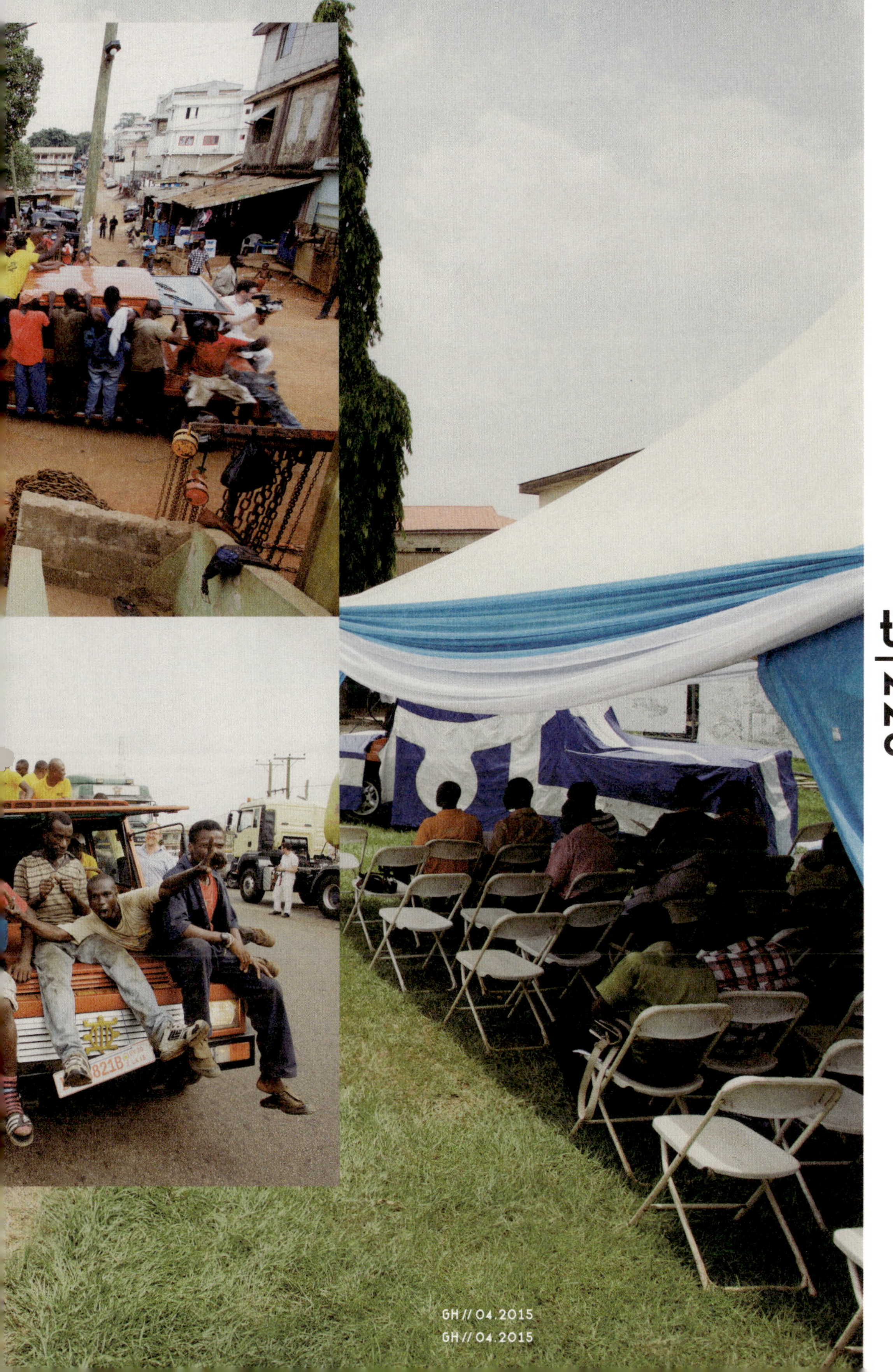

GH // 04.2015
GH // 04.2015

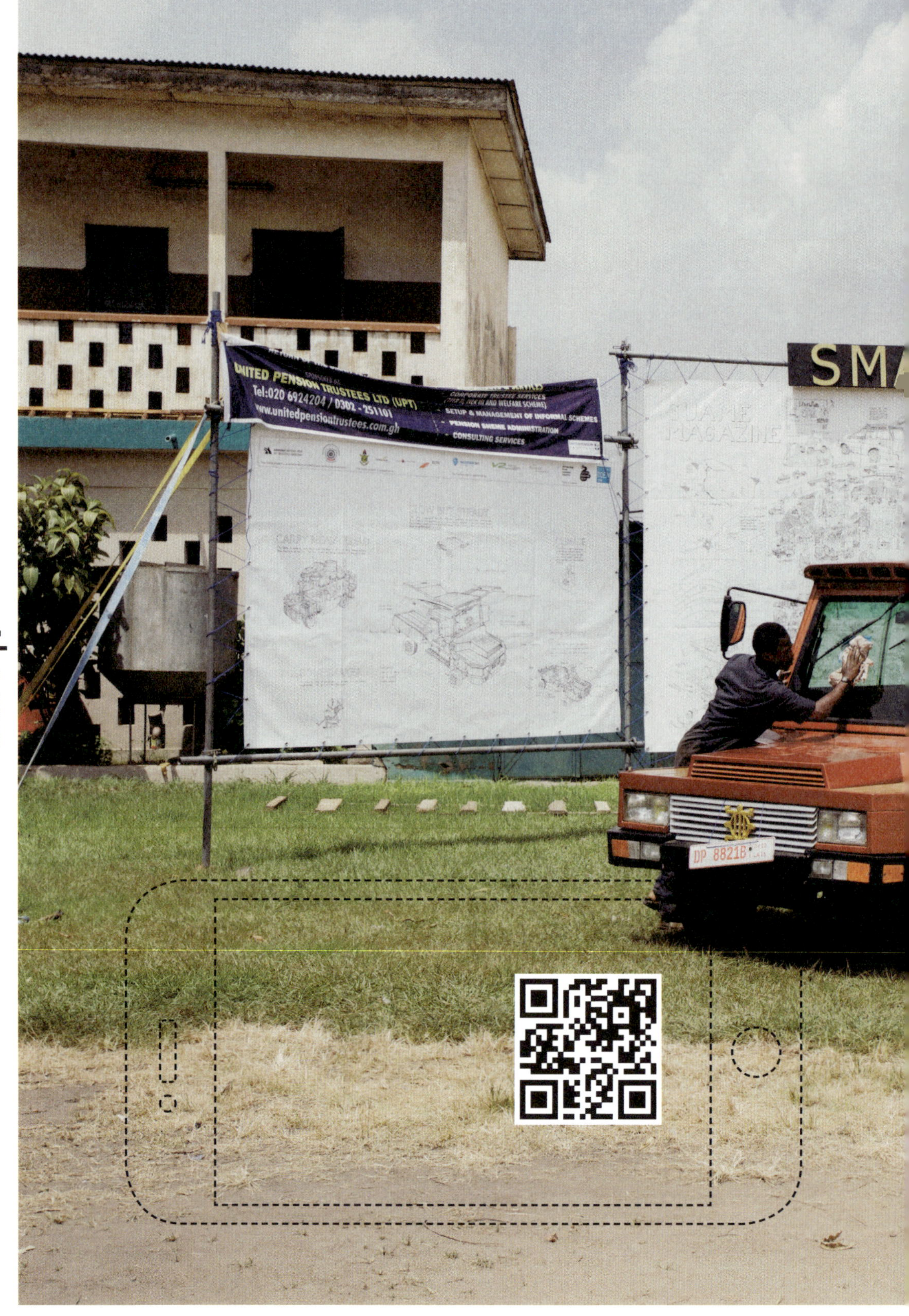

226 | t1

Exhibition of the Turtle project at the ITTU workshop,
26 April – 1 May 2015.

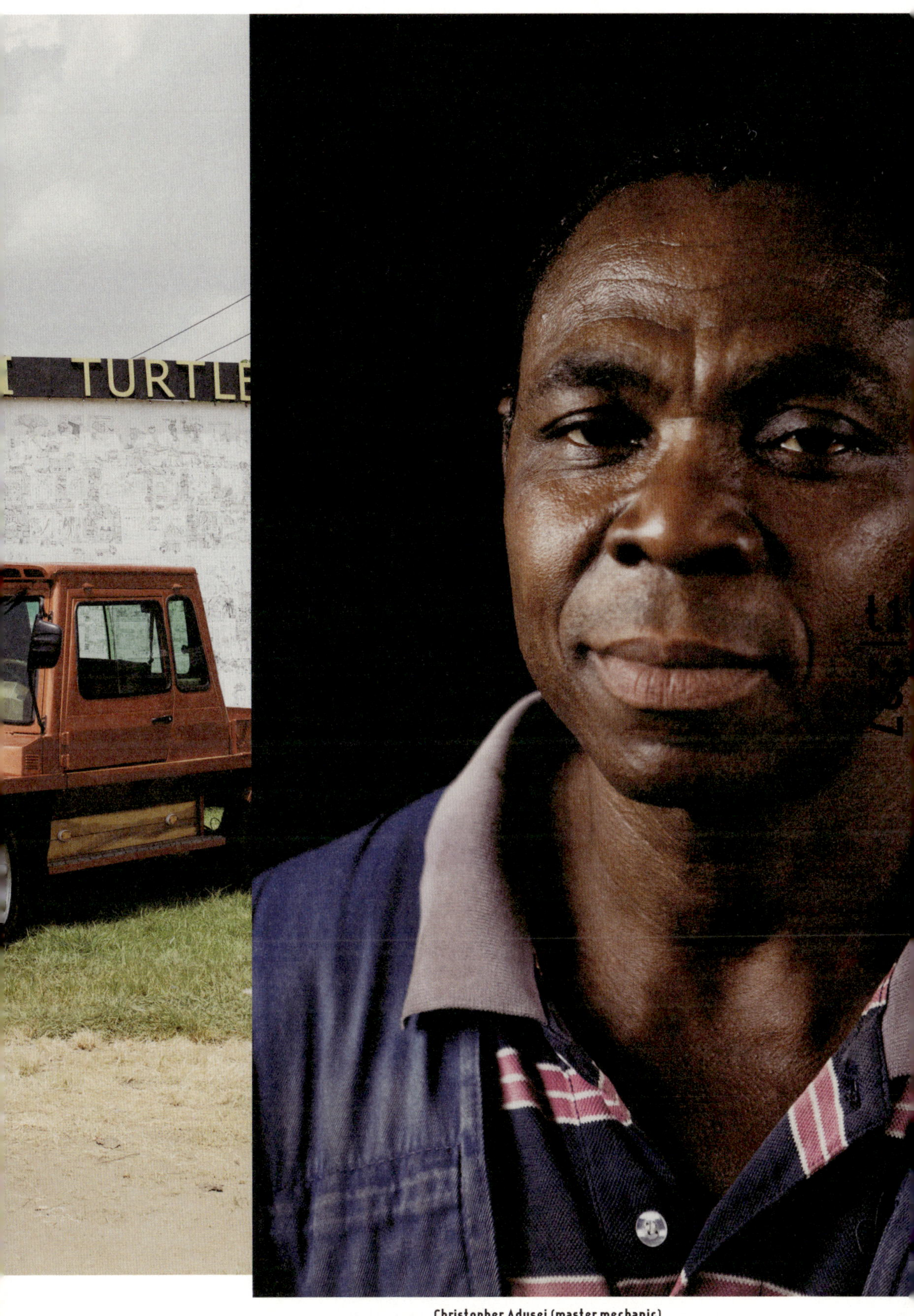

Christopher Adusei (master mechanic)

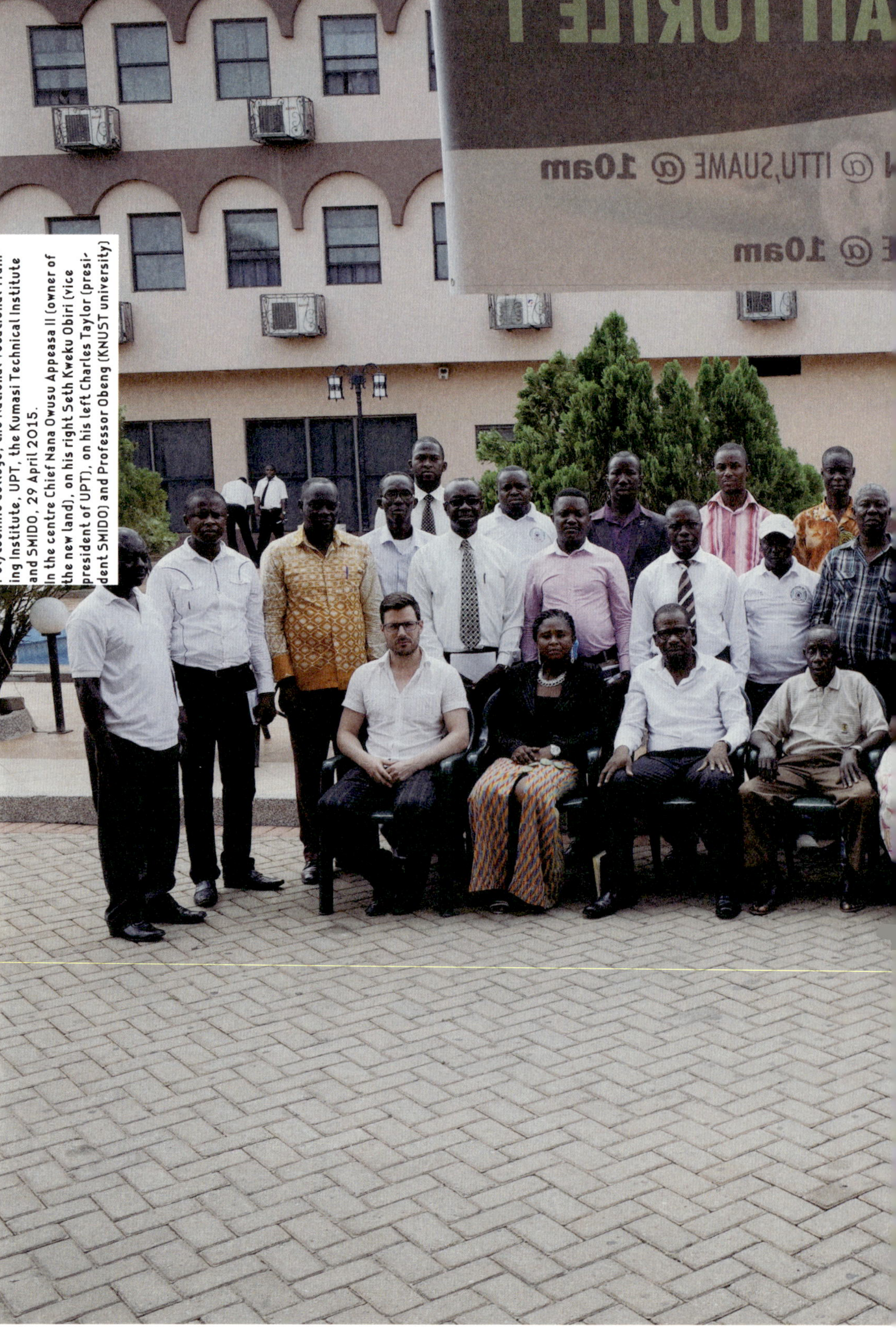

Conference at the Miklin Hotel about the future of the Turtle 2 with among others representatives from the government, the KNUST University, ITTU, the Polytechnic College, the National Vocational Training Institute, UPT, the Kumasi Technical Institute and SMIDO, 29 April 2015.
In the centre Chief Nana Owusu Appeasa II (owner of the new land), on his right Seth Kweku Obiri (vice president of UPT), on his left Charles Taylor (president SMIDO) and Professor Obeng (KNUST university)

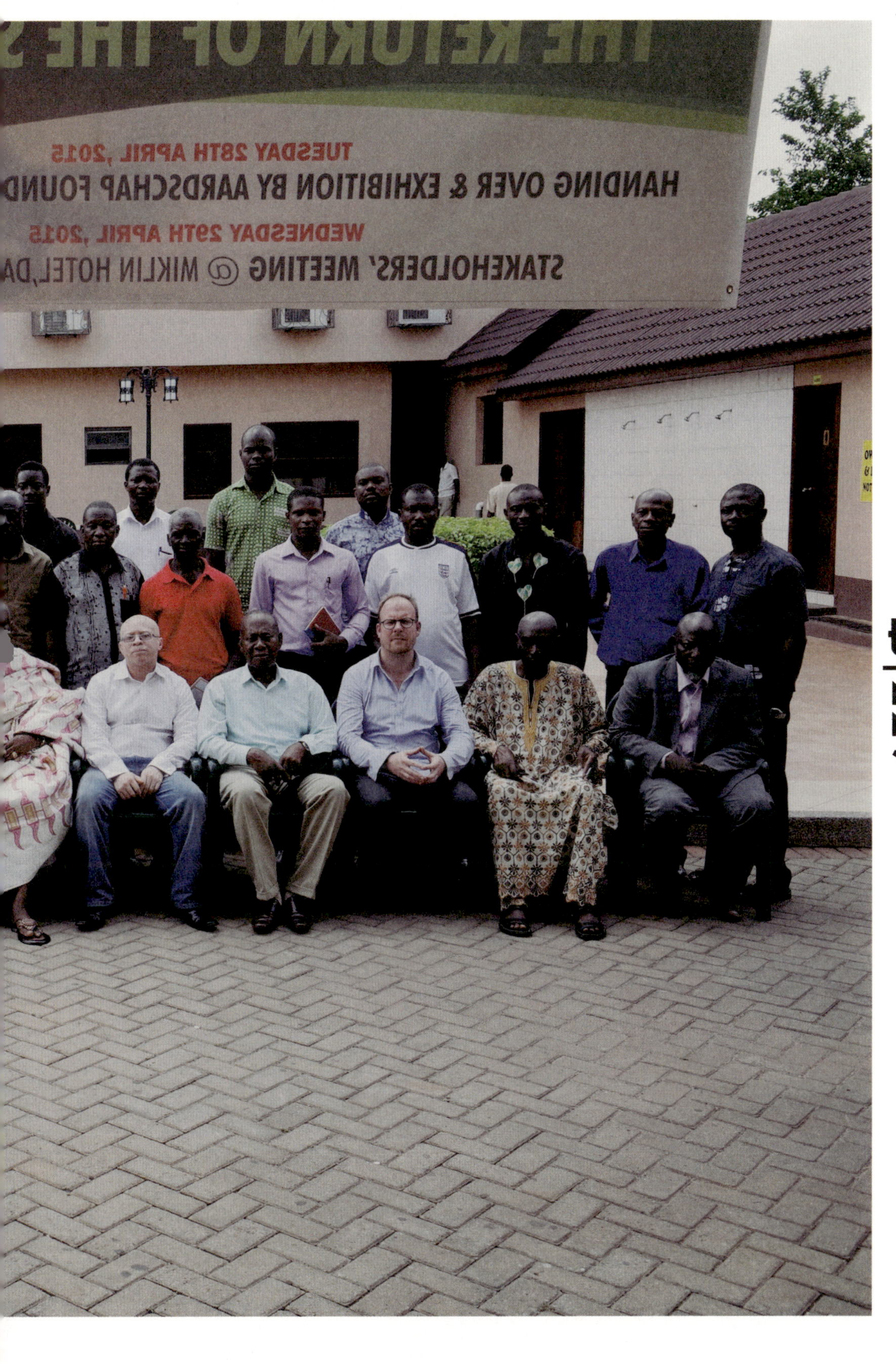
THE RETURN OF THE S
TUESDAY 28TH APRIL ,2015
HANDING OVER & EXHIBITION BY AARDSCHAP FOUND
WEDNESDAY 29TH APRIL ,2015
STAKEHOLDERS' MEETING @ MIKLIN HOTEL,DA

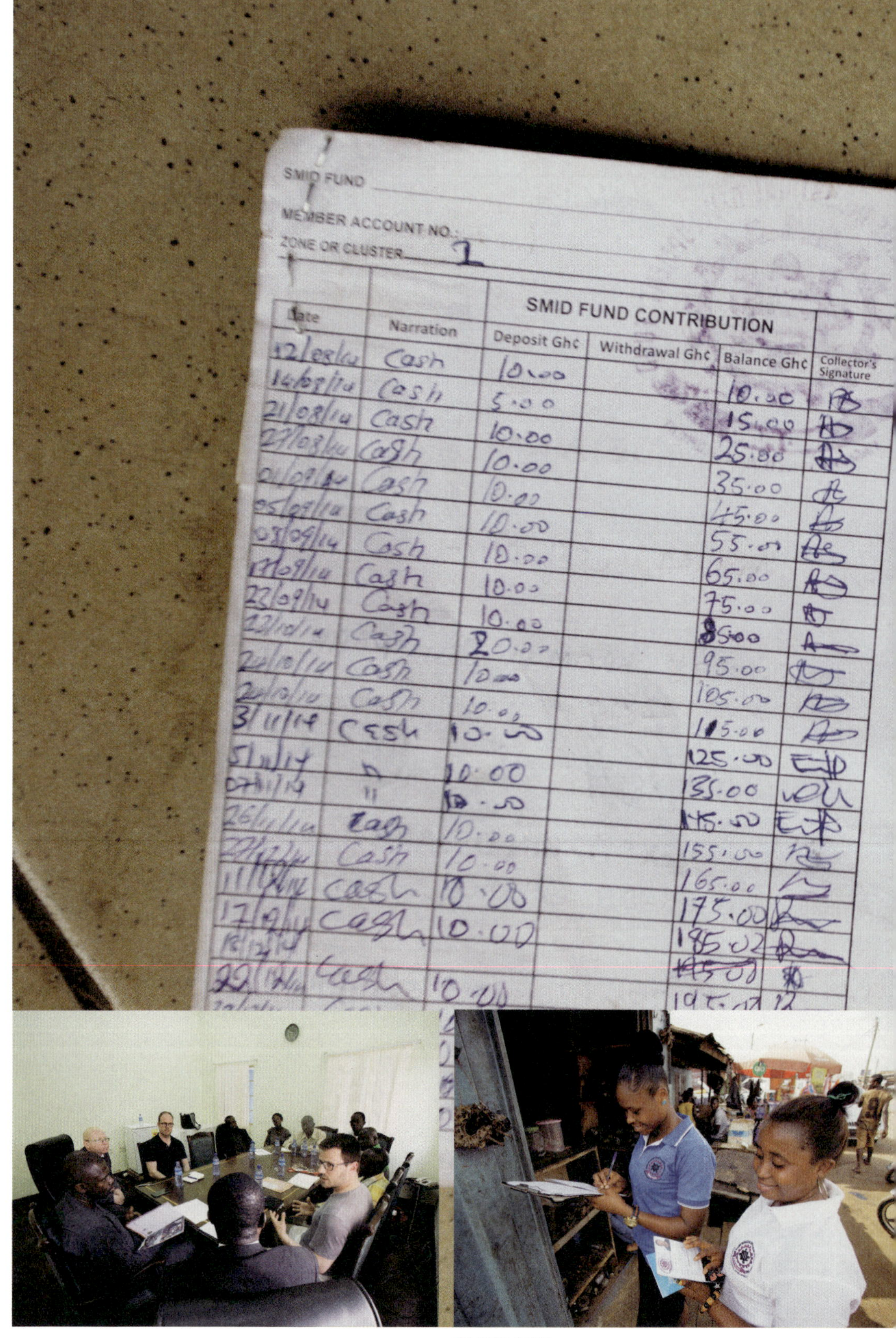

L: Meeting with the UPT board.
R: The UPT collection team collects money for the SMID pension fund in Old Suame.

GH // 04.2015

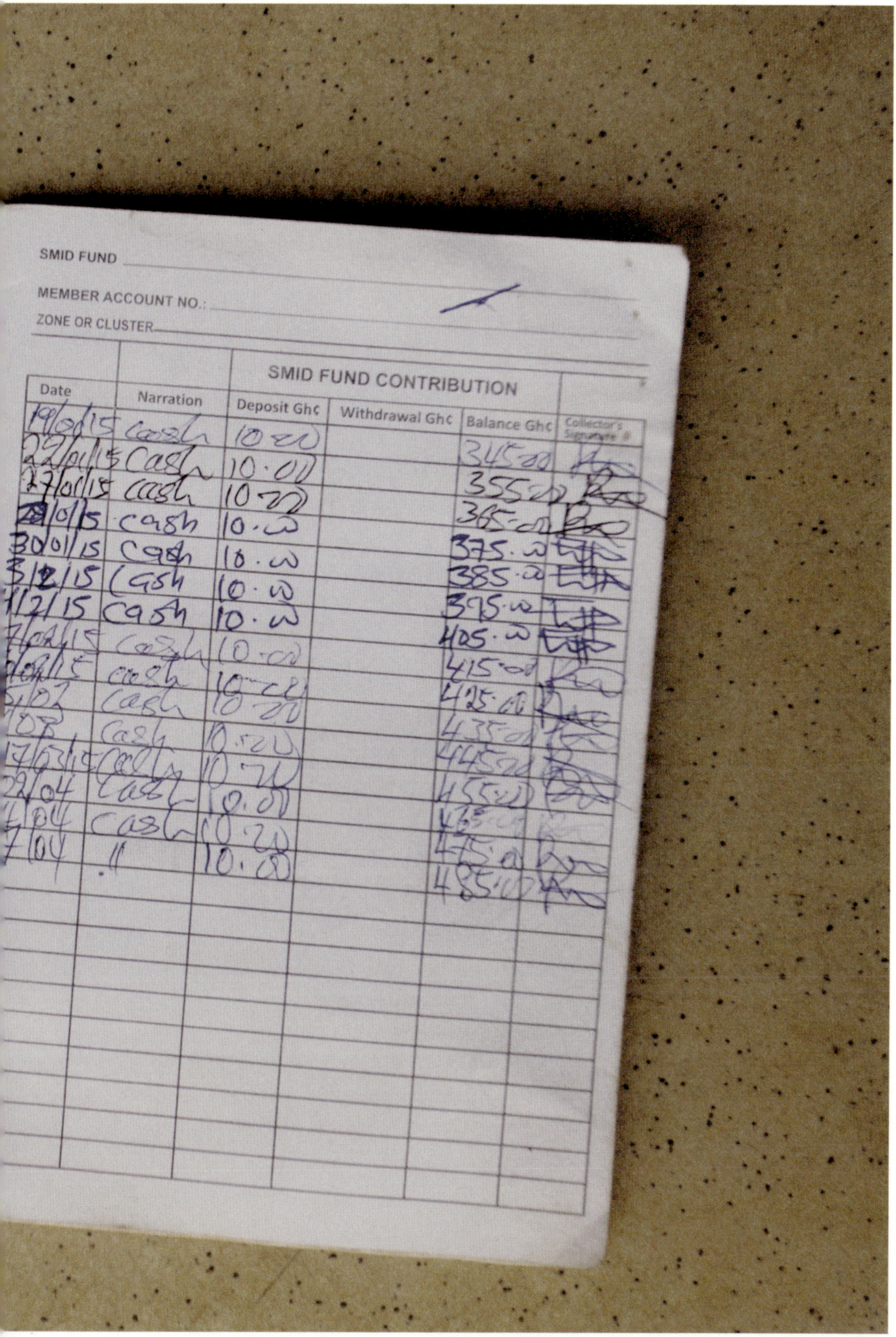

SMID FUND

MEMBER ACCOUNT NO.:

ZONE OR CLUSTER

Date	Narration	SMID FUND CONTRIBUTION			
		Deposit Gh¢	Withdrawal Gh¢	Balance Gh¢	Collector's Signature
19/01/15	cash	10.00			
22/01/15	Cash	10.00		345.00	[illegible]
27/01/15	cash	10.00		355.00	[illegible]
[illegible]/01/15	cash	10.00		365.00	[illegible]
30/01/15	cash	10.00		375.00	[illegible]
3/2/15	Cash	10.00		385.00	[illegible]
[illegible]/2/15	cash	10.00		395.00	[illegible]
[illegible]/02/15	cash	10.00		405.00	[illegible]
[illegible]/02/15	cash	10.00		415.00	[illegible]
[illegible]/02	cash	10.00		425.00	[illegible]
[illegible]/03	cash	10.00		435.00	[illegible]
17/03/15	cash	10.00		445.00	[illegible]
22/04	cash	10.00		455.00	[illegible]
[illegible]/04	cash	10.00		465.00	[illegible]
7/04	"	10.00		475.00	[illegible]
				485.00	[illegible]

t1 | 231

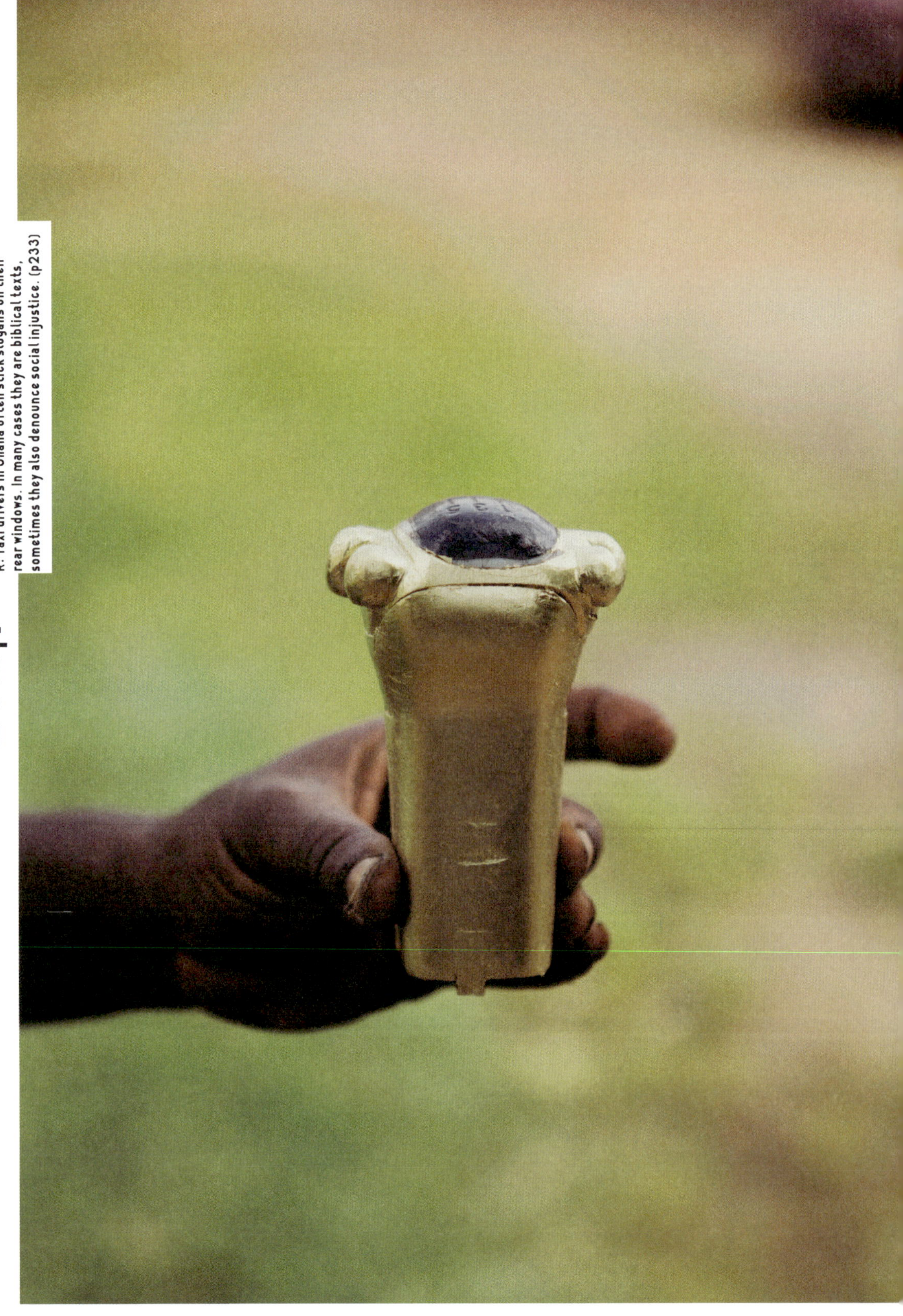

L: The Turtle's gear stick, made by Daniel Ekow (master armourer).
R: Taxi drivers in Ghana often stick slogans on their rear windows. In many cases they are biblical texts, sometimes they also denounce social injustice. (p233)

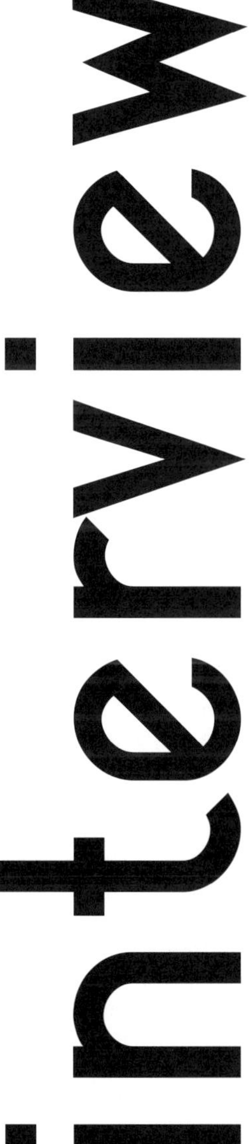

Warna Oosterbaan meets Melle Smets and Joost van Onna on April 4, 2016
Melle Smets (1975) and Joost van Onna (1976) know each other from nursery school. One became a visual artist, the other a criminologist. "We always kept in touch, and we had always planned to do something together," says Smets. The opportunity presented itself when Smets went to the United States in 2011 for a project and tacked on a trip with Van Onna. Along the way, they visited Detroit and were astounded to see the ruins of the auto industry there. "We kept talking about how dangerous it is to put all your eggs in one basket."[1]

It was an issue that went on 'simmering' in both their minds. Smets – who was working on mobility in the Netherlands among other things – wanted to seek out the other end of the spectrum. Were you meant to be for the Western system or against? Was there another way of structuring your economy? That is where Smets and Van Onna's ideas converged. After having lived in South America for years and through his work as a criminologist, Van Onna was interested to find out how people organise their lives without government protection or formal rules. Can one learn anything from a world is which very little is regulated?

Interesting questions, but Smets and Van Onna did not immediately see how to translate them into a productive project. "Then I read a book by the British historian David Edgerton, The Shock of the Old," says Smets. "He argues that important innovations often develop by accident. And he mentioned the industrial cluster in Suame Magazine, Ghana, as an example of a robust system where discarded cars from all over the world are tropicalised."[2]

Maybe we should go and visit that place, Smets and Van Onna thought. "We went, and immediately fell for it. We found a partner, the Suame Magazine Industrial Development Organization (SMIDO), who was willing to build a car with us." But not before they had first made a tedious round of sponsors, donors and potential partners. In the end, they found 15 organisations that were willing to support the project, including the Kwame Nkrumah University in Kumasi, Royal Dutch Burger group and the Centrum Beeldende Kunst Rotterdam. They were ready to get started.

Did you first try to figure out how it worked over there in Suame Magazine? Van Onna: "Actually, that is exactly what we did not want to do. Suame was our field of research. Everything that was going to happen, would give us new insights and therefore be

1 See for example, Wright, R. 2005. *A Short History of Progress.* Edinburgh: Canongate Books.
2 Edgerton, D. 2011. *The Shock of the Old.* New York: Oxford Press.

valuable. It was an experiment in the real world, with an open end. We had no preconceived ideas for the design of the car either. We wanted it to be determined by the surroundings and local preferences and circumstances. That would also make the experiment most fitting to Suame. Learning by doing, that was our slogan, just like the apprentices learn their skills in the workshops. You understand the social system by getting involved in it, not by being a fly on the wall, particularly in Suame Magazine."[3]
Smets: "We were naive outsiders, which had its advantages. When there was a conflict, we were the lightning conductors: they could blame us and that would be the end of it. But we only found that out later."

Was it easy, once you started understanding the place? Van Onna: "At a certain point you start to get a better understanding of the place. Suame is a fickle world. For example, 'putting pressure' as a way of getting something done. Who pays the bill? Who puts energy into a project? You cannot always resolve those questions by drawing up a planning schedule and making agreements. It is a game, and you have to learn to play it. Sometimes by ignoring people, or by presenting them with a fait accompli, or simply by imposing your own view. On the last day, we had to leave in a hurry as the Turtle had to be taken to the port. We had organised a minivan because there was quite a group coming along. But Philip insisted on a different van; he said the tyres were worn out. For some reason he was not into the whole plan. We reacted rather bluntly, which was out of character for us. Sometimes arguments are pointless in such situations; they won't get you anywhere. We told him: 'Good or bad tyres, we're off.' We had a boat and a plane to catch."
Smets: "You also learn how to bluff – like that time I said we had no money for a generator because I felt SMIDO should pay up. We learnt those things simply by doing. The process of learning what you can and cannot do is endless though and keeps repeating itself. Like the time Philip corrected my planning board by erasing all the deadlines. It doesn't work, he said, everyone will think there is plenty of time left."

Was it a revelation for you, to see how people in Suame solve problems? Smets: "Initially we were in disbelief. It seemed like people were not taking any initiative and just waiting around to see what might happen. In the West, we are taught that if you do not invest, you will end up empty handed. In Suame it is different. It is a fickle society, where you never know exactly what could happen tomorrow. You're always waiting for your chance and you have to seize the opportunity when it comes along. That constant uncertainty makes it hard to count on anything. To us, the waiting looked like laziness, but it wasn't. It is about investing your energy at the right moment."
Van Onna: "The lack of formal structures means that Suame's informal society is mainly built on the underlying social fabric. And up to a point, it works surprisingly well. For example, there is not much violence in Suame Magazine. Social structures like the master-apprentice system form the backbone of the neighbourhood. It keeps the "angry young men" in check. It works like a village. No one is unemployed. There is always some odd job to be done and children easily get a job through an aunt or uncle. The same goes for the church: beyond its religious function, it has an important role as a safety net for people in need."
Smets: "On the other hand, there is a quagmire of social obligations. The only way to get things done is through personal relations. Doing someone a favour is a way of building up credit that you can draw upon later. You learn to anticipate the opportunities that come along. It is pointless to think about the future too much. That means that running a successful business in Suame Magazine is rather reactive."

That system was a disadvantage for you? Smets "Yes, but on the other hand you learn a lot from it. You realise the extent to which we are always thinking about the future. We are always thinking about what we are going to do, instead of focusing on what is happening now and where we are."
Van Onna: "Many things actually work very well. It is incredible to see what the mechanics and artisans of Suame achieved in 12 weeks under very challenging conditions – not just local conditions, but also the project brief. We had no preconceived plan or design for the car; we often chose the hard road (e.g. building a car made up of different brands); and the team that built the car had never worked together before. For instance, I thought their method of "sharing ideas" was brilliant. It involved people of the same rank discussing their ideas for as long as needed until they reached a consensus. It was perhaps not the most efficient way of building a car, but it was a nice solution to the problem of having several masters in our workshop and, as a result, no real hierarchy."

There were a couple of moments when things looked very gloomy. Did you ever think: let's just quit? Smets: "No, the research kept us going. The outcome was open-ended. Even if it was going to end in failure, we had to describe and examine why that had happened. And of course we also became part of the social system. We actually developed great admiration

3 *Sharing Ideas and Putting Pressure. "Criminological Insights from action-research in Informal Entrepreneurship in the Largest Car-related Industrial Cluster in the World".*
Cahiers Politiestudies, 29: 147-170.

›r the everyday optimism of people in Suame. It is an ıcredible battle for survival, to keep all the balls in the ir every day. When things were not going our way, we ied to follow their example."

id they also learn something from you? Van nna: "They complimented us – though not on our bilities as car builders, because those left a lot to be esired. But they liked the fact that we collaborated, ıey always praised that."
mets: "Joost and I often consulted each other. /e had an idea and we would discuss it and arrive t a conclusion. In a way it was like "sharing ideas". hey picked up on that straight away. And we kept ur promises. When the mechanics and sheet metal orkers did overtime, we could not always pay them nmediately, because the banks were closed. But then ıey got their pay the next day. That does not always appen in the world of Suame. You make agreements n the basis of trust, there is no written proof. That is hy business deals are often sealed with handshakes nd group photos. Contracts are drawn up, but how o you enforce them in a world like Suame? nfortunately, everyone has seen cases where people reak the unwritten rules. For instance, when we did ot get our money back for the rear axle we returned. /e had good contacts and were able to resolve it. ut if you're poor, or not part of a strong group, you're ı trouble."

ow do you see the future of Suame Magazine? mets: "The biggest problem is that very little is egulated. Everything runs on human energy, which all over the place. That makes it very difficult to ollaborate according to a plan, which means that hen you want to build something as complicated s a car, everything has to run smoothly. Before you ıow it, something you had not factored in gets in the ay, like the fact that you have to work with a specific pholsterer because he is part of the group. And so you annot start working with the upholsterer you chose."
an Onna: "It is a fickle and unpredictable world. ven more so if you have left your own village, your orkshop, your network, or your church – then it is a ıngle where you have to make your own way. You can nly put pressure on people if you have built up the ght contacts. The master-apprentice system can be starting point, and then you have to figure out how to uild upon that."
mets: "If you want to make something like the Turtle, ɔu need a common goal, but also the knowledge and ıe means to organise the process. The institutes with ıe capacity to do this have to work together, but that is ot happening now."
an Onna: "You can't just rely on individuals to make it happen. The same is true in the Netherlands actually. The "participation society" only works in neighbourhoods that already have strong social capital. Otherwise the government continues to play an important role."

So a second Turtle will be difficult? Van Onna: "The people in Suame Magazine are very good at a number of things. They are already building all sorts of things. Welding machines, wheelbarrows, top pieces for gas canisters – they are brilliant at those kinds of things. Dealers from across West Africa go there to buy these parts. But it is still risky to invest there. Building a workshop is a gamble, because the land rights are not well regulated.[4]
If you build a nice workshop, you can be sure that someone is going to turn up to claim the land on which you built your investment. That is why Suame remains reactive and small scale. At Wageningen University people asked us: "Why would you even consider building a car there? Wouldn't it be better to think of something simpler?"
Smets: "Of course they had a point. But the strength of building a car is not the product; it is the story, people's learning process. During the building process, people started to see the capacities and strengths of the Magazine community. "Tropicalisation", i.e. the transformation of industrially produced cars into low-tech off-road vehicles – is a radically different way of applying technology. It is a powerful idea that would otherwise have remained abstract. By building more Turtles, you can train and empower new generations to refine and develop this process. You don't have to be able to read or write to learn how to build Turtles.

But how exactly? Smets: "You can go two ways. The first option: make the industrial product simpler. We visited a factory on the coast that was being run by an Indian and where they produced bolts, nuts and leaf springs. Those are relatively simple products, but still, it was not easy to keep such a mass-production factory running. Machinery often broke down and spare parts were slow to arrive. You can also choose a different tack, like the one Azongo was advocating. Establish a training system, teach basic skills. The product can be complex, as long as the production process is well organised. We are convinced that that is possible.
So that means basing your thinking on human organisation, not on the simplification of technology."
Van Onna: "We more or less chose that route, we tried to initiate a process. Our idea was that participating in building this kind of car can be like a master's project, which gives you access to further education. And the building process is a crossroads, where people from different disciplines and of different skill levels meet and get to know each other. But it is still difficult. There is a kind of training centre, the SMATI, where they

4 Ubink, J.M. 2008. *In the Land of the Chiefs. Customary Law, Land Conflicts, and the Role of the State in Peri-rban Ghana.* Leiden: Leiden University Press.

teach English language and repair techniques. But if apprentices need money, they don't go to the training centre; they go and look for an odd job instead."

Is it an African problem that it is hard to get things of the ground? Van Onna: "Research shows that similar problems and patterns arise in any area that is poor and where the government is weak. So it is not a cultural issue or an African problem. The parallels are bigger than the differences. On the other hand, there are cultural aspects to the way things work in Suame Magazine. To me, poor farmers in Peru are more organised and they have a much more collectivistic attitude. Some researchers have a historical explanation for this: the Incas organised their society in an almost communist structure. I saw much less of that capacity for organisation in Suame. But I was often reminded of an interview I read with Jean Marc Ndjofang, one of the world's top draughts players. He is from Cameroon. He said that Western players are especially good at the opening moves. They are endlessly trying to precalculate the game. But an African makes his move based on a gut feeling, on intuition; he improvises. And those are the qualities that African players deploy in the end game, when the board is a lot less predictable and that is when they shine. That is why they often beat Western players. I recognised that strength in Suame. To run a successful business in Suame Magazine, you have to constantly anticipate what lies ahead. It is like being a skipper at sea: you don't stay on course with a planning schedule and contracts, but with experience, knowledge of your surroundings, intuition and guts."

Would there be a market for a Turtle-like car in Ghana? Smets: "It's hard to say. We did not do any market research. But if you think of what people can afford there, between €2,000 and €5,000 – you cannot build a car for that price. We spent around €8,000 on the Turtle 1. You have to be able to compete with the global offer. As long as it is cheaper to import a wreck for a couple of thousand euros and get it fixed for a couple of hundred euros, it is a losing battle. Making a vehicle is precision work, and that is more suited to an industrial process. And let's be honest, anyone who manages to save up enough money would rather get a real SUV than the kind of car that we built."

What did you learn from the project? Van Onna: "The contrasts between self-organisation and formal systems. Self-organisation is social; it takes life as it comes. It is a healthy attitude to life that fits with mankind's social nature. But self-organisation has its limits and in daily life it is difficult for weak parties to survive in that kind of system. If you go the other route, if you start collaborating, rationalising and formalising, you have to make a sacrifice: you have to give up freedom. In our world with all its certainties, we have been trained from a young age to plan ahead. You know that if you invest, you will be rewarded in the end. That is quite different in an informal world where the future is so uncertain."
Smets: "The building of the Turtle taught us that the informal world is, paradoxically, a restrictive system – almost diametrically opposed to our romantic idea of freedom. In fact, our formal system, with its rules and institutions, offers a lot of freedom. It enables society to channel and ritualise all sorts of elementary processes. It is reassuring and also gives confidence, so that there is time left for more complex things, like building an auto industry."

You have unleashed something over there, created expectations. How do you see your responsibility? Smets: "We didn't know what we were getting into, we couldn't do much more than build the car to the best of our ability. But the story developed a positive dynamic, through the publicity and because of the king's appearance. When we went back to the Netherlands we had two options. We could have said: "Thank you and goodbye." But we chose a different path. We stuck to our commitment. We were certainly sceptical as to whether this showcase car could lay the foundation for a fully fledged car industry, but we still wanted to take the challenge seriously. That is why we set up a promotional tour and explored whether we could further develop the idea in Europe. We talked to training institutes and organisations in the field of development aid. We drew up a plan, which we presented to potential stakeholders in Europe and Ghana. The opportunities to take it to the next level are available, but it is not up to us to make it happen. In the end, it was not our dream to establish a car brand."
Van Onna: "We had a business agreement with SMIDO from the start, and we stuck to it. They are responsible businessmen, we had objectives and so did they; we clearly discussed that from the beginning. They have to take this further if they want to. They have the capacity for it."
Smets: "That is also why we brought the Turtle back to Ghana; it is theirs. If we had kept it – which was an option as it is formally ours – then it would probably have ended up as an art installation. But it does not belong in a museum; it is a car."

elected bibliography

e Soto, H. 1989. *The Other Path: The visible Revolution in the Third World.* ew York: HarperCollins.

e Soto, H. 2000. *The Mystery of Capital: hy Capitalism Triumphs in the West and ils Everywhere Else.* New York: Basic ooks.

lgerton, D. 2011. *The Shock of the Old.* ew York: Oxford Press.

art, K. 1973. *Informal Income pportunities and Urban Employment Ghana,* Journal of Modern African udies, 11: 61-89.

aarsma, T., H. Maart, P. Richards, & . Wals. 2011. *The Role of Materiality in pprenticeships: the Case of the Suame agazine, Kumasi, Ghana.* Journal of ocational Education & Training, 63: 59-449.

ahoda, M., P.F. Lazarsfeld, & H. Ziesel. 971. *Marienthal. The Sociography of n Unemployed Community.* London: ansaction Publishers.

ebenberg, L. 1990. *The Art of Tracking. he Origin of Science.* Claremont: David hilip Publishers.

yaaba-Aweeba Azongo. 2013. *The egional Investment Gateway Project.*

euwirth, R. 2012. *Stealth of Nations: The lobal Rise of the Informal Economy.* New ork: Random House.

nna, van J.H.R. 2013. *Sharing ideas en utting pressure. Criminologische inzichten 't actie-onderzoek naar informeel ndernemerschap in de grootste autowijk r wereld* (Sharing Ideas and Putting ressure. Criminological Insights om action-research in Informal ntrepreneurship in the Largest Car-elated Industrial Cluster in the World). ahiers Politiestudies, 29: 147-170.
tichting Aardschap. 2015. *S.M.A.T.I. urtle 1. Action Research. Ideas for a Local ar Manufacturing Industry in Suame.*

uame Industrial Development rganisation. 2012. *Building Prospects for rosperity.*

bink, J.M. 2008. *In the Land of the hiefs. Customary Law, Land Conflicts, and he Role of the State in Peri-rban Ghana.* eiden: Leiden University Press.

Venningsted-Torgard, R., P. Schulz chovsbo, B. Ballisager & J. Wegener onde. 2013. *Suame Magazine. Light ndustrial Living.* Retrieved from: https:// l.dropboxusercontent.com/u/11586293/ uame%20Magazine.pdf

Vright, R. 2005. *A Short History of rogress.* Edinburgh: Canongate Books.

Turtle Team

Researcher
Joost van Onna (1976) studied social psychology and criminology. He currently works as a criminologist (Netherlands Public Prosecutors Office) and is preparing a PhD thesis at the VU University of Amsterdam on criminal development and (non-) compliance to laws. He is fascinated by the functioning and strength of informal self-regulating (economic) systems, an interest he developed through his work, his thesis research and after having lived in South America for several years.

Artist
Melle Smets (1975) studied OK5/art and public space at ArtEZ Academy in Arnhem. As an 'archaeologist of the present' Smets explores and interprets society by organising expeditions to contemporary landscapes. The expeditions find their reflection in visual art projects, lectures, publications and workshops. Smets is the founder of Stichting Aardschap and is currently affiliated to the Sandberg Institute, where he heads the temporary Master's programme, The System D Academy.

Photographer and film-maker
Teun Vonk (1986) studied photography at the Royal Academy of Art in The Hague. His work focuses on the relationship between the individual and the group. Vonk is currently exploring interaction from the perspective of the personal atmosphere within architectonic installations.

Production Team
Eva van Ginhoven, press & media, co-funding & web design;
Pascal de Man, web design & realisation;
Trafic, storage & maintenance Turtle

Project management SMIDO
Charles Taylor - president
Nyaabe-Aweeba Azongo - consultant
Reuben Konlan - communications
George Amankwah - former president

Technical supervision
Albert Cophie Wornenor (Dr Waco)

Assistant technical supervision
Philip K. Kwarteng

Mechanics
Eliaia Abew
Sidik Adramani
Daniel Appiah Adjeilum
Christopher Adusei
Appiah Boateng
Desmond
Seth Frimpong
J.K. Mensah
Kofi Owusu (Osu)

Painters
Atta Agyemah
Kwame Degraft
S. K. Appiah Kubi (Besto)
Debora Nyarko
Thomas Owusu

Upholsterers (Liners)
Yaya Adama
Joseph Arthur Atta
Kwame Degraft
Yaw

Electricians
James
Lamus Kofi Musah
Shiabu Nabiridih Rashidi
Justice Jamal Saeea
Francisco Yeboah

Bodyworkers
Abdul Razak Abubakar
Daniel Owusu
Apomasu Kofi Stevenson
Sulomon Osei Yeboah

All round
Samuel Ampiah (Sami)
Daniel Ekow
Francis Kuyol
Antipem Charles Ofori

Carpenter
Murphy Martey Cudjoe

Part	Original brand & type	Shop Suame Magazine
Accelerator	Nissan Urvan	Manko Sons Enterprises
Air shaft	Locally produced in Suame Magazine	Montals Enterprise
Antenna	Unknown	Yebochea Enterprise
Automotive battery	Mutulu	Glorious Monarch Autoparts Enterprise
Bolts & nuts	Unknown	God is Able - Bolts & Nuts
Brake pedal	Toyota Hiace	Olala Brakes
Bumper	Locally produced in Suame Magazine	Bras workshop Unknown
Car seats	Mercedes Sprinter	Not By Might Nor Power But By My Spirit
Chassis	Toyota Land Cruiser 2	Japan Motor House Enterprise
Clutch pedal	Toyota Hiace	Olala Brakes
Cross member	Locally produced in Suame Magazine	The Blood of Jesus Blacksmith
Dashboard control box	Mercedes	IB-TEC Enterprise
Dashboard cover	Locally produced in Suame Magazine	Carpenter Muffmat Enterprise
Door handles	Mazda, Mercedes, Renault	Fran-Gee Ent.
Door rubbers	Locally produced in Suame Magazine	Isaac Enterprise
Door locks	Mazda, Mercedes, Renault	Fran-Gee Ent.
Drive shaft	Nissan, Mercedes	Isaac Enterprise
Electric fan	Opel Vectra	Josat Motors
Electronics and wiring	BMW	Rose Wiring Electrics
Engine	SsangYong engine 2,8 litre, 5 cylinder	Okess Enterprise
Firewall	Locally produced in Suame Magazine	D&A (Daniel Owusu & Abdul Razak Abubakar)
Foot boards	Locally produced in Suame Magazine	Fra Fra Scrap Market
Frame	Locally produced in Suame Magazine	Master Sulomon Osei Yeboah
Front axle	Nissan Trade	Enkasa Enterprise
Front springs	Locally produced in Suame Magazine	Boakye Yiadom Ent.
Fuel tank	Mazda	Big Sasruku Enterprise
Gearbox (electric)	Mercedes Sprinter	All Shall Pass Enterprise
Gearbox (manual)	Mercedes Sprinter	John Boat Enterprise
Hammer, iron saw, tools	Locally produced in Suame Magazine	Boatmod Enterprise
Headlights	Volvo	God is King Lights & Horns
Hinges	Chrysler	Fra Fra Scrap Market
Horn	Morris	God is King Lights & Horns
Interior lights	Locally produced in Suame Magazine	Plastic smith (James Backlight)
Interior upholstery	Locally produced in Suame Magazine	Uphostery master (Atta Joseph Arthur)
Logo mould	Locally produced in Suame Magazine	Abu-Dia company
Mudflaps	Locally produced in Suame Magazine	Mudflaps (Master Owusu)
Muffler	Mitsubishi	Tommy Pipe House
Paint	Sunburst Orange Metallic	Kusi Brempong Ent.
Petrol	Unknown	In God We Trust Filling Station
Radiator	Ford, Opel	Josat Motors
Resonator	Mazda	Tommy Pipe House
Rear axle	Nissan Patrol	Enkasa Enterprise + Christ is King Enterprise
Rims	Toyota	Alviant Rims & Tyres
Roofing sheets	Made in China	Jehova Alone is Enough Ent.
Rubber joints	Locally produced in Suame Magazine	Master Iddrisu Rubber Company Business Cen
Shock absorbers	Made in China	Kai Prempeh Enterprise
Side indicators	Locally produced in Suame Magazine	Plastic smith (James Backlight)
Side mirrors	KIA Ceres	Buddhistman Mirrors
Spring extensions	Locally produced in Suame Magazine	Nyame Ye Kese
Springs	Automotive Springs Tema Lt.	Automotive Springs Tema Lt.
Steel plates	Tata Steel India	Ben Owusu co. ltd.
Steering column	KIA	Afrokiko
Steering port	Toyota	Nana Agyed Poku & Sons
Storage box	Locally produced in Suame Magazine	D&A (Daniel Owusu & Abdul Razak Abubakar)
Tyres	Unknown	Alviant Rims & Tyres
Windows	KIA Ceres, Toyota van	Osofo Appiah car glass
Windshield wipers	Opel	Yebochea enterprise

ap coordinates	Reference Number
P-14	NIS-315
J-12 / AK-12	SM-315
M-13 / AN-13	UNK-053
M-14	MUT-493
P-13	UNK-036
P-14 / AQ-14	TOY-313
Q-13 / AQ-14	SM-104
K-13	MER-456
T-13	TOY-351
P-14 / AQ-14	TOY-005
P-11	SM-822
N-14 / AO-14	MER-034
T-12	SM-415
L-13	SM-735
N-13	SM-164
L-13	MAZ-367 + MER-462 + REN-876
N-13	NIS-167 + MER-325
N-14	OPE-400
Q-13	BMW-312
S-14	SSY-285
M-11	SM-315
Q-12	SM-426
Q-12	SM-385
R-13 / AR-14	NIS-402
P-12	SM-631
R-12 / AR-13	MAZ-876
P-13 / AP-14	MER-525
Q-13	MER-482
O-13	SM-530
P-14	VOL-159
Q-12	CHR-319
P-14	MOR-934
L-12 / AL-13	SM-986
J-13 / AK-13	SM-512
J-11	SM-831
ew Suame	SM-145
O-12	MIT-194
O-12	UNK-964
L-12 / AM-12	UNK-218
N-14	FOR-256
O-12	MAZ-457
R-13 / AR-14 (enkasa) + AQ-13/AQ-14 (Christ)	NIS-245
N-13 / AN-14	TOY-396
M-13 / AM-14	CHI-413
L-11	SM-369
M-14 / AN-14	CHI-994
L-12 / AL-13	SM-21
N-12 / AN-13	KIA-424
P-12	SM-341
	SM-320
S-12	SM-502
Q-14	KIA-356
N-12	TOY-334
M-11	SM-138
N-13 / AN-14	UNK-402
Q-14	KIA-011
M-13 / AN-13	OPE-961

Photo caption syntax

Example: TOY-351 // GH // AT-13 // 03.2013 part reference number // country code // map coordinates // date

Part reference numbers

BMW: BMW / CHI: Made in China / CHY: Chrysler / FOR: Ford / KIA: KIA / MAZ: Mazda / MER: Mercedes / MIT: Mitsubishi / MOR: Morris / MUT: Mutulu / NIS; Nissan / OPE: Opel / REN: Renault / SM: Suame Magazine / SSY: SsangYong / TOY: Toyota / UNK: Unkown / VOL: Volvo

QR codes & videos

Scan code with smartphone QR reader app to view videos

Acknowledgements

The Turtle Project is the proverbial child of many fathers. First of all, we would like to thank the artisans of Suame Magazine and the people at SMIDO, ITTU and the KNUST University, as well as our Dutch partners. Three people in the Netherlands made important contributions to the project, each in their own way. Firstly, Bram Esser: he was there during our first expeditions to Suame in 2012, and during the project he carried out research in the neighbourhood by doing an apprenticeship with Master Desmond. He soon acquired the nickname Suame Jesus because of his tall lanky figure and his wild hairdo. He described his experiences in the essay *Auto-Recycling in Ghana*, that was published in the monthly magazine Streven on 9 December 2013. Bram knew a lot about the neighbourhood and made important contacts for us. As a teacher at the Rietveld Academy and a supervisor of the Dutch students, Cynthia Hathaway was very important for the student programme. Her ideas and her love of cars and technology were a great source of inspiration to us. Finally, it is important to mention Tijs van den Boomen, who wrote the long read *Turtle 1, de auto uit Afrika* from an independent journalistic perspective. It was partly thanks to the efforts of his publisher, Fosfor, that we were able to generate publicity for the Turtle Project.

Partners in Ghana

Suame Magazine Industrial Development Organization, (SMIDO), Kumasi (Ghana).
Kwame Nkrumah University of Science and Technology Kumasi (KNUST), departments of Painting and Sculpture and Mechanical Engineering, Kumasi (Ghana).
Embassy of the Kingdom of the Netherlands, Accra (Ghana).

Partners in the Netherlands

Stimuleringsfonds Creatieve Industrie, Rotterdam.
Centrum Beeldende Kunst, Rotterdam.
Stichting Doen, Amsterdam.

Sponsoring

Royal Burger Group, Rotterdam, NL.
Africa Express Line, Kent, UK.
Compagnie Fruitière, Marseille, FR.
Xelvin BV, Alkmaar, NL.
UPT, Accra, GN.
Supermaritime Group, Tema, GN.
Sivoko, Automotive Springs Ltd., Tema, GN.

Donors

C.H. Bakker, Joep Beckers, Ellen van den Berg, D.M. Boots, Studio Dara (D. Schonkeren), Jurr van Diggele, Maurits Hertzberger, Geke Hop, Jeroen, Sietske de Jong, Thierry Karsemeijer, Sophie van de Kerkhof & Jeen Berting, Mart van de Kerkhof & Tineke de Beer, Van de Laar Voet & Zorg, Bas Leurs, Marijke & Maud, Van Onna-Timmerbrink family, Vicky & Martha van Onna, Hatice Özgul, Arne Padt & friends, REBOND (Jan Dirk de Jong), Derk Runhaar, P. Smets & M. Smets-Servais, H. Koot and R. Smets, Luuk Smits, Freek Spruijt, Bureau Timmermans, Mischa Tol, Jet Vonk, J.J. Vonk & M.A. Prince, Rob Groot Zevert and anonymous donors.

Partners Research Programme

Gerrit Rietveld Academy Amsterdam (Department Designlab).
Willem de Kooning Academy Rotterdam (Department Fine Art).
Xelvin BV, Alkmaar.
HAN Automotive, Arnhem/Nijmegen
V2_, Institute for the Unstable Media, Rotterdam.
Rijksdienst voor het Wegverkeer, (RDW) Lelystad.

Thank you

Florence van Berckel, Jeroen van Bergeijk, Kodua Boakye, Arno Boers, Asher Boersma, Lejo Buning, Mr. Crossman, Erik van Dam, Michel van Dartel, Ramon va Dijk, Rolf Engelen, Yesuenyeagbe Fiagbe, Christiaan Fruneaux, Edwi Gardner, Ernst Gleijm, Maaike Gouwenberg, Genevieve Herange Lieve Heylen, Michael Huijser, Amponsah Boadi Japhet, Dirk-Jan de Jong, Michelle Kasprzak, Stein van Kervel, Kissiedu, Harm Krale, Frank Appiah Kubi, Michael Kuijl, Joris Lindhout, Marcia Luyten, Evert Nieuwenhuis, Kevin Overtoom, Monique Sanders & Lútsen Zijlstra, Peter Michiel Schaap, Marnix Segers, Laurens Snoek & co, Kwaku Boafo Tweneboah, Arjan van Vliet, Aunt Vicky, Hugo de Vocht, Bob Vos, Lukas Wolzak, and the participant in the expert meetings.

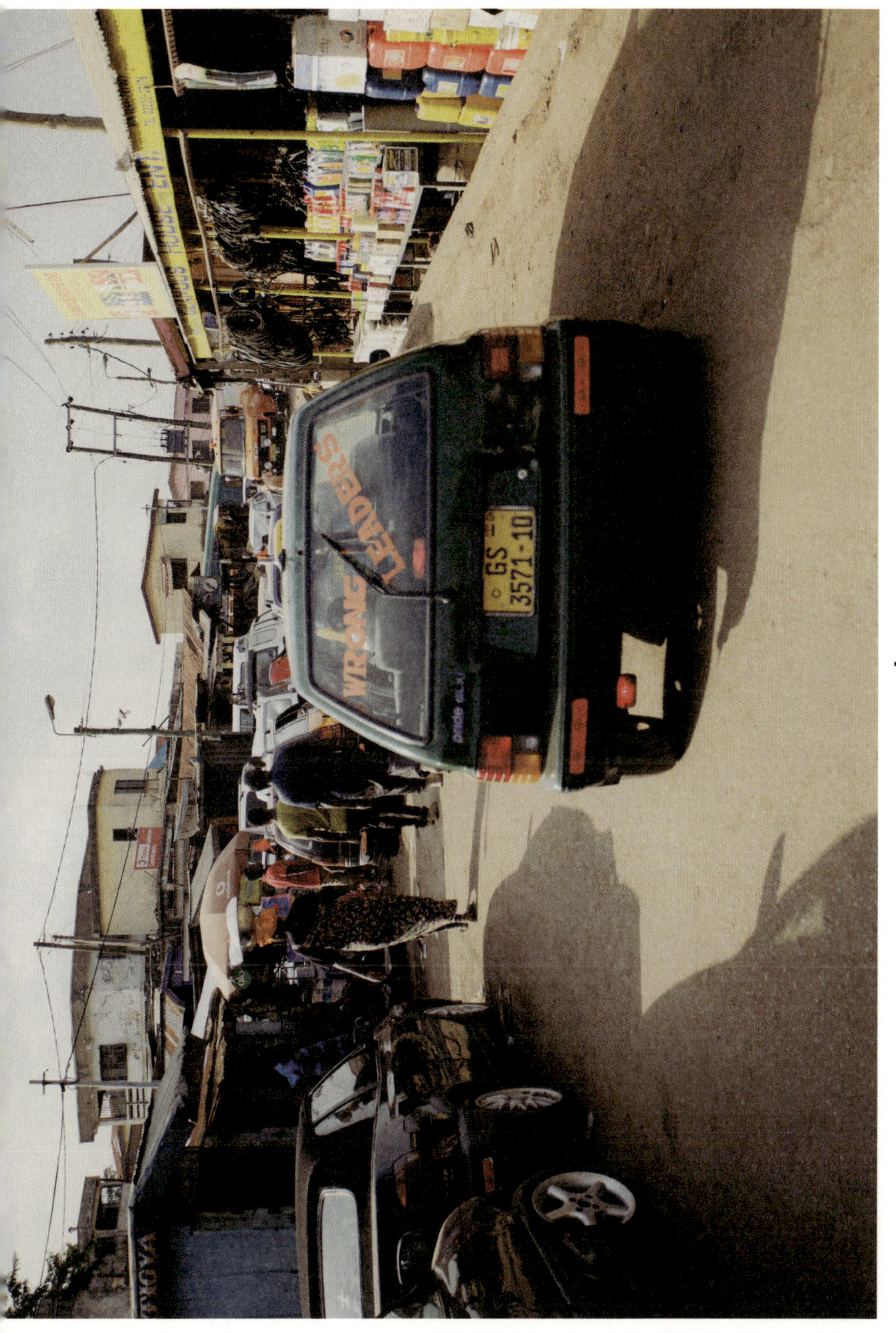

t1|233

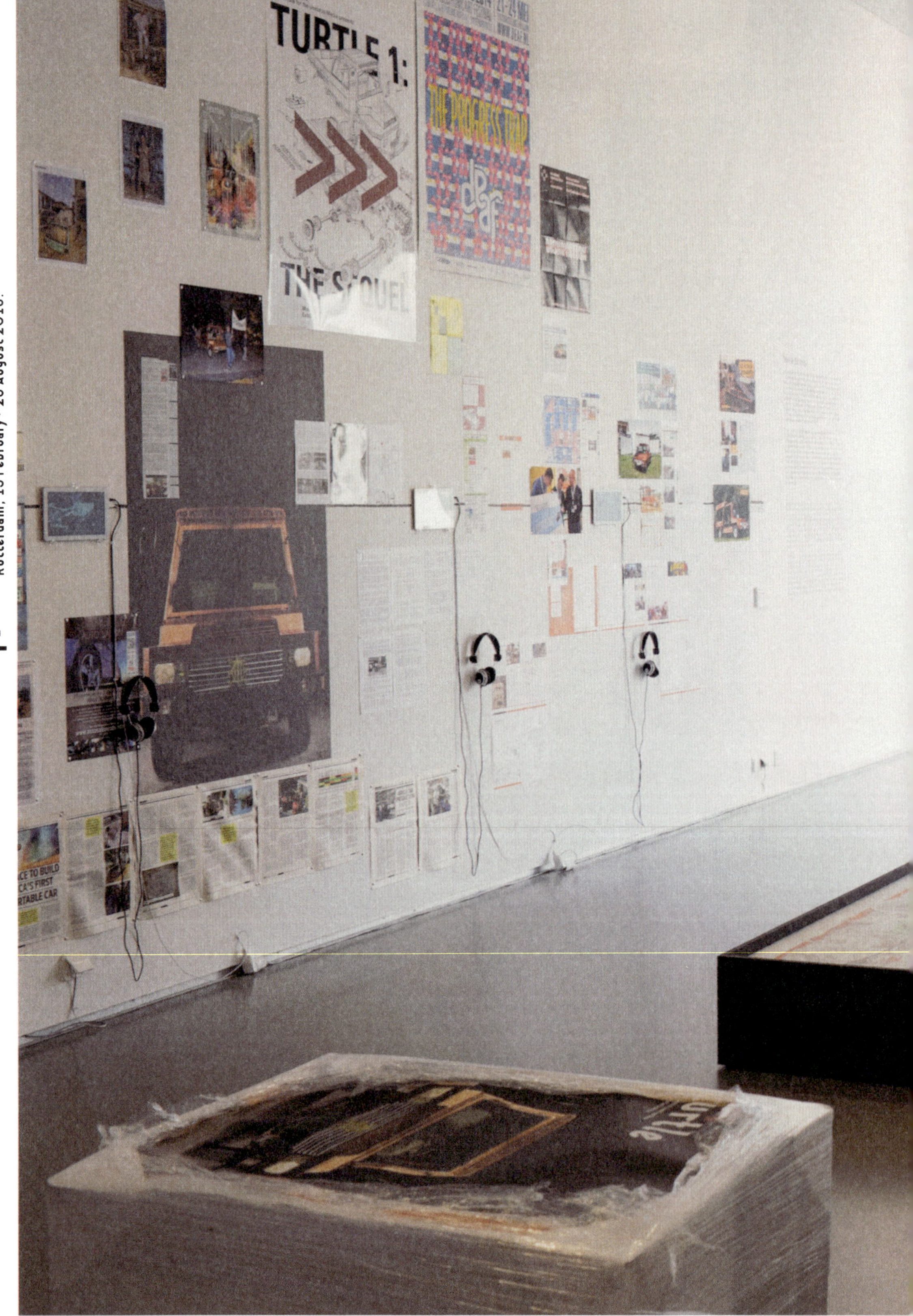

Turtle 1 presentation at group exhibition Project Rotterdam, Museum Boijmans van Beuningen, Rotterdam, 13 February - 28 August 2016.

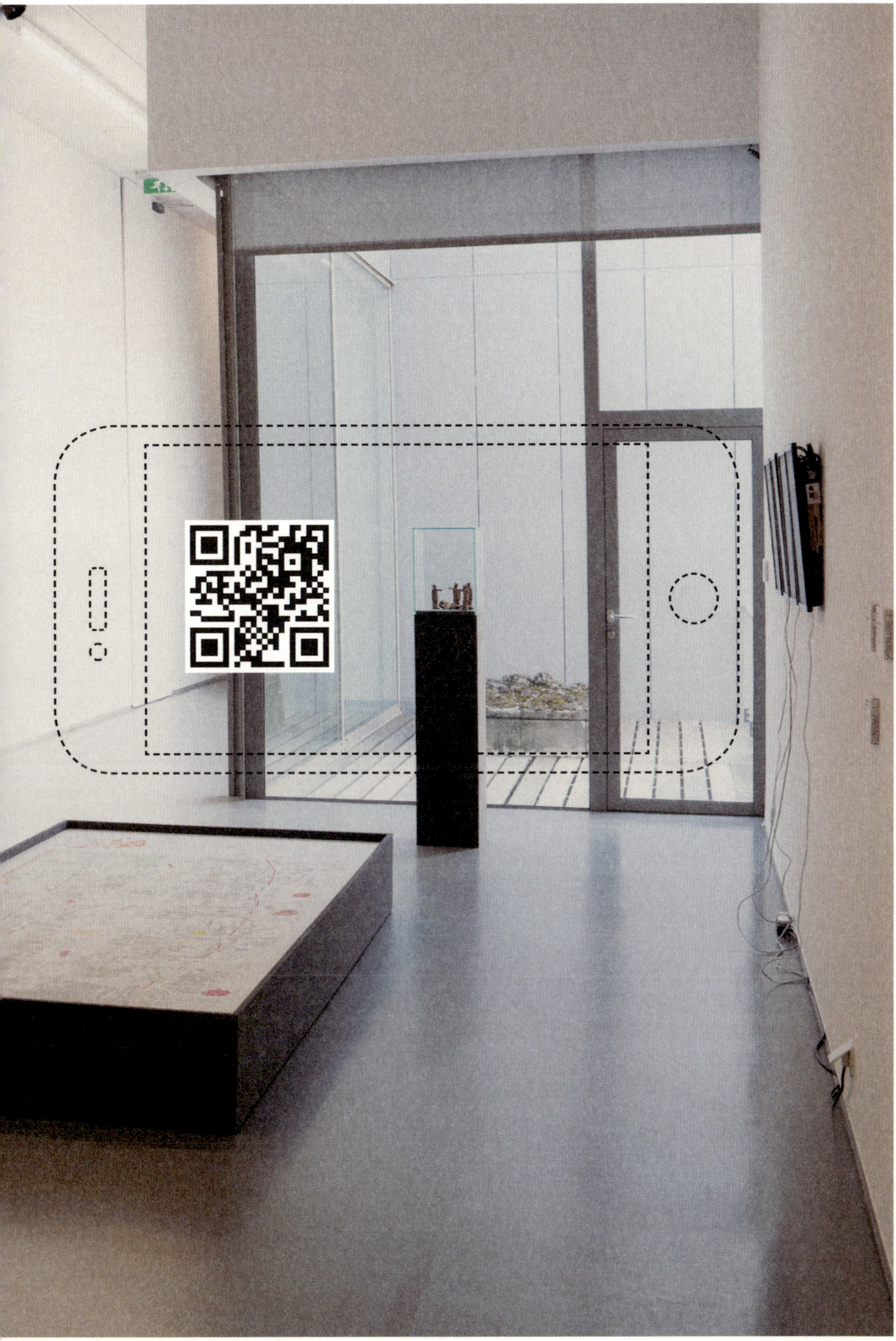

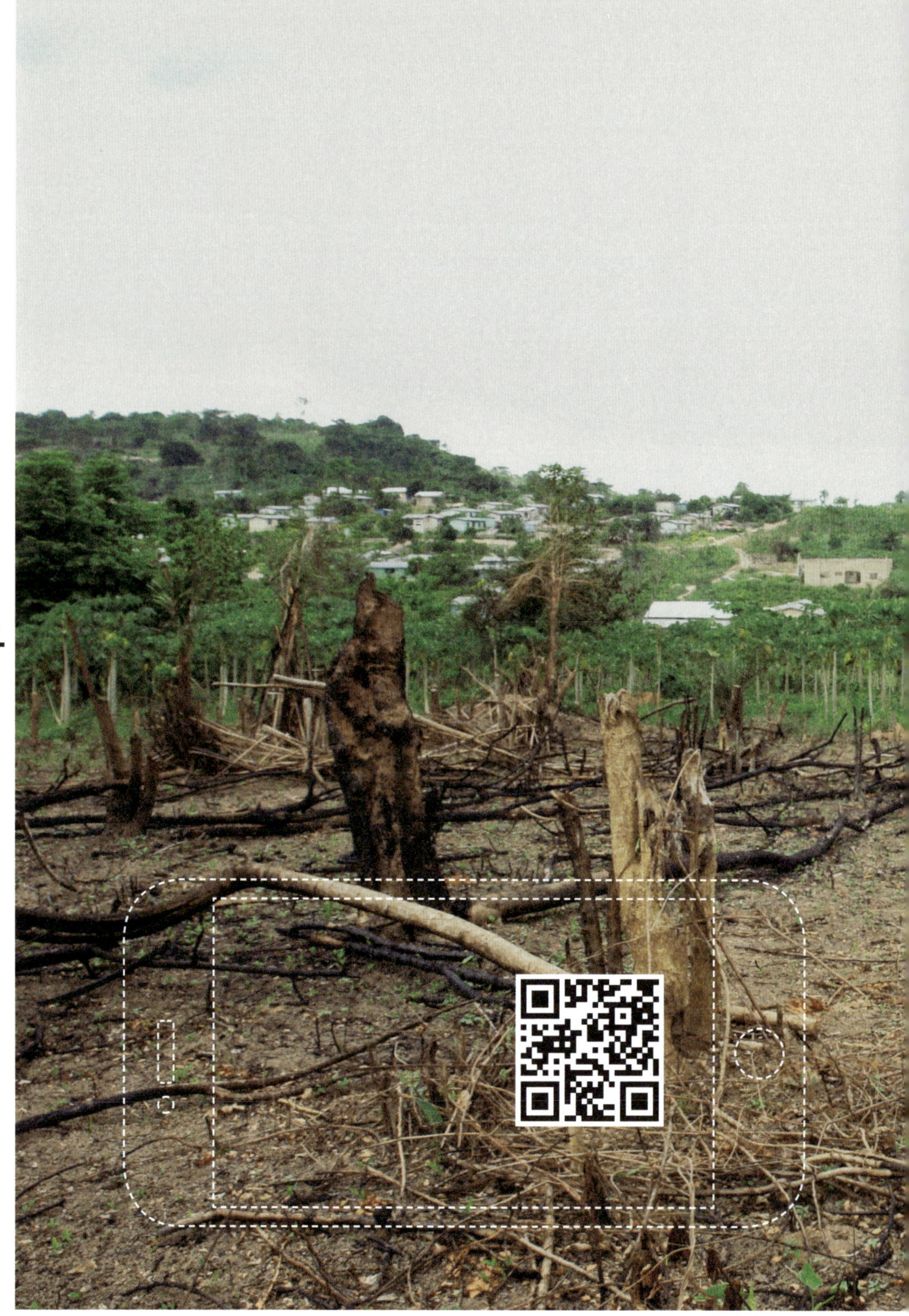

The New Land in 2015. This is the piece of land where a new and improved Suame Magazine is to be built.

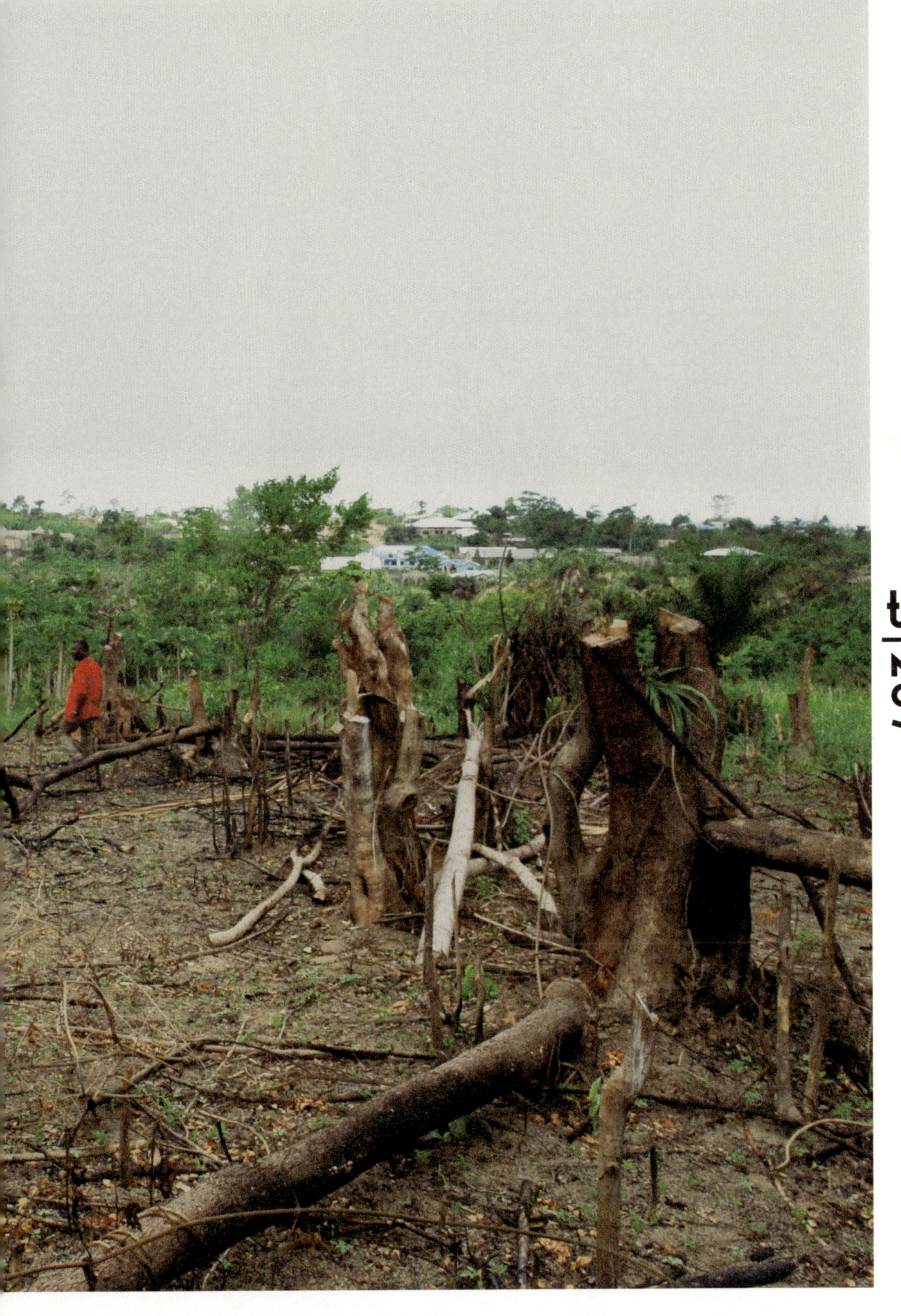

The Turtle 1 is stored in Dr Waco's workshop, waiting for what lies ahead, 15 April 2016.

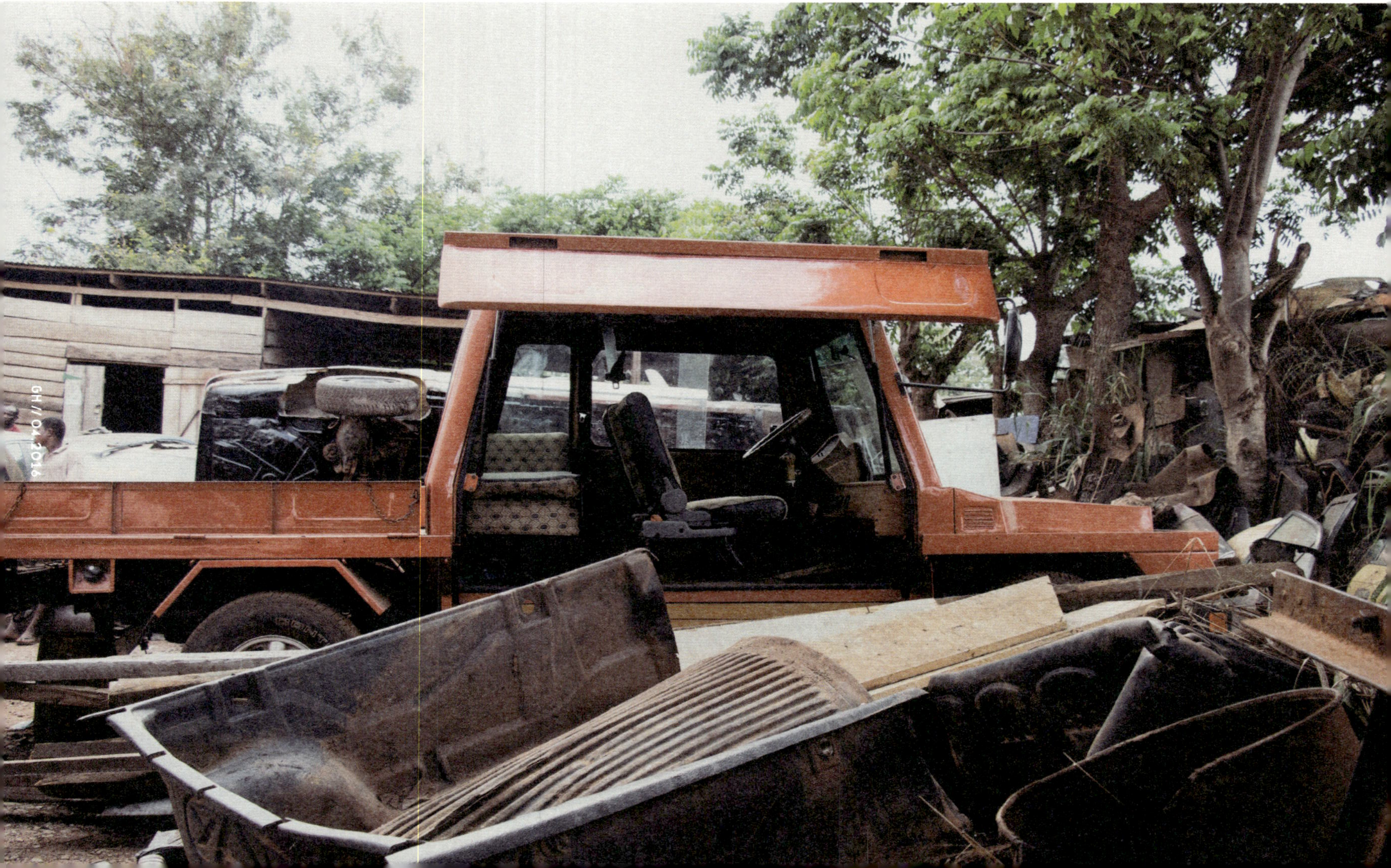

GH // 04.2016